Rabbinic Authority

Volume 6

Rabbinic Authority

The Vision and the Reality

Beit Din Decisions in English

Volume 6

RABBI A. YEHUDA (RONNIE) WARBURG

URIM PUBLICATIONS
Jerusalem • New York

Rabbinic Authority: The Vision and the Reality –
Beit Din Decisions in English, Volume 6

by A. Yehuda (Ronnie) Warburg

Editor: Rabbi Dov Karoll

Typeset by Juliet Tresgallo

Printed in Israel

First Edition

ISBN: 978-965-524-381-9

Library of Congress Control Number: 2013492287

Urim Publications, P.O. Box 52287, Jerusalem 91521 Israel

www.UrimPublications.com

רב דוד באבד, פוסק מפורסם של המאה התשע עשרה מעביר לנו מסורה שקיבל:
"מריש כל אמינא מה ששמעתי מפי הגאון רבי באריש רפפורט . . . שהיה מקובל מפי רבו הגאון נודע בשערים האבד"ק לובלין, בבוא לפניו איזה שאלה, מקודם הי' שוקל בשכלו על אמיתת העניין לפי שכל האנושי האיך הוא, ואם נראה לו לפי שכל האנושי שהדבר אמת, אז הוא מעיין עפ"י חוקי תוה"ק מה משפטו – וכן הוא אצלי, בבוא לפני שאלת עגונה וכדומה, אם ברור הדבר בעיני לפי השכל ודעת בני אדם שהדבר אמת, אז אנכי מיגע א"ע למצוא צד היתר עפ"י חוקי ומשפטי תוה"ק וכו'" (שו"ת חבצלת השרון ב:כ"ח)

Rabbi Dovid Babad, a renowned 19th century authority communicates to us the following *mesorah* that he received:

"I heard from *ha-Gaon* Rav Barish Rappaport . . . that he had a *mesorah* from his Rav, *ha-Gaon* Noda Bashearim, ha-Av Beit Din of Lublin, that upon receiving a question to address, he would first weigh in his mind the truthfulness of the matter according to what human reason dictates and if in his estimation human reason the matter is true, then he will delve into *Halakhah* to arrive at a decision." (Teshuvot Havatzelet Ha-Sharon 2:28)

"כל רב בישראל רוצה בתקנת בנות ישראל ויודע גודל המצוה להתירה מעיגון והאיסור הגדול לעגן כשהיה בידו לתקן ולא תיקן"(רב משה פיינשטיין, אגרות משה אה"ע א:קי"ז)

"Every *rav* in *Yisrael* wants to promote the welfare of the daughters of *Yisrael* and he is aware of the greatness of the *mitzvah* to free her from *igun* and it is a major prohibition "to leave a wife in chains" if one has the ability to address the situation and does not resolve it." (Rabbi Moshe Feinstein, Iggerot Moshe EH 1:117)

"וכל מי שמתיר עגונה אחת בזמן כאילו בנה אחת מחורבות ירושלים העליונה"
(הב"ח, שו"ת בית חדש החדשות סימן ס"ד)

"Freeing one *agunah* is like rebuilding one of the ruins of the ruins of the heavenly Jerusalem"
(Rabbi Yoel Sirkes, Teshuvot Bayit ha-Dash ha-Hadashot 64)

"הנני מסכים . . . להתיר האישה מכבלי העיגון . . . ויען שמבואר בתשובת ב"ח החדשות . . . כי מי שמתיר עגונה אחת בזמן הזה כאלו בנה אחת מחורבות ירושלים העליונה . . . וכן נדחקתי לגמור התשובה ביום הצום על חרבן בית תפארתנו [תשעה באב]"

(הרב שלום שבדרון, שו"ת מהרש"ם א:פ"ד)

"I agree to free a woman from the chains of *igun* since it states in Teshuvot ha-Bah "freeing one woman is like rebuilding the ruins of the Heavenly Jerusalem" therefore I pushed myself to finish the *teshuvah* (the ruling) on the fast day which commemorates the destruction of our glorious temple [=*Tisha be-Av*]"
(Rabbi Shalom Schwadron, Teshuvot Maharsham 1:84)

Contents

Foreword from Volume 1

IN REFERRING TO THE highest level of truth finding in a judicial proceeding, our Sages make use of the phrase *hadan din emet la amitoe*. What is being conveyed here is that knowledge of the law is not sufficient to render a verdict of truth. In order for the *dayan* to arrive at the correct verdict the **precise** facts of the case must be discovered as well.

A beit din panel is not only thoroughly versed in the relevant halakhot, but it is well equipped by virtue of educational background and professional work experience to grasp the reality on the ground. This entails a relentless commitment to relevant fact finding, taking nothing at face value, and understanding the implications of the facts for commercial behavior of the parties.

A second characteristic of the halakhic-judicial process dealing with monetary matters consists of the documentation that must accompany the decision that the panel hands over to the litigants at the conclusion of the proceedings the claims of plaintiff, as well as the respondent's rebuttals and counterclaims must be meticulously recorded. Next, a thorough discussion of the issues from a halakhic perspective is presented. Finally, the decision is rendered and this decision is demonstrated to have flowed from the halakhic discussion.

Rabbi Dr. A. Yehuda Warburg has assumed a vital role in implementing its vision of a "double level" of truth in the Beit Din of America and on other panels. In the present work *Rabbinic Authority: The Vision and the Reality,* Rabbi Warburg presents a number of his judicial rulings. For two of these judgments, the present work draws from Rabbi Warburg's contributions to *Hakirah* in which he enhanced his rulings with further refinements. What stands out in these decisions is the halakhic framework, legal perspective and "reasoned opinions" Rabbi Warburg sets up to support his decisions.

For a number of decades I have been involved on an ad hoc basis as a *dayan,* including serving on judicial panels for the *Beit Din of America.* In this capacity I have often crossed paths with Rabbi Warburg and served together with him on the same judicial panel. In each panel we served together, Rabbi Warburg's outstanding Torah scholarship is always in evidence. Its *sine qua non* is a Torah scholarship motivated by a perfectionist's drive to achieve new vistas in advancing the "double dimension "of truth that stands as the ideal for the judicial process.

R. Dr. Aaron Levine, *z"l*
19 Adar 1, 5771
February 23, 2011

Preface

THE PRESENT VOLUME IS the sixth in a series of volumes intended as an introduction to a subject perhaps unfamiliar to many—rabbinic authority in our *halakhic* sources. The subtitle, "The Vision and the Reality", points to the themes being addressed in this work. In addressing the "*halakhic* vision" of rabbinic authority,[1] we will primarily focus our attention upon the issue of the modern-day *agunah*, the wife who is unable to receive her *get* due her husband's recalcitrance.[2]

1. As we know, *Halakhah* distinguishes between the theoretical halakhah, which emerges from an abstract study of the sources of *Halakhah*, and the halakhah that is applied in a particular factual context, i.e., *halakhah le'ma'aseh*. See Talmud Bavli *Bava Batra* 130b and Talmud Yerushalmi *Beitza* 2:1 (R. Yohanan's statements). However, whereas "the vision" portion of the presentation deals with the decisions of authorities memorialized in the literary sources of Halakhah, "the reality" portion of our presentation focuses upon the *halakhic*-judicial rulings of a *beit din*.

2. The modern-day *agunah* is to be distinguished from the classical *agunah*. Clearly, *get* recalcitrance is not only a modern phenomenon. Already in the Middle Ages, the phenomenon existed in both the Ashkenazic and Sephardic communities. See *Resp. Ha-Rashba* 1:860-861; *Resp. Ha-Rosh* 43:8, 13; *Resp. Ha-Tashbetz* 1:1, 132; *Resp. Ha-Rivash* 57; *Mordekhai, Ketubot* 186; *Resp. Maharil Ha-Hadashot* 206; *Resp. Maharik*, shoresh 26, 29, 71; *Resp. Maharam Mintz* 11.

It is a matter of dispute whether one requires one individual Jew, a rabbi or a *beit din* of three in order to address matters of *igun*. For this debate, see *Resp. Terumat Ha-Deshen, Pesakim U-Ketavim* 139; *Rema, Shulhan Arukh Even Ha-Ezer* 17:39; *Helkat Mehokeik, Shulhan Arukh, Even Ha-Ezer* 17: 78; *Beit Shmuel, Shulhan Arukh, Even Ha-Ezer* 17:124; *Bi'ur Ha-Gra, Shulhan Arukh, Even Ha-Ezer* 17 (131); *Arukh Ha-Shulhan, Even Ha-Ezer* 17:118; R. Hayyim Pelaggi, *Resp. Hikekei Lev*, Even Ha-Ezer 57; *Resp. Mahari Ha-Kohen, Even Ha-Ezer* 3; *Resp. Va-Ya'an Avraham* 28; *Sha'agat Aryeh*, Kol Shahal 13 (end);*Resp. Minhat Ani* 65; *Resp. Seder Eliyahu Rabba Ve-Zuta*, 125–126; *Mar'ot Ha-Tzovot, Even Ha-Ezer* 17 (158); *Atzei Arazim, Even Ha-Ezer* 17 (165); Z.N. Goldberg, *Lev Mishpat*, vol. 1, 149-150.

Should a hearing be conducted by a single rabbi, there is a controversy whether

Some of our lines of inquiry will be the following: How does *Halakhah* understand the undertaking of marriage via the transfer of the ring from a Jewish man to a Jewish woman (the execution of the *kinyan kiddushin*)? Does the transfer connote that the man owns his prospective spouse? If not, how does one view this transfer?

In chapter two, in the event of a husband's get recalcitrance, may we only seek solutions from Torah luminaries who are "Torah giants" (*gedolei ha-dor*) or may we authorize credentialed rabbinic authorities to address this matter of voiding a marriage? This chapter originally appeared in Hebrew in the Tevet 5784 issue of *Hama'ayan.*

One of the techniques to void a marriage is to inquire whether there are grounds for arriving at a decision that the marriage was established based upon a mistake (*kiddushei ta'ut* – loosely translated as a marriage in error). Next, in chapter three, we examine if a husband intentionally or unintentionally fails to disclose to his prospective spouse prior to marriage that he had a major flaw ("*mum gadol*") such as being impotent, unwilling to have children, gay, mentally dysfunctional, or being a criminal. In the second portion of this chapter, In contradistinction to *kiddushei ta'ut,* where one focuses upon the past – namely, when there was a mistake at the time of the consummating the marriage in the

---

testimony submitted to the rabbi should be in the presence of three rabbinic arbitrators (*dayanim),* namely a *beit din.* See *Helkat Mehokeik,* op. cit.; *Taz, Shulhan Arukh, Even Ha-Ezer* 17:56 and *Resp. R. Akiva Eiger, Mahadura Kamma* 123 cited by *Pithei Teshuvah, Shulhan Arukh, Even Ha-Ezer* 17 (155); *Resp. Hatam Sofer, Even Ha-Ezer* 2:130; *Seder Eliyahu Raba Ve-Zuta,* op. cit.; *Mar'ot Ha-Tzovot,* op. cit.; *Atzei Arazim,* op. cit.; *Pithei Teshuvah, Shulhan Arukh, Even Ha-Ezer* 17 (152) in the name of *Brit Avraham*; *Arukh Ha-Shulhan,* op. cit.; *Hazon Ish, Even Ha-Ezer* 27:9; *Lev Mishpat,* op. cit.

Implicit in our understanding, should a rabbi be allowed to address such matters, he must have the credentials to be an arbiter, no different than being a decisor in *halakhic* ritual law but he is not viewed as a *beit din.* See *Hiddushei Ha-Granat,* Nezikin 195. Furthermore, in accordance with Rabbi Michel Epstein, rabbinic approval must be sought prior to the rabbi issuing a *teshuvah* (a responsum) in *igun* matters. See *Arukh Ha-Shulchan, Even Ha-Ezer* 17:139, 255.However, many decisors disagree with his view. See this writer's *Rabbinic Authority: The Vision & the Reality* (hereinafter: *Rabbinic Authority*), vol. 3, 256-262.

Based upon the foregoing, should there be grounds for get coercion, Halakha only empowers a beit din rather than an individual Jew. See *Tumim* 1:1, 3:1; *Ketzot Ha-Hoshen* 3:1; *Netivot HaMishpat* 3, *Biurim* 1, *Meshoveiv Netivot* 3; *Resp. Hatam Sofer* 4:54; *Imrei Bina Dayanim* 9; *Ohr Sameah, Mamrim* 4:3.

On the other hand, after a decision has been handed down, it is incumbent upon every Jew of our covenant faith community to assist the husband to fulfill the mitzvot. See *Resp. Hatam Sofer, Hoshen Mishpat* 177.

form of an undisclosed grave preexisting personality and/or medical or psychological disorder and consequently, the marriage may be voided retroactively – when one invokes an *umdana demukhah* (a major assessment of expectations – hereinafter: *umdana*) as a grounds for voiding a marriage, we are focusing on a future occurrence, i.e. one that transpired after the creation of the marriage. Are there grounds to void such a marriage (*bittul kiddushin*[3]) which is a marriage in error or marked by an *umdana* and under what conditions can it be done?

Part 5 of the U.K. Serious Crime Act 2015, entitled "Protection of Children and Others," contains a section on Domestic Abuse. Article 76 of that section which came into force on December 29, 2015, addresses coercive control or controlling behavior in an intimate or family relationship. In other words, violence perpetrated towards a spouse is not limited to physical violence and emotional and verbal abuse. Violence towards a spouse is also characterized by the attempts of the abuser to control the wife and to limit her actions. Manifestation of control in general, and prevention of the formation of contacts outside the family, criticism of the way a wife dresses, prevention of access to financial information and demanding that she account for herself in particular, cause tension, shouting, cursing, and trading insults at a higher rate than that typical of couples who live together without violence. Insofar as an English court decides in a particular case that *get* refusal constitutes an instance of coercive control on the part of the husband, and sentences him to a set period of imprisonment in accordance with the above legislation, does the criminal process against the *get* refuser affect the validity of the executed *get*? In other words, the threat of prosecution would seemingly result in a coerced *get*. The halakhic examination of the English legislation was originally addressed in Hebrew in *Emunat Itecha*, Nissan 5783.

3. We are examining the notion of voiding (*bittul kiddushin*) rather than annulling (*hafka'at kiddushin*) a Jewish betrothal (loosely translated throughout the monograph: a Jewish marriage). See this writer's *Rabbinic Authority*, vol. 3, 135, n. 1. See also, File no. 905457/10, Tel Aviv-Yaffo Regional Beit Din, September 11, 2017, which astutely distinguishes between the two concepts. Cf. Rabbi Hayyim Berlin who utilizes both concepts interchangeably in the same responsum. See *Resp. Nishmat Hayyim* 126.

There are arbiters who utilize the term of annulling a marriage when in actuality the marriage is being voided. As such, in their minds there is one type of annulment which nullifies *a priori* the act of *kiddushin* and there is a second type of annulment which is predicated upon the notion that the *kiddushin* actually was established and *ex post facto* arbiters are empowered to annul it. See Rabbi S. Cohen, "*Get* Coercion in Contemporary Times," (Hebrew) 11 *Tehumin* 195, 199 (5750).

The question that emerges in chapter four is whether the execution of a *get* under these conditions is deemed halakhically a coerced *get.* In our decision titled, "A Dead Marriage: The Halakhic and Legal Aftermath," we address the significance of two sample *beit din* rulings which allow a couple to execute a *get* without running afoul of the strictures of a forced *get* (*get me'useh*) due to the coercive control legislation. This chapter originally appeared in 27 *Hakirah* (2019) and appears here with their permission.

We move from our discussion of "the vision" of the rabbinic authority regarding issues of family matters (*Even Ha-Ezer*) into "the vision" of the rabbinic authority concerning commercial (*Hoshen Mishpat*) issues. Chapters five through nine respectively, deal with an introduction to the varying avenues of establishing an acquisition agreement and an obligatory agreement, collaborative reproduction, unscrambling the conundrum of halakhic parentage through the prism of the norms of halakhic adoption and the ownership and market of human tissue in American law and Halakhah. Chapters six and twelve have appeared respectively in 32 *Hakirah* (2022) and 17 *Dine Yisrael,* 1993-1994. Additionally, chapters eight and nine have appeared respectively in *And You Shall Surely Heal: Albert Einstein College of Medicine Synagogue Compendium,* and they appear here with their permission.

Finally, we offer an application and ramifications of the doctrine, "the law of the land is the law" and the norm, "there is no agent to commit a wrong," which serve as the basis for a *beit din* ruling. The significance of this ruling lies in the fact that as members of the Jewish covenant community we are under certain conditions dutybound to comply with the norms of civil law as well as the dictates of Halakhah.

Just as a halakhic authority must perform his due diligence to search for a reasoned solution, similarly, an *agunah* must persist in identifying a *beit din* or rabbinic authority who will afford her relief. Even if an *agunah* received a reply from a *beit din* or a rabbi that *Halakhah* affords no solution for her being chained (*igun*), nonetheless, many authorities permit her to revisit her case by submitting it to another rabbi or *beit din.* Lest one challenge this conclusion based upon the Talmudic rule regarding prohibitions (*issurim*), "if a scholar prohibited something, his colleague has no authority to permit it after it already has been forbidden"[4] this rule may either be inapplicable in contemporary times[5] or it may be that

4. Talmud Bavli *Berakhot* 63b; *Avodah Zarah* 7a. See further, this writer's *Rabbinic Authority, vol. 1,* 35, at n. 65.

5. *Arukh Ha-Shulhan, Yoreh Deah* 242:63; *Resp. Maharsham* 9:79.

"a matter of *agunah*" is an exception to this norm.[6] An *agunah* being forced to remain alone is untenable and therefore she should continue to seek out rabbinic authority who hopefully can address her situation.

In this volume, we have included thirteen cases inspired by reasoned opinions handed down on various rabbinic and *beit din* panels. In each presentation, we offer a rendition of the facts of the case. Subsequently, there is an analysis of the *halakhic* issues emerging from the case, followed by a *psak din*, a decision rendered by the *beit din* panel. To preserve the confidentiality of the parties involved in these cases, all names have been changed, and some facts have been changed or deleted. Realizing the controversial nature of some of the cases dealt with in this volume, we are keenly aware of Rabbi Yosef Karo's ruling and admonition that a scholar must refrain from permitting a matter which the community views as being prohibited[7]. Yet, on the basis of a well-trodden *mesorah*, such judgments can be rendered provided that reasons are given for one's position. [8] As such, we have offered reasoned opinions for our decisions.

Both components of this monograph, namely "the vision" and "the reality" of rabbinic authority, have benefited immensely from live interactions as well as telephone and e-mail communications that I had and continue to have with various rabbinical authorities in Israel who serve or served as rabbinic arbitrators (*dayanim*) in the regional rabbinical courts (*battei din*) and Beit Din ha-Rabbani ha-Gadol, the Supreme Rabbinical Court in the Chief Rabbinate network of *battei din*. As *dayanim* who 24/6 immerse themselves in "the sea of the Talmud" ("*the yam ha-Talmud*"), novella (*sifrei hiddushim*) restatements *(sifrei pesak)* and responsa *(teshuvot)*, listen to parties' claims and counterclaims, and hand down reasoned decisions primarily in the area of divorce, their insights and advice have been immeasurable.

Hopefully our presentation will educate our community regarding the parameters and scope of rabbinic authority in general and "shatter the silence" surrounding the various techniques towards confronting the matter of "*igun*" in particular.

---

6. *Resp. Sha'arei De'ah* 100; *Resp. Millu'ei Even* 29 (end); *Resp. Heikhal Yitzhak, Even Ha-Ezer* 2:45.

7. *Shulhan Arukh, Yoreh Deah* 242:10.

8. *Shakh, Shulhan Arukh, Yoreh Deah* 242:17; *Ba'air Hetev Shulhan Arukh, Yoreh Deah* 242:12; *Arukh Ha-Shulchan, Yoreh Deah* 242:25; *Dibrot Moshe, Ketubot, vol. 1, 244-245.*

I Rabbinic Authority
The Vision

Chapter 1

The Nature of the *Kinyan* of *Kiddushin*: A Mode of Acquisition or Obligation?

1. The Nature of *Kiddushin* and *Nissu'in*

What are the building blocks which establish this consensual agreement to establish a marital relationship? Recognizing that marriage consists of two separate acts, an act of betrothal, (*kiddushin*) and marriage (*nissu'in*) respectively, Rabbi Norman Frimer and Professor Dov Frimer note:[1]

> In practical terms, *kiddushin* as the primary state of Jewish marriage can be... normatively constituted through the presence of five halakhic elements... At the helm stands intention (*kavanah*). But intention for what purpose? Two divergent directions emerge... According to one authority, the intent of the couple must be for at least the most minimal and natural characteristics of the marital experience... That decision, however, must also include the stipulation that the wife shall be exclusively related to her husband and prohibited to all others. From this intent of intimacy (*leshem ishut*) will then flow all other authority which will bestow legitimacy and direction upon the formal ceremony and simultaneously form the foundation of the *kiddushin*. The other view finds the natural standard utterly inadequate... What, then, shall be the normative canon for *kavanah*? It must be for the intent of biblical betrothal (*lekiddushei Torah*) or *leshem kiddushin*... a conscious awareness that the ceremony must be in faithful fulfillment of the hallowed imperatives of Jewish law (*kedin*).

---

1. Norman Frimer and Dov Frimer, "Reform Marriages in Contemporary Halakhic Responsa," 21:3 *Tradition* (1984), 7, 9-11. Hebrew terms have been translated by this author.

> ...the intention to marry must be visibly objectified, in order both to articulate as well as to inculcate the core ideas of that *kavanah.* Jewish tradition, therefore, devised two more patterns of action to achieve tangibility. One of them was the *amirah* (declaration*)*, an official verbal declaration of marital *kavanah* to be made directly by the groom to his bride in a formal and public style... The other act... was the *netinah,* giving, initiated again by the groom and complemented by the parallel *kabbala,* receipt, by the bride. These sequential acts of "give and take" involve an object... traditionally a ring ...
>
> But not only must these facets of *kavanah* be shared between bride and groom. Normally, the halakhah also demands... *ratson* (consent*)* – a fourth element, involving the couple's voluntary assent to all parts of the betrothal *(erusin)...*
>
> Finally, a Jewish marriage must be witnessed by at least two qualified witnesses *(edim),* whose responsibility is two-fold. When necessary, they... can help establish the facts and certify the... degree of compliance with the prerequisites of Jewish marriage law. Yet, even more critical is their role... who by their very presence and participation at the ceremony constitute the validity of the act of betrothal *(ma'aseh kiddushin).*

In short, the subjective marital intentions of the Jew and Jewess are translated into reality via verbal articulation and modes of concretization of this intent under the scrutiny of witnesses and in the presence of an officiating rabbi and public assemblage for the expressed purpose of establishing a consensual marital union.

The question arises whether the act of *kiddushin* initiated by the prospective husband is to be identified as an act of acquisition of a prospective wife and places this acquisition squarely within the ambit of other property transactions recognized by Halakhah?

The opening chapter of Mishnah Kiddushin teaches us:

> A woman is acquired in three ways ...She is acquired with money, or with a document, or through conjugal relations...
>
> An Israelite servant is acquired with money or with a document...
>
> A Canaanite slave is acquired with money, and with a document, and by performing tasks for his owner (*hazakah*)...
>
> A large animal is acquired by transfer (*mesirah*) from seller to buyer, and the small one by lifting (*hagbahah*), these are the

> words of Rabbi Meir and Rabbi Eliezer. And the Sages say a small animal is acquired by pulling (*meshikhah*)...
>
> Property which has security (real estate) is acquired by money, by a document and by taking hold (of the land). Property which does not have surety is acquired with property which has security with money, with a document and by taking possession.

At first glance, the common denominator of these differing relationships, marriage and nonmarriage alike, is that ownership is established by different forms of acquisition, and the acquisition of a wife is within the ambit of other property transactions. *Ipso facto,* we may seemingly conclude that upon the consummation of the act of *kiddushin,* the wife becomes the property of her husband.[2] The unity of the linguistic usage of the Hebrew word acquired ("*nikneit*") and the modes of acquisition mentioned throughout the five passages of the Mishnah seemingly conveys to us that the proprietary interest of the husband is identical to that of the Israelite servant and the Canaanite servant as well as the acquisition of animals and different types of property.[3]

The parallel between marriage and other property transactions persists in later Talmudic discussions. For example, the Talmudic source for undertaking the duty (*kinyan*) via the medium of money for establishing *kiddushin* is derived from the Biblical verse, "I will give the money for the field."[4] Elsewhere, the Talmud equates a servant to a woman. In accordance to Rabbi Meir and Rabbah, a servant has no powers of executing a *kinyan* distinct from his master, nor a wife distinct from her husband.[5] More significant, it is the money itself in which it changes hands at the time of the *kiddushin* which the Talmud records in the following fashion:[6] According to Ulla, if a daughter of a Jew is betrothed to a Jew from the priestly class (a *kohen*), she is, according to Biblical law, permitted to eat a priestly tithe (*terumah),* as stated, "if a priest buy any soul, the purchase of his money, he may eat out of the *terumah*."[7] In other words, the wife is "the purchase of his money (*kinyan kaspo*)."

In short, these various passages seem to convey the notion that the

---

2. Whether the validity of the financial obligations stems from the essence of *kiddushin* or is derivative from the act of *kiddushin,* and the ramifications of this distinction, is beyond the scope of our presentation.

3. See also Mishnah *Gittin* 1:4-6.

4. Talmud Bavli, *Kiddushin* 4b, citing *Bereshit* 23:13.

5. *Kiddushin* 23b.

6. *Ketubot* 57b.

7. *Vayikra* 22:11.

establishment of *kiddushin* is to be viewed minimally as a monetary acquisition of the wife by the husband and maximally as an acquisition of the wife's body by the husband no different than the acquisition of chattel.

2. The Nature of *Kinyan Kiddushin*

The threshold question is how does the vehicle of symbolically undertaking an obligation (a *kinyan)* function in halakhic commercial relations? For example, undertaking an obligation via the medium of money (*kinyan kesef*) regarding a sales transaction may be construed in two different ways. One conception is that money is being given by the buyer to the seller in exchange for receiving an item.[8] Consequently, since the donor doesn't require anything including money in exchange for the gift, therefore *kinyan kesef* isn't needed to receive a gift.[9] On the other hand, if *kinyan kesef* is viewed as a sales transaction as a means of effectuating a transfer,[10] then the act of gifting does mandate a *kinyan.*[11]

Another example of *kinyan kesef* is *kiddushei kesef* whereby the groom, in the presence of two eligible witnesses, transfers to his prospective spouse money or its equivalent which has the value of a *perutah* for the purpose of *kiddushin,* halakhic engagement. One approach is that the money represents the value of the *kiddushin.*[12] In other words, the wife must derive pleasure from the transfer. Consequently, if the groom gives

---

8. *Sma, Hoshen Mishpat* 190:1-2; *Netivot Ha-Mishpat, Hiddushin* 190:3; Afikei *Yam* 16 (11) in the name of R. Hayyim Ozer; R. Shkop, *Hiddushei R. Shimon Ha-Kohen*, 2.

9. *Responsa* (hereinafter: Resp.) *Ha-Mabit* 1:350; *Perisha, Hoshen Mishpat* 241:1 in the name of Tur; *Minhat Asher*, second ed. 5779, Bereshit, Hayei Sara, 40.

10. Executing a *kinyan kesef* involves the giving of money for symbolic reasons. See *Taz, Hoshen Mishpat* 190:2; *Sha'arei Hayyim* 1(2); *Afikei Yam*, supra n. 8. Cf. others who argue that the giving of money entails exchanging money for the sake of purchasing an item. See *Sma, Hoshen Mishpat* 190:1.

For earlier treatments of the nature of *kinyan kesef* and *kinyan kiddushin*, see Y. Ehrenberg, "The Law of *Kinyan* and the Monetary *Kinyan* – The Similarity & the Difference" (Hebrew), 4 *Meisharim*, 5764; A. Cohen, "Kiddushei Kesef," (Hebrew) 4 *Meisharim* 5766; G. Kornberg, "*Kinyan* Forever: The Link and Applicability to *Kinyan* & *Kiddushin*," (Hebrew), 3 *Netiva* 578; A. Saksonov, "*Kiddushin* as a *Kinyan* – The Establishment of a Link or an Obstacle from the World," (Hebrew), 8 *Asif* 292, 5783.

11. *Tosafot Ha-Rid, Kiddushin* 13a; *Divrei Yehezkel* 39:4.

12. *Piskei Ha-Rosh, Bava Metzia* 1:48; *Avnei Milluim* 29:2. For a critique of this position, see *Minhat Asher*, supra note 9.

a gift to his prospective wife on the condition that it is returned to him, she is not deemed engaged (*mekudeshet*).[13] A woman will also not be engaged if the groom waives a loan that she is obligated to him, due to the fact that she isn't deriving pleasure presently at the time of the transfer.[14] However, in commercial transactions, a gift with a condition to return as well as a loan may be utilized as a *kinyan kesef*. Furthermore, if in the presence of two eligible witnesses, the prospective husband hands over to his bride a deed written on forbidden foods (*issurei hana'ah*) which states the name of the parties and the *kiddushin* formulae (*kiddushei shtar*), the *kiddushin* is invalid because the bride is prohibited from deriving pleasure from the deed.[15]

Maimonides has described historically, a contrasting approach for a *kinyan* in marriage when he states:[16]

> Prior to the giving of the Torah, a man would encounter a woman in the marketplace; if he and she desired each other, he would bring her into his home and would have relations with her and she became his wife. Once the Torah was given, Israel were commanded that if the man would like to marry the woman, he ought to undertake the duty to marry her (*yikneh*) in the presence of witnesses and afterwards he would take her as a wife...

If the execution of *kidddushin* is to be viewed as acquiring the woman, what was the difference between the situation prior to the Sinaitic revelation and afterwards? Clearly, Maimonides is teaching us that the Torah was seeking to replace the prevailing custom of matrimony based solely upon mutual love and affection and "take her as a wife".[17] What is the meaning to "take her as a wife"?

Relying implicitly upon precedential opinion,[18] R. Osher Weiss notes:[19]

13. *Mishneh Torah, Hilk. Ishut* 8:24.

14. *Mishneh Torah Hilk. Ishut* 5:13, 24; *Avnei Milluim* 28:15-16. On the other hand, in a sales transaction where what is required is the transfer of money rather than the recipient deriving pleasure, a transaction can be finalized with a loan. See *Mishneh Torah, Hilk. Mekhirah* 7:4.

15. *Resp. Ha-Rashba* 1:603.

16. *Mishneh Torah, Hilk. Ishut* 1:1.

17. R. M. Avraham, "Does *Kiddushin* Confer Ownership," (Hebrew), 31 *Akadamut* 2019, 117, 119. See infra n. 29.

18. Supra n. 10.

19. File no. 1126792/1, Netanya Regional Beit Din, October 1, 2017.

> The engagement of a woman is different according to our holy Torah than as accepted in the entire modern world. According to Jewish law, the man acquires the woman in exchange for the ring that he gives her as *kiddushei kesef*... and the entire *kiddushin* is initiated by him, but we require her consent... and truthfully the money of betrothal (*kesef kiddushin*) does not entail an exchange but rather an act of *kinyan.*

To state it differently, whereas the establishment of marital relations among non-Jews is established upon the engagement of intimacy (*kinyan ishut*), marriage of Jews is consummated upon the execution of a symbolic legal act, namely *kinyan kesef* or a bona fide deed (*kinyan shtar).* As the Jerusalem Talmud expounds:[20]

> We learnt that a woman is acquired in three ways: either by money, a deed or by intercourse with regard to Jews. With regard to non-Jews? Rabbi Abahu... says. It states, "You shall die for the woman you have taken, as she is married to her husband" (*Bereshit* 20:13)...

Just as *kinyan kesef* is viewed in a sales transaction as a means of effectuating a transfer,[21] similarly, upon undertaking the *kiddushin* obligation, one utilizes a *kinyan*. Our understanding of the notion of *kinyan* teaches us the meaning via a comparison, in the Talmud, of the act of *kiddushin* with the purchase of Ephron's field by Avraham, our forefather. The biblical term taking ("*kihah*") is utilized regarding both relationships, and just as money served as the means in the sale of the field, analogously, the transfer of money is a vehicle for consummating a halakhic engagement. As Nahmanides aptly observes:[22]

> Since her body is not acquired (by her husband – AYW) via possession (*hazakah*)... It is only derived from the common term '*kihah*' that we learn that *kesef* is a medium of *kinyan* in *kiddushin*. There is no intention of comparing a woman with a field.

---

20. Talmud Yerushalmi, *Kiddushin* 1:1. See also, *Bereshit Rabbah, Parsha* 18, Verse 24; *Even Ha-Ezel, Hilk. Ishut* 4:16, 6:1.

21. Supra, n. 10.

22. *Hiddushei Ha-Ramban, Kiddushin* 3a, s.v. *li'me'utei*. For similar reasoning, see *Tosafot Kiddushin* 3a, s.v. *ve'isha*.

In other words, *kiddushei kesef* is an example of a *kinyan kesef. Kiddushei kesef* entails giving money to the prospective wife, and as the Talmud notes, this is one of the means of actualizing '*kihah*' similar to the '*kihah*' regarding the conveyance of the field.[23] Nevertheless, the nature of the *kinyan* in marriage is different from the nature of the *kinyan* of a field. Whereas *kinyan* regarding the purchase of a field entails a proprietary acquisition, the *kinyan* of marriage involves an obligation (a *hithayevut).* In short, the term *kinyan* in matters of *kiddushin* is a borrowed term from a *kinyan* employed in monetary matters, which may mean undertaking an obligation, and under certain conditions the *kinyan* entails an acquisition.[24]

To state it differently, it seems that one should not draw inferences from civil law to ritual law. As the Talmud states:[25]

> We may not infer ritual law from civil law (*issura mimamona la yalfinan)*

Nevertheless, as we mentioned, the Talmud drew an analogy between the taking ("*kihah*") concerning the conveyance of a field to the "*kihah*" in *kiddushin.* Moreover, such inferences from civil law to ritual law were drawn in other Talmudic passages.[26] And some post-talmudic commentators have raised the contradiction between these passages and the Talmudic rule of "ritual law is not derivative from civil law" (*issura mimamona la yalfinan).*[27] Nonetheless, such inferences may be executed on the condition that the authority is aware of the substantive differences between ritual issues and monetary matters.[28] As such, in

23. Talmud Bavli, *Kiddushin* 2a; *Minhat Asher*, supra n. 9. Nevertheless, as R. Weiss notes, *kessef kiddushin* concerning other halakhot will be different from *kinyan kessef.* See *Minhat Asher*, supra n. 9.

24. Whereas in *kiddushin,* the function of *kinyan* serves to undertake an obligation, in financial matters *kinyan* may serve as a mode of acquisition as well as undertaking an obligation. For the dual role of *kinyan* concerning monetary matters, see chapter 5 in this monograph; B. Lifshitz, *Employee, Contractor-Acquisition and obligation in Contract,* (Hebrew): 1993, pp. 12-23; I. Warhaftig, *Undertaking in Jewish Law,* (Hebrew), Jerusalem:2001, pp. 7-8. For the linguistic grounds for the dual meaning of *kinyan,* see B. Lifshitz, *Law and Action: Terminology of Obligation and Acquisition in Jewish Law,* (Hebrew) Jerusalem: Bialik Institute, 2001, pp. 218-219.

25. Talmud Bavli, *Berakhot* 19b; *Ketubot* 40b.

26. Talmud Bavli, *Kiddushin* 6b; *Yevamot* 115b; *Bava Kama* 37b; *Bava Metzia* 20b.

27. *Tziyun Le-Nefesh Hayyah, Berakhot* 19b; *Pnei Yehoshua, Berakhot* 19b, *Bava Metzia* 27a.

28. *Yad Malachi* 43; *Resp. Hakham Tzvi* 134. See further Eliav Shochetman,

our case, the *kinyan* of *kiddushei kesef* entails an obligation (*hithayevut*) rather than an act of acquisition (*hakna'ah*) which in certain instances will be performed by a *kinyan kesef*.

The emerging question is: what is the purpose of the *kinyan* of *kiddushei kesef*? Clearly, based upon a review of Talmudic and post-talmudic sources, others have shown that the husband receives no proprietary interest in his wife's body.[29]

"On Analogy in Decision Making in Jewish Law and the Foundation of Law Act", (Hebrew) 13 *Shenaton Ha-Mishpat Ha-Ivri* 307 (1987).

29. On the one hand, a Jewish husband is entitled to various monetary rights vis-à-vis his wife, which is known in halakhic nomenclature as "*shi'budim.*" For example, when a wife receives an income from her property known as *nikhsei melug* such as rent or interest from capital, it belongs to the husband. Or under certain conditions, the earnings of the wife from her own exertion (*yegi'a kappeha*) derived from work (*ma'aseh yadeha*- the wife's handiwork) belong to the husband. See Mishneh Torah, Hilk. Ishut 12:1-3.

However, on the other hand, the husband receives no proprietary interest in his wife's body. See Abraham Rutta, *Dina De-Malkhuta Dina*, 1939; R. K. Kahana, *The Theory of Marriage in Jewish Law*, Leiden: Brill, 1966, pp. 5-14, 26-55, 80-95; R. N. Rothstein, "The Nature of *Kiddushin* and its *Kinyan*," (Hebrew), *Nezer Ha-Torah*, Av 5770, pp. 52-110; R. Z. Gartner, *Kefiyah Be-Get*, pp. 32-33; R. M. Ehrenreich, "*Kiddushin – Kinyan* or *Ma'aseh*?" (Hebrew) *Eretz Hemdah*, pp. 29-43; R. E. Shochetman, "Engaged, not Acquired," (Hebrew) 223 *Nekuda*, March 1999, pp. 36-44; R. Avraham, supra n. 17; R.Y. Ushinski, *Orhot Mishpat* vol. 1, pp. 40-53; R. D. Wolf, *Minha Le-Aharon*, 5765, pp. 18-31; M. Avraham, Kesef and Kinyan Kesef: Halakhic Ramifications at Col. 525 (Hebrew) at https:mikyab.net.

In fact, some authorities explicitly or implicitly reject the notion that a husband has a proprietary interest in his wife. See *Tosafot, Kiddushin* 7b, s.v. *hetzyekh*, (Cf. *Tosafot, Bava Batra* 48b, s.v. *kadish be'biah*); Ran on Rif, Gittin 9a, s.v. vekatva (Cf. Ran on Rif, Ketubot 9b); *Hiddushei Ha-Ra'ah, Kiddushin* 2a; *Hiddushei Ha-Ramban, Kiddushin* 5b, s.v. *ha natan, Kiddushin* 16b, s.v. *zot omeret, Bava Metzia* 46a, s.v. *hakhi ka'amar, Gittin* 38b, s.v. *gufeih*; *Resp. Ha-Rashba Ha-Meyuhasot LeRamban* 284; *Hiddushei Ha-Rashba, Kiddushin* 3a, s.v. *li'me'utei halifin*, 6b: s.v. *amar Abaye, Bava Batra* 48b, s.v. *ella*; *Hiddushei Ha-Ritva, Kiddushin* 2a, s.v. *ketiv hacha*, 7a, s.v. *arev*, s.v. *mi dami*; *Perush R. Avraham Min Ha-har, Nedarim* 15b; *Resp. Ha-Rivash* 385; *Resp. Ein Yitzhak* 1, *Even Ha-Ezer* 16; *Avnei Milluim*, Resp. 17, *Even Ha-Ezer* 42 (1); *Resp. Helkat Yoav* 1, *Even Ha-Ezer* 4; *Resp. Birkat Shlomo* 12 (31); *Hiddushei R. Shimon Shkop, Kiddushin* 9; *Resp. Divrei Yatziv, Even Ha-Ezer* 56 (3); *Resp. Iggerot Moshe, Even Ha-Ezer* 1:117; *Resp. Avnei Nezer, Even Ha-Ezer* 123:9; R. Herzog, *Pesakim Ve-Ketavim* 6, 207-210,8, 916 (Cf. *Pesakim Ve-Ketavim* 7, 833-834); *Peri Moshe* 60; *Minhat Asher, Kiddushin* 8, 22. Cf. *Tosafot Rosh Kiddushin* 5a.

For the utilization of the word *kinyan* in another fashion by some of the early arbiters, see A. Saksonova, supra n. 10, 296-298.

For the requirement of two witnesses to attest to the designation of the woman as the prospective wife to the exclusion of all others rather than as a vehicle to transfer the woman into the man's domain akin to a piece of property, see *Hiddushei*

On the contrary, the Talmud states:[30]

> What does the rabbinical terminology the man betroths (*mekadesh*) – connote? That he (the man – AYW) prohibits her to all (men – AYW) as consecrated-prohibited for secular use (*hekdesh*).

Ha-Ramban, Kiddushin 65b; *Hiddushei Ha-Ritba Kiddushin* 65b and *Hiddushei Ha-Rashba* 65b.

Moreover, the execution of *kinyan issur* for establishing personal status (*ishut*) during the act of *kiddushin* (see infra text accompanying n. 34) is implemented through a *kinyan* of money. Therefore, the *kinyan issur* is defined by the Talmud *Ketubot* 57b as the acquisition of money (*kinyan kaspo*). See *Shitah Mekubetzet, Ketubot* 57b; *Avnei Milluim*, op. cit.

For a discussion of Ran, *Nedarim* 30a, s.v. *ve-ishah* which seemingly contends that during the transfer of the *kiddushei kesef* the prospective wife is passive and thus is acquired by the husband, see infra n. 31 and this writer's *Rabbinic Authority*, vol. 5, pp. 103-104.

Finally, addressing the *beit din* plea known as *kim li*, i.e. it is established for me [that the law is in accordance with a particular authority, who favors my position], Professor Menahem Elon explains, "The plea is grounded on the basic principle that the burden of proof is on the claimant...the claimant must prove the facts that entitle him to recover from the defendant...if there are conflicting opinions as to the law, one in favor of the plaintiff and the other in favor of the defendant, the latter can argue that in his view, the opinion that favors him is correct, and thus nothing can be taken from his possession unless it is affirmatively proved that the view favoring his position is correct...". See Menahem Elon, *Jewish Law: History, Sources and Principles*, JPS, 1994, 1282. In other words, in monetary matters, the defendant possesses the money (*muhzak be'mamon*). However, concerning prohibitions (*issurim*) such as marriage, a wife is not the monetary asset of the husband, rather she is in her own domain (*reshut*). See Ran on Rif, *Gittin* 3a, s.v. *ve-katvu*; *Shakh, Tokfo Kohen* 127; *Resp. Hemdat Shlomo, Orah Hayyim* 18:32; R. Herzog, *Pesakim Ve-Ketavim* 6, 207-210; *Piskei Din Rabbanayim* 10:241, 245, 12:229, 231-232, 13:352, 354-355; File no. 467862/1, Netanya Regional Beit Din, 11 Shevat 5771. Cf. *Resp. Hatam Sofer, Hoshen Mishpat* 177 (3); *Pesakim Ve-Ketavim* 8, 915 in the name of R. Y. Kalmas; *Resp. Ateret Shlomo* 36-37.

For further contemporary analysis whether *get* coercion is understood as separation of a husband from his spouse who *belongs* to him, see Amihai Radzyner, "*Kim Li* Claim in *Get* Coercion" (Hebrew) 35-36, *Dinei Israel* 397, 418-420 (5782). Clearly, our presentation rejects the view that a husband has a proprietary interest in his wife. However, others disagree. See *Resp. Hatam Sofer, Hoshen Mishpat* 177 (3). Cf. *Hiddushei Hatam Sofer, Gittin* 2a; *Kuntres Coercion of Imprisonment*, 75-82; Kuntres of *Get* Coercion, 46; *Piskei Din Rabbanayim* 12:229, 231-232.

30. Talmud Bavli *Kiddushin* 2b; *Shulhan Arukh, Even Ha-Ezer* 27: 1; *Beit Shmuel*, ibid. 4.

In other words, she is prohibited to the entire world. Alternatively, it means that the consequence of executing the *kinyan kiddushin* is that the engaged woman is designated for a particular man.[31] The execution of *kiddushei kesef* confers upon the woman the status of a married woman (an *eishet ish*). The consummation of the act of *kiddushin* creates a halakhic-personal tie between the parties which can be only dissolved by divorce via the giving of a *get,* or the death of either party. The act of *kiddushin* not only prohibits cohabitation between the wife and the husband[32] but also does not bring about the mutual rights and duties between the couple. The change in their personal status in terms of permitting cohabitation accompanied by all the mutual rights and duties as a married couple is created by the act of marriage (*nissuin*) which transpires either when the couple is in seclusion (*yihud*) after the marriage ceremony (*hupah*) or when they enter the marital home and live together.[33]

---

31. *Tosafot Kiddushin* 2b, s.v. *de'asar lah.*

Moreover, a precondition that the man may perform the act of *kiddushin* is that is the woman is willing to accept the transfer of the *kiddushei kesef.* See Rashi, *Kiddushin* 44a, s.v. *kiddushin mi'da'atah*; Ran, *Nedarim* 30a, s.v. *ve'isha*; R. S. Shkop, *Hiddushei R. Shimon Shkop, Kiddushin* 1; *Avnei Milluim* 27:6; *Mishnat Shlomo, Kiddushin* 2; R. Rothstein, supra n. 29, pp. 68-71. In Talmudic parlance, concerning the act of *kiddushin,* the woman has *semikhut da'at* (akin to "a meeting of the minds"). See *Ketubot* 56b, 82b; *Kiddushin* 48a. Consequently, based upon the woman's consent, should a man intentionally or unintentionally fail to disclose prior to their marriage a major defect (a *mum gadol*) that existed; under certain conditions the *kiddushin* may be voided and the wife may be freed without the execution of a *get.* In other words, she could argue that her consent to the marriage was predicated upon being unaware of the major flaw, and was thus undermined by it. See File no. 870175/4, Haifa Regional Beit Din, December 25, 2014.

32. *Shulhan Arukh, Even Ha-Ezer* 55:1, 6.

33. *Beit Shmuel, Even Ha-Ezer* 55:4; *Bi'ur Ha-Gra, Even Ha-Ezer* 55:9; Rema, *Even Ha-Ezer* 55:2; *Helkat Mehokeik, Even Ha-Ezer* 55:9; Rema, *Even Ha-Ezer* 61:1.

If there is no marital relationship (*ishut*) (i.e., only the act of *kiddushin* was consummated as occurred in the time of the Mishnah and Talmud, where the marriage transpired 12 months after the *kiddushin*), there is no obligation to pay maintenance until the couple is married. Hence a husband has no duty to support a wife who refuses to engage in sexual relations (*moredet*) or is found to be an adulteress. See *Tur* and *Beit Yosef, Even Ha-Ezer* 77; *Shulhan Arukh, Even Ha-Ezer* 77:2; *Piskei Din Rabbanayim* (hereafter: PDR) 4:1557, 162. As R. Moses Sofer declares: "If spousal maintenance is absent, there is no marital relationship *(ishut)*." See *Resp. Hatam Sofer, Even Ha-Ezer* 131. In other words, due to the violation of the status of being a married woman which was conferred upon her at the time of *kiddushin,* a husband's monetary obligation established subsequently by the act of marriage is voided.

On the other hand, though the monetary duties and rights of the couple only

This matter can be summed up by referencing a similar question that was posed to R. Naphtali Tzvi Berlin (Netziv) of Volozhin, where an inquirer requested of R. Berlin regarding the *kinyan* of a woman to her husband, what does this mean and for what purpose. In response, R. Berlin states:[34]

> Biblically, a man has no *kinyan* vis-à-vis his wife except for *ishut* (designation for intimacy – AYW) and notwithstanding *ishut,* a husband has no *kinyan.*

To state it differently, *kesef kiddushin* is, in actuality, the undertaking of a prohibition (a *kinyan issur*).

3. *Kinyan Kiddushin* and *Kinyan Kessef* are Two Sides of the Same Coin

To understand the import of this halakhic–metaphysical fact that she is

---

emerge with the act of marriage, there is a halakhic-legal tie (*agida bei ketzat*) created between the man and the woman with the consummation of *kiddushin*, see Tur and *Beit Yosef, Even Ha-Ezer* 69; *Helkat Mehokeik, Shulhan Arukh, Even Ha-Ezer* 69:12. The tie emerges after the execution of the *kinyan issur* which generates the status of being a married woman. As such, after the execution of *kiddushin,* should a man state that he has no interest in receiving the privilege of benefiting from a particular financial right of his prospective spouse, therefore he is empowered to renounce the right (*siluk*) before he receives the benefit. See *Resp. Ha-Rashba* 1:960, 2:132; Rema, *Even Ha-Ezer* 92:1; *Taz, Hoshen Mishpat* 209:4; Cf. *Resp. Bah* 124 who disagrees with this view.

34. *Resp. Meishiv Davar* 4:35 (and 5:72). See also *Beit Ha-Behirah, Kiddushin* 2a; *Ohr Sameach, Hilk. Ishut* 4:2; *Resp. Avnei Nezer, Even Ha-Ezer* 135:17; *Resp. Mahaneh Hayyim* 1:65; *Resp. Helkat Yoav, Even Ha-Ezer* 2; *Avnei Milluim* 42:1; *Hiddushei Ha-Rim, Kiddushin* 2a; *Resp. Seridei Eish, Kiddushin* 13; *Minhat Asher, Kiddushin* 8. Whereas R. Berlin conceptualizes the *kinyan* as an obligation of a prohibition (a *kinyan issur*) relying upon *Avnei Milluim*, Resp. 17, others argue that we are dealing with an obligation and a prohibition. See R. S. Shkop, *Hiddushei R. S. Shkop, Kiddushin* 11; R. Y. Gustman, *Kuntresei Shiurim, Kiddushin, Shiur* 1; R. Rothstein, supra n. 24, p. 63. Subsequently, in the same responsum, R. Berlin agrees with the others. Cf. *Hazon Ish, Hoshen Mishpat, Bava Kamma* 23 (28) who identifies intimacy in marriage as *kinyan ishut.*

However, with the conferral of the status of becoming married, the husband is entitled to certain financial rights. See supra n. 28. Should the husband refuse to engage in intimacy with his wife, there is a debate whether he is halakhically divested of these rights. See *Beit Ya'akov, Shulhan Arukh, Even Ha-Ezer* 77:2; *Netivot Ha-Mishpat* on *Sefer Meisharim* 23:10; PDR 1:239, 245.

identified as a designated woman for a particular man (a *mekudeshet*),[35] let's briefly review a decision handed down on October 1, 2017, by the Netanya Regional Beit Din, a *beit din* (rabbinical court) which functions in the network of the rabbinical courts (*battei din*) under Israel's Chief Rabbinate.[36] Let's see how *kesef kiddushin and kinyan issur are two sides of the same coin.*

The background of the case is the following: The female petitioner proceeded to the *beit din* in order to verify her status as a Jewess. In order to verify her Jewishness, the petitioner's mother was summoned to the *beit din*. During the proceeding, the petitioner's mother recounted that she was married Jewishly in a country under Communist rule to her first husband during 1989, and subsequently, in 1990, he immigrated to Israel. Shortly thereafter, the petitioner's mother civilly divorced her first husband and a *get* (a writ of Jewish divorce) failed to be executed. Subsequently, she immigrated to Israel and engaged in relations with a Jewish man, and she gave birth to the petitioner. Given that the petitioner's wife never received a *get*, she was still married to her first husband. As such, siring a child from an incestuous relationship, i.e., namely a forbidden relationship, labels her daughter as a halakhic bastard (a *mamzeret*).[37] The issue is whether the petitioner may be recognized by the Jewish community.[38] Clearly, if Halakhah recognizes the validity of the original *kiddushin*, should the petitioner marry the second Jewish man or another Jew, the marriage would be null and void.

Given that resolving the petitioner's personal status hinges upon the validity of her mother's initial *kiddushin*, the *beit din* inquired whether the *kiddushin* was executed properly. If it was executed properly, then the petitioner is a halakhic bastard (a *mamzeret*), whereas if the act of *kiddushin* was invalid, then the couple was never married and the petitioner was not tainted by halakhic bastardy (*mamzerut*).

Following an inquiry, the *beit din* concluded that the officiating rabbi at the *kiddushin* (*mesadeir kiddushin*) was ignorant regarding the norms of Halakhah. As a result, numerous halakhic doubts emerged regarding the validity of the *kiddushin*. Firstly, given the centrality of having nonrelatives to establish that the act of *kiddushin* transpired,[39] it was

35. J. D. Bleich, "The Metaphysics of Property Interests in Jewish Law: An Analysis of *Kinyan*," 43 *Tradition*, 49, 50 (2010); Avraham, supra n. 17, p. 118.

36. File no. 1126792/1.

37. Mishnah *Kiddushin* 3:12

38. *Devarim* 23:3.

39. *Shulhan Arukh, Even Ha-Ezer* 42:5; *Beit Shmuel, Even Ha-Ezer* 42:16; *Helkat Mehokeik, Even Ha-Ezer* 42:12.

unclear whether relatives served as witnesses at the ceremony. Secondly, even assuming that nonrelatives served as witnesses, there exists Ritva's view that in the absence of designating the witnesses, if both eligible and ineligible witnesses are present under the wedding canopy, that the testimony is invalid.[40] Thirdly, even if they were nonrelatives, there is a fear that they were sinners and therefore disqualified to give testimony. On the other hand, possibly these men are to be subsumed in the halakhic category of "a baby that was kidnapped by non-Jews" (i.e., a Jew without a formal Jewish education who transgressed the Shabbat by working lest he could not support his family). However, in our case the witnesses were well aware of the warnings of the Torah, including the submitting of false testimony. Fourthly, there is doubt if the couple understood that the act of *kiddushin* is implemented through the giving of the ring or *kesef* by the man to the woman accompanied by the recitation by the man of a *kiddushin* formula, or if they viewed it merely as part of the ceremony. Finally, there is a doubt whether the ring or *kesef* was given by the man to the woman before his recitation of the *kiddushin* formula. In short, emerging from our case there are five factual doubts regarding the validity of the *kiddushin*.[41] In sum, the various requirements which impart validity to the execution of the *kinyan kesef* and confer the status of *eishet ish* may have not occurred. As such, the talmudic prerequisite prior to marriage of "that he prohibits her to all as *hekdesh*" may have not materialized through this couple's act of *kiddushin*. In effect, the *kinyan issur* which is supposed to confer the status of *eishet ish* upon the petitioner's wife never materialized through the *kiddushei kesef* performed by her husband.

Concerning where there is a doubt regarding a matter, the rule is that in a biblical (a *de'oraita*) matter a stringent approach is required, whereas a lenient approach is indicated in rabbinic (*de-rabbanan*) matter.[42] That being said, what is considered a doubt regarding halakhic betrothal (a *safek kiddushin*)? Clearly, we are well aware of the stringency related to the prohibition of *eishet ish* which serves as the primary reluctance to invalidate a *kiddushin* and invoke the concept of *safek kiddushin*. However, the policy to act stringently in a *safek kiddushin* is not a necessary derivative from the rule that in a *de'oraita* (biblical) matter a

40. *Hiddushei Ha-Ritva*, *Gittin* 18b, *Kiddushin* 43a.

41. The Hebrew word *safek* means doubt. Halakhah distinguishes between an uncertainty as what the Halakhah ought to be (*safek de'dina*) and a doubt concerning a factual uncertainty (*safek de'metzi'ut*). Our case deals with the latter type of doubt.

42. Talmud Bavli, *Betzah* 3b; *Avodah Zarah* 7a.

stringent approach is mandated. In contradistinction to this rule, there is a rule that we operate with a factual-halakhic presumption regarding a particular fact or state of affairs (a *hazakah*). As such, argues the Netanya Beit Din, if there is a factual doubt regarding the validity of the *kiddushin,* we presume that the woman's earlier status as an unmarried woman (a *penuyah*) still exists on a biblical level.[43] In other words, the *kinyan issur* which entails the man's duty to engage in intimacy with his spouse disappears. Relying implicitly on precedential opinion,[44] the *beit din* relied upon this line of reasoning as a supporting argument (a *senif)* in arriving at their judgment. Secondly, relying upon numerous authorities[45], the *beit din* contends that once you have a double doubt (*sefek sefeika)* and operate with the presumption that she is an unmarried woman, then if there is a suspicion of *mamzerut,* one can permit the petitioner to marry. Furthermore, concludes the Netanya Beit Din, since she is a *safek mamzer* and she is prohibited rabbinically, she can marry.

4. Conclusion

In conclusion, our presentation reflects the words of the late Israeli Supreme Court Justice Moshe Silberg who incisively observes:[46]

> In the Talmudic dialectic there is no distinction – from the standpoint of the delimitation of concepts and their manner of functioning – whether the issue under discussion deals with money matters, or whether it deals with Temple property or Levitical purity... One... finds... all the well-established procedural details that one finds in the order of Damages (tort law – AYW) and the order of Women (family law – AYW) – the same dialectic, the same approach, the same conception, the same classification...

The interweaving of the "legal" (the employment of the *kinyan* denoting an obligation) and the "religious" (the conferral of the status of the prohibition of being a married woman) in the concept of *kinyan issur* provides

43. Ran on the Rif, *Kiddushin* 5b; *Mishneh Le-Melekh, Mishneh Torah, Hilk. Tumat Tzara'at* 2:1; *Resp. Masat Binyamin* 50; *Resp. R. Akiva Eiger* 1:37.

44. *Resp. Maharashdam, Even Ha-Ezer* 11; *Resp. Ha-Ridvaz* 1:56.

45. See responsa cited in *Resp. Yabia Omer*, 6, *Even Ha-Ezer* 6:5, 7.

46. M. Silberg, *Talmudic Law and the Modern State,* N.Y.: The Burning Bush Press, 1973, pp 65-66.

an example of *kiddushei kesef* in general and of the dynamics of *safek kiddushin* in particular.

Addendum

Based upon the foregoing, the act of *kiddushin* confers the status upon the woman that she is a married woman (an *eishet ish*), which subsequently will be transformed into one of the husband's duties upon the completion of the act of marriage (i.e. cohabitation) rather than the execution of the *kinyan* of *kiddushei kesef* serving as a means for acquiring ownership of one's spouse.

As such, the dignity of human beings (*kevod ha-beriyyot)* ought to be one of the governing halakhic norms in our social relations.[47] Thus, a husband has a duty to respect his wife as a member of the human race. Additionally, as a husband it is incumbent upon him to respect her more than he respects himself.[48] Whereas various halakhic guidelines have been established relating to the duty of *kevod ha-beriyyot,* there is a paucity of sources practically detailing how to demonstrate in positive terms one's respect for one's wife. Clearly, spousal respect requires intimate and individualistic answers that emerge from the singularity of persons and their relationships to each other, as well as their fused existence. It seems that Halakhah has left it up to the husband to determine how to translate into practical terms respect for his spouse.

On the other hand, there are specific acts of dishonor, of demeaning a wife's persona, such as threatening to assault her or actual battery, which entail a diminution of her honor as a person.[49] Consequently,

47. Talmud Bavli, *Berakhot* 19b; *Shabbat* 94b; *Bava Kamma* 79b; *Menahot* 37b–38a; Talmud Yerushalmi, *Berakhot* 6b; *Kilayim* 32a.

48. Talmud Bavli *Shabbat* 59b; *Bava Metzia* 59a; *Yevamot* 62b; *Nedarim* 51a; *Hullin* 84b; *Shulhan Arukh Hoshen Mishpat* 228:3.

49. *Resp. Maharam of Rothenburg,* Cremona Edition, 291; *Resp.Ha-Rashba Ha-Meyuhasot La-Ramban,* 102; *Resp. Ha-Rashba* 4:113; *Resp. Binyamin Ze'ev,* 88; *Beit Yosef, Tur, Even Ha-Ezer* 74; *Sefer Ha-Agudah, Ketubot* 172; *Resp. Hayyim Ve-Shalom* 2:36; *Resp. Perah Matteh Aharon* 1:60. Cf. numerous *authorities* who sanction wife-beating in order to prevent the commission of a transgression (*le-afrushei me-issura*), should a wife be delinquent in fulfilling her marital duties or needlessly curses her husband. See *Resp. Terumat Ha-Deshen* 218; *Resp. Ha-Ridvaz* 888; *Mishneh Torah, Hilk. Ishut* 21:10; *Rema, Shulhan Arukh Even Ha-Ezer* 154:3. Whether such conduct is permissible today is beyond the scope of our presentation. Suffice it to say that there are authorities who prohibit assaulting a wife. Furthermore, even verbal violence is prohibited, See Talmud Bavli, *Bava Metzia* 59a; *Resp. Ha-Tashbetz* 2:8.

just as battery (*habbala*) involves transgressing a negative Torah commandment,[50] similarly, spousal battery is a violation of *habbala*[51] and is subject to criminal sanctions.[52] In short, whereas Halakhah has given latitude for a husband to determine how to translate his duty of spousal respect into practical behavior, nonetheless, in situations of violating her persona by means of assault, Halakhah sets out guidelines for how to address such behavior.

The seriousness of the *prohibition (issur)* of battery expresses itself in a husband's liability for injuring his wife while engaging in conjugal relations (*onah*).[53] The duty of a husband to engage in *onah* is *mi-deoraita.*[54] Lest one argue that engagement in a *mitzvah* exempts one from responsibility from injury caused during its performance, Halakhah states otherwise.[55] Hence, Hazon Ish contends that engagement in the *mitzvah* of *onah* does not serve as a defense.[56] Even if the husband unintentionally injured his wife due to losing self-control, i.e., *ones,* nevertheless, regarding any assault against another person, a person is always deemed forewarned (*adam mu'ad le-olam*)[57]

Consequently, it is no surprise that numerous authorities argue that it is the husband's responsibility to foresee the possibility of potential injury and therefore, if injury nevertheless transpired, he is negligent.[58] Similarly, a husband who argues that he lost self-control and therefore

50. *Devarim* 25:3; *Maimonides, Sefer ha-Mitzvot, mitzvat lo ta'aseh* 300; *Shulhan Arukh, Hoshen Mishpat* 420:1.

51. *Shulhan Arukh, Even Ha-Ezer* 154:3, *Rema,* ad locum. Moreover, the batterer is invalid to be a witness in a *beit din* proceeding. See *Shulhan Arukh, Hoshen Mishpat* 34:4; *Resp. Mahari Weil,* 28,87; *Resp. Ha-Mabit,* 1:291; *Resp. Maharit,* vol. 2, *Even Ha-Ezer* 43.

52. *Beit Yosef, Tur, Even Ha-Ezer* 154; *Darkhei Moshe, Tur, Even Ha-Ezer* 154:20.

53. *Shulhan Arukh, Even Ha-Ezer* 63 (end), Hoshen Mishpat 421:12

54. *Shemot* 21:10; *Tur, Even Ha-Ezer* 69; *Shulhan Arukh, Even Ha-Ezer* 69:6.

55. Talmud Yerushalmi, *Bava Kamma* 6:13; *Shulhan Arukh, Yoreh Deah* 340, *Hoshen Mishpat* 418:12; *Resp. Havot Yair,* 207; *Resp. Be'er Sarim,* 1:10. For exceptions to the rule, see *Mishneh Torah, Hilk. Hovel u-Mazik* 6:8; *Shulhan Arukh Hoshen Mishpat* 359:4.

56. *Hazon Ish, Bava Kamma* 11:21.

57. *Shulhan Arukh, Hoshen Mishpat* 378:1; *Hazon Ish,* supra n.56. Cf. *Tosafot, Bava Kamma* 27a, s.v. *u-Shemuel amar*; *Tosafot, Bava Metzia* 42a, s.v. *amar Shemuel.*

Should a husband unintentionally abstain from conjugal relations and his spouse becomes emotionally distressed regarding the situation, he violates Halakhah. See *Resp. Maharam Alsheich* 40; *PDR* 18:1, 20 (R. Elyashiv); File no. 860977-1, Netanya Regional Beit Din, *Plonit v. Ploni,* May 20, 2013. Cf. *Resp. Ha-Mabit* 3:131 in the name of *Maimonides.*

58. *Piskei Ha-Rosh, Bava Kamma* 2:10.

assaulted his wife will also be held responsible for his behavior. As Shulhan Arukh, *Sma,* and R. Shlomo Luria note,[59] if a husband is liable for any injury caused to his spouse during *onah, a fortiori,* should he force her to have conjugal relations against her will, he has committed *"habbala"* and he is therefore liable in tort (*nezikin)* damages.[60] A husband must control his desires and neither injure his wife nor rape her under any circumstances. Moreover, neither the establishment of marriage nor a mutual agreement between spouses to sanction a husband's assault of his wife, even for her own personal enjoyment, may serve as grounds for a husband's exemption from liability for any ensuing damage.[61] Any agreement between two individuals to be a subject of battery is prohibited.[62] *A fortiori,* he should not force himself upon his wife.[63] In sum, according to Halakhah – a wife is a person rather than a piece of chattel.

---

59. *Shulhan Arukh, Hoshen Mishpat* 421:12; *Sma, Hoshen Mishpat* 421:20; *Yam Shel Shlomo, Bava Kamma* 3:21.

60. *Hazon Ish, Hoshen Mishpat* 19:2; *Resp. Divrei Yaziv, Even Ha-Ezer* 77:3. Even if the injury was unintentional, he is liable for *nezek* and *tza'ar*. See Talmud Bavli, *Menahot* 49a; Talmud Yerushalmi, *Gittin* 5:5; *Kesef Mishneh, Mishneh Torah, Hilk. Ma'aholot Asurot* 13:28; *Resp. Hatan Sofer, Hoshen Mishpat* 24; *Shulhan Arukh, Even Ha-Ezer* 83:1.

Though one is exempt from liability for shame (*boshet)* if one unintentionally rapes one's wife (see *Tur, Hoshen Mishpat* 421; *Shulhan Arukh, Hoshen Mishpat* 421:12, *Sma, Shulhan Arukh, Hoshen Mishpat* 421:20), nonetheless meting out damages for shame as a punitive measure (*migdar milta*), is permissible. See *Shulhan Arukh, Hoshen Mishpat* 420:38.

For the prohibition against spousal rape, see *Mishneh Torah, Hilk. De'ot* 5:4, *Hilk. Ishut* 14:8, 15:17, 21:12; *Tur, Even Ha-Ezer* 25, *Shulhan Arukh, Orah Hayyim* 240:3, *Even Ha-Ezer* 25:2; *Magen Avraham Shulhan Arukh, Orah Hayyim* 240:7; *Beit Shmuel, Orah Hayyim* 77:4; *Resp. Divrei Yatziv, Even Ha-Ezer* 77.

If a wife is rebellious (a *moredet* who refuses to engage in conjugal relations) it is subject to debate whether coercion is permissible. See *Mordekhai, Kiddushin* 530; *Atzei Arazim, Even Ha-Ezer* 25:1; *Piskei Ha-Rosh, Ketubot* 5:34 in the name of *Rabbeinu Tam*; *Tosafot Rid, Ketuvot* 64a; *Mabit, Kiryat Sefer, Hilk Ishut* 14.

61. *Resp. Revid Ha-Zahav* 42:3.

62. Talmud Bavli, *Bava Kamma* 93a; *Resp. Ha-Rosh* 68:10; *Shulhan Arukh, Hoshen Mishpat* 421:12. Nonetheless, though there exists a prohibition to agree to be a victim of battery, should battery occur with the consent of the victim, the batterer will be exempt from liability. See *Bava Kamma*, op. cit.; *Tosafot Ketubot* 56b, s.v. *harei* in the name of R. Elhanan,

63. *Taz, Divrei David, Devarim* 6:17 ("since the body of the wife belongs to her"); *Shulhan Arukh, Orah Hayyim* 240:3, *Even Ha-Ezer* 25:2

Chapter 2

Who Has the Authority to Void a Marriage: Giants of the Generation (*Gedolei Ha'dor*) or Qualified Rabbinic Authorities?

ON 5 TAMMUZ 5778 (June 18, 2018), the Haifa Regional Beit Din, a *beit din* (a rabbinical court) under Israel's Chief Rabbinate composed of Rabbis Avraham Shloush, Daniel Edrei and Samuel Hazan, handed down a majority opinion supported by Rabbis S. Amar and B.Z. Boyaron which invalidated the two designated witnesses who testified that the act of *kiddushin* (Jewish betrothal ceremony) actually happened and who by their presence at the ceremony usually impart validity to the act of engagement. In short, in the wake of a husband's *get* recalcitrance the marriage was voided by the *beit din* and thus, she was able to remarry without the execution of a writ of Jewish divorce (a *get).*[1] Less than a year later, ten Israeli rabbis submitted written opinions explaining their halakhic (Jewish legal) opposition to that judgment.[2]

One of the critics was Rabbi Avraham Sherman, a retired *dayan* (a

1. In other words, the case addresses whether one can void a halakhic betrothal (*bittul kiddushin*), which we are loosely labeling voiding a marriage rather than annul a halakhic betrothal (*hafka'at kiddushin*). See this writer's *Rabbinic Authority: The Vision & the Reality – Beit Din Decisions in English* (hereinafter: *Rabbinic Authority*), vol. 3, p. 135, n. 1. See also; File no. 905457/10, Tel Aviv-Yaffo Regional Beit Din, September 11, 2017, which astutely distinguishes between the two concepts. For an elucidation of the difference between these two concepts, see *Rabbinic Authority*, vol. 5, 325-326.

There are authorities who utilize the term of annulling a marriage when in actuality the marriage is being voided. As such, in their minds there is one type of annulment (which we label voiding) which nullifies a priori the act of *kiddushin,* and there is a second type of annulment which is predicated upon the notion that the *kiddushin* actually was established and ex post facto arbiters are empowered to annul it. See R. She'ar Y. Cohen, "*Get* Coercion in Contemporary Times," (Hebrew) 11 *Tehumin* 195, 199 (5750).

2. Opposition papers were bound into a pamphlet entitled *Al Shever Bat Ami,* Adar 1 5779, third edition.

rabbinic arbitrator) from the Beit Din ha-Rabbani Hagadol in Jerusalem. In short, given the fact that the three *dayanim* (rabbinic arbitrators) who served on this case were not Torah giants according to R. Sherman they were invalid to either address the issue and/or render a decision regarding this matter of personal status.[3]

In this essay we will present the support for the view that only Torah giants are authorized to void a marriage, and in opposition to this posture we will submit the dissenting opinion, and attempt to resolve this issue.

1. Those Who Advocate that Only Torah Giants Possess the Authority to Void a Marriage

a. The Rabbinic Legislation of a Conditional *Kiddushin*

Among the possible precedents that support this view,[4] R. Sherman argued that there was a major late nineteen century precedent which offered reasoning to corroborate his posture. In 1884, legislation was enacted in France which established that its judges would address a marital dispute and should the spouse's (or spouses') arguments be valid reasons

3. *Al Shever Bat Ami*, 43-52. For an expansive treatment of this topic, see Avraham Sherman, "The Authority of the Torah Giants in Matter of Personal Status and Conversion" (Hebrew), 30 *Tehumin* 5770, 163. Furthermore, R. Yosef Henkin argues that only Torah giants may void the marriage of a classical *agunah* in a situation of *umdana*. See *Otzar Haposkim*, vol. 4, 354.

4. For the requirement to enlist the authority of *gedolei ha'dor* regarding resolving classical *agunah* cases where the husband is missing, see *Resp. Ha-Rivash* 377; *Resp. Bah* 79; *Resp. Sam Hayyei* 53; *Resp. Hemdat Shlomo Even Ha-Ezer* 33.

Alternatively, one can review the above responsa and arrive at the conclusion that this is a practice (a *nohag*) rather than a requirement for a rabbinic arbiter to enlist the approval of Torah giants. See infra, n. 56.

Seemingly, R. Mordekhai Breisch agrees with this position, see *Resp. Helkat Ya'akov, Even Ha-Ezer* 38. Upon closer scrutiny, he invoked their authority only due to the fact that the rabbis in his day would only act stringently and therefore there was a need to have *gedolei ha'dor* address the situation due to their readiness to render a decision based upon lenient opinions. In fact, in a subsequent ruling, R. Breisch clearly states that being a rabbinic authority (a *moreh horo'ah*) suffices when dealing with an issue of *get* recalcitrance (*igun*). See *Resp. Helkat Ya'akov, Even Ha-Ezer* 58.

For a failure to distinguish between a *moreh hora'ah* and a *gadol hador* and thus draw erroneous conclusions regarding the position of certain authorities regarding our issue, see R. A. Sherman, "The Exclusive Jurisdiction of Torah Giants and its Authorities in Matters of Conversion and *Get* Recalcitrance" (Hebrew), *Kenes Ha-dayanim* 5769, 178, 181.

for executing a divorce, they would be authorized to dissolve the marriage even against the husband's will, and the man and woman were free to remarry. In light of this new legislation of civil divorce and in the wake of instances where wives in the French community became *agunot* due to their inability to receive a *get* from their husbands, upon the counsel of Rabbi Eliyahu Hazan of Alexandria, Egypt,[5] in 1887 some members of the French rabbinate introduced the solution of a conditional marriage where the husband would state to his spouse:[6]

> You are betrothed to me, should the civil judges divorce us and I will not give you a divorce in accordance to the religion of Moshe and Yisrael, this betrothal shall not be effective.

In short, the execution of this *kiddushin al tenai*, conditional marriage,[7] and the implementation of this conditional marriage in effect results in the voiding of the marriage and obviates the need for a *get*.

Rabbi Michal Weil of France and formerly "Grand Rabbi" of Algiers suggested that wives would be considered *halakhically* divorced based upon a constellation of factors: namely the power of the rabbinate to annul the betrothal (*hafka'at kiddushin*), recognition of a civil divorce as well as reliance upon the opinions of Rabbi Akiva and Rabbi Shimon ben Gamliel which validated a Jewish divorce executed in non-Jewish courts.[8] Various renowned rabbis from different lands, including Chief Rabbi Zadok Kahn of Paris, Rabbi Shalom Schwadron, Rabbi Elhanan Spektor,[9] and Rabbi Naftali Tzvi Berlin of Yeshivat Volozhin opposed in writing the propriety of such a solution.[10] At the request of Rabbi Hayyim Grodzinsky, Rabbi Yehuda Lubetsky of Paris, France, accompanied by the assistance of Rabbi Moshe Weiskopf of Paris, France, who collected over thirty letters from rabbinical authorities who rejected this

5. *Resp. Talumot Lev 3:49.*

6. *Ein Tenai Be'Nissu'in, p. 4.*

7. Formally speaking the condition is linked to the establishment of *kiddushin*, betrothal. However, today, as is the case for centuries the act of marriage (*nissu'in*), marriage transpires "on the heels of the act of *kiddushin*," therefore we are addressing simultaneously the issue whether we can condition the validity of the *nissu'in*. See *Resp. Terumat Ha-Deshen* 223; *Resp. Hikrei Lev Even Ha-Ezer* 58 in the name of Rosh. Consequently, it is unsurprising that the collection of the letters which addresses the propriety of the French conditional *kiddushin* executed at the time of *kiddushin* is entitled *Ein Tenai be'Nissu'in*.

8. A. Freiman, *Seder Kiddushin Ve-Nissu'in*, Jerusalem, 1964, p. 389, n. 1.

9. *Ein Tenai Be'Nissu'in, p. 4.*

10. *Resp. Meishiv Davar* 3:49.

solution as well as others, accompanied by the signatures of dozens of rabbis who opposed the *tenai,* their response was published in 1930 in a book entitled *Ein Tenai be'Nissu'in.*[11]

In addition to the halakhic objections to this rabbinic enactment communicated by some of the above cited rabbis who are *gedolei ha'dor,*[12] Rabbi Sherman cites the objection of R. Menachem Krakowski, Vilna *dayan,* who states the following:[13]

> This matter, which deals with a married woman and halakhic bastardy (*mamzerut*), one cannot say that this a matter which relates to only France, the place of the authors of the legislation but also to the entire world, to all of Israel from one end of the land to the other end of the land obviously. I don't understand at all how the French Rabbis legislated this matter without asking the giants of Israel, the giants of the generation throughout the scattered lands of the Diaspora...

In other words, this situation is a public matter and in the wake of the absence of normative Halakhah as reflected in the classical restatements of the *Mishneh Torah, Shulhan Arukh* and commentaries, one requires a broad comprehension of Halakhah, and as such this dictates that the inquiry and its resolution be performed by the greatest Torah scholars. Analogously, voiding a marriage which entails freeing a wife without a *get* relates to the entire Jewish world, consequently R. Sherman argues such issues ought to be resolved by Torah giants.

Consequently, it is unsurprising that Rabbi Hayyim Grodzinsky, a *gadol ha'dor* in his own right and opponent of annulling marriages,[14] said that if there are reasons for the above legislation which have yet to be publicized; it is incumbent that the reasoning be communicated to R. David Friedman, a *gadol ha'dor* and a presiding *dayan* of Pinsk-Karlin communities for his evaluation.

In sum, the authority of Torah giants is not limited to this issue of a conditional marriage but extends to situations of the classical *agunah* where the husband's whereabouts are unknown.[15] To state it differently,

11. For a review of the halakhic and meta-halakhic reasoning memorialized in these letters, see this writer's *Rabbinic Authority,* vol. 4, pp. 21-43.

12. See this writer's review, ibid.

13. *Ein Tenai Be'Nissu'in, p. 20.*

14. *Ein Tenai Be'Nissu'in, p. 16.*

15. *Rivash,* supra n. 4; *Bah,* supra n. 4; *Sam Hayyei,* supra n.4; *Hemdat Shlomo,* supra n. 4.

in effect the scope of the authority of a Torah giant extends beyond addressing the propriety of a rabbinic enactment and enters into the realm of that which is forbidden and that which is permissible (*issur ve-heter*) which encompasses voiding a marriage regardless as to whether we are dealing with a conditional marriage or a marriage which was established by invalid witnesses.

The emerging question is: on what basis did these *dayanim* of the Haifa Regional Beit Din void the marriage and on what grounds did these rabbis reject their ruling? Clearly, we are dealing with a matter of voiding a marriage and seemingly, we require such a matter to be resolved by *gedolei ha'dor*. And it is not our impression that these arbiters are recognized as *gedolei ha'dor*. And should a few have earned such recognition, what about the other rabbis and *dayanim* – how could they engage in voiding a marriage or object to voiding it?

b. The Source for the Authority of Torah Giants to Void a Marriage and Their Scope

Furthermore, elaborating upon the Biblical verse, "According to the Torah that they instruct you... you shall not deviate (*lo tasur*) from the word they shall tell you, neither to the right nor to the left," R. Aharon Ha-Levi of Barcelona, Spain, observes:[16]

> And this divine commandment is applicable during the time that the Supreme Rabbinical Court is in Jerusalem... And this duty encompasses to do in every period the directive of the arbitrator. In other words, the giant Scholar... And one who transgresses this and fails to listen to the advice of renown individuals of his generation in matters of Torah wisdom as they instruct, nullifies this positive commandment.

Following in the footsteps of R. Aharon Ha-Levi, R. Sherman states:[17]

16. *Sefer Ha-Hinnukh, Mitzvah* 495. See also *Mitzvah* 496. Cf. *Resp. Yesh Ma'ayan* 13; R. Chajes, *Torat Neviim, Ma'amar Lo Tasur*; *Resp. Meishiv Davar* 43; *Kovetz Shiurim, Kuntres Divrei Soferim*, 2:3-4; *Resp. Helkat Ya'akov Yoreh De'ah* 17 in the name of *Havot Yair*; R. Perlow, *Sefer Ha-Hinnukh*, Machon Yerushalayim ed., *Mitzvah* 495, note 3 in the name of all early authorities (*Rishonim*).

17. Sherman, supra n. 3, at 165.

Addressing the case of a get from a man in a permanent vegetative state whose wife was permitted to remarry by the Safed Regional Din composed of qualified rabbinic authorities, following in the footsteps of Rabbi Sherman, Rabbi M. Mordekhai

> Since the majority of Scholars and Torah giants of the generation observe who the giants are in their generation, and Jewish community in its entirety perceive them as the ones (i.e., the Torah scholars – AYW) who determine which individuals are renowned Torah authorities, therefore their decision is determinative. As a result, these renowned decisors on their own became the rabbinical court of the Jewish community and the Jewish communities, Torah scholars, rabbinical courts and rabbis are subservient to them (i.e., the rabbinical court – AYW).

The Torah giants are those who have the exclusive jurisdiction to address matters of marriage, divorce and conversion which impact the Jewish community. In Rabbi Sherman's mind, they are the individuals who determine issues of civil divorce, *mamzerut,* rabbinical legislation relating to marriage and divorce, voiding marriage and accepting mitzvot during conversion.[18] They derive their authority and power not from institutional advancement, but from rabbinic and communal acceptance.

Farbstein of Hebron Yeshiva in Jerusalem writes a letter to the three dayanim and states:

> It appears that you did not understand the purpose of my public statement on this matter. The intent was not to discuss the halakhic details with you but to express my anguish and protest on the great wrong of the three rabbinical court judges who are not among the leading scholars of our generation and arrogantly decided to rely on their own judgment to permit a married woman [to marry another man] in a way that none of our great rabbis have ever done, and to publicize the matter only after the fact. Realize that even great leaders of the generation, like R. Akiva Eiger, and others, did not rely on themselves–they made their rulings conditional on the approval of other Torah authorities. Before you actually issued the get, you should have written your conclusions and reasoning, and sent them to some of the leading halakhic authorities of the generation for approval.

18. *Piskei Ha-Rosh, Bava Kamma* 9:5; *Yam shel Shlomo, Bava Kamma* 9:6-7; *Shulhan Arukh, Hoshen Mishpat* 2:1, Rema, ad. locum.; *Resp. Maharik, shoresh* 188; *Resp. Hatam Sofer, Even Ha-Ezer* 1:108; File no. 1313311/7, Be'air Sheva Regional Beit Din, March 21, 2023, in the name of R. Yeruham, *Mordekhai, Maharbil, Resp. Re'im, Resp. Sheil u-Meishiv, Resp. Hatam Sofer,* and *Maharam Schick.*

Certain matters which deal with the maintenance of public order are subject to debate whether lay judges are sufficient, or one requires a Torah giant to address the matter. See this writer's *Rabbinic Authority,* vol. 2, 88, n. 41.

2. Those Who Argue that Every Qualified Rabbi May Void a Marriage

To state it differently, in the wake of the lapse of the presence of the Supreme Rabbinical Court (the Sanhedrin) prior to the closure of the Talmud, R. S. Daichovsky argues that the resolution of halakhic issues was continued in the hands of the rabbinic arbiters (*morei hora'ah).*[19] On the other hand, R. Sherman contends that the Supreme Rabbinical Court was replaced by *gedolei ha'dor* who possessed exclusive jurisdiction to address matters in marriage, divorce and conversion which impact the entire Jewish community such as addressing the propriety of civil marriage, halakhic bastardy, rabbinic legislation dealing with marriage and divorce, voiding a marriage and acceptance of *mitzvot* in a proper fashion during conversion. Who were these Torah giants? R. Sherman states:[20]

> Since the majority of Torah scholars and Torah giants of the generation observe who are the giants are in their generation, and the Jewish community in its entirety perceive them as the ones (i.e., the Torah scholars – AYW) who determine which individuals are renowned Torah authorities, therefore their decision is determinative. As a result, these renowned decisors on their own became the rabbinical court of the Jewish community...

Though there are no extant records of lists of Torah giants in our communities throughout the generations, nevertheless, in numerous instances in the writings of Torah scholars one will find identification of a certain authority as a *gadol ha'dor* or *gadol Yisrael* (a renowned decisor of Israel). For example, R. Y. Spektor, R. D. Friedman of Karlin, R. M. Feinstein, R. Z. Frank and R. O. Yosef have been respectively identified

---

19. S. Daichovsky, "*Da'at Torah in Halakhah*" (Hebrew), 30 *Tehumin* 174, 5770. See also, S. Daichovsky, "The Duty to Comply with Torah Scholars in Contemporary Times" (Hebrew), 6 *Kevodah shel Torah*, 60-65.

For the Talmudic and post-talmudic precedent for this position, see Talmud Bavli *Berakhot* 4b, *Eruvin* 21b, *Yevamot* 20a; Maimonides, *Sefer Ha-Mitzvot, shoresh* 1 (Cf. *Mishneh Torah, Hilk. Mamrim* 1:1-2); *Resp. Ha-Rashba* 2:322; *Sefer Ha-Hinnukh*, supra n. 16; *Resp. Havot Yair* 126 (Cf. *Resp. Helkat Ya'akov Yoreh Deah* 17:2); *Resp. Noda Be-Yehudah*, 2 *Even Ha-Ezer* 120; *Resp. Radakh, Bayit* 22, *Heder* 14; *Resp. Hayyim Be-Yad*, 1; *Resp. Hikkekei Lev*, 2, *Hoshen Mishpat* 14. For additional sources, see supra n. 16.

20. Sherman, supra n. 3.

by Torah scholars as *gedolei ha'dor.*[21] Additionally, R. S. Schwadron and R. E. Klatzkin have been labeled by a Torah scholar as *gedolei Yisrael.*[22] As noted by R. Sherman, once an individual is identified by a Torah scholar (or by many Torah scholars) as a Torah giant, subsequently the community endorses their approval by viewing him as a Torah giant and they become the authority(ies) to address certain issues which affect the entire Jewish community. In other words, we are referring to a *gadol ha-dor* who is bona fide Torah scholar endowed with judicial authority and thus readily distinguishable from the popular understanding of a *gadol ha'dor* memorialized in Talmudic and post-Talmudic sources as an individual who has been chosen by a sect of the Orthodox Jewish community as their communal leader.[23]

In sum, jurisdiction to render a judgment regarding the propriety of the act of *kiddushin* resides in the hands of Torah giants who are qualified rabbinic authorities who possess knowledge which spans the four

21. *Resp. Ein Yitzhak,* Introduction, Machon Jerusalem ed.; *Ein Tenai Be'Nissu'in,* p.28; *Resp. Tzitz Eliezer* 18:63; *Resp. Minhat Asher* 1:84.

22. *Minhat Asher,* supra n. 21.

23. Regarding a Torah giant as a Torah scholar, see *Sefer Ha-Hinnukh,* supra n. 16; *Resp. Re'em* 57; *Shulhan Arukh Hoshen Mishpat* 2; *Resp. Noda Be-Yehuda, Mahadura Tinyana, Hoshen Mishpat* 1; *Yam shel Shlomo, Bava Kamma* 10:10; *Hazon Ish, Emunah U-Bitahon,* chapter 30. See further supra n. 3 and M. Sagron, *No'am Amorei,* 5. For Torah giants dealing with communal matters, see H. Sha'anan, *"Da'at Torah",* (Hebrew) 12 *Tehumin* 5751, 171.

For the judicial capacity of a Torah giant, see *Piskei Ha-Rosh, Bava Kamma* 9:5, *Sanhedrin* 3:41; *Mordekhai Sanhedrin* 709; *Yam shel Shlomo, Bava Kamma* 9:7; *Resp. Maharik, shoresh* 163; *Bah, Tur Hoshen Mishpat* 2, s.v. *vekatav*; *Shulhan Arukh Hoshen Mishpat* 2:1, *Rema,* ibid.; *Gidulei Terumah, Sha'ar* 62:6; *Re'em,* op. cit.

Concerning the popular understanding of a *gadol ha'dor* as a communal leader see Talmud Bavli *Pesahim* 49b; *Sotah* 12a; *Kiddushin* 32b; *Resp. Ha-Rosh* 85:5-6; *Shulhan Arukh Even Ha-Ezer* 2:6; Rema, *Hoshen Mishpat* 290:1; *Bi'ur Ha-Gra, Hoshen Mishpat* 290:7.

Regarding his authority to establish a halakhically valid custom (*minhag*), see *Resp. Yabia Omer,* 1 *Orah Hayyim* 40(14), 2, *Orah Hayyim* 25(9), 3 *Orah Hayyim* 34, 5, *Orah Hayyim* 9(5), 43(9), 10, *Orah Hayyim* 21(8).

Concerning his authority in matters of guardianship (*apotro'pos*) see *Resp. Ha-Rosh* 85:5-6; *Rema, Hoshen Mishpat* 280:1; *Resp. Maharashdam Hoshen Mishpat* 424.

For additional sources regarding the two types of a Torah giant, see *No'am Amorei,* op. cit.; File no. 884268/1, Supreme Rabbinical Court, November 13, 2019.

Finally, in our contemporary setting there is no one rabbi who possesses power to impose their halakhic opinions on other individuals and/or communities. As R. Feinstein notes, the notion of one overarching community does not exist. See *Resp. Iggerot Moshe, Orah Hayyim* 1:159.

sections of *Shulhan Arukh* and are endowed with extensive reasoning skills.[24] Again, given R. Sherman's view, on what basis did these *dayanim* of the Haifa Regional Beit Din feel authorized to void the marriage and on what grounds did these other ten rabbis feel empowered to reject their ruling?

To fully understand what is transpiring here, we need to present another model of rabbinic authority who decides Halakhah. We may extrapolate from the Talmudic description of the ordination of Rav and Rabbah bar Hana that the right to adjudicate that which is forbidden and that which is permitted (*issur ve-heter*) is the right to teach or to provide guidance (*lehorot*).[25] Consequently, it is unsurprising to find continuous usage in rabbinic literature of the term, "a student who has attained the ability to issue rulings". As R. Yosef Karo states:[26]

> A student who has not attained the ability to render judgments and nevertheless does so, this is an evil, primitive fool.... Any Torah scholar who has attained the ability to render judgments and does not – this individual withholds Torah and places stumbling blocks before the public...

"The ability to render judgments" is powerfully articulated earlier by R. Asher b. Yehiel (better known by the acronym: Rosh) in the following fashion, and subsequently endorsed by Rema:[27]

24. For an understanding of the skills of a qualified rabbinic authority, see *infra*, text accompanying notes 24-39.

25. Contemporary Ashkenazic rabbinic ordination is defined as receiving permission from your rabbi to rabbinate. See Talmud Bavli *Sanhedrin* 5a-b; *Resp. Ha-Rivash* 271; *Rema, Yoreh Deah* 242:14.

26. Talmud Bavli *Sotah* 22a; *Tur Yoreh Deah* 242, *Hoshen Mishpat* 10; *Shulhan Arukh, Yoreh De'ah* 242:13-14, Rema, ad. locum.; *Tur Hoshen Mishpat* 10; *Shulhan Arukh Hoshen Mishpat* 10:3; *Bi'ur Ha-Gra Yoreh Deah* 242:24.

See *Mishneh Torah, Hilk. Talmud Torah* 5:3-4; *Resp. Ha-Rashba* 1:253; *Resp. Maharashdam, Hoshen Mishpat* 1:10; *Resp. Hikrei Lev, Orah Hayyim* 96; *Resp. Hemdah Genuzah*, 47-51; *Resp. Sheilat Ya'avetz* 1:5.

Lest one contend that one requires practical experience in rendering decisions by observing an experienced rabbi (see *Torat Rabbi Yisrael Mi-Salant*, 150), note that no such requirement is memorialized in *Shulhan Arukh*. Nevertheless, upon issuing any decision including a ruling which is not found in the *Shulhan Arukh* or another major compendium (a *hora'ah* – see *Shulhan Arukh Yoreh Deah* 242:8), the arbiter must possess fear of God lest he respond incorrectly. See *Pri Megadim, Mishbetzot Zahav, Orah Hayyim* 143; *Resp. Iggerot Moshe*, introduction, *Even Ha-Ezer* 2:11.

27. *Piskei Ha-Rosh, Sanhedrin* 4:6; *Tur Hoshen Mishpat* 25 (end); *Rema, Hoshen Mishpat* 25:1. For a similar definition of a Torah scholar as an individual who is

> When two giants disagree regarding a ruling in Halakhah, the *dayan* should not say that I will resolve according to how I please, and if he did that –the judgment is a lie. Rather, if he is a renowned scholar – knowledgeable, with developed analytical reasoning skills and knows how to resolve in pursuance to one opinion through clear and proper proofs – such is permissible. Even if another scholar has resolved in another matter, the scholar can rebut his words with proofs and overrule him... And if he isn't qualified (a *bar hakhi*), one may not exact payment (based on his judgment) in a case of doubt...

The *dayan* is not entitled to choose one of the views in an arbitrary fashion, and if he does his decision is considered false. In Rosh's words, only if he is a "*bar hakhi* (qualified)," or "a student who has attained the ability to issue a ruling" does he have the authority to choose. Does that mean that everyone may rule for himself? Clearly a person who is bereft of halakhic knowledge ("*gamir*"), analytical reasoning skills ("*savir*") and/or incapable of arriving at a position grounded in "clear and proper proofs" cannot render a judgment for himself. For example, given that some of the techniques to void a marriage in the case of a husband's *get* recalcitrance require a keen understanding of over one hundred responsa (*teshuvot*) in family law (*Even Ha-Ezer*), a Jew who has earned rabbinic ordination in the Diaspora, where his study focused on the laws of ritual slaughter, dietary laws, honoring one's parents and Torah scholars, charity, circumcision, visiting the sick and mourning (*Yoreh Deah*) and/or in commercial matters and a few portions of family law (*Hoshen Mishpat* and *Even Ha-Ezer*), would need to have completed additional study in order to be qualified to render rulings in voiding marriages in general and a husband's *get* recalcitrance in particular. Completion of his formal studies in rabbinic ordination would not suffice!

As the Talmud and post-Talmudic authorities explain, an individual who engages in matters of ritual law must be knowledgeable (*gamir*) and

---

eminent in learning distinct from the rest of the community rather than eminent from other Torah scholars, see *Shakh, Yoreh Deah* 244:2 and *Tokfo Kohen* 93. In fact, *Shakh* cites Rosh in support of his position .For additional endorsements of Rosh's position without utilizing the term "*bar hakhi,*" see *Tosafot Bava Batra* 62b, s.v. *itmar*; Rabbeinu Yonah and *Nimmukei Yosef, Bava Batra* 62b; *Resp. Terumat Ha-Deshen* 352; Maharshal, *Yam shel Shlomo*, Introduction to *Bava Kamma* and *Hullin*; Maharal, *Netiv Ha-Torah* 15; *Kovetz Shiurim, Bava Batra* 378; *Sheilot U-Teshuvot Hitoreirut Le-Teshuva* of Rav Shimon Sofer, Introduction; *Resp. Iggerot Moshe Yoreh Deah* 1:101, 3:88.

possessive of cogent reasoning skills (*savir*).[28] In the words of the *Shakh* (*Yoreh Deah* 242:8):

> If he is a *bar hakhi* (one with the ability) to know, decide, understand and instruct, then a judge has only what his own eyes see....

As R. Ya'akov Emden notes:[29]

> A student who needs to be knowledgeable of and possess the reasoning of his teacher is prohibited from ruling... since he has not attained the ability to rule.

Consequently, a qualified rabbi who can arrive at a decision based upon the submission of proofs and upon his own view, need not invoke the rules of decision-making such as: concerning Torah law one follows the stringent opinion and in a rabbinic matter one follows the lenient view.[30]

Should he possess these credentials, he can disagree with his predecessors from earlier generations, provided he brings proofs for his opinion that are accepted by his contemporaries.[31] Others contend that he must be a well-known rabbi in order to disagree with his predecessors.[32] Some argue that the arbiter must advance proofs (or sources unknown to the earlier arbiters[33]) rather than logic as the basis for disagreeing

---

28. Talmud Yerushalmi *Terumot* 5 (end), *Avodah Zarah* 2:9; Talmud Bavli *Horayot* 2b.; *Piskei Ha-Rosh, Sanhedrin* 1:2 in the name of R. Sherira Gaon; *Tur, Hoshen Mishpat* 3. The interplay between the dynamic of tradition *(mesorah)* and innovation (*hiddush*) in the halakhic decision-making process is beyond the scope of our presentation. See this writer's *Rabbinic Authority*, vol. 1, pp. 53-63.

29. *Sheilat Ya'avetz, supra* n. 26.

30. R. Y. Karo, Introduction to *Beit Yosef*; Yam *shel Shlomo, Bava Kamma* 2:5; *Rema, Hoshen Mishpat* 25:2; *Shakh, Yoreh Deah* 242:8, *Hoshen Mishpat* 37:25; *Pri Hadash, Orah Hayyim* 496:11; *Resp. Noda Be-Yehudah, Mahadura Kamma, Yoreh Deah* 55. Compare *Urim Ve-Tumim, Hoshen Mishpat* 25; *Resp. Maharik, shoresh* 159.

Should he submit proofs to corroborate his view, he is labeled "a *gadol be-Torah.*" See *Arukh Ha-Shulhan Hoshen Mishpat* 25:12. Moreover, under such circumstances, his view may be accepted even if it represents a minority of scholars. See *Resp. Minhat Yitzhak* 5:51.

31. Rosh, supra n. 27; *Rema*, supra n. 27.

32. *Pri Hadash*, supra n. 30.

33. *Sheilat David, Kuntres Hiddushin*, 73.

with the decisors of the past.[34] However, if the authority corroborates the logical reasoning by submitting acceptable proof, we listen to his view.[35] Clearly, a review of the responsa will demonstrate that one can disagree with a Torah giant such as R. Yosef Karo, author of the *Shulhan Arukh*, the classical restatement of Halakhah who relied upon the Rif, Maimonides and the Rosh.[36]

Implicit in this position is that a Torah scholar may overrule under certain conditions (e.g., submission of compelling proofs or halakhic works which were disseminated in the community supporting the Torah scholar's posture) someone who may be greater than him or his predecessor.[37] Finally, under certain conditions a qualified authority may rely upon a minority opinion in a biblical (*d'oraita*) matter such as the prohibition of an *eishet ish*, a married woman.[38] In effect, we are dealing

---

34. *Resp. Ha-Rashba* 2: 322; *Resp. Pnei Yehoshua Yoreh Deah* 34; *Resp. Maharam Mi-Lublin* 135.

35. Rema, *Yoreh Deah* 242:36. Consequently, a qualified rabbinic authority that advances logical reasoning or submits proofs from a halakhic work may *permit* a matter which is viewed by the community as a prohibition. See *Shakh, Yoreh Deah* 242:17. Implicitly, the presumption is that upon hearing the proofs or the reasoning, other qualified authorities will concur with his position. See R. M. Feinstein, *Dibrot Moshe*, 1 *Ketubot*.

36. *Resp. Hut Ha-Meshullash* 9; *Resp. Rid* 62; R. Karo, Introduction to *Beit Yosef*; *Hazon Ish, Hoshen Mishpat, Likkutim* 1; *Resp. Minhat Yitzhak* 9:150; *Resp. Helkat Ya'akov, Even Ha-Ezer* 56; *Resp. Havatzelet Ha-Sharon, Even Ha-Ezer* 28; *Resp. Iggerot Moshe, Orah Hayyim* 1:109, *Yoreh De'ah* 3:88. Netziv of Volozhin, *Ha'amek Davar, Devaim* 1:1; R. Avraham Sofer in the name of R. Elyashiv, *Nishmat Avraham*, Introduction, vol. 4, 14. *A fortiori*, one Torah giant may overrule the ruling of another Torah giant.

See *Resp. Iggerot Moshe, Orah Hayyim* 4:68; *Resp. Tzitz Eliezer* 13:38, 18:63; *Resp. Mishneh Halakhot* 8:136-137. Cf. *Resp. Terumat Ha-Deshen* 241.

37. See *Resp. Terumat Ha-Deshen, Pesakim Ve-Ketavim* 238; Rema, *Yoreh De'ah* 242:3; Maharshal, Introduction to *Yam shel Shlomo; Noda Be-Yehudah*, supra n. 30; *Pri Hadash*, supra n. 30; *Hazon Ish, Kilayim*, 1, letter; *Resp. Mishneh Halakhot* 8:137; *Resp. Iggerot Moshe*, Introduction to Orah Hayyim, *Orah Hayyim* 1:109, *Yoreh Deah*, supra n. 36.

38. *Ohr Zarua*, 2, *Sukkah*, 306; *Resp. Ha-Rashba* 1:253 (as understood by *Resp. Ha-Rashbash* 513); *Bah, Yoreh Deah Kuntres Aharon, Psak be-Hanhagot Hora'ah ve-Issur Ve-Heter*; *Resp. Re'eim* 2:5; *Resp. Mayim Amukim* 2:5 in the name of Rabbi Eliyahu Mizrahi; *Resp. Tumat Yesharim* 209 in the name of *Mahara Yerushalmi*; *Resp. Maharam Alshakar* 26 (end); *Get Pashut, Kelalim* 6; *Taz Yoreh Deah* 293:4, *Even Ha-Ezer* 17:15; R. Zweig, *Resp. Ohel Moshe, Mahadura Tinyana* 123:2; *Resp. Seridei Esh* 1:90, 3:25; *Resp. Yabia Omer* 8, *Orah Hayyim* 34, vol. 10, *Yoreh Deah* 43; R. Aharon Lichtenstein, "The Human and Social Factor in Halakhah," 36 *Tradition*, 2002, pp. 1, 11, n. 30.

with a qualified *moreh hora'ah* who possesses the ability to overrule predecessors as well as contemporaneous decisors.

Lest one claim that the Halakhah is reduced to the arbiter's whims, there are guidelines for overruling a contemporary decisor which guarantee the integrity of the decision-making process. For example, under certain conditions one must follow the view of the wiser authority provided he submits proofs for his opinion.[39] Secondly, some decisors contend that in light of Torah giants of earlier generations, a *moreh hora'ah* must refrain from an autonomous judgment even if he has compelling proofs to support his opinion.[40] Furthermore, "The books... are our masters" mandates that all halakhic works that were disseminated in our community by our predecessors must be examined prior to rendering a decision. To state it differently, whereas there are numerous sources relating to rendering a halakhic judgment before one's rabbi, today these guidelines are inapplicable due to the absence of the institution a guiding rabbi (a *rav muvhak*) and halakhic books are viewed as our teachers. As such, our arbiters are unable to render autonomous judgments of leniency should the authors of these works have adopted stringencies.[41]

In the absence of a qualified decisor or an arbiter who has no proofs to support a particular view, the ordained individual would address the resolution of the issue based upon one of the following five principles of decision-making (*kelalei hora'ah*):[42]

Cf. other authorities who rely upon a minority opinion only in a *de'rabbanan*, a matter of Rabbinic law. See *Resp. Ha-Rashbash* 513 in the name of Tashbetz and Ran; Rema, *Hoshen Mishpat* 25:2; *Helkat Mehokeik, Even Ha-Ezer* 17:31; *Shakh, Yoreh De'ah* 242, *Pilpul be-Hanhagot Hora'ot Issur Ve-Heter*; *Resp. R. Akiva Eiger, Mahadura Kamma* 122; Resp. *Iggerot Moshe, Orah Hayyim* 1:51(1), *Even Ha-Ezer* 4, 83(1).

39. Talmud Bavli *Avodah Zarah* 7a; *Resp. Ha-Rosh* 94:5; Rashba, supra n. 25; Rema, *Hoshen Mishpat* 25:2.

40. *Resp. Maharik, shoresh* 84, 159; R, Yosef Karo, Introduction to *Beit Yosef*; *Get Pashut, Kelal* 5; *Urim Ve-Tumim Hoshen Mishpat* 25.

41. A. Ha-Kohen of Lunel, *Orhot Hayyim, Hilk. Talmud Torah*, ch. 21; *Resp. Terumat Ha-Deshen* 2:241; Rema, *Hoshen Mishpat* 25:2; Rema, *Yoreh Deah* 242:30; *Lehem Mishneh, Hilk. Talmud Torah* 5:4; *Resp. Shevut Ya'akov* 2:64; *Resp. Yabia Omer*, 4, *Hoshen Mishpat* 1:6. See further, this writer's *Rabbinic Authority*, vol. 1, 33-34, nn. 62-63.

42. Rules 1-2 and 4-5 have been culled from *Resp. Ha-Rashba* 253 and rule 3 has been extrapolated from *Resp. Terumat Ha-Deshen* 2:241 and *Rema, Shulhan Arukh, Hoshen Mishpat* 25:1. Cf. R. Elisha Aviner, "The Principles of Instructions in Halakhot of Doubt" (Hebrew), 19 *Ma'aliyot* 5759, 145, 152-166, who advances other halakhic sources for rules 1 and 4-5.

1. The Halakhah is in accordance with the superior one in wisdom and in the number of students i.e., the number of students following his instruction or in age.[43]
2. The Halakhah is following the *mara d'atra*, i.e., the accepted rabbi in the community.[44]
3. The Halakhah is in accordance with the stringent rulings found in the books that have spread in the community.[45]
4. In a controversy between a majority and a minority, we follow the majority opinion.[46]
5. In the event that one cannot resolve a pending issue based upon the above decision-making rules, the matter would be determined – in biblical matters, in pursuance to the stringent view, and concerning rabbinic matters we ought to follow the lenient opinion.[47]

The common denominator of the Haifa *dayanim* and their detractors is that they all earned formal ordination (*hasmakha le'rabbanut*) combined with supplementary education in voiding marriage and were therefore authorized as qualified *morei hora'ah* to render rulings in the matter of ritual law in general and voiding marriages in particular.[48] Thus, R. Moshe Soloveitchik maintains that a decisor who does not have the status of being ordained is:

> Essentially a reference guide, providing reliable information

43. *Avodah Zarah, supra n. 39.*

44. *Resp. Ha-Rashba, supra n. 26, 1:1190; Resp. Ha-Ran* 48; *Resp. Ha-Rivash* 256; *Pri Hadash*, supra n. 30. See further, this writer's *Rabbinic Authority*, vol. 1, pp. 21-53.

45. Rema, *Hoshen Mishpat* 25:1; this writer's *Rabbinic Authority*, vol. 1., p. 34, n. 62.

46. *Tosefta Berakhot* 4:15; Mishnah *Eduyot* 1:5; Maimonides, *Sefer Ha-Mitzvot* 175.Cf. others who contend that the rule to follow the majority is limited to resolving issues within the confines of a rabbinical court proceeding and cannot be extended to intergenerational disputes. See *Beit Yosef, Hoshen Mishpat* 13 (end) in the name of Rashba; *Get Pashut, Kelalim, kelal* 1, 5. See further this writer's *Rabbinic Authority*, vol. 1., 24, nn. 29-30, vol. 3, 247, n. 21. Secondly, this rule is applicable only where both authorities are of equivalent stature. See Rashba, supra n.26. However, if the minority is of greater stature than the majority, their position is determinative. See *Resp. Yabia Omer*, 2, *Hoshen Mishpat* 3(5) in the name of Nahmanides, Hinnukh and Rashbatz.

47. *Avodah Zarah*, supra n. 39.

48. *Resp. Ha-Rivash* 271, 350; *Resp. Radach* 18; *Rema, Yoreh De'ah* 242:2.

> about what the tradition and its sources, properly understood and interpreted, state; but it is they (the ordained – AYW), rather than he, that bind authoritatively.[49]

The Haifa case is not the only case where authorities addressed whether there were grounds to void a marriage. There is a well-trodden tradition (*mesorah*) that opines that voiding a marriage resides in the hands of qualified *morei hora'ah*. How does one seek a solution to the matter of modern-day *igun* (a woman chained to a marriage due her husband's *get* recalcitrance)? Rabbi David Babad, a renowned nineteenth-century decisor, communicates to us the following:[50]

> I heard from ha-Gaon Rabbi Barish Rappaport... that he had a tradition from his Rav, ha-Gaon Noda Ba-shearim, ha-Av Beit Din of Lublin, that upon receiving a question to address, he would first weigh in his mind the truthfulness of the matter according to what human reason dictates and if in his estimation human reason the matter is true, then he will delve into Halakhah to arrive at a decision.

By invoking this tradition which addresses the mission of "a *mo'reh hora'ah*" in rendering a ruling, twentieth century Torah giants Rabbis Ya'akov Breisch and Yitzhak Weiss convey to us that resolution of all cases, including classical *agunah* questions where the husband is missing, is within the purview of a qualified rabbinic authority rather than only to be addressed by a Torah giant.[51] R. Maharam Schick, R. Aryeh Heller, and R. Sinai Sapir are among others who invoke the assistance of "a qualified *mo'reh hora'ah*" to resolve an *igun* situation.[52] Consequently, implicitly following the tradition of R. Rappaport, it is unsurprising that in contemporary times, panels of Israeli *dayanim* who serve under the Beit Din Rabbani of the Chief Rabbinate, who are not viewed as Torah giants by our community in general and by other rabbis in particular, have addressed this issue of voiding a marriage and *without even raising in their judgments the possibility that there was a jurisdiction issue.*[53]

49. R. Aharon Lichtenstein, *Leaves of Faith: The World of Jewish Learning,* N.Y., 2004, 293.

50. *Resp. Havatzelet Ha-Sharon* 2:28.

51. *Resp. Helkat Ya'akov Even Ha-Ezer* 56; *Resp. Minhat Yitzhak* 9:130.

52. *Resp. Maharam Schick* 110; *Resp. Sha'agat Aryeh Ve-Kol Shahal* 2-3; *Resp. Minhat Ani* 65.

53. *Piskei Din Rabbanayim* 3:225, 10:241, 15:1, 20:239; File no. 1-14-1393,

Similarly, it is no surprise that the rabbis who were critical of the above cited Haifa Regional Beit Din of June 18,2018, did not raise any jurisdictional issue regarding the propriety of the dayanim in voiding a marriage.

Lest one contend that seeking solutions to matters of *igun* (*get* recalcitrance) is to be relegated to Torah giants, R. Yitzhak ben David of the nineteenth century exclaims:[54]

> If every Torah scholar would refrain from responding and exclaim, "how can I enter this flame of a mighty blaze due to the severity of the prohibition of illicit relations (*ervah*)?"... each man, a minor one like a great one, is obligated to seek with candles,

---

Jerusalem Regional Beit Din, March 5, 2003; File no. 1-22-1510, Beit Din ha-Rabbani ha-Gadol, September 7, 2004; File no. 306044470-21-4, Jerusalem Regional Beit Din, June 10, 2008; File no. 2433-21-1, Beit Din ha-Rabbani ha-Gadol, February 3, 2010; File no. 589138/2, Haifa Regional Beit Din, June 7, 2011; File no. 861252/1, Beit Din ha-Rabbani ha-Gadol, January 23, 2012; File no. 373701/10, Tel Aviv-Yaffo Regional Beit Din, March 12, 2012; File no. 271091/10, Netanya Regional Beit Din, July 2, 2012; File no. 861974/1, Tzfat Regional Beit Din, January 21,2013; File no. 917387/1, Jerusalem Regional Beit Din, November 17, 2013; File no. 914652/2, Petah Tikvah Regional Beit Din, March 24, 2014; File no. 861974/2, Tzfat Regional Beit Din, May 20,2014; File no. 996047/2, Beit Din ha-Rabbani ha-Gadol, December 25,2014; File no. 870175/4, Haifa Regional Beit Din, December 29,2014; File no. 1011498, Be'air Sheva Regional Beit Din, May 10, 2015; File no. 818315/7, Be'air Sheva Regional Beit Din, September 21, 2015; File no. 1061015/2, Haifa Regional Beit Din, February 16, 2016; File no. 1068330/1, Haifa Regional Beit Din, January 12, 2017; File no. 932006/1, Be'air Sheva Regional Beit Din, February 1, 2017; File no. 1097040/10, Haifa Regional Beit Din, June 6, 2017; File no. 905457/10, Tel Aviv-Yaffo Regional Beit Din, September 11, 2017; File no. 1064682/4, Jerusalem Regional Beit Din, September 12, 2017; File no. 1097040/10, Haifa Regional Beit Din, November 6, 2017; File no. 989812/1, Haifa Regional Beit Din, February 2, 2018 (*mamzerut*); File no. 1227676/1, Ashdod Regional Beit Din, August 1, 2019; File no. 1294108/1, Be'air Sheva Regional Beit Din, June 13, 2021; File no. 1310757/1, Be'air Sheva Regional Beit Din, July 13, 2021; 1305851/13, Rehovot Regional Beit Din, April 3, 2022; File no. 1376869/1, Jerusalem Regional Beit Din, July 19, 2022; File no. 1356578/1, Jerusalem Regional Beit Din, July 19,2022; File no. 1376874/1, Tel Aviv- Yaffo Regional Beit Din, April 25, 2023.

Even File no. 870175/4, op. cit. and File no. 1294108/1, op. cit. which offer the most comprehensive and systematic presentations of the various controversies regarding the propriety of techniques to void a marriage, do not address whether there is a jurisdiction issue.

54. *Resp. Divrei Emet* 9. See also *Resp. Ha-Rosh* 51:2; *Resp. Terumat Ha-Deshen, Pesakim Ve-Ketavim* 139; *Resp. Maharashdam, Even Ha-Ezer* 43-44; *Resp. Nivhar Me-Kesef* 63; *Resp. Pnei Moshe* 2:130, 3:15. As we mentioned, regardless of one's rabbinic stature, an arbiter must possess the credentials to render decisions in marriage and divorce.

> a careful search in holes and cracks, possibly he will find relief for the benefit of the daughters of Israel to save them from *igun*.

In fact, commencing with the Middle Ages and until contemporary times, numerous rabbis and rabbinical courts alike, both in the lands of our dispersion and in Eretz Yisrael, have propelled themselves "to enter this flame" and have rendered decisions that have offered solutions for the modern-day *agunah* as well as the classical *agunah*.

In sum, whereas an imperative authority has the right or power to act and expect compliance to his authority, an epistemic authority is an authority in a particular field, but he does not possess any right to command. Essentially, an imperative authority is "in authority," while an epistemic authority is simply "an authority".[55] The halakhic positions outlined above regarding the nature of rabbinic authority can be described accordingly. On one hand, R. Avraham Sherman argues that a Torah giant is the only one authorized to void a marriage and therefore he is "in authority," and R. Sherman would consider a qualified *moreh hora'ah* as "an authority," but unable to render a judgment and void a marriage.[56] On the other hand, numerous rabbis have pointed out that both a qualified *moreh hora'ah* and a Torah giant are empowered to void a marriage and thus they are both "in authority".[57]

In conclusion, whereas the minority opinion permits only Torah giants to render judgments such as voiding a marriage due to public policy considerations, such as its impact upon the entire Jewish community in

55. Richard T. De George, *The Nature and Limits of Authority*, Kansas: 1985, 27, 63.

56. See Sherman, supra n. 2, at 167.

57. Whether a decision of a *moreh hora'ah* which voids the marriage requires the endorsement of "a second opinion" is subject to controversy. The majority of arbiters view it as a practice (a *nohag*). See this writer's *Rabbinic Authority*, vol. 3, pp. 256-262, vol. 4, 161.For examples of some contemporary decisors who required an endorsement of a *moreh hora'ah* prior to voiding a marriage, see *Resp. Ohel Moshe* 2:123; *Resp. Yabia Omer* 9, *Even Ha-Ezer* 36; *Resp. Minhat Avraham* 2:10; *Resp. Ha-Shavit* 7:20.

For others who required the endorsement of Torah giants, see *Resp. Maharsham* 1:14, 6:160, 8:239; *Resp. Minhat Asher* 1:73, 3:85.

The number of *morei hora'ah* required to address an issue of marriage and divorce in general and voiding a marriage in particular is beyond the scope of our presentation. See R. S.Z. Gartner, *Kefiyah Be-get*, pp. 25-44; R. Z.N. Goldberg, *Lev Mishpat* 1, pp. 149-150; this writer's *Rabbinic Authority*, vol. 3, p. 12, n. 3, vol. 5, p. 271, n. 1.

general and the family in particular,[58] the majority view empowers qualified rabbinic arbiters to address issues relating to marriage, divorce and conversions based upon an understanding of the Talmudic sources as interpreted by post-Talmudic authorities and the guidelines for arriving at decisions as outlined above.

Addendum:

The following question was posed to Rabbi Moshe Feinstein, he responded to it in 1934, and it was published in *Iggerot Moshe* (*Yoreh Deah* 1:101) in 1959.

> My dear friend you ask how is it possible to rely on new views such as I have expressed, in particular when they are against certain *aharonim*? Do you think that there is an end and limitation – Gd forbid! – to Torah? Do you think that contemporary halakhic decisors can only express the views that have previously been published? Do you feel that if a question comes up that has not been previously discussed and published in a book – that we should not issue an opinion – even though we understand the issue and are capable of expressing an opinion? In my humble opinion, it is prohibited to say such a thing. There is no question that it is still possible for Torah to expand and develop even in our times. Therefore, there is an obligation for all those who are competent to make halakhic

58. For example, one of the concerns which lead rabbinic authorities to be reluctant to engage in voiding marriages is the fear that the public will err, thinking that a married woman is exiting her marriage without the execution of a *get*. Relying upon this perception, a wife may remarry without receiving a *get* and have children who would be *mamzerim* (halakhic bastards). For a recognition of this fear in other contexts, see Rashi, *Mahadura Kamma, Shitah Mekubetzet Ketubot* 73b, s.v. *tzerikha get*; *Lehem Mishneh, Hilk. Ishut* 4:10; *Resp. Ahiezer* vol. 1, *Even Ha-Ezer* 27 (3, 5); *Resp. Ein Yitzhak* 1, *Even Ha-Ezer* 24; *Resp. Devar Eliyahu* 48.

Whereas *Taz* (*Orah Hayyim* 585:5 and *Yoreh Deah* 117:1) contends that an arbiter cannot prohibit what the Torah permits, however, for purposes of protecting certain institutions such as the family the imposition of punitive measures (*le'migdar milta),* one may forbid what the Torah allows. See *Re'eim,* supra n. 23; R. Aharon Maged, *Sefer Beit Aharon,* 8, pp. 158-160. As we have presented, whether a Torah giant or a qualified authority may render such judgments regarding marriage, divorce and conversion is subject to debate.

For other examples of prohibitions based upon public policy considerations, see A. Frimer and D. Frimer, "Women's Prayer Services – Theory and Practice, Part 1," 32 *Tradition* 5, 39, 60-63 (1998).

decisions, to rule on all matters that come to them to the best of their ability after solid research in the Talmud and authorities with the use of clear reasoning and proper proof. Even if this results in something new which has not been previously discussed in the halakhic works. Furthermore, even if this has been previously discussed, there is no question that an arbiter needs to understand it fully and to clarify it in his mind before he issues a ruling. He should not issue a ruling simply because he saw an authoritative source expressing such an opinion. This is the same as mechanically deriving from one's notes that the Talmud (*Sotah* 22a) condemns: Tannaim who teach Halakhah from their notes without paying attention to the reasons behind them destroy the world. Even if these rulings are occasionally against the views of *Aharonim* – so what? There is no question that we have the right to disagree with *Aharonim* and also sometimes against particular views of certain *Rishonim* when we have clear-cut analysis and especially also correct reasons. On such matters, our Sages (*Bava Batra* 131a) say, "A judge can only rely on what he sees." This ability to disagree is in those situations where the ruling doesn't go against the well-known decisors of the *Shulhan Arukh* whose views have been accepted everywhere. On a related matter it is said, "They have left us room to be creative." This is in fact the approach of the majority of the responsa literature of the *Aharonim* when they decide practical halakhic issues. However, one should not be arrogant in making halakhic rulings, and it is necessary to show restraint as much as possible. However, in a situation of great need and surely in a situation where a woman is an *agunah* as in our present case – there is no question that we are obligated to issue a ruling when it seems that we have the basis for a permissive judgment. Furthermore, it is prohibited for us to have humility and cause a Jewish woman to remain an *agunah* or to cause someone to violate a prohibition or even to cause someone to lose money. *Gittin* (56a) says that the humility of Rav Zecharya ben Avkulas caused the Temple to be destroyed. Why does the Talmud blame his humility? What does this have to do with his humility? Maharetz Chajes gives a proper explanation to this matter which is truly in agreement with what I have said. Therefore, we are forced to make halakhic rulings in practice when we have convincing proofs and clear understanding, and especially in cases of *agunah* such as this. We need to remove the obstacles.

In the foregoing responsum, Rabbi Feinstein writes:

> However, in a situation of great need and surely in a situation where a woman is an *agunah* as in our present case – there is no question that we are obligated to make ruling when it seems that we have the basis for a permissive judgment... we are forced to make halakhic rulings in practice when we have convincing proofs and clear understanding and especially in cases of *agunah* such as this. We need to remove the obstacles.

Clearly, Rabbi Feinstein argues that halakhic issues in general and agunah matters in particular are to be resolved by qualified *morei hora'ah*. Moreover, it should be noted that Rabbi Feinstein responded to the petitioner when he was in his forties, at which point it is likely that he was not yet known as a Torah giant. Nonetheless Rabbi Feinstein argues in his responsum that an ordained and halakhically educated rabbi may address such issues.[59]

As Rabbi Feinstein concludes elsewhere:[60]

> Every *rav* in Yisrael wants to promote the welfare of the daughters of Yisrael and he is aware of the greatness of the *mitzvah* to free her from *igun* and it is a major prohibition "to leave a wife in chains" if one has the ability to address the situation and does not resolve it

59. There are other instances where he contends that the halakhic decision-making process was in the hands of credentialed decisors rather than Torah giants. See Resp. *Iggerot Moshe, Orah Hayyim* 1, Introduction, *Yoreh Deah* 3:88; *Dibrot Moshe, Shabbat* 11.

Clearly, when Rabbi Feinstein ruled regarding the special halakhic decision-making responsibility of great Torah scholars, he explicitly mentioned them. See *Resp. Iggerot Moshe, Orah Hayyim* 4:39. The fact that he failed to mention them in his responsa indicates that he is dealing with qualified *morei hora'ah.*

60. *Resp. Iggerot Moshe Even Ha-Ezer* 1:117.

Chapter 3

The Parameters of Marital Intimacy

1. Common Law Conception of Marital Intimacy

The origins of the common law definition of the nature of the marriage can be traced to Blackstone's Commentaries on the Law of England. William Blackstone articulated the doctrine as follows:[1]

> By marriage, the husband and wife are one person in law; that is, the very being or legal existence of the woman is suspended during the marriage, or at least is incorporated and consolidated into that of the husband; under whose wing, protection, and cover she performs everything; and is therefore called... feme-covert... her condition during her marriage is called her coverture. Upon this principle of a union of person in husband and wife, depend all the legal rights, duties, and disabilities, that either of them acquire by the marriage.

For centuries, common law gave husbands rights in their wives' properties and earnings and proscribed wives from contracting, filing suit, or holding property in their own names. Essentially, wives were bereft of legal capacity. This common law of marriage, a relic of feudalism,[2] persisted from the late Middle Ages to the late nineteenth century where state legislation was enacted that gave married women, similar to other

1. W. Blackstone, *Commentaries on the Law of England Oxford,* (1768), 1:422, 430-431. For an earlier articulation of this idea, see *The Lawes Resolution of Women's Rights*, London, 1632 reprinted in M. Bloomfield, *American Lawyers in a Changing Society, 1776-1876*, Cambridge, Mass. (1976), 94-95.

See further this writer's "A Comparative Analysis of a Wife's Capacity to Pledge her Husband's Credit for Domestic Necessaries in Anglo-American Law and Jewish Law," 13 *The Jewish Law Annual* 213 (2000).

2. L. Kanowitz, *Women and the Law: The Unfinished Revolution* 35 (1969).

individuals, rights to own, buy and sell property as well as make contracts.[3] Yet, the marital unity view remained providing rules for marital partners which include marital property rules,[4] inheritance laws[5] and special tax rules.[6] A wife could not be convicted of most crimes "if she committed a prohibited act jointly with (her husband), or while he was present," and as of 1980, rape in states with a marital rape exemption still could not be prosecuted.[7]

Many rules have changed to treat spouses as individuals with legal capacity within the marriage unit. For example, in many states, spouses may now sue one another for torturous behavior, credit opportunities must be accorded to married women in their own names and a husband's permission is not mandated for a wife's abortion decision.[8]

Prior to the above articulation of the nature of marriage,[9] in the early eighteenth century, Sir Matthew Hale, a former Chief Justice of the King's Bench in England states the following:[10]

> But the husband cannot be guilty of a rape committed by himself upon his lawful wife, for by their mutual matrimonial consent and contract the wife hath given up herself in this kind unto her husband, which she cannot retract.

In other words, given that, in the words of Blackstone, "the existence of the woman is suspended during the marriage, or at least is... consolidated into that of the husband," therefore we can begin to understand the marital rape exemption.

As Jill Hasday states in 2000:[11]

---

3. N.Y. Gen. Oblig. Law, sections 3-301,-315 (McKinney 1978); Okl. Stat. Ann. Tit. 32 Section 15 West 1976); H. Clark, The Law of Domestic Relations Section 2.2, at 222-223 (1968).

4. M. Glendon, *State, Law and Family* 140-181 (1977).

5. M. Glendon, supra note 4, at 279-280, 282-284.

6. M. Glendon, supra note 4, at 178.

7. R. Perkins, On Criminal Law 910-918 (2d edition 1969); Glasgow, The Marital Rape Exemption: Legal Sanction of Spousal Abuse, 18 *J. Family L.* 565, 582 (1980).

8. W. Prosser, The Law of Torts Section 122 (4th ed, 1971); Equal Credit Opportunity Act, 15 U.S.C. Sections – 691-1691e (1976); Planned Parenthood of Missouri v. Danforth 428 U.S. 52, 67-71 (1976)

9. See supra n. 1

10. M. Hale, *The History of the Pleas of the Crown*, Philadelphia: R. Small, 1st Am. Ed. 1847 (1736), 629.

11. J. Hasday, "Contest and Consent: A Legal History of Marital Rape," 88 *California Law Review* 1484-1486 (2000).

> Reform of the criminal exemptions has been... fragmentary. A majority of states still retain some form of the rule exempting a husband from prosecution for raping his wife. Some states require a couple to be separated at the time of the injury... Some only recognize marital rape if it involves physical force and/or serious physical harm. Some provide for vastly reduced penalties if a rape occurs in marriage, or create special procedural requirements for marital rape prosecutions....

Even more recently, reform of the criminal exemption continues to be fragmentary, as Kennedy Holmes notes in 2021:[12]

> Instead of repealing spousal exemptions through the legislative compromises, states create categories of loopholes including (1) punishing spousal rape separately, (2) barring marriage as a defense only to rape in the first degree, (3) permitting a marriage defense in cases of statutory rape, or (4) limiting the exemption...
>
> Even though progress has been made, due to the loopholes and failed repeal efforts, married women are still at a disadvantage in their access to justice...

2. Halakhic View of Intimacy

To understand the nature of halakhic intimacy, there is a need to briefly present the building blocks for establishing marriage.

What are the building blocks which establish this consensual agreement to establish a marital relationship? Recognizing that marriage consists of two separate acts, the act of betrothal (*kiddushin*) and marriage (*nissu'in*) respectively, Rabbi Norman Frimer and Professor Dov Frimer note:[13]

> In practical terms, *kiddushin* as the primary state of Jewish marriage can be... normatively constituted through the presence of five halakhic elements... At the helm stands intention

12. K. Holmes, "Shining another Light on Spousal Rape Exemptions: Spousal Sexual Violence Laws in the #MeToo Era" 11 *UC Irvine Law Review* 1230-1231 (2021).

13. Norman Frimer and Dov Frimer, "Reform Marriages in Contemporary Halakhic Responsa," 21 *Tradition* (1984), 7, 9-11.

> (*kavanah*). But intention for what? Two divergent directions emerge... According to one authority, the intent of the couple must be for at least the most minimal and natural characteristics of the marital experience... That decision, however, must also include the stipulation that the wife shall be exclusively related to her husband and prohibited to all others. From this intent of intimacy (*leshem ishut*) will then flow all other authority which will bestow legitimacy and direction upon the formal ceremony and simultaneously form the foundation of the *kiddushin*. The other view finds the natural standard utterly inadequate... What, then, shall be the normative canon for *kavanah*? It must be a halakhic marriage (*lekiddushei Torah)* or for the purpose of marriage (*leshem kiddushin)*... a conscious awareness that the ceremony must be *kedin*, in faithful fulfillment of the hallowed imperatives of Jewish law...
>
> ...the intention to marry must be visibly objectified, in order both to articulate as well as to inculcate the core ideas of that *kavanah*. Jewish tradition, therefore, devised two more patterns of action to achieve tangibility. One of them was the statement (*amirah)*, an official verbal declaration of marital *kavanah* to be made directly by the groom to his bride in a formal and public style... The other act... was the giving (*netinah)*, initiated again by the groom and complemented by the parallel receipt (*kabalah*), by the bride. These sequential acts of "give and take" involvc an objcct... traditionally a ring....
>
> But not only must these facets of *kavanah* be shared between bride and groom. Normally, the Halakhah also demands... a will (*ratson)* – a fourth element, involving the couple's voluntary assent to all parts of the *erusin* (betrothal – AYW)....
>
> Finally, a Jewish marriage must be witnessed by at least two qualified witnesses (*edim)*, whose responsibility is two-fold. When necessary, they... can help establish the facts and certify the... degree of compliance with the prerequisites of Jewish marriage law. Yet, even more critical is their role... who by their very presence and participation at the ceremony constitute the validity of an act of betrothal (*ma'aseh kiddushin)*.

In short, the subjective marital intentions of the Jewish man and Jewish woman are translated into reality via verbal articulation and modes of concretization of this intent under the scrutiny of witnesses and in the presence of an officiating rabbi and public assemblage for the expressed purpose of establishing a consensual marital union.

However, seemingly other rabbinic sources advance the notion that the act of marriage is nonconsensual. The Torah teaches us:[14] "When a man taketh a wife..." and the Talmud explains exegetically, "When a man taketh a wife, and not when [a woman] taketh [a man]."[15] Moreover, at the beginning of Chapters 1 and 2 of Mishnah *Kiddushin* respectively, we read: "The man betroths" and "the woman is acquired." In other words, as opposed to sale in which the money is handed over in consideration of the object that was acquired, here, in *kiddushin*, the money is given an act of undertaking an obligation(s) (a *kinyan*) of a prospective husband toward his prospective wife. According to the literal interpretation of the Torah and the Mishnah, the man executes the act of undertaking a duty through *kiddushin* vis-à-vis the woman, the prospective spouse is passive, and negates her mind and her will in the face of her husband, and seemingly the wife is being acquired by the husband. This appears to be the case according to the well-known words of Ran who elucidates:[16]

> Since the Torah said, "When a man takes a woman," and it did not say, "When a woman be taken to be with a man," she has no legal capacity to transfer herself into his legal jurisdiction. Rather, in agreeing to be taken in marriage by the man, she negates her own will and mind and is then considered as ownerless property (*hefker* – AYW) vis-à-vis her husband. At that point, the husband transfers her into his domain, hence the act of "taking someone in *kiddushin*" can only be executed by a man and never by a woman.

However, if one examines closely the words of Ran and other authorities, one sees that an act is required on the part of the woman, whereby she negates her will with respect to the act of *kiddushin*.[17] Lest one construe the Ran's words as suggesting that the consummation of *kiddushin*

14. *Devarim* 24:1.

15. Talmud Bavli *Kiddushin* 4b.

16. *Nedarim* 30a, s.v. ve-ishah.

17. *Hiddushei R. Shimon Shkop, Kiddushin* 1; *Sha'arei Yosher* 7:12; *Kehillot Ya'akov, Kiddushin* 7 (Comments); *Mishnat Shlomo, Kiddushin* 2; File 870175/4, Haifa Regional Beit Din, 7 Tevet 5775; *Minhat Asher, Kiddushin* 1.

In other words, whereas the man establishes the *kiddushin* via the execution of a *kinyan*, the woman must accept (*kabalah*) the money in order to finalize the *kiddushin*. See *Minhat Asher, Kiddushin* 20.

entails that the man is acquiring a monetary asset, namely his spouse, nothing could be further from the truth. As Ran notes elsewhere:[18]

> The woman is not the asset of the husband.... The couple must be aware of the fact that the act of *kiddushin* is executed.

Relying upon precedent,[19] contemporary authorities and/or writers concur with the Ran that the husband possesses no proprietary interest in his wife's body.[20]

Though there is no proprietary interest in the woman's body, nonetheless *kiddushin* generates an acquisition of a prohibition (*kinyan issur*), namely that a married woman is prohibited to the world except to her husband, rather than being a monetary acquisition (a *kinyan mamon*) similar to owning chattel.[21]

---

18. *Ran on Rif, Gittin* 9a, s.v. *ve-katuv*.

19. In fact, some authorities explicitly reject the notion that a husband has a proprietary interest in his wife. See *Ran on Rif, Gittin* 9a, s.v. *vekatva* (Cf. *Ran on Rif, Ketubot* 9b); *Hiddushei Ha-Ra'ah, Kiddushin* 2a, *Resp. Helkat Yoav* 1, *Even Ha-Ezer* 4; *Hiddushei Ha-Ramban, Kiddushin* 9a; *Hiddushei Ha-Rashba, Kiddushin* 3b, s.v. *li'me'utei halifin* , 6b: s.v. *amar Abaye, Bava Batra* 48b; *Hiddushei Ha-Ritva, Kiddushin* 2a, s.v. *ketiv hakha*; *Perush R. Avraham Min Ha-Har, Nedarim* 15b; *Resp. Ha-Rivash* 385; *Resp. Ein Yitzhak* 1, *Even Ha-Ezer* 16; *Avnei Milluim*, Resp. 17, *Even Ha-Ezer* 123:9; R. Herzog, *Pesakim Ve-Ketavim* 6, 207-210,8, 916 (Cf. *Pesakim Ve-Ketavim* 7, 833-834); *Pri Moshe* 60; *Minhat Asher, Kiddushin* 8, 22. Cf. *Tosafot Rosh Kiddushin* 5a; *Avnei Milluim*, Resp. 17, *Even Ha-Ezer* 42(1), *Resp. Birkat Shlomo* 12(31); *Hiddushei R. Shimon Shkop, Kiddushin* 9; *Resp. Divrei Yatziv, Even Ha-Ezer* 56(3); *Resp. Iggerot Moshe, Even Ha-Ezer* 1:117; *Resp. Avnei Nezer, Even Ha-Ezer* 123:9; R. Herzog, *Pesakim Ve-Ketavim* 6, 207-210, 8, 916 (Cf. *Pesakim Ve-Ketavim* 7, 833-834); *Pri Moshe* 60; *Minhat Asher, Kiddushin* 8, 22. Cf. *Tosafot Rosh Kiddushin* 5a.

20. See Abraham Rutta, *Dina De-Malkhuta Dina*, 1939; R. K. Kahana, *The Theory of Marriage in Jewish Law*, Leiden: Brill, 1966, pp. 5-14, 26-55, 80-95; R. N. Rothstein, "The Nature of *Kiddushin* and its *Kinyan*" (Hebrew), *Nezer Ha-Torah*, Av 5770, pp. 52-110; R. Z. Gartner, *Kefiyah Be-Get*, pp. 32-33; R. M. Ehrenreich, "*Kiddushin* – *Kinyan* or *Ma'aseh*?" (Hebrew), *Eretz Hemdah*, vol. 2, pp. 29-43; R. E. Shochetman, "Engaged, not Acquired" (Hebrew), 223 *Nekuda*, March 1999, pp. 36-44; R. Y. Ushinski, *Orhot Mishpat* vol. 1, pp. 40-53; R. D. Wolf, Minhah Le-Aharon, 5765, pp. 18-31; M. Avraham, *Kesef and Kinyan Kesef: Halakhic Ramifications* at Col. 525 (Hebrew), at https:mikyab.net.

21. See Talmud Bavli *Kiddushin* 2b; *Tosafot Kiddushin* 2b, s.v. de'asar; *Hiddushei Ha-Ramban, Kiddushin* 16a, s.v. *zot omeret*; *Hiddushei Ha-Ritva, Kiddushin* 15a, s.v. *mokheir atzmo*; *Hiddushei Ha-Rashba, Gittin* 75a, *Nedarim* 15a; *Beit Shmuel Even Ha-Ezer* 27:4; *Resp. Meishiv Davar* 4:35; *Resp. Ein Yitzhak* 1, *Even Ha-Ezer* 16; *Resp. Mahaneh Hayyim* 2, *Even-Ha-Ezer* 44; *Avnei Milluim* 44:4; *Sha'arei Yosher, Sha'ar* 5, *Perek* 22; *Resp. Heikhal Yitzhak Even Ha-Ezer* 1:25(32).

On the other hand, the *kiddushin* is created via the acquisition of money (*kinyan kesef*).[22] In other words, *kiddushin* is established by the transfer of money (e.g., a ring) from the man to the woman which symbolizes the undertaking by the man of his marital duties vis-à-vis his prospective wife based upon mutual consent rather than a medium of acquisition. Furthermore, whereas a sales transaction executed via the transfer of money (a *kinyan kesef*) between the buyer and the seller is for the purpose of payment, in a matter of *kiddushin*, the transfer of an item of monetary value (*sha'veh kesef*) is a symbol for establishing intimacy (*kinyan ishut*).[23]

The notion of intimacy is predicated upon the dignity of human beings (*kavod ha-beriyyot*), which is a governing halakhic norm in our human relations.[24] For example, the sanction to execute a marriage on Shabbat for a single man who hasn't fulfilled the *mitzvah* of siring children is based upon the halakhic doctrine the dignity of human beings.[25] In other words, *kavod ha-beriyyot* is not limited to the prevention of physical harm but extends to cases of emotional injury such as embarrassment to a single man and woman who have a pressing need (*she'at ha-dehak*) to marry and start a family. Thus, a husband has a duty to respect his wife as a member of the human race. Emotional abuse is decried by the authorities.[26] Additionally, as a husband, it is incumbent upon him to respect her more than he respects himself.[27] As an Israeli rabbinical court states:[28]

> A wife is not the acquisition of her husband, "for life she is given and not for pain." There is no place for distinguishing between a wife and a friend, and as the words of Rema state, "it is a sin like striking a friend".... On the contrary, in relation to one's wife, the

22. *Resp. Avnei Millium* 17.

23. *Seridei Esh, Kiddushin* 13, 31.

Consequently, the execution of this *kinyan issur* and the resulting status of the woman becoming a married woman (*eishet ish*) preempts another man from executing the act of *kiddushin* with this woman.

24. Talmud Bavli *Berakhot* 19b, *Shabbat* 94b, *Bava Kama* 79b, *Menahot* 37b–38a; Talmud Yerushalmi, *Berakhot* 6b, *Kilayim* 32a.

25. *Resp. Ha-Rema* 125; *Rema, Orah Hayyim* 339:4.

26. Talmud Bavli *Bava Metzia* 59a; *Resp. Binyamin Ze'ev* 88; *Resp. Ha-Tashbetz* 2:8.

27. Talmud Bavli *Shabbat* 59b, *Yevamot* 62b, *Ketubot* 61a, *Nedarim* 51a, *Bava Metzia* 59a, *Sanhedrin* 76b, *Hullin* 84b; *Mishneh Torah, Hilk. Ishut* 15:19; *Shulhan Arukh, Hoshen Mishpat* 228:3.

28. File no. 4927-21-1, Petah Tikvah Regional Beit Din, 6 Tishrei 5765.

husband is obligated to love her and respect her more than the duty concerning his friend.

Whereas various halakhic guidelines have been established relating to the duty of *kavod ha-beriyyot*, there is a paucity of sources practically detailing how to demonstrate in positive terms one's respect for one's wife. Clearly, spousal respect requires intimate and individualistic answers that emerge from the singularity of persons and their relationships to each other, as well as their fused existence. It seems that Halakhah has left it up to the husband to determine how to translate into practical terms respect for his spouse.

On the other hand, there are specific acts of dishonor, of demeaning, of demeaning a wife's persona, such as threatening to assault her or actual battery, which entail a diminution of her honor as a person.[29] Consequently, just as battery *(habala)* involves transgressing a negative Torah commandment,[30] similarly, spousal battery is a violation of *habala*[31] and is subject to criminal sanctions.[32] In short, whereas Halakhah has given latitude for a husband to determine how to translate his duty of spousal respect into practical behavior, nonetheless, in situations of violating her persona by means of assault, Halakhah sets out guidelines for how to address such behavior. The seriousness of the prohibition of battery expresses itself in a husband's liability for injuring his wife while engaging in conjugal relations (*onah*).[33]

29. Resp. Maharam of Rothenburg, Cremona ed. 291, Prague ed. 81,927; *Resp. Ha-Rashba ha-Meyuhasot la-Ramban*, 102; *Resp. Ha-Rashba* 4:113; *Resp. Binyamin Ze'ev*, supra n. 28; *Beit Yosef, Tur, Even Ha-Ezer* 74; *Sefer Ha-Agudah, Ketubot* 172; Rema, *Even Ha-Ezer* 154:3; *Resp. Hayyim Ve-Shalom* 2:36; *Resp. Perah Mateh Aharon* 1:60. Cf. numerous decisors who sanction wife-beating in order to prevent the commission of a transgression (*le-afrushei me-issura*), should a wife be delinquent in fulfilling her marital duties or needlessly curses her husband. See *Resp. Terumat Ha-Deshen* 218; *Resp. Ha-Ridvaz* 888; *Mishneh Torah, Hilk. Ishut* 21:10; Rema, *Even Ha-Ezer* 154:3. Whether such conduct is permissible today is beyond the scope of our presentation. Suffice is to say that there are authorities who prohibit assaulting a wife under these circumstances.

30. *Devarim* 25:3; Maimonides, *Sefer Ha-Mitzvot, mitzvat lo ta'aseh* 300; *Shulhan Arukh, Hoshen Mishpat* 420:1.

31. *Shulhan Arukh, Even Ha-Ezer* 154:3, *Rema*, ad locum. Moreover, the batterer is invalid to be a witness in a *beit din* proceeding. See *Shulhan Arukh, Hoshen Mishpat* 34:4; *Resp. Mahari Weil*, 28 and 87; *Resp. Ha-Mabit*, 1:291; *Resp. Ha-Maharit*, 2, *Even Ha-Ezer* 43.

32. *Beit Yosef, Tur, Even Ha-Ezer* 154; *Darkhei Moshe, Tur, Even Ha-Ezer* 154:20.

33. *Shulhan Arukh, Even Ha-Ezer* 63 (end); *Shulhan Arukh, Hoshen Mishpat* 421:12.

The duty of a husband to engage in *onah* is grounded in a biblical imperative (*mi-deoraita*).[34] Lest one argue that engagement in a *mitzvah* exempts one from responsibility from injury caused during sexual intercourse, Halakhah states otherwise.[35] Hence, Hazon Ish contends that engagement in the *mitzvah* of *onah* does not serve as a defense.[36] Even if the husband unintentionally injured his wife due to losing self-control, i.e., *ones*, nevertheless, regarding any assault against another person, a person is always deemed forewarned and thus liable (*adam mu'ad le-olam*).[37] Should a husband unintentionally abstain from conjugal relations and his spouse becomes emotionally distressed regarding the situation, he still violates Halakhah.[38]

Consequently, a husband is proscribed from preparing a prenuptial agreement which releases himself from his duty to perform conjugal relations[39] due to the fact that such abstention from relations engenders "*tza'ar*," pain for his wife and/or is understood as entailing "the *ikar ha-nissuin*", the essence of marriage.[40] Notwithstanding the view of

---

34. *Shemot* 21:10; *Tur, Mekhilta* of R. Yishmael, *Mishpatim* 3, ed. Horowitz-Rabin 258-259; *Even Ha-Ezer* 69; *Shulhan Arukh, Even Ha-Ezer* 69:6.

Alternatively, it is derived from logical inference. See Birkat Ha-Netziv on *Mekhilta*, op. cit. It is the wife's right to engage in conjugal relations and the husband's obligation to satisfy the wife in this regard.

Though the source for the duty to engage in conjugal relations has been stated with reference to the husband (see *Shemot*, op. cit.; Talmud Bavli, *Ketubot* 47b), however this obligation is equally incumbent upon the wife. See Talmud Bavli, *Ketubot* 63a, *Nedarim* 15b; *Shulhan Arukh Even Ha-Ezer* 77:2-3. As Rashba notes, the couple is mutually bound regarding conjugal relations as a necessarily implied incident of marriage. See *Hiddushei Ha-Rashba, Nedarim* 15b. Cf. Netziv of Volozhin's position that the wife's obligation is derivative of her being bound to the husband for intimacy. See *Resp. Meishiv Davar* 4:35.

35. Talmud Yerushalmi, *Bava Kama* 6:13; *Shulhan Arukh, Yoreh Deah* 340, *Hoshen Mishpat* 418:12; *Resp. Havot Yair*, 207; *Resp. Be'er Sarim*, 1:10. For exceptions to the rule, see *Mishneh Torah, Hilk. Hovel U-Mazik* 6:8; *Shulhan Arukh, Hoshen Mishpat* 359:4.

36. *Hazon Ish, Bava Kama* 11:21.

37. *Shulhan Arukh, Hoshen Mishpat* 378:1; *Hazon Ish*, supra n. 36. Cf. *Tosafot, Bava Kama* 27a, s.v. *u-Shemuel amar*; *Tosafot, Bava Metzia* 42a, s.v. *amar Shemuel.*

38. *Resp. Maharam Alsheikh* 40; *Piskei Din Rabbanayim* (hereinafter: PDR) 18:1, 20 (R. Elyashiv); File no. 860977-1, Netanya Regional Beit Din, Plonit v. Ploni, May 20, 2013. Cf. *Resp. Ha-Mabit* 3:131 in the name of Maimonides.

39. *Hiddushei Ha-Ramban, Bava Batra* 126b, s.v. *harei zu mekudeshet*. Alternatively, it is viewed as *mehilah*, waiving her right to engaging in relations. See *Shitah Mekubetzet, Ketubot* 56a in the name of Rashba.

40. Rashi, *Kiddushin* 19b; Ramban, supra n. 39; Ramban, *Sefer ha-Zekhut, Ketubot* 26 (on Rif).

Talmud Yerushalmi and a few decisors,[41] adopting the Talmud Bavli's position,[42] the majority of authorities invalidate such a condition due to the fact that it is "*matneh al mah sha-katuv ba-Torah*," it is a stipulation in variance to the Torah.[43] In short, the performance of "*onah*" is one of the foundations of a halakhic marriage and consequently a husband cannot decide to unilaterally opt out of it.[44]

Consequently, it is of no surprise that numerous arbiters argue that it is the husband's responsibility to foresee the possibility of potential injury and therefore, if injury nevertheless transpired, he is considered negligent.[45] Similarly, a husband who argues that he lost self-control and therefore assaulted his wife will also be held responsible for his behavior. As Shulhan Arukh, Sma, and R. Shlomo Luria note,[46] if a husband is liable for any injury caused to his spouse during *onah, a fortiori,* should he force her to have conjugal relations against her will, he has committed "*habala*" and he is therefore liable for tort (*nezikin*) damages.[47] A

---

41. Talmud Yerushalmi, *Ketubot* 5:7 and *Bava Metzia* 7:7; *Hiddushei Ha-Ritva, Kiddushin* 19b, *Bava Metzia* 51a and *Bava Batra* 126b; *Mordekhai Ketubot* 213 and *Bava Metzia* 369.

42. Talmud Bavli *Ketubot* 56a, *Kiddushin* 19b, *Bava Metzia* 94a

43. Rashi, *Ketubot* 56a; Rashbam, *Bava Batra* 126b; Ramban, supra n. 39; *Mishneh Torah, Hilk. Ishut* 12:7; *Tur Even Ha-Ezer* 38:12–13; *Shulhan Arukh* and Rema *Even Ha-Ezer* 38:5. 49.

44. Though if a wife requests (or possibly sets a condition) before the marriage (or possibly during the marriage) that her husband refrain from performing *onah*, assuming the husband has fulfilled the mitzvah of having children, there are authorities who will validate this arrangement. See *Mishneh Torah, Hilk. Ishut* 15:1, *Shulhan Arukh Even Ha-Ezer* 76:6; *Mishneh le-Melekh, Mishneh Torah Hilk. Ishut* 6:10; *Perishah, Tur Even Ha-Ezer* 76:17; *Hagahot Rabbi Akiva Eiger, Shulhan Arukh Even Ha-Ezer* 76:1; *Resp. Shoeil u-Meishiv* 3:108.

Clearly, if the husband unintentionally causes pain by failing to engage in *onah* properly such as being impotent, sexually dysfunctional or being imprisoned, he is in contravention of Halakhah, and such situations may serve as grounds for obligating or coercing a *get*. See *Shulhan Arukh Even Ha-Ezer* 76:13; *Resp. Alsheikh* 60; *Resp. Ha-Ridvaz* 4:118; *Resp. Oneg Yom Tov* 168; PDR 12:96, 116.

45. *Piskei Ha-Rosh, Bava Kamma* 2:10. See Y. Sinai & B. Shmueli, "The Water Reached the Soul" (Hebrew), 6 *Moznei Mishpat* 5767, 318-332; this writer's *Rabbinic Authority*, vol. 2, 84-101.

46. *Shulhan Arukh, Hoshen Mishpat,* supra n. 27; *Sma, Shulhan Arukh, Hoshen Mishpat* 421:20; *Yam Shel Shlomo, Bava Kama* 3:21.

47. *Hazon Ish, Hoshen Mishpat* 19:2; *Resp. Divrei Yatziv, Even Ha-Ezer* 77:3. Even if the injury was unintentional, he is liable for injury and pain. See Talmud Bavli *Menahot* 49a; Talmud Yerushalmi, *Gittin* 5:5; *Kesef Mishneh, Mishneh Torah, Hilk. Ma'akhalot Asurot* 13:28; *Resp. Hatan Sofer, Hoshen Mishpat* 24; *Shulhan Arukh, Even Ha-Ezer* 83:1. Though one is exempt from liability for shame if one

husband must control his desires and neither injure his wife nor rape her under any circumstances. Moreover, neither the establishment of marriage nor a mutual agreement between spouses to sanction a husband's assault of his wife even for her own personal enjoyment may serve as grounds for a husband's exemption from liability for any ensuing damage.[48] Any agreement between two individuals to be a subject of battery is prohibited.[49] *A fortiori*, he should not force himself upon his wife. In fact, normative Halakhah outlaws spousal rape,[50] as said behavior entails "stealing her body."[51]

That being said, the emerging issue is whether a wife is entitled to divorce herself from her husband the rapist. Maimonides's reply is:[52]

> A woman who withholds marital intimacy from her husband is called a *moredet* ("a rebellious woman"). She is asked why she has rebelled. If she answers: "Because I am repulsed by him and I cannot voluntarily engage in relations with him," her husband should be compelled to divorce her immediately. For she is not like a captive, [to be forced] to engage in relations with one she loathes.

As such, coercing a *get* (*kofin le-garesh*) by a *beit din* may entail flogging or imprisonment. In terms of Halakhah,[53] assuming that legally this sanction could be applied; there are arbiters who subscribe to Maimonides's posture that advancing a repulsion plea justifies mandating *get* coercion.[54]

---

unintentionally rapes one's wife (see *Tur, Hoshen Mishpat* 421; Sma, supra n. 40), nonetheless meting out damages for shame as a punitive measure (*migdar milta*), is permissible. See *Shulhan Arukh, Hoshen Mishpat* 420:38.

48. *Resp. Revid Ha-Zahav* 42:3.

49. *Bava Kama* 93a; *Resp. Ha-Rosh* 68:10; *Shulhan Arukh, Hoshen Mishpat* 421:12. Nonetheless, though there exists a prohibition to agree to be a victim of battery, should battery occur with the consent of the victim, the batterer will be exempt from liability. See *Bava Kamma*, op. cit.; *Tosafot Ketubot* 56b, s.v. *harei* in the name of R. Elhanan.

50. Talmud Bavli *Eruvin* 100b; *Mishneh Torah, Hilk. De'ot* 5:4, *Hilk. Ishut* 14:8, 15:17, 21:12; *Tur, Even Ha-Ezer* 25, *Shulhan Arukh, Orah Hayyim* 240:3, *Even Ha-Ezer* 25:2; *Magen Avraham, Shulhan Arukh, Orah Hayyim* 240:7; *Beit Shmuel, Shulhan Arukh, Even Ha-Ezer* 77:4; *Teshuvot Resp. Divrei Yatziv, Even Ha-Ezer* 77.

51. *Divrei David, Devarim* 6:17.

52. *Mishneh Torah, Hilk. Ishut* 14:8

53. This level is distinguishable from the rabbinic legislative level (*takanah*).

54. *Resp. Hut Ha-Meshullash, Tur Shelishi* of R. Tawah, 34 in the name of Rabbeinu Gershom; *Mordekhai Ketubot* 185 in the name of Rabbeinu Hananel (Cf.

In such circumstances, others reject *get* coercion.[55] On the other hand, there are some decisors who would *obligate* a *get*.[56]

The implicit premise of the above opinions is predicated upon the assumption that the sole issue is whether or not one may coerce a *get*, as well as whether there is a duty to give a *get*. However this is not the case. One of the reasons for divorcing a man (*ilot gerushin*) is because he causes his spouse to violate prohibitions (*oveir al dat Moshe*) such as engaging in conjugal relations during her menstrual period.[57] Clearly, a husband may only have intercourse with his wife's consent;[58] to fail to desist from spousal rape after a wife entreats her husband to cease from such behavior is unconscionable. Under such circumstances, a victim of spousal rape in and of itself may entail an infraction of battery (*habala*). As Rabbi Karo and Rabbi Shlomo Luria rule, a husband is liable for any injuries caused during consensual intercourse,[59] *a fortiori* should he force her to have relations against her will he has committed battery, and is liable for damages.[60] Whether an act of spousal rape without any attendant harm would constitute *habalah* is subject to debate.[61] The

---

Tosafot Ketubot 64a, s.v. *aval* in the name of Rabbeinu Hananel; *Sefer Ha-Yashar* of R. Tam 24 in the name of Rashbam; *Piskei Ha-Rosh Ketubot* 5:34 in the name of Rashbam; *Mishneh Torah, Hilk. Yibbum* 2:15 in the name of Ra'avad; *Tosafot Gittin* 84b in the name of Ri; *Resp. Ha-Tashbetz* 2:256; *Resp. Shoeil U-Meishiv, Mahadura* 3, 1:350.

Some authorities will coerce a *get* if circumstances demonstrate that there is a clear pretext (*amatla mevureret*). See this writer's *Rabbinic Authority*, vol. 6, 197-201.

55. R. Tam, *Sefer Ha-Yashar, Resp.* 24; *Piskei Ha-Rid, Ketubot* 63b; *Ba'al Ha-Maor*, Alfasi, 27a; Ran, Alfasi, *Ketubot* 27b; *Resp. Ha-Rashba* 1:573, 1192, 1335 (Cf. *Resp. Ha-Rashba* 2:276); *Hiddushei Ha-Ramban Ketubot* 63b; *Hiddushei Ha-Ritva Ketubot* 63b (Cf. *Beit Ha-Behirah Ketubot*, Sofer ed. 269 in the name of Ritva); *Resp. Mahari Bruna* 211; *Resp. Maharil Ha-Hadashot* 189; *Resp. Maharshal* 41; *Resp. Zera Anashim, Even Ha-Ezer* 36; *Resp. Maharashdam Even Ha-Ezer* 135; *Resp. Torat Emet* 186; *Hazon Ish Even Ha-Ezer* 69:1.

56. Rema, *Even Ha-Ezer* 77:3, *Yoreh Deah* 228:20; *Resp. Tzitz Eliezer* 4, 21:8, 5:26:3 in the name of Rema and Gaon of Vilna.

57. Rema, *Even Ha-Ezer* 154:3; *Arukh Ha-Shulhan Even Ha-Ezer* 154:17; PDR 6:221–222; 11:327.

58. Talmud Bavli *Eruvin* 100b; *Mishneh Torah, Hilk. Issurei Bi'ah* 21:12, *Hilk. Ishut* 15:17; Ra'avad, *Ba'alei HaNefesh, Sha'ar Ha-Kedushah* 122; *Shulhan Arukh, Even Ha-Ezer* 25:2. See also *Beit Shmuel, Shulhan Arukh, Even Ha-Ezer* 77:4; *Resp. Maharit*, 1:5; *Teshuvot Yaskil Avdi* 6:25. Cf. *Atzei Arazim* 25:1.

59. *Shulhan Arukh Hoshen Mishpat* 421:12; *Shulhan Arukh Hoshen Mishpat Sma*, 421:10; *Yam shel Shlomo Bava Kama* 3:21. See further this writer's *Rabbinic Authority*, vol. 2, 81–102.

60. *Hazon Ish Hoshen Mishpat* 19:2; *Resp. Divrei Yatziv Even Ha-Ezer* 77:3.

61. *Sefer Ravan, Eruvin* 159; *Tosafot Nidah* 12a; *Ra'avyah* 3:994; *Ohr Zarua* 1,

bottom line is that spousal rape entails a prohibition and consequently such a husband is *oveir al dat Moshe.*

Based upon the foregoing understanding of halakhic intimacy, Rabbi O. Yosef rules that there are grounds to coerce a *get.*[62] Among the reasons that he gives are the following: Firstly, a woman in our generation may succumb to engaging in illicit affairs lest a *get* be delivered to her. Secondly, sitting in jail today is not to be equated to physically coercing a husband to give a *get.* Furthermore, in the event the couple is separated we should take into consideration Rabbi H. Pelaggi's posture that if the couple has been separated for at least eighteenth months and there are no prospects to restore domestic tranquility (*shalom bayit*), *get* coercion is a proper sanction.[63] Furthermore, Maimonides's view regarding grounds for *get* coercion when a wife is advancing a repulsion plea (*ma'is ali*) is subscribed to by others, and as such does not represent a minority view.

3. Conclusion

The first prominent modern argument for the marital rape exemption, the claim from privacy, posits that there is something inherent in the nature of the relationship between husband and wife that makes halakhic intervention inappropriate, misguided, and ultimately self-defeating. It contends that the marital relation depends on intimacy protected from outside scrutiny, intimacy that could not survive if the law intervened to investigate and prosecute marital rape charges.

This notion of marital privacy dates back to the nineteenth century where the North Carolina Supreme Court states the following:[64]

> If no permanent injury has been inflicted, nor malice, cruelty, nor dangerous violence shown by the husband, it is better to draw the curtain, shut out the public gaze, and leave the parties to forget and forgive.

The "drawing of the curtain" and the consequent privatization of law allowed a couple to engage in spousal rape and supported a woman's

Nedarim 20b; *Piskei Ha-Rosh Eruvin* 10:13. Cf. Talmud Bavli *Nedarim* 15b

62. *Resp. Yabia Omeir*, 3 *Even Ha-Ezer* 18-20.

63. For a recent exposition of a rejection of this posture and/or interpreting this view as requiring an obligation to give a *get* rather than *get* compulsion, see File no. 32292/3, Ashdod Regional Beit Din, February 13, 2023.

64. State v. Oliver 70 N.C. 60 (1874).

right to control use of her sexual organs and thus engage in abortion and use of contraceptives.[65]

In addition to keeping the public out, drawing the curtain keeps the couple in the marital home. As such, the couple is required to resolve their issues on their own. When a couple is able on their own to resolve differences, a greater mutual respect might be expected than if the couple proceeds to court for resolution. Litigating in court may only permanently accentuate the differences between the spouses and may make their ultimate resolution more difficult.

Given that a couple can end up in either a *beit din* or court to address issues of the propriety of marital intercourse, seemingly the net result is identical. But, in fact the circumstances can be quite different. Whereas in common law, we are dealing with a couple who may have engaged in spousal rape and in certain jurisdictions there may be a marital exemption for this conduct, in Halakhah we are addressing a case of marital intimacy which ought to be marked by the husband's respect towards his wife and his wife's consent to engage in intercourse.[66] In this event, should the wife be injured due her spouse's behavior during intimacy, the husband is responsible.[67] Whereas, as we have observed, marital intimacy according to Halakhah provides guidelines for proper behavior, common law sanctions spousal rape. As Jill Hasday aptly observes:[68]

> In the first half of the nineteenth century, courts were almost completely silent on the question whether marital rape could even be cruelty. The one notable case on the subject during this period, *Shaw v. Shaw*,[69] suggested that wives would encounter extreme difficulty in establishing the claim.

To state it differently, whereas common law endorses privatization of the law due to the norms of marital privacy, Halakhah is a religious legal system which provides guidelines for marital living in general and intimacy in particular.

---

65. Prince v. Massachusetts, 321 U.S. 158,166 (1944); Poe v. Ullman 367 U.S. 497 (1961); Griswold v. Connecticut 381 U.S. 479,495 (1965); Cotner v. Henry 394 F. 2d. 873 (7th Circuit 1967); Loving v. Virginia, 388 U.S. 1 (1967); Eisenstadt v. Baird 405 U.S. 438 (1972); Roe v. Wade 410 U.S. 113 (1973); Planned Parenthood of Missouri v. Danforth 428 U.S. 52 (1976)

66. See supra text accompanying nn. 30-44.

67. See supra text accompanying nn. 45-51.

68. See supra n. 10, at 1465.

69. 17 Conn. 189 (1845).

Chapter 4

The Status of a Married Woman as a Businesswoman, Property Owner & Participant in the *Beit Din* Process

AS WE MENTIONED IN chapter 3, the origins of the common law definition of the nature of the marriage can be traced to Blackstone's Commentaries on the Law of England. William Blackstone articulated the doctrine as follows:[1]

> By marriage, the husband and wife are one person in law; that is, the very being or legal existence of the woman is suspended during the marriage, or at least is incorporated and consolidated into that of the husband; under whose wing, protection, and cover she performs everything; and is therefore called... feme-covert... her condition during her marriage is called her coverture. Upon this principle of a union of person in husband and wife, depend all the legal rights, duties, and disabilities, that either of them acquire by the marriage.

One scholar described the effects of this loss of legal capacity as follows:[2]

> To secure this unity the law starts with the assumption that the wife's legal existence becomes suspended or extinguished during the marriage state.... she cannot earn herself, nor in general, contract, sue or be sued in her own right; and this because she is not, in legal contemplation, a person....

1. W. Blackstone, *Commentaries on the Law of England Oxford,* (1768), 1:422,430-431.For an earlier articulation of this idea, see *The Lawes Resolution of Women's Rights,* London, 1632 reprinted in M. Bloomfield, *American Lawyers in a Changing Society,1776-1876,* Cambridge, Mass. (1976),94-95.
2. J. Schouler, *Marriage, Divorce, Separation and Domestic Relations* (6th ed. 1921), vol.1, section 5.

More recently expressing the "civil death" of a married woman, the idea was well captured by Professor Lawrence Friedman:[3]

> Essentially, husband and wife were one flesh; but the man was the owner of the flesh.

Professor Gila Stopler observes:[4]

> All (American – AYW) states have chosen to perpetuate the English common law doctrine of coverture, thereby incorporating essentially a highly discriminatory religious view of women into their laws.

On one hand, Professor Stopler's presentation of the receptivity of the unity doctrine requires more elaboration when dealing with the marital rape exemption, i.e., a husband could not be prosecuted for raping his wife. Since the late 1970's several U.S. states have partially or completely abolished the exemption through legislation and judicial decisions.[5] With the advent of the 1980s and 1990s, the majority continue to permit marital rape, by criminalizing only first-degree rapes and permitting spousal rape prosecutions when the parties are living apart and/or divorced or separated.[6] As of early 2023, 12 states have loopholes such as classifying the crime as Class B felony rather than a Class A felony, focusing on marital rape that occurs against an incapacitated person or one who is drugged, or participating in therapy sessions as a replacement for punishments.

---

3. L. Friedman, *A History of American Law*, N.Y. 1973, 184. One of the ramifications of invoking the "unity" doctrine is the recognition of the marital rape exemption law that preempts prosecuting a husband for marital rape of his wife. See further, this writer's *Rabbinic Authority: The Vision and the Reality* (hereinafter: *Rabbinic Authority*), vol. 2, 185-186.

4. "A Rank Usurpation of Powers" – The Role of Patriarchal Religion and Culture in the Subordination of Women, 15 *Duke J. of Gender Law and Policy* 365, 386 (2008).

5. L. Siegel, "The Marital Rape Exemption: Evolution to Extinction," 43 *Cleveland State Law Review* 352-353 (1995).

6. M. Hilf, "Marital Privacy and Spousal Rape," 16 *New England Law. Review* 31-32 (1980); A. Dailey, "To Have and to Hold: The Marital Rape Exemption and the Fourteenth Amendment, 99 *Harvard Law Review* 1258-1259 (1986); R. West, "Equality Theory, Marital Rape, and the Promise of the Fourteenth Amendment," 42 *Florida Law Review* 46-47 (1990); J. Hasday," Contest and Consent: A Legal History of Marital Rape" 88 *California Law Review* 1375-1376, 1501-1502, (2000).

On the other hand, Professor Stopler's assertion that the theory of coverture is grounded in religion is well founded. Addressing the first marriage recorded in the Torah, we are told:[7]

> That is why a man leaves his father and his mother, and cleaves to his wife: and they become one flesh.

Clearly, whether a wife is devoid of legal capacity cannot be attributed to the exegetical interpretation of a Biblical verse whereby a wife's identity merged into the existence of her husband. One must delve into the literary and legal sources of Halakhah in order to ascertain whether a wife possesses halakhic capacity.

Generally, people view Halakhah as religious in nature and therefore it is their understanding that this religious tradition deals with relations between God and man such as the laws of prayer, Shabbat and Festivals and the laws of *kashrut* (rabbinical certification of food). However, the literary and legal sources of Halakhah embody a religious *legal* system, a system which has been in existence for over three thousand years which has its adherents both in Israel as well in the Diaspora, in countries outside of Israel. As such, Halakhah encompasses the range of subjects characteristic of all modern legal systems – civil matters such as contracts, torts, agency, labor relations, domestic relations; criminal matters such as criminal law, criminal procedure, and public and administrative law.

The literary sources of Halakhah comprise the following:

1. The Bible, which includes the Five Books of Moses, the writings of the Prophets, and the Hagiographa.
2. The Mishnah, which was composed from the first century to 220 C.E. – the first restatement of Halakhah.
3. The Babylonian and Jerusalem Talmuds, composed between 220 C.E. to the end of the fifth century, C.E. – the classical exposition of Halakhah.
4. From post-talmudic period until today, Halakhah was and continues to be recorded in the following authoritative legal sources:
   a. *Perushim* (commentaries) and *hiddushin* (novella) which are discursive critical investigations of the Talmud.
   b. *Sifrei Psak* – restatements of Halakhah

7. *Bereshit* 2:24.

c. *She'elot u Teshuvot* (responsa literature) – There are over three hundred thousand juridical authorities' decisions on Halakhic queries of litigants, judges, communal leaders and other individuals. The responsa literature is very similar to our case law.

Jewish legal arbiters have at their disposal five tools for arriving at a legal decision: *midrash* (canons of interpretations entailing an exegetical interpretation of passages in the Bible); *takanah* (legislation which is authored by an arbiter[s] or by the Jewish community[ies]); *minhag* (custom); *ma'aseh* (precedent) which is persuasive rather than binding and *sevarah* (halakhic logic) such as "*hekesh,*" analogical reasoning.

Unlike a western legal system which functions institutionally in accordance with a tripartite division of authority, namely an executive, legislature and judiciary, the Halakhic system embodies an executive authority and a judicial-legislative authority. In other words, an arbiter is empowered to both interpret the Halakhah as well as to legislate under certain conditions.[8]

The purpose of this presentation is to examine both the literary as well as legal sources of Halakhah in order to determine whether the inception of a halakhic marriage preempts a wife's identity and therefore, "she cannot earn herself, nor in general, contract, sue or be sued in her own right."

How does Halakhah view the legal capacity of a married woman acquiring property, executing contracts, and managing her life financially? Describing the three-fold classification of a wife's property, Professor Ben Zion Schereschewsky, former Supreme Court Justice in Israel, observes:[9]

> Dowry or *"nedunyah"* means all property of whatever kind brought by the wife to the husband upon their marriage... those assets of the wife which she of her own free will entrusts to her

8. For further discussion regarding the literary and legal sources of Halakhah, see Menachem Elon, *Jewish Law; History, Sources and Principles*, Philadelphia: The Jewish Publication Society, 1994, 275-1007.

9. B. Z. Schereschewsky, "Dowry" in M. Elon (ed.), *The Principles of Jewish Law*, Jerusalem: 1975, 390-392.

For a comparative analysis of the halakhic property regime with the community property and common law matrimonial property systems, see N. Rakover, "Property Relations between Spouses" (Hebrew), Jerusalem: 1970; A. Rosen-Tzvi, *The Law of Matrimonial Property* (Hebrew), Jerusalem:1982, 121-134.

> husband's responsibility... *"nikhsei tzon barzel"*... is a term derived from a name of a transaction in which one party entrusts property on certain terms, the latter undertaking responsibility... for the return of the capital value of the property at the time of his receipt thereof... Upon dissolution of the marriage, this obligation of the husband is governed by the rule that any appreciation or depreciation in the property is his.... *Melog* property is property of which the principal remains in the wife's ownership but the fruits thereof are taken by the husband, so that he has no responsibility... in respect of the principal, both its loss and gain being only hers, and upon dissolution of the marriage such property returns to the wife.... This category embraces all the property of the wife falling outside the category of *"nikhsei tzon barzel"* (except for a third category described below – AYW)... whether brought by her at the time of entering the marriage, or acquired thereafter, e.g. by way of inheritance or gift.... A third category is property of the wife concerning which the husband has no rights at all, neither to the principal nor the fruits thereof. This includes property acquired by her after the marriage by way of gift, the donor having expressly stipulated that it be used for a specific purpose... or that it be used for any purpose of her choice without her husband having any authority... or property given to her as a gift by her husband.

The ramification of halakhic matrimonial property law was described in the following fashion:[10]

> Therefore, if a wife who is managing her husband's property now holds property in her name that she amassed after the marriage, it is presumed that the property, although in her name, is really property that she amassed for her husband. The deeds should have been in her husband's name, since she was using her husband's money to purchase property since her own money had been turned over to her husband at the time of the marriage.

Although marriage does not affect a husband's property, a wife's property is impacted by marriage. Though the title to the wife's *melog* property (movables and immovables) and *tzon barzel* property of immovables resides with her, the husband has exclusive rights to its management,

10. E. Quint, *A Restatement of Rabbinic Civil Law,* Northvale, NJ, 1991, 163-164.

income, and profits, to be used for "the comfort of the home."[11] Any expenses incurred are the husband's sole responsibility.[12] The term "comfort of the home" is not intended to limit the husband's right in the fruits of *nikhsei melog* but rather to define the manner of the husband's use of this property.[13] Moreover, the husband as breadwinner of the family is responsible for economic support, while the wife is entrusted with domestic and child care services. Hence, similar to common law, a married woman in Halakhah is dependent upon her husband. Having limited assets subject to her power of disposition,[14] in numerous situations, a wife is factually incapable of satisfying any debt or liability Halakhah might have imposed upon her and permitted her to incur.

This does not mean however that Halakhah denies capacity to a wife, similar to the status of a minor or a mentally deficient individual (a *shoteh*). In fact, dispositive arrangements regarding property relations can be effected between a husband and a wife.[15] For example, how does Halakhah deal with a married woman who pledges credit? A wife, like an unmarried woman who borrows funds for engaging in a commercial transaction, is liable for repayment of the loan. Secondly, in a locale where women are accustomed to participating in commercial transactions, if a couple contracted jointly as co-borrowers, the law of joint and several liability is applicable.[16] Pursuant to Halakhah, the liability is "joint" in that both the wife and the husband may be joined to render

---

11. Talmud Bavli *Ketubot* 80b; *Tur Even Ha-Ezer* 85; *Shulhan Arukh, Even Ha-Ezer* 85:17, *Helkat Mehokeik*, ad. locum. 41, *Beit Shmuel*, ad. locum. 38.

12. *Shulhan Arukh Even Ha-Ezer* 88:7, *Beit Shmuel*, ad. locum.11, *Helkat Mehokeik*, ad. locum. 11,14; *Piskei Din Rabbanayim* 8:281-282.

13. *Piskei Din Rabbanayim* 2:95-96.

14. Though there is a Talmudic principle, "what a wife acquires, the husband acquires" (Talmud Bavli *Gittin* 77a and *Nazir* 24b), nonetheless, a wife may amass assets in one of two ways:

(1) Property may be acquired by her during marriage through a gift (with proper stipulation) and it is entirely hers. See *Shulhan Arukh Even Ha-Ezer* 85:11.

(2) Alternatively, assets acquired by a wife which are unknown to her husband remain under her control. See *Shulhan Arukh Even Ha-Ezer* 90:11.

15. Talmud Bavli, *Kiddushin* 19b, *Bava Metzia* 51a, 94a, *Ketubot* 56a, *Bava Batra* 126b; *Shulhan Arukh Even Ha-Ezer* 38:5, 69:6; *Bi'ur Ha-Gra Even Ha-Ezer* 93:6; Rema, *Hoshen Mishpat* 344:1.

However, the value of the *ketubah* (*ikar ketubah*) and the wife's inheritance by the husband are not subject to private ordering. See *Shulhan Arukh Even Ha-Ezer* 66:3, 9; *Helkat Mehokeik, Even Ha-Ezer* 69:12; *Shulhan Arukh, Hoshen Mishpat* 209:8, Rema.

16. *Sma, Hoshen Mishpat* 77:25; *Shakh, Hoshen Mishpat* 77:30; R. M. Jaffe, *Hoshen Mishpat* 77:11.

repayment of the loan; it is "several" in that each borrower is liable for fifty per cent of the loan transaction. And it is "joint and several" in that no co-borrower's liability is extinguished until the creditor's claim is completely satisfied, that is, the husband and wife are guarantors for each other.[17] Having limited assets subject to her power of disposition, a wife may be incapable of satisfying the debt. Therefore, in the absence of the existence of a wife's assets, the "rule of joint and several obligations" guarantees that a creditor may proceed against her husband.[18]

What happens in the following multifarious situations when dealing with a wife who is a businesswoman running the family business (*noseit ve'notenet be'tokh ha'bayit*)[19]? A wife borrows money at the customary rate of interest while her husband is out of town. Upon his return, the husband refuses even to repay the principal, contending that she borrowed the money without his consent. Or a couple rents a house. In the midst of one rental period, the husband traveled out of town and the wife returned to her mother's home and sublet the house to a third party. Upon his return, the husband asserts the right to return to his home. The husband argued that since she was prohibited to sublet it without his permission, the husband claimed his right to the home. Finally, a situation where a wife manages the domestic affairs due to her husband's illness, can the wife contribute large sums of money to charity without his permission?

Implicitly relying upon Rashi,[20] Rabbi Eliezer ben Natan (known by the acronym: Raban), a twelfth century Tosafist of Germany, states the following:[21]

---

17. *Shulhan Arukh Hoshen Mishpat* 77:10; R. Jaffe, supra n. 16.

18. Upon becoming a widow or a divorcee, she is obligated to repay the debt. See *Shulhan Arukh Hoshen Mishpat* 132:1.

19. On one hand, the words *be'tokh ha'bayit* allude to the wife's responsibility to perform all the domestic work involved in running a household. And her work (*ma'aseh yadeha*) is performed in exchange for her husband's economic support (*mezonot*). See Talmud Bavli *Ketubot* 47b, 58b, 107b; *Tur Even Ha-Ezer* 69; *Shulhan Arukh Even Ha-Ezer* 69:4. On the other hand, the words *noseit ve'notenet* alludes to a wife who engages in business. See Mishnah *Shevuot* 7:8; *Tiferet Yisrael, Mishnah Shevuot* 7:8; Talmud Bavli *Shevuot* 45a; Talmud Bavli *Bava Batra* 52b; infra notes 18, 21 and 22; *Resp. Maharsham* 2:30.

20. Talmud Bavli *Shevuot* 48b.

21. *Resp. Raban* 115.

This view reflects the historical passage of a wife from one who resides in the marital home to participating in commercial living. See E. Urbach, *Ba'alei Ha-Tosafot, their History, Writings and Methods*, (Hebrew), Tel Aviv: 5714, 151; J. Katz, 31 *Kiryat Sefer* 14, 5716; this writer's, "A Comparative Analysis of a Wife's Capacity to

> Today all women are administrators (*apitropsot*) of their husbands' properties and an administrator is an agent (a *shaliah*)... therefore all her business dealings are done as his agent...

A similar response was suggested by Rabbi Shlomo ben Shimon Duran (better known by the acronym: Rashbash), a fifteenth century Sephardic legist who stated the following:[22]

> There are locales where women do as they please with their husband's assets... and no one protests. Consequently, she is like his agent; and he cannot say,"I appointed you as my agent only for my benefit," since it is customary for them to do as they please. Thus, if the husband later wishes to void the transaction, he may not, since at the inception of the transaction the wife contracted with his consent.

However, as noted by Rabbi Jacob of Lisa, though she is the agent of her husband, nevertheless, if he signs off that she should be relied upon, then in the absence of her husband she is obligated to pay any outstanding debt.[23]

Subsequently, Rabbi Jacob Reicher, an eighteenth century authority notes:[24]

> We have found that a married woman has obligated herself if she transacts affairs in her house and the husband must pay; it is as if the husband appointed agents. And this is the agreement of most decisors, like the view of Mordekhai... Shakh... Helkat Mehokeik...

Others concurred with Raban's posture in its entirety,[25] or limited its application to small debts, where the husband may potentially derive

---

Pledge her Husband's Credit for Domestic Necessities in Anglo-American Law and Jewish Law,"13 *The Jewish Law Annual* 236-237, 2000.

22. *Resp. Ha-Rashbash* 91.

23. *Netivot Ha-Mishpat, Hoshen Mishpat* 77, *Biurim* 11. See also, *Resp. Nahal Yitzhak* 77 (4); *Resp. Ateret Devorah, 2 Even Ha-Ezer* 48.

24. *Resp. Shevut Ya'akov* 1:155.

25. *Mordekhai, Bava Kamma* 8:87-88; *Hagahot Maimononiot, Hil. Hovel U-Mazik* 4:3.

benefit from the transaction, or should her husband protest that he never authorized her to act in his name, then she is not deemed an agent.[26]

In short, notwithstanding certain circumstances, the majority of arbiters subscribed to the notion that the wife is the agent of the husband. In contrast to common law, being an agent imparts halakhic recognition of the wife's capacity.[27] Under such an arrangement of being an agent, a merchant would extend credit and sell to a married woman, relying on the fact that should she refuse to pay, Halakhah would charge these purchases to the husband. Under such circumstances, the halakhic discussion would resolve upon the extent that the husband is liable for his wife's commercial dealings, included but not limited to loan transactions.[28]

However, there may be instances where a wife may singlehandedly operate her husband's affairs. Rabbi Ovadiah Hadaya, a twentieth century Israeli *dayan,* addresses a situation in which a woman supported a Torah scholar with large sums of money and the scholar subsequently discovered that the disbursement of these funds was done without the permission of the woman's husband. Here, we are dealing with a different type of *noseit ve'notenet be'tokh ha'bayit.* Describing the wife as an owner rather than merely managing the husband's property as an agent, Rabbi Hadaya elucidates:[29]

> It is clear from his actions that he allows her to be involved in trade and use the assets just as a person would use his own property. He brought the items to the store while she was the manager, whom all the customers viewed as the owner. Therefore, his actions demonstrate that she was serving not merely in capacity as a manager, but as an owner, and since without her he could not do anything in the business, she is permitted to use

26. *Resp. Ha-Rosh* 13:1, 39:8; *Yam Shel Shlomo, Bava Kamma* 8:29; *Shakh, Hoshen Mishpat* 96:9; *Resp. Shoeil U-Meishiv,* 2nd ed., 2:18; *Resp. Ha-Mabit* 190; *Arukh Ha-Shulhan Hoshen Mishpat* 96:8; *Resp. Iggerot Moshe, Even Ha-Ezer* 1:103.

27. For some of the sources which demonstrate the significance of an agent possessing capacity, see Mishnah *Terumot* 4:4, *Eruvin* 3:2, *Kiddushin* 2:1, *Gittin* 1:1; Talmud Bavli *Eruvin* 31b, *Meilah* 21a; *Shulhan Arukh Even Ha-Ezer* 141:35; *Resp. Hatam Sofer Orah Hayyim* 20; *Netivot Ha-Mishpat Hoshen Mishpat* 182, *Biurim* 2. For additional sources, see N. Rakover, *The Jewish Law of Agency in Legal Proceedings* (Hebrew), Jerusalem: 5732, 11-29; M. Wygoda and H. Zafri, *Agency* (Hebrew), Jerusalem: 2014, 4-25.

28. Rema *Even Ha-Ezer* 86:2, 96:6 and *Resp. Ha-Maharik, shoresh* 189, who reject a husband's liability for his wife's debts which were incurred due to her active involvement in commercial trade. Cf. *Shakh Hoshen Mishpat* 62:8.

29. *Resp. Yaskil Avdi* 5 *Yoreh Deah* 36.

> his property just as a person would use his own, and he cannot protest against what she has already done. Clearly he would have to agree to anything she asked of him, because if he would be opposed, she could refuse to run the store and he would not be able to make a living.

A wife will not claim a portion of the profits which accrued in a business since her work (*ma'aseh yadeha*) is performed in exchange for her husband's economic support (*mezonot*).[30] Consequently, the wife relies upon the monetary value of her *ketubah* that will be paid to her at the time of divorce or becoming a widow.[31]

However, as aptly noted by Dayan Uriel Lavi, presiding *dayan* on the Jerusalem Regional Beit Din, in contemporary times *noseit ve'notenet be'tokh ha'bayit* is often to be understood as a wife who is a partner in the marriage.[32] As Dayan A. Sharezee states:[33]

> Even though the act of establishing marriage has not changed, and it will never change... nonetheless, in monetary matters there are changes and continue to be major changes, due to a change in mentality and social mores... The unifying force of all these changes is the improvement of the position of women and the transformation of her being a wife to being a full partner, or almost a complete one... in sustaining the home, and the husband being transformed into a partner whose rights and monetary obligations have undergone a change.

Certain elements of marriage have not changed, despite changes in society. Thus, the creation of *kiddushin* remains a consensual agreement that designates a particular woman for a particular man and prohibits her to all others.[34] Subsequently, the act of marriage entails a husband's monetary obligations such as spousal support. At the same time, as we mentioned earlier in our presentation, private ordering of financial matters may be permitted. Thus, although many of the wife's assets are owned by the husband,[35] Halakhah allows spouses to determine their

30. See supra n. 17.
31. See supra n. 21.
32. *Ateret Devorah*, supra n. 21.
33. *Mehalkhei Mishpat*, p. 95.
34. Talmud Bavli *Kiddushin* 2b; *Shulhan Arukh Even Ha-Ezer* 26, 37-39, 43 and 44.
35. See supra, text accompanying notes 9-10.

own business relationship provided that any agreements between the couple complies with proper form (e.g., a *kinyan*) and does not violate any prohibitions such as the interdict against taking interest (*ribbit*).

As such, under certain circumstances a marriage may be viewed as a commercial partnership, a position subscribed to by R. I. Herzog, R. I. Graubard, R. S. Daichovsky, R. U. Lavi as well as others.[36] Implicit in their position is the precedent that *noseit ve'notenet be'tokh ha'bayit* applies to most women.[37] Consequently, at the inception of marriage, upon a man's undertaking various duties to his spouse memorialized in the *ketubah*, there can be an obligation to establish various monetary matters in accordance with halakhic partnership law.[38]

Clearly, a man and woman alike who have executed a partnership

---

36. *Pesakim Ve-Ketavim* 9, *Hoshen Mishpat* 33; *Resp. Havalim Ba-Ne'imim* 5, *Even Ha-Ezer* 34; R. S. Daichovsky, "The Halakhot of Marital Partnership: The Law of the Kingdom" (Hebrew), 18 *Tehumin* 18, 5758; *Ateret Devorah*, supra n. 21.

For additional authorities who endorse this position, see this writer's *Rabbinic Authority*, vol. 1, 184-186.

37. *Resp. Ha-Rashba* 1:957; *Piskei Ha-Rosh Bava Batra* 355; Rema *Hoshen Mishpat* 62; PDR 2:289, 3:188.

38. Some authorities require that the couple must sign an agreement that explicitly states that their marriage is based upon an economic partnership. See *Resp. Maharival* 2:23; Y. Ariel, "The Modern Family Unit-Halakhic Implications" (Hebrew), 22 *Tehumin* 129, 145, 5762.

For the ramifications of establishing such a partnership, see *Beit Yosef, Hoshen Mishpat* 176, *Perisha*, ad. locum; *Shulhan Arukh, Hoshen Mishpat* 176:3; *Taz, Hoshen Mishpat* 176; *Resp. Ha-Ridvaz* 1:380; *Resp. Hatam Sofer Hoshen Mishpat* 96; *Netivot Ha-Mishpat* 176:5; *Resp. Divrei Hayyim* 1, *Hoshen Mishpat* 26,28; *Mishpat Shalom* 176; File no. 9061-21-1, Netanya Regional Beit Din June 26, 2006; File no. 14850-1, Ashdod Regional Rabbinical Court, September 19, 2010; File no. 347562-1, Tel Aviv- Yaffa Regional Rabbinical Court, September 13, 2011; File no. 842067/5, Supreme Rabbinical Court, May 29,2017; File no. 1228979/5, Tel Aviv-Yaffa Regional Beit Din, January 10,2023.

Alternatively, Hazon Ish suggests a different avenue to establish halakhic partnership and states the following:

> The law of the kingdom (civil government – AYW) determines the expectation of people. Since we customarily abide by the law of the kingdom under certain prescribed conditions, the law influences people, who then decide to rely on civil law.... Therefore, when we (the *beit din* – AYW) apply secular law, we are in actuality following our Halakhah rather than their laws. See Sanhedrin, Likkutim 16:1

In other words, there is an implicit expectation (*umdana*) that the terms of the economic partnership will be based upon civil partnership law. See further, this writer's *Rabbinic Authority*, vol. 1, 184-186, 189-193.

agreement concerning property own their particular share(s) in the property, provided that the location of the share(s) is specified in the agreement. Therefore, if the partner sold his portion or gave it as a gift, the transfer of ownership is valid.[39] However, during the time that the property is under the partner's ownership he is permitted to use it, provided the use is acceptable by the community.[40] However, should the partner coerce the other partners to divide the partnership, it is valid.[41]

What happens if the purchase of the marital home is bankrolled by the wife and the registration is recorded in land registration arrangement, such as the Israeli *reshum ba-tabu* under the names of the wife and husband? As we know, some will contend that we establish ownership based upon the party(ies) who paid for the purchase rather than the parties who are registered.[42] Other authorities will argue that whomever registered is the owner(s) of the property.[43]

Seemingly, the wife gifted half of the home to her husband and the parties are co-partners in the ownership of the home. One could negate his ownership right since his portion was given it as a gift contingent upon the condition that the marriage would continue. Or possibly there was no intention to give a gift but the title registration was given in equal portions only to avert fighting with the opposing side. Therefore, given the pending divorce, the expectation (*umdana*) is that the gift is null. Secondly, he has rights in the home since he consumes the fruits of her property (*perot nikhsei melog*) rather than receiving a right of ownership in her home.[44]

The question is who is the owner of the home, and does the title registration of the couple establish an equal partnership in the property? The

39. *Tosafot, Sukkah* 42b, s.v. *ella*; *Ohr Zarua Bava Batra* 41; *Resp. Ha-Rosh* 99:3; *Piskei Ha-Rosh Bava Metzia* 9:21; *Resp. Ha-Rashba* 1:935, 3:148; *Resp. Maharam of Rothenberg*, Cremona ed. 25; *Hiddushei Ha-Ran Bava Batra* 126b; *Resp. Ha-Rashbash* 68, 79; *Tur Hoshen Mishpat* 218:19; *Resp. Ha-Mabit* 1:25.

40. *Resp. Maharah Ohr Zarua* 151; *Yad Ramah Bava Batra* 8:97; *Piskei Ha-Rosh Bava Batra* 3:70; *Resp. Maharam Di Boton* 54; *Tur Hoshen Mishpat* 161:7; *Shulhan Arukh Hoshen Mishpat* 161:5; *Rema Hoshen Mishpat* 214:7; *Resp. Avkat Rakhel* 104, 114; *Resp. Sha'agat Aryeh* 91; *Resp. Torat Emet* 125; *Resp. Maharshah* 1:115.

41. *Hazon Ish Bava Batra* 6:17; *Beit Zevul* 1:34 (2).

42. *Resp. Ha-Rashba* 1:957; *Resp. She'erit Yosef* 75.

43. *Resp. Ha-Rosh* 96:4; *Shulhan Arukh Hoshen Mishpat* 60:12, Rema *Hoshen Mishpat* 62:1. See further, *Yad Yehudah, Shulhan Arukh Even Ha-Ezer* 69-88, 370-374.

44. Mishnah *Ketubot* 79a; *Resp. Ha-Rashba* 2:307; *Helkat Mehokeik Even Ha-Ezer* 85:41, *Beit Shmuel*, ad. locum. 103. And with his demise, the wife recovers the entire ownership of the home.

threshold question is whether title registration without the undertaking of ownership via a symbolic act (i.e., *kinyan*) and executing an agreement, constitutes a *kinyan* for the acquisition of the property for the party who is registered? The title registration is a commercial custom in order to have a record of the execution and set up the arrangement between the seller and purchaser(s) rather than a *kinyan*.[45] Registry of the home does not establish equal partnership in the property and is not an indication of written acquisition (a *shetar kinyan*) but rather demonstrative proof (*shetar ra'yah*) that the marital home is the wife's property (*nikhsei melog*) accompanied by the husband's usufruct property (*kinyan perot*).[46]

Espousing a diametrically opposing position, there are arbiters who argue that title registration either entails the undertaking of an obligation (*ma'aseh kinyan*) based upon mercantile custom (a *kinyan situmta*) or is effective due to being grounded in "the law of the kingdom is the law" (*dina de'malkhuta dina*).[47] As such, since the wife registered the home in the land registry that fifty per cent is in the husband's name, the husband received half of its value based upon the execution of a *kinyan* and the norms of civil law. Should the home be sold, each party would receive fifty per cent of its market value, even if the home is registered only in the husband's name.[48]

Regardless of which view is endorsed, the wife possesses property or receives funds from possessing property. Clearly, contemporary Halakhah rejects the recognition of "double *ketubah*" (*kefel ketubah*), namely that she is awarded the value of her *ketubah* while receiving upon her divorce property and/or funds based upon balancing the value of her assets (*izun nekhasim*).[49]

Finally, according to common law, a tort committed by one spouse against the other does not generate a cause of action in favor of the

45. *Erekh Shai Hoshen Mishpat* 60:12; *Arukh Ha-Shulhan Hoshen Mishpat* 60:21; *Resp. Rav Pealim* 2 *Even Ha-Ezer* 16; *Ha-Gahot Tur* 8; *Hazon Ish Hoshen Mishpat Likkutim* 16:9; *Mishpat Ke-Halakhah*, p. 591 in the name of *Sim Shalom* 278.

46. Talmud Bavli *Bava Batra* 139b; *Tur Even Ha-Ezer* 85; *Shulhan Arukh Even Ha-Ezer* 85, *Helkat Mehokeik*, ad. locum. 3.

47. Talmud Bavli *Bava Metzia* 74a; *Piskei Ha-Rosh Bava Metzia* 38; *Resp. Ha-Rivash* 478; *Shulhan Arukh Hoshen Mishpat* 201:1-2, *Shakh*, ad. locum 1 in the name of *Bah*; *Knesset Ha-Gedolah, Hoshen Mishpat* 190; *Piskei Din Rabbanayim* 1:283, 6:377-384. Rema *Hoshen Mishpat* 68:1, 369:8; *Resp. Hatam Sofer* 142; *Resp. Reim Hoshen Mishpat* 13.

48. File no. 956318/1, Jerusalem Regional Beit Din, March 21, 2016.

49. U. Lavi, Z. Luz-Aluz, and N. Gertler, *Kenes Ha-Dayanim* 5777, 275-298.

injured spouse due to the theory of unity or coverture, namely their separate identities merged upon marriage. As such, a wife having no legal identity could neither sue nor be sued and the husband was responsible for her torts.[50]

On the other hand, based upon a biblical decree (*gezarat hakatuv*),[51] a woman is invalid as a witness.[52] Even if she is trustworthy, she is invalid to serve as a witness.[53] In other words, a woman's invalidation is not attributed to the undermining of her integrity. Clearly, as we will see, her trustworthiness may be relied upon in certain circumstances. Her invalidation is based upon a biblical decree.[54]

A review of some authorities will show that the unavailability of eligible witnesses in a situation will not sanction ineligible witnesses to testify. As Maimonides states:[55]

> One should not think... that women or children should be permitted to testify that one person has injured another person... This is not so. No individual will ever be mandated to pay compensation for the testimony of witnesses unless the witnesses are eligible to testify in other cases.

Others endorse this posture.[56]

Citing in his *Darkhei Moshe* commentary on the *Tur*[57] well-known authorities such as Rabbeinu Gershom, Rabbeinu Tam, Mordekhai, *Kolbo*, R. Kolon, R. Isserelein and *Agudah*, Rabbi Moshe Issereles in his glosses on the *Shulhan Arukh* elucidates the following:[58]

---

50. Jewell v. Porter & Rolfe, 31 N.H. 34, 38 (1855); Bassett v. Bassett, 112 Mass. 99,100 (1873); Thompson v. Thompson, 218 U.S. 611, 31 S. Ct. 111,54 L.Ed. 1180 (1910); Sargeant v. Fedor, 130 Atl. 207 (N.J. Sup. Ct. 1925); Gray v. Gray, 87 N.H. 82,174 Atl. 508 (1934).

For the state of American law subsequent to the Congressional legislative passage of the nineteenth century Married Woman's Property Acts, see C. Schneider & M. Brinig, *An Invitation to Family Law*, West Publishing: 1996, 142-161.

51. *Devarim* 19:17

52. *Shulhan Arukh Hoshen Mishpat* 35:14.

53. *Resp. Zikhron Yehudah* 88; *Resp. Maharik, shoresh* 70.

54. E. Shochetman, *Civil Procedure in Rabbinical Courts* (Hebrew), Jerusalem: 5771, 815.

55. Maimonides, *Mishneh Torah, Hil. Nizkei Mamon* 8:13.

56. *Resp. Ha-Rashba* 2:182, 5:139; *Resp. Ha-Ritva* 183; *Piskei Ha-Rosh Bava Kama* 1:19; *Shulhan Arukh Hoshen Mishpat* 408.

57. *Hoshen Mishpat* 35. See also, *Netivot Ha-Mishpat* 35, *Hiddushin* 19.

58. *Hoshen Mishpat* 35:14

> And all those who are ineligible are so even in those situations where there are no eligible men available to testify. This is according to Halakhah. But there are those who claim that there is ancient legislation (*takanah*) that in a place where there are usually no eligible men present, such as to testify that a woman had worn certain attire and therefore they belong to her, and men will usually not notice such things, the woman is trusted in her testimony.... even a woman herself or a relative or a minor child is eligible in matters of assault... or other controversy..., since it is not possible to prepare in advance eligible witnesses in these matters.

For the purpose of awarding damages, in the absence of a batterer's admission, optimally there ought to be two male witnesses of majority age who can attest to the occurrence of the event.[59] In the absence of two male witnesses of majority age, ineligible witnesses such as women may testify in situations dealing with assaults and insults.[60] Additionally, in a situation where men are not present, a woman may testify that another woman's husband was still alive in order to establish ownership of the attire, whether in the deceased husband's estate or belonging to the widow.[61] In other words, a distinction is being drawn between testimony (*edut*) and a presumption of credibility (*ne'emanut*). Whereas some decisors require testimony and reject the application of the rabbinic legislation,[62] there are authorities who endorse a presumption of credibility and recognize the legislation.[63]

The precedent for Rabbi Moshe Issereles's posture, argues Gaon of Vilna, may be found in the Talmudic case of a midwife who may testify which child is a Kohen, which is a Levi, which a Gibeonite, which is a bastard, in situations where there is no contest.[64] To state it differently, in the absence of witnesses, permission for a woman to testify in a tort

---

59. *Devarim* 19:15; *Tur Hoshen Mishpat* 408; *Shulhan Arukh Hoshen Mishpat* 408:1.

60. *Resp. Maharam Mintz* 6; *Tumim Hoshen Mishpat* 35:9; *Resp. Nodah Be-Yehudah, Mahadura Tinyana, Hoshen Mishpat* 58; *Resp. Mishneh Halakhot* 5:269; File no. 4564-24-1, Netanya Regional Court, Shevat 8, 5766.

61. *Resp. Terumat Ha-Deshen* 353.

62. Rashba, supra n. 53; *Resp. Ha-Rosh* 52:2; *Yam Shel Shlomo Bava Kamma* 1:41; *Resp. Beit David Hoshen Mishpat* 66; *Mishkenot Ha-Roim* Entry Ayin (65); *Resp. Hikkei Lev Yoreh Deah* 47.

63. Supra nn. 60-61.

64. Talmud Bavli *Kiddushin* 73b; *Bi'ur Ha-Gra Hoshen Mishpat* 35:28.

matter may be derived from an issue of personal status. In fact, in the absence of witnesses there are situations of personal status where a woman's submission of testimony is permissible. For example, in the absence of witnesses, a midwife may testify which child is the firstborn, a woman may testify that she was kidnapped and not raped, and a woman may testify that she was once married and is now unmarried.[65]

In conclusion, whereas the seventeenth century common law theory of the unity of a person (i.e., a married woman) as it relates to the right to contract or own property has disappeared, Halakhah, from its very inception until contemporary times, viewed a married woman as a businesswoman, property owner and a participant in the *beit din* process, namely a plaintiff, defendant and in the absence of witnesses, as a witness in tort and ownership matters as well as issues of personal status.[66]

---

65. *Mordekhai, Yevamot* 6:117.

For additional situations where Halakhah accepts invalid testimony such as a woman's testimony, see this writer's *Rabbinic Authority*, vol. 2, 93-99.

66. Though Halakhah recognizes the notion *ishto kegufo* (lit. "his wife is as himself"), the concept is applied overwhelmingly in matters of ritual Halakhah, such as limiting a husband's intercourse to one woman to the exclusion of others, in a few cases of testimony, one instance of torts, one case of labor relations and one situation of agency. See Talmud Bavli *Sanhedrin* 58a, *Encyclopedia Talmudit*, vol. 2, entry: *ishto kegufo* and this writer's *Rabbinic Authority*, vol. 2, 186-187. A review of these instances would demonstrate that this halakhic concept applies in situations which stress the psychological unity of the marriage rather the impingement of the wife's halakhic rights such as executing contracts or acquiring property.

Chapter 5

The Propriety of Voiding a Marriage via *Kiddushei Ta'ut* and *Umdana*: Varying Opinions

I. Kiddushei Ta'ut

1. The Difference Between Voiding a Marriage and Annulling a Marriage

One of the solutions increasingly offered by many authorities to address the situation known as the plight of the modern-day *agunah*, whereby a husband refuses to grant a *get*, a writ of Jewish divorce to his wife, is for a *beit din* or an arbiter (*posek*) to engage in voiding the marriage ("*bittul kiddushin*").[1] One of the avenues to void the marriage is based

1. *Kiddushin* entails the man giving a ring to his prospective wife and reciting the words of betrothal in the presence of two eligible witnesses.

The term annulling a marriage ("*hafka'at kiddushin*") is to be distinguished from voiding a marriage ("*bittul kiddushin*"). Whereas *bittul kiddushin* is predicated upon the conclusion that there never was a *kiddushin* and entails various techniques to void a marriage such as *kiddushei ta'ut* or by invalidating the establishment of *kiddushin* where there were no witnesses present during the ceremony or the witnesses were invalid for the *kiddushin*. On the other hand, marital annulment is premised upon a bona fide *kiddushin*. See also, File no. 905457/10, Tel Aviv-Yaffo Regional Beit Din, September 11, 2017, which astutely distinguishes between the two concepts.

However, upon examination, the term marital annulment is sometimes utilized in a case that may be subject to voiding a marriage. See *Responsa* (hereinafter: Resp.) *Nishmat Hayyim* 87 (126); *Resp. Maharsham* 6:159. As such, in their mind there is one type of annulment which nullifies *a priori* the act of *kiddushin* and there is a second type of annulment which is predicated upon the notion that the *kiddushin* actually was established, and *ex post facto* arbiters are empowered to annul it. See Rabbi S. Cohen, "*Get* Coercion in Contemporary Times," (Hebrew) 11 *Tehumin* 195, 199 (5750).

Moreover, though the term ***kiddushin*** refers to establishing **betrothal**, for our presentation we are loosely translating it as marriage.

upon an error in the initial creation of the marriage known as a mistaken betrothal ("*kiddushei ta'ut*") as it relates to grave preexisting flaws in the husband's personality prior to the marriage. According to certain authorities, assuming certain conditions are obtained, the wife is free to remarry without receiving a *get*. The purpose of this presentation is to clarify the varying approaches towards the permissibility of invoking *kiddushei ta'ut* as a vehicle to void a marriage in the wake of a husband's *get* recalcitrance and thus free a wife from her marriage without receiving a *get*.

2. The Definition and Scope of a Mistaken Transaction

Any transaction regarding which people agree that the presence of a particular defect serves as grounds to nullify the transaction constitutes a mistaken transaction.[2] The majority of people must consider this matter as a defect in order for it to serve as grounds to void a transaction.[3] Analogously, the majority of men consider certain defects in women as grounds for voiding a marriage (*kiddushei ta'ut*).[4]

Finally, *jurisdiction to void a marriage lies in the hands of qualified rabbinical authorities, not necessarily exclusively Torah giants*. See supra chapter 2.

Should a *beit din* fail to summon the husband to a hearing regarding the matter of the get, American Orthodox rabbis ought to function as arbiters of prohibitions and permissibility ("*moreih hora'ah*"), and rabbinic courts ought to function as arbiters of prohibitions and permissibility, addressing the wife's inquiry as to whether there are grounds to give a get. For a rabbi functioning as a *moreh hora'ah*, see infra chapter 11.

In other words, one may resolve this question of whether a husband is obligated to give a get to his wife or are there grounds to void a marriage, as these are "halakhot of prohibitions and permissibility" ("*issur ve-heter*"). See *Helkat Mehokeik, Even Ha-Ezer* 17:78; *Taz, Even Ha-Ezer* 17:56; *Pithei Teshuvah, Shulhan Arukh Even Ha-Ezer Seder ha-Get* 6, 8; *Resp. R. Akiva Eiger, Mahadura Kamma*, 123; *Resp. Sha'agat Aryeh* 13; *Rabbi Z. N. Goldberg, Lev Mishpat* 1, 149-150.

For a description of the other three techniques to void a marriage, see this writer's, *Rabbinic Authority: The Vision and the Reality* (hereinafter: *Rabbinic Authority*), vol. 3, 134-176, 231-269; vol. 4, 143-298; vol. 5, 38-305.

2. *Resp. Ha-Rif* 153; *Piskei Ha-Rosh, Bava Metzia* 4:15; *Mishneh Torah, Hilk. Mekhirah* 15:5; *Shulhan Arukh, Hoshen Mishpat* 232:6; *Resp. Divrei Rivot* 300; *Resp. Maharshakh* 1:19; *Resp. Ha-Mabi*t 2:127.

3. *Bi'ur Ha-Gra, Hoshen Mishpat* 232:11.

4. Ran (according to Rif pagination) *Ketubot* 33a; *Helkat Mehokeik, Shulhan Arukh, Even Ha-Ezer* 39:1; *Resp. Malbushei Yom Tov* 4; *Piskei Din Rabbanayim* 5:193, 196. For the most comprehensive and systematic treatments of this technique to void a marriage, see File no. 870175/4, Haifa Regional Beit Din, December 29, 2014, and File no. 1294108/1, Be'air Sheva Regional Beit Din, June 13, 2021.

Implicitly relying upon earlier authorities,[5] a mistaken transaction (*mekah ta'ut*) is memorialized in *Shulhan Arukh* in the following fashion:[6]

> If one sells another land, a slave, a domestic animal, or other moveable property, and a defect, which the buyer did not know, is found in the purchase, a buyer may return it… since this sale was based upon a basic error, provided that the buyer did not use the object after he became aware of the defect.

3. The Propriety of a Husband Advancing a Claim for *Kiddushei Ta'ut*

Shulhan Arukh states:[7]

> If one betroths a woman on the condition that she has no blemishes and blemishes were subsequently discovered,… she is deemed not betrothed… If he betroths a woman without explicitly stating any preconditions (*stam*) and it was discovered later that she has blemishes that invalidate women… she is betrothed due to a doubt.

In other words, upon discovering a flaw in the woman, though he initially was concerned about the defect, he didn't want to marry her. However, if he remained silent about the defect and didn't make any prior stipulation, she is betrothed to him.[8] On a biblical level, she retains

---

Even if the husband stipulated that the marriage shall be without defects in his wife, if people do not consider these defects as grounds for "an error in the marriage", there would be no basis to void the marriage. See *Shulhan Arukh*, Even Ha-Ezer 39:1.

5. Alfasi, supra n. 2; Rosh, supra n. 2; *Mishneh Torah*, supra n. 2. See also, *Resp. Divrei Rivot* 300; *Resp. Maharshah* 1:19; *Resp. Ha-Mabit* 2:127.

6. *Hoshen Mishpat* 232:3. Even if the buyer failed to inspect the item prior to his purchase and the seller sold it to him without stipulating a condition, he is not empowered to void the transaction due to an error in the sale. See *Sma, Hoshen Mishpat* 232:10. Moreover, even if the buyer observed the defect and he remained silent, he can retract his consent to the purchase provided he did not use the item. *A fortiori* if the buyer could have inspected and failed to inspect the item, the transaction is void. See *Pithei Teshuva, Hoshen Mishpat* 232:1 in the name of *Mishneh Le-Melekh*.

7. *Even Ha-Ezer* 39:3, 5.

8. *Helkat Mehokeik, Even Ha-Ezer* 39:9.

her status as being unmarried (*p'nuyah*), however, rabbinically she is prohibited to remarry without receiving a *get*.[9] Given that we are dealing with a betrothal which is in doubt, the wife must return the money she received from her husband for the betrothal.[10] Alternatively, either the doubt is linked to the above uncertainty – whether in the scheme of the wife's personality the defect was significant or the rabbinic concern that people should not err and think that a married woman leaves her husband without a *get*.[11] For example, should a wife, prior to her marriage, fail to disclose to her spouse that she is barren (*ailonit*), then according to certain opinions, the betrothal is valid and she requires a *get* upon separation from her husband,[12] whereas according to others she requires a *get* rabbinically or due to doubt.[13] The underlying logic for requiring a *get* according to the aforesaid views is that it is more difficult to void a marriage based upon a fundamental error in the sale (*mekah ta'ut*) relating to undisclosed flaws of his wife since the husband always has the capacity to divorce his wife.[14]

In bold contrast to the above views, numerous arbiters contend that being barren is a major defect since it undermines the purpose of a halakhic marriage – to sire children and fulfill the duty of propagation – and therefore upon the discovery of such an error the *kiddushin* is

---

9. Ran on Rif Kiddushin 5b; *Responsa Maharashdam Even Ha-Ezer* 11, 13; *Resp. Maharik, shoresh* 169. Cf. others who argue that on a biblical level her status has been undermined. See *Resp. Ha-Maharit* 1:41.

The implicit premise in this note, as well as the balance of our presentation in this monograph, is that the *Shulhan Arukh* is a compendium of halakhic rulings. See *Shulhan Arukh Hakdama*; *HaMapa, Hakdama*; *Resp. Ginat Veradim, Even HaEzer* 4:30. For additional examination whether the *Shulhan Arukh* was intended as a work of Halakhah, see A. Storch, "Was the *Shulhan Arukh* Intended to Be a Code of Jewish Law?" 33 *Hakirah* 309, Spring 2023.

10. *Shulhan Arukh, Even Ha-Ezer* 50:1. Given that the money is returned, the emerging question is: how did she become betrothed to her husband. See *Resp. R. Akiva Eiger, Mahadura Tinyana* 55; *Resp. Maharam Schick* 74.

11. *Beit Shmuel, Even Ha-Ezer* 39:16. For antecedents to this latter approach, see Rashi, *Mahadura Kamma, Shitah Mekubetzet, Ketubot* 73b; *Lehem Mishneh, Hilk. Ishut* 4:10; *Resp, Ahiezer, Even Ha-Ezer* 27 (3); *Resp. Ein Yitzhak*, 1, *Even Ha-Ezer* 24.

12. *Mishneh Torah, Hilk. Ishut* 4:10.

13. *Hiddushei Ha-Ritva, Yevamo*t 2b in the name of R. Tam; *Tosafot Yevamot* 2b in the name of R. Bourgvilain.

14. *Resp. Noda Be-Yehudah, Mahadura Tinyana, Even Ha-Ezer* 80; *Resp. Iggerot Moshe, Even Ha-Ezer* 1:79. Cf. *Resp. Ahiezer* 1, *Even Ha-Ezer* 10; *Resp. Dvar Yehoshua* 3:20.

invalid, and under certain conditions one does not require a *get*.[15] Dating back to the time of the *Tanaim*,[16] other matters such as a wife behaving in a lunatic fashion which is strange in the eyes of most people may be a defect which invalidates the act of *kiddushin*, and under certain conditions one does not require a *get*.[17] Major flaws in the wife's persona which were undisclosed prior to the marriage under certain conditions may serve as grounds for *kiddushei ta'ut* and void the marriage.[18]

4. The Propriety of a Wife Advancing a Claim for *Kiddushei Ta'ut*

Can a wife similarly claim that her husband failed to disclose a major defect(s) prior to their marriage, and should he refuse to give a *get* the marriage would be voided?[19]

Clearly, according to the Talmud,[20] regarding a defect of which the wife was unaware, either she is required to have a *get* executed on a rabbinic level lest the community say that the woman is departing her marriage without a *get*, or there is a doubt if the *kiddushin* is void since there are people who don't care about a flaw, therefore she is betrothed due to doubt (a *safek kiddushin*).[21]

---

15. *Tosafot Yevamot* 2b, s.v. *oh*; *Piskei Ha-Rosh, Yevamot* 1:3, *Ketubot* 7:10; *Hiddushei Ha-Rashba Gittin* 46b; *Shulhan Arukh Even Ha-Ezer* 44:4; *Resp. Noda Be-Yehudah, Mahadura Tinyana Even Ha-Ezer* 50; *Avnei Milluim, Even Ha-Ezer* 39:9; *Resp. Imrei Yosher* 2:159; *Resp. Iggerot Moshe, Even Ha-Ezer* 1:79 in the name of *yesh omrim*.

16. *Tosefta Ketubot* 7:9.

17. *Resp. Oneg Yom Tov* 1, *Even Ha-Ezer* 4.

18. *Shitah Mekubetzet, Ketubot* 72b in the name of Rivash and Maharit; *Resp. Avnei Nezer, Even Ha-Ezer* 2:176; *Resp. Helkat Yoav* 24; *Resp. Beit Ha-Levi* 3:4. Cf others who argue that it remains a doubt concerning the *kiddushin* (*safek kiddushin*) and consequently the marriage cannot be voided. See *Resp. Yeshuot Malko, Even Ha-Ezer* 3.

19. Clearly, drawing an analogy from a matter of Hoshen Mishpat (i.e., sales transaction) to an issue of Even Ha-Ezer (i.e., act of betrothal) does not imply that betrothal for marriage (*kiddushin*) is to be construed as a form of acquisition, akin to a monetary transaction. See supra chapter 1, "The Nature of the *Kinyan* of *Kiddushin*: A Mode of Acquisition or Obligation?". See supra text accompanying note 14.

20. Talmud Bavli *Ketubot* 73b.

21. *Pithei Teshuvah, Even Ha-Ezer* 38:14, in the name of *Hatam Sofer*; *Resp. Ahiezer* 3:19. Nevertheless, the *Resp. Beit HaLevi* 3 notes that we derive the scope of a husband's defects from the scope of a wife's defects as enumerated in the Talmud. See also *Beit Shmuel* EH 154:2. Given the talmudic sanction of *hekesh* (analogical reasoning), one may infer the scope of a husband's major defects from those possessed by a spouse. Regarding this technique, see this writer's *Rabbinic Authority,*

Rabbi Menashe Klein exclaims:[22]

> And in the novella of... Rabbi Joseph Henkin... it states: since we never heard or know from the time of the Talmud that a marriage would be voided due to a defect, in particular after *kiddushin* was executed, and everywhere and every time when there were questions such as these and they always required a *get*... and one cannot void a marriage even if the defect was clear and the other party was unaware of it.

Though arbiters who authored restatements such as Rif, Maimonides, Rosh, *Tur* and *Shulhan Arukh* failed to invoke *kiddushei ta'ut* regarding defects undisclosed by a *husband* prior to their marriage as a technique to void a marriage under certain conditions where the husband refuses to give a *get*,[23] and/or we are dealing with a doubt in the *kiddushin*, similar to a man who is unaware of his wife's flaw;[24] nonetheless, there were numerous authorities who recognized this technique.[25]

---

vol. 1, 53-57.

22. *Resp. Mishneh Halakhot* 17:46.

23. *Resp. Yeriot Shlomo* 1:8; R. Y. Henkin, *Perushei Ivra*, 1:42 (41-43); *Resp. Helkat Ya'akov* 3:114; *Resp. Beit Avi* 3:135.

In fact, pursuant to some authorities, on a biblical level we recognize there is a valid argument for *kiddushei ta'ut* for a woman. However, rabbinically we require the execution of a *get* lest the public err in their thinking that a woman goes free without the execution of a *get*. See *Resp. Ein Yitzhak, Even Ha-Ezer* 1:24; *Resp. Tzemah Tzedek* 114, 134.

24. *Beit Shmuel, Even Ha-Ezer* 39:2.

25. There are over 40 decisors who have employed this technique to void a marriage. See this writer's *Rabbinic Authority*, vol. 3, 141, n. 10.

The following question arises: If the man had simply misrepresented to the woman during their courting days that he promised that he would treat her children of her first marriage properly or would support her, would his statement be construed *halakhically* as a misrepresentation, and therefore a case of "*kiddushei ta'ut*"? Or is the fact that he had a track record, namely of mistreating his own children from his first marriage and failing to support his first wife, serve as the grounds for viewing his promise as a misrepresentation and consequently a situation of "*kiddushei ta'ut*"? In the absence of any past history of mistreating his own children from his first marriage or failing to support his wife, various later authorities (*Aharonim*) conclude that given that he could have changed his mind, his failure to keep his word to act properly would be viewed as grounds for voiding a marriage based upon error. See *Atzmot Yosef, Kiddushin* 62a; *Resp. Helkat Yo'av, Even Ha-Ezer* 25; *Resp. Hatam Sofer, Even Ha-Ezer* 3:82.

5. *Kiddushei Ta'ut*: The Absence of a Meeting of the Minds

Seemingly, the plausible position is that the technique of *kiddushei ta'ut* concerning flaw(s) undisclosed by the husband before the marriage will be ineffective. As Dayan Maimon Nahari notes,[26] the Torah teaches us,[27] "When a man takes a wife..." and the Talmud explains exegetically, "When a man takes a wife, and not when a woman takes a man."[28]

Furthermore, at the beginning of Chapters one and two of Mishnah Kiddushin respectively, we read: "The man betroths" and "the woman is acquired". In other words, as opposed to a sale in which the money is handed over in consideration of the object that was acquired, here in *kiddushin*, the money is given as a medium for undertaking an obligation(s) (a *kinyan*) of a prospective husband toward his prospective wife.

According to the literal interpretation of the Torah and the Mishnah, the man executes the undertaking of a duty through the consummation of the act of *kiddushin* which entails that the woman be passive, negating her mind and will in the face of her prospective husband and resulting seemingly in the wife being acquired by the husband. This appears to the conclusion according to the well-known words of Ran who elucidates the following:[29]

> Since the Torah said, "When a man takes a woman," and it did not say, "When a woman be taken to be with a man," she has no legal capacity to transfer herself into his halakhic jurisdiction. Rather, in agreeing to be taken in marriage by the man, she negates her own will and mind and is then considered as ownerless property (*hefker* – AYW) vis-à-vis her husband. At that point, the husband transfers her into his domain, hence the act of "taking someone in *kiddushin*" can only be executed by a man and never by a woman.

However, if one examines closely the words of Ran and other authorities, argues Dayan Nahari, one sees that an act of *kinyan* is consummated whereby she negates her will and mind with respect to the act of *kiddushin*.[30] Consequently, if somebody coerces a woman to engage

26. File no. 870175/4, supra n. 4.
27. *Devarim* 24:1.
28. Talmud Bavli *Kiddushin* 4b.
29. *Hiddushei Ha-Ran, Nedarim* 30a, s.v. ve-ishah.
30. *Hiddushei R. Shimon Shkop, Kiddushin* 1; *Sha'arei Yosher* 7:12; *Kehillot*

in the act of *kiddushin*, the *kiddushin* is invalid since her will and mind are absent from consummating the act.[31] One requires the meeting of the minds (*gemirat da'at*) between the man and the woman in order to finalize the act of *kiddushin*. Therefore, in the wake of emergence of an error in a sales transaction, the transaction is null and void due to the lack of the meeting of the minds. Analogously, if an error emerges in the act of *kiddushin* such as the wife being unaware prior to their marriage of the defect(s) of her prospective husband, under certain conditions the marriage is void due to the absence of the meeting of the minds.[32] In short, there is a basis for recognizing *kiddushei ta'ut* as a vehicle to void marriage when dealing with a husband's defect(s).[33]

The implication of our reasoning is that the absence of the meeting of the minds (*gemirat da'at*) of the couple may generate *kiddushei ta'ut* which serves as the basis for engaging in voiding the marriage regardless of whether the husband intentionally or unintentionally failed to disclose the flaw to his wife prior to the marriage.[34]

To state it differently, via the consummation of *kiddushin*, the woman is designated exclusively to one man and is prohibited to every other man.[35] The emergence of *kiddushin* is predicated upon "a meeting of the minds" which entails an act of undertaking an obligation (*peulah*

Ya'akov, Kiddushin 7 (comments); *Mishnat Shlomo, Kiddushin* 2; *Minhat Asher, Kiddushin* 1, 20. In fact, elsewhere Ran notes that "the woman is not the asset of the husband." See Ran on Rif, *Gittin* 9a, s.v. *ve'katvu*.

31. Talmud Bavli *Bava Batra* 48b; *Mishneh Torah, Hilk. Ishut* 4:1.

32. *Mishneh Torah, Hilk. Mekhirah* 17:2; *Hazon Ish Even Ha-Ezer* 56:9, 77:6; R. S. Shkop, *Shiurei Roshei Yeshivot Lita*, 90; *Resp. Beit Ha-Levi* 3:3; *Resp. Helkat Yo'av Even Ha-Ezer* 25; *Makor Hayyim, Be'iurim* 448:9; *Moreshet Moshe, Bava Metzia* 60:4; *Resp. Beriti Shalom* 5:15; *Hazon Ish, Even Ha-Ezer* 56:9; *Resp. Minhat Shlomo* 1, 80:9; *Hiddushei Ha-Gra al Ha'shas, Yevamot* 93 Cf. others who contend that there is an implied condition in the sales transaction that there will be no defect. See infra n. 36.

33. For the analogy between *mekah ta'ut* and *kiddushei ta'ut* in the words of some early authorities (*Rishonim*), see *Hiddushei Ha-Rashba, Ketubot* 72a; *Magid Mishneh, Hilk. Mekhirah* 15:3 in the name of Rambam; Resp. *Ha-Ri Megash* 129; Resp. Ha-Rosh 33:1; Beit Ha-Behirah, *Yevamot* 2b.

34. *Resp. Sha'arei Tzion 2, Even Ha-Ezer* 20 (22-25). Cf. *Resp. Even Shoham Even Ha-Ezer* 57 and *Resp. Rav Pe'alim* 1, *Even Ha-Ezer* 8 who contend that the applicability of *kiddushei ta'ut* is limited to a situation of a husband who intentionally failed to disclose prior to the marriage that he possessed a defect.

35. *Kiddushin* 2b; *Tosafot, Kiddushin* 2b; *Beit Shmuel Even Ha-Ezer* 27:4.

However, intimacy between the two may only commence when they marry each other (*nissuin*) and commence with certain duties between them. See *Mishneh Torah, Hilk. Ishut* 10:1; *Shulhan Arukh Even Ha-Ezer* 55:1, 6.

kinyanit).[36] There are multifarious situations such as the establishment of *kiddushin* under duress and deception, borrowing a ring for the *kiddushin* ceremony, breach of promise, rape and adultery which must be addressed prior to being accorded the status of a betrothed.

Conceptually, from the moment a woman is betrothed (a *mekudeshet*) this status may only be removed with the issuance of a *get*,[37] or given that *kiddushin*, similar to a transaction, was established via a *kinyan* – under certain conditions we can void the marriage based upon the husband's failure to disclose to his wife a fundamental flaw in his personality. As such, *kiddushin* possesses a dual dimension: its prohibitive nature (an *issur*), as well as an undertaking of a duty which leads to the establishment of *kiddushin*. Whereas a wife is unable to advance a plea of *kiddushei ta'ut* based upon its prohibitive nature; however, such an argument may be claimed based upon the *kinyan* aspect of *kiddushin*.[38]

In sum, utilizing rabbinic nomenclature, there is no meeting of the minds, which is the vehicle to establish the act of undertaking an obligation (*ma'aseh kinyan*) such as *kiddushin*.

6. *Kiddushei Ta'ut*: A Violation of an Implied Condition

Seemingly, the above line of reasoning as the basis for voiding a marriage due to implementing the technique of *kiddushei ta'ut* has limited application. As aptly noted by the Jerusalem Regional Beit Din:[39]

36. *Hiddushei Ha-Ramban, Kiddushin* 5b, 7a; *Hiddushei Ha-Rashba, Kiddushin* 6a, *Bava Batra* 48b; *Hiddushei Ha-Ritva* 7a. For the wife's requirement of what is transpiring (*da'at*) in the execution of *kiddushin*, see *Hiddushei Ha-Rashba, Kiddushin* 2b, s.v. *tanna*, *Meiri, Kiddushin* 2b, s.v. *harbei*.

37. *Mishneh Torah, Hilk. Ishut* 11:2-3; *Shulhan Arukh Even Ha-Ezer* 26:3.

38. A. Sakasonov, "*Kiddushin* as a *Kinyan* – The Establishment of a Link or a Hindrance from the World?" (Hebrew), 8 *Assif* 5783, 292, 293-298, 312. Clearly, the existence of the *kinyan* aspect, as we argue, does not presume that the man possesses a proprietary interest in his spouse.

Whether the *issur* transpires before or after the *kinyan* or emerges simultaneously to it is subject to debate. Secondly, whether *kinyan* exists at all concerning *kiddushin*, refers to the prohibition or of the monetary nature is subject to controversy. See *Tosafot Kiddushin* 7a, b, *Hiddushei Ha-Ramban Gittin* 9a; *Resp. Zekhor Yitzhak* 1:23; *Resp. Ha-Tashbetz* 2:67; *Avnei Millium*, Resp. 17, 28:21, 31; *Mishnat Aharon Gittin* 30; *Hiddushei Ha-Gra Issurei Biah* 13; *Resp. Helkat Yoav Even Ha-Ezer* 6; *Pri Megadim, Orah Hayyim* 339.

See further concerning the dual nature of the act of *kiddushin* (*issur* and *kinyan*) in R. Datnair, "*Kinyan* and *Hekdesh* in *Kiddushin*, (Hebrew) 8 *Assif* 5783, 204.

39. File no. 1066559/12, Jerusalem Regional Beit Din, March 27, 2020. See also Beit Ha-Levi, supra n. 32.

> Those who argue that a mistaken transaction is void due to the absence of the meeting of the minds which is integral to the undertaking of the duty (*kinyan*) rather than due to the condition are addressing whatever was present at the time of the execution of the sale. However, when the defect only appears *after* the sale has been nullified as a result of this flaw... it is based upon the clear expectation (the *umdana*) that there exists a condition regarding the transaction.

However, certain decisors contend that a sale in error (*mekah ta'ut*) is grounded in the violation of a condition (a *tenai*) rather than the absence of undertaking an obligation. To state it differently, despite the prohibition of "a married woman," nonetheless, in pursuance to the above view, we may invoke here the mechanism of "an error in marriage" and void the marriage based upon an implied condition (rather than an explicit condition) formulated in accordance with the halakhot of conditions (*mishpetei ha-tena'im*), i.e., an implied condition.[40]

Consequently, there are authorities who have voided the marriage by invoking *kiddushei ta'ut* as it relates to defects which emerge after the onset of the marriage based upon, "had I known my husband would have acted towards me such during the marriage I never would have married" (*umdana demukhah* – a major assessment of expectations).[41]

On the other hand, there are arbiters who oppose utilizing *umdana* as a technique to void a marriage.[42]

---

40. Rashi, *Ketubot* 73b, s.v. *de'amar*; *Resp. Avnei Nezer* 255; *Ohr Sameah, Hilk. Ishut* 10:2, 11:11; *Resp. Birkat Retzeh* 14; *Resp. R. Akiva Eiger* 2:51, 106; *Resp. Beit Yitzhak Hoshen Mishpat* 64; *Hafla'ah, Ketubot* 73a.

Given that the act of *kiddushin* is executed by the husband and the wife consents, some contend that a wife cannot stipulate a condition since she doesn't execute the act of *kiddushin*. See R. Hayyim Soloveitchik on *Rambam, Hilk. Yibbum and Halitzah* 4:16; *Kovetz He'arot* 76. However, given that the wife is empowered to stipulate a condition regarding her *kiddushin*, said conclusion is incorrect. See *Shulhan Arukh Even Ha-Ezer* 38:24, 35, 39.

41. *Nimmukei Yosef, Shitat Kadmonim, Kiddushin* 49b, s.v. *le'nikhsei*; *Resp. Maharam of Rothenberg*, Prague ed. 993, 1022 (*halitzah* -in theory); R. Meir Posner, *Tzal'ot Ha-Bayit* 6; *Resp. Zikhron Yehonatan*, 1, *Yoreh Deah* 5; *Resp. She'eilat Moshe, Even Ha-Ezer* 2; *Resp. Avnei Hefetz* 30.

Alternatively, we are dealing with a wife's declaration, "had I known my husband would have acted towards me such during the marriage I never would have married" (*umdana demukhah* – a major assessment of expectations). *The implicit assumption is that the umdana is construed as a ta'ut*. See *Ra'avyah, Resp. U-Biurei Sugyot* 1032.

42. *Resp. Avodat Gershuni* 35; *Resp. Beit Yitzhak* 1:106; *Resp. Nishmat Hayyim*

7. The Validity of Invoking the Presumption *"Tav Le-Meitav Tan Do"*

Do all obligations executed prior to the *kiddushin* need to be fulfilled?

As Rabbi Yehoshua Reich of Efrat, Israel, aptly notes:[43]

> As Rashbam elucidates:[44]
>
>> The marriage-broker who serves as guarantor does not intend to comply with his duty to repay the debt guarantee; his intention is to facilitate the couple's marriage. The woman does not lose anything [by his defaulting] since "it is better to live as two together rather than to live alone". Consequently, he acts for her benefit by serving as a guarantor.

Dissenting from Rashbam's position, Rabbi Natan Gestetner explains:[45]

> Consequently (following Rashbam's logic – AYW) it is legitimate for someone to deceive a woman by saying that he will guarantee her *ketubah* (i.e., the value of the *ketubah* – AYW) even though in reality he has no intention of committing himself to serve as a guarantor. The deceit is justified since it is for her benefit; and in any case, loses nothing, for it always is preferable to be married than single, even if as a result, her *ketubah* is at risk.
>
> However, in my opinion this is incorrect, for surely no woman is prepared to lose her *ketubah,* which is her right.... The presumption that "it is better to live as two together rather than to

---

126, 129; *Resp. Noda Be-Yehudah, Mahadura Kamma, Even Ha-Ezer* 85, *Mahadura Tinyana, Even Ha-Ezer* 80; *Resp. Hatam Sofer, Even Ha-Ezer* 1:82; *Resp. Ahiezer* 3:19; *Resp. Heikhal Yitzhak, Even Ha-Ezer* 2:25.

As we know, the view of R. Y. Karo as recorded in *Beit Yosef, Even Ha-Ezer* 42:1 is that *umdana* cannot be utilized as a vehicle to void a marriage. Given that in the *Shulhan Arukh,* R. Karo does not address the issue, we may conclude that he retained his position memorialized in *Beit Yosef.* See *Resp. Asher Le-Shlomo* 13; *Resp. Yismah Lev Ovadiah, Leket Teshuvot* 1; *Resp. Emek Yehoshua,* 1 *Even Ha-Ezer* 13-14; *Resp. Mikveh Ha-Mayyim* 2 *Hashmatot* 10. Cf. *Resp. Divrei Mordekhai* 19.

43. International Beit Din, ruling no. 261.

44. Talmud Bavli *Bava Batra* 174b, s.v. *mitzva.*

45. *Resp. Le-Horot Natan* 5:102.

> live alone" is not strong enough to override this basic right, and no woman will consent to be married unless her husband provides halakhically binding coverage for her *ketubah*.

In sum, there is a controversy whether the above presumption ("*tav le-meitav tan do mi-le-meitav armalu*") overrides the right of a guarantor of the value of the *ketubah*.

That being said, what then prompted the above debate whether this technique of *kiddushei ta'ut* could be utilized to void a marriage? Does the above presumption override a woman's discovery of a husband's flaw(s) in her marriage? Dealing with a childless widow, the Talmud states:[46]

> A childless widow whose lot falls for *yibum* (levirate marriage) consideration before a brother-in-law who is afflicted with a severe skin disease (boils) [and is physically repulsive to her – AYW] should be released without *halitzah* [the ceremony in which the brother-in-law renounces his duty to marry his sister-in-law and releases her to marry anyone of her choosing] because she did not betroth herself in marriage to her brother-in-law with this in mind.

However, rejecting the wife's reasoning, the Talmud cites Reish Lakish's ruling approvingly:

> In that case we can attest that a woman is ready to accept any conditions (provided she is married to her first husband)… for Resh Lakish stated: it is better to live as two than to remain in widowhood ("*tav le-meitav tan do mi-le-meitav armalu*").

Consequently, given that marrying a brother-in-law who is afflicted with boils is preferable to remaining a widow, therefore her first marriage cannot be considered a *mekah ta'ut*. As such, Tosafot extrapolates that in all situations where a husband exhibits major defects, a wife cannot argue that there is a *mekah ta'ut* because she prefers living with any man

46. Talmud Bavli *Bava Kamma* 110b-111a.For other contexts where the presumption is invoked, see *Yevamot* 118b, *Ketubot* 75a, and *Kiddushin* 7a.

In the absence of grounds for coercing a *get* regarding a specific plea for divorce (*ilat gerushin),* the presumption is inapplicable. See *Resp. Ein Yitzhak* 1, 24:41; *Resp. Ahiezer* 27; *Resp. Iggerot Moshe Even Ha-Ezer* 1:79.

even if there exists a danger in the future that she will be forced to live with her brother-in-law who is afflicted with a skin disease rather than live a life of spinsterhood.[47]

In effect, Reish Lakish's presumption, which in Aramaic is termed "*tav le-meitav tan do mi-le-meitav armalu,*" has been understood as an ontological and existential fact rather than linked to cultural, sociological and psychological factors – the latter of which would result in the inapplicability of this presumption in certain contexts.[48]

Consequently, it is unsurprising to find the following observation of *Rabbi Osher Weiss,* a contemporary authority and *dayan*:[49]

> Our scholars have distinguished between defects in a wife where we presume that we are dealing with *kiddushei ta'ut* and defects in a man that we say *tav le-meitav tan do mi-le-meitav armalu.* And regarding this question the Bah and Beit Shmuel are in dispute. According to the Bah (Section 154) regarding defects found in a man one should not void the betrothal (loosely translated: the marriage – AYW) since they said *tav le-meitav tan do mi-le-meitav armalu.* However, pursuant to Beit Shmuel (ibid. subsection 2) even his defects if unknown to her are halakhically analogous to her defects if unknown to him. And see Beit Meir who concurs with the Bah's view...[50]

In other words, according to R. Weiss, for Bah one cannot draw an equation between a wife's defects and a husband's defects regarding grounds to void a marriage. On the other hand, for Beit Shmuel, one can analogize from one to the other.[51] Moreover, the reason that Bah distinguishes

47. *Tosafot, Bava Kamma* 110b; Rashi, *Kiddushin* 41a, *Bava Kamma* 111a; *Resp. Ein Yitzhak,* 1 *Even Ha-Ezer* 24, *Anaf* 5; *Resp. Even Yakarah, Mahadura Tlita'a* 53.

48. R. J. Soloveitchik, "Surrendering to the Almighty," *Light,* 17 Kislev 5736 (1976), 11-15, 18.

49. *Resp. Minhat Asher,* 1:85(2).

50. *Hazon Ish, Even Ha-Ezer* 69:23 also agrees with Bah.

51. If a certain flaw in the wife's physiological makeup or psyche is viewed as a major defect (*mum gadol*), similarly, such a defect may be labeled a major flaw in the husband's makeup. See *Tosafot Ha-Rid, Ketubot* 74a; *Shitah Mekubetzet, Ketubot* 72a in the name of Rivash and Maharit; *Resp. Ha-Rosh* 42; *Resp. Maharam, Ketzarot* 77; *Resp. Maharhash* 33; *Beit Yosef, Hoshen Mishpat* 232:4 in the name of *Magid Mishneh; Bi'ur Ha-Gra, Hoshen Mishpat* 232:9; *Beit Shmuel, Even Ha-Ezer* 117:24, 154:2; *Resp. Seridei Eish* 3:33; *Resp. Yabia Omer,* 8, *Even Ha-Ezer* 3 (16); *Resp. Helkat Ya'akov* 3:114; *Resp. Har Tzvi, Even Ha-Ezer* 2:180-181.

between the two situations is due to whether one invokes the aforesaid presumption or not.[52]

Therefore, it is unsurprising to find that many arbiters who prohibit implementing the method of *kiddushei ta'ut* rely upon this Talmudic presumption as one of the grounds for their position.[53] On the other hand, a review of the responsa reveals that in multifarious situations, authorities argue that we encounter a *mekah ta'ut* that rebuts the presumption and allows the wife to remarry without the giving of a *get*. For example, in accordance with Havot Yair, the *tav le-meitav* presumption is based upon the wife's desire to engage in sexual relations with her husband.[54] Consequently, it is unsurprising that some authorities invoke *kiddushei ta'ut* in situations where it can be established that already prior to the marriage the husband is sexually impotent, refuses to have children or is a homosexual.[55]

Furthermore, a cursory glance of the responsa memorialized in Otzar Ha-Poskim and elsewhere shows that the *tav le-meitav* presumption is not limited to the sexual underpinning of the relationship but equally applies to instances where the matrimonial bond becomes severely compromised by a husband's major flaws such as mental dysfunction, criminal behavior, misrepresentation, and religious nonobservance that preexisted the marriage and only were discovered after the onset of the marriage.[56]

In short, the invoking of *mekah ta'ut* is predicated upon rebutting

52. See also, File no. 1169128/2, Petah Tikvah Regional Beit Din, March 4, 2020. However, according to *Bah*, even concerning a wife's defects one requires a *get* due to the fact that the husband was aware of the defect and was unconcerned. Similarly, regarding a husband's flaws a *get* is required due to the fact that the wife was aware of the flaw and was unconcerned.

53. *Resp. Ha-Tashbetz* 1:1; *Beit Ha-Levi*, supra n. 32; *Resp. Shevut Ya'akov* 1:101; *Beit Meir Even Ha-Ezer* 154:1; *Hazon Ish Even Ha-Ezer* 69:23; *Perushei Ivra*, supra n. 23; *Yeriot Shlomo*, supra n. 23.

Even though in certain circumstances, the *tav le-meitav* presumption was inapplicable, some decisors opposed voiding a marriage based upon *kiddushei ta'ut*. See *Resp. Hatam Sofer* 4, *Even Ha-Ezer* 2:150; *Resp. Helkat Ya'akov Even Ha-Ezer* 85; *Resp. Minhat Yitzhak* 7:122.

54. *Resp. Havot Yair* 221. See also, *Resp. Radakh, Bayit* 9.

55. *Resp. Beit Av* 7:27; R. Goldberg, *Koah De-heteira*; *Resp. Iggerot Moshe Even Ha-Ezer* 1:79, 4:13, 52, 113.

56. *Otzar Ha-Poskim, Even Ha-Ezer* 39:16-17; *Resp. Shoeil U-Meishiv, Mahadura Kamma* 1:151,197, *Mahadura Tlitaah* 61; *Resp. Mahari Ha-Cohen* 13; *Resp. Birkat Retzeh* 107; *Resp. Sheilot Moshe, Even Ha-Ezer* 2 (59); *Resp. Ein Yitzhak*, 1, *Even Ha-Ezer* 24(41).

the *tav le-meitav* presumption. Obviously, rebutting this presumption is based upon the discovery of a major defect in the husband's persona by halakhic decisors.[57]

---

57. Regarding medical issues such as impotence and epilepsy, the determination of it being a major defect is placed in the hands of physicians. Consequently, halakhic authorities invoke the professional opinion of the latter prior to arguing that we are dealing with a major defect. See *Resp. Ahiezer* 19; *Resp. Maharsham* 3:16; *Resp. Dvar Eliyahu* 48; *Resp. Iggerot Moshe, Even Ha-Ezer* 1:19, 162, 3:47, 4:52; *Resp. Dvar Yehoshua* 3:20; *Resp. Minhat Yitzhak* 7:127; *Resp. Minhat Asher* 1:73, 88. One may trust the physician's records of his patients. See R. Elyashiv, *Kenes Ha-Dayanim,* 5773, 21. Concerning trusting physicians, see *Resp. Ha-Rosh* 102:9, *Tur, Hoshen Mishpat* 232:13; *Shulhan Arukh, Hoshen Mishpat* 232:16.

Concerning a mentally dysfunctional individual (a *shoteh*), halakhic arbiters sought a physician who rendered his professional opinion regarding the severity of the flaw. See *Resp. Maharsham* 7:95, 8:239; *Resp. Malbushei Yom Tov Even Ha-Ezer* 4; *Sefer Minhat Avraham* 2:11-12; *Resp. Har Tzvi* 1:14, 22:180; *Resp. Beit Avi, Ezer Avraham* on *Even Ha-Ezer,* 1:14; File no. 1-14-1393, Jerusalem Regional Beit Din, March 5, 2003; File no. 870175/4, supra n. 4; File no. 1168319/2, Supreme Rabbinical Court, August 5,2019.

However, in certain circumstances, observing a person may be halakhically sufficient to label him mentally dysfunctional. See *Resp. Maharsham* 6:159, 160.

Finally, in the absence of corroborating evidence that a defect existed prior to the marriage; notwithstanding Rabbi Aaron Walkin's judgment that one is proscribed from voiding a marriage when it isn't clear that sexual impotence preexisted the marriage (see *Resp. Zekan Aharon* 2:104), we respectfully disagree. *Mahariz Enzel* and others argue that we may invoke the presumption (the *hazakah*) that in fact he was impotent or gay prior to the marriage. See *Resp. Mahariz Enzel* 35; *Resp. Iggerot Moshe, Even Ha-Ezer* 4:113. For biological determinants linked to homosexuality such that consequently we may assume that even before the marriage the husband was gay, see this writer's *Rabbinic Authority,* vol. 3, p. 155, n. 45. Precursors to a disease such as schizophrenia that existed prior to the marriage may suffice to allow for voiding the marriage, see File no. 870175/4, supra n. 4.

Interestingly, addressing the case of a husband who reneged on a premarital condition to refrain from his assaulting his spouse, *Shirat Ha-Levi* 14 invokes *kiddushei ta'ut* without even verifying that such a flaw existed prior to the marriage. One suggestion is that if a defect is noted suddenly after the marriage and it is clear that this flaw predated the marriage, then we can conclude that the situation is a case of *kiddushei ta'ut* without further verification. See *Hiddushei Ha-Ramban, Yevamot* 2b.

Based upon this line of reasoning, we can understand that it was sufficient for R. Feinstein that it was proven that the husband was impotent on his wedding night. Therefore, despite the fact that the *kiddushei ta'ut* could not be corroborated to exist before the marriage, the marriage may be voided. See *Resp. Iggerot Moshe Even Ha-Ezer* 4:52. However, in another scenario, R. Feinstein requires doctors to corroborate that the husband was impotent prior to the marriage before employing the technique of *kiddushei ta'ut* to void the marriage. See *Resp. Iggerot Moshe Even Ha-Ezer* 1:79.

8. The Preconditions for Invoking the Technique of *Kiddushei Ta'ut*

Prior to invoking *kiddushei taut* as a vehicle for voiding a marriage, three preconditions need to apply:

1. Obviously, the *dayan* must be astute and keenly aware of the slippery slope and therefore be very cautious as to what constitutes a grave, latent defect, lest one undermine the institution of marriage. Consequently, though certain types of behavior or diseases such as temper tantrums, stinginess, and diabetes may impact upon marital stability, nonetheless such flaws would generally fail to be classified as a major defect that may potentially, under certain conditions, be grounds for a *kiddushei ta'ut.*

There is a tradition that the scope of *get* compulsion is defined by a list of specific grounds enumerated in the Mishnah and Talmud.[58]

Alternatively, unwilling to rely upon a closed list, we may receive definitional guidance for understanding the nature of the flaw from the words of Rabbi Refael Shlomo Daichovsky, a retired *dayan* from the Beth Din Ha-Rabbani Ha-Gadol. Addressing the situation of a Yemenite man who married two women while living in Yemen and subsequently moved to Israel, R. Daichovsky states the following:[59]

> The entire subject of defects is linked to the opinion of people and their absence of mental readiness to accept a deplorable situation regarding their spouses... A defect is not limited to the realm of individual physiology; also a behavioral defect such as being a pimp would obligate the giving of a *get*... In the western world it is a degradation for the woman to share her bed with another woman. And a husband who would marry a second

Finally, in a situation of a major flaw which may serve as grounds to coerce a *get*, the presumption is inapplicable. See *Ein Yitzhak*, supra n. 23.

58. See *Tosafot, Ketubot* 70a, s.v. *yotzi*; *Mishneh Torah, Hilk. Ishut* 15:7; *Piskei Ha-Rosh, Yevamot* 6:11; *Resp. Ha-Rosh* 17:6; (Cf. *Piskei Ha-Rosh Ketubot* 4:3); *Mordekhai Ketubot* 194; *Hiddushei Ha-Ramban, Ketubot* 63b; *Hiddushei Ha-Rashba, Ketubot* 64a; *Resp. Ha-Rashbash* 93; *Tur, Even Ha-Ezer* 154 in the name of Rosh; *Resp. Mahari Bruna* 211; *Shulhan Arukh, Even Ha-Ezer* 154:5, 21; *Resp. Ha-Ridvaz* 4:108 (1180); *Bi'ur Ha-Gra, Shulhan Arukh, Even Ha-Ezer* 154:50; *Resp. Zekan Aharon* 149; *Hazon Ish, Ketubot* 69:23. For additional sources, see *Rabbinic Authority*, vol. 5, 299, n. 78.

59. File no. 1-22-1510, Supreme Rabbinical Court, September 7, 2004.

> wife would be obligated a *get* not only because of the *herem* of Rabbeinu Gershom (the prohibition against bigamy with its attendant sanction of excommunication – AYW) but also due to the degradation and the defect that is involved (in this second marriage – AYW).... Here (in Israel – AYW) the matter is a major embarrassment as a major defect.

Similarly, Rabbi Shlomo Amar argues regarding battery of a wife:[60]

> In contemporary times, we need to be very stringent regarding the assaulting of one's wife since every well-mannered and intelligent man is embarrassed by this (conduct – AYW) and a woman cannot tolerate this, and it is a major embarrassment today compared to earlier times... a man who batters his wife is deemed as being disgusting and abhorrent in his wife's eyes... to the extent that she cannot live with him.

Addressing the grounds for a release from a levirate marriage (*halitzah*)[61] due to a missing brother-in-law, upon a wife's discovery after marriage that her husband is sexually impotent, Rabbi Y. Spektor writes:[62]

> We see that this is a severe flaw because the majority are particular about this... and the Halakhah concerning all defects... is that it depends on the agreement of the citizenry as it is elucidated in Hoshen Mishpat 232:6...

On the other hand, addressing the grounds for voiding a marriage where

60. *Resp. Shema Shlomo* 1 *Even Ha-Ezer* 15.

61. When a husband dies without having offspring, there is a duty upon the original husband's brother to marry his sister-in-law (*yibum*). Normative Halakhah mandates a ceremony entitled *halitzah* where the brother-in-law (*yavam*) renounces his duty to marry his sister-in-law and releases her to marry anyone of her choosing.

62. *Resp. Ein Yitzhak*, 1 *Even Ha-Ezer* 24. Even if the wife possesses a flaw that the husband is concerned about does not mean that there are grounds to void the marriage. Should a husband fail to discover the flaw during the marriage, and it is discovered after his death, there is a debate whether there are grounds to void the marriage. See *Tosafot Yevamot* 2a, s.v. oh, 56a, s.v. *meit*; *Hiddushei Ha-Ran, Ketubot* 35a; *Shulhan Arukh, Even Ha-Ezer* 39:1; *Beit Shmuel, Even Ha-Ezer* 39:4; *Avnei Milluim* 39:3; *Mikneh*, 39:13, 38:31; *Resp. Kovetz Teshuvot* 4:155; *Resp. Even Yisrael* 9:133; R. Litke, *Piskei Din*, 12.

the wife discovers after marriage that her husband is sexually impotent, Rabbi Moshe Feinstein advances another rationale:[63]

> Since it is clear and straightforward that he isn't capable of engaging in intercourse, which is the primary component of intimate relations, for this is the reason why a bride enters the wedding canopy.... Therefore, it is clear that an individual who is not capable of intercourse is the greater defect... and one does not have to submit proofs for this...

Therefore, in accordance with R. Feinstein, though insanity, pre-existing impotence and homosexuality are not recorded in the Talmud as defects, the principle of *kiddushei ta'ut* is applicable and can be invoked under such conditions.[64] In short, the severity of the defect is determined by reason and logic.

On the other hand, Rabbi Hayyim Berlin – the son of the renowned Rabbi Naftali Zvi Berlin – lambasts those authorities who engage in reason and logic as an avenue to void a marriage by stating:[65]

> One cannot imagine the damage and the breaches that can emerge from this in our dissolute generation... they will begin comparing one matter to another one – in the beginning, they will permit based upon assessed expectations (*umdanot*)... they will permit (to remarry – A.Y.W.) every wife whose husband who has traveled overseas to America or Africa... And afterwards they will permit... if a person will promise a certain amount of dowry and subsequently it will be discovered... that he cannot keep his promise, they will say, "in her mind she would not have submitted to this marriage"... and halakhic bastards (*mamzerim)* will multiply in Israel.

Alternatively, in contrast to Rabbis Amar's and Daichovsky's approach, there is a tradition (*mesorah*) which posits that the imposition of coercion will determine the severity of the defect. If the particular behavior of the husband dictates a *beit din* ruling of *get* coercion,[66] then under cer-

63. *Iggerot Moshe,* supra n. 57.

64. *Iggerot Moshe,* supra n. 57; *Even Ha-Ezer* 1:80; *Even Ha-Ezer* 4:113

65. *Nishmat Hayyim,* supra n. 1. Cf. *Resp. Iggerot Moshe, Hoshen Mishpat* 2:74 who is unconcerned about the slippery slope argument.

66. Halakhah recognizes three levels of *get* coercion. The lowest level is moral

tain conditions voiding a marriage is possible. However, if the particular behavior doesn't require *get* coercion, then voiding a marriage will not be an option. In the former case, in the presence of *get* coercion we are addressing a major blemish. In the latter case, which is dealing with the absence of *get* coercion, we are dealing with a minor flaw. As Rabbi Yitzhak E. Spektor, a leading decisor of nineteenth century Lithuania states:[67]

> ...in the case of impotence, we are compelled to acknowledge that there is no doubt at all as to whether she would have accepted, because this blemish is one that most everyone – or at least, most women – would object to; so we compel the husband to give a divorce. And it follows that this is a defect for which a marriage will be voided.

Subsequently, focusing upon a wife who was not aware prior to marriage that her husband was impotent, and he failed to give her a *get*, Rabbi Moshe Feinstein, a twentieth century arbiter, rules that there are grounds to coerce a *get*. As R. Feinstein and others opine, given the absence of the legal ability to impose *get* coercion today, under certain

---

pressure, known as coercion by words ("*kefiyah bidevarim*"). See *Tosafot, Ketubot* 70a, s.v. *yotzi*; *Shulhan Arukh, Even Ha-Ezer* 71:1; *Resp. Ha-Ridvaz* 4:157 (1228). The intermediate type of coercion is financial pressures, known as enforcing an order, such as an increase for spousal support ("*kefiyah derekh bereirah*"). See *Pithei Teshuva Even Ha-Ezer* 154:8 in the name of *Beit Meir*; *Gevurot Anashim* 48; Ridvaz, op. cit.; *Resp. Ha-Mabit* 1:76. The most severe form of coercion is whipping and imprisonment (coercion via *sho'tim*). See Talmud Bavli *Ketubot* 77a; *Gittin* 88b; *Resp. Ha-Rivash* 127; *Resp. Ha-Rashba* 5:242; *Resp. Darkhei Noam Even Ha-Ezer* 53; Ridvaz, op. cit.; *Resp. Heikhal Yitzhak, Even Ha-Ezer* 1:1-2; *Resp. Yabia Omer*, 3 *Even Ha-Ezer* 20.

Consequently, if the particular behavior of the husband dictates a *beit din* ruling of *get* coercion, then under certain conditions voiding a marriage is possible. In the event that the decisor (see supra n. 60) fails to specify the type of coercion, then we may assume that any one the three forms of coercion may be a precondition for voiding a marriage.

If the husband fails to mention a defect such as pedophilia prior to the marriage, then there are grounds for *get* compulsion. See *Beit Shmuel, Even Ha-Ezer* 117:24; *Resp. Ohr Gadol* 5:2; *Resp. Ein Yitzhak, Even Ha-Ezer* 2:35 (34); *Resp. Hatam Sofer, Even Ha-Ezer* 1:117. Cf. *Resp. Galya Masekhet, Kuntres Aharon* 5; *Hafla'ah, Ketubot, Kuntres Aharon* 18; *Hazon Ish, Ketubot* 69:23; *Resp. Maharsham* 3:327.

67. *Ein Yitzhak*, supra n.62.

conditions one may invoke *kiddushei ta'ut* and thus free the woman to remarry without a *get.*[68]

Moreover, the presumption of "*tav le-meitav tan do mi-le-meitav armalu*" may not be invoked if the wife advances the argument of *kiddushei ta'ut,* predicated upon a defect which may be grounds for *get* coercion.[69]

Is it possible that the *kiddushin* will be voided based upon *ta'ut* even if the spouse fails to raise the argument of a mistaken transaction? To state it differently, is the claim of *kiddushei ta'ut* a halakhic argument and therefore doesn't require the invoking of said claim, or is it a personal claim and if the spouse fails to advance it, then there is no consequence in terms of *kiddushei ta'ut*? Regarding commercial transactions, some argue that the transaction becomes void due to the assumption (*anan sahadi*) that there is a condition that the transaction is bereft of a defect. Therefore, the buyer must raise his concern about the defect.[70] Others contend that the voiding due to error is not based upon a stipulation but rather an absence in the meeting of the minds in establishing the undertaking of a commitment (*ma'aseh kinyan*).[71] The identical controversy exists regarding where a marriage may be voided due to error where the spouse has not raised his/her objection to the defect.[72]

2. In order to invalidate the act of *kiddushin*, it must be clear that the defect existed prior to the marriage, and that the wife was unaware of it prior to the marriage.

Regarding the trustworthiness of the wife stating that she was unaware

68. *Beit Ha-Levi,* supra n. 32; *Resp. Iggerot Moshe, Even Ha-Ezer* 1:79 (5); *Resp. Har Tzvi Even Ha-Ezer* 1:133, 2:81; *Resp. Yabia Omer,* vol. 3, *Even Ha-Ezer* 20, vol. 9, *Even Ha-Ezer* 38; *Minhat Avraham* 2:10; *Kovetz Teshuvot* 4:152 (a possibility); R. Y. Goldberg, *Ellu She'kofin Le'hotzi,* 121, n. 36.

Interestingly enough, *Beit Shmuel* and *Hazon Ish* did not arrive at this conclusion. However, they rule that a case of *kiddushei ta'ut* obligates *get* coercion. See *Beit Shmuel, Even Ha-Ezer* 154:2; *Hazon Ish, Even Ha-Ezer, Ketubot* 69:23; *Resp. Har Tzvi, Even Ha-Ezer, Gittin* 181 in the name of Bah.

69. *Birkat Retzeh,* supra n. 55; *Ein Yitzhak,* supra n. 62; *Iggerot Moshe,* supra n. 55.

70. Ran, *Avodah Zarah,* Chapter 1 (4b on the pages of Rif); *Hiddushei Ha-Ritva, Bava Batra* 136a; *Resp. Ha-Ri Megas* 129; *Sefer Hayashar* 653; *Resp. Beit Yitzhak, Hoshen Mishpat* 64; *Resp. Divrei Malkiel* 2:85.

71. Supra n. 32.

72. *Tosafot, Yevamot* 2b; *Beit Ha-Levi,* supra n. 32; *Resp. Dvar Yehoshua* 1:71; *Resp. R. Akiva Eiger, Hilk. Pesah* 448:9; *Avnei Milluim* 39:3; R. Grossman, *Resp. Knesset Yisrael* 4; *Resp. Kovetz Teshuvot* 1:159.

of her husband's flaw prior to the marriage, Rabbi Osher Weiss, a contemporary Israeli *dayan,* rules as follows:[73]

> Since there is a doubt concerning the essence of the *kiddushin,* it is to be construed as if she isn't a married woman and therefore "one witness is trustworthy regarding prohibitions" in "a matter of licentiousness" (*davar she'be'ervah*) when it is bereft of the status of being prohibited, in accordance with the view of the Maharik, shoresh 72. Similarly, thus is the view of Tosafot in Gittin 2b, s.v. havei...
>
> Though seemingly the majority of arbiters disagree with this position, and in pursuance to their opinion a single witness cannot be trusted in "a matter of licentiousness" even it is devoid of the status of being prohibited, as it is explained in the words of Ramban... in the words of Rashi... and as in Rashba... seemingly we one must be stringent in this matter... However, renowned later authorities tended to be lenient and that is what was written in the Resp. of Noda Be-Yehudah in many places. See in Mahadura Kamma 54... 59... 38... 43.... And they are worthy these pillars of the world, Noda Be-Yehudah, Hayyei Adam and... Rabbi Akiva Eiger to rely upon them in an hour of emergency...

Notwithstanding the position that women today are "licentious" and therefore they are untrustworthy,[74] the above posture of R. Weiss was affirmed by other authorities.[75]

---

73. *Resp. Minhat Asher* 1:73 (3)

74. *Mordekhai, Kiddushin* 542 in the name of Maharam; *Beit Yosef, Even Ha-Ezer* 17 in the name of *Orhot Hayyim; Resp. Mahari Weil* 22; *Resp. Ha-Ridvaz* 4:118; *Resp. Maharam Alshakar* 89. Cf. others who reject this posture. See *Resp. Maharbi*l 3:102; *Resp. Maharlbah* 33; *Drisha, Even Ha-Ezer* 154; *Gevurat Anashim* 67; *Resp. Ein Yitzhak, Even Ha-Ezer* 2:34; *Resp. Yabia Omer* 4, *Even Ha-Ezer* 11. If a *beit din* trusts her words, *ex post facto* if she got married based on that ruling, she may remain in the marriage. See *Bah, Even Ha-Ezer* 17; *Beit Shmuel, Even Ha-Ezer* 17:4; *Helkat Mehokeik, Even Ha-Ezer* 17:4; *Resp. Ein Yitzhak, Even Ha-Ezer* 1:30.

Whether she is trustworthy in regard to her allegation that her husband raped her is subject to debate. See *Resp. Edut Be-Ya'akov* 36; *Resp. Yaskil Avdi* 5, *Even Ha-Ezer* 69; *Resp. Mishpat Tzedek* 59. Cf. *Hiddushei Ha-Ritva Ketubot* 23a; *Resp. Ha-Ridvaz* 3:406-407; *Sdei Hemed Ha-Shalem, Gerushin* 1:12; *Piskei Din Rabbanayim* 4:342, 345.

75. *Resp. Beit Avi Even Ha-Ezer* 3:135 (4) in the name of Ran, Tosafot, Rosh, Rivash, and Maharik.

In short, we trust what the wife alleges in *beit din* regarding her unawareness concerning the existence of a husband's major flaw prior to the marriage. As we mentioned earlier, the determination of its existence and severity has been left in the hands of physicians and health care professionals for their determination.[76]

3. Upon a wife's awareness of the major latent defect that her husband may have intentionally or unintentionally failed to disclose, she must decide to leave the marriage. Whether she must immediately leave the marriage or not is subject to debate.[77]

For those who permitted remaining together upon discovery of a latent flaw, a reasonable explanation was required by the *beit din*. And once the explanation ceased to be applicable, then Halakhah demanded that the wife immediately leave him. Addressing the case of a mother of two children who, during the span of seven years was living with a psychologically dysfunctional husband before separating from him, Dayan Ben Tzion Boaron, serving at that time as a *dayan* on the Supreme Rabbinical Court in Jerusalem, Israel, astutely notes:[78]

> And one cannot say that since she lived with him seven years and had two children and observed the defect, she forgave him. That is not the case, since in these matters one cannot comprehend the disease in clear terms for an extended period of time because sometimes due to her love she explains his anger and anxiety... (she views it – AYW) as a temporary psychological state and she craves and hopes that his situation will improve. In

76. See supra text accompanying note 57.

77. *Mishneh Torah, Hilk. Ishut* 25:11, *Tur* and *Beit Yosef, Even Ha-Ezer* 154, Rema, *Shulhan Arukh Even Ha-Ezer* 154:1; *Helkat Mehokeik, Even Ha-Ezer* 39:9; *Beit Shmuel Even Ha-Ezer* 39:16; *Resp. R. Akiva Eiger, Mahadura Tinyana* 51,106, *Resp. Shemesh U-Magen* 3, *Even Ha-Ezer* 27:4, *Even Ha-Ezer* 94 and *Piskei Din Rabbanayim* 6:221, 223 who mandate immediate departure from the marriage. And if intimacy (*ishut*) transpired, neither spouse can claim that he/she was unaware of the defect. See *Shulhan Arukh Even Ha-Ezer* 117:10.

Others may sanction remaining for a time, provided there is a reasonable explanation for staying there. See *Tashbetz*, supra n. 49; *Resp. Maharsham* 3:16, 77, 6:160; *Ein Yitzhak*, supra n. 61; *Resp. Be'eirot Ha-Mayim Even Ha-Ezer* 1; *Hazon Yehezkel* on *Masekhet Zevahim, Even Ha-Ezer* 8; *Resp. Dvar Yehoshua* 71; *Resp. Iggerot Moshe, Even Ha-Ezer* 3:45, 48, 4:113; *Resp. Minhat Asher* 1:73 (4), 2:72; File no. 1-14-1393, Jerusalem Regional Beit Din, March 5, 2003.

78. *Resp. Sha'arei Tzion* 3, *Even Ha-Ezer* 4.

> particular, when a person regularly takes medicine, there are periods when he is relaxed and quiet. Such is the situation in particular after he explodes and then becomes relaxed and pleads for forgiveness....

His observations of human nature and their significance in terms of voiding a marriage have precedents in earlier authorities.[79]

Similarly, Rabbi Osher Weiss argues that remaining with her husband after discovery of a defect does not prevent a wife from later claiming that that was a mistaken marriage. As he notes:[80]

> Given that we are witnesses [to the fact that], the reactions of people differ. It is very common that when a person discovers defects in a spouse, he does not react immediately for various reasons, sometimes due to distress and shock, and sometimes in order to preserve his sanity or in order to consider how not to hurt the feelings of the spouse, and this is not proof that he has pardoned or that he does not care...
>
> But it appears that even though she surely regretted her marriage, in any case she was prepared to try, to see if matters could be sorted out by effort, etc., but when all these attempts failed, we return to the original finding, namely that this is a case of mistaken *kiddushin*...

In short, based upon the foregoing, given the particular circumstances of the case, it will depend on whether there are reasonable explanations for a wife's delay in bolting the marriage due to the major defect.

One frequent case which has been addressed in the responsa is if the wife explicitly agreed prior to her marriage to deal with her future husband's sickness (*savrah ve-kiblah*). Subsequently, with the onset of the marriage, she discovers that the illness has become more severe than expected and she is unwilling to deal with it. As R. Trani, R. M. Arik and Sanzer Rebbe contend, a disease which by its very nature is subject to change and may become more severe, one cannot say *savrah ve-kiblah.*[81]

Others contend that we focus upon whether we are dealing with a major defect (a *mum gadol*) or not. Consequently, if we are dealing with

79. *Resp. Maharsha*m 3:16; *Resp. Ohr Gadol* 5:12; *Resp. Avnei Ha-Ephod* 117:15.
80. *Resp. Minhat Asher* 1:73 (4).
81. *Resp. Ha-Mabit* 3:212; *Resp. Divrei Hayyim* 1:51; *Resp. Imrei Yosher* 2:119.

a major disease, one cannot say *savrah ve-kiblah.*[82] Rabbi M. Feinstein argues similarly when he states:[83]

> Since craziness is a major defect, and even if she remains for fifteen months, we can claim that there were various delays rather than say that she accepted to remain his wife, and *savrah ve-kiblah.*

Addressing mental dysfunction, R. Aryeh Leib Horowitz similarly states:[84]

> The logic that he accepted (the disease – AYW) is inapplicable to a defect that is constant.... However, the sickness of mental incompetence changes from one period to another. Therefore, it is a possibility that in the condition that he knew (her – AYW) prior to the marriage he accepted, and the craziness that emerged with her afterwards he couldn't tolerate, and therefore one cannot say he accepted it.

Regarding a wife who became crazy, R. Tzvi Hirsch Orenstein observes:[85]

> When there is a change, one can say, "it is unacceptable to me."

In contemporary times, this posture was concretized in various Israeli rabbinical court decisions.[86] All the aforesaid rulings deal with grave defects concerning a wife. Two Israeli rabbinical decisions apply this conclusion dealing with a wife's defects to a husband's flaws and stated that such a conclusion is considered acceptable by the authorities.[87]

In short, the concept of *savrah ve-kiblah* is inapplicable when dealing with an illness that changes with the passage of time.

However, does the rule of acquiescence (*savrah ve-kiblah*) apply when

82. *Resp. Maharik Ha-Hadashim* 24; *Resp. Har Tzvi, Even Ha-Ezer* 2:181; *Resp. Beit Ha-Levi* 3:4; *Resp. Ahiezer Even Ha-Ezer* 27:3

83. *Resp. Iggerot Moshe, Even Ha-Ezer* 4:45.

84. *Resp. Harei Besamim, Mahadura Tinyana* 72.

85. *Birkat Retzeh,* supra n. 56.

86. File no. 912/51, Ma'aleh Adumim Regional Beit Din,15 Tammuz 5753; File no. 895985/1, Netanya Regional Beit Din, 28 Ellul 5774; File no. 81261/11, Be'air Sheva Rabbinical Court, 25 Ellul 5775; File no. 1129170/1, Jerusalem Rabbinical Court, 2 Nissan 5778.

87. *Piskei Din Rabbanayim* 21:279, 283; 17 *Shurat Ha-Din* 123 (5770).

the husband employs bodily pain vis-à-vis his spouse? May she waive (*mehilah*) bodily pain? Pursuant to the Talmud and Shulhan Arukh:[88]

> If a person says to a friend – "hit and wound me on the condition that you will exempt (from liability)" and his friend maimed him, he is exempt.

Despite the fact that agreeing to being assaulted entails a violation of the prohibition of maiming (*havalah*), if the friend complied with the condition – the condition is valid, and he is exempt from paying for the injury. To state it differently, there is a difference between the prohibitive result and the halakhically illegal obligation.

The question is whether a person can stipulate such a condition which will produce bodily pain? Rabbi Asher ben Yehiel (Rosh) observes:[89]

> A condition is invalid if it sanctions a friend's bodily harm which engenders pain.

Rivash concurs with his conclusion.[90] In contradistinction to some decisors,[91] the majority of legists rule that one is proscribed from stipulating a condition regarding conjugal relations, since abstention from conjugal relations engender pain for the wife.[92]

Finally, some claim that a wife sanctioning bodily harm in a continuous fashion such as receiving physical abuse or permitting spousal rape would constitute a waiver, an example of *savrah ve-kiblah* and is prohibited.[93] However, others contend that one cannot assume that continuous domestic violence is acceptable by the wife, a situation of *savrah ve-kiblah.*[94]

---

88. *Bava Kamma* 93a; *Shulhan Arukh, Hoshen Mishpat* 421:12.

89. *Resp. Ha-Rosh* 68:10.

90. *Resp. Ha-Rivash* 484.

91. *Tosafot Ketubot* 56a; *Hiddushei Ha-Ritva Bava Batra* 126b; *Darkhei Tur, Even Ha-Ezer* 38:8; *Beit Shmuel, Even Ha-Ezer* 69:5.

92. *Mishneh Torah, Hilk. Ishut* 6:10 (Cf. *Mishneh Torah, Hilk. Ishut* 14:7); *Tur Even Ha-Ezer* 38, 69; *Shulhan Arukh Even Ha-Ezer* 38:5; 69:6, 76:11. See further this writer's *Rabbinic Authority*, volume 5, pp. 147-155.

93. *Resp. Shoeil U-Meishiv, Mahadura* 1, 1:197.

94. *Mishneh Le-Melekh, Hilk. Ishut* 15:1; *Lehem Mishneh, Hilk. Ishut* 15:1; *Resp. Ha-Maharik, shoresh* 107. See this writer's *Rabbinic Authority*, vol. 5, 271-305 which deals with a case of a wife who is a victim of Stockholm syndrome.

9. Conclusion

In conclusion, according to Rabbi Yosef Baer Soloveitchik and Rabbi Yitzhak Elhanan Spektor, though on a biblical level one may void a marriage based upon *kiddushei ta'ut,* since nevertheless rabbinically a wife may not exit without the execution of a *get,* in practice they refrained from voiding a marriage under these conditions.[95] In effect, this position argues for a *get le'humra,* as a precautionary stringency.[96] To void a marriage and thus free a woman to remarry without the execution of a *get* serves as a slippery slope; endangering the integrity of all marriages.[97]

Nonetheless, as Rabbi Moshe Feinstein notes, in situations where it is clear that she is an *agunah,* one is not required to rabbinically remain an *agunah* one's entire life, and therefore voiding a marriage would be permissible.[98] In short, the plight of a young woman who desires to remarry has been aptly described by numerous arbiters as an emergency situation (a *she'at ha-dehak*) and has been construed as a *post facto* situation (*be-di'avad*) – as if she has already married someone else. Moreover, a minority opinion may be relied upon in such a situation even if the matter entails a Biblical injunction, such as the prohibition of a married woman, provided that the rabbinic decisor is superior in wisdom and in the number of students i.e., the number of students following his instruction or in age.[99]

---

95. *Beit Ha-Levi,* supra n. 32; *Ein Yitzhak,* supra n. 52.

96. *Shulhan Arukh, Even Ha-Ezer* 39; 5; *Helkat Mehokeik, Even Ha Ezer* 35:9; *Resp. Ahiezer 1, Even Ha-Ezer* 27.

97. *Nishmat Hayyim,* supra n. 1; *Resp. Divrei Yatziv, Even Ha-Ezer* 16; R. S.Z. Urbach, "In the Matter of Annulling a Marriage," (Hebrew) *Torah She-Ba'al Peh* 36, 48 (5734).

98. *Resp. Iggerot Moshe Even Ha-Ezer* 1:79, 80. See also Rabbi Y. Abramsky, *Hazon Yehezkel on Masekhet Zevahim, Even Ha-Ezer* 8; File no. 870175/4, supra n. 4. For further analysis of these contrasting views, see this writer's *Rabbinic Authority,* vol. 3, pp. 169-176.

99. Mishnah *Eduyot* 1:5-6; *Resp. Ha-Rashba* 1:253; *Resp. Ma'sat Binyamin* 44; *Resp. Re'eim* 1:36 cited by *Taz, Shulhan Arukh, Even Ha-Ezer* 17:10; *Resp. Ginat Veradim* 3:6; *Resp. Sha'arei Tzion* 14; R. Aharon Lichtenstein, "The Human and Social Factor in Halakhah," 36 *Tradition,* 2002, 1, 3-4, 6-7.

See further *Resp. Helkat Ya'akov, Even Ha-Ezer* 38; *Resp. Yabia Omer,* 7, *Even Ha-Ezer* 8, 17, *Even Ha-Ezer* 36:10 (*halitzah*), 38(5) (marriage), who contends that one may rely upon a minority opinion in a case of dire need and even regarding a Torah law given that the doctrine of majority rule is only valid when all parties are sitting together such as a *beit din* proceeding. See *Resp. Ha-Rashba* 2:104; *Get Pashut, Kelalim* 1. For different explanations for the nonapplicability of this doctrine, see *Yam shel Shlomo, Bava Kamma* 10:10; *Resp. She'elat Ya'avetz* 1:157; *Urim Ve-Tumim,*

Finally, a woman is entitled, more than a man, to have a marriage voided based upon *kiddushei ta'ut*. The rationale for this conclusion is that the man may always divorce his wife and he can marry another woman with the permission of 100 rabbis residing in three lands. However, the woman neither may divorce him without his consent nor marry another man.[100]

As noted by *Rabbi Moshe Feinstein*:[101]

> One does not rush to void a marriage, one attempts to obtain a *get*.

As such, it is important for every *beit din* to address this matter, either by procedurally obligating a *get* (*hiyyuv get*), or by directing the husband to give a *get* (*mitzvah le'garesh*), or by recommending it to be given (*hamalatzah le'garesh*).[102]

In the event that the *beit din* obligated that the *get* ought to be given and the husband refused to give it, then the beit din *ought* to investigate and deliberate whether there are grounds to void the marriage. Should there be a basis to void the marriage and the arbiter(s) refuses, *R. Feinstein* states:[103]

> It is a major prohibition "to leave a wife in chains" if one has the ability to address the situation and does not resolve it.

Final Thoughts

As we mentioned, one of the reasons that some arbiters oppose invoking kiddushei ta'ut as an avenue to void a marriage is due to *halakhic* logic (*sevara*), namely to avoid a public perception that a married woman may be freed without the execution of a *get*.

Kitzur Tokfo Kohen, 123-124; *Hazon Ish, Hilk. Kilayim* 1.

100. *Yam shel Shlomo, Ketubot* 75a; *Resp. Noda Be-Yehudah, Even Ha-Ezer Mahadura Tinyana*, 80 (in theory rather than practice); *Resp. Seridei Esh, Even Ha-Ezer* 27:4; *Resp. Iggerot Moshe, Even Ha-Ezer* 1:79; Resp. Minhat Avraham 2:10.

101. *Mesorat Moshe*, vol. 1, 419.

102. For the significance and the differences of these types of divorce enforcement, see this writer's *Rabbinic Authority*, vol. 5, 306-323.

Regarding the significance of incorporating these different divorce enforcements into the *beit din* procedure in order to solve *get* recalcitrance issues, see supra chapter 4.

103. *Resp. Iggerot Moshe, Even Ha-Ezer* 1:117.

Furthermore, as we noted earlier, Rabbi Hayyim Berlin – the son of the renown Rabbi Naftali Zvi Berlin – lambasts those authorities who engage in reason and logic as an avenue to void a marriage by stating:[104]

> One cannot imagine the damage and the breaches that can emerge from this in our dissolute generation… they will begin comparing one matter to another one – in the beginning, they will permit based upon assessed expectations(*umdanot*)… they will permit (to remarry – AYW) every wife whose husband who has traveled overseas to America or Africa… And afterwards they will permit… if a person will promise a certain amount of dowry and subsequently it will be discovered… that he cannot keep his promise, they will say, "in her mind she would not have submitted to this marriage"… and *mamzerim* will multiply in Israel.

In short, halakhic logic teaches us that there is a need to educate the community of the importance of execution of a *get* under certain prescribed circumstances, and to avoid the slippery slope of voiding a marriage where there was no basis to proceed down this avenue. Consequently, it is unsurprising, that as we mentioned earlier, Rabbi Menashe Klein exclaims:[105]

> And in the novella of… Rabbi Joseph Henkin… states: since we never heard or know, from the time of the Talmud, that a marriage would be voided due to a defect, in particular after *kiddushin* was executed, and everywhere and every time when questions such as these arose, they always required a *get*… and one cannot void a marriage even if the defect was clear and the other party was unaware of it.

Therefore, pursuant to this position, there are those who mandate the giving of a *get*. Seemingly, invoking *halakhic* logic entails a biblical mandate.[106] As the Talmud exhorts us in a few places, "What need is there for

104. *Nishmat Hayyim*, supra n. 1. Cf. *Resp. Iggerot Moshe, Hoshen Mishpat* 2:74 who is unconcerned about the slippery slope argument.

105. *Resp. Mishneh Halakhot*, supra n. 22.

106. *Kol Kitvei Maharatz Hayot, Siman* 1; *Pnei Yehoshua, Berakhot* 35a, s.v. *ella sevarah.*

a biblical verse? It is a *sevara* (the view may be based upon reasoning)".[107] Upon further reflection, since the *get* is being given on rabbinic grounds, we are dealing with imposing a stringency in order to protect the undermining of the status of a married woman lest a husband leave his spouse without giving a *get.* As such we are dealing here with invoking *halakhic* reasoning which is rabbinically mandated.[108]

Nevertheless, as we discussed elsewhere,[109] there is adequate proof that one may under certain conditions void a particular marriage. Consequently, in accordance with arbiters such as Rashba and Rabbi O. Yosef who contend that with the submission of proof we may set aside the *halakhic* reasoning of earlier authorities, the above *halakhic* logic may be rejected.[110]

However, we would like to submit additional proof to substantiate the view of those authorities who endorse under certain conditions to void a marriage involving a get-recalcitrant husband. As we explained, implicitly relying upon earlier authorities,[111] a mistaken transaction (*mekah ta'ut*) is concretized in Shulhan Arukh in the following fashion:[112]

> If one sells another land, a slave, a domestic animal, or other moveable property, and a defect, which the buyer did not know, is found in the purchase, a buyer may return it even if a number of years (have lapsed since the transaction), since this sale was

107. Talmud Bavli *Berakhot* 4b; *Ketubot* 22a; *Bava Kamma* 46b. Consequently, R. Yehezkel Landau argues that only if the Talmud states, "What need is there for a biblical verse? It is a *sevara* (the view may be based upon reasoning)," then the sevara is biblically mandated. See *Tzlah, Berakhot* 4b.

However, one may not rely upon a sevara in order to sanction engaging in a biblical prohibition. See *Resp. Yabia Omer,* 9, Introduction.

108. Resp. *Shevut Ya'akov* 3:135; *Tzlah, Berakhot* 35a.

109. See this writer's *Rabbinic Authority,* vol. 3, 134–176, 231–333; vol. 4, 143–298 and vol. 5, 233-248, 278-305 and in this chapter.

110. *Resp. Ha-Rashba* 2:322 and *Resp. Yabia Omer,* 7 *Orah Hayyim* 33 (2), vol. 9, Introduction, 10, *Orah Hayyim* 55 (13).

111. Alfasi, *Bava Metzia* 30b; *Piskei Ha-Rosh, Bava Metzia* 4:15; *Mishneh Torah, Hilk. Mekhirah* 15:3.

112. *Hoshen Mishpat* 232:3.

Even if the buyer failed to inspect the item prior to his purchase and the seller sold it to him without stipulating a condition, he is not empowered to void the transaction due to an error in the sale. See *Sma, Hoshen Mishpat* 232:10. Moreover, even if the buyer observed the defect and he remained silent, he can retract his consent to the purchase provided he did not use the item. *A fortiori* if the buyer could have inspected and failed to inspect the item, the transaction is void. See *Pithei Teshuva, Hoshen Mishpat* 232:1 in the name of *Mishneh Le-Melekh.*

> based upon a basic error, provided that the buyer did not use the object after he became aware of the defect.

And numerous authorities have applied the model of the halakhot of a mistaken transaction for rescinding a sale (*mekah ta'ut*) due to an error towards defining a major flaw (a *mum gadol*) concerning *kiddushei ta'ut* where a husband, prior to the marriage, failed to disclose his major defect, and under certain conditions, the marriage was voided.[113]

Though the role of reasoning by analogy (*hekesh*) is an integral ingredient in rendering a decision,[114] seemingly the invoking of halakhic logic here is proscribed due to the Talmudic rule, "one does not learn prohibitions from monetary matters".[115] As the Talmud states:[116]

> How can one deduce a prohibition from a monetary matter?

Said conclusion is reached by the Talmudic sage R. Amram due to the need to be stringent concerning the doubt relating to the woman being married.[117]

Consequently, invoking of halakhic logic to apply a model from the universe of commercial matters (mistaken sales transaction) to the universe of marriage (error in marriage) which entails prohibitions is seemingly out of place. To state it differently, it would seem that the halakhic logic advanced by those who opposed voiding a marriage trumps the halakhic logic employed by the supporters who argue that *kiddushei ta'ut* is a valid technique to void a marriage. However, upon examination there are at least a dozen Talmudic passages accompanied by post-Talmudic interpretations which conclude that one may learn a halakhah dealing with a monetary matter and apply it to the halakhic

113. For the analogy between *mekah ta'ut* and *kiddushei ta'ut* in the words of some *Rishonim,* see *Hiddushei Ha-Rashba, Ketubot* 72a; *Magid Mishneh, Hilk. Mehirah* 15:3 in the name of Maimonides; *Resp. Ha-Ri Megash* 129; *Resp. Ha-Rosh* 33:1; *Beit Ha-Behirah, Yevamot* 2b. See this writer's *Rabbinic Authority,* vol. 3, 151-157.

If a certain flaw in the wife's physiological makeup or psyche is viewed as a major defect and may be subjected to voiding the marriage similarly, such a defect may be labeled a major flaw in the husband's makeup. See supra n. 47.

114. Talmud Bavli *Bava Batra* 130b; *Resp. Ha-Rosh* 55, 78:3; see this writer's *Rabbinic Authority,* vol. 1, 53-57.

115. Talmud Bavli *Berakhot* 19b.

116. Talmud Bavli *Bava Metzia* 20b.

117. Rashi *Gittin* 34a; *Tosafot, Bava Metzia* 20b, s.v. *issura mi'mamona; Resp. Ein Yitzhak,* 2 *Even Ha-Ezer* 54:29.

issue relating to a prohibition.[118] Consequently, it is unsurprising that the model of the halakhot of a mistaken transaction for rescinding a sale (*mekah ta'ut*) due to an error is applied to defining a major flaw (a *mum gadol*) concerning *kiddushei ta'ut* where a husband prior to the marriage failed to disclose his major defect and, under certain conditions, the marriage was voided.[119]

II. Umdana

In contradistinction to *kiddushei ta'ut*, where one focuses upon the past – namely, when there was a mistake at the time of the consummating the marriage in the form of an undisclosed grave preexisting personality and/or medical or psychological disorder and consequently, the marriage may be voided retroactively – when one invokes an *umdana demukhah* as a grounds for voiding a marriage, we are focusing on a future occurrence, i.e., one that transpired after the creation of the marriage.[120] For example, "had I known that my husband would have been physically abusive to me or would become mentally dysfunctional during our marriage, I never would have married him" may serve as illustrations of a wife invoking *umdana demukhah*, which we hereafter label for the sake of the presentation simply as '*umdana*.'

For an *umdana* to be effective, there is a precondition that it depends upon the consent of both parties. For example, a sales transaction entails the agreement of both parties, i.e., "*taluy be-da'at shneihem*",[121] the seller and the buyer. The voiding of the sale with the appearance of a defect subsequent to purchase would be predicated upon the fulfillment of two conditions:

1. The buyer would not have consummated the deal if he had realized that the item would be defective within a reasonable time.

---

118. See R. A. Walkin, *Beit Aharon* 9, 189-190; E. Shochetman, "On Analogy in Decision Making in Jewish Law & the Foundations of Law Act," (Hebrew), 13 *Shenaton Ha-Mishpat Ha-Ivri*, 307, 327-336, 1988.

119. However, clearly there are instances where one cannot deduce a forbidden norm from a monetary matter including issues of divorce. See Shochetman, supra n. 118, 340-344.

120. For our conceptual distinction between *kiddushei ta'ut* and *umdana*, see *Resp. Ohr Sameach* 2:29; *Resp. Sheilot Moshe, Even Ha-Ezer* 2 and *Resp. Zikhron Yehonatan*,1, *Yoreh Deah* 5.

121. *Tosafot Ketubot* 47b, s.v. *shelo*; *Netivot Ha-Mishpat* 230:1. Cf. *Tosafot, Yevamot* 45b, s.v. *me*.

2. The seller would negotiate the sale contingent upon the utility of the item being sold.

To state it differently, the voiding of the sales transaction is dependent upon the existence of both the seller's and buyer's implied conditions.[122] And pursuant to Rabbis Yosef B. Soloveitchik and Aaron Levine, to void the sale based upon utilizing *umdana*, one requires an explicit condition (*tenai*) and the agreement of both parties concerning the condition, and in the absence of an explicit condition – we require the employment of an *umdana*.[123]

The requirement of "*taluy be-da'at shneihem*" as a precondition prior to invoking an *umdana* equally applies to marriage, which is based upon the consent of both the man and the woman.[124] Consequently, it is unsurprising that the *umdana* of each spouse may be identical. For example, if both are committed to a Torah lifestyle, and someone told the couple that one of the spouses would renounce religion and become a Reform Jew during the marriage, clearly most couples would never marry under such conditions. However, in the wake of the husband becoming irreligious and refusing to give a *get*, though his wife may argue the *umdana*, "had I known that he would become a Reform Jew I never would have married him," there may be grounds to oppose voiding the marriage for five reasons: Firstly, we are dealing the stringency of a married woman. Secondly, there is the Talmudic presumption, "it is better to live as two together rather than to live alone" (*tav le-meitav tan do mi-le-meitav armalu*}, and hence there is no predisposition to sever marital ties. Thirdly, it is difficult to establish *umdanot* regarding a matter of personal status.[125]

---

122. For the establishment of each implied condition emerging from the invoking of the *umdana*, see Talmud Bavli *Ketubot* 55a; *Bava Batra* 146b. Consequently, according to the Talmudic sage R. Meir, one must examine whether the *umdana* mentions both the affirmative and the negative, akin to a double condition (*tenai kaful*). See *Resp. Mahari Ha-Kohen, Even Ha-Ezer* 13.

123. *Resp. Beit Ha-Levi* 3:3; *Avnei Hefetz*, supra n. 41.

124. *Tosafot Rosh, Ketubot* 47b; *Tosafot Bava Kamma* 110b, s.v. *de'ada'ata; Mishneh Le'Melekh, Hilk. Ze'khiyah U-Mattana* 6:1; *Beit Meir, Tzalot Habayit* 1:6; *Resp. Hakham Tzvi* 41; *Resp. Noda Be-Yehudah, Mahadura Kamma Yoreh Deah* 69; *Resp. Divrei Hayyim* 1, *Even Ha-Ezer* 3; *Resp. Kokhav Me-Ya'akov* 1:41; *Resp. Avodat Ha-Shem Yoreh Deah* 7; *Resp. Minhat Shai* 1:94; *Resp. Ginat Veradim, Hoshen Mishpat* 49; *Resp. Maharshakh* 2:45; *Resp. Mahari ben Lev* 2:45; *Resp. Pnei Moshe* 1:62; *Resp. Shoeil U-Meishiv, Mahadura Tlitai* 1:61.

125. Talmud Bavli *Bava Kamma* 111a; *Resp. Maharam of Rothenberg*, Prague ed., 4:993; Rema, *Even Ha-Ezer* 42:1; *Bi'ur Ha-Gra, Even Ha-Ezer* 42:4; *Resp. Hatam Sofer* 3, *Even Ha-Ezer* 1:85; *Arukh Ha-Shulhan Even Ha-Ezer* 42; *Resp. Mishpetei*

And, in fact some authorities concurred with this conclusion regarding an apostate Jew.[126] Other arbiters rejected invoking *umdana* as a vehicle to void marriages in dealing with specific medical, psychological, and/or behavioral disorders of a husband who refuses to give a *get*.[127]

Furthermore, as Rabbi Yehezkel Landau observes:[128]

> Regarding a man we do not declare that "with this understanding he was not married" (*ada'ata dehaki lo kidshah nafshah*), since he has not incurred much of a loss, since he can divorce her when he desires and is able to marry another one. However, a woman – she neither can divorce nor marry another – it is correct to say, "with this understanding she was not married".

Though Rabbi Landau states that the aforementioned judgment is "in theory and not in practice," nonetheless, at the end of the responsum he emphatically arrives at the conclusion that practically speaking, *umdana* is not a halakhic option and therefore the woman will remain an *agunah* as long as she does not receive a *get* from the apostate![129]

Finally, after a marriage, a *get* is mandated. Said conclusion is based upon the Talmudic presumption, "man is not wont to cohabitate licentiously" (*ein adam oseh be'ila beilat zenut*), and is endorsed by post-Talmudic authorities.[130] Were the marriage viewed as void from its inception, all acts of intimacy which transpired during the marital

---

Uzziel Even Ha-Ezer 2:49; *Resp. Kol Mevaseir* 1:29; File no. 1294108/1, Be'air Sheva Regional Beit Din, June 13, 2021.

126. *Resp Maharsham* 2:110; *Resp. Avnei Tzedek, Even Ha-Ezer* 56.

127. *Resp. Avodat Ha-Gershuni* 235; *Resp. Beit Yitzhak* 1:106; *Resp. Nishmat Hayyim* 129; *Resp. Noda Be-Yehudah, Mahadura Kamma, Even Ha-Ezer* 85, *Mahadura Tinyana, Even Ha-Ezer* 80; *Resp. Hatam Sofer, Even Ha-Ezer* 82; *Resp. Oholei Aharon* 2:44; *Resp. Ahiezer* 3:19; *Resp. Heikhal Yitzhak, Even Ha-Ezer* 2:25.

Regarding the view of Rabbi Karo, it is clear from his commentary on the Tur that he rejected *umdana* as a vehicle to void a marriage. See *Beit Yosef, Even Ha-Ezer* 42:1. Though he didn't memorialize his view in the *Shulhan Arukh*, nonetheless we assume that he did not retract his position. See *Resp. Asher Le-Shlomo* 13; *Resp. Yismah Lev Ovadaya, Leket Teshuvot* 1; *Resp. Emek Yehoshua* 1, *Even Ha-Ezer* 13-14; *Resp. Mikveh Ha-Mayyim* 2, *Hashmatot* 10.

128. *Resp. Noda Be-Yehudah, Mahadura Tinyana Even Ha-Ezer* 80.

129. File no. 905457/10, Tel Aviv-Yaffo Regional Beit Din, September 11, 2017. See also, *Resp. Iggerot Moshe, Even Ha-Ezer* 1:79.

130. Talmud Bavli *Gittin* 81a; *Ketubot* 72b, 74a; *Yevamot* 110a; *Shulhan Arukh, Even Ha-Ezer* 149; *Bi'ur Ha-Gra, Even Ha-Ezer* 38, 44; *Shulhan Arukh, Even Ha-Ezer* 28:16, 31:9, 155:20.

relationship would post facto be deemed illicit and equated with prostitution. As such, from the husband's perspective it was a legitimate marriage. Absent an express stipulation by the wife at the inception of the marriage, it can be assumed that she waived any objection to the defect, wanting the marriage to occur, including the disorder or defect which was discovered after the marriage ensued.[131] Though there are arbiters who claim that the above presumption applies to men and women alike,[132] the majority of decisors argue that the presumption is inapplicable to a woman and therefore there is no implicit assumption,[133] and thus even in the face of a severe defect – the woman is willing to continue to being married to her husband.[134]

Despite the foregoing, others subscribe to implementing the mechanism of *umdana* to void a marriage regarding a husband's behavior identifying with the position, "he has not incurred much loss since he can divorce her when he desires and is able to marry another one".[135] Secondly, upon invoking *umdana* in order to void the marriage, the explicit presumption is that "*tav le-meitav tan do mi-le-meitav armalu*" is rebuttable.[136] Moreover, in the absence of an agreement between the parties prior to the marriage, if the wife wants to dissolve the marriage and her husband steadfastly refuses, under certain conditions we may employ an *umdana* to void the marriage.[137]

The voiding of the marriage via the mechanism of *umdana* is done retroactively due to the existence of a condition which is not articulated by a party in accordance with the halakhot governing conditions. When something newly emerges after the onset of the marriage concerning the husband's behavior; it is clear that the wife did not want to marry him

131. A. Hacohen, *The Tears of the Oppressed*, N.Y. 2004, 84-85.

132. Ra'avad, *Mishneh Torah, Hilk. Gerushin* 10:19; Ran, *Kiddushin* 25b according to pagination of Alfasi; *Resp. Hayyim shel Shalom* 2:81; *Resp. Tzitz Eliezer* 1:27.

133. *Resp. Shoeil U-Meishiv, Mahadura Kamma*, 1:1; *Resp. Ha-Maharitz* 247; *Resp. Shevat Zion* 71; *Resp. Hikrei Lev, Even Ha-Ezer* 57; *Resp. Iggerot Moshe, Even Ha-Ezer* 1:79.

134. Though said conclusion is advanced by Rabbi Taubes concerning a case of *kiddushei ta'ut* (see *Resp. Hayyim shel Shalom* 2:81), the same ought to apply in a situation of *umdana*.

135. *Resp. Ahiezer, Even Ha-Ezer* 27:4; *Resp. Iggerot Moshe, Even Ha-Ezer* 1:79.

136. *Sheilot Moshe*, supra n.120; *Resp. Birkat Retzeh* 107; *Beit Ha-Levi*, supra n. 123.

137. In other words, an *umdana* applies not only with two parties but equally with one party, e.g., a wife who is unhappy with the marriage and the husband refuses to give a *get*. See *Tosafot*, supra n. 123; *Noda Be-Yehudah*, supra n. 124; Hakham *Tzvi*, supra n. 124.

and it is as if an implied condition was violated.[138] In other words, the marriage is void due to the husband's nonfulfillment of the condition. As Rabbi Asher ben Yehiel, known by the acronym *Rosh*, observes:[139]

> For if [the wife] had wanted to stipulate at the time of the betrothal that if [the husband] would die prior to being married to her, then the betrothal would be voided, so she would not find herself bounded to his leper brother, the husband would not have objected. Consequently, it is deemed as if she had declared such a condition.

---

138. Numerous decisors mandate that a condition must comply with the halakhot of conditions (*mishpetei ha-tena'im*) in matters of marriage and divorce due to the fact that we are dealing with a matter of prohibition (i.e., the prohibition of being with a married woman). See *Resp. Ha-Rif* 31; *Rashbam, Bava Batra* 137b, s.v. *ve'im lav*; *Mordekhai, Succah* 758. Nevertheless, in certain circumstances Halakhah will validate an implied condition. See *Tosafot Ketubot* 97a, s.v. *zavin*; *Tosafot Gittin* 75a, s.v. *le'afukei*; *Resp. Iggerot Moshe Even Ha-Ezer* 4:121 (end); B. Lifshitz, *Promise: Obligation and Acquisition in Jewish Law* (Hebrew), Jerusalem: 1988, 138, n. 106. In other words, despite the fact that we are dealing with the prohibition of "a married woman," nonetheless, we may invoke here, in accordance with various decisors, the mechanism of the clear expectation and void the marriage based upon an implied condition of marriage. See *Resp. Maharam of Rothenberg*, Prague ed. 1022; *Resp. Maharam Mintz* 105; *Sheilat Moshe*, supra n. 120; *Resp. Torat Hessed, Even Ha-Ezer* 20(6).

Cf. R. Michael Abraham, "Voiding a Marriage Due to a Major Expectation" (Hebrew), *Mavoi Satum*, 5774.

139. *Shittah Mekubetzet* in the name of *Tosafot Ha-Rosh, Bava Kamma* 110b. See also *Resp. Ha-Rosh* 34:1; *Resp. Terumat Ha-Deshen* 223; R. Shkop, *Sha'arei Yosher* 5:18. Cf. *Darkhei Moshe, Even Ha-Ezer* 157:5 in the name of Mahari Bruna.

However, some authorities contend that this matter is dealing with "*kiddushei ta'ut*". See *Resp. Ra'avyah* 1032; *Resp. Me'il Tzedakah* 2 and 4; *Resp. Tzemah Tzedek* 322; *Resp. Shoeil u-Meishiv, Mahadura Kamma* 1:197, *Mahadura Tlitai*, 61; *Mahari Ha-Kohain*, supra n. 122; *Avnei Hefetz*, supra n. 123; *Resp. Har Tzvi Even Ha-Ezer* 2:180. In other words, the formulation of the *umdana* would be the following: "had I known that my husband possessed a major defect (*mum gadol*), I never would have married him." See *Zikhron Yehonatan*, supra n. 123, at subsection 17.

The difficulty in linking the *umdana* of *ada'ata de-hakhi lo kidshah nafshah* to an error which predated the marriage is due the fact that the *umdana* relates to a husband's behavior which emerges after the onset of marriage and is not linked to anything prior to the marriage. In other words, since one didn't know the future at the inception of the marriage, it is impossible to categorize the case as one of *kiddushei ta'ut*. See A. Westreich, "'*Umdena*' as a Ground for Marriage Annulment: Between Mistaken Transaction and Terminative Condition," *Jewish Law Association Studies* XX, 330, 339 (2010). See *Sha'arei Yosher*, op. cit.

For example, if a woman is preparing to marry a man who has a brother who suffers from cancer, she weighs all the possibilities: either her husband will die without children, in which case she may be obligated to marry her brother-in-law (levirate marriage), or that he will sire a child. By marrying this sick man, she indicated that she didn't care what will happen insofar as a concern regarding the dissolution of the marriage.[140] In other words, she surrendered her right to void the marriage if her husband dies. In short, the implied condition was established due to the exercise of an *umdana* which uncovers the stipulation.[141] Secondly, when there is a major assessment of expectations (an *umdana demukhah*), we may rely upon the *umdana* of one individual and do not require an explicit acknowledgment from both people that we are dealing with a marriage subject to being voided.[142]

What type of behavior may we subsume under an *umdana*? The famed nineteenth century Galician authority, Rabbi Shaul Nathanson, observes that in the absence of being authorized to coerce a *get* both legally and therefore halakhically, consequently he concludes that one may under certain conditions utilize *umdana* and void a marriage.[143] Others have concurred with his view.[144] In other words, as Rabbi Meir Posner aptly notes, prior to invoking an *umdana,* one must be assured that there exists grounds to coerce the husband to give a *get.*[145] For example, if a wife exclaims, "had I known that he was going to be an apostate Jew (a *mumar*) I wouldn't have married him!" In fact, there are decisors who would coerce a *get* in such a case.[146] Given that there are arbiters who would coerce a *get* in such a situation, in the absence of this means of divorce enforcement, according to certain authorities, the marriage may be voided under these conditions via the avenue of *umdana.*

These grounds of compelling the issuance of a *get* by a *beit din* are mentioned in the Mishnah and Talmud.[147] After the close of the

140. However, others argue that one may invoke the *umdana* even regarding an infrequent situation. See *Re'em*, supra n. 129; *Resp. Shoeil U-Meishiv, Mahadura Kamma*, 1, 98.

141. *Tosafot, Kiddushin* 49b, s.v. *devarim she'balev*; *Piskei Ha-Rosh, Ketubot* 11:9; *Mahari Ha-Kohen*, supra n. 121.

142. *Avnei Hefetz,* supra n. 41.

143. *Shoeil U-Meishiv,* supra n.124. See also, *Shoeil U-Meishiv Mahadura Tlitai,* supra n. 124.

144. *Resp. Ramatz, Orah Hayyim* 15(4).

145. *Tzalot Ha-Bayit,* supra n. 41.

146. *Mordekhai, Gittin* 450; *Resp. Terumat Ha-Deshen* 228; *Beit Yosef, Even Ha-Ezer* 154 in the name of *Orhot Hayyim*; *Rema, Even Ha-Ezer* 154:1.

147. Mishnah *Ketubot* 7:9-10; Mishnah *Nedarim* 11:12; *Ketubot* 63b,

Talmudic period, the question arises whether a *beit din* may compel a husband to deliver a *get* to his wife in circumstances not mentioned in the Mishnah and/or Talmud. One approach is that one compels a *get* on the condition that the particular ground is mentioned in the Mishnah and/or the Talmud.[148] Others claim that the list may be expanded based upon drawing inferences by way of analogical reasoning (*hekesh*) to encompass other instances not mentioned in the Mishnah and/or Talmud.[149] In sum, the scope of the *umdana* is dependent upon one's position regarding whether one can mandate *get* enforcement concerning a behavior which is not mentioned in the Mishnah and/or Talmud.

In the event of a particular case where *get* coercion is not an option, can one employ *umdana* as a basis for voiding the marriage? We now must address the issue of whether there is a basis to coerce a *get* in a situation where a husband is a batterer. One approach, which first appears in the writings of Ohr Zarua, Rabbeinu Simhah and is espoused by others, is to issue a compulsion order in the wake of a husband who assaults and insults his wife.[150] A contemporary rationale for *get* coercion

75-76a,77a-b; *Yevamot* 65b.

148. Rashi, *Yevamot* 65b, s.v. *hu amar*; *Tosafot, Ketubot* 70a, s.v. *yotzi*; *Tosafot, Yevamot* 64a, s.v. *yotzi*; *Mishneh Torah, Hilk. Ishut* 15:7; *Piskei Ha-Rosh, Yevamot* 6:11; *Resp. Ha-Rosh* 17:6, 42:1 in the name of Ra'avyah, 43:3 (Cf. *Piskei Ha-Rosh, Ketubot* 4:3, 5:34; *Resp. Ha-Rosh* 43:6); *Mordekhai Ketubot* 194; *Hiddushei Ha-Ramban Ketubot* 63b; *Hiddushei Ha-Rashba Ketubot* 64a; *Resp. Ha-Rashba Ha-Me'yuhasot Le-Ramban* 138; *Sefer Meisharim, Netiv* 23, *Helek* 8 in the name of Rashba; *Tur Even Ha-Ezer* 154 in the name of Ramah; *Beit Ha-Behirah, Ketubot* 63a; *Resp. of Maharam of Rothenberg*, Prague ed., 946; *Hagahot Maimoniyot, Hilk. Ishut* 25:4; *Resp. Ha-Rashbash* 93; *Tur* 154 in the name of Rosh; *Resp. Mahari Bruna* 211; *Shulhan Arukh Even Ha-Ezer* 154:5, 21; *Resp. Binyamin Ze'ev* 1:88; Rabbi A. Ha-Levi, *Resp. Ha-Ridvaz* 4:108 (1180), 1331 (260); *Resp. Be'air Sheva* 61; *Resp. Mekor Barukh* 17; *Resp. Emunat Shmuel* 8; *Resp. Ha-Maharit, Even Ha-Ezer* 2:14; *Resp. Maharshakh* 3:42; *Bi'ur Ha-Gra, Shulhan Arukh Even Ha-Ezer* 154:50, 65; *Tosafot Yom Tov, Tur Even Ha-Ezer* 154; *Pithei Teshuvah, Shulhan Arukh Even Ha-Ezer* 154:7, 29; *Resp. Hakham Tzvi* 1; Rabbi Eliyahu Ha-Levi, *Resp. Zekan Aharon* 149; *Hazon Ish, Ketubot* 69:23.

149. *Piskei Ha-Rosh, Ketubot* 5:34; *Resp. Ha-Rosh* 42:1; *Resp. Ha-Rivash* 241; *Resp. Ha-Tashbetz* 2:8, 180; *Sefer Ha-Agudah, Yevamot* 77; *New Resp. Ha-Maharik* 2; *Resp. Maharam Alshakar* 73; *Resp. Rashbash* 383; *Resp. Ha-Ridvaz* 4:157. For the role of analogical reasoning in halakhic decision-making, see E. Shochetman, supra n. 115; this writer's *Rabbinic Authority*, vol. 1, 53-57, vol. 5, 315-323, 324-350.

In the wake of a debate whether *get* coercion can be mandated, one is prohibited from issuing a compulsion order lest it be deemed a coerced *get* which is null and void according to the majority of authorities. See this writer's *Rabbinic Authority*, vol. 2, 30, note 11.

150. *Resp. Ohr Zarua* 3, *Bava Kamma* 161; *Resp. Maharah Ohr Zarua* 127 in

is articulated by an Israeli dayan who teaches us:[151] *get* coercion is due the destruction of family life by the husband as a result of his behavior rather than due to the acts of abuse, and the wife is therefore entitled to demand a *get.*

Responding to this posture of Ohr Zarua and Rabbeinu Simha, *Rabbi Yosef Karo* in Beit Yosef demurs, stating:[152]

> We cannot rely on their words... to coerce... since it is not mentioned by any one of the renowned authorities.

In light of the view of the Beit Yosef's predecessors who argue that since the Mishnah and/or Talmud failed to explicitly mention that spousal battery is a ground for divorce (*ilat gerushin*) which mandates *get* coercion, a *beit din* may not issue a compulsion order.[153] And this view was subsequently established in Rabbi Karo's Shulhan Arukh.[154] Yet, Rabbi Karo concurs that a husband may be obligated to give a *get.*[155]

Therefore, the rationale for the opposition to coercing a husband who

---

the name of Rabbeinu Simha and Rabbeinu Menahem; *Beit Yosef Tur Even Ha-Ezer* 154 in the name of Rabbeinu Simha; *Resp. Maharam of Rothenberg*, Prague ed., 927; *Resp. Ha-Rashba* 1:693 (Cf. Resp. *Ha-Rashba* 7:477); *Darkhei Moshe, Tur Even Ha-Ezer* 154:16 in the name of Rabbi Shemarya; *Resp. Binyamin Ze'ev* 88 in the name of Ri and Rabbeinu Tam; *Resp. Maharshakh* 2:130; *Resp. Hatam Sofer Even Ha-Ezer* 2:60; *Arukh ha-Shulhan Even Ha-Ezer* 154:15; *Resp. U-Mitzur Devash Even Ha-Ezer* 10; *Resp. Hina Ve-Hisda* 3, *Ketubot* 77a. See also the opinion of a contemporary of Rabbi Karo, *Beit Shmuel Shulhan Arukh Even Ha-Ezer* 154:24 and *Helkat Mehokeik, Shulhan Arukh, Even Ha-Ezer* 154:18 in the name of Maharshal and *Resp. Noseh Ephod* 32. Whether *Resp. Ha-Tashbetz* 2:8 aligns himself with this view is subject to debate. See *Yad Aharon Even Ha-Ezer* 154; *Resp. Maharsham* 5:38; *Resp. Va-Yomeir Yitzhak, Even Ha-Ezer* 135.

151. PDR 1:5, 13. See also PDR 1:333, 338; File no. 30138-21-2, Beit Din Rabbani ha-Gadol, July 28, 2008; *Resp. Mishpatekha Le-Ya'akov*, vol. 6, Siman 4, 108.

152. *Beit Yosef, Tur Even Ha-Ezer* 154:3.

153. Rashi, *Yevamot* 65b, s.v. *hu amar*; *Tosafot, Ketubot* 70a, s.v. *yotzi*; *Tosafot Yevamot* 64a, s.v. *yotzi*; *Tosafot Ketubot* 70a, s.v. *yotzi*; *Piskei Ha-Rosh, Yevamot* 6:11; *Resp. Ha-Rosh* 42:1 in the name of Ravyah, 43:3; *Resp. Ha-Rashba Ha-Meyuhasot Le-Ramban* 138; *Sefer Meisharim, Netiv* 23, *Helek* 8 in the name of Rashba; *Hiddushei Ha-Ramban, Ketubot* 77a; *Hiddushei Ha-Rashba, Ketubot* 77a; *Hiddushei Ha-Ritva*, ad locum; Ran on Alfasi, *Ketubot* 36a; *Resp. Ha-Rivash* 127; *Semag*, Positive Commandment 48; *Resp. Mahari Bruna* 211; *Resp. Ha-Ridvaz* 4:1331 (260); *Shulhan Arukh, Even Ha-Ezer* 154:5, 21; *Bi'ur ha-Gra Shulhan Arukh Even Ha-Ezer* 154:50, 65; *Resp. Be'er Sheva* 61; *Be'air ha-Golah, Shulhan Arukh, Even Ha-Ezer* 77:6; *Hazon Ish, Ketubot* 69:23; R. Eliyahu Ha-Levi, *Resp. Zekan Aharon* 10, 149.

154. *Shulhan Arukh, Even Ha-Ezer* 154:21 in the name of yesh omrim.

155. *Beit Yosef, Tur Even Ha-Ezer* 74 (end) citing Nahmanides' responsum.

is a batterer to give a *get* is based upon their understanding that the resultant *get* is deemed "a coerced *get*" ("a *get me'useh*") and consequently it is invalid. Consequently, should the wife remarry relying upon this *get* and have children, the offspring would be labeled as halakhic bastards (*mamzrerim*). Since a halakhic bastard is the product of an incestuous relationship, the fact that the *get* was invalid means that in effect she was still married to her first husband when she had children from her "second marriage." In the wake of Beit Yosef's posture, Darkhei Moshe rules:[156]

> I don't see his words [as valid] at all because it is worthwhile relying upon the *Geonim*, a *fortiori* given that Ramban and Maharam [also] agree in their responsa concerning assaulting a wife (that it is a grounds for to obligate a *get* – AYW) and they brought clear proofs to their words, and logic agrees with them. And the fact that it isn't mentioned by the earlier authorities (i.e., the reason that spousal battery is not mentioned in the Talmud as a ground for a *get* – AYW), one possibly could say that it was obvious in their eyes... and it did not happen in their days (that the phenomenon of spousal battery was less common – AYW)....

Numerous decisors subscribe to Beit Yosef's and Darkhei Moshe's posture that one cannot coerce a husband who assaults his wife to give a *get*.[157]

Though there are authorities (*Poskim*) who claim that in situations where the spousal assaults are frequent and life-threatening to the wife, there are grounds to coerce the husband to give a *get*,[158] clearly in

156. *Darkhei Moshe, Tur, Even Ha-Ezer* 154:21.

157. *Resp. Ha-Ridvaz* 3:888 (447), 4:157 (1228); *Resp. Binyamin Ze'ev*, in the name of Ri and R. Tam; *Resp. Lehem Rav* 31; *Resp. Maharshakh* 2:130; *Resp. Mishpat Tzedek* 1:59; *Resp. Perah Matteh Aharon* 1:60; *Resp. Masat Moshe* 1, *Even Ha-Ezer* 17; *Resp. Mohari Ha-Levi* 9; *Resp. Rabbi Akiva Eiger* (in manuscript) *Even Ha-Ezer* 55; *Resp. Mishneh Halakhot* 14:146; *Resp. Noseh Ha-Ephod* 32:15.

158. *Resp. Hut Ha-Meshullash, Tur* 3, 35; *Resp. Ha-Rashba* 4:311; Rema, *Shulhan Arukh Even Ha-Ezer* 154:3 in the name of "some say" (*yesh omrim*); *Matteh Aharon*, supra n. 157; *Resp. Yafeh le-Lev* 8, *Even Ha-Ezer* 154 (5); *Resp. Yismah Lev Even Ha-Ezer* 11; *Resp. Va-Yomer Yitzhak* 1, *Even Ha-Ezer* 135; *Resp. Shoshanim le-David* 2:20; *Resp. Tzitz Eliezer* 6:42; *Resp. Amudei Mishpat* 1:12; *Piskei Ha-Rosh, Ketubot* 7:19.

Cf. others who reject *get* coercion even under these circumstances. See *Mishpat Tzedek*, supra n. 157; *Resp. Beit Aharon Even Ha-Ezer* 3, *Siman* 8; *Mishneh*

situations where the assaults are infrequent and non-life threatening, and therefore there is no basis for *get* coercion, seemingly there ought to be no grounds to void a marriage.

Upon inquiry, we encounter responsa which demonstrate that in cases of acts of criminality perpetrated by the husband which the wife only became aware of during the marriage, should a husband be *get* recalcitrant, there would be permission to void the marriage based upon the technique of *umdana*. As Rabbi Aharon Levine, head of the *beit din* in nineteenth century Rzeszow, observes:[159]

> One may add a further consideration to our argument regarding this case, namely, that in light of the fact that we now know that the husband is a despicable criminal engaged in human trafficking, his marriage has been voided, notwithstanding its formal validity. There can be no doubt that had she known of these activities, she would never have consented to marry him. They constitute an *umdana*, i.e., a compelling circumstantial presumption in favor of voiding the marriage. This is analogous to the case cited in Bava Kamma 106b (correction: 110b – AYW) regarding a levirate wife whose levir is suffering from a serious skin disease. The Talmud suggests that in such circumstances, the levirate wife may claim that she is no longer bound by the levirate bond, since she would never have married her husband had she known that this situation would arise in the future; hence, her original marriage has now been voided. The reason that the Talmud rejects this claim is the adage of Resh Lakish that "women will accept defective men rather than remain unmarried." This adage is, however, inapplicable in our case, since by virtue of his criminal activities the husband's life is constantly in danger, and the couple lives in constant fear and dread. Moreover, what woman could be expected to live with such a despicable and loathsome person? There can be no doubt that she would never have knowingly consented to marriage in these circumstances and this case is a classic one for the application of the *umdana* principle. Now, it is true that Hatam Sofer (Resp. Even Ha-Ezer 82) rejected *umdana* as a basis for voiding a marriage, but the reason was

Halakhot, supra n. 157. Clearly, the need to act stringently and avoid the strictures of a "*get me'useh*" underlies this position. See *Gevurat Anashim* 44.

159. *Avnei Hefetz*, supra n. 123. See also, *Resp. Mahari Hakohen* 13 (71b).

> because of the weak nature of the *umdana* in that case, i.e., the husband told the wife that he was rich and he turned out to be poor, and that he was a learned man but he turned out to be an ignoramus. The weakness of the *umdana* lies in the fact that he may very well have been rich but, in the meantime, he lost his fortune. Likewise, he was once learned but, in the meantime, he forgot his learning. At the most, the marriage in this type of case is of doubtful validity. In our case, however, the *umdana* is strong and powerful and free from all doubt as to the absolute unacceptability of the marriage on the part of the wife. Hence, we rule that she would never have consented to marry had she known the facts about her husband.

Since it became clear during the marriage that the man who betrothed the woman who was one of those who engaged in the white slave trade business, the *kiddushin* were valid yet it was of no value, since there is a great *umdana* indicating that "on this understanding she did not marry him."

Alternatively, both Torat Hayyim and Minhat Shai argue that we can employ *umdana* in situations which do not occur frequently, such as domestic violence, and the wife therefore did not expect it to occur.[160]

Finally, in the event that the *umdana* is identical for both the husband and wife, then we may conclude that there is a basis to void the marriage via the *umdana*.[161]

In conclusion, there are decisors who will invalidate a marriage via the implementation of *umdana*.[162] Other legists will refrain from voiding a marriage based solely upon *umdana*.[163] Finally, given that rulings

---

160. *Torat Hayyim, Bava Kamma* 110a-b; *Resp. Minhat Shai* 53.

161. *Resp. Tiferet Tzvi* 4.

162. *Resp. Maharam of Rothenberg,* Prague ed.,993, 1022 (*halitzah* – in theory); R. Meir Posner, *Resp. Tzal'ot Ha-Bayit* 2; *Zikhron Yehonatan,* supra n. 120; *Resp. Hessed Avraham, Mahadura Tinyana, Even Ha-Ezer* 55; *Resp. Radakh* 9; *Resp. Meshivat Nefesh, Even Ha-Ezer* 73, 76–77; *Resp. Torat Hessed, Even Ha-Ezer* 20:6 (*halitzah*); *Resp. Divrei Malkiel* 4:100; *Resp. Maharsham* 7:95; *Resp. Re'eim,* 68; *Resp. Sho'eil u-Meishiv, Mahadura Kamma,* 1: 61,198; *Avnei Hefetz,* supra n.123; *Resp. Divrei Hayyim* 1, *Even Ha-Ezer* 3; *Resp. Radad* (Meisels), *Even Ha-Ezer* 40; *She'eilot Moshe,* supra n. 120; *Resp. Ohel Moshe Mahadura Kamma* 62, *Mahadura Tlitai* 123; *Resp. Sheilat Yitzhak* 174, 186; *Resp. Har Tzvi, Even Ha-Ezer* 1:79, 2:133; *Resp. Iggerot Moshe, Even Ha-Ezer* 4:121 (a *halitzah* case accompanied by an argument for *kiddushei taut*); *Resp. Sha'arei Ezra,* 4 *Even Ha-Ezer* 26; *Tzvi Tiferet,* supra n. 161; *Ha-Ramatz* supra n. 144.

163. *Mahari Ha-Kohen,* supra n. 122; *Resp. Iggerot Moshe, Even Ha-Ezer* 4:121;

regarding a *halitzah* situation[164] (which entails an "*issur lav*" – a prohibition whose violation is punishable by lashes) are not treated halakhically as stringent as a marriage case (which involves "*karet*"- divine punishment by premature death), due to the fact that the *halitzah* case neither involves a violation of one of the prohibited sexual relations ("*davar she'be'ervah*")[165] nor being a married woman thus prohibited to others ("*eishet ish*"), and therefore it may not serve as a precedent for matrimonial situations – numerous arbiters nonetheless clearly derive conclusions from *halitzah* situations and apply them to marriage cases in matters of *umdana* as well as *kiddushei ta'ut*.[166] In other words, even though a widow waiting for her deceased husband's brother to perform *halitzah* (a *shomeret yavam*) is biblically prohibited to anyone else and her personal status is not as stringent as the status of a married woman who is biblically prohibited to anyone else, one may nonetheless apply *halitzah* rulings to marriage cases. In short, despite the fact that

---

File no. 861974/2, Tzfat Regional Beit Din, June 23, 2014 (R. Uriel Lavi's opinion).

164. The ceremony in which the brother of a married man who dies without children, upon whom the duty of levirate marriage applies, renounces his duty to marry the woman whose husband dies without children.

165. There are three different definitions of "a matter of licentiousness." One definition is any testimony concerning a matter which emerges from illegitimate intercourse of a married man is considered "a matter of licentiousness." See *Tosafot Gittin* 2b, s.v. *eid ehad ne'eman*; *Sefer Ha-Yashar* pp. 83; *Resp. Noda Be-Yehudah, Mahadura Kamma, Yoreh Deah* 55. *Resp. R. Akiva Eiger* 125 in the name of *Netivot*. A second alternative is that "a matter of licentiousness" is defined as any testimony that changes the status of a man as it relates to a matter of prohibition and permission (*issur ve'heter*); see R. S. Shkop, *Sha'arei Yosher, Sha'ar* 10, *Perek* 10. Finally, some propose that any testimony regarding a person rather than an object is viewed as "a matter of licentiousness." See *Resp. Avnei Nezer, Hoshen Mishpat* 20; *Mahaneh Ephraim, Hilk. Edut* 13.

166. *Hazon Yehezkel, Masekhet Zevahim, Even Ha-Ezer* 8; *Sheilat Moshe*, supra n. 120; *Resp. Har Tzvi, Even Ha-Ezer* 1:95, 99. Even though a *shomeret yavam* is biblically prohibited to anyone else and her status is not as stringent as the status of a married woman who is biblically prohibited to anyone else, one may nonetheless apply *halitzah* rulings to marriage cases equally in matters of *kiddushei ta'ut*. See *Yevamot* 119a (Rava's dictum); *Resp. Terumat Ha-Deshen* 250; *Resp. Noda Be-Yehudah, Mahadura Tinyana Even Ha-Ezer* 66 (end) and compare with *Mahadura Kamma Orah Hayyim* 21; *Hazon Yehezkel*, op. cit.; *Har Tzvi*, op. cit.

Cf. *Resp. Torat Hessed, Orah Hayyim* 29; R. Safran, *Resp. Rabaz* 88 (3) and *Resp. Iggerot Moshe, Yoreh Deah* 2:46 who would reject such an application of *halitzah* rulings to marriage situations in light of the stringency of the status of a married woman.

Whether one can utilize the *halitzah* ruling to conclude that one can equally void the marriage of a husband who is impotent is open to much debate.

halitzah doesn't entail an infraction of being a married woman (the *issur of eishet ish*), pursuant to some authorities – one can release the wife without the performance of *halitzah,* and such a ruling may be a halakhic precedent to void a marriage.

Chapter 6

Criminal Proceedings Against a Jew in a Non-Jewish Court for *Get* Refusal: The Effect on the Validity of the *Get*

PART 5 OF THE U.K. Serious Crime Act 2015, entitled "Protection of Children and Others," contains a section on "Domestic Abuse." Article 76 of that section – which came into force on 29 December 2015 – addresses coercive control or controlling behavior in an intimate or family relationship.[1]

In other words, violence towards a spouse is not the exclusive province of a violent husband who resorts to physical violence and emotional and verbal abuse. Violence towards a spouse is also characterized by the attempts of the abuser to control the wife and to limit her actions. Manifestation of control in general, and prevention of the formation of contacts outside of the family, criticism of the way a wife dresses, prevention of access to financial information and demanding that she account for herself in particular, cause tension, shouting, cursing and trading insults at a higher rate than that typical of couples who live together without violence, all fall into this category.

Controlling relationships are defined by Professor Evan Stark, as quoted in an English judgment, as follows:[2]

> In coercive control, abusers deploy a range of non-consensual, non-reciprocal tactics, over an extended period to subjugate or dominate a partner rather than merely to hurt them physically.

---

1. In light of the above legislation on February 21, 2022, for the first time, a man who refused to give his wife a *get* (i.e., a writ of Jewish divorce) has been convicted on a charge of coercive control. Despite the threat that he would be sentenced to imprisonment, the husband refused to give his wife a *get,* and on April 1, 2022, he was sentenced to be imprisoned for eighteen months.

A similar legislative proposal (A347) is pending in front of the New York Standing Committee on Codes.

2. Regina v. Challen (2019), EW CA 916, Court of Appeal.

> Compliance is achieved by making victims afraid and denying basic rights, resources, and liberties without which they are not able to effectively refuse, resist or escape demands that militate against their interests.

Insofar as an English court decides in a particular case that *get* refusal constitutes an instance of coercive control on the part of the husband, and sentences him to a set period of imprisonment in accordance with the above legislation, does the criminal process against the *get* refuser affect the validity of the *get*?

It is well-known that if a husband gives his wife a *get* under coercion, the *get* is void.[3] Therefore, if he is imprisoned until he gives the *get*, and he gives the *get* in order to secure his release from prison, the *get* is void.[4] Apparently, on the basis of the above, if the court in England sentences a person to prison on a conviction for the criminal offence of coercive control over his wife, and he then gives the *get*, the *get* will be void as being coerced! In other words, the husband and wife must agree to divorce. Therefore, if a husband gives his wife a *get* against his will in order to be released from prison (i.e., coercion) or if *he was threatened to be imprisoned*, the *get* is void.[5]

The question arises: is there a halakhic basis for compelling a *get* by means of a criminal process in a non-Jewish court?

In accordance with the Biblical passage (*Deut.* 24:1), "...he writeth her a bill of divorcement and giveth it in her hand, and sendeth her out of his house," the *Mishnah*[6] and the authorities state that a man may not divorce his wife except of his own free will.[7] It is clear that the *get* must

---

3. *Mishneh Torah, Hilk. Gerushin 1:1; Shulhan Arukh, Even Ha-Ezer* 134:7. For additional authorities, see infra n. 8 and see this writer's *Rabbinic Authority*, vol. 3, p. 30, n. 11.

4. *Responsa* (hereinafter: Resp) *Ha-Rashba* 2:276; *Resp. Ha-Rivash* 232; *Resp. Mas'at Binyamin* 22. There is a *mesorah* (a tradition) that if a *beit din* threatened to imprison him or threatened to extradite him to the government where there is a fear that they will imprison him, and he gave the *get* to avoid incarceration, the *get* is null and void. See Rashba, op. cit.; *Arukh Ha-Shulḥan Even Ha-Ezer* 134:22; *Resp. Rabbenu Bezalel Ashkenazy* 15. *A fortiori* (*kal ve-ḥomer*) if the government itself would threaten to prosecute him if he doesn't give a *get*.

5. Talmud Bavli *Gittin* 88b; *Shulḥan Arukh, Even Ha-Ezer* 134:7; *Beit Shmuel*, ad. loc. 13; Rashba, supra n. 4; *Resp. Rabbenu Betzalel Ashkenazy* 15; *Arukh Ha-Shulḥan Even Ha-Ezer* 134:22.

6. M. *Yevamot* 13:1.

7. *Mishneh Torah, Hilk. Gerushin* 1:1–2; Rashbam, *Bava Batra* 48a, s.v. *ve-ken atah omer*.

be given with the consent of the husband, and a *get* that is given without the husband's volition is void.[8]

On the other hand, the Mishnah states:[9]

> A *get* compelled by a Jewish [court] is valid, but [if he was compelled] by gentiles, [it is] invalid. But with regard to the gentiles, they may beat him [at the request of the *beit din*] and say to him: Do what the Jews are telling you, and it is a valid [divorce].

And the Talmud states:[10]

> And similarly, you find [this *halakhah*] with bills of divorce, [that when the court rules that he must divorce his wife] they coerce him until he says, I want [to divorce my wife]. [The *gemara* rejects this proof as well.] But perhaps there it is different, because it is a *mitzvah* to listen to the statement of the Sages.

In other words, although under certain conditions the husband is compelled to give his wife a *get*, his consent to accept the judgment of a *beit din* is effective for the purpose of considering the *get* to have been given "of his own free will."

Maimonides' explanation of this matter is well known and incisive:[11]

> When a man whom the law requires to be compelled to divorce his wife does not desire to divorce her, the *beit din* should have him beaten until he consents, at which time they should have a *get* written. The *get* is acceptable. This applies at all times and in all places.

---

8. There is a controversy amongst the decisors as to whether a coerced *get* is biblically or rabbinically invalid. According to the majority of authorities, a coerced *get* is null and void. See this writer's *Rabbinic Authority*, vol. 3, p. 30, note 11.

However, there is a minority opinion, that *be-di'avad* (ex post facto) the execution of the *get* under duress is valid. See *Mishneh Torah*, infra n. 11; *Ḥiddushei Ha-Ran, Bava Batra* 48a; *Resp. Be'er Yitzḥak, Even Ha-Ezer* 1:10 (3); *Resp. Ḥatam Sofer, Even Ha-Ezer* 2:174; *Resp. Ma'aseh Ḥiyah* 24.

On the other hand, according to biblical law, a woman may be divorced against her will. See *Tosefta Ketubot* 12:3; Talmud Bavli *Gittin* 78a. As is known, in pursuance to Rabbeinu Gershom's medieval enactment, a wife may be divorced only if she consents. See *Resp. Ha-Rosh* 42:1.

9. M. Gittin 9:8.

10. Talmud Bavli *Bava Batra* 48b.

11. *Mishneh Torah, Hilk. Gerushin* 2:20.

> Similarly, if gentiles beat him while telling him: "Do what the Jews are telling you to do," and the Jews have the gentiles apply pressure on him until [he consents] to divorce his wife, the divorce is acceptable...
>
> Why is this *get* not void? For he is being compelled – either by Jews or by gentiles – [to divorce] against his will [and a *get* must be given voluntarily].
>
> Because the concept of being compelled against one's will applies only when speaking about a person who is being compelled and forced to do something that the Torah does not obligate him to do – e.g., a person who was beaten until he consented to a sale, or to give a present. If, however, a person's evil inclination presses him to negate [the observance of] a *mitzvah* or to commit a transgression, and he was beaten until he performed the action he was obligated to perform, or he dissociated himself from the forbidden action, he is not considered to have been forced against his will. On the contrary, it is he himself who is forcing [his own conduct to become debased]. With regard to this person who [outwardly] refuses to divorce [his wife] – he wants to be part of the Jewish people, and he wants to perform all the *mitzvot* and eschew all the transgressions; it is only his evil inclination that presses him. Therefore, when he is beaten until his [evil] inclination has been weakened, and he consents [to the divorce], he is considered to have performed the divorce willfully.

It is emphasized in Maimonides' ruling that in a case in which the husband is compelled to give his wife a *get*, he must say, "I want it." Even though there are circumstances in which the halakhic system allows for the *get* to be compelled,[12] succumbing to the pressure becomes consent to give the *get*.[13]

In short, a *get* compelled by a *beit din* is valid, but compulsion of the *get* by a non-Jewish court is invalid.

---

12. M. *Ketubot* 7:9–10.

13. And others concur with Maimonides's rationale for his ruling. See *Tosafot, Bava Batra* 48a, s.v. *alima maha*; Rashbam, *Bava Batra* 48a, s.v. *dilma*; *Resp. Ohr Zarua* 754; *Resp. Maharaḥ Ohr Zarua* 126; *Resp. Ha-Tashbetz* 2:68; *Resp. Yakhin U-Boaz* 2:21; *Resp. Ha-Mabit* 1:76; *Resp. Ein Yitzḥak* 2:46; *Resp. Ḥavot Yair* 55; *Shulḥan Arukh, Ḥoshen Mishpat* 205:1. Compare *Ḥiddushei Ha-Ramban, Yevamot* 53b, s.v. *ha de-amar Rava*; *Ḥiddushei Ha-Ritva, Ketubot* 64a; *Resp. Ha-Ridvaz* 4:1228; *Resp. Maharik, shoresh* 63.

In the event that the *beit din* ruled to compel the *get* in a particular case, does compulsion of the *get* by non-Jewish courts invalidate it? Tur, *Even ha-Ezer* 134, cites a dispute between his father, the Rosh, and the Ramah regarding the law in the case of a non-Jewish court that compels a man to give a *get*, when that court did not state, "Do what the Jews are telling you." In such circumstances, is the *get* valid or not? Tur rules:[14]

> If a *beit din* compels him through the non-Jewish court, and they say to him, Do what the Jewish court tells you, and they compel him, then the *get* is valid, and Ramah wrote that they must use those words. But if the non-Jews compel him and say to him, Give a *get*, even though they have been told by a *beit din* to compel him, the *get* is invalid. And is it not clear to my father, the Rosh, that because the *beit din* instructs the non-Jewish court to compel him, even if the non-Jewish court says, "Give a *get*," the *get* is valid.

The focus of the disagreement between the Rosh and Ramah is explained clearly by Dayan Uriel Lavi, Presiding Dayan of the Jerusalem Regional Beit Din:[15]

> Ramah and Rosh were in disagreement concerning a case in which a *beit din* ruled that the husband is to be compelled to divorce, and subsequently the non-Jewish court compelled him to give a *get* by virtue of their law, doing so independently, and not in order to comply with the ruling of the Jewish court. Ramah holds that because the non-Jewish court is not compelling the husband as an agent of the *beit din*, the *get* is not valid. According to the Rosh, however, because prior to the compulsion the *beit din* had already ruled that he is to be compelled to divorce, then whosoever enforces this compulsion, including the non-Jewish court, will be considered the long arm of the *beit din*, even if they have not said as much.

In other words, according to Ramah it is possible for a non-Jewish court to enforce the ruling to compel the *get* issued by a *beit din*, on condition that the former says, "Do what the Jewish court rules." As opposed to this, according to Rosh, it is sufficient that the non-Jewish court compel,

14. *Even Ha-Ezer* 134.
15. File 622918, Jerusalem Regional Beit Din, 4 Sivan 5777.

on its own initiative and unrelated to the ruling of the *beit din*, provided that the *beit din* has issued a ruling to compel the *get*.[16]

R. Yosef Karo resolved the dispute as follows:[17] "And if the *beit din* compelled him through the Cuthites [Samaritans] and the Cuthites

16. The position of Rosh dovetails with the general principle in *Ḥoshen Mishpat* that it is permissible to enforce a judgment issued by a *beit din* via a non-Jewish court. See *Resp. Ha-Rashba Ha-Ḥadashot* 204; *Tur, Ḥoshen Mishpat* 2; *Drisha* ad. loc.; *Sefer Me'irat Einayim, Ḥoshen Mishpat* 26:5; *Beit Yosef, Ḥoshen Mishpat* citing *Sefer Ha-Terumot*; *Resp. Ḥatam Sofer, Ḥoshen Mishpat* 3; *Bi'ur Ha-Gra, Ḥoshen Mishpat* 26:2; *Resp. Maharsham* 1:89; *Resp. Ha-Elef Lekha Shlomo* 4, *Ḥoshen Mishpat* 3; *Resp. Beit Avi* 4:169; *Kovetz Teshuvot* 1:180; File no. 846913, Haifa Regional Beit Din, 18 Sivan 5777 citing Rabbis Elyashiv and Shlomo Zalman Auerbach. In other words, a *hekesh* (an analogy) may be drawn between the halakhah relating to divorce and the halakhah concerning a civil matter. In other words, regardless of whether a *beit din* ruling is handed down regarding a matter of ritual law or a monetary matter, we may utilize the services of a non-Jewish court to enforce the judgment. See *Beit Yosef, Ḥoshen Mishpat* ad loc.; *Bi'ur Ha-Gra, Ḥoshen Mishpat* ad loc. Cf. *Resp. Be'er Yitzḥak, Even Ha-Ezer* 10.

To state it differently, Halakhah distinguishes between employing an agent regarding the performance of a religious obligation, concerning the performance of an undertaking (*kinyan*) or a sale where one requires an agent and agency for the purpose of enforcing a *beit din* ruling such as *get* enforcement which is viewed like "the act of a monkey" (*ma'aseh kof*). See *Shulḥan Arukh, Ḥoshen Mishpat* 188:1; *Resp. Ḥatam Sofer, Oraḥ Ḥayyim* 201; *Resp. Ḥelkat Yoav* 3; *Resp. Iggerot Moshe, Even Ha-Ezer* 1:256; *Kefiyah Be-Get,* 99. Regarding the former type of agency, a non-Jew cannot serve as an agent for a Jew. See Talmud Bavli *Gittin* 23b, *Kiddushin* 41b; *Resp. Ha-Ritva* 39. On the other hand, the second type of agency may be employed by a non-Jew for a Jew.

Consequently, we therefore can understand why Maharil Diskin and R. Shmuel Gartner argue that formally speaking, the non-Jewish court does not serve as an agent for the *beit din*. See *Resp. Maharil Diskin, Pesaḥim* 52 (5); *Kefiyah Be-Get,* 96–99.

Alternatively, there is the opinion that the woman is the agent of the *beit din*. See Kefiyah Be-Get, 85–86, n. 54. Since agency may be established by verbal agreement between the principal and the agent (see *Shulḥan Arukh, Ḥoshen Mishpat* 182:1), in our situation there ought to be communication between the *beit din* and the woman concerning directing the non-Jewish court to address *get* coercion in accordance with its laws.

Finally, as R. Meir Arik notes, the non-Jewish court addresses the matter upon its own initiative and in effect becomes the agent of the *beit din*. It is as if the *beit din* directs the court to coerce the husband to give a *get*. See *Kefiyah Be-Get* 85. The implicit premise of this position is that the principal, namely the *beit din*, may authorize the court to be its agent in its absence. See *Shulḥan Arukh, Even Ha-Ezer* 120.

For the precedent that a *dayan* may serve as an agent (*shaliah*), see Talmud Bavli *Gittin* 88b, *Bava Kamma* 84b.

17. *Shulḥan Arukh, Even Ha-Ezer* 134:9.

whip him and say, 'Do what the Jewish court tells you,' it is considered as if the *beit din* compelled him."

A straightforward reading of the language of R. Yosef Karo would seem to indicate that his ruling favors the opinion of Ramah;[18] however, the glossators of the Shulhan Arukh understood that R. Karo was ruling in accordance with Rosh, and that his mention of the declaration of the Cuthites was not necessarily the ruling he adopted.[19]

The question is whether, according to the approach of Rosh, every compulsion of a *get* carried out by the non-Jewish courts by virtue of their laws (i.e., that *get* refusal is an example of coercive control) will be considered as compulsion on the part of the *beit din*.

In Kovetz Sha'arei Torah, several of the contemporary authorities deliberated on the law applicable to a husband who refuses to appear in court in a divorce suit, where his wife claims and can prove that he is a eunuch, and she asks whether she can sue for divorce in a non-Jewish court that will compel him to divorce her according to their laws: would the *get* be valid?

An answer to this question may be found in the words of *R. Joseph Shalom Halevi Faigenbaum*, who decided in accordance with the opinion of Rosh:[20]

> Indeed, according to both Rosh and Tur, and this seems to be the opinion of the Beit Shmuel at the end of 134:15, and in accordance with what we said, viz., that it turns on the above-mentioned distinction, he was correct in his ruling, for this is [also] the ruling of Rema in Orah Hayyim 11 and 32 and see there Magen Avraham 11, and Siftei Kohen, Yoreh Deah 271:5, that even if the *beit din* said nothing at all, the *get* is valid, and only beyond what is required did he say that the *beit din* should give some help. In any case, in the present case it is clear that also according to the words of Rosh and those who support his view, the *get* is not valid. This is because when the State authorities compel him to divorce, this is not due to the laws of Israel but is rather in accordance with their own conventional State law,

---

18. This is also the opinion in *R. Betzalel Ashkenazy*, supra n. 4; *Resp. Ha-Rid* 55; *Resp. Ha-Rashbash* 339; *Resp. Oneg Yom Tov* 128 citing several *Rishonim* (early authorities).

19. *Beit Shmuel, Even Ha-Ezer* 134: 15; *Sma, Even Ha-Ezer* 26:5. In contemporary times, R. Shmuel Gartner is of the opinion that "the decisive majority of Rishonim" endorsed the view of the Rosh. See *Kefiyah Be-Get*, pt. 14, 145.

20. *Kovetz Sha'arei Torah*, pt. 3, *kuntres* 11:63,173 ff.

> which aims to save the oppressed from the oppressor. And even should it emerge that a law to divorce has its antecedents in Jewish law, this would not help, because what we need is that the compulsion be attributed to the *beit din*. But if the non-Jewish court administers the beating in light of its own procedure, as is pointed out by Ran, unless the beating is given specifically on the basis of a directive of the *beit din* in accordance with Jewish law, it is not effective [for the purpose of a valid *get*]. Even if the non-Jew says to the husband: Do as the Jews command you, according to the law of the Torah, this will not result in a valid *get*.

From what R. Faigenbaum writes, it emerges that if a *beit din* compels the husband to give a *get* to his wife, the *get* is not valid if the non-Jewish court then compels him to do so by virtue of their own laws. This is so even if the non-Jewish court says, "Do what the Jewish court orders according to Jewish law" – the *get* is not valid.

R. Meir Arik, author of Resp. Imre Yosher and Minhat Pittim, disagrees with R. Faigenbaum:[21]

> Surely the *beit din* can designate the wife herself to be an agent, who will compel the husband through the non-Jewish courts, and in that case the *get* would be valid because she is an agent of the *beit din*, and what she does is as if the *beit din* did it. Therefore, the *beit din* should issue a ruling that the matter be considered by the State court, and if what she says is true, he is obligated to divorce her, and it is valid, because the State compulsion is due to the wife being an agent of the *beit din*.

R. Ya'akov Shor agreed:[22]

> It is clear to me that in fact, as long as the *beit din* orders that he must divorce his wife, and they warn him that if he does not comply they will allow the wife to sue him under their [non-Jewish] laws to force him to divorce her, then even though their compulsion is not by virtue of the orders of the *beit din*, but by virtue of conventional State law, the *get* is a valid compelled *get*

21. *Kovetz Sha'arei Torah*, pt. 4, *kuntres* 15, 25 ff.; *Kovetz Sha'arei Torah*, pt. 4, 34:2, 68ff.

22. *Kovetz Sha'arei Torah*, pt. 4, 34, pp. 68.

under Jewish law, and it is acceptable *ab initio* as if he divorced her in a *beit din.*

In accordance with the position of R. Arik and R. Shor, together with the adoption of Rosh's approach, if the *beit din* ruled that the husband must give a *get* and he refused, and he was compelled by a non-Jewish court to divorce, even if not by virtue of the ruling of the *beit din* but rather by virtue of State law, the *get* is valid *ab initio*. This is also the opinion of the late R. Leibes, formerly a rabbi in Brooklyn, NY.[23]

In light of the above, in order to eliminate the possibility that a *get* that is given due to a criminal proceeding in the non-Jewish court will be deemed a coerced *get* and therefore invalid, bringing charges against a *get* refuser in a non-Jewish court should be pursued only in the above cumulative circumstances:

1. From a procedural point of view, a *beit din* is permitted to decide on a matter of divorce with the participation of both spouses, or in the presence of the wife alone, on condition that the husband was summoned to the *beit din* and refused to appear for the hearing in the *beit din.*[24]

23. *Resp. Beit Avi* 4:169 (14).

24. *Resp. Ha-Rashbash* 46; *Resp. Ramah Me-Fano* 86; *Resp. Ha-Mabit* 1:76, 2:138; *Resp. Lev Mavin, Even Ha-Ezer* 130; *Resp. Mishpatim Yesharim* 1:436; *Resp. Maharsham* 6:161; *Resp. Avnei Nezer, Even Ha-Ezer* 238; R. Yo'ezer Ariel, *Laws of Borerut* (Heb.), 302; R. Dr. Eliav Shochetman, *Procedure in the Rabbinical Courts* (2 ed., Heb.) 521–522; R. Abraham Debaremdiker, *Book of Procedure* (Heb.) 1:59; this writer's *Rabbinic Authority*, vol. 4, 216, note 2.

A review of the above rulings will demonstrate that we can conduct a hearing in the absence of a husband for two reasons. First, in a matter of personal status (*ishut*), we may convene a hearing in the absence of a party provided both parties were summoned to the hearing. Secondly, in a situation of *igun*, under certain conditions we may conduct a *beit din* proceeding in the absence of the husband. Cf. the opinion of Rabbis Elyashiv and U. Lavi who contend that the convening of a *beit din* proceeding for matters of marriage and divorce require the presence of both parties. See *Kefiyah Be-Get*, Introduction; *Resp. Kovetz Teshuvot* 1:181, 3:202; File no. 865704/1, Safed Regional Beit Din, 12 Iyar 5777; R. Lavi, *Resp. Ateret Devorah* 3:87.

Furthermore, in the absence of the husband at a hearing, a *beit din* may hear the submission of evidence by witnesses insofar as it relates to matters of personal status. See *Resp. Ohalei Ya'akov* 27 in the name of Meiri and Ridvaz; *Resp. Ha-Rivash Ha-Ḥadashot* 14 in the name of Ramah; *Resp. Ha-Rashba* 4:200; *Resp. Ha-Tashbetz* 2:19; *Resp. Ha-Rashbash* 46, 287; *Resp. Maharshal* 33; *Resp. Ha-Ridvaz* 70; *Resp. Avnei Nezer Even Ha-Ezer* 30, 123, 124; *Resp. Noda Be-Yehudah, Mahadura Kama, Even Ha-Ezer* 72 (Cf. with no. 92); *Resp. Karnei Reim* 1:4; *Yeshuot Ya'akov*

2. The lack of legal and therefore halakhic capacity of *batei din* outside of Israel to render a compulsion *get* order does not prevent them from issuing an order for compulsion, with a proviso that the compulsion will be enforced only by means of the non-Jewish courts and in accordance with their laws. In other words, the decision of the *beit din* must be in accordance with the facts of the case that require compulsion of the *get*, and nothing more!
3. **Prior** to filing a claim for coercive control in the secular court, the *beit din* must convene and issue a ruling to obligate a *get* (*hiyyuv get*).[25]

Even Ha-Ezer 42; *Resp. Ḥelkat Ya'akov, Even Ha-Ezer* 1:4; *Resp. Ḥatam Sofer, Even Ha-Ezer* 1:84; *Resp. Ha-Maharnah* 1:68; *Piskei Din Rabbanayim* (hereinafter: *PDR*) 6:266, 281.

In the event that one deals with an *agunah*, the situation is characterized as "an hour of emergency" and as such is halakhically viewed as if it were ex post facto and therefore, evidence in matters related to personal status may be submitted in the absence of the husband. See *Maharnah*, op. cit. Cf. *Rema, Shulḥan Arukh Even Ha-Ezer* 11:4, *Ḥoshen Mishpat* 28:15; *Resp. Ha-Rema* 17; *Beit Shmuel, Shulḥan Arukh, Even Ha-Ezer* 11:16; *Resp. Maharshal* 11; *Resp. Mas'at Binyamin* 106; *Resp. Panim Meirot* 1, *Even Ha-Ezer* 104; *Resp. Maharashdam Even Ha-Ezer* 21, 27; *Resp. R. Akiva Eiger* 99. For further discussion, see S. Shilo, "Testimony in the Absence of a Party in Matrimonial Matters," (Hebrew) 5 *Shenaton Ha-Mishpat ha-Ivri* 321 (1978).

Whether it is essential to turn to a *beit din* or whether a scholar(s) who is an expert in *Even ha-Ezer* and *Ḥoshen Mishpat* may issue a ruling regarding marriage and divorce such as coercing and obligating a *get* is subject to debate amongst the authorities. See *Yam Shel Shlomo, Bava Kamma* 3:9; *Ketzot Ha-Ḥoshen* 3:1–2; *Netivot Ha-Mishpat, Ḥoshen Mishpat* 3:1; *Resp. Yehudah (Gordin), Even Ha-Ezer* 51:2; *Resp. Ma'aseh Ḥiya* 24; *Resp. Ḥatam Sofer, Even Ha-Ezer* 2:64–65, *Ḥoshen Mishpat* 177; *Resp. Avnei Nezer, Even Ha-Ezer* 167:1; *R. Z.N. Goldberg, Lev Mishpat* 1:149–150; this writer's *Rabbinic Authority*, vol. 5, 232, note 1.

25. In the Diaspora where, generally speaking, rabbinical courts refrain from issuing a ruling of obligating the giving of a *get*, our presentation demonstrates the significance of a *beit din*'s acute need to issue this type of ruling in order to address the plight of the *agunah* who is seeking relief via the services of a non-Jewish court.

There is a minority of authorities who argue that rendering a judgment to obligate the giving of a *get*, similar to coercing a *get*, runs afoul of the strictures of a coerced *get* (a *get me'useh*). See *Ḥazon Ish Even Ha-Ezer* 99:2; *Teshuvot Resp. Yabia Omer* 2 *Even Ha-Ezer* 10; R. Shimshon S. Karelitz, *Resp. Ateret Shlomo* 1:32 (6) in the name of Rashba and Rivash; *PDR* 7:201, 204 (Rabbi Elyashiv in the name of Rosh); File no. 8211227/2, Jerusalem Regional Beit Din, December 12, 2013; File no. 1083672/1, Haifa Regional Beit Din, January 25, 2018.

However, the majority of authorities, including but not limited to the majority of the Israeli rabbinical courts under the network of Israel's Chief Rabbinate, issue decisions of obligating a *get*. Consequently, the rabbinical courts in the Diaspora

4. If the husband refuses to give a *get*, a "*heter arkha'ot*" – permission to turn to a non-Jewish court – must be obtained in order to bring a criminal action in the non-Jewish court to compel the *get*. The purpose of the action is to prove that *get* refusal constitutes an instance of coercive control that occurred in the course of the marriage. In other words, a precondition of bringing this action in a non-Jewish court is that the *beit din* issued a judgment ordering that the *get* (*hiyyuv get*) be given.
5. If the husband gave the *get* in order to prevent an indictment under the above law, the *get* is valid.

In light of all the above, a judgment issued by a *beit din* together with enforcement through a criminal process in the English court may save Jewish women living in England from the state of *igun*, and this can help prevent serious violations of Jewish law pertaining to married women, as well as preventing the proliferation of *mamzerim* [bastards under Jewish law] in Israel – May the Lord save us!

Addendum 1

A new law on coercive control (California Family Code 6320) became effective on January 1, 2021. According to the new law, among the remedies available to victims of domestic violence is that the courts may consider such behavior as a factor in determining child custody and visitation privileges as well as calculating the amount and duration of spousal support.[26] Prior to a court's determination that *get* recalcitrance

---

should follow the procedure adopted by the above Israeli rabbinical courts as well as by numerous decisors. See *Tosafot, Ketubot* 70a, s.v. *yotzi* in the name of Rabbeinu Ḥananel; *Tosafot, Yevamot* 64a, s.v. *yotzi*; *Piskei Ha-Rosh, Yevamot* 6:11; *Resp. Maharam of Rothenberg*, Prague ed., 946; *Ḥiddushei Ha-Ran, Ketubot* 77a; *Resp. Ha-Rashba* 7:477; *Resp. Ha-Rivash* 127; *Resp. Ha-Tashbetz* 2:68; *Semag*, Positive Mitzvah 48 (end); *Ḥiddushei Ha-Ritva, Ketubot* 77a; *Tur* and *Beit Yosef, Even Ha-Ezer* 70, 154; *Shulḥan Arukh, Even Ha-Ezer* 70:3, 154:3, 21; *Rema, Yoreh De'ah* 228:20, *Even Ha-Ezer* 154:21; *Arukh Ha-Shulḥan, Even Ha-Ezer* 154:20; *Shakh, Gevurat Anashim* 29; *Pithei Teshuvah, Even Ha-Ezer* 154:15; *Resp. Ha-Maharit* 1:113; *Resp. Noda Be-Yehudah, Mahadura Tinyana* 90; *Resp. Nosei Ha-Ephod* 32:18; PDR 1:141 (R. Elyashiv's opinion). See further, this writer's *Rabbinic Authority*, vol. 5, pp. 306–324.

26. Prior to adjudicating matters of spousal support, child support and parenting arrangements in a non-Jewish court, one is required to receive "*heter arkha'ot*," permission to proceed to non-Jewish court to deliberate end-of-marriage issues.

Whether one must receive halakhic permission from a *beit din* or whether a *hora'ah* (an instruction) of a scholar who is an expert in *Even Ha-Ezer* and *Ḥoshen*

is an example of coercive control, a *beit din* must have ruled that in theory the circumstances dictate that a *get* ought to be coerced. However, in practice, given that legally and therefore halakhically the imposition of *get* coercion is an impossibility, the *beit din* must have handed down a ruling that the husband is obligated to give a *get* and acknowledge that the court is following their law. In effect, with the existence of such a rabbinic judgment, a civil court order will not impact the integrity of any subsequent execution of a *get*. See *R. Tobol, Resp. Mar'ot Yesharim* 29. As we explained earlier, in effect the civil court is serving as a *shaliah*, an agent of the *beit din*. For further discussion, see *Kefiyah Be-Get*, supra note 18, 85, 87, 99–100.

Finally, whereas we are dealing with the halakhic validity of *get* coercion by a non-Jewish court, the NY *Get* Law stated that the party initiating a divorce proceeding in the civil courts must certify that he or she has removed any "barrier to remarriage" as defined in that law. However, this statute is limited, for it only withholds a civil divorce but cannot compel a *get*. As such, we have refrained from examining the NY *Get* Law in our presentation.

Addendum 2

Below please find a sample *beit din* decision which serves as a vehicle for a victim of *get* recalcitrance to file a claim pursuant to the coercive control legislation without running afoul of the strictures of a coerced *get*. In other words, the *beit din* judgment must be issued prior to filing a claim in secular court addressing whether there are grounds to indict for coercive control behavior.

Avraham v. Miriam

FACTS OF THE CASE

Avraham and Miriam were married on July 3, 2001. Since October 2018 the couple has been separated. To date, Avraham refuses to give Miriam a *get*. We convened a hearing with the parties.

Mishpat suffices in order to be permitted to litigate in a non-Jewish court is subject to debate. See *Shulḥan Arukh, Ḥoshen Mishpat* 26:2; *Resp. Maharil Diskin* 13; *Resp. Shevet Ha-Levi* 4:183. See further, this writer's *Rabbinic Authority*, vol. 1, 154, note 160.

DISCUSSION

Based upon information submitted at the hearing, there are no prospects for *shalom bayit*, marital reconciliation. Given that Avraham and Miriam have been separated for more than 18 months, Avraham is obligated to give a *get* to Miriam.

R. Pelaggi, a renowned Sephardic authority rules:[27]

> In general.... When *Beit Din* realizes that they are separated for a long time and they cannot be reconciled.... We have to make an effort to separate them from each other and he should give a *get* in order that they not sin grievously.... And my time frame, in case of dispute [between] wife and husband... and 18 months have passed...*Beit Din*... should force him to give a divorce...

We concur with R. Pelaggi, that there are grounds to coerce a *gett* (see also *Piskei Din Rabbaniyim* 9:145, 152, 15:145, 158-159, 18:71,81; File no. 8025/1, Ashdod Regional Beit Din, 1, 21, 2016). However, in contemporary times in the Diaspora we cannot coerce a *get*. **Therefore, we obligate Avraham to give a *get* immediately**. See also *Iggerot Moshe, Yoreh Deah* 4:15(2).

Should Miriam file a claim against *get* recalcitrance as an example of coercive control in marriage under English law, in accordance to Rabbi Meir Arik, Rabbi Yaakov Shor and others, we acknowledge that the court in general is following their law and their norms of coercion in particular, and the ensuing *get* will be valid. See *Kovetz Shaarei Torah*, Section 4, Kuntres 15, 34, pp.69ff: File no. 622918/19, Jerusalem Regional Beit Din, May 29, 2017; File no. 846913/2, Haifa Regional Beit Din, June 12, 2017.

27. Resp. Hayyim Ve-Shalom 2:112. See also Resp. Hayyim Ve-Shalom 2:35.

Chapter 7

An Introduction to the Varying Avenues of Establishing An Acquisition Agreement (*Hakna'ah*) and an Obligatory Agreement (*Hit'hayevut*)

1. Negotiating in Good Faith

The threshold question is whether the Halakhah of obligations (*hith'ayevut*) imparts any consequence to resolving in one's mind to act in a certain fashion via-a-vis another individual.[1] Is there a halakhic-moral norm which mandates that we follow *the dictates of our mind and heart* and is there a halakhic consequence for failing to abide by this halakhic-moral norm? Is every member of our covenantal Jewish community obliged to follow "the resolution of the mind and heart," or are only certain members of our community bound by it?

The Talmud expounds:[2]

> Our Rabbis taught: A person who buys herbs in the market and picks out and places down, even the entire day, does not acquire possession (of the herb).... If he has resolved in his mind to buy it, he acquires possession.... Does one acquire possession... because he resolved in his mind to purchase? R. Hoshaia responded: We are dealing here with a God-fearing man like R. Safra, for example who applied to himself (the verse), *And spoke truth in his heart.*

An individual who is God fearing (a *ye'rei shamayim*) that resolved in

1. Whether resolving in one's mind to give a donation (*tzedaka*) entails the execution of a vow (a *neder*) is subject to debate and beyond the scope of this presentation. See *Shulhan Arukh, Hoshen Mishpat* 212:8, *Rema*, ad.locum. Similarly, invoking a vow to impart credence to a promise is beyond the scope of our presentation. See *Sifra*, Horowitz ed., *Bamidbar*, 153, 200.

2. Talmud Bavli *Bava Batra* 88a. See also, Talmud Yerushalmi, *Sheviit* 10:9.

his mind to purchase herbs, acquires them under circumstances that another person would not acquire the herbs. As Meiri notes:[3]

> The practice of pious individuals (*Hasidim*) to comply with their words... and some pious people... resolve from their hearts without pronouncing it with their mouth...
>
> Halakhically, we may say that he is engaging in the personality trait of saintliness ("*middat hasidut*").[4] Though the Talmud here does not describe such an individual as one who is engaging in saintly conduct, nonetheless, in other Talmudic passages such conduct between man and man comports with the standard of saintliness.[5] Such behavior is directed to saints only [6] and the minute he resolves to purchase it in his mind and picks it up, he acquires the object and must not change his mind.[7]
>
> This recognition of accepting one's thoughts to acquire an object or perform an action extends equally to one's promises to one's fellowman. Following in the footsteps of various Tannaitic and Amoraic traditions,[8] normative Halakhah states:[9]

---

3. *Sefer Beit Ha-Behira*, Bava Metzia 49a. See also, *Sheiltot Ahai Gaon, Bereshit, Parshat Vayehi* 36:3; Rashi, *Makot 24a*, s.v. *R. Safra*.

4. However, the Talmud in *Shabbat* 120a distinguishes between a saint and a God-fearing man. See also *Responsa* (hereinafter: Resp.) *Iggerot Moshe, Hoshen Mishpat* 1:58.

Compliance with one's words is contingent upon the matter being permitted according to Halakhah. For example, there is a prohibition for two individuals to agree to have their differences resolved in a secular court. In other words, even if the parties execute a *kinyan* (symbolically undertaking an obligation), Halakhah proscribes them from resolving their issues in a secular court. See *Mishneh Torah, Hilk. Sanhedrin* 26:7; *Shulhan Arukh, Hoshen Mishpat* 22:2, 26:1, 3.

However, if the parties agreed to proceed to secular court where one side is entitled to an award in accordance with civil law (and not Halakhah) and executed a *kinyan;* it is subject to debate whether a *kinyan* is effective. See *Sma, Hoshen Mishpat* 22:15, 26:11; *Taz, Hoshen Mishpat* 61:6.

5. Talmud Bavli *Shabbat*, supra n. 4; *Bava Metzia* 52b; *Hullin* 120a.

6. *Mishneh Torah, Hilk. Nahalot* 6:11. Whether this standard is to be equated to "the spirit of the Sages is not pleased with him" we leave as an open question.

7. *Shulhan Arukh, Hoshen Mishpat* 200:11; *Bi'ur Ha-Gra, Hoshen Mishpat* 200:34. Cf. others who contend that this standard is applicable only if he picked up the object in order to purchase it. See Hazon Ish, Likkutim, Hoshen Mishpat 11; *Mahaneh Ephraim, Kinyan Ma'ot* 10.

8. *Mekhilta, Parshat Beshalach* 15; *Sheviit* 10:9; *Tamid* 28a; *Nidah* 70b; *Shabbat* 31a.

9. *Shulhan Arukh, Orah Hayim* 156:1.

> Afterwards he will pursue his affairs... and should negotiate in good faith.

2. The Constitutive Elements of an Acquisition Agreement

Negotiating in good faith exhibits itself in multifarious situations. Dating back to Talmudic times, the classic corpus of Halakhah expounds:[10]

> R. Kahane was given money (in advance) for the purchase of flax. Subsequently, flax appreciated, so he appeared in front of Rav and said, "deliver the (amount of) flax in accordance with the amount of money that you received". He responded to him, "but as for the remainder, it is a verbal transaction, and a verbal transaction does not constitute a breach of faith. Since it has been stated: A verbal transaction: Rav rules that it entails a breach of faith. R. Yohanan states it does entail a breach of faith.

Relying upon R. Yohanan's view, the *Shulhan Arukh*, the classic restatement of Halakhah, states:[11]

> When one conducts and finalizes commercial transactions utilizing words only (the agreement not being finalized by a formal act of undertaking a duty [*kinyan*]), that individual should be faithful to his word.... Whoever withdraws from this type of transaction is deemed a faithless person. Rabbinical scholars are not favorably disposed toward him, though he is not to be given a formal condemnation.[12]

---

10. Talmud Bavli *Bava Metzia* 49a.
11. *Hoshen Mishpat* 204:7, Rema, ibid., 11.
12. In the words of the Sages, "*ein ruah Hakhamim nohah hei'menu*", i.e., the spirit of the Torah scholars is displeased with him. See Rashi, *Bava Metzia* 49a, s.v. *aval amru hakhamim*; *Mishneh Torah, Hilk. Mekhirah* 7:8.

Whether the person is to be labeled a wicked person (a *rasha*) is subject to debate. See *Resp. Maharam of Rothenberg*, 153, Prague ed. 949 in the name of Rivam; *Resp. Maharam Mintz* 101; *Shakh, Yoreh Deah* 264:7; *Taz, Yoreh Deah* 264: 5; *Resp. Betzeil Ha-Hokhmah* 5:159; *Shitah Mekubetzet, Bava Metzia* 49a, s.v. *od*, in the name of Ra'avad. If we accept the majority view that he is to be labeled a wicked person, then he will be invalidated to give testimony in a *beit din* proceeding. See *Sma, Hoshen Mishpat* 34:7; *Resp. Har Ha-Carmel* 36. Cf. *Resp. Divrei Yehezkel* 8.

This position was adopted by Rif, Maimonides, Meiri, Rosh, Tur, and Rema.[13]

The question emerges: what happens if the seller and buyer arrive at a price for the transaction and after their agreement there was a price change, and one party wants to retract his consent to the transaction? There exists a minority view of authorities that the person is only deemed faithless (*mehusar amanah*), when the price continues to reflect the parties' agreement.[14] However, according to the majority opinion, under all circumstances, regardless of whether the price has increased or not, upon retraction he is deemed faithless.[15]

There are various understandings of the dispute between Rav and R. Yohanan which shed light upon the concept of imparting trust, reliance (*histamkhut da'ata/ de-samkha da'ataihu*) towards establishing obligations.[16] Is the invoking of faithlessness due to the prohibition of deception, or is the prohibition of retraction due to the damage done to the other person who hoped for the agreement to be fulfilled?[17]

R. Naftali Tzvi Berlin responds:[18]

---

13. Alfasi, *Bava Metzia* 49a; Maimonides, supra n. 12; *Sefer Beit Ha-Behira, Bava Metzia* 49a; *Piskei Ha-Rosh* 4:12; *Tur, Hoshen Mishpat* 204:11; Rema, *Hoshen Mishpat* 204:14.

14. *Ba'al Ha-Maor, Bava Metzia* 49a, page 72 on pages of Alfasi; *Piskei Ha-Rosh,* supra n. 13; *Sma, Hoshen Mishpat* 204:12; *Bi'ur Ha-Gra, Hoshen Mishpat* 204:18.

15. Nahmanides, pages of Alfasi, *Bava Metzia* 29a, 44a; *Tosafot, Bava Metzia* 49a, s.v. *domeh*; *Nimmukei Yosef, Bava Metzia* 49a, pages of Alfasi in the name of Ran and Rashba; *Hiddushei Ha-Rashba, Bava Metzia* 49a; *Mordekhai, Bava Metzia* 311; *Magid Mishneh, Hilk. Mekhirah* 7:8; *Beit Yosef Hoshen Mishpat* 204; *Shulhan Arukh, Hoshen Mishpat* 204:7, Rema, ibid.; *Resp. Hatam Sofer, Hoshen Mishpat* 102 (cf. *Resp. Hatam Sofer, Yoreh Deah* 246); *Resp. Maharsham* 2:125; *Resp. Maharshag* 3:113; *Resp. Betzeil Ha-Hokhmah* 5:175.

Prior to invoking the claim that the individual is *mehusar amanah*, the parties need to have agreed upon a price. See supra n. 11; *Beit Ha-Behirah, Bava Metzia* 48a. Should the market price change after their agreement and one wants to retract his promise, it is subject to debate whether *mehusar amanah* is applicable. See Rema, *Hoshen Mishpat* 204:11.

16. The term *histamkhut daat* has two meanings in the Talmud: One understanding is *gemirat da'at* which means consent and the other meaning is trust and reliance. For the former meaning as prerequisite for the validity of the act of *kiddushin* (loosely translated: marriage), see *Ketubot* 82b; *Kiddushin* 48a.

17. Whether the act of faithlessness is a biblical prohibition or a rabbinic proscription is subject to debate. See Rashi, *Ketubot* 86a, s.v. *periat ba'al hov mitzva*; *Ba'al Ha-Maor, Bava Metzia* 29b pages of Alfasi; *Minhat Hinnukh, Mitzva* 259 (1); *Minhat Petim, Hoshen Mishpat* 204:11. Cf. *Piskei Ha-Rosh, Bava Metzia* 4:12; *Resp. Ranah* 1:118.

18. *Sheiltot Ahai Gaon*, supra n. 3, *Sheiltah* 36 (2).

> R. Yohanan argues that since the other party is relying upon the promise of the opposing party therefore his reneging constitutes faithlessness. And Rav contends that since the party did not expect the price to increase, he is permitted to change his mind, and this isn't deemed a lie that he retracted since the agreement of the parties was not under such circumstances.

On the other hand, R. Moshe Feinstein offers another understanding of the controversy between Rav and R. Yohanan which deals with the efficacy of a promise.[19] There is a halakhic mandate that interpersonal relations be governed by good faith (*hin tzedek*). As we know, the Torah obligates us in measuring weights and measures by exhibiting good faith regardless of whether the measure of capacity is large or small.[20] Analogously, as the Talmud observes, if a person makes a commitment, he should carry it out based upon the imperative of engaging in good faith (*hin tzedek*) and "the remnant of Israel shall do no wrong." And if he initially had no intention to fulfill his promise, he violates the two aforementioned good faith requirements.[21] As we mentioned, though in accordance with Rav, if there was a price increase he can retract his promise, however in pursuance to R. Yohanan, since the articulation of a promise caused the buyer to consent to the agreement, therefore, the seller is dutybound to keep his promise even if he didn't expect the price to increase.[22] To state it differently, Halakhah views promise-keeping as aligning oneself with the fulfillment of a religious norm rather than compliance with a norm of natural law, institutional moral norm, or moral norm established by social convention.

To state it differently: As Hazon Ish aptly notes:[23]

19. *Resp. Iggerot Moshe, Hoshen Mishpat* 1:58.

20. *Vayikra* 19:36.

21. Talmud Bavli *Bava Metzia*, supra n. 10; *Mishneh Torah, Hilk. Deot* 2:6; *Kiddushin* 45b; Rashi, *Bava Metzia*, op. cit.; *Sma, Hoshen Mishpat* 204:12; *Ohr Zarua* 3, *Bava Metzia* 149; *Sha'arei Teshuva, Sha'ar* 3, 183; *Mordekhai, Bava Metzia* 84, *Siman* 312 in the name of Maharam; *Beit Yosef, Yoreh Deah* 264.

Whereas the *hin zedek* imperative obligates compliance with one's promise, "the remnant of Israel shall do no wrong" teaches us that if an individual retracts his promise, he has committed a sin. See R. Z.N. Goldberg, "The Validity of an Obligation to Sell in a Preliminary Agreement," (Hebrew) 12 *Tehumin* 279, 291-292, 5751.

22. This understanding of the dispute is predicated upon Rashi's interpretation of the controversy. See Rashi, *Bava Metzia* 49a, s.v. *shelo yedabeir, ela she'yehei.*

23. *Hoshen Mishpat* 22. See also, *Hazon Ish, Bava Kamma* 21 (5); *Even Ha-Ezer* 38:7. See also, *Resp. Tuv Ta'am Ve'daat, Mahadura* 3, 2:146; *Tziyunim Le'torah* 39; R. Wasserman, *Kovetz Shiurim* 430. Cf. *Resp. Nodah Beyehudah, Mahadura Kamma,*

> The major principle in undertaking obligations (*kinyanim*), the primary purpose of undertaking an obligation is that he must firmly resolve in his heart to sell the item to his friend and his friend must have intention to acquire it.

In halakhic nomenclature, there is a requirement of the seller's and buyer's resolution to transfer an object, i.e., *gemirat da'at*.[24]

However, a concrete articulation of the parties' firm resolve to undertake an obligation is generally insufficient to finalize a purchase. As such, there is a second requirement which entails the symbol of this mutual resolution, namely the execution of a formal act known as a *kinyan* (a symbolic act to undertake an obligation) to transfer objects.[25] In

---

Hoshen Mishpat 28, who contends that the parties' resolution to acquire an object is contingent upon the enactment of scholars.

24. Talmud Bavli *Yevamot* 52b; *Kiddushin* 26a; *Tur Hoshen Mishpat* 189, *Beit Yosef*, ibid., *Bah*, ibid.; *Avnei Milluim* 27:9; *Sha'arei Yosher, Sha'ar* 7, *Perek* 12; *Resp. Tuv Taam ve-Da'at* 1:269; *Tziyunim La-Torah* 39; *Resp. Ramatz, Yoreh De'ah* 76; *Resp. Devar Yehoshua*, vol. 3, *Hoshen Mishpat* 13 (3).

Gemirat da'at is determined objectively in accordance to the assessment of rabbinic authorities. See *Hiddushei Ha-Ramban, Kiddushin* 26a; *Hiddushei Ha-Ran, Kiddushin* 13a.

25. *Mishneh Torah, Hilk. Mekhirah* 1:1, 5:12-13; *Piskei Ha-Rosh, Bava Batra* 4:12; *Shulhan Arukh, Hoshen Mishpat* 189:1. The physical act of *kinyan* such as acquisition by deed or money (*kinyan shtar* or *kinyan kesef*), or barter (*halifin*) is usually performed by the buyer and the seller remains passive and consents to the transaction. See Mishnah *Bava Metzia* 4:2.

However, there are situations recognized by Halakhah where an oral commitment suffices to transfer ownership even without the execution of a *kinyan*. See *Ketubot* 102b; *Tosafot, Ketubot* 102b, s.v. *aliba*; *Tosafot Bekhorot* 18b, s.v. *aknuyei*; *Hiddushei Ha-Rashba, Bava Kamma* 102b, s.v. *ha de'amar R' Abba*; *Ran on Rif, Kiddushin 8b*; *Mishneh Torah, Hilk. Zekhiyah U-Mattanah* 6:15; *Resp. Noda Be-Yehudah, Mahadura Kamma, Hoshen Mishpat* 27-28; *Resp. Shoeil U-Meishiv, Mahadura Tlita'a* 1,223; *Ketzot Ha-Hoshen* 313:1; *Resp. Maharsham* 2:224, 3:318; See supra, *Rabbinic Authority*, vol. 2, 307-330; *Pesakim Ve-Ketavim Hoshen Mishpat* 111; *Resp. R. Akiva Eiger*, 1:37; *Resp. Beit Ephraim, Yoreh Deah* 66; *Resp. Tuv, Ta'am Ve'da'at*, supra n. 24; *Hazon Ish, Hoshen Mishpat* 21:5, 22. Cf. *Resp. Maharam Lublin* 31. Whether the act of *kinyan* is the final stage prior to ownership transfer or is proof of *gemirat da'at* to execute the transfer is subject to debate. See *Minhat Asher, Bava Batra* 46:1, 2, 4.

The inability to transfer a nonexistent object is either because neither party has the *gemirat da'at* to execute the transfer or because the transfer lacks the substance to satisfy the conferral of a halakhic status (a *halot*). See R. Tam, *Sefer Ha-Yashar* 592; *Resp. Maharam Mintz* 35; *Resp. Noda Be-Yehudah, Mahadurah Tinyana, Even Ha-Ezer* 54; *Resp Beit Yitzhak, Yoreh Deah* 2, *Kuntres Aharon* 12; *Resp. Divrei Nehemiah, Even Ha-Ezer* 36.

other words, the execution of a *kinyan* entails the transfer of ownership (*hakna'ah*). Furthermore, in dealing with a nonexistent object (*davar shein bo mamash*) one is unable to transfer an object via a *kinyan* and when addressing a situation where the object is not in possession (*davar she'eno be-reshuto*) it is halakhically construed as an object which is not in this world (*davar she'lo ba le'olam*) and under either condition the execution of a *kinyan* will be ineffective.[26] Finally, the Talmud states that the execution of a *kinyan* between two partners for the express purpose of dividing a plot of land equally between them, talmudically labeled as a *kinyan devarim* (a verbal promise to do something in the future), is null and void.[27] Since the presence of a corporeal estate (*davar sheyesh bo mamash*) requirement is a condition for the effectiveness of the *kinyan*, consequently a promise to perform a future action such as to pay, to build, to buy, and to sell is bereft of this element, an agreement to divide up land is halakhically ineffective.[28]

---

26. Concerning the inability to sell a *davar she'lo ba le'olam*, or to establish an obligation of a monetary nature in the future when it entails his domain *(reshut)*, see *Mishneh Torah, Hilk. Mekhirah* 22:1; *Resp. Ha-Tashbetz* 3:147, *tur* 2:13; *Levush Hoshen Mishpat* 209; *Shulhan Arukh, Hoshen Mishpat* 209:4; *Shakh Hoshen Mishpat* 209:4. Cf. *Gidulei Terumah, Sha'ar* 64, vol. 1, ot 2.

Regarding the mandate to transfer proprietary rights via an existing object, see *Mishneh Torah, Hilk. Mekhirah* 5:14, 22:13-14; *Shitah Mekubetzet, Bava Batra* 147b, s.v. *amar Rava; Resp. Maharam of Rothenberg*, Prague ed. 949; *Resp. Ha-Rosh* 102:10; *Shulhan Arukh, Hoshen Mishpat* 212:1, *Rema*, ibid.; *Biur Ha-Gra, Hoshen Mishpat* 264:13.

Concerning the view that an object not in the seller's possession is to be equated to an object which is not in this world, see Talmud Bavli *Yevamot* 93a; *Mishneh Torah, Hilk. Mekhirah* 22:5; *Shulhan Arukh, Hoshen Mishpat* 209:5, 211:1. The logic of the equation is that both circumstances are viewed as a deficiency in establishing a meeting of the minds. See *Resp. Maharash Tzeror* 13.

Finally, if the object is not in the seller's possession at the time of the agreement, the seller is entitled to retract his promise. See *Mishneh Torah, Hilk. Mekhirah* 22:8; *Resp. Ha-Tashbetz* 3:147; *Shulhan Arukh, Hoshen Mishpat* 60:6, 209:4.

27. Talmud Bavli *Bava Batra* 3a; *Shulhan Arukh, Hoshen Mishpat* 157:2, 203:1, 245:1-2; *Sema Hoshen Mishpat* 209:4; *Shakh Hoshen Mishpat* 60:24, 207:1. See supra n. 31.

28. *Mishneh Torah, Hilk. Mekhirah* 5:14; *Resp Ha-Rashba* 2:41; *Resp. Ha-Rosh* 12:3, 102:10; *Resp. Maharam Mintz* 17; *Shulhan Arukh, Hoshen Mishpat* 157:2; Rema, *Hoshen Mishpat* 203:1; *Rema, Yoreh Deah* 264:1; *Resp. Ne'eman Shmuel* 110; *Resp. Maharhash, Hoshen Mishpat* 1:79.

Even if the promise entails a future action and a *kinyan* has been executed, it is halakhically unenforceable in terms of the halakhah of obligations. See *Resp. Ha-Rashba* 2:41; *Shulhan Arukh, Hoshen Mishpat* 157:2; Rema, *Hoshen Mishpat* 203:1; *Taz, Hoshen Mishpat* 203:1; *Shakh, Yoreh Deah* 264:7; *Netivot Ha-Mishpat, Hoshen*

In short, if cases where a promise is missing one of the foundational prerequisites for transferring ownership, namely the absence of the execution of a *kinyan*, the absence of an existent object, or the lack of possession of the object, or an agreement to behave in a certain fashion in the future, Halakhah mandates compliance, lest one be deemed a *mehusar amanah* and be in violation of the good faith requirement (*hin tzedek*) or "the remnant of Israel shall do no wrong".[29] Yet, in all four instances, noncompliance with the agreement under these circumstances may be halakhically unenforceable by a *beit din* due to the fact that the transfer of ownership has failed to transpire.[30]

Mishpat 203, *Hiddushin* 5.

For solutions to validate an agreement with a future action, see *Beit Yosef, Hoshen Mishpat* 195:20, 22 in the name of Rashba and Ramban; Rema, *Hoshen Mishpat* 212:1; Rema, *Hoshen Mishpat* 171:1.

29. Regarding the situation of transferring an object which is not in the world, some authorities claim that that a promisor who retracts his words is labeled a *mehusar amanah.* See *Rashbam, Bava Batra* 69b; *Hiddushei Ha-Rashba, Bava Batra* 69b; *Tosafot Bava Metzia* 77a in the name of R. Tam; *Resp. Maharam Mintz* 35; *Resp. Terumat Ha-Deshen* 320; *Shakh, Yoreh Deah* 264:7. Cf. *Piskei Ha-Rosh, Bava Batra* 4:12 (Cf. Resp. Ha-Rosh 102:10). See *Minhat Petim* 209 who rejects this position. However, halakhically-morally he must keep his promise.

Failure to comply with his promise regarding an object not in his possession at the time of the agreement deems the promisor a *mehusar amanah.* See Rashbam, op. cit.; Rashba, op. cit.; *Resp. Radam, Hoshen Mishpat* 11; *Imrei Binah,* Laws of Halva'ah, 51 in the name of Rashbam and *Terumat Ha-Deshen.*

If the seller reneges on an agreement which entails a future action, we can curse him. See *Resp. Toafot Re'em* 6.

Concerning a promise dealing with a nonexistent object, some arbiters claim that a promisor who retracts his words is labeled a *mehusar amana.* See *Shulhan Arukh, Yoreh Deah* 264:1; *Resp. Hatam Sofer Yoreh Deah* 246; *Resp. Iggerot Moshe Hoshen Mishpat* 1:58.

Noncompliance of a promise involves a violation of "the remnant of Israel shall do no wrong". See *Bava Metzia* 106b; *Sha'arei Teshuva Le-Rabbeinu Yona, Sha'ar* 3, 6:183.

The implicit premise of the foregoing is that some will contend that *mehusar amana* transpires only when the promisor articulated his thoughts in the promisee's presence. See *Shulhan Arukh Ha-Rav, Hoshen Mishpat, Hilk. Mekhirah U-Matana* 6; *Minhat Petim Hoshen Mishpat* 204 in the name of *Hafla'ah*; *Resp. Helkat Yoav* 30. However, others argue that even if the promise was articulated in the promisee's absence, we are dealing with a situation of *mehusar amana.* See *Resp. Hatam Sofer Yoreh Deah* 297, *Arukh Ha-Shulhan Yoreh Deah* 305:22.

30. Whereas, a halakhic norm is enforceable by a *beit din,* compliance with a halakhic-moral norm is dependent upon volition. Whether a *mehusar amana* may be coerced to comply with his promise is subject to debate. On one hand, there are authorities who argue that coercion is a remedy. See *Rashi, Ketubot* 86a; *Mordekhai,*

Moreover, an agreement which is missing one of the foundational ingredients for transferring ownership between parties, namely the execution of a *kinyan*, the presence of an existent object, or the possession of the object, have been all labeled by rabbinic authorities as "a *kinyan devarim*".[31] Yet, as we stated, Halakhah mandates compliance of the agreement lest one be deemed a *mehusar amanah* and be in violation of a good faith requirement. The foregoing is dealing with an agreement of acquisition where a person possesses all the rights in a particular asset, and in exchange for money transfers all the rights to another person such as a sales transaction, a gift, partnership in an asset, and an employment agreement.

Based upon the foregoing, where no payment has been made, and the seller articulates an oral commitment to sell realty or personalty to a prospective buyer, and should either party renege on the agreement under the following circumstances, he is stigmatized as a *mehusar amana.* Does the undertaking of a promise create an obligatory agreement? Given that no act of acquisition entailing transfer of ownership, i.e., *kinyan.* has been executed between the parties, technically either party may withdraw from consummating the agreement. Furthermore, even if a *kinyan* was executed, should the promise entail transferring title of something not yet in existence (i.e. *davar she'lo ba la'olam*) during the time of the transaction, such as an item which has not been produced or not in possession (*eno bi-reshuto*) or if there is an agreement to behave in a certain fashion in the future such as to divide up land, the promisor must comply with the agreement lest he be labeled as *mehusar amana.*[32]

Bava Metzia 451 in the name of *Ittur*; *Resp. Pri Yitzhak* 1:51. However, numerous authorities disagree with this opinion. See *Mishneh Torah, Hilk. Mekhirah* 7:8; Mordekhai, *Bava Metzia* 4:312; *Resp. Maharam of Rothenberg*, Prague ed. 949; *Resp. Ha-Tashbetz* 1:94; *Resp. Maharam Mintz* 101; *Sma, Hoshen Mishpat* 216:14; *Resp. Ein Yitzhak*, 1:34 (37).

Even if the promise is unenforceable by a *beit din*, nonetheless, the public may proclaim and shame him that he has reneged on an oral commitment. See Mordekhai, *Bava Metzia* 4:451; *Resp. Maharam Mintz* 39,101; *Sefer Ha-Agudah, Bava Metzia* 66; R. Schwadron, *Mishpat Shalom, Hoshen Mishpat* 204. Whether we can label him a wicked person is subject to debate. See supra n. 12.

31. For a sample of said description in the classic restatements of Halakhah, see *Mishneh Torah, Hilk. Mekhirah* 5:14; *Shulhan Arukh, Hoshen Mishpat* 203:1; Rema, ibid.; *Shulhan Arukh, Hoshen Mishpat* 157:2; Rema, *Hoshen Mishpat* 206:4. See supra n. 27.

32. Rashbam, *Bava Batra* 69b, s.v. *ve'i lo zavin leh*; *Tosafot, Bava Metzia* 66b, s.v. *hatam zevini* in the name of Rabbeinu Tam; *Piskei Ha-Rosh, Bava Batra* 4:12 (Cf. *Resp. Ha-Rosh* 102:10); *Maharam of Rothenberg*, supra n. 12; *Resp. Maharam Mintz*

3. The Constitutive Elements of an Obligatory Agreement

What is the conceptual difference between an acquisitive agreement (*hakna'ah*) and an obligatory agreement (*hit'hayevut*)? If someone sells a house, he is now deemed the seller. On the other hand, if he obligates himself to sell a house, the house still remains in the ownership of the seller, until he sells it to the purchaser. The ramifications of this distinction emerge if the house is damaged while it is in the seller's possession. If the damage transpired after the undertaking of the obligation (*kinyan*), the seller loses since the damage happened while it was in his possession. However, if there was an obligation unaccompanied by an act of undertaking the duty then the purchaser may change his mind since the damage happened while the house was in the seller's possession.

What is the Halakhah when addressing the undertaking of an agreement in the form of an obligation (*hit'hayevut*) or a duty grounded in Halakhah (*min hadin*) such as tort obligations? Similar to an agreement of acquisition, among the foundational prerequisites for establishing an agreement of obligation between parties is the requirement of the execution of a *kinyan*, the presence of an existent object, and the possession of the object. For example, obligating oneself to sell an object, utilizing the language of *hit'hayevut* establishes a duty to sell the object.[33]

35; *Resp. Terumat Ha-Deshen* 320; *Shulhan Arukh, Yoreh Deah* 264:1; *Nahalat Shiva* 29; *Resp. Hatam Sofer, Yoreh Deah* 246; *Resp Maharam Schick, Yoreh Deah* 306; *Arukh Ha-Shulhan, Yoreh Deah* 264:12; *Resp. Iggerot Moshe, Hoshen Mishpat* 1:58. Cf. *Resp. Ha-Rosh* 102:10; *Minhat Petim, Hoshen Mishpat* 209:5.

On the other hand, if the item was in existence, however it was not in the seller's possession during the time of the transaction, he must fulfill his promise and transfer it to the buyer. See *Hiddushei Ha-Ritva, Bava Batra* 69b; Ra'avad, *Mishneh Torah, Hilk. Mekhirah* 24:13. For further discussion, see R. Y. Fleischman, *Sefer Mishpetei Yosher* vol. 1, 386-393.

33. *Beit Yosef, Hoshen Mishpat* 206:2 in the name of Rashba (Cf. *Resp. Ha-Rashba* 1:1142); *Resp. Maharit* 69; *Resp. Perah Matteh Aharon* 2:9. However, the actual asset doesn't actually become transferred to the individual. See *Beit Yosef* in the name of Rashba, op. cit.

In the absence of employing "a word of obligation," a promise accompanied by a *kinyan* will be ineffective. See Rashba, op. cit. Others such as *Resp. Ha-Mabit* 2:26 in the name of *Resp. Ha-Rashba* 1:1142 contend that such a promise mandates compliance.

Conversely, one cannot purchase an item by obligating oneself, since the money he obligated himself remains in the purchaser's domain and as such, the seller does not receive anything during the period of the execution of the *kinyan*. See *Hiddushei Ha-Ritva, Kiddushin* 8b, s.v. *manah*; *Hiddushei Ha-Rashba, Kiddushin* 8b, s.v. *manah*. Cf. *Ritva, Kiddushin* 8b, s.v. *amar Raba*.

Nevertheless, the effectiveness of the obligation is contingent upon the execution of a *kinyan* in the presence of witnesses,[34] incorporating the *hit'hayevut* in a deed *(shtar)*[35] or the executing of action which follows the practice (*minhag*) and one obligates oneself in accordance with it.[36] Whether the obligation is effective depends on whether the obligor is dutybound to personally accept liability should the object be lost – will he reimburse the value to the obligee.[37] Secondly, if he promised to sell

---

34. *Resp. Mahara Sasson* 133 in the name of Rif; *Mishneh Torah, Hilk. Mekhirah* 8:7; *Shulhan Arukh, Hoshen Mishpat* 40:1, 60:6; *Ketzot Ha-Hoshen* 40:1.

35. *Mishneh Torah, Hilk. Mekhirah* 11:15.

36. *Rema, Hoshen Mishpat* 129:56; *Sma, Hoshen Mishpat* 129:15; *Hagahot Imrei Barukh, Hoshen Mishpat* 201. One example of a practice becoming enforceable is acquisition by *situmta* (a mode of acquisition practiced in a given locale), see *Bava Metzia* 74a. The halakhot of *situmta* have been invoked not only with regard to methods of acquisition but equally to modes of obligations such as "I will give" known as "*kinyan ei'tein*". See *Resp. Hatam Sofer Hoshen Mishpat* 66; *Resp. Maharshag* 3:113.

Employing the language of "I will give" does not impact the validity of the agreement since the usage of this term is invalid due to the fact that it is directed towards the future and is construed as a promise and therefore the execution of a *kinyan* will not validate said agreement. However, if there is a practice that upon executing a *kinyan* he was undertaking the payment of the debt such as by signing off on the agreement, the agreement is valid. See *Bava Metzia* 74a; *Hagahot Imrei Barukh Hoshen Mishpat* 201; *Resp. Divrei Hayyim Hoshen Mishpat* 2:26; *Piskei Din Rabbanayim* (hereinafter: *PDR*) 4:279 (R. Elyashiv's opinion), 8:302, 9:228; *Resp. Tzitz Eliezer* 16:3; *Resp. Har Tzvi Yoreh Deah* 252. Cf. *Hazon Ish, Hoshen Mishpat* 16:11. Others argue that under such circumstances no *kinyan* has been executed. Nonetheless, we coerce him to comply with his promise. See *Beit Shmuel, Even Ha-Ezer* 51:10. See further, *Meishiv Mishpat* 36.

Finally, though "I will give" does not impact the validity of the agreement since the usage of this term is invalid since it is directed towards the future and is construed as a promise and therefore the execution of a *kinyan* will not validate said agreement, nonetheless, it is prohibited to sign off on such agreement. For the infraction of a prohibition under these circumstances, see *Yoma 4b; Rashi, Yoma 4b*, s.v. *she'hu*; *Sha'arei Teshuva* of R. Yonah, *Sha'ar* 3, 225; *Meiri, Sanhedrin* 31a; *Resp. Shevet Ha-Levi* 4:220.

37. *Ketzot Ha-Hoshen* 60:7, 206:1; *Netivot Ha-Mishpat* 203:4. For example, if there is an agreement to sell a house, whereas the Ketzot mandates that the buyer undertakes personal liability to purchase the house, for *Netivot*, the buyer is liable given that the agreement is halakhically construed as a monetary obligation. See *Shulhan Arukh Hoshen Mishpat* 60:6. Numerous arbiters adopted the *Netivot's* posture. See PDR 4:279, 6:322; R. Herzog, *Pesakim Ve-Ketavim* 9, Hoshen Mishpat 26. Accordingly, R. Elyashiv argued that one may rely upon *Netivot's* view and extract money based upon this agreement. See R. Cohen, *Emek Ha-Mishpat* 1, p. 67. In other words, a monetary obligation establishes a new halakhic situation, namely that the buyer has assumed a monetary obligation. See R. S. Shkop, *Sha'arei Yosher*,

utilizing the words "I will pay", it remains a debate whether the obligation is effective or not.[38] Nevertheless, some will argue that retracting this agreement allows the community to curse him.[39] Alternatively, if he promises to sell employing the words, "I obligate myself now *(me'akhshav)* to sell" and executes a *kinyan*, the agreement is valid since he is obligating himself now, i.e., he is selling the actual asset now to the other person.[40]

Another example: if he utilizes the term, "I will sell," it means that we are dealing with an obligation to behave in a certain fashion in the future, and according to certain authorities, such an agreement in the form of an obligation would be a *kinyan devarim*.[41] Moreover, if the asset

---

Sha'ar 5, *Perek* 2.

38. Whether this is an example of "a *kinyan eitein*" and it will be effective is subject to controversy. See *Tur, Hoshen Mishpat* 157; *Hiddushei Ha-Ramban Bava Batra* 175b; *Beit Yosef Hoshen Mishpat* 206 in the name of Rashba and *Ittur*; *Beit Yosef Hoshen Mishpat* 245 in the name of Rama, Tashbetz and Ramban; *Shulhan Arukh, Hoshen Mishpat* 245:1-2, Rema, ibid., 157:4.207:13; *Resp. Mahara Sasson* 133; *Resp. Lehem Rav* 147. For a contemporary discussion of this dispute, see PDR 11:131; R. Goldschmidt, *Ezer Mishpat* 26.

Alternatively, some construe this obligation either as a financial obligation which is valid, or they viewed it as an obligation to behave in the future in a certain fashion which is bereft of halakhic significance. See *Tur, Hoshen Mishpat* 157:20, *Beit Yosef*, ibid; *Shulhan Arukh, Hoshen Mishpat* 60:6. See infra n. 40.

39. *Tur* and *Shulhan Arukh, Hoshen Mishpat* 204; *Resp. Toafot Re'em Hoshen Mishpat* 6; *Resp. Beit Yitzhak, Hoshen Mishpat* 41.

40. In effect, to recognize a transaction which will transpire in the future, Halakhah posits the notion of *meshabed nafshei* (he sells himself) via the execution of a *kinyan* and utilizing the word "*me-akhshav*" (retroactive to now) benefit has accrued and the transfer takes place now and it is effective! See *Bava Metzia* 47a; *Bava Batra* 2a, 106b, 173b, 174b; *Tosafot, Ketubot* 54b, s.v. *af al pi*; *Tosafot Yevamot* 93a, s.v. *kenuyah lekha me'akhshav*; *Hiddushei Ha-Ritva Kiddushin* 7a, s.v. *arev*, *Bava Batra* 173b; Rashbam, *Bava Batra* 131a, s.v. *amar leih R. Papa*; *Piskei Ha-Rosh Ketubot* 1; *Shulhan Arukh, Hoshen Mishpat* 206:1, 245:4; *Resp. Ha-Mabit* 2:26; *Resp. Mishpat Tzedek* 3:84; *Resp. Mahara Sasson* 133. See supra n. 25 and B. Lifshitz, "Consideration in Jewish Law" 8 *The Jewish Law Annual* 115 (1989).

Clearly, an obligation exists where the obligor is dutybound to personally accept liability should the object be lost, and he will reimburse the value to the obligee. See supra n. 37. However, as noted by R. Z. N. Goldberg, with a *kinyan eiten* where his assets are not placed as a lien, any execution of *kinyan* will be ineffective and it will be deemed a promise which ought to be fulfilled. See, Goldberg, supra n. 21, 281.

41. *Tosafot Bava Batra* 3a, s.v. *kinyan devarim be'alma hu*; *Tosafot Ketubot* 54a, s.v. af al pi; *Piskei Ha-Rosh, Bava Batra* 1:1, 3; *Shulhan Arukh, Hoshen Mishpat* 245:1; *Resp. Lehem Rav* 193; *Resp. Maharash Ha-Levi, Hoshen Mishpat* 5; *Pithei Hoshen, Kinyanim* 13:20. Cf. *Tur Hoshen Mishpat* 157 in the name of *Yad Ramah*; *Sma, Hoshen Mishpat* 60:18; *Shakh*, ibid. 24 who argue that an agreement of "I obligate myself

is a nonexistent object, even if the agreement is marked by obligation and a *kinyan* has been executed, the agreement is invalid.[42] On the other hand, if he *obligates* himself to sell to another individual an asset which is not present in the world, the agreement is valid, provided that a *kinyan* was executed.[43] In other words, whereas in the context of an obligation dealing with an asset absent from the world the agreement is valid;[44] however, when dealing with an acquisition of an asset(s), we found the agreement to be invalid.[45] Similarly, one may obligate another individual concerning an asset which is not in his possession, provided a *kinyan* was executed.[46]

In short, an agreement of obligation is valid, provided a *kinyan* was executed.[47] Even an obligation established by mercantile custom (*kinyan*

---

with a *kinyan* to give (or sell) to an individual" will be effective. On the other hand, one cannot obligate oneself to transfer ownership of an item due to the fact that that the money that he obligated is still in the buyer's possession and therefore the seller will not receive anything from the buyer during the execution of a *kinyan*. See *Hiddushei Ha-Ramban, Kiddushin* 8b, s.v. *manah*; *Hiddushei Ha-Rashba, Kiddushin* 8b, s.v. *manah*.

Conversely, if the execution of the *kinyan* is to prevent the execution of a specific act, it has no validity and is labeled a *kinyan devarim*. See *Resp. Maharah Ohr Zarua* 251; *Resp. Maharashdam, Hoshen Mishpat* 274; *Resp. Maharam of Lublin* 108; *Resp. Perah Matteh Aharon* 13-14.

Such an obligatory agreement fails to be binding for two reasons. Firstly, in the absence of "committing oneself" (*meshabed nafshei*) *now*, by transforming oneself into a debtor now, one cannot endow a commitment that will occur in the future with halakhic validity. See *Gittin* 13b, 49b; *Bava Kamma* 40b; *Bava Metzia* 94a; *Bava Batra* 175a; *Resp. Ha-Tashbetz* 1:94; *Resp. Ha-Rashba* 2:87, 3:20; *Resp. Ha-Rema* 278; *Resp. Ha-Mabit* 3:31; *Maharashdam*, op. cit.; *Resp. Maharsham* 2:18; this writer's *Rabbinic Authority*, vol. 2, 253-264. Moreover, to effectively undertake an obligation it must be predicated upon something that is tangible, i.e., possessing height, width and depth (*davar she-yesh bo mamash*). See *R. Hai Gaon, Mekah U-Memkar, Sha'ar* 2.

42. *Shulhan Arukh, Hoshen Mishpat* 212:1; *Sma, Hoshen Mishpat* 243:19; *Arukh Ha-Shulhan, Hoshen Mishpat* 60:11; *Resp. Divrei Hayyim Hoshen Mishpat* 31. Cf. *Petah Ha-Bayit* 38 in the name of *Perah Matteh Aharon* who raises a doubt concerning this matter.

43. *Shulhan Arukh, Hoshen Mishpat* 60:1, *Sma*, ad. locum.18; *Shakh*, ad. locum. 26; Rema, *Hoshen Mishpat* 209:4; *Resp. Maharashdam, Hoshen Mishpat* 28, 333; *Resp. Divrei Rivot* 319; *Resp. Panim Meirot* 2:8. Cf. *Resp. Ranah* 1:66 in the name of *Tosafot*; *Resp. Maharshakh* 1:103.

44. *Resp. Ha-Ramban* 7, 9; *Resp. Ha-Rashba* 3:65; *Sefer Ha-Terumot* 43:4; *Sefer Mesharim*, 17; *Resp. Maharbil* 2:37-38; *Shulhan Arukh, Hoshen Mishpat* 210:6; *Resp. Maharashdam, Hoshen Mishpat* 28; *Resp. Maharit 2, Hoshen Mishpat* 69.

45. See supra n. 26.

46. See supra n. 42.

47. Talmud Bavli *Bava Metzia* 94a; *Hiddushei Ha-Ritva*, ibid., s.v. *be'mai*

situmta) is valid.[48] However, even in the absence of the execution of a *kinyan situmta,* failure to fulfill one's promissory obligation, R. Karo rules:[49]

> When one conducts and finalizes commercial deals employing words only, that individual ought to keep his word, though the purchase price has not been taken, or a purchaser's mark on the assets.... whoever withdraws from this type of transaction, whether buyer or seller... is considered a person bereft of faith (*mehusar amanah*). Rabbinical authorities are not disposed towards him...

4. The Status of a Preliminary Agreement and the Modern-Day Contract

Let's provide an example of a transaction which entails *an obligation to sell* which is memorialized in a preliminary agreement (*zikhron devarim*)? The seller obligates himself to sell a house to the buyer. A *zikhron devarim* is executed between the two parties which states that the seller obligates to sell to the buyer and the buyer obligates himself to buy a car from the seller. Subsequently, the seller retracts his offer and the buyer demands from the seller to fulfill his obligation. The emerging question is whether the articulation of the obligation may mandate the seller's compliance to sell or is it to be halakhically construed as a *kinyan devarim* (a verbal promise to do something in the future) such that the preliminary agreement is meaningless? For Ketzot Ha-Hoshen, one is proscribed from obligating a particular asset, rather one must obligate a sum of money since it is a financial obligation residing upon the obligor.[50] On the other hand, Netivot Ha-Mishpat argues that one can obligate oneself to sell an asset and the obligation to sell may reside upon the obligor (a *shi'bud* upon himself) and consequently the obligation that is

bi'devarim in the name of Ra'avad.

48. Talmud Bavli *Bava Metzia* 74a; see sources infra n. 58; *Meishiv Mishpat* 36. If a deed (*shtar*) of obligation was written, the execution of the *kinyan* must be stated at the end of the deed. See *Shulhan Arukh, Hoshen Mishpat* 60:6.

49. *Shulhan Arukh, Hoshen Mishpat* 204:7. See further, *Shakh, Yoreh Deah* 264:7, *Taz,* ad. locum. 5.

50. *Ketzot Ha-Hoshen* 203:2; *Hagahot Imrei Baruch, Hoshen Mishpat* 201, 203; PDR 4:279.

memorialized in the preliminary agreement is effective.[51] Most authorities adopt the approach of Netivot Ha-Mishpat.[52] Consequently, if he obligates himself to sell to another individual an asset which is not present in the world, his obligation to sell would be effective.[53] On the other hand, assuming an authority should rule in accordance with Ketzot Ha-Hoshen, should a *kinyan* be executed after the parties signed the agreement, the seller's intent was to sell the asset.[54] Should the preliminary agreement state, "I will sell to you," the emerging question is whether this verbalization, an example of "*kinyan eitein*" (undertaking an obligation of 'I will give'), is halakhically effective or not. This issue is subject to controversy.[55] Alternatively, it is viewed as an obligation to behave in the future in a certain fashion which is bereft of halakhic significance.[56]

Moreover, an obligation memorialized in a modern-day contract, albeit an agreement which isn't drafted in halakhic terminology, nonetheless has been recognized as a *kinyan situmta* (a legal undertaking recognized by mercantile custom) which either is grounded in practice (*minhag*) or the law of the land (*dina de'malkhuta dina*).[57] In other words, *kinyan situmta* not only applies to modes of transferring ownership.

---

51. *Netivot Ha-Mishpat* 203:6.

52. *Imrei Binah, Dinei Halva'ah* 51.

53. *Shulhan Arukh, Hoshen Mishpat* 60:6; *Sma*, ibid. 18.

54. Rashi *Ketubot* 83a; Rashbam *Bava Batra* 42b-43a; *Resp. Ha-Rashba* 2:301; *Beit Yosef, Hoshen Mishpat* 195:20; *Shulhan Arukh, Hoshen Mishpat* 60:6; Rema, *Hoshen Mishpat* 212:1.

55. See supra n. 38.

56. See supra n. 38.

57. Mordekhai, *Shabbat* 472-473 in the name of Rabbi Yehiel of Paris and Maharam; *Resp. Ha-Rivash* 105, 128, 345; *Resp. Ha-Rashba* 2:268; *Resp. Maharam of Rothenberg*, Prague ed. 537; *Piskei Ha-Rosh Bava Metzia* 5:72; *Tur, Hoshen Mishpat* 42, 201:3; *Shulhan Arukh, Hoshen Mishpat* 42:15, 201:1-2; Rema, *Hoshen Mishpat* 61:5; *Yam shel Shlomo, Bava Kamma* 5:37; *Resp. Maharashdam Hoshen Mishpat* 380; *Ketzot Ha-Hoshen* 126:3; *Resp. Divrei Malkiel* 4:139; *Resp. Tzemah Tzedek Hoshen Mishpat* 201:1; *Resp. Beit Yehudah*, vol. 1, 23; PDR 3:368-369, 4:198; *Resp. Tzitz Eliezer* 16:53.

For recognition due to the governing civil law, see *Resp. Shoeil U-Meishiv, Mahadura Kama*, 1:18 in the name of Maharshal.

Clearly, there are instances where custom will not serve as a medium to validate a particular transaction. This matter is beyond the scope of our presentation. See *Netivot Ha-Mishpat* 201:1; *Sma, Hoshen Mishpat* 201:4; *Erekh Lehem Hoshen Mishpat* 201:1.

Some argue that it is a derivative of an act of transfer by dint of a nominal exchange (*kinyan halifin*) See *Resp. Dvar Avraham* 1:1 (3); *Hokhmat Shlomo, Shulhan Arukh, Hoshen Mishpat* 123 (end); *Hiddushei Maharit, Kiddushin* on Rif 3:1.

Well over two dozen *aharonim* (later authorities) and contemporary decisors recognize the efficacy of a modern day contract to be an example of the execution of a *kinyan* (*situmta*).[58] Halakhic validity of the contract is contingent upon the document being recognized by civil law.[59] And even if the contract focuses upon a matter which is not in this world (*davar she'lo ba le'olam*), the contract would be valid.[60]

---

58. *Resp. Maharil, Pesakim* 126; *Resp. Maharashdam, Hoshen Mishpat* 380; *Resp. Maharshakh* 3:8; *Resp. Hatam Sofer, Hoshen Mishpat* 66; *Resp. Maharsham* 5:25, 35; *Resp. Maharshag* 3:113. For additional responsa see Ron Kleinmann, *Methods of Acquisition and Commercial Customs in Jewish Law*, (Hebrew), Keterpress, 2013, 257-258.

Furthermore, a *kinyan situmta* establishes a contractual obligation such as a duty to sell. See *Meshoveiv Netivot* 60:10; *Resp. Mishpatekha Le-Ya'akov* 2:9; I. Warhaftig, *Ha-Hit'hayevut*, Jerusalem: 2001, 188. The modern-day contract entails a *halakhic obligation* between the buyer and seller to execute a sales transaction rather than a transfer of actual ownership between the two parties. See S. Rosenberg, "The preparing of contracts," (Hebrew), *Ha-Yashar Ve-ha Tov*, 36, 39-40 (5769). Consequently, though halakhically the parties are obligated to execute a sale, nevertheless, the ownership has only been transferred *halakhically* via the contract based upon "the law of the land" rather than the halakhah of obligations. See supra, text accompanying n. 59. Others argues that the effectiveness of the contract is based upon custom *(minhag)*. See *Resp. Ha-Rivash* 105; *Hagahot Imrei Barukh, Shulhan Arukh Hoshen Mishpat* 201, 203.

59. *Netivot Ha-Mishpat* 201 in the name of *Maharshal; Resp. Mishpatekha Le-Ya'akov* 3:5 (4); PDR 12:279, 291, 18:108, 112.

Consequently, though among the requirements is that the paper and the ink of the agreement (the *shtar kinyan)* belong to the seller and the agreement must be written on parchment that can't be erased (see *Ketzot Ha-Hoshen* 191:1 and *Shulhan Arukh, Hoshen Mishpat* 42:1), nonetheless given that the modern-day contract is halakhically valid as a *situmta* which is enforceable by civil law, these requirements may be foregone.

Furthermore, the execution of a credit card transaction entails payment for an item rather than being a halakhic avenue undertaken by the purchaser to receive title of the item. Consequently, this type of transaction is not an example of a *kinyan situmta*. Moreover, even though he is obligated to pay money in the credit card transaction, however, the seller never received any money at the time of the execution of the sale. See *Hiddushei Ha-Ramban, Kiddushin* 8b, s.v. *manah*; *Hiddushei Ha-Rashba, Kiddushin* 8b, s.v. *manah*. Cf. *Hiddushei Ha-Ritva, Kiddushin* 8b, s.v. *amar Raba; Resp. Ohela Shel Torah*, 479; Ya'akov Hildesheim, *The Laws of Kinyan in Modern Business* (Hebrew), Jerusalem: 5778, 84, 98-99. According to this view, though legally in the U.S. one cannot acquire an item via a credit card, nonetheless since it is customary to acquire via a credit card therefore the sale has validity as a *kinyan situmta*. For another solution, see Kleinmann, supra n. 58, 248, n.10.

60. *Mordekhai, Shabbat* 472-473 in the name of Maharam; *Resp. Ha-Rosh* 12:3, 13:20; *Pithei Teshuva Hoshen Mishpat* 201:2 in the name of *Hatam Sofer Hoshen Mishpat* 66; *Resp. Maharshal* 36; *Resp. Divrei Hayyim, Hoshen Mishpat* 2:26; *Resp.*

In contrast to the validity of a preliminary agreement and a modern-day contract being recognized as an example of *kinyan situmta*,[61] will the giving of a deposit without the signing of a document be considered an example of *kinyan situmta*? The reply to this question depends up whether the community has adopted such a practice. If the practice exists, then submitting a deposit will be viewed as an example of a *kinyan situmta*.[62] On the other hand, in the absence of such a custom, a deposit is not deemed an example of *kinyan situmta*.[63]

5. Promise-keeping Based Upon Induced Reliance

In Halakhah, is there an additional ground for promise-keeping based upon the argument that the promisor caused harm by induced reliance which entails trust,[64] and that is what creates the binding nature of the promise? Is the violation of a reliance-based duty actionable in a *beit din* (i.e., a tort obligation) or is it akin to a promissory obligation, a

---

Maharsham 1:47; *Resp. Maharam Schick* 41. Compare Mordekhai, ibid., in the name of Rabbi Yehiel of Paris; *Resp. Ha-Ridvaz* 1:278; *Yam shel Shlomo, Bava Kamma* 8:60; *Ketzot Ha-Hoshen* 201:1; *Resp. Rabbi Akiva Eiger, Mahadura Kamma* 134. For contemporary arbiters and additional later authorities who debate this point, see *Resp. Yabia Omer* 9, *Even Ha-Ezer* 27:11; PDR 3:368, 5:264; *Resp. Kovetz Teshuvot* 1:199,209. According to the majority of authorities, *kinyan situmta* is effective in a matter of *davar she'lo ba le'olam*. See *Resp. Beit Yitzhak, Hoshen Mishpat* 60.

61. However, according to Rabbi Z. Nechemia Goldberg, since the signing of a *zikhron devarim* is in order to obligate the seller or buyer in civil court, the net result is that the preliminary agreement is not executed due to the will of merchants but rather to enforce it in civil court. Therefore, a *zikhron devarim* is not a *kinyan situmta* on a biblical level. See Rabbi Z.N. Goldberg, supra n. 21, 290

Moreover, given that a contract is executed after the writing of a preliminary agreement, consequently the sale is consummated upon the writing of the contract. See *Taz, Even Ha-Ezer* 50:12, *Beit Shmuel*, ad. locum. 15; *Resp. Rabbi Akiva Eiger, Tinyana* 75. Compare *Beit Shmuel, Kuntres Aharon Even Ha-Ezer* 12; *Resp. Noda Be-Yehudah, Mahadura Tinyana, Yoreh Deah* 148; *Tiv Kiddushin* 50:17; *Otzar Ha-Poskim, Even Ha-Ezer* 50:44 (3).

However, if the preliminary agreement is accompanied by a clause that it was executed in the presence of a respected *beit din (beit din hashuv)* and from now (*me'akhshav*), even *Taz* will validate the agreement. See *Resp. Maharsham* 3:127.

62. *Resp. Maharsham* 5:37; *Resp. Rabbi Akiva Eiger, Mahadura Kamma* 134; *Resp. Avnei Nezer Yoreh Deah* 405:11.

63. *Resp. Mayim Hayim*, vol. 2, *Hoshen Mishpat* 5; *Resp. Maharam Schick Hoshen Mishpat* 61.

64. Talmud Bavli *Kiddushin* 59a; *Bava Metzia* 16a.

toothless tiger, providing no *beit din* relief? Responding to our question, the Talmud instructs us:[65]

> If someone gives money to his friend to serve as his agent to go and purchase wine for him during the season while the price was low. And he was negligent and failed to buy it, the law is that he has to pay him wine according to the low price....

Here, the promisee relied on the promisor and incurred losses because he is liable for failing to keep his commitment (his *hit'hayevut*) to purchase the wine. Despite the absence of the execution of a *kinyan,* the Talmud concludes that the promisor is liable to compensate for the harm suffered. When he accepted the assignment, the promisor agreed that the promise would be reimbursed for damages, including profit loss.[66]

The dominant approach emerging from this Talmudic passage is that compensation resulting from a breach of an induced-reliance obligation is because the promisor explicitly agreed at the time the agreement was executed to reimburse the promisee for such loss resulting from failure to consummate the wine purchase.[67] In other words, in the absence of said agreement in the above situation mentioned in the Talmud, any harm suffered from reliance would be unrecoverable. Reliance of the promisee upon the oral commitment of the promisor does not engender monetary liability.[68]

In short, one ought to keep a promise regardless of whether it induces reliance or not. To state it differently, in reneging of a promise, the promisee is frequently harmed because he relied on the fulfillment of the promise. Concerning compliance with the promise, however, harm is irrelevant. One is halakhically-morally obliged to fulfill the promise qua promise, i.e. the religious duty of promise-keeping regardless of whether the promisee has detrimentally relied on the promise or not.

65. Talmud Bavli *Bava Metzia* 73b.

66. Rabbeinu Tam, *Bava Metzia* 74a; *Piskei Ha-Rosh Bava Metzia* 9:4, 7; *Hiddushei Ha-Ramban, Bava Metzia* 104a; Mordekhai, *Bava Kamma* 9:114-115; *Shulhan Arukh, Hoshen Mishpat* 328:2; *Resp. Maharash Enzel* 6:62; *Resp. Maharashakh* 1:167.

67. *Hiddushei Ha-Ritva, Bava Metzia* 73b in the name of Ri; *Hiddushei Ha-Rashba*, ibid.; Ran, ibid.; *Nimmukei Yosef*, ibid.

68. *Hiddushei Ha-Rashba, Bava Metzia* 73b; *Piskei Ha-Rosh, Bava Metzia* 5:69; *Netivot Ha-Mishpat (Biurim), Hoshen Mishpat* 176:31, 183:1; *Resp. Hatam Sofer, Hoshen Mishpat* 168; *Hazon Ish, Bava Kamma* 22:1; *Mishpat Shalom, Hoshen Mishpat* 176:4.

The binding nature of the promise is independent and free-standing, separate from the induced-reliance duty.

However, in pursuance to R. Aaron b. Joseph ha-Levi (known by the acronym: Ra'ah),[69] even in the absence of execution of a *kinyan*, promissory reliance will engender monetary liability even if the promisor did not agree to assume liability. As *Ra'ah* observes:

> Here (Bava Metzia 73b), even though the agent did not contractually agree to assume liability [for failure to fulfill his promise], since the principal gave him money with which to purchase merchandise, and the principal would have either purchased it himself or arranged for another to do so had not the agent promised to do so, and the principal relied upon him and gave him the money based upon the reliance; for that reason the agent is liable to pay the loss caused by the reliance on his promise.

His position consists of four propositions. Firstly, one does not require an agreement that explicitly stipulates that consequential damages are recoverable. Secondly, in the absence of such an agreement of obligation, by giving money to the agent to effectuate a wine purchase at a place where the market price was lower than others give, the promisee relied upon the promisor's compliance. The third proposition is that the words of the promisor serve as the medium of inducing reliance by the promisee.

Finally, it is the benefit (*be-hahi hana'ah*) created by the reliance that establishes a surety relationship (*arevut)* between the two individuals rather than the norm of promise-keeping that endows validity to the agreement.[70] Just as a guarantor's obligation to compensate is created

69. Though numerous authorities identify the authorship of this view with Ritva, in fact Ritva, *Hiddushei Ha-Ritva Ha-Hadashim, Bava Metzia* 73b is citing Ra'ah, his teacher. See I. Brand, "Ha-Nosei Ve-Noten Bi'Devarim: Between Contractual Obligation and Tortuous Reliance," (Hebrew) 24 *Mehkarei Mishpat* 5, nn. 107, 122-124 (2008).

For an examination of Ra'ah's position, see this writer's "The Theory of Efficient Breach: A Jewish Law Perspective" in ed. Aaron Levine, *Judaism and Economics*, pp. 347-348, Oxford University Press: 2010.

70. In other words, the duty of the guarantor is established due to the benefit derived from trust. See *Bava Batra* 173b; *Hiddushei Ha-Ramban, Ketubot* 101b; *Resp. Maharik, shoresh* 181; *Ohr Zarua, Bava Batra* 244; *Resp. Imrei Yosher* 2:55; *Resp. Shoeil U-Meishiv, Mahadura Kamma, Helek* 1, 163; *Bi'ur Ha-Gra, Hoshen Mishpat* 209:32.

Alternatively, the benefit is a form of *kinyan*, or it substitutes for another *kinyan*.

by the trust that is engendered by the creditor's conviction that he will comply with his promise and the guarantor will compensate him in case the borrower defaults on his loan, should an individual be negligent and fail to purchase the wine at a lower price for another person as promised, akin to a guarantor (*arev*), he is liable to indemnify him for any ensuing loss for violating a reliance-induced duty[71] as well as transgressing a promissory obligation.[72] In other words, the *arev's* obligation to pay is in exchange for the benefit of trust enjoyed by the creditor that in the event that the debtor cannot remit the monies, the *arev* will pay the debt to the creditor.[73] In modern Rabbinic Hebrew, this duty is known as "*hit'hayevut mi'din arev*," a person who requests of another to take his own money and transfer it to a third party, thereby obligating himself as a guarantor to pay said money.[74]

Though Ra'ah's posture is unacceptable for many *Rishonim* (early authorities),[75] there are authorities who endorse his approach in other contexts.[76] For example, the liability of an unpaid bailee (a *shomer hinnam*) to the owner for proven negligence is due to the owner's trust that the bailee (the promisor) will guard his object.[77] Another example is a person who verbally hires another individual for employment, and prior to beginning work he retracts the offer; given that there was work available elsewhere, he is obligated to pay the amount he promised.[78] As Nahmanides elucidates:[79]

See *Hiddushei Ha-Ramban Kiddushin* 7a; *Hiddushei Ha-Ritva, Kiddushin* 7a; R. Y.E. Spektor, *Nahal Yitzhak, Hoshen Mishpat* 40.

71. A breach of a reliance-induced obligation involves the violation of "the remnant of Israel shall do no wrong nor speak falsehood." See Or Zarua, *Resp. Ohr Zarua* 1:748; *Piskei Ha-Rosh, Hullin* 3:34.

72. See supra nn. 21 and 30.

73. *Hiddushei Ha-Rashba, Kiddushin* 6b; Mordekhai, *Bava Metzia* 370 in the name of Maharam; *Resp. Shoeil U-Meishiv, Mahadura* 2, *Helek* 1, 70.

74. For the scope of *hit'hayevut mi'din arev*, see B. Kahane, *Guarantee Law* (Hebrew), Jerusalem: 1991, pp. 78-90.

75. *Hiddushei Ha-Rashba, Bava Metzia* 73b, s.v. *meshalem*; *Piskei Ha-Rosh, Bava Metzia* 5:69; Mordekhai, *Bava Kamma* 9:114-115; *Hiddushei Ha-Ran, Bava Metzia* 73b, s.v. *meshalem*.

76. Mordekhai, *Bava Metzia* 370, in the name of Maharam, 3:707; *Resp. Maharik, shoresh* 181; *Resp. Maharashdam, Hoshen Mishpat* 380; *Beit Yosef, Hoshen Mishpat* 207; Rema, *Hoshen Mishpat* 14:5; *Resp. Avnei Nezer, Even Ha-Ezer* 207.

77. *Resp. Ha-Ritva* 199; *Resp. Shoeil U-Meishiv, Mahadura* 4, *Helek* 3, 143; *Erekh Shai, Hoshen Mishpat* 291:5; *Mahaneh Ephraim, Hilk. Arev* 1.

78. Talmud Bavli *Bava Metzia* 76b.

79. *Hiddushei Ha-Ramban, Bava Metzia*, ibid.

> Even though...here we are dealing with words, we are obligated to pay... since he relied upon him...

However, other authorities argue that if the promise relies upon the promisor's explicit words in a situation of incurring lost profits (*meni'at revah),* he is exempt from paying.[80]

On the one hand, one may view *arevut* as an example of undertaking an obligation (*hit'hayevut*) as a guarantor to pay money to a creditor upon default of a loan, the benefit (*be-hahi hana'ah*) created by the reliance establishing a surety relationship (*arevut)* between the two individuals.[81] On the other hand, others such as Ra'ah view the loan default as a situation where the guarantor caused a loss to the creditor and therefore the guarantor is dutybound based upon the halakhah of torts (*nezikin*) to reimburse the creditor for his loss.[82] To state it differently, the focus is upon the promisor who is obligated to pay his fellow man for harm incurred rather than the promise created by agreement of obligation, namely *arevut,* which is grounded in induced reliance.

The invoking of the halakhah of torts is not limited to the matter of *arevut* but extends itself to a retraction of a promise. For example, relying upon Maharam of Rothenberg, *Rema* rules:[83]

> If someone tells his friend that they should adjudicate in another place, and he responded: "Go there and I will follow you," and he proceeded there and the second one did not follow him – he must pay him all his expenses.

And Rema's invoking of the halakhah of torts is predicated upon the fact that the promisee relied upon his promise. As such, various well-respected authorities cite Rema's ruling in order to emphasize the reliance which emerged from the person's explicit promise to adjudicate in a certain place. For example, if the time for a wedding was finalized and

80. *Netivot Ha-Mishpat* 333:3; *Resp. Maharash* 4:100; *Resp. Divrei Malkiel* 5:125.

81. Talmud Bavli *Bava Batra* 174b; *Kiddushin* 7a; *Mishneh Torah, Hilk. Mekhirah* 11:15; *Bah, Hoshen Mishpat* 129:3; *Shakh, Hoshen Mishpat* 40:7; *Mahaneh Ephraim, Arevut* 1; *Resp. Avodat Ha-Gershuni* 117; *Resp. Havot Yair* 128; *Dibrot Moshe, Bava Metzia* 2, pp. 486-487; *Bava Batra* 173b.

82. *Nimmukei Yosef, Bava Batra* 81a; *Mirkevet Ha-Mishneh* on *Rambam, Hilk. Malveh Ve-Loveh* 25:7.

83. Mordekhai, *Sanhedrin* 707 in the name of Maharam; *Rema, Hoshen Mishpat,* supra n. 77.

the groom failed to appear, the groom is liable to pay for the wedding expenses.[84] Similarly, if a couple set a date for proceeding to execute a *get* and the wife came from afar to accept the *get* and the husband didn't appear, the arbiter concludes that the husband is responsible to pay for his wife's outlay of expenses.[85]

In effect, "Go there and I will follow you" is conceptually identical to the Talmudic case of "showing a dinar to a money-changer" who proffers advice and is liable for any ensuing damages should his advice be acted upon.[86] As the Talmud teaches us:[87]

> If one shows a dinar to a money-changer (in order to determine whether it is good so that he may accept it, and the money changer says it is good), but it turns out to be bad – one *baraita* states that if he is an expert, he is absolved from liability, while if he is a layman, he is liable. However, another *baraita* states he is liable regardless of whether he is an expert or a layman.

Post-Talmudic decisors have expounded upon various indicators which demonstrate the client's reliance upon the investor's advice. One suggestion is that the reliance factor is satisfied if the client explicitly states that he is relying upon the investment advice.[88] Another approach is to calibrate the reliance factor based upon the advisor's financial expertise. The greater the degree of expertise, the greater the presumption that the customer will rely upon his advice. Consequently, a financial planner who earned a license in financial planning may be classified as an expert (a *mumheh*)[89] and be exempt from liability unless there was negligent misrepresentation.[90]

---

84. *Pithei Teshuvah, Hoshen Mishpat* 14:15 in the name of *Resp. Havot Yair* 168.

85. *Resp. Nodah Be-Yehudah, Mahadurah Tinyana, Even Ha-Ezer* 90.

86. *Be'air Eliyahu* 14:31. Alternatively, the obligation of compensation is grounded in the concept of indirect cause (*garmi*) in accordance with Ritzva's posture (*Tosafot, Bava Batra* 22b) that this is a frequent loss. See *Bi'ur Ha-Gra, Hoshen Mishpat* 14:30-31. Pursuant to *Sma, Hoshen Mishpat* 386:2, *Rema, Hoshen Mishpat* 386:2 endorsed Ritzva's position and in effect explains *Rema, Hoshen Mishpat*, supra n. 76.

87. Talmud Bavli *Bava Kamma* 99b.

88. *Resp. Ha-Tashbetz* 2:174.

89. The burden of proof to demonstrate a planner's expertise lies with the planner. See *Mishneh Torah, Hilk. Sekhirut* 10:5; *Resp. Beit Ha-Levi* 3:20 (2).

90. *Netivot Ha-Mishpat Hoshen Mishpat* 306:12; *Shakh, Hoshen Mishpat* 306:12. Cf Maharam Barukh who argues that an expression of reliance will trump the investor's advice. See *Shakh*, ibid. and this writer's "The Tort of Negligent

Others contend that apparent reliance which may be distilled from the surrounding circumstances of the situation rather than an explicit reliance statement suffices to engender liability.[91] Finally, some maintain that the determining factor is "the pecuniary interest." In other words, if the investment advisor receives money for his advice, he becomes liable.[92] According to numerous authorities, this is a relevant yardstick to establish reliance only regarding an expert advisor.[93]

In short, there are four criteria for assessing the reliance factor involving proffering investment advice and thus creating a fiduciary relationship between the parties: an explicit expression of reliance, apparent reliance based upon the circumstances, the expertise of the advisor and payment to the advisor for his services.

This posture of viewing a breach of a promise and its damages as tortuous (*hezek*) extends itself to the issue of whether there is liability for damages when a marital engagement is broken. As *Maimonides* states:[94]

> My teachers have ruled that if it is the custom of the land that each man (upon betrothal – *kiddushin*) should make a feast for his friends... and he follows the custom of all [local] people [in holding such a feast] and then she retracts, she must refund his expenses, because she has caused him to spend his money; and whoever causes another to lose money must pay for it.

In a critical annotation, *Ra'avad* states:[95]

> My teachers have ruled that if it is the custom of the land... I do not concur with his teachers regarding this matter. This indirect causation is akin to seeds in the garden that did not grow, concerning which one pays (only) the expenses. The principle of the matter (applicable here) is: (in the case of) monetary loss indirectly caused by the money's owner, even though someone caused him (to incur the loss), that person is exempt from liability.

Misrepresentation of Investment Planning: A Comparative Analysis," 19 *The Jewish Law Annual* 141 (2011).

91. *Shulhan Arukh Hoshen Mishpat* 306:6, Rema, ibid.

92. *Arukh Ha-Shulhan Hoshen Mishpat* 306:13. See further, this writer's *Rabbinic Authority*, vol. 2, 117-147.

93. *Piskei Ha-Rosh Bava Kamma* 9:16.

94. *Mishneh Torah, Hilk. Zekhiyah U-Matanah* 6:24.

95. Ibid.

In other words, whereas according to Maimonides, breach of a promise to marriage is actionable, according to Ra'avad, damages are not recoverable.[96] Though a minority of decisors concur with Ra'avad's posture, most authorities agree with Maimonides.[97]

In conclusion, *the Talmud* teaches us:[98]

> Raba stated: When a man enters for judgment (in the next world), he is asked: Did you deal faithfully (honestly), did you allocate time for learning, did you engage in procreation, did you hope for salvation, did you engage (in the acquisition of) knowledge, did you understand one thing from another?

In sum, on the one hand, an obligation between two parties to transfer ownership in the future is characterized by the Talmud as a *kinyan devarim* and is understood by the decisors as an example of the ineffectiveness of a *kinyan* in the absence of *davar she'yesh bo mamash.*[99] On the other hand, a person may *obligate* himself monetarily and will consequently be required to pay.[100] In other words, the monetary duty isn't a promise to execute a future action but rather a change of the legal condition now, i.e., from this moment there is a monetary obligation upon the obligor to the obligee.[101] Furthermore, if an individual

96. This interpretation of the dispute is predicated upon two assumptions. First, though the controversy focuses on reimbursement for the outlaying of a wedding feast, the stated positions relate to compensation for all engagement and wedding-related expenses. Secondly, though this dispute centers on a betrothed woman, who violates her *kiddushin,* clearly the controversy extends to situations where an engaged man or woman breaks the engagement known as *shiddukhin.* For this explicit and sometimes implicit understanding of this difference of opinion, see *Resp. Ha-Tashbetz* 2:166; *Resp. Ha-Ridbaz* 1:329 and 4:234; *Resp. Mahari Zahalon* 262.

97. *Shulhan Arukh, Even Ha-Ezer* 50:3. For a discussion of whether reliance in the law of obligations may serve as grounds for recovery rather than a ground for relief in accordance with the law of torts, see this writer's "Breach of a Promise to Marry," 17 *The Jewish Law Annual* 267, 274-277, 2007, reprinted in this writer's *Rabbinic Authority,* vol. 4, 62-74.

98. Talmud Bavli *Shabbat* 31a.

99. Supra n. 32. See also Sma, *Shulhan Arukh, Hoshen Mishpat* 157:5; *Netivot Ha-Mishpat, Hoshen Mishpat* 157:4. For alternative understandings as to why an obligation to act in a certain fashion is unenforceable, see this writer's *Rabbinic Authority,* vol. 4, 65, note 18.

100. *Mishneh Torah, Hilk. Mekhirah* 11:15; *Shulhan Arukh, Hoshen Mishpat* 60:6.

101. Sha'arei *Yosher, Sha'ar* 5, Perek 2. For further implications of our understanding, see D. Bass, *Keter,* vol. 1, 44-46, 1996.

promises something which is intangible and therefore is not subject to the execution of a *kinyan,* such as a wife who promises to invite a guest to the house, or a couple that agrees that each will be responsible to cook for the household, failure to comply with one's promise entails untrustworthiness and therefore is a violation of Halakhah.[102]

Finally, if a broker promises to his client, prior to commencing with his negotiation, an amount of compensation which exceeds the prevailing practice, there is an ongoing debate as to whether he must pay the entire amount that was promised. Some say that the entire fee must be paid, provided it was clear at the time of undertaking the obligation (where a *kinyan* was not executed) there was no intent to joke with him.[103] Others demur and argue that he was joking (*hashatah*) and therefore, one must compensate only the prevailing customary amount.[104] In fact, even if an individual performs a benefit for another without being asked; the beneficiary must pay.[105]

The common denominator of this array of questions asked in heaven is directed at the duty of a member of the covenantal Jewish community to pursue the improvement of the world (*tikkun olam*). The issue of engaging with integrity is the first question. Clearly, Raba is teaching us that the pursuit of honesty is of primary importance.[106] Our foregoing is a brief presentation of the varying avenues of how one engages with honesty in general, and validating our promises in particular, via the halakhot of transferring ownership as well as the halakhot of obligations, torts and the norms of custom.

Whether an obligation to sell an item or for an employee or independent contractor to engage in work is deemed a *kinyan devarim,* we leave as an open question.

102. *Beit Yosef, Yoreh Deah* 264 in the name of Maharam; *Shulhan Arukh, Yoreh Deah* 264:1; *Resp. Hatam Sofer, Yoreh Deah* 246; *Resp. Iggerot Moshe, Yoreh Deah* 1:58.

103. *Resp. Hikrei Lev, Hoshen Mishpat* 135.

104. *Mordekhai, Bava Kamma* 10:172 in the name of R. Simha; *Resp. Ha-Tashbetz* 3:20; *Resp. Maharashdam Even Ha-Ezer* 212; *Resp. Bah* 28; *Resp. Ha-Mabit* 2:56; *Resp. Imrei Yosher* 1:97. Cf. *Resp. Ha-Rosh* 64:3, 105:2; Rema, *Hoshen Mishpat* 246:17 (Cf. Rema, *Hoshen Mishpat* 363:10); *Resp. Ha-Rema* 86; *Resp. Beit Yitzhak, Hoshen Mishpat* 76.

105. *Hiddushei Ha-Rashba, Nedarim* 33b; *Responsa Ha-Rashba* 4:125; *Hiddushei Ha-Ran, Ketubot* 107b; *Resp. Ha-Rema, Hoshen Mishpat* 264; *Resp. Maharam Alsheikh* 70 in the name of many arbiters; *Resp. Terumat Ha-Deshen* 317; *Resp. Mahari Ha-Levi* 103; *Resp. Doveiv Mesharim* 1:42.

106. *Bah, Tur Orah Hayyim* 155. Compare the sequence of questions in *Sanhedrin* 7a; *Tosafot Sanhedrin,* ad. locum, s.v. *ela; Mishneh Torah, Hilk. Talmud Torah* 3:5; *Tur Orah Hayyim* 155-156; *Beit Yosef, Tur Orah Hayyim* 155.

Chapter 8

Collaborative Reproduction: Unscrambling the Conundrum of Legal and Halakhic Parentage

An American Legal View

In the opening lines of her book *Science at the Bar,* Sheila Jasanoff, Pforzheimer Professor of Science and Technology Studies at Harvard University, writes:[1]

> American political culture derives its distinctive flavor as much from faith in scientific and technological progress as from a commitment—some might even say an addiction—to resolving social conflicts through law. These powerful cultural predilections have brought the institutions of science and technology into turbulent confrontations with the legal system.... discoveries in the biological sciences have revolutionized our ability to manipulate the basic processes of life so as to fight infertility, aging, hunger and disease.

The intersection of science and law in general, and the advent of reproductive technology beginning in the late 1970s in particular, have wreaked havoc on the legal notions of parenthood.

The new noncoital reproduction options—traditional surrogacy and gestational surrogacy—raise the issue of determining legal parentage. The most common surrogacy arrangement pertains to an infertile couple, often due to the wife's infertility. In order for such a couple to have a child who is genetically related to one of them, the couple seeks the services of another woman, known as a surrogate mother. The surrogate agrees to conceive a child through artificial insemination of the

1. Sheila Jasanoff, *Science at the Bar: Law, Science & Technology in America,* Cambridge, 1995, 1-2.

husband's sperm and carry the child to term. Upon birth, the surrogate agrees to relinquish her parental rights and transfer custody of the child to the father. In most cases, a formal adoption of the child by the wife is required. A second type of arrangement entailing embryo transfer, which may be utilized in cases where a woman is fertile but is unable to carry a child to term. In this situation, the father and genetic mother may conceive an embryo through in vitro fertilization (hereinafter: IVF) and then have it implanted in the surrogate's womb. The surrogate would carry and give birth to the child. In this situation, the surrogate bears a gestational relationship to the child. Whereas in the traditional surrogacy arrangement, the surrogate is using her egg and another man's sperm, in the gestational surrogacy pattern, the surrogate carries the child to term using the wife's egg and husband's sperm implanted in her uterus. In this arrangement, the egg donor, i.e., the wife, and the genetically related father intend to raise a child who enjoys a genetic and gestational bond with another woman, i.e., the surrogate. In the traditional surrogacy scenario, the genetically related father and the wife who is genetically and gestationally unrelated to the child intend to raise a child who enjoys a gestational tie with the surrogate. In either of these arrangements, the contracting couple agrees to pay a fee to the surrogate and reimburse her for any medical expenses associated with the pregnancy. When both the genetic and gestational parents desire custody of the child, how should motherhood and fatherhood be defined? The fragmentation of biological maternity by artificial insemination and IVF obliges one to take a Solomonic approach, asking in an either/ or fashion: Which mother is the child's mother? Is it the genetic, gestational, or the unrelated intending mother? Which father is the child's father? Is it the sperm donor, the unrelated intending father, or the surrogate's husband? Does the law simultaneously recognize more than two individuals as parents of the child?

This essay attempts to arrive at the differing conceptions of parenthood emerging from American law that settle claims to parentage posed by the genetic parents, the gestational surrogate of the child, and the intended parents. Though some jurisdictions have promulgated statutory schemes,[2] most have not, leaving courts to resolve these surrogacy arrangements by following common law presumptions, by identifying genetic and gestational bonds, or by invoking contract principles or the

2. See e.g., ARK. CODE ANN. SEC. 9-10-201 (1998); N.H. REV. STAT. SEC. 168-B:23 (1994); UTAH CODE ANN. SEC. 76-7-204 (Michie 1995) & WIS. STAT. SEC.69.14 (1) (h) (West 1999).

child's best interests standard. The varying judicial responses will be viewed within the context of the voluminous legal scholarship which has sought rules to determine legal parenthood. This article then evaluates a number of definitional standards of the term "parent" in adoption and collaborative-reproduction arrangements between Jews as suggested by contemporary discussions in Jewish law.

The most famous case involving traditional surrogacy is the New Jersey Superior Court[3] and New Jersey Supreme Court[4] opinions In re Baby M. The case involved a surrogate arrangement entered into between William Stern, the biological father, and Mary Beth Whitehead, a gestational host. Mr. Stern and his wife contracted with Mrs. Whitehead, wife of Richard Whitehead and mother of two children, to donate her egg, have it fertilized in vitro with Mr. Stern's sperm, carry the child to term, and relinquish her rights upon birth. In return, the Sterns agreed to pay her $10,000 and to assume all her medical expenses. Upon birth, the surrogate changed her mind, absconded to Florida with the child, and sued for maternity. After apprehending the Whiteheads, the Sterns commenced with a custody claim in New Jersey family court requesting the enforcement of the preconception surrogacy agreement. The opinion of Judge Sorkow, before whom the case was heard in the New Jersey Superior Court, proceeded from the assumption that there were two competing families offering dual-parent care, and two "mothers" prepared to accept responsibility for the child. The court began by stating:[5]

> Justice, our desired objective, to the child and the mother, to the child and the father, cannot be obtained for both parents. The court will seek to achieve justice for the child. This court's fact finding and application of relevant law must mitigate against the heartfelt desires of one or the other of the natural parents.

In short, the court initially recognized that the claims of Mr. Stern and Mrs. Whitehead were based on biological grounds rather than legal entitlement. Pursuant to statute N.J.S.A. 9:17–44, given Mr. Whitehead's refusal to consent to the artificial insemination of his wife, paternity was accorded to Mr. Stern, the sperm donor, who was genetically related to the child. Although maternity can be severed into various components, apart from her stated intent in the surrogacy contract to relinquish

3. 217 N.J. SUPER 313, 525 A. 2D 1128 (1987).
4. 109 N.J. 396, 537 A. 2D 1227 (1988).
5. Baby M, supra n. 3, at 1132.

parental rights upon the child's birth, Mrs. Whitehead, by all of the other criteria that aid in determining parenthood, appears to be the one. She is genetically and gestationally related to the child; she expressed a post-birth intention to serve as a mother, and her reluctance to surrender her child would lead the court to conclude that she is a mother in fact, if not in law.

Yet the court depicts Mrs. Whitehead in the following manner:[6]

> Mrs. Whitehead has been found too enmeshed with the infant child and unable to separate her own needs from those of the child. She tends to smother the child with her presence even to the exclusion of access by her other two children. She does not have the ability to subordinate herself to the needs of this child. The court is satisfied that... Mrs. Whitehead is manipulative, impulsive, and exploitive.

In the words of one legal commentator,[7] the court construed her maternalistic feelings as having "run amok." As evidence for her maternal unfitness vis-à-vis her child, the court referred to her breach of the preconception agreement.[8] Despite the surrogate's gestational bond and post-birth intent to raise the child, the court invoked the legal standard of "the best interests of the child" and concluded that she was unfit to raise this child.[9] Consequently, all of her parental rights were terminated and permanent custody was awarded to Mr. Stern and mandated adoption by Mrs. Stern, who were lauded as "credible, sincere and truthful people."[10] Though the court treated the dispute as a custody battle between a father and mother, employing the standard of the child's best interests, nevertheless Judge Sorkow focused upon the surrogacy arrangement itself. Given that the drafters of state statutory schemes did not contemplate this type of an agreement, the court concluded that legislation governing adoption and baby-selling could not apply to the Baby M scenario. Hence, contract principles, constitutional rules, and *parens patriae*, which he termed a "viable independent standard for termination

6. Ibid., at 1170.
7. Janet Dolgin, *Defining the Family* (New York, 1997), 123.
8. Baby M, supra n. 3, at 1169.
9. However, the court admitted that she was a fit mother to raise her older children. Baby M, supra n. 3, at 1140 & 1170.
10. Ibid. at 1170. See also ibid. at 1167–70.

of parental rights,"[11] were utilized to resolve the case.[12] Since the Sterns invested time, energy, and emotion in finding the gestational host and initiating pregnancy in reliance on her promise, the court argues that the preconception intentions of the parties should be respected; hence, one cannot justify the reneging decision of the surrogate after giving birth. In effect, the court upheld the validity of the agreement.[13]

Mrs. Whitehead appealed to the New Jersey Supreme Court and was granted certification.[14] The court affirmed the trial court's custody award to Mr. Stern, but it reversed the trial court's termination of Mrs. Whitehead's parental rights by invalidating the surrogate contract and the order allowing Mrs. Stern to adopt the child. The case was remanded to the trial court for a determination of the surrogate's visitation rights. Whereas the trial court upheld the surrogacy contract, the Supreme Court chose to invalidate the agreement on statutory and public policy grounds.[15] Rather than suggesting a new legal framework addressing the surrogacy arrangement, the court noted that "the factual issues confronted and decided by the trial court were the same as if Mr. Stern and Mrs. Whitehead had had the child out of wedlock, intended or unintended."[16]

Following in the footsteps of the trial court findings, the Supreme Court concurred that the biological delineation of family provides the bright-line definition, i.e., Mr. Stern is the legal father, and Mary Whitehead is the genetic and gestational mother. Consequently, in treating the arrangement as analogous to private placement adoption, the court terminated Whitehead's maternal rights and awarded custody to Mrs. Stern. Applying the paradigm of adoption to the surrogacy arrangement, the court then proceeded to view the contract, in essence, as baby selling, which is prohibited by New Jersey statute.[17]

---

11. Baby M, supra n. 3, at 1171.

12. Ibid. at 1157, 1159, 1166.Whether specific performance of the surrogate's surrender obligation is to be enforced, see Margaret Radin, "Market Inalienability," and 100 *Harv. L. Rev.* 1849, 1921–36 (1987) and Note, "Rumpelstiltskin Revisited: The Inalienable Rights of Surrogate Mothers," 99 *Harv. L. Rev.* 1936, 1954 (1986).

13. However, this excludes the provision purporting to give Mr. Stern control over abortion. Ibid. at 1159. Some have argued that the recognition of the contract was cloaked in the garb of the child's best interests standard. See Judith Areen, "Baby M Reconsidered", 76 *Georgetown L.J.* 1741, 1751 (1988).

14. In the Matter of Baby M, supra n. 4.

15. Ibid. at 1240–1244, 1246–1248, 1250.

16. Ibid. at 123.8.

17. Ibid. at 1240. If payment to obtain a child is illegal, then payment for adoption and egg and sperm donation should equally be outlawed. See Richard Posner,

At first blush, surrogacy and adoption are similar, and therefore adoption statutes could possibly govern the outcome of surrogacy disputes. Both surrogacy and adoption provide for the termination of parental rights and surrender of child to an individual who is not the legal parent. Additionally, issues of revocability and child's best interests are major concerns in both types of arrangement.

However, to assert that there exist certain common fact patterns and standards emerging from these arrangements is to ignore certain distinctions that argue in favor of treating the situations differently. Rejecting the analogy, one commentator observed:[18]

> In surrogacy (1) the intended father is in most cases the biological father; (2) through their surrogacy contract the intended parents accept responsibility for the child from the moment of conception, thus protecting the interests of the child in having a secure home regardless of impairment in the child or of any changes of circumstances among the adults involved... and (3) there is less duress on the woman who agrees to give up the child, since she makes her decision even before conception and is typically a married, secure woman with children of her own. In contrast, the woman who gives up the child for adoption is most often an unmarried teenager for whom this is her first pregnancy (as does the biological father), and who lacks the financial resources to take care of the child.

Despite these differences as well as others,[19] the court treated the surrogacy contract as a subsection of adoption and construed the adoption statutes to arrive at these conclusions, even if the statutory language dictated otherwise.[20] Utilizing the child's best interests standard for custody award and adoption placement, the Supreme Court agreed with the trial court that awarding custody to the Sterns was in the child's best interests. However, this standard did not apply to the termination of the surrogate's parental rights. According to New Jersey adoption law, in the absence of intentional abandonment, parental neglect, or parental

---

"The Regulation of the Market in Adoptions," 67 *B.U.L.* 59, 71 (1987). Cf. the trial court's conception of the arrangement as a contract for gestational services rather than a contract for the sale of a baby. See Baby M; supra n. 3, at 1157.

18. Elliot Dorff, *Matters of Life and Death* (Philadelphia, 1998), 65.

19. Girardeau Spann, "Baby M & and the Cassandra Problem," 76 *Georgetown L.J.* 1719, 1728 (1988).

20. Baby M, supra n. 4, at 1240–46.

unfitness, parental rights could not be terminated.[21] The surrogate's behavior did not satisfy statutory requirements; therefore, her rights could not be terminated.[22] Given the surrogate's retention of her parental status and the illegality of the contract providing for the surrogate's contractual relinquishment of parental rights, Mrs. Stern was precluded from adopting Baby M and this in effect furnished the grounds for Mrs. Whitehead's claim for visitation.[23]

Though parenthood based upon biology was clearly defined in Baby M, technological advances permit the separation of biological motherhood into its genetic and gestational components, two claims to parenthood that have defined natural motherhood since time immemorial. Johnson v. Calvert,[24] a case similar to Baby M, except that the surrogate bears no genetic bond to the child, was the first case litigated where two women submitted conflicting claims to motherhood grounded on their biological connections to a child. In this case, Anna Johnson, a single mother, was hired as a surrogate to gestate an embryo created with the gametes provided by a married couple. Mark and Crispina Calvert. Pursuant to the contract, upon birth of the child, Johnson was to surrender parental rights to the Calverts. A few months prior to the child's birth, the parties appeared in court disputing the child's parentage. All three California courts that heard the Johnson case ruled in favor of the Calverts, but for different reasons.

At trial, given their genetic connection, the court recognized the Calverts as the baby's parents:[25]

> Who we are and what we are and identity problems particularly with young children and teenagers are extremely important. We know that there is a combination of factors. We know more and more about traits now, how you walk, talk, and everything else, all sorts of things that develop out of your genes, how long you're going to live, all things being equal, when your immune system is going to breakdown, what diseases you may be susceptible to. They have upped the intelligence ratio of genetics to 70 percent now.

21. Ibid. at 1242, 1251–52.
22. Ibid. at 1251–1252.
23. In a subsequent proceeding, Mrs. Whitehead was awarded visitation rights. See In re Baby M, 225 N.J. Super. 267, 542 A. 2d 52 (Ch. Div. 1988).
24. 81 P. 2d 776 (Cal. 1993).
25. Johnson v. Calvert, No. x-1633190, slip op. at 8 (Cal. App. Dep't. Super. Ct. Oct. 22, 1990).

The court found Crispina Calvert to be the baby's "genetic, biological and natural mother" and Mark Calvert to be the baby's natural father, while Anna Johnson was "a gestational carrier" who was like a foster parent knowing that one day the natural mother may regain custody of her child.[26]

The appellate court affirmed, finding statutory authority regarding the parent-child relationship rather than biological truths that the Calverts were the parents.[27] Relying upon a provision of the Uniform Parentage Act (UPA), incorporated into the California Civil Code, that allows a man and a woman to be deemed "natural" parents based upon blood tests which indicate genetic similarities between the individual and child provided the basis for the California Court of Appeals to affirm the trial court's findings.[28]

However, the Supreme Court acknowledged that either a genetic function or a gestational function could serve as grounds for declaring natural maternity under California law.[29] In the absence of a legislative preference for either biological contribution and the invocation of biological truths in favor of a particular woman, the Supreme Court declared that the agreement was not "on its face, inconsistent with public policy,"[30] and relied on the contract to determine the parties' intentions.

As the court observed:

> Although the Act recognizes both genetic consanguinity and giving birth as means of establishing a mother and child relationship, when the two means do not coincide in one woman, she who intended to procreate the child—that is, she who intended to bring about the birth of a child that she intended to raise as her own—is the natural mother under California law.[31]

Pursuant to the statute, both women demonstrated viable claims based on genetic or gestational contributions toward establishing legal motherhood. Since there was no clear legislative preference for either claim and California recognizes only one mother,[32] the court concluded that the preconception intents of the Calverts was the dispositive factor, and

26. Ibid. at 5–6, 17.
27. Anna J. v. Mark C., 286 Cal. Rptr. 369, 373 (Ct. App. 1991).
28. Ibid. at 373–74.
29. Johnson v. Calvert, 851 P. 2d 776, 780–781 (Cal. 1993).
30. Ibid. at 783.
31. Ibid. at 782.
32. Ibid.

Johnson became the facilitator of the couple's intent. Had Johnson expressed her intentions to raise the child prior to negotiating the surrogacy contract, the Calverts would have withdrawn from the arrangement.[33]

George Annas, a leading bioethicist, has criticized the reasoning of Johnson v. Calvert:[34]

> [The Johnson] opinion contributes little to the resolution of whether the genetic or the gestational mother should be considered the legal mother of a child. Calling the genetic mother the "natural" mother simply begs the question; it does not answer it.... In human reproduction men contribute only genes; women contribute both genes and gestation. The question is what rules society should adopt now that these maternal contributions can be separated.

To argue that the Johnson court failed to provide a solution for gestational surrogacy arrangements shows an unwillingness to admit that the court held that preconception intentions determine legal parentage.

What, in fact, were the parameters of the court's reasoning? Adopting a contractual paradigm, was the court enthroning individual autonomy in collaborative reproduction decision-making and abandoning the traditional biological connections to the child? Was the court formulating a rule that the preconception intentions of a genetic mother will be recognized over the changed intentions of the gestational mother? The majority opinion had, in Judge Kennard's view, decided to rely upon intent to identify the Calverts as legal parents without considering Johnson's interests:[35]

> [I]n making the intent of the genetic mother who wants to have a child the dispositive factor, the majority renders a certain result preordained and inflexible in every case: as between an intending genetic mother and a gestational mother, the genetic mother will, under the majority's analysis, always prevail. The majority recognizes no meaningful contribution by a woman who agrees to carry a fetus to term for the genetic mother beyond that of mere employment to perform a specified biological

33. Ibid.

34. George Annas, "Using Genes to Define Motherhood – The California Solution," 326 *New Eng. J. Med.* 417, 419 (1992).

35. Johnson v. Calvert, supra n. 29, at 797–798.

> function.... The gestational mother's biological contribution of carrying a child for nine months and giving birth is likewise an assumption of parental responsibility.

In fact, this conclusion is a misrepresentation of the majority opinion. The court observed that "under our analysis, in a true 'egg donation' situation, where a woman gestates and gives birth to a child formed from the egg of another woman with the intent to raise the child as her own, the birth mother is the natural mother under California law."[36] In other words, if the gestational mother had been the intending mother, she would have been deemed the child's natural parent.

The next year, with Johnson as its backdrop, the New York Court of Appeals decided McDonald v. McDonald, which scrutinized parentage in the context of gestational surrogacy and recognized the gestational mother as the natural mother because she was the intending mother.[37]

In the words of the court: [38]

> In the case at bar, we have a true "egg donation" situation, and we find the reasoning of the Supreme Court of California on this issue to be persuasive. Accordingly, the Supreme Court, Queens County, correctly held that in the instant "egg donation" case, the wife, who is the gestational mother, is the natural mother of the children, and is, under the circumstances, entitled to temporary custody of the children with visitation to the husband.[39]
> In short, the McDonald holding and the majority opinion of Johnson convey the rule "that courts should look to intentional parentage to resolve an apparent biological 'tie' but not to grant parentage to someone lacking any biological connection to the child involved."

In one case, the courts may choose the genetic mother as the legal parent due to her intent to raise the child, and in the other the gestational mother may be chosen as the intended mother. Following in the footsteps of Johnson, the McDonald court refused to evaluate the case from

36. Ibid. at 782, n. 10.

37. 608 N.Y. S. 2d 477 (N.Y. App. Div. 1994).

38. Janet Dolgin, "Choice, Tradition, & the New Genetics: The Fragmentation of the Ideology of the Family," 32 *Conn. L. Rev.* 523, 538 (1999–2000). See also, Dolgin, supra n. 7, at 185–187.

39. Supra n. 37 at 480.

the child's perspective and thus rejected the application of the child's best interests standard to resolve maternity disputes in gestational surrogacy cases.[40]

This framework for invoking intentional parentage within the context of biological parenthood continued to garner support in In re Marriage of Moschetta.[41] In a case involving a traditional surrogacy arrangement, Robert Moschetta, the genetic father, and his wife, Cynthia Moschetta, contracted with a surrogate who was to be inseminated with Robert's sperm, and who consented in exchange for $10,000 to carry the fetus to birth and surrender the baby to the Moschettas. Aware of the couple's marital problems while she was in labor, the surrogate changed her mind regarding the arrangement. After the birth of the baby, Mrs. Moschetta filed for divorce and demanded custody of the baby. Finding no question about biological parenthood to settle, in short, no "tie to break,"[42] the Court recognized Mr. Moschetta and the surrogate as the legal parents and awarded them joint and physical custody. Arguing for Cynthia's maternity in order to preclude having to share custody of his baby with the surrogate, Mr. Moschetta contended that Cynthia had received the baby into her home and therefore should be declared its mother. Refusing to establish parentage based upon the parties' intentions sans reference to biological bonds, the court found no genetic or gestational ties between Cynthia and the baby. Consequently, Cynthia could not be deemed the mother of this child. Finally, the court declined to enforce the surrogacy contract, which was incompatible with the state's adoption laws.[43] In effect, in the absence of a biological connection, Cynthia was not deemed a legal parent. Attempting to unearth the biological criteria for parenthood in statutory law, the court noted:[44]

> [T]he framework employed by Johnson v. Calvert of first determining parentage under the Act is dispositive of the case before us. In Johnson v. Calvert our Supreme Court first ascertained parentage under the Act; only when the operation of the Act

---

40. McDonald, supra n. 37, at 480 & Johnson, supra n. 35, at 782, n. 10. In fact, some states adopt this standard for custody determination rather than for parentage determination. See e.g., UTAH CODE ANN. SEC. 76-7-204 (1995) & WASH. REV. CODE ANN. SEC. 26.09. 191; 26.09187 (3) (West 1997). Cf. Id. 799, 801 (Kennard, J., dissenting).

41. 30 Cal. Rptr. 2d 893 (Cal. Ct. App. 1994).

42. Ibid. at 896.

43. Ibid. at 894–895.

44. Ibid. 895.

> yielded an ambiguous result did the court resolve the matter by intent as expressed in the agreement. In the present case, by contrast, parentage is easily resolved in Elvira Jordan [the surrogate] under the terms of the Act. Here, apropos the language in Johnson v. Calvert... the two usual means of showing maternity—genetics and birth—coincide in one woman.

Though the above-discussed cases premise maternity upon either biology, biology coupled with pre-conception intent of the parent, or adoption, the Buzzanca case, involving a gestational surrogacy arrangement, posited a type of parentage ab initio that lacks any biological connection to the child.[45] In that case, Mr. and Mrs. Buzzanca contracted with a surrogate to gestate an embryo created from anonymous donors. The couple separated, and Mrs. Buzzanca claimed maternity. The identities of the genetic donors were unknown, the surrogate declined to claim the baby, and the Buzzancas, the intending parents, were not biologically related to the baby. Expanding the Johnson intent standard, the court argued that they were the intending parents, despite the absence of biological ties to the baby.[46] Their parentage, i.e., intending parents, was established by their arrangement for the surrogate to become pregnant through the utilization of an embryo created by anonymous donors.[47]

Finally, the court concluded that intending parents serve the best interests of the child and consequently custody should be awarded to the intending parents.[48] This two-pronged approach of initially defining intentional parentage and then arriving at a custody determination based on the child's best interests originated in Johnson. As the court observed:[49]

> The mental concept of the child is a controlling factor of its creation, and the originators of that concept merit full credit as conceivers. The mental concept must be recognized as independently valuable; it creates expectations in the initiating parents of a child, and it creates expectation in society for adequate performance on the part of the initiators as parents of the child.

---

45. In re Marriage of Buzzanca, 72 Cal. Rptr. 2d 280 (Cal. Ct. App. 1998).

46. Ibid. at 288–290. For the court's misreading of the Johnson holding, see Janet Dolgin, "An Emerging Consensus: Reproductive Technology & the Law," 23 *Vermont L. Rev.* 225, 250, n. 166 (1998).

47. Ibid. at 288.

48. Ibid. at 293.

49. Ibid. at 293.

In place of the biological parentage paradigm and "adoption default model" applied by the courts in other cases of collaborative reproduction, Buzzanca applied an intentional-parent construct to be determined apart from the biological facts while simultaneously serving the child's best interests.

The varying paradigms at work in these cases of reproductive technology have been aptly summarized elsewhere: [50]

> There are three... models on which society and the law ground parentage. One model permits the transfer of parentage from one parent or set of parents to another. This sort of parentage does not follow automatically from a child's birth. The second assumes parentage follows automatically from the nature of the biological case. Finally, the third model presumes parentage at the moment of a child's birth, but as the result of legal (cultural) presumptions and not as the result of assumptions about nature itself.... Thus, there are two paradigms for determining a child's parentage ab initio. One predicates parentage on reproductive facts. The other predicates parentage on presumptions about some social aspect of familial relationships. The sort of parentage ab initio constructed in Johnson and expanded in Buzzanca is presumptive, not biological parentage.

Biological parentage and presumptive parentage are the pole stars for understanding the court decisions emerging from the various collaborative reproduction cases.

Upon further examination, the emerging yardstick of presumptive parentage is reflective of America's "habits of the heart"— Tocqueville's expression for the amalgam of traits essential to our national character and its impact upon the transformation of American family law during the last thirty years. As Robert Bellah and his colleagues, for example, have observed:[51]

---

50. Dolgin, supra n. 46, at 259.

51. Robert Bellah et al., *Habits of the Heart* (New York, 1985), 85, 89–90. The truth, as Oscar Wilde said, "is rarely pure and never simple" (Wilde, *The Importance of Being Earnest*, Act I); hence, to explain the transformation in family law in terms of a single overarching factor is destined to fail. Thus, this interpretation does not purport to explain all of the strands of family law. However, this line of thought will be helpful in explaining the trend in the emerging definition of parenthood within the context of collaborative reproduction.

> Tocqueville... saw the family, along with religion and democratic political participation, as one of the three spheres that would help us to moderate our individualism.... Much has changed since Tocqueville's day.... Given the enormous American emphasis on independence and self-reliance... the survival of the family, with its strong emphasis on interdependence and acceptance, is striking... the network of kinship has narrowed and the sphere of individual decision has grown.... The sphere of individual decision within the family is growing. For one thing, it is no longer considered disgraceful to remain unmarried.... Further, no one has to have children. Finally, one can leave a marriage one doesn't like. Divorce as a solution to an unhappy marriage, even a marriage with younger children, is far more acceptable today than ever before.

In short, the shift from a familial to contractual orientation has laid the groundwork for family members to view themselves "as a collection of individuals united temporarily for their mutual convenience and armed with rights against each other."[52] In the legal context, this perception has been translated into private ordering of behavior. This "privatization process"[53] has led to the development of prenuptial and post-nuptial arrangements, treating married persons as separate individuals, and a shift from fault-based to no-fault divorce. Marriage has been redefined as the pursuit of individual fulfillment, and parenting has been reconceptualized as an opportunity for individual happiness rather than viewed in terms of its value to society and promoting child welfare. Finally, the traditional nuclear family has been challenged by consensual alternatives to marriage, such as cohabitation and same-sex marriages and the emergence of intimate contract ordering.[54]

The recognition of surrogacy contracts reflects the extension of the trend in family law toward privatization of family issues. In fact, this shift has not gone unchallenged. There is an ongoing debate in legal scholarship whether a contractual paradigm should be applied to establishing

---

52. Carl Schneider, "Moral Discourse and the Transformation of American Family Law," 83 *Michigan L. Rev.* 1803, 1859 (1985).

53. See Frances Olsen, "The Family and the Market: A Study of Ideology and Legal Reform," 96 *Harvard Law Review* (1983), 1474; Jana Singer, "The Privatization of Family Law," 1992 *Wisconsin Law Review*, 1443, 1446–1449; Lenore Weitzman, *The Marriage Contract* (New York, 1981).

54. Gregg Temple, "Freedom of Contract & Intimate Relationships," 8 *Harv. J. L. & Pub. Pol'y* 121 (1985).

parentage in the context of reproductive technology.[55] Following in the footsteps of the legal scholars who propound the adoption of a contractual model, the majority opinion in Johnson v. Calvert invokes intent-based motherhood, championing preconception intentions. As the court noted, the contract model is premised upon the notion that the interests of the genetic mother and the gestational mother as reflected in their preconception agreement are explicit, bargained for, and relied upon.

For Johnson, legal parenthood is awarded to the contracting parents, or as the literature would identify them, the intending parents who have intended to bring the child into this world. Addressing the parties' intentions, the court found that but for the Calverts' actions, the baby would not exist. Relying upon the analysis of Hill,[56] a proponent of the intentionalist theory, the court invoked the "but for causation argument" and claimed that "the child would not have been born but for the efforts of the intended parents."[57] Hence, the intended parents as against any others would be accorded parental status. At the core of this intent theory is that the intending mother should be afforded parenthood because she orchestrated the procreative process and the honoring of the agreement gives rise to certain expectations. Aside from the instrumental role of the intended mother and the concomitant expectations engendered upon reliance on the agreement, the existence of intent vests feelings

55. For those who advocate a family law model, see Martha Field, *Surrogate Motherhood* (Boston, 1988); Carl Schneider, "Surrogate Motherhood from the Perspective of Family Law," 13 *Harv. J.L. & Public Pol'y* 125 (1990); Alexander Capron & Margaret Radin, "Choosing Family Law over Contract Law as a Paradigm for Surrogate Motherhood," 16 Law, *Medicine & Health Care,* 34 (1988); Barbara Rothman, *Recreating Motherhood: Ideology and Technology in a Patriarchal Society* (New York, 1989); Margaret Brinig, "A Maternalistic Approach to Surrogacy: Comment on Richard Epstein's Surrogacy: The Case for Full Contractual Enforcement," 81 *Va. L. Rev.* 2377 (1995). For the contractual model advocates, see Andrea Stumpf, Note, "Redefining Mother: A Legal Matrix for New Reproductive Technologies," 96 *Yale L.J.* 187 (1986); June Carbone, "The Role of Contract Principles in Determining the Validity of Surrogacy Contracts," 28 *Santa Clara L. Rev.* 581 (1988); John Hill, "What Does It Mean to be a "Parent"? The Claims of Biology as the Basis for Parental Rights," 66 *N.Y.U. L. Rev.* 353 (1991); Richard Epstein, Surrogacy, "The Case for Full Contractual Enforcement," 81 *Va. L. Rev.* 2305 (1995).

56. Hill, supra n. 55, at 41.

57. Johnson, supra n. 29, at 782. For a critique of this argument, see Melinda Roberts, "Good Intentions & a Great Divide: Having Babies by Intending them," 12 *Law & Philosophy*, 287, 312–315 (1993).

of motherhood between her and the baby. Relying upon the words of Stumpf,[58] Johnson explained,[59]

> The mental concept of the child is a controlling factor of its creation, and the originators of that concept merit full credit as conceivers. The mental concept must be recognized as independently valuable; it creates expectations in the initiating parents of a child, and it creates expectations in society for adequate performance on the part of the initiators as parents of the child.

Giving effect to contractual intent lays the groundwork for the development of a mothering relationship accompanied by a societal expectation of parental responsibility vis-à-vis the child.

However, as Justice Kennard noted in her dissent, it is inappropriate to examine family law through the lens of tort law, property law, and contract law. The opinion asserted unhesitatingly that the conceiving of a child mentally is invoking the realm of intellectual property-ownership rights akin to an individual who conceives of an invention.[60] In short, the Johnson holding, in the words of Dolgin, seems to obliterate the long-standing difference in Western culture between relationships based in status and relationships based in contract, because it seems to merge the family with the world of business and commerce, to define family relations as negotiable ties between otherwise unconnected, autonomous individuals.[61]

In effect, for Kennard, the shift from a familial orientation to a contract framework lends credence to Hafen's characterization that "ours is the age of the waning of belonging."[62] This atomism critique, which decries the focus on the individual, his psychic fulfillment, and the commodification of human relationships, and advances the need to develop "belonging"-type relationships that stem from the reservoirs of strength

58. Stumpf, supra n. 55, at 196.

59. Johnson, supra n. 29, at 783.

60. Johnson, supra n. 29, at 795–797 (Kennard J., dissenting).

61. Janet Dolgin, "Just a Gene: Judicial Assumptions about Parenthood," 40 U.C.L.A. 637, 692 (1993). The interplay of status and contract in the panoply of court decisions in collaborative reproduction is a recurring theme in Dolgin's writings. See Dolgin, supra n. 7, at 63–93, 259–260 & Janet Dolgin, "An Emerging Consensus: Reproductive Technology & the Law," 23 *Vermont L. Rev.* 225 (1998).

62. Bruce Hafen," Individualism & Autonomy in Family Law: The Waning of Belonging," 1991 *B.Y.U. L. Rev.* 1 (1991).

and compassion we carry within ourselves, resonates either as a communitarian or a feminist agenda.

As Marsha Garrison observes, "while communitarian thinkers are a diverse group, they uniformly favor a de-emphasis on abstract individual rights; they tend to emphasize the individual's embeddedness in various communities of interests, such as the family."[63] For feminists, the values of care, commitment, and responsibility must replace "the norms of the marketplace."[64] Hence, the surrogacy contract represents the commodification of a woman's procreative capacity and undermines her identity and personhood.[65]

Whether, to some degree, legal scholars have overstated the extent to which the introduction of a contractual approach in family law has contributed to the development of marriage as an institution of self-fulfillment and gratification rather than commitment and interconnectedness is subject to debate,[66] however, the underlying significance of Johnson and the subsequent holdings lies elsewhere. As will be shown, these cases address the broader debate regarding the proper role of contractual intent in establishing parenthood in multifarious situations.

The writings of John Hill and Margorie Shultz, which serve as the backdrop for these cases and have been the most influential in advocating a theory of parenthood based upon intentionality, set clear

63. Marsha Garrison, "An Evaluation of Two Models of Parental Obligation," 86 *Cal. L. Rev.* 41, n. 205 (1998). For communitarian critiques of the increased contractualization of family law, see Schneider, supra at note 52; Milton Regan, Jr., "Market Discourse & Moral Neutrality in Divorce Law," 1994 *Utah L. Rev.* 605, 620, 627; Mary Glendon, *Abortion & Divorce in Western Law* (Boston, 1987), 112–119; Martha Minnow, "Forming Underneath Everything That Grows: Toward a History of Family Law," 1985 *Wis. L. Rev.* 819, 894 (1985. Margaret Brinig aptly notes that "much of the communitarian literature... sets a mood rather than providing an agenda." Margaret Brinig, "Status, Contract, & Covenant," 79 *Cornell L. Rev.* 1573, 1573 (1994).

64. Minnow, supra n. 63, at 885–889; Katherine Bartlett, "Re-Expressing Parenthood," 98 *Yale L.J.* 293, 311–312 (1988). For attempts to demonstrate the compatibility of contract and commitment, see Margaret Brinig & Steven Crafton, "Marriage & Opportunism," 23 *J. Legal Studies,* 869, 873 (1994); Lloyd Cohen, "Marriage, Divorce, & Quasi Rents: or 'I Gave Him the Best Years of My Life,'" 16 *J. Legal Studies,* 267, 272–273 (1987); Marjorie Shultz, Address at the Law & Society Association Annual Meeting (June 17, 1994) where Shultz points out that "intention and contracting is a primary way to build relationships."

65. Margaret Radin, "Market-Inalienability," 100 *Harv. L. Rev.* 1849, 1932 (1987). See also, Cass Sunstein, "Incommensurability & Valuation in Law," 92 *Mich. L. Rev.* 779, 850 (1994).

66. Jennifer Wriggins, "Marriage Law & Family Law: Autonomy, Interdependence, & Couples of the Same Gender," 41 *B.C. L. Rev.* 265, 278–285 (2000).

parameters for the application of this intent model.[67] Professor Hill, for example, argues that "what is essential to parenthood is not the biological tie between parent and child but the preconception intention to have a child, accompanied by the undertaking of whatever action is necessary to bring a child into the world."[68] Though Hill weighs and rejects various arguments in according priority to genetic or gestational parents over the claims of intentional parents, nevertheless, the model does not govern in all cases. As Hill states:[69]

> Intentionality acts as a trump for the intended parents when conflicting claims are made by parties who have contributed biologically to the creation of the child. Intentionality, however, is not the only way to acquire parentage. Where no party has intended to create a child, as in the case of the unplanned child, there are no intentional parents. Thus, the claims of the biological parents would take precedence.

For Hill as well as for Shultz,[70] the model is relevant only in cases of collaborative reproductive agreements. Adopting this regnant view of the limited application of the intent rule, Johnson, McDonald, and Moschetta looked to intentional parentage to trump a biological tie but not to award parentage to someone lacking any biological connection to the child. However, Buzzanca demurred, relying on the notion of intent, moved beyond the parameters of these holdings and the influential writings of Shultz and Hill, and allowed parenthood to be determined apart from biological ties. In short, Buzzanca views parenthood as a functional status, rather than one derived from biology or legal entitlement.

---

67. Hill, supra n. 55; Marjorie Shultz, "Reproductive Technology and Intent-Based Parenthood: An Opportunity for Gender Neutrality," 1990 *Wisconsin Law Review,* 297.

68. Hill, ibid. at 414.

69. Hill, ibid. at 387. This bargained-for-intention which is determinative of legal parenthood is predicated upon a formal contract rather than a mere gratuitous promise upon which the intent parent relied. See Hill, id. 387, n. 184, 415–416; Dolgin, supra n. 61, at 259. Cf. Marsha Garrison, "Law Making for Baby Making: An Interpretive Approach to the Determination of Legal Parentage," 113 *Harv. L. Rev.* 835, 862, n. 128 (1999–2000). Additionally, the intended parents must have utilized "morally permissible measures," such as refraining from kidnapping and willingness to provide "minimally adequate conditions to be able to raise and care for the child." See Hill, ibid. at 356, n. 12.

70. Shultz, supra n. 67, at 324. See also, Shoshana Hillers, "A Labor Theory of Legal Parenthood," 110 *Yale L. J.* 691, 703 (2001).

Adopting this approach has led courts[71] and legal scholarship[72] to limit the rights of parents who have failed to accept responsibility for their children and to grant "parental" rights to nonparents who are intending parents.

In effect, pursuant to this perspective, all types of nontraditional family relationships potentially could be granted the status of marital families by the courts and legislatures. In effect, parenthood is to be viewed, like adoption, as "essentially the factitious creation of blood relationships between persons who are not so related."[73] The ties between the adopted child and his natural parents are severed, and the adoptive parents have all the rights and responsibilities of a biological parent, including a duty to support the child. Similarly, an adopted child has all the rights of a biological child, including the right to inherit.[74] Analogously, reproductive technology, by separating the biology of parenthood into various components, has allowed the emergence of a notion of parentage focusing on relationships rather than biological ties and defined these relationships as legally equivalent to the status of biological parenthood.

---

71. Ira Ellman, Paul Kurtz, and Elizabeth Scott, *Family Law: Cases, Text, Problems* (3rd Ed. 1998), 724–728; Harry Krause, Linda Elrod, Marsha Garrison, and J. Oldham, *Family Law: Cases, Comments & Questions* (4th ed. 1998), 700–02, 710–11.

72. Katharine Bartlett, "Rethinking Parenthood as an Exclusive Status: The Need for Legal Alternatives When the Premise of the Nuclear Family has Failed," 70 *Va. L. Rev.* 879, 902–19 (1984); Note, "Looking for a Family Resemblance: The Limits of the Functional Approach to the Legal Definition of Family," 104 *Harv. L. Rev.* 1640, 1643–50 (1991); Nancy Polikoff, "The Child Does Have Two Mothers: Redefining Parenthood to Meet the Needs of Children in Lesbian-Mother and Other Nontraditional Families," 78 *Geo. L.J.* 459 (1989–1990); Leslie Harris, "Reconsidering the Criteria for Legal Parenthood," 1996 *Utah L. Rev.* 461, 480; Dolgin, supra n. 7, at 226.

73. Huard, "The Law of Adoption: Ancient & Modern," 9 *Vanderbilt L. Rev.* 743 (1956). Forty-three years later, the law continues to structure adoption "in imitation of biology." See Elizabeth Bartholet, *Family Bonds: Adoption, Infertility and The New World of Child Production* (Boston, 1999), 93, 170; Radhika Rao, "Assisted Reproductive Technology & the Threat to the Traditional Family," 47 *Hastings L. J.* 951, 957 (1996); Shultz, supra n. 55, at 320. However, statutory prohibitions against incestuous marriages do not apply to adoptive relationships. See Missouri ex rel. Miesner v. Geile, 712 F. Supp. 1061 (Mo. Ct. p. 1988); Israel v. Allen, 577 P. 2d. 762 (Colo. 1978); Bagnardi v. Hartnett, 366 N.Y. S. 2d 89 (Sup. Ct. 1975). Secondly, the unwillingness to erase the biological past is indicated by the trend of unsealing adoption records as well as a move towards open adoptions in which biological and adoptive parents are involved in jointly parenting a child. See Marsha Garrison, supra n. 69, at 890–891.

74. Homer Clark, *The Law of Domestic Relations*, Minn. 1968, 602. On the other hand, most states have legislated severing the right of inheritance from natural parents. See 2 C.J.S. Adoption of Persons Section 146 (1972 & Supplement 2001); Little v. Smith, 943 S.W. 2d 414 (Tex. 1997).

Both adoption and the emergence of functional parenthood from various holdings dealing with collaborative technology have attempted to mirror as closely as possible the natural family via a system of legal regulations.

A Jewish Legal View

Does Jewish law impart recognition to the notion of functional parenthood? Let us focus upon Jewish adoption law and its normative implications for collaborative reproductive technology. Without addressing the entire range of ties between adoptive parents and their adopted child, let us briefly deal with the question of support (*mezonot*) of an adoptive child, the most frequently discussed issue during the last fifty years in Jewish adoption law.[75]

The support obligation is a monetary obligation which creates a monetary debt upon the obligor vis-à-vis the obligee.[76] The *Rishonim* (a designation given to 11th–15th century decisors) advanced four possible modes of establishing this monetary obligation: by means of effectuating a *kinyan*, i.e., a symbolic act for undertaking an obligation; by signing a *shtar*, i.e. a bona fide deed; by transferring money; or by a prescribed verbal commitment in the presence of witnesses. The normative opinion allows for the creation of a monetary obligation either by submitting a *shtar* to the obligee or by a verbal commitment.[77] Advocating the employment of a *shtar* in 1957, R. Eliezer Goldschmidt, an Israeli rabbinical court *dayan* (an arbitrator of Jewish law) drafted a document to be utilized by adoptive parents in obligating themselves to

---

75. Rabbinical Court Decision 2323/1951 (unpublished); Barukh Ezrachi, "The Dimensions of Obligation in Child Adoption," (Hebrew), 4 *Noam* 94 (1961); Moshe Findling, "Child Adoption," (Hebrew), 4 *Noam* 63 (1961); Abraham Rudner, "Child Adoption & The Duty to Support a Friend," (Hebrew), 4 *Noam* 61 (1961); Mordekhai Hakohen, "Adoption According to Jewish Law," (Hebrew), 48 *Sinai* 204 (1961); Ben Zion Uziel, *Responsa* (hereinafter: Resp.) *Shaarei Uziel*, 2: Gate 39, Chapter 1; 3 *Piskei Din Battei Din Harabbanayim* (hereinafter: PDR) 109; 4 PDR 374; Ido Divon, "Obligations of Child Support in Adoption," (Hebrew), 9 *Dinei Israel* 183 (1978–80); R. Herschel Schachter, "Adoption in Jewish Law," *Yeshiva University Chavrusa, April 1982*; Shlomo Daichovsky, "The Parental Obligation to Support Adoptive Children," (Hebrew), 15 *Tehumin* 278 (1994).

76. *Shulhan Arukh Hoshen Mishpat* 60:6; R. Shimon Shkop (Lithuania and U.S., 1860–1940), *Shaarei Yosher*, Gate 5, Chap. 2.

77. For an overview of the early authorities (*Rishonim)* regarding this matter, see Ezrachi, id. & Divon, supra n. 75. For the normative position, see *Shulhan Arukh Hoshen Mishpat* 40:1.

support and educate their adoptive children. In effect, the *shtar* serves as a concrete articulation of the parties' firm resolve to undertake the obligation (i.e., *gemirat da'at*).[78] The incorporation of a support obligation in a *shtar* poses a difficulty. Seemingly, according to Maimonides,[79] maintenance is to be categorized as a matter which is an undefined sum, i.e., *davar she'eino katzuv*. In other words, although the adoptive parent may obligate himself to maintain the child for a specific time, the amount of support is not specified. Consequently, the obligor is bereft of firm resolve to obligate himself in support. Hence, such an agreement should be invalidated. However, given the fact that most decisors disagree with this position,[80] therefore, such a maintenance agreement, despite its undefined nature, is halakhically effective.

Alternatively, some decisors contend that according to Maimonides, should the obligor receive something in exchange for undertaking the obligation, one has transformed a unilateral obligation into a bilateral obligation, which will be legally effective in an agreement with a provision providing for an "undefined sum" of the duty.[81] Consequently, citing the Talmudic dictum "*behahi hana'ah de... gamar umesha'bed nafsheh*," i.e., "regarding the benefit he receives... he resolves to undertake the obligation," a rabbinical court concludes that the benefit accrued by the adoptive parent in raising this child serves as an essential building block, imparting validity to the *shtar* or verbal commitment for the support obligation.[82] Here, in the *beit din's* words, the efficaciousness of the benefit

---

78. For the text of the agreement, see Daichovsky, supra n. 75, at 291. For a proposed modification of the document, see Itamar Warhaftig, *Undertaking in Jewish Law* (Hebrew) (Jerusalem, 2001), 500–503. For the efficacy of a *shtar* without an accompanying *kinyan*, see R. Moses Maimonides (Egypt: 1135–1204) *Mishneh Torah Hilk. Mekhirah* 11:15, *Shulhan Arukh Hoshen Mishpat* 40:1.

79. *Mishneh Torah Hilk. Mekhirah* 11:16.

80. R. Shabbetai Rapaport (Poland, 1621–1662), *Shakh Shulhan Arukh Hoshen Mishpat* 60:12; 3 PDR 109, 110–120; 363, 365–66; 4: 193, 198; 289, 298–300; 11: 240. Cf. 9 PDR 251; 11:252; Rudner, supra n. 75. at 64, n. aleph.

81. R. Judah Rosanes (Turkey, 1657–1729), *Mishneh Lemelekh, Mishneh Torah, Hilk. Mekhirah* 11:16; R. Aryeh Loeb Heller (Poland, 1745–1813), *Ketzot Ha-Hoshen Hoshen Mishpat* 60:2; R. Jacob Lorberbaum (Poland, 1760–1832), *Netivot Ha-Mishpat Hoshen Mishpat* 60:3: R. Abraham Eisenstadt (Poland, 1813–1868), *Pithei Teshuvah Shulhan Arukh Hoshen Mishpat* 60:3 in the name of the *Urim Ve-Tumim*. According to R. Yom Tov Ishbili (Spain, 1250– 1330), *Ritva, Ketubot* 101b, Maimonides's position cannot be understood in this manner. In fact, one of his responsa contradicts this interpretation. See *Resp. Rambam*, No. 114. For an attempt to resolve this seeming contradiction, see 3 PDR 109, 119–120.

82. 3 PDR 109, 118; Daichovsky, supra n. 75, at 282.

For the meaning of the expression *behahi hana'ah*, see Shamma Friedman,

is "akin to money." In other words, the psychological benefit functions like a *kinyan*, similar to the operation of the transfer of money (*kinyan kessef*).[83]

However, is there a basis for enforcing a support obligation in cases where the adoption document fails to address the issue of maintenance? As we mentioned, to impart halakhic force to an agreement creating obligations requires that it is objectively evident that the parties involved have firmly resolved to finalize the agreement. A formal symbolic act attests to the presence of *gemirat daat* or contributes to the realization of *gemirat daat*.[84] Adopting this framework, evidence of *gemirat daat* can be obtained by means of verbal consent alone, sans consummation by means of a *kinyan*. For example, owing to the benefit that parents derive from matrimonial ties, i.e., *hana'ah*, the parents of a prospective groom and bride firmly resolve to bind themselves without a formal *kinyan* to certain premarital monetary obligations.[85] Analogously, owing to the benefit of adoption, the parents firmly make up their mind and, without the implementation of a *kinyan*, become obligated in supporting their adoptive child.[86] The *hana'ah* that the parents derive from adoption is sufficient motivation to bind them to their promises and obviates the necessity of a *kinyan*. Adoption is an example of a situation in which a verbal agreement can effectuate a contract. According to certain

"Hana'ah & Acquisitions in the Talmud," 3 *Dine Israel* 115 (1972); Berachyahu Lifshitz, *Promise: Obligation & Acquisition in Jewish Law* (Hebrew), Jerusalem, 1988, 209–19; Warhaftig, supra n.78, at 60, 88, 375–383, 425–426.

83. Ezrachi, supra n. 75, at 117. For the antecedents for this premise, see *Ritva, Kiddushin* 6b; R. Moshe ben Nahman (Spain, 1140–1270), Nahmanides, *Kiddushin* 7b; R. Isaac Herzog (Israel, 20th cent.), *Pesakim U-Ketavim – She'elot U-Teshuvot Bedinnei Hoshen Mishpat* 9:111 & *Resp. Nahal Yitzhak* 40:3–4, 6; R. Isaac Herzog, *The Main Institutions of Jewish Law* (New York, 1965), vol. 1, 146– 147.

84. For an overview of decisors and academic scholars who espouse this view, see Ron Kleinman, *Merchant Customs (Lex Mercatoria) Relating to Methods of Acquisition in Jewish Law: Kinyan Situmta* (Hebrew) (Ramat Gan, 2000), Unpublished Dissertation, 106–110. For an alternative explanation, see Kleinman, ibid. 123–125; Shillem Warhaftig, *The Jewish Law of Contract* (Hebrew) (Jerusalem, 1974), 2.

85. Talmud Bavli *Ketubot* 102a; R. Jacob Tam (France: 1100– 1171), *Tosafot Ketubot* 102a, s.v. *aliba*. Whether the ascertaining of this pleasure is grounded in rabbinic legislation or *umad hadaat*, i.e., a presumption, is subject to debate. See R. Menahem b. Solomon Meiri (Provence, 1249–1316), *Meiri, Kiddushin* 9b: R. Ezekiel Landau (Prague: 1713–1793), *Resp. Nodah Be-Yehudah, Mahadura Kamma, Hoshen Mishpat* 27–28. For additional sources, see Warhaftig, supra n. 78, at 375–383, 421–426; Kleinman, supra n. 84, at 111–120.

86. Ezrachi, supra n. 75, at 94, 111, 148; Daichovsky, supra n. 75, at 280–281.

decisors, the mere existence of *gemirat daat* predicated upon the presence of benefit without a verbal commitment may suffice to create this obligation.[87]

The invoking of *gemirat daat* without an accompanying *kinyan* is predicated upon the assumption that one can expand the cases of "benefit" to be utilized as a yardstick to ascertain *gemirat daat* beyond the situations enumerated in the Talmud.[88] Following in the footsteps of his father, Hazon Ish contended that the efficacy of such an agreement was limited to the cases mentioned in the Talmud.[89] Hence, adopting this approach preempts the application of these grounds for enforceability of the obligation.

In the absence of a written adoption arrangement or in dealing with an arrangement which fails to provide for maintenance, are there additional grounds for enforceability? One suggestion is that the adoptive parental duty provides an example of the creation of an obligation based upon surety (*arevut*).[90] Generally speaking, in a conventional surety, an individual guarantees to pay the obligation of another person. The creditor must proceed first against the principal debt in order to satisfy the debt; and failing that, he is then allowed to recover payment from the guarantor. The creditor's willingness to loan the money is grounded upon reliance on the surety's promise to repay the loan. Since the guarantor receives *hana'ah* in being trusted by the creditor, a surety's obligation does not require a *kinyan* to be valid.[91] However, according to certain authorities,[92] this surety relationship is recognized even in the absence of the guarantor's agreement to repay the money. The factor which is instrumental in giving validity to this repayment obligation is the guarantor's feeling of responsibility to avoid causing a financial loss to the individual who relied upon and trusted in him. Hence, despite the absence of a surety agreement, the psychological benefit engendered by the creditor's trust obligates him. Analogously, since the adoptive child

87. Daichovsky, supra n. 75, at 281.

88. For a listing, see R. Abraham Karelitz (Israel, 1878–1953), *Hazon Ish, Bava Kamma* 21:5; *Resp. Heikhal Yitzchak* 40: *Anaf* 3–4.

89. *Hazon Ish, Bava Kamma* 22 & 21:5. See also, R. Isaac b. Sheshet (Spain: 14th cent.), *Resp. Ha-Rivash*, no. 129; 5 PDR 289, 297.

90. Daichovsky, supra n. 75, at 285.

91. Talmud Bavli *Bava Batra* 173b. For the invoking of the reliance element without adopting the *arevut* principle, see *Resp. Mishpetei Uziel, Even Ha-Ezer* 4.

92. *Hiddushei Ha-Ritva Ha-Hadashim Bava Metzia* 73b; 75b; R. Solomon ben Adret (Spain: 1235–1310), *Shittah Mekubbetzet, Bava Metzia* 118a; *Netivot Ha-Mishpat Hoshen Mishpat* 306:6; 3 PDR 18, 30.

could have been adopted by another family who would have provided food and clothing, consequently implied in the adoption proceeding is the adoptive parent's willingness to assume the support duty, a conventional responsibility incurred by all adoptive parents. This adoptive parental willingness to support is akin to an *arev* who feels responsible for the adoptive child's trust and reliance upon him. Hence, the adoptive parent has an obligation to support his adoptive child.

However, numerous authorities reject this special institution of *arevut* based upon an obligation.[93] Second, even if one recognizes the efficacy of this type of *arevut*, R. Farbstein, a contemporary decisor, argues that adoption cases must be distinguished from conventional monetary agreements.[94] For example, if one forwards money to an individual to engage in a commercial transaction for their mutual profit and the person fails to execute his assignment, pursuant to the above opinion, the individual has a right to collect consequential damages due to his reliance on the promisor's words. In the words of one decisor, "the promisee relied upon him and gave him money upon reliance; he therefore is obligated to compensate him for the incurred loss from relying upon the promise; due to the benefit he resolves to obligate himself, like a guarantor."[95] Since he relied upon his promise to engage in the transaction, the resulting damage occurred. Consequently, the promisor is obligated to reimburse the promisee for damages, similar to a guarantor who is obligated to make repayment. In effect, the lost profits arising from inactive capital generate a monetary right to compensatory damages. Adoption, to the contrary, is dealing with a child who is the beneficiary of a gift rather than exercising a monetary right. Hence, the surety arrangement cannot be extended to cover cases of adoption.

Alternatively, the argument has been advanced that the adoptive parental responsibility of support involves the fulfillment of an obligation (a *hiyuv*), namely the duty of charity (*tzedakah*).[96] Given the fact that *tzedakah* entails monies without determinate plaintiffs (*mammon*

---

93. R. Isaac b. Samuel (France: 12th cent.), *Tosafot Ha-Ri, Shittah Mekubbetzet*, id.; R. Asher b. Yehiel (Spain: 1250–1327), *Piskei Ha-Rosh, Bava Metzia*, 5:69; R. Mordekhai b. Hillel Ha-Kohen (Germany, 1240–1298), *Mordekhai, Bava Kamma*, 9: 114–115; R. Moses Margoliot (Lithuania, 18th cent.), *Pnei Moshe*, Talmud Yerushalmi *Bava Metzia* 5:3.

94. Daichovsky, supra n. 75.

95. Ritva in the name of his teacher, supra n. 92. For an elucidation of this position, see this writer's "The Theory of 'Efficient Breach': A Jewish Legal Perspective" in *Judaism and Economics* (Aaron Levine ed., Oxford 2010).

96. 3 PDR 109,116; Cohen, supra n. 75; Daichovsky, supra n. 75, at 286–287.

she'ain lo tov'in),[97] failure to donate is not justiciable. Whereas, for example, the failure to repay a loan gives rise to the claim and initiation of legal proceedings by a plaintiff (*zekhut teviyah*), the evasion of one's *tzedakah* obligation gives an adoptive child no legal redress against a recalcitrant parent who fails to furnish support. As the Israeli Rabbinical Court notes, "The obligation of *tzedakah*... is an obligation upon the individual, but he is not obligated to the recipient.... There is a general obligation of *tzedakah*... without a creditor to whom he is duty-bound to pay his obligation."[98] Despite the absence of a determinate recipient, the *Beit Din* explains, that a deserving and needy individual can approach the *Beit Din*, and as "a father of orphans"[99] it can compel an adoptive parent to fulfill his *tzedakah* obligation.[100] Aside from the issue of the absence of a plaintiff in the context of a *tzedakah* obligation, the scope of the duty is quite limited. Clearly, amounts of *tzedakah* were fixed at a tithe, limiting the potential donation. Second, the donor's and recipient's financial conditions become relevant factors. An adoptive parent may be obligated to provide support only after providing for his or her own needs.[101] Or if the adopted child is financially independent, there would be no obligation to give *tzedakah*.[102] Hence, there will be numerous situations where an adopted child will be bereft of clothing and food and become a public charge, dependent upon communal charity funds.[103] In sum, the underlying premise of these varied solutions for obligating an adoptive parent to support his adopted child[104] is that adoption does not

97. Talmud Bavli *Bava Kamma* 36b & 93a; *Hullin* 103b.

98. 1 PDR 145, 154–155.

99. Talmud Bavli *Gittin* 37a & *Bava Kamma* 37a.

100. PDR, supra n. 98.

101. *Shakh, Shulhan Arukh Yoreh Deah* 240: 5, 248:1; R. Moses Isserles (Poland, 1525–1572), *Rema* YD 251:3.

102. *Resp. Mishpetei Uziel, Even Ha-Ezer* 74; 2 PDR 301;4: 7; 7:136, 149–151.

103. TB *Nedarim* 65b; *Shulhan Arukh Yoreh Deah* 257:8.

104. Others have suggested that upon an adoptive parent's consent to an adoption, the parent has accepted all the secular legal responsibilities vis-à-vis the adopted child, including maintenance. See Nahum Rakover, "Adoption in Mishpat Ivri," (Hebrew) 11 *Deot* 55 (1960); Schachter, supra n. 75; Daichovsky, supra n. 75, at 285. Another suggestion is that upon the child's entrance into the adoptive parent's domicile, the parent becomes automatically obligated to support the child. See Daichovsky, supra n. 75, at 285, n. 3. According to all these approaches, there is an implicit assumption that upon reaching majority and becoming an individual of financial means, the adoptive child needs not reimburse his adoptive parents for their financial outlay of his living expenses. Though this conclusion seems to contradict the ruling in *Shulhan Arukh Hoshen Mishpat* 290:24, nevertheless, see *Rema, Yoreh Deah* 253:5 & *Resp. R. Akiva Eger, Pesakim* 147.

reflect the "factitious creation of blood relationships between persons who are not so related."[105] As *R. Gedaliah Felder* observes:[106]

> The Jewish family is built from its inception upon a natural foundation. Based upon a blood tie and unlike ancient nations who accepted a stranger into the family, adopted him and his rights were identical to the rights of a son, this approach is foreign to Jewish law.

Had adoption reflected the natural parent-child tie, there would be a similar support obligation as exists with regard to the nuclear family; a duty not contingent upon resolving certain contractual issues via the means of a *kinyan, gemirat daat, ha'anah,* employing a special *arevut* arrangement, or applying the norms of *tzedakah*. In short, the adoptive parent-child relationship is reflective of the halakhot of obligation and *tzedakah* rather than anchored in biology.[107] Given our conceptual understanding of the Jewish view of adoption, does contemporary Halakhah recognize functional parenthood as the defining yardstick for establishing legal parentage within the context of collaborative reproductive arrangements between Jews? Does "intending parenthood" as envisioned by Johnson and its progeny find any support in our contemporary Jewish legal tradition? To unravel the answer to this question, we shall address whether there exists a support obligation of offspring collaboratively reproduced either through artificial insemination utilizing the husband's semen, i.e., AIH, or artificial insemination utilizing

105. Huard, supra n. 73.

106. *Resp. Nahalat Zvi*, vol. 1, p. 180.

107. While attempting to structure adoption support law upon these varying grounds, the system simultaneously did not sever the ties between the natural parents and the adoptive child. Hence the requirement of open adoption records, see R. Joseph Henkin (U.S., 1880–1973), *Resp. Ibra* 2:72; R. Menashe Klein (U.S., 21st cent.) *Resp. Mishneh Halakhot* 4: 167, 170; For extenuating circumstances which allow the adoptive parent to conceal the natural parents' names from their adoptive child, see *Resp. Iggerot Moshe, Yoreh Deah* 1: 162; R. Samuel Werner (Israel: 20th cent.), *Resp. Mishpetei Shmuel, Mahadura Tinyana*, 3. For an excellent overview demonstrating that Jewish legal authorities recognized that biological ties between the adoptive child and his natural parents are not severed while simultaneously creating an adoptive relationship without treating it identical to a biological tie, see Nili Maimon, *The Laws of Child Adoption* (Hebrew) (Tel Aviv, 1994), 510–588.

For the applicability laws of privacy with a woman who is not your wife or halakhic daughter (*yihud*), see *Resp. Iggerot Moshe Even Ha-Ezer* 4:64; *Resp. Tzitz Eliezer* 6:40 (21).

another man's semen, i.e., AID. Both types of insemination involve the emission of semen into the female genital tract without sexual intercourse. Our analysis will establish the relationship between paternity and child maintenance within the context of collaborative reproduction. Does this relationship reflect the adoptive parent's ties to his adopted child? Subsequently, we will address contemporary approaches defining maternity in reproductive technology.

One of the frequently cited sources addressing this problem is the comment of the thirteenth-century French decisor R. Peretz b. Elijah of Corbeille, the author of the Hagahot Semak:[108]

> A woman may lie on her husband's sheets but should be careful not to lie on sheets which another man slept lest she become impregnated from his sperm. Why are we not afraid that she becomes pregnant from her husband's sperm and the child will be conceived of a menstruating female [niddah]? The answer is that since there is no forbidden intercourse, the child is completely legitimate [lit. kosher] even from the sperm of another.... However, we are concerned about the sperm of another man because the child may eventually marry his sister.

108. Cited by R. Yoel Sirkes (Poland, 1561–1650), *Bah, Tur Yoreh Deah* 195; R. Samuel Halevi (Poland: 1586–1667), *Turei Zahav, Yoreh Deah* 195:7; R. Samuel b. Phoebus (Poland, 17th cent.), *Beit Shmuel, Even Ha-Ezer* 1:10; R. Moshe Lima (Lithuania, 1605– 1658), *Helkat Mehokeik, Even Ha-Ezer* 1:8; *Mishneh Lemelekh, Mishneh Torah, Hilk. Ishut* 15:4. Though the above decisors concur that the child so conceived is legitimate ab inito, nevertheless there are various extant manuscripts of the *Hagahot Semak* which indicate that a child conceived sine concubito is a "son of a menstruant," and after the fact, i.e., *be-di-avad,* the child is legitimate. See R. Hayyim Joseph Azulai (Israel: 1724–1806), *Birkei Yosef, Even Ha-Ezer* 1:14; R. Joshua Boaz (Italy: 16th cent.), *Shiltei Gibborim Shevuot,* the beginning of chapter 2; Joseph Green, Artificial Insemination (Hebrew), 5 *Sefer Assia* 112, 114–116 (1986). Cf. with others who contend that according to the Birkei Yosef the child has no father. See Michael Corinaldi, "The Legal Status of a Child Born from Artificial Insemination from an Alien Donor or a Donated Ovum" (Hebrew), 18–19 *Shenaton Hamishpat Haivri* 295, 302–303 (1992–1994). For the impact of extant manuscripts upon the validity of the above decisors' rulings, see generally R. Ovadia Yosef (Israel, contemporary) *Resp. Yabia Omer Even Ha-Ezer* 2:1, subsection 10; R. Shlomo Z. Havlin, "Trends in the Publication of the Books of *Rishonim*" (Hebrew), 8 *Hamaayan* 36 (1968); Moshe Bleich, "The Role of Manuscripts in Halakhic Decision-Making," 27 *Tradition* 22 (1993); Yaakov Spiegel, *Chapters in the History of the Jewish Book: Scholars and Their Annotations* (Hebrew) (Ramat Gan, 1996), 479–514. The translation of the excerpt from *Hagahot Semak* has been culled from Fred Rosner, *Modern Medicine and Jewish Ethics* (New York, 1986) 93–94.

Whether or not a woman can, in fact, be impregnated by sperm while lying on bed sheets, R. Peretz recognizes the empirical possibility of *conception sine concubito*. Second, the offspring is considered legitimate even if the wife were forbidden to her husband on account of her status of ritual impurity, i.e., menstruating.[109] The majority of decisors subscribe to this position, and due to the creation of the paternal ties, the father is obligated to support the child.[110]

However, R. Peretz demurs in the case of a couple who resort to AID, i.e., insemination from the semen of an anonymous donor, not the husband; a situation reminiscent of the traditional surrogacy arrangements. Though AID is not to be equated with adultery due to the absence of sexual intercourse, nevertheless there is a concern that an incestuous relationship may develop at a later date when the child will marry his own sibling. In addition to the concern regarding a future consanguineous marriage, there are numerous halakhic moral considerations which have been expressed:[111]

> From a psychological point of view, AID is detrimental to the marriage, for it makes the husband feel deficient and lacking function. The couple may thus become estranged, thereby frustrating the whole purpose of allowing AID which is to create conjugal harmony.... In the halakhic literature, we find many expressions of spiritual opposition to the act itself. Some of the authorities have termed AID ugliness, abomination, prostitution and licentiousness.... Should AID be permitted, there arises the grave moral fear that semen of one donor, or a group of donors, may be used to "produce" a whole generation, justified on the eugenic grounds of improving the strain. This would lead to genetic selection, which is detrimental to the institution of the family.... There are some authorities who forbid AID because of the halakhic problems which would arise should it be

---

109. *Resp. Iggerot Moshe, Even Ha-Ezer* 2:18.

110. Isaac Indig, "Maintenance Obligation in Cases of Artificial Insemination," (Hebrew), 2 *Dine Israel* 83, 85–99 (1971); R. J. David Bleich, *Contemporary Halakhic Problems*, vol. IV (New York, 1995), 240, n. 9; For dissenting opinions, see Indig, id.; Rosner, supra n. 108, at 96–97; Bleich, op. cit.

111. Moshe Drori, *Artificial Insemination, in Jewish Law & Current Problems* ed. Nahum Rakover (Jerusalem, 1984), 203, 210–212. *Resp. Iggerot Moshe, Even Ha-Ezer*, 1: 71, 2:11; R. Yehiel Weinberg (Switzerland, 20th cent.), *Resp. Seridei Esh* 3:5; *Resp. Mishpetei Uziel Even Ha-Ezer* 19; R. Ovadiah Hadayah (Israel, 20th cent.) *Resp. Yaskil Avdi*, 5, *Even Ha-Ezer* 10; *Resp. Tzitz Eliezer* 3:27; 9:51 and many others.

> permitted. Thus, for example, a woman who was a real adulteress could claim that she had conceived by artificial insemination, or a woman undergoing AID might be brought to real adultery with the donor.

Nevertheless, if the procedure is implemented, R. Peretz concludes, the child is legitimate, a position accepted by various contemporary decisors.[112] Others have argued that the implantation of a stranger's semen even without sexual intercourse constitutes adultery plain and simple, and the offspring is considered a halakhic bastard (*mamzer*) or a "doubtful *mamzer*."[113] Whereas in other legal systems a child born out of wedlock where no capital crime has been committed has the status of a bastard, in Jewish law there must be an incestuous act involving a capital crime in order to be labeled a *mamzer*.[114] In other words, those authorities who accorded the child the status of a *mamzer* or a *safek* (doubtful) *mamzer* have expanded the concept of halakhic bastardy (*mamzerut*). The status of *mamzerut* is created by a child who is born from the union of any individuals who cannot consummate a valid marriage as well as from individuals involved in an adulterous relationship.[115]

Regardless of whether one considers the child perfectly legitimate or a *mamzer*, the common denominator of the various opinions is that the donor of the sperm is obligated to provide maintenance for the offspring. However, the nature of the obligation may differ. The sources of child maintenance can be based upon either rabbinic legislation or the norms of *tzedakah*. *Mezonot* based upon rabbinic enactment is a direct obligation of the father to his child which is absolute and unconditional, irrespective of the financial situation of the father or of the children. A *tzedakah* obligation, on the other hand, as we mentioned, is conditional on the financial ability of the father to provide for the child and the inability of the child to provide for himself.[116] If *mezonot* is based on the norms of *tzedakah*, it is questionable whether the child has legal standing to sue. As an Israeli Rabbinical Court observes:[117]

---

112. R. Menachem Kirschenbaum (twentieth cent.), *Resp. Menahem Meshiv* 2:26; R. Yehoshua Baumol (U.S., 1880–1948), *Resp. Emek Halakhah* 1:68; *Resp. Mishpetei Uziel Even Ha-Ezer* 19; *Resp. Iggerot Moshe, Even Ha-Ezer* 1:10, 71 & 2:11.
113. Indig, supra n. 110, at 100–104; Rosner, supra n.108, at 96–97.
114. Talmud Bavli *Yevamot* 45b; *Shulhan Arukh Even Ha-Ezer* 4:13.
115. J. David Bleich, *Bioethical Dilemmas* (New York, 1998), 248–249.
116. 1 PDR 145, 156–157.
117. PDR, ibid.

> If the obligation is out of charity, one who is able is obliged to give, but this is an obligation applying to him and he is not indebted to the recipient. Even if he is obligated to give charity to a specific person, as in the case of a father to his son... it is not indebtedness to the son.

On these grounds, the son is bereft of legal standing to sue his father.

Adopting the first approach, which recognizes the legitimacy of offspring who are a product of AID, inexorably leads to the conclusion that the *mezonot* obligation is a direct one. On the other hand, if the product of this collaborative reproduction arrangement is accorded the status of a *mamzer* or a *safek mamzer*, there is a dispute regarding the source of the *mezonot* duty, whether it is based upon rabbinic legislation or *tzedakah*.[118] In short, this obligation, whether direct or based upon *tzedakah*, is engendered by paternity, regardless of the child's personal status. However, we are dealing with an anonymous donor of semen; hence the identity of the father is unknown. Unable to trace his father's whereabouts, the child will be bereft of food and clothing. The question arises whether the husband of the wife who provided the gametes, conceived, and gave birth to the child becomes obligated to maintain the child. Regardless of whether one views AID as adultery or not, the wife requires the husband's prior consent before undergoing the procedure.[119]

---

118. *Shakh, Shulhan Arukh Hoshen Mishpat* 87:57; 1 PDR 145, 156–157; 2 PDR 154. Cf. R. Israel Isserlein (Germany: 15th cent.), *Resp. Terumat Ha-Deshen, Pesakim* 37 who expresses a doubt regarding this conclusion.

119. Clearly, if the procedure is subsumed in the category of adultery (see text accompanying n. 113), then obtaining of the husband's consent cannot nullify the prohibition. A husband's consent to continue living with his adulterous wife is no defense, as per 1 PDR 5, 12. See Joseph Green, "Artificial Insemination in Case Law & Legislation in the State of Israel," (Hebrew) 5 *Sefer Assia* 125, 127, n. 9 (1986). Despite the irrelevancy of the husband's consent regarding the impropriety of the act, nevertheless authorities concur, that the wife is bound to her husband by a lien regarding conjugal relations (*shi'bud*).

See this writer's "Solomonic Decisions in Frozen Preembryo Disposition: Unscrambling the Halakhic Conundrum," 36 *Tradition* 31, 37, n. 8 (2002) and "Spousal Emotional Stress: Proposed Relief for the Modern Day *Agunah*," 55 *The Journal of Halacha and Contemporary Society* 49, 54, n. 14 (2008). Without her husband's consent, her participation in this procedure constitutes an infringement of the lien. See *Resp. Iggerot Moshe Even Ha-Ezer* 1:71; R. Eliezer Waldenberg (Israel, contemporary) *Resp. Tzitz Eliezer* 13:97; Unpublished Haifa Regional Rabbinical Court Decision cited in Green ad. locum, 133. Whether a wife's undertaking this procedure without her husband's prior consent is grounds for divorce, see R. Mordechai Breisch (Switzerland: 1895–1977), *Resp. Helkat Yaakov* 1:24; *Resp. Tzitz Eliezer* 9:51;

In the absence of his consent, the husband is exempt from child support.[120]

Given the absence of a paternal tie to the child, what are the grounds for obligating the husband in child support? There are two possible bases for the duty. First, it could be construed as an implied condition of marriage. The wife desires the procedure in the belief that the offspring represents her last remaining opportunity for genetic motherhood—in Talmudic parlance, "wanting a staff to lean on and a spade for burial."[121] In contemporary times, this woman's cause of action has been understood as a means to contribute to her psychological as well as her material well-being.[122] However, this cause of action will not serve as a defense if the wife undergoes the procedure without her husband's consent.[123] Due to his consent, she is willing to remain married to him and views her continued commitment in exchange for her husband's readiness to support the offspring produced from the insemination process. Alternatively, a more far-reaching position is evidenced in the 1977 decision of a Haifa Regional Rabbinical Court. Predicating its decision upon the position that AID is not considered adultery, the Beit Din notes: Since he has agreed to the procedure, therefore all the obligations that flow from this fact accord him the status of a guarantor (*arev*), and clearly under these circumstances all the ingredients that obligate an *arev* exist.[124] Given the absence of a *kinyan* and an explicit commitment to child support, one contemporary writer questions the efficacy of this *arevut*.[125] However, as we discussed in our examination of the varying frameworks for establishing a support duty for an adoptive child,

13:97; R. Shmuel Halevi Wosner (Israel: contemporary) *Resp. Shevet Halevi* 3: 175; R. Isaac Weiss (Israel, contemporary) *Resp. Minhat Yitzchak* 4:5; *Resp. Iggerot Moshe, Even Ha-Ezer* 1:71.

120. In fact, R. Waldenberg advances the notion that the absence of consent to the adulterous act of AID is an infringement of his *shi'bud*, resulting in child support exemption. See *Resp. Tzitz Eliezer* 13 97:4. For the exemption of child support and the wife's medical expenses in cases of a husband's refusal to consent to the procedure, see *Resp. Iggerot Moshe Even Ha-Ezer* 1:10 (end); 71.

121. Talmud Bavli *Yevamot* 65b; Y. Goldberg, *Ellu Kofin Le-Hotzi,* Jerusalem: 5773, 305-322.

122. 1 PDR 8; 4: 356. Cf. Nahmanides, *Milhamot, Yevamot* 20b, s.v. *veod hu.*

123. *Resp. Tzitz Eliezer* 13:97.

124. Green, supra n.119, at 133. Clearly, he is not the father of the offspring and therefore there exists no *mezonot* obligation similar to a natural father's duty. See *Taz, Even Ha-Ezer* 1:8; R. Malkiel Tenenbaum (Poland, 19th cent.), *Resp. Divrei Malkiel* 4:107; *Resp. Sreidei Esh* 3:5.

125. Id. at 133, n. 38.

hana'ah can create an *arevut* which will mandate a support obligation.[126] As in the case of the adoptive child, the obligation is a product of the relations between the adoptive parents; similarly, in our issue at bar, the duty materializes due to spousal ties. As the Haifa Beit Din observes, in the case of a recalcitrant husband, the wife as the plaintiff is submitting a claim for *mezonot* based upon the halakhic norms of obligations vis-à-vis her husband rather than representing the child as a guardian ad litem enforcing a direct obligation owed by the husband to the child.[127]

As one contemporary scholar argues:[128]

> The court did not base the husband's support liability on his direct commitment to support the child... instead, the court held that the husband is obligated to pay the mother for supporting the child. A direct obligation to support the child would be invalid for two reasons. First, at the time the husband consented to the AID procedure, the child was obviously not yet conceived. Most authorities hold that an obligation made to one who did not exist at the time of the obligation was made is not valid. Second, under Jewish law, to become valid a transaction generally requires the performance of a formal act (*kinyan*). No such act was performed, and therefore no valid agreement was made in this case.

The systemic limitations of a possible direct duty vis-à-vis the child, i.e., the absence of a *kinyan* and obligee at the inception of the obligation, serve as the grounds for the nonapplicability of the direct duty. Consequently, the support obligation emerged as a result of the husband's acceding to his wife's request to undergo the procedure. Hence, there exists a husband's duty to his wife to pay for the child's expenses.

In sum, paternity is established based on biology rather than parental intent. In the framework of collaborative reproduction, whether it is AIH or AID, the sperm donor becomes the legal father of the offspring, regardless of his personal status in the eyes of Jewish law.[129] In

126. Supra text accompanying nn. 84–92.

127. Green, supra n. 119, at 134, n. 39.

128. Chaim Povarsky, "Regulating Advanced Reproductive Technologies: A Comparative Analysis of Jewish & American Law," 29 *U. Toledo L. Rev.*, 409, 444 (1998).

129. R. Shlomo Z. Urbach, "Artificial Insemination" (Hebrew), 1 *Noam* 145 (1958); *Resp. Minhat Yitzchak* 1:50; 4:5; Cf. *Birkei Yosef*, supra n. 108; R. Menachem Kasher, *Torah Shelemah*, 17, Addendum, 4:16; *Resp. Tzitz Eliezer* 9:51; 15:45;

effect, reproductive noncoital arrangements reflect coital reproduction, wherein paternity is created biologically on the basis of having provided the sperm in the context of sexual intercourse either with one's marital partner or with one with whom he has been involved in an adulterous or incestuous relationship. In the absence of paternity, as in the case of the husband in an AIH procedure, support is based on the halakhah of obligations or the norms of *tzedakah* rather than a direct duty imposed by the system. Regarding the duty of maintenance, the husband in AIH and an adoptive parent possess identical obligations.

In contrast to determining paternity, with the advent of reproductive technology, the answer to the question of who is the child's mother, depending on the context, is not so easily resolved. Regarding traditional surrogacy, such as the Baby M and Moschetta cases, where the genetic and gestational mothers are identical, maternal parentage is clear-cut. However, in situations where there is implantation of an embryo or a fetus from a genetic mother to a surrogate mother, the issue of maternity becomes more complex. In such cases of gestational surrogacy, numerous contemporary decisors have raised the question of maternity, i.e., whether the genetic mother, the gestational mother, or both the genetic and gestational mothers are considered the halakhic mother of the resulting child. As in numerous other instances, contemporary authorities resort to the use of analogical reasoning and legal logic, i.e., *sevara*. Earlier halakhic sources are scrutinized to determine the relevant rules and these are then applied to the new situation. As the Hazon

Waldenberg, "Test-Tube Babies" (Hebrew), 5 *Sefer Assia* 84, 89–90 (1986). Despite the fact that Jewish law emphasizes biological identity, status and lineage, nevertheless, one of the rationales advanced by arbiters who construe AIH as a form of adultery indicates that countervailing considerations will sever the father's biological status. According to the Talmud (Talmud Bavli *Yevamot* 23a, 98b; *Kiddushin* 17b), upon conversion and intermarriage, all familial relationships are severed based upon the rule of *afkerei rachmanah le'zar'eh* (hereinafter: *afkerei*), the legal system abandons the sperm. Analogously, in our case and relying upon the precedent-setting responsum of R. Menachem Fano (1548–1620) *Resp. Rama Mefano* 116, authorities argue that *afkerei* dictates that a woman's insemination by another man (AID) severs any genealogical relationship between the sperm donor and the child. See *Resp. Emek Halakha* 2:10; *Resp. Tzitz Eliezer* 9:51; 15:45, *Sefer Assia*, ibid. at 305; Corinaldi, supra n. 108, at 305. For an additional example of the implementation of "*afkerei*" in artificial insemination, i.e., postmortem sperm implantation, see *Resp. Noda Be-Yehudah, Mahadura Kamma Even Ha-Ezer* 69; R. Urbach, supra n. 129, at 155; R. Moshe Hershler, Halakhic Problems of Test-Tube Babies, in *Halakha & Medicine* (ed. M. Hershler), Jerusalem: 1980, 207, 214–215. R. Shaul Yisraeli (Israel, 20th cent.), *Resp. Havot Binyamin* 3: p. 686–687; Yitzchak Breitowitz, "Halakhic Alternatives in IVF—Pregnancies: A Survey," 14 *Jewish Law Annual* 29, 91–94 (2003).

Ish observes: "one cannot make a distinction between explicit rules and those which are not explicit. Indeed, no rules are not explicit, for everything is explicit in our Torah."[130] Jewish law responds to the challenge in accordance with its own inner logic and on the basis of its prescribed methods, procedures, and canons of interpretation, relying on its own sources to resolve this question.

Among present-day legists there is a heated discussion concerning this problem. Rabbis Shlomo Goren and Itamar Warhaftig regard the genetic mother as the legal mother. In accordance with a tannaitic source[131] cited by both the Jerusalem and Babylonian Talmuds:[132]

> There are three partners in the creation of man: the Holy One, his father, and his mother. The father contributes the semen from which the child's bones, sinews, nails, the brain, and the white in his eye are formed. The mother contributes the red from which the skin, flesh, blood, hair, and the black of the eye are formed. And the Holy One contributes the spirit and the breath, facial features, eyesight, hearing, the power of speech... understanding and intelligence.

Upon fertilization, fatherhood and motherhood are defined genetically and the womb of the surrogate mother is merely a medium for growth of the embryo.[133] The significance of conception can be demonstrated from the ritual law that the milk of an animal possessing a physical defect in one of its organs (a *treifa*) is not included the prohibition of mixtures of meat and milk. As R. Akiva Eiger states:[134]

> It is questionable whether the milk of a *treifa* is included in the prohibition, according to the principle that a *treifa* cannot give birth, and hence is unable to be a mother. See Sanhedrin 69a

130. *Sefer Hazon Ish, Hoshen Mishpat, Likkutim* 16:1.

131. A tannaitic source is one of the sources of Jewish law which was recorded between the first century C.E. and 220 C.E.

132. Talmud Yerushalmi *Kilayim* 8:3; Talmud Bavli *Niddah* 31b. R. Goren, *Torat Harefuah* (Hebrew) (Jerusalem, 1999), 271.

133. Itamar Warhaftig, "The Validity of a Surrogate Agreement" (Hebrew), 16 *Tehumin* 181, 185 (1997) & "Establishment of Maternity: Addendum," (Hebrew) 5 *Tehumin* 268–69 (1984).

134. R. Akiva Eiger, *Shulhan Arukh Yoreh Dea*h 87:6. Translation is culled from R. Zalman N. Goldberg, "Maternity in Fetal Transplants," in *Crossroads: Halacha & the Modern World* (ed. E. Rosenfeld, Alon Shvut, 1987), 71, 72.

> (where the Talmud excludes from the halakhot of the rebellious son one who has reached the majority three months earlier, as he is considered to be a [potential] father and not a son. He is capable of impregnating a woman from when he attains majority, and after three months the pregnancy is evident, at which time, he is called a father.) This implies that the father of an embryo is considered to be a father. Similarly, in our case, the *treifa* is capable of being a mother, since she can conceive, although she cannot deliver (see Shakh Yoreh Deah 57:45). The mother of the embryo is also considered a mother. However, it is possible that the parent of an embryo is considered a parent only if the embryo will be delivered in the future. A *treifa*, however, who cannot deliver, is not considered to be a mother while pregnant. Subsequently, I discovered that the Issur Veheter (31:14) ruled that the milk of a *treifa* is included in the Torah prohibition of milk-meat because it was impregnated before she became a *treifa*, she is capable of delivering even when a *treifa*. Accordingly, the milk of an animal born a *treifa* will not be included in the prohibition.

According to this line of reasoning, motherhood is established by conception. Hence, in a gestational surrogacy arrangement, the genetic mother is the legal mother. In contrast, earlier twentieth-century arbiters such as Rabbis Binyamin Weiss and Yekutiel Kamelhar found corroboration for the rejection of genetics as determinative in the laws of plant grafting.[135] The fruits of a tree are forbidden as *orlah* during its first three years of growth. The Talmud Sotah 43b adds a caveat that a fruit of a seedling grafted onto the mature tree loses its halakhic status and is not considered *orlah.* Analogously speaking, in our issue at bar, the offspring of a fertilized ovum implanted in a surrogate assumes the identity of the nurturing woman rather the genetic mother. However, R. Yaakov Ariel contends that the *orlah* analogy is flawed. Whereas the seedling, upon being grafted, loses its identity, the fetus is distinct and eventually will exit the surrogate's womb and therefore one could claim

135. R. Binyamin Weiss, *Resp. Even Yekarah* 3:29; R. Yekutiel Kamelhar, *Hatalmud Umada'ei Hatevel* (Lemberg, 1908), 44–45. Though both respondents are applying the laws of plant grafting to ovarian transplants, the analogy equally applies to gestational surrogacy. See J. David Bleich, *Contemporary Halakhic Problems* (New York, 1977), 107–108.

that it assumes identity from the woman who is the gamete provider.[136] The absence of the offspring's identity is underscored by the Talmudic statement that a fetus less than forty days old is "mere water."[137] Hence, argue R. Ahron Soloveichik, R. Shaul Yisraeli, R. Mordechai Halperin, and R. Yehoshua Ben-Meir,[138] the lack of identity implies the absence of legal parentage. Even though genetics is the basis of fatherhood, the birth mother is the legal mother. Seemingly, this source seems to be dispositive regarding this issue. However, numerous decisors argue that an embryo during the first forty days of gestation may acquire property and inherit.[139] Hence, the recognition of legal capacity is not conditional upon the embryo's future development. Analogously, one could argue that the establishment of parenthood is not contingent upon a particular stage of fetal development.

Third, the rejection of genetics as a determinant of motherhood emerges from the Talmudic law of conversion, a frequently cited argument in favor of those legists who invoke birth as the determinant of maternity.[140] The Talmud observes:[141]

> Twin brothers who are converts or emancipated slaves do not

136. R. Yaakov Ariel, "Artificial Insemination & Surrogacy" (Hebrew), 16 *Tehumin* 171, 177 (1997).

137. Talmud Bavli *Yevamot* 69b.The legal significance of this description of the formation of the embryo, for purposes of the halakhot of priestly tithes (*teruma*) and abortion is beyond the scope of this presentation.

138. R. Moshe Soloveichik, "The Law of Test-tube Babies," (Hebrew) 100 *Ohr Hamizrach* 122, 125 (1980) in the name of R. Ahron Soloveichik; R. Shaul Yisraeli, Resp. Havot Binyamin 2:68 R. Mordechai Halperin, "Modern Perspectives on Halachah & Medicine," in *Medicine & Jewish Law* (ed. F. Rosner, New York, 1990), 175; R. Yehoshua Ben-Meir, "Legal & Genetic Parenthood in Jewish Law," 12 *Jewish Law Annual* 153, 165–166 (1997).

139. R. Menahem Hameiri, citing "the majority of commentators" in *Sefer Bet Ha-Behira* Tractate *Bava Batra* 141a; Maimonides, *Mishneh Torah, Hilk. Mekhirah* 22:10; R. Joseph Caro, *Beit Yosef, Hoshen Mishpat* 210 in the name of the *Ittur*; Sma *Hoshen Mishpat* 210:4 in the name of the *Tur* and *Shulhan Arukh*.

140. R. Moshe Hershler, "Halakhic Problems with Test-Tube Babies" (Hebrew), in *Halakha & Medicine* (ed. M. Hershler, Jerusalem, 1980), 316; R. Zalman N. Goldberg, "Fetal Implants" (Hebrew), 5 *Tehumin* 248, 252 (1984); R. Abraham Kilav, "Test-Tube Babies"(Hebrew), 5 *Tehumin* 260, 261 (1984), R. Moshe Hershler, "Test-tube Babies in Jewish Law" (Hebrew), in *Halakha & Medicine* (ed. M. Hershler, Jerusalem, 1985), 90, 93.

141. Talmud Bavli *Yevamot* 97b. The translation is culled from Goldberg, Fetal Implants, supra n. 134, at 74.

> perform *yibum* or *halitzah* [for each other],[142] nor is one prohibited [from marrying] the other's widow. (Rashi—Even if the [first] marriage was contracted after the conversion, as a convert is like a newborn child and therefore he does not have the relationship of brotherhood, even [with a child] from the same mother.) If their conception was before conversion and their birth after conversion, they do not perform *yibum* or *halitzah* (Rashi—Because *yibum* is dependent on the father's side, and they do not have a father), but are prohibited from marrying each other's widow (Rashi— ...because of the prohibition of the wife of a brother on the mother's side, as the mother is like any Jewess who bears children).

Based upon the Talmudic rule that "a non-Jew who converts is akin to a newly born child,"[143] an individual who converts to Judaism legally severs all of his non-Jewish familial ties for purposes of Jewish law. Nevertheless, the twin brothers who were conceived by a non-Jewish woman who converted during her pregnancy are considered brothers from their common maternal lineage and are proscribed from marrying each other's wives. Given that upon conversion all previously established familial ties are legally severed, why are the twin brothers obligated to refrain from marrying each other's wives? Obviously, the brothers never converted but are Jewish due to being born from a Jewish mother. The filial relationship is reestablished at the time of birth. As Rashi observes, "the mother is like any other Jewess who bears children."[144] Since at the time of birth the mother was Jewish, her offspring are Jewish and are therefore obligated to refrain from incestuous relationships. Accordingly, birth rather than conception establishes parenthood. Analogously, the legal mother in a gestational surrogacy arrangement is the surrogate mother.

At first glance, it would appear that this source resolves our question. In fact, it is corroborated by various Talmudic dicta which indicate that a child conceived by a non-Jewish woman who converted during

142. *Yibum* is levirate marriage (*Devarim* 25:5) of the widow of a man who died childless and is survived by a brother. He is obligated to either marry her or renounce his duty by means of a ceremony called *halitzah*, literally, removing a shoe, severing the bond between the brother-in-law and the sister-in-law.

143. Talmud Bavli *Yevamot* 22a, 62a, 97b; *Bekhorot* 47a. For the notion that the process of conversion by means of circumcision and immersion in a ritual bath, i.e., *mikveh*, is viewed legally as a physical transformation, see *Tosafot, Sanhedrin* 68b, s.v. katan.

144. R. Solomon b. Isaac (France, 1040–1105) *Yevamot* 97b, s.v. *aval hayavin*.

pregnancy is exempt from conversion and that such a child is obligated in various laws of the firstborn.[145] Here again, birth establishes maternity, with attendant obligations mandated for the Jewish offspring. Second, implicit in this understanding of the twin-brothers passage is that only the pregnant woman undergoes conversion and the child is born as a full-fledged Jew. Various legists argue[146] that this line of reasoning is in consonance with the majority opinion[147] that *ubar yerekh imo*, literally, the fetus is its mother's thigh. Since the fetus is viewed as an integral part of the mother, therefore, upon her conversion, she becomes a Jewess and the child is born as a Jew. However, if one contends that *ubar lav yerekh imo*, literally, the fetus is not its mother's thigh, then the fetus possesses its own legal identity. Hence, the fetus, while in his mother's womb undergoes his own independent conversion.[148] Consequently, there is no compelling reason to claim that the child's lineage to his mother is established at birth rather than at conception. Pursuant to this line of reasoning, logic dictates that maternity is determined by conception. Alternatively, one can argue that only with regard to the Talmudic cases which explicitly raise the issue of *ubar yerekh imo* or *lav yerekh imo* ought this controversy be of concern. However, in Talmudic cases such as the twin brothers which fail to invoke this dispute, one must refrain from introducing it.[149] Hence, there is no compelling reason for us to

145. Talmud Bavli *Yevamot* 78a, *Bekhorot* 46a.

146. R. Yehiel Epstein (Belarus, 1829–1908), *Arukh Ha-Shulhan Hoshen Mishpat* 268:1; R. Aryeh Leib Heller (Galicia, 1745–1813), *Avnei Millu'im Even Ha-Ezer* 13:4; R. Zvi Pesach Frank (Israel, 20th cent.) *Resp. Har Tzvi Yoreh Deah* 223–224.

147. In addition to over a dozen sources cited by Abraham Steinberg, *Encyclopedia of Jewish Medical Ethics* (Hebrew) Jerusalem, 1996), 125–126, n. 178, see *Arukh Ha-Shulhan Hoshen Mishpat* 268:11; R. David b. Zimra (Egypt and Israel, 16th cent.) *Resp. Ha-Ridbaz* 1:188. Maimonides' stance regarding this issue is unclear. For a listing of numerous commentators who attempt to clarify his position, see Steinberg, id., and R. A. Eiger, *Derush Vehiddush Ketubot* 11:1.

148. Given the fact that the fetus is in its natural state of development, i.e., in utero, the mother and the fetus underwent conversion by the same immersion. See Talmud Bavli *Yevamot* 78a. This conclusion is predicated upon the fact that the mother's body is not an interposition with the fetus. See R. A. Eiger, supra n. 147, at s.v. *vehatosfot*. Upon birth, the male child will require circumcision in order to finalize his status as a convert. See Nahmanides, *Hiddushei Ha-Ramban Yevamot* 47b; Rashba, *Hiddushei Ha-Rashba Yevamot* 47b. For the ramifications of the status of this newly born uncircumcised child, see R. Naftoli Tropp, *Hiddushin Ketubot*, No. 28; *Hiddushin Yevamot*, No. 11. Cf. with Ritva, *Hiddushei Ha-Ritva Yevamot* 47b who argues that the fetus in his mother's womb is like a female who requires immersion only.

149. Elyakim Ellenson, "The Fetus in Halakhah" (Hebrew), 66 *Sinai* 20, 28–29 (1970).

explain this Talmudic dictum in light of this controversy. Nonetheless, the analogy between the pregnant gentile woman who converted and our situation of gestational surrogacy is flawed. Implicit in the employment of this analogy is that one can extend the norm governing the twin-brothers case, which is predicated upon one set of fact patterns, to our fact pattern, i.e., surrogacy, which is similar in relevant respects. Regarding the conversion case, based upon the rule that "a convert is akin to a newly born child," all his natural ties have been legally severed, including to his mother, a gamete provider. In effect, his only biological mother is the one who brought him into this world. Though in terms of reality, his gestational mother is identical with the conceiving mother, nevertheless for purposes of Halakhah, based upon his newly born status as a convert, it is a different mother. Hence, in such a situation, birth establishes maternity. On the other hand, in a gestational surrogacy arrangement, the child has two mothers, a genetic mother and a gestational one, and maternity may possibly be determined by the genetic one.[150] Therefore, R. Levi Halperin argues that in the case of the offspring of a fertilized ovum of a Jewish couple which is implanted in a surrogate and carried to term, maternity (as well as paternity) is determined by genetic origin.[151] In fact, it has been contended that even though conversion annuls familial ties, it cannot erase the biological fact that the birth mother is identical to the genetic mother in the conversion scenarios. In other words, the inference from the conversion situation is that in order for maternity to be based upon parturition, the gestational mother must have been the genetic mother. The conversion scenario proves that the establishment of maternity based upon birth is contingent upon the reality of genetics rather than that parturition is the sole determinant of maternity.[152] Hence, the laws of conversion cannot serve as an analogy to demonstrate that the gestational surrogate is the legal mother of the child.

In sum, the common denominator of these proofs is either that a particular source offers a clear answer to our question, such as R. Akiva Eiger's observation regarding the law of *treifa*, or the source is open to analogy and counter-analogy, as in the cases of plant grafting

150. R. Yaakov Ariel (Israel, 21st cent.), "Artificial Insemination & Surrogacy," 16 *Tehumin* 171, 175 (1997).

151. R. Levi Halperin (Israel, 21st cent.) *Resp. Ma'asheh Hoshev*, 3:37.

152. R. Ezra Bick, "Ovum Donations: A Rabbinic Conceptual Model of Maternity, 28 *Tradition* 28, 29 (1993). Cf. J David Bleich, Maternal Identity Revisited," 28 *Tradition* 52 (1994).

and conversion. Interestingly enough, we find sources that invoke the possibility that both conception and parturition are determinants of maternity, i.e., dual-motherhood. For example, in summarizing a Talmudic source, suggestive of a theory of dual-motherhood as propounded by Professor Low,[153] R. Bleich observes:[154]

> Analogously speaking, is fetal development to be determined by the conceiving mother, similar to the stalk's growth in its initial location which is determinative or by the gestational mother which is akin to the additional grain growth after transplantation which is determinative? Since regarding the case of the grain, the Talmud leaves the situation open and rules that the stringencies of both identities must be invoked, similarly, in a surrogacy arrangement; the fetus should be regarded as having two mothers.

Though all these sources do not address our issue explicitly, the common denominator is that contemporary legists substantiate their claims by distilling the literary sources of the tradition by employing logic and analogical reasoning in order to arrive at their positions.

Given our overview of their thought processes which indicate the intrinsic difficulties with each posture, it is not surprising to find a minority of decisors argue logically, without recourse to precedent, that the fetus is bereft of a natural mother (and equally a biological father). In fact, cognizant of this unique approach to our question, R. Bleich summarizes this approach and reacts to it on purely logical grounds. R. Bleich observes:[155]

> R. Eliezer Waldenberg, Ziz Eliezer, XV, no. 45, has advanced the novel view that… a child born of an in vitro fertilization has neither a father nor a mother…. Rabbi Waldenberg's reasons, which are not based upon cited precedents or analogy to other halakhic provisions, are three in number: (1) fertilization in the course of in vitro procedure occurs in an "unnatural"

153. Prof. Zev Low, "Test-Tube Baby: The Status of a Surrogate Mother," (Hebrew) in 2 *Emek Halakha* 163, 165–169 (1989).

154. Bleich, supra n. 110, at 254–255. For an additional source underwriting this theory, see Bleich, id. 257.

155. Bleich, id. 238–239. For a similar approach to R. Waldenberg's, see R. Yehudah Gershuni, "The First Test-Tube Baby in the World According to Halakha" (Hebrew) 27 *Ohr Hamizrach* 15 (1979).

> manner through the intermediacy of a "third power" extraneous to the father or mother, i.e., the Petri dish. (2) Conception occurs in a manner "that has no relationship to genealogy." (3) In natural reproduction the ovum remains "attached" to the body and is fertilized therein. Maternal identity is consequent solely upon fertilization that occurs while the ovum is yet attached to the mother's body. Thus, upon "severance" and removal of the ovum from the mother's body any genealogical relationship between the ovum and the mother is destroyed.... In response to the first argument it must be stated that the Petri dish is not a "third power" and in no way contributes biologically or chemically to the fertilization process. It is simply a convenient receptacle... in which fertilization may occur. Rabbi Waldenberg's second argument... is entirely conclusory. In order to demonstrate that no maternal relationship exists, some evidence or argument must be presented that would serve to demonstrate that genealogical relationships are generated solely in utero. Whatever cogency the third argument may have is lost if it is recognized that parturition, in and of itself, establishes a maternal relationship.

This give-and-take based on logical argumentation without resorting to source citation adds an additional dimension to the heated debate regarding the determinants of maternity. Essentially, whereas the other contemporary decisors utilize analogical reasoning to arrive at their conclusion, R. Waldenberg extrapolates the unperceived association, the unifying characteristic which informs the myriad of details, to articulate the concept which underlies the many disparate facts. For the Netziv, decision-making is a reflection of an ongoing process of employing either sheer untrammeled logic, i.e., *pilpul,* or analogical reasoning, i.e., *medama milta lemilta.*[156] Our discussion regarding the definition of maternity reflects the exercise of both types of reasoning. In sum, the absence of a clear-cut answer to our issue has allowed legists to resort to the use of analogies and counter-analogies from such diverse areas of the legal system as the laws of conversion, plant grafting, dietary laws,

156. *Ha'amek Davar, Shemot* 34:1, *Bamidbar* 15:33, and *Devarim* 10:6. See this writer's *Rabbinic Authority,* vol. 1, 53-57.

agricultural law,[157] animal husbandry law,[158] and inheritance law,[159] and to the employment of sheer logic to establish a determinant of maternity,[160] and animal genealogy to define maternal parenthood.[161] In the absence of a clear-cut determinative answer to our question and/or in light of the emergence of counter analogies from the heated discussions regarding this matter, authorities have even attempted to yield a halakhic solution based upon various *aggadic* sources, an obviously problematic approach, generally speaking.[162]

Contemporary discussions regarding collaborative reproduction reflect our understanding of contemporary Jewish adoption law. The severance of parenthood into genetic, gestational, and intentional

157. R. *Goldberg*, supra n. 140, at 257–258; *Goldberg*, supra n. 134, at 74–75; *Ma'asheh Hoshev*, supra n. 151, at 35; *R. Ariel*, supra n. 150, at 176.

158. R. *Goldberg*, supra n. 134, at 74–75; R. Ezra Bick, "Maternity in Fetal Implants," in *Crossroads: Halacha & the Modern World* (ed. E. Rosenfeld: Alon Shvut, 1987), 79, 82–84.

159. *Ma'aseh Hoshev*, supra n. 151, at 35.

160. *R. Waldenberg*, supra n. 155.

161. *Ma'aseh Hoshev*, supra n. 151, at 35–36.

162. During the last ninety years, moving beyond the conventional canons of halakhic methodology, legists attempted to arrive at solutions based upon the use of *aggadic* statements, an obviously problematic approach. See listing in Bleich, supra n. 152, 54–55. In addition, see Bick, supra n. 152, at 38–43 and many others. For an attempt to develop a halakhic conceptual model of maternity based upon aggadic statements, see R. Ezra Bick supra n. 152. For a scathing critique for adopting this methodology, see Bleich, supra n. 152, at 55–56. For the lack of authoritativeness of *aggadah*, see Talmud Yerushalmi *Hagigah* 1:8, *Peah* 2:4, *Horayot* 3:5; R. Sherira Gaon (Pumbedita: 968–1004), *Otzar Hageonim, Hagigah*, Resp., 48–49, R. Hai Gaon (Baghdad, 939–1038), *Otzar Hageonim Berakhot, Teshuvot*, 357; *Otzar Hageonim, Berakhot, Commentaries* 135; *Otzar Hageonim Hagigah, Commentaries*, 69; Maimonides, *Moreh Nevukim*, Introduction (end); R. Yair Bachrach (Germany, 1638–1702) *Resp. Havot Yair*, 124; *Resp. Nodah Be-Yehudah, Tinyana Yoreh Deah* 161; *Resp. Yabia Omer*, 1 *Yoreh Deah* 4, s.v. *ivra*. For additional sources, see Yaakov Elbaum, *Lehavin Divre Hakhamin* (Hebrew) (Jerusalem, 2000), 13–41; Berachyahu Lifshitz, "Aggadah & its Role in the History of the Oral Law," (Hebrew), 22 *Shenaton Hamishpat Haivri* 233 (2003). Cf. R. Judah b. Bezalel (Prague, 1525–1609), Sefer *Be'er Hagolah* (Jerusalem, 1971), 6, p. 135. However, according to certain authorities, absent any Talmudic dicta to the contrary, one can derive norms from aggadic statements. See R. Yaakov Reicher (Austria, 18th cent.), *Resp. Shevut Yaakov* 2:178; R. Menashe Klein, *Resp. Mishneh Halakhot* 2:44; R. Zvi Hirsch Chajes, *Darkei Ha-Hora'ah*, sec. 2 in *Kol Kitvei Maharatz Hajes* (Jerusalem, 1958) 1;251. Regarding our issue, there is no explicit Talmudic source contradicting the *aggadic* statements. In fact, the interpretation of certain sources will corroborate these *aggadic* conclusions. Hence, the utilization of a*ggadah* to arrive at a normative conclusion would be permissible.

components creates indeterminancy of parentage. The Jewish legal response to this indeterminancy is to recognize "biologism" rather than functional and intentional parenthood as the yardstick for establishing legal parentage. Hence, some decisors contend that genetics determine motherhood, others look to parturition; others argue parturition, which is contingent upon genetic makeup; others propound a dual-motherhood theory, and some insist that collaborative technology undermines biologism and conclude that the child is bereft of legal parentage. In short, the significance of biology is paramount in the definition of familial relationships (maternal as well as paternal), whether established by coital reproductive or collaborative reproduction.

Concluding Remarks

Cases like Marvin, Baby M, and their respective progeny give one the opportunity to participate in the ongoing debate about what marriage in society should be.

> Cases are not neatly packaged in the categories established by legislative or judicial rules but exhibit surprising configurations of their own, bringing to the surface hitherto unseen tensions and contradictions in our social life and culture. The legal case is always a narrative; and as a narrative... can always be a way of testing the presuppositions of the culture, forcing to the bright center of the mind difficulties we wish to push back into the twilight.[163]

How would intending parenthood redefine or reconstitute parenting? To what degree has the privatization process, which involves private norm creating and private decision-making, impacted upon collaborative reproduction technology?[164]

Our review of the holdings in collaborative reproduction technology reflects the legal uncertainty about the comparative significance of biological criteria vs. contractual criteria in establishing legal parentage. Whereas some courts continue to affirm the longstanding yardstick of biology, others have advocated the employment of the universe of contract to expand the definition of parenthood.[165] As we pointed out,

163. James White, *When Words Lose Their Meaning*, 265 (Chicago, 1984).
164. See supra, text accompanying n. 63.
165. See supra, text accompanying nn. 3–71.

the decisions invoking contract principles have served as grounds for acknowledging the paradigm of the nuclear family but also legitimate non-nuclear relationships that share the essential characteristics of traditional relationships.[166]

In contrast to the role of contractual ordering in American domestic relations, the implementation of private ordering in Jewish family law functions quite differently. The laws of lineage, i.e., *yuhasin,* including the laws of legal parentage, are grounded upon the norms of the Jewish legal system rather than heredity and genetics. Hence, in certain situations the system will impart recognition to genetic facts of procreation, while in others the system will sever the link due to certain normative considerations.[167]

As we saw, maternity is based upon biology rather than intent. Regarding paternity in collaborative reproduction, whether it is AIH or AID, the sperm donor becomes the legal father of the offspring, regardless of his personal status in the eyes of the system.[168] All of his monetary obligations vis-à-vis his child are a function of his status as a father. What is the status of the husband who consented to the AID procedure? In contrast to Jewish law, numerous American jurisdictions have adopted in whole or in part Section 5 of the Uniform Parental Act, which provides that the husband who consents to the AID procedure is treated as if he were the natural father and donor of the semen.[169] In effect, by designating the husband as the legal father and by denying the identity of the sperm donor, there is a conscious attempt to place this technologically created family into the traditional family defined by blood, marriage, or adoption. For Jewish law, the husband is viewed as akin to an adoptive parent whose monetary obligations, such as child support vis-à-vis his wife's offspring, are grounded upon the law of obligations or the norms of *tzedakah.*[170] These monetary duties are recognized even in the context of AID, which is prohibited by Jewish law. Even though a husband's consent to allow his spouse to be impregnated by a donor will not legitimate the procedure in the eyes of Halakhah, the system will either impart validity to the husband's monetary duties or infer the existence of these duties vis-à-vis the offspring emerging from this procedure. However, in contrast to American law, in Halakhah

166. See supra, text accompanying n. 72.
167. See supra, text accompanying n. 128.
168. See supra, text accompanying n. 112–115.
169. Povarsky, supra n. 128, at 435.
170. See supra, text accompanying nn. 119–128.

there is a distinction between the technologically formed family and the traditional one. The husband who consents to an AID procedure, despite his duties vis-à-vis the child created by artificial insemination, is not recognized as his legal father.

The Jewish legal system is reluctant to grant legal validity to parenthood established by intent, choice, and commitment. However, at the same time, the system recognizes that in cases of parentage based upon collaborative reproduction of the undertaking of agreements which emerge from the implementation of this technology, these are to be recognized and require the Jew of the covenant-faith community to comply with the obligations created by the execution of these agreements.[171]

171. See supra, text accompanying nn. 108–128.

Chapter 9

The Ownership and Market of Human Tissue

THE SALE OF HUMAN tissue[1] shares many characteristics with standard market exchanges, and the participants in such transactions have interests that fit into the rubric of property rights. The purpose of this essay is to analyze how property interests in human tissue are treated in American law and contemporary Halakhah.

American Law

Human Tissue: Property Interest or Privacy Interest?

Recent decades have seen the emergence of a medical process known as in vitro fertilization (IVF), a form of reproductive technology that enhances an infertile couple's ability to procreate. In IVF, eggs are surgically retrieved from a woman's ovaries and fertilized in a laboratory with the sperm of her husband or a donor. Subsequently, this preembryo, or extra-corporeal embryo, is implanted into the uterine wall to bring about pregnancy. The implantation of too many preembryos may create multiple births, and couples therefore often consider cryopreservation, a procedure that freezes the unused preembryos for future use.

IVF and cryopreservation pose questions with respect to ownership and disposition of these preembryos. Is a frozen preembryo to be viewed as property? Can preembryos be legally discarded? If they are discarded and a couple advances a subsequent claim for the frozen preembryos, do the parents have a cause of action against the clinic that physically destroyed the preembryos?

1. As used here, the term "human tissue" includes any organs, tissues, fluids, cells, or genetic material within the human body, except for waste products such as urine and feces.

The case of *Del Zio v. Presbyterian Medical Center*[2] resulted from the first known attempt to perform IVF. To bypass Mrs. Del Zio's damaged fallopian tubes, the Del Zios agreed to participate in an experimental procedure in which the husband's sperm and the wife's egg were mixed. A physician at the medical center, upon becoming aware of the existence of the created preembryos, ordered them destroyed without consulting the Del Zios or their physician. The Del Zios sued for conversion[3] and emotional distress due to the loss of this reproductive material. The court's instructions to the jury were that a determination for either the emotional distress claim or the conversion claim was sufficient to award damages. Consequently, although the jury awarded damages based upon the infliction of emotional distress, the judge surmised that the jury may actually have concluded that damages for the conversion claim were included in the damages awarded for emotional stress. It is thus unsurprising that some legal commentators viewed this decision as recognition of frozen preembryos as property.[4]

A second case involving the ownership of a cryopreserved egg is *York v. Jones*.[5] The couple in this case underwent three IVF procedures at a clinic in Virginia. After the third failure, one of the preembryos was frozen for future use. Subsequently, the couple decided to undergo treatment at a different clinic in California. Despite repeated requests from the Yorks, the Virginia clinic refused to transfer the preembryo, and the couple therefore sued in court. Although the parties had signed a cryopreservation agreement that precluded the clinic from retaining the preembryos, the clinic argued that the agreement did not allow transfer of the preembryo to another clinic. The court disagreed and noted that the pre-freeze agreement had established a bailor-bailee relationship,

2. *Del Zio v. Presbyterian Medical Center*, 74 Civ. 3588 (S.D. N.Y. Nov. 14, 1978).

3. Conversion is defined as "[a]n unauthorized assumption and exercise of the right of ownership over goods or personal chattels belonging to another, to the alteration of their condition or the exclusion of the owner's rights;" *Black's Law Dictionary* 300 (5th ed., 1979).

4. Kathryn Lorin, "Alternative Means of Reproduction: Virgin Territory for Legislation," 44 *La. L. Rev.* (1984), 1641, 1670; Michelle F. Sublett, "Frozen Preembryos: What are They and How Should the Law Treat Them?," 38 *Cleveland St. L. Rev.* (1990), 585, 598-9; John Robertson, "Reproductive Technology and Reproductive Rights: In the Beginning: The Legal Status of Early Preembryos," 76 *Va. L. Rev.* (1990), 437, 459, 515-17; Judith Fischer, "Misappropriation of Human Eggs and Preembryos and the Tort of Conversion: A Relational View," 32 *Loyola of Los Angeles Review* (1999), 381, 394. Cf. Deborah Walther, "'Ownership' of the Fertilized Ovum in Vitro," 26 *Fam. L. Q.* (1992-1993), 235, 240.

5. *York v. Jones*, 717 F. Supp. 421 (E.D. Va. 1989).

which imposed upon the bailee an obligation to return the bailment – that is, the preembryo – should the Yorks desire to use the preembryo to initiate pregnancy at another facility. By construing the agreement as a bailment contract, the court, following in the footsteps of *Del Zio*, clearly recognized the Yorks' property interest in the frozen preembryo.[6]

In short, *Del Zio v. Presbyterian Medical Center* and *York v. Jones* construe preembryos as property; however, the holdings fail to elucidate what this classification means. It certainly seems overly simplistic to equate body parts with tangible property or physical possessions.[7]

In *Moore v. Regents of the University of California*,[8] the California Supreme Court did not directly address IVF or cryopreservation. Nonetheless, this case has potential implications for classifying preembryos as property. The court found that the plaintiff failed to have a cause of action for conversion against the physicians who used cells that had been removed from his spleen to create a cell line for commercialization without his knowledge or consent. The *Moore* court held that to support a cause of action for conversion, one must possess title to the property and expect to retain possession of it.[9] Since Moore did not expect to retain possession of his spleen after removal, he did not have an ownership right in this body part. Numerous commentators interpret the *Moore* holding as establishing that excised human cells can never be classified as property and that research participants, such as Moore, possess no property rights in their tissue or the commercial products developed therefrom.[10] Furthermore, society's need for biomedical research and the development of new medical products outweighs the interests of research participants, which would likely cause the biotechnology sector to flounder.[11]

6. Ibid., 424, 427. In the event of divorce, the agreement provided that the ownership of the preembryos would be determined in a "property settlement."

7. There are certain similarities, such as theft and larceny laws, which are applicable to their misappropriation. See ibid., 489; John Robertson, "Assisted Reproductive Technology and the Family," 47 *Hastings L. J.* (1996), 911, 919.

8. *Moore v. Regents of the University of California*, 793 P. 2d 479 (Cal. 1990), cert. denied, 499 U.S. 936 (1991).

9. Ibid., 488-9.

10. Lynne Thomas, "Abandoned Frozen Preembryos and Texas Law of Abandoned Personal Property: Should There be a Connection?," 29 *St. Mary's L. J.* (1997-1998), 255, 281-4; Fischer, supra n.4, 404-9; E. Richard Gold, *Body Parts: Property Rights and the Ownership of Human Biological Materials* (Washington D.C., 2007), 19-40.

11. *Moore*, supra n.8, 495-6.

However, as Professor Radhika Rao aptly notes:[12]

> *Moore* is capable of at least three different constructions, all of which can be reconciled with the idea that spleens might sometimes constitute property. First, it is possible that the court's refusal to recognize Moore's conversion claim stems from the intuition that body parts cannot be property so long as they are contained within a living human being. If so, the court could have recognized Moore's ownership of his spleen at the point that it was detached from his body without thereby rendering his whole person a form of property. A second possible reading is that, even if the spleen was initially Moore's property, it had been essentially abandoned by its "owner," for whom the diseased organ bore little value, and hence became capable of appropriation by another. Finally, the court implicitly may have held that body parts once removed from a person return to the public commons available to all and become a form of community property.

In other words, although a spleen may not be the property of the donor, it may become the property of the medical researchers.

Thirteen years later, in *Greenberg v. Miami Children's Hospital,*[13] the court held that not only is human tissue not the donor's property, but that genes are also the property of the researchers who isolated them and the hospital that was granted a patent for the isolation. Despite the differences between the *Greenberg* holding and the *Moore* holding, the common denominator is the absence of clear criteria for establishing what characterizes property in regard to human tissue.

Thorough analysis of property as it relates to human tissue must include the examination of the decision in *Davis v. Davis,*[14] which involved a dispute between a woman and her husband. The woman desired to use the couple's frozen preembryos to have a child, while her husband opposed her use of the preembryos. Consequently, each sought custody of the preembryos in court. Although the wife initially wanted the

12. Radhika Rao, "Property, Privacy, and the Human Body," 80 *B. U. L. Rev.* (2000), 360, 374-5.

13. *Greenberg v. Miami Children's Hospital,* 264 F. Supp. 2d 985 (S.D. Florida, 2003).

14. *Davis v. Davis,* 842 S.W. 2d 588 (Tenn. 1992), cert. denied, 507 U.S. 911 (1993).

preembryos implanted in herself, during litigation, she changed her mind and wanted to donate them to a childless couple. Unlike in *York*, the Davises had no executed written agreement providing for disposition of the preembryos in the event of a dispute or divorce. The court concluded that the frozen preembryos are neither persons nor property, but rather occupy a middle ground entitling them to "special respect" because of their potential for human life:[15]

> It follows that any interest [of the biological parents] in the preembryos in this case is not a true property interest. However, they do not have an interest in the nature of ownership to the extent that they have decision-making authority concerning disposition of the preembryos, within the scope of policy set by law.

The *Davis* court stressed that the progenitors' interest was "not a true property interest," but rather entailed engaging in "decision-making authority" limited to policy considerations.[16]

As Professor John Robertson observes:[17]

> [A] property interest in gametes must exist, regardless of whether an action for conversion will lie. The term "property" merely designates the locus of dispositional control over the object or matter in question. The scope of that control is a separate matter and will depend upon what bundle of dispositional rights exist with regard to that object.

For Robertson, preembryos are not to be equated with tangible objects, and, as the court stated in *Davis*, human tissue is not "a true property

15. Ibid., 597.

16. After arguing that the decisional authority regarding the disposition of the preembryo resides with the gamete providers, the court sought to determine how to deal with disputes between the parties. In the absence of any existing prior agreement, if either party's intention is not ascertainable or if there is a dispute about preembryo disposition, then the court must weigh the "relative interests" of a party wishing to use or deny the other the use of the preembryos. The *Davis* court took the position that the husband's right to avoid being a father outweighs the wife's interest in donating the preembryos to another couple where unwanted parenthood would place a possible financial and psychological burden upon Mr. Davis. Consequently, the court awarded custody of the preembryos to the husband on the ground that "the party wishing to avoid procreation should prevail." See ibid., 604.

17. John Robertson, "Posthumous Reproduction," 69 *Ind. L. J.* (1994), 1027, 1038.

interest." But ownership is not the same as sole dominion over property. Instead, property is best thought of as a "bundle of rights" possessed by individuals vis-à-vis objects, including, inter alia, the right to possess one's property, the right to use it, the right to exclude others from its use, and the right to transfer ownership by gift or sale.[18] The application of the property designation to preembryos is solely to describe who has the right to make decisions about preembryo disposition,[19] and the logical candidate is the gamete provider. If we afford preembryos "special respect," this does not mean that the gamete providers are bereft of decision-making regarding their preembryos. On the contrary, disposition of preembryos being accorded special respect can be governed by contracts.

Hecht v. *Superior Court*[20] involved a dispute over custody of sperm deposited in a sperm bank by the deceased partner of the plaintiff. In addressing the issue of whether the ownership of the sperm could be transferred from one person to another via the execution of a will, the *Hecht* court, invoking both *York* and *Davis*, classified the sperm as "property" for the limited purpose of probating a will. A few years later, in *Kass v. Kass*,[21] which involved a dispute between a divorced couple over frozen preembryos, the court again focused upon the dispositional authority of the gamete providers and enforced preembryo contracts.

Endorsing the idea that a preembryo is deserving of "special respect," in *AZ v. BZ*,[22] the court applied the *Davis* court's logic of balancing procreational interests in preembryo disposition disputes. The court recognized the wife's trauma in enduring multiple IVF procedures, while stressing that a balance must be struck between her right to procreate and her husband's right not to procreate. The fact that the wife was capable of undergoing IVF again or adopting, and therefore was not limited to using the preembryos under dispute, weighed heavily against her in the balancing process. Regarding the husband, the court realized that

18. Ibid.

19. Robertson, supra n. 4, 454-5, 455 n. 48; Stephen Munzer, *A Theory of Property* (Cambridge, 1990), 16-17, 56. Rather than focusing on dispositional authority, Munzer argues that people do not own their bodies, but rather have limited property rights in them. Since the law proscribes consumption or destruction of one's body, this indicates that people do not own their bodies in the fashion that we own a desk or a chair. See ibid. 41-43.

20. *Hecht v. Superior Court*, 20 Cal. Rptr. 2d 275 (Cal. Dist. Ct. App. 1993).

21. *Kass v. Kass*, 696 N.E. 2d 174,179 (N.Y. 1998).

22. *AZ v. BZ*, Mass. Law. Weekly No. 15-008-96, slip op. (Mass. Prob. & Family Ct., March 25, 1996).

this was a situation of unwanted parenthood accompanied by financial burdens. Consequently, the court declined to authorize the preembryo transfer to the wife.

In both *Davis v. Davis* and *AZ v. BZ,* since the issue of resolving disputes relating to preembryos is one of decision-making authority, the special respect and dispositional authority need not be mutually exclusive. Thus, for both courts, there is no reason why decisions of disposition cannot be made without a high degree of respect for the frozen preembryo.

The cases cited above represent the ongoing debate among legal commentators regarding whether the issue of property rights to human tissue, such as preembryos, ought to be framed in terms of property,[23] special respect,[24] or control.[25]

In bold contrast to the aforementioned approaches, another position maintains that the human body is subject to privacy rights. The right to refuse medical treatment and the right to abortion have been grounded in the constitutional right to privacy.[26] Similarly, whereas property can

---

23. For arguments that human tissue possesses characteristics that satisfy some of the criteria for establishing rights in tangible property, see Roy Hardiman, "Comment, Toward the Right of Commerciality: Recognizing Property Rights in the Commercial Value of Human Tissue," 34 *U.C.L.A. L. Rev.* (1986), 207, 218; Patricia Martin and Martin Lagod, "The Human Preembryo, the Progenitors, and the State: Toward a Dynamic Theory of States, Rights and Research Policy," 5 *High Tech. L. J.* (1990), 257, 261; Alise Panitch, "Note: The Davis Dilemma: How to Prevent Battles over Frozen Preembryos," 41 *Case W. Res. L. Rev.* (1991), 543, 553; Philip Prygoski, "The Implications of *Davis v. Davis* for Reproductive Rights Analysis," 61 *Tenn. L. Rev.* (1994), 609, 609 n.2; Helen S. Shapo, "Frozen Preembryos and the Right to Change One's Mind," 12 *Duke J. Comp. & Int'l L.* (2002), 75, 76, n.3.

For others who argue that the body should not be treated as property, see Rao, supra n.12, 365; Stephen Munzer, "An Uneasy Case Against Property Rights in Body Parts," 11 *Soc. Philosophy and Policy Rev.* (1994), 259; idem., supra n.19; Leon Kass, *Toward a More Natural Science* (1985), 283.

24. See Robertson, supra n.4, 450 n.37; Kristine Luongo, "Comment: The Big Chill: *Davis v. Davis* and the Protection of Potential Life," 29 *New Eng. L. Rev.* (1995), 1011, 1023.

25. For arguments for a property-based notion of control over one's body parts, see Mary Danforth, "Current Topic in Law and Policy: Cells, Sales, and Royalties: The Patient's Right to a Portion of the Profits," 6 *Yale Law & Policy Review* (1988), 179, 191-5; Bonnie Steinbock, "Sperm as Property," 6 *Stanford L. & Policy Rev.* (1995), 57, 66; Julia Mahoney, "The Market for Human Tissues," 86 *Virginia Law Rev.* (2000), 164, 201.

26. *In re Quinlan*, 355 A. 2d 647, 663 (N.J. 1976); *Cruzan v. Missouri*, 497 U.S. 261 (1990); *Roe v. Wade*, 410 U.S. 113 (1973); *Planned Parenthood v. Casey*, 505 U.S. 833, 928 (1992).

be separated from "the owner" and be sold on the market, privacy is integrated into the body and defines one's personal identity. Thus, for example, a right to individual and familial privacy may be violated by publication of genetic information without the person's consent.[27]

Commodification

There is more at stake in the biomedical research of human tissues than simply saving life or avoiding death. Vexing ethical and policy questions are raised in the professional literature, including an individual's right or ability to commodify his body – that is, to transform it into a commodity. Invoking the legal status of property with regard to the body or its uses and parts is problematic because it threatens many values, including the right to privacy and respect for the sanctity of human life. To characterize human tissue as property implies that it can be sold and bought on the market; the right to commodify one's body is derived from a property right in one's body.

As Elizabeth Anderson writes:[28]

> To say that something is properly regarded as a commodity is to claim that the norms of the market are appropriate for regulating its production, exchange and enjoyment. To the extent that moral principles or ethical ideals preclude the application of market norms to a good, we may say that the good is not a (proper) commodity.

Conceptualizing property in terms of tangible objects and arguing that reproductive and genetic materials should have the same legal status as a table or doorknob is repugnant in the eyes of many. Commodifying excised human materials threatens our human dignity.[29] As one commentator noted, "the body is one of the last places of sanctuary from a commodified world."[30] On the other hand, if property is viewed as a

27. Rao, supra n.12.

28. Elizabeth Anderson, "Is Women's Labor a Commodity?," 19 *Philosophy and Public Affairs* (1990): 71-72.

29. Margaret Jane Radin, "Property and Personhood," 34 *Stanford L. Rev.* (1982), 957, 1014-15; idem., "Market-Inalienability," 100 *Harvard L. Rev.* (1987), 1849, 1852, 1885.

30. Elizabeth Blue, "Redefining Stewardship over Body Parts," 21 *Journal of Law and Health* (2007-2008): 75, 86.

question of control,[31] the greater the degree of freedom and autonomy over one's assets, the greater is the respect accorded to the individual. Analogously, people who exercise some measure of control over their human materials enhance, rather than diminish, their human dignity. The notion that the human body is intimately bound up with the exercise of dispositional authority resonates in the words of Harvard law professor and former Solicitor-General Charles Fried: [32]

> Moral personality consists, as Kant said, of the capacity to choose freely and rationally… Now, a claim to respect for physical and intellectual integrity implies a claim to the conditions under which a sense may develop of oneself as a free, rational, and efficacious moral being…

The underlying Kantian idea is that an individual's control over one's persona, including one's body and its parts, is essential to freedom or autonomy.

In sum, there is a difference of opinion regarding whether or not marketing human issue entails commodification.

Halakhah

Human Body and Tissue: Property Interest or Dispositional Authority?

What is the Halakhah's perspective on a Jew's ownership of his body? R. Shlomo Yosef Zevin approaches this question by analyzing the agreement made between Shylock and Antonio in Shakespeare's *The Merchant of Venice*, in which Antonio's debt would be paid off with a pound of flesh (apparently an acceptable form of paying damages upon reneging on a contract according to Venetian law). R. Zevin argues that since God owns everything, including our bodies, one is proscribed from inflicting physical harm upon his own body or that of others (*havalah*).[33] Consequently, the Venetian agreement would be unenforceable.[34]

The notion that one's body does not belong to him resonates in many

31. See supra n. 25.

32. Charles Fried, Right and Wrong (Cambridge, 1978), 123,142. See also Leon Kass, "Organs for Sale? Propriety, Property and the Price of Progress," 107 *Public Interest* (1992), 72.

33. *Shemot* 19:5; *Devarim* 10:14; *Berakhot* 35a.

34. Shlomo Yosef Zevin, *Le-Or Ha-Halakhah* (Tel Aviv, 5717), 318.

realms of commercial matters (*Hoshen Mishpat*) including the collection of an outstanding monetary debt from a borrower.[35] One of the possible avenues for collecting an outstanding debt is coercing an individual to hire himself to engage in work in order to pay off his debt. On the one hand, the purpose of the coercion is for the debtor to engage in work in order for the creditor to recover his monies. But is such coercion tantamount to deprivation of personal freedom, bordering on enslavement? Does the creditor have a legal right to demand of a borrower to find gainful employment in order to satisfy the debt? Some opinions, such as *Rosh*, *Tur*, and *Shulhan Arukh*, contend that such coercion is prohibited.[36] In the words of *Rosh* and *Sma*, "We are the servants of God and not the servants of other servants."[37]

Rabbi Ephraim Navon (*Mahaneh Ephraim*) argues, however, that if a debtor undertakes a duty to work in order to satisfy his debt, the commitment should not be construed as a form of enslavement as a result of his loss of autonomy. While the debtor agrees to satisfy his debt by engaging in work, whether the employment will be personally performed by him or by third parties remains his choice.[38] Other legists permit such coercion regardless of whether such a stipulation has been made.[39] If the parties stipulate to such an arrangement and the agreement complies with laws of obligations, *Perishah* would validate it.[40]

Another possible means of debt collection is imprisonment. Maimonides rejects this approach as illegal, enjoining the creditor to refrain from entering the debtor's premises to collect a debt.[41] *Rosh* affirms Maimonides's view and argues that the Torah does not generally deprive a person of his personal freedom. Even if the borrower and creditor explicitly stipulated that imprisonment would result upon failure to satisfy the debt, such a condition is null and void, as it relates to one's persona

35. Some of the sources for our ensuing discussion have been culled from Menahem Elon, *Freedom of the Debtor's Person in Jewish Law* (Hebrew) (Jerusalem, 1964).

36. *Responsa (hereinafter: Resp.) Ha-Rosh* 78:2; *Tur, Hoshen Mishpat* 97:28-30; *Shulhan Arukh, Hoshen Mishpat* 333:3.

37. *Rosh*, ibid.; *Sma, Hoshen Mishpat* 97:29. Similarly, a Jew neither owns a non-Jewish slave nor acquires from a non-Jew the rights to excise parts of a body of a non-Jewish slave; see *Gittin* 19a, 21b; Rashi, ad loc., s.v. *lo efshar*; *Yevamot* 46a.

38. *Mahaneh Ephraim, Hilk. Sekhirut Po'alim* 2.

39. *Resp. Maharam Mi-Rothenburg* (Cremona ed.) 146. Rif and R. Yehuda Barzilai, cited by Maharam, argue that although an individual cannot be coerced to find employment, he is nonetheless obligated to work.

40. *Perishah, Hoshen Mishpat* 99:19.

41. *Mishneh Torah, Hilk. Malveh Ve-Loveh* 2:1; *Resp. Ha-Rambam* (Blau ed.) 410.

(*tenay she-ba-guf*).[42] Similarly, Rashba writes, "A man's body is not to be enslaved... for imprisonment... Rather, he is indebted to his creditor and his assets are a surety..."[43] This view was endorsed by *Tur, Shulhan Arukh*, and others.[44]

Nevertheless, numerous decisors validate imprisonment in situations in which a borrower fails to pay his debts.[45] One of the rationales offered is that such a person violates the *mitzvah* of paying one's debts.[46] As such, Halakhah sanctions imprisonment as a form of coercion to effectuate a debtor's compliance. While endorsing the *Shulhan Arukh's* opposition to imprisonment for a debtor who cannot pay, *Rema* rules that a debtor who has the financial ability to pay and is simply attempting to conceal his assets (such as through fraudulent conveyance) may be incarcerated.[47]

Thus, the question of whether one may deprive a debtor of his personal freedom through imprisonment or coercion to engage in gainful employment is the subject of debate.[48] R. Zevin aptly observes that some decisors maintain that even though the human body belongs to God, Halakhah allows an individual to be deprived of his personal freedom by another individual, such as an employer, or an institution, such as a prison.[49]

Offering a contrasting perspective, R. Shaul Yisraeli contends that man actually retains co-partnership over his body with God. Although *havalah*, self-inflicted harm or assault of another person, is clearly forbidden,[50] implying that an individual is not the owner of his own body, R.

---

42. *Resp. Ha-Rosh* 68:10.

43. *Resp.Ha-Rashba* 1:1069.

44. *Tur, Hoshen Mishpat* 97: 28; *Shulhan Arukh, Hoshen Mishpat* 97:15; *Maggid Mishneh, Hilk. Malveh Ve-Loveh* 25:14; *Leket Yosher, Yoreh Deah 79-80.*

45. Resp. *Ha-Rivash* 484; Resp. *Maharashdam, Hoshen Mishpat* 390; Resp. *Ranah* 58; *Yam Shel Shlomo, Bava Kamma* 8:65; *Bah, Hoshen Mishpat* 97:28; Resp. *Ha-Ridvaz* 1:60; *Sma, Hoshen Mishpat* 107:10. For additional concurring opinions, see Elon, supra n.35, 164-237.

46. *Ketubot* 86a; *Pesahim* 91a; Rashi, ad loc.; *Rivash*, ibid.

47. Rema, *Hoshen Mishpat* 97:15.

48. This diversity of opinion as to whether denying an individual a degree of his freedom is a form of enslavement informs the issue of whether a husband can be obligated to engage in work in order to pay spousal support (*mezonot isha)* as well as the question of whether an employee (*po'eil)* who works by the hour, has the right to withdraw from his work without liability for losses incurred.

49. After examining this debate, R. Zalman N. Goldberg concludes that such a view is difficult to comprehend. See R. Zalman N. Goldberg, "Acts of Acquisitions in the Sale of Kidneys" (Hebrew), 30 *Tehumin* (5770): 108, 112.

50. *Bava Kamma* 91b; *Tosafot*, ad loc., s.v. *ela hai*; *Shulhan Arukh, Hoshen Mishpat* 424:1.

Yisraeli defines ownership differently. Despite God's ownership rights, so to speak, there is broadly speaking, "a bundle of rights" that may be exercised by man, within certain halakhic parameters to be sure, with respect to one's bodily tissue: principally, the right to possess it, to exclude others from removing it, and donate and/or sell it to another individual.[51]

How, then, would Halakhah approach a dispute between a couple regarding preembryo disposition? What would happen if a happily married Jewish couple agreed to participate in an IVF program and there is no evidence that they signed a preembryo agreement? If the couple, now divorced, dispute who has authority over disposition of the preembryos – the wife yearning for implantation and the husband objecting to implantation, arguing that the financial burden of unwanted fatherhood should not be mandated without his consent – with whom would the Halakhah side?

Understanding the halakhic nature of marriage is crucial background to this question. *Kiddushin*, the act of halakhic engagement, itself may be said to be a consensual agreement,[52] as it establishes a personal status of a woman designated for a particular man and prohibited to all others *(mekudeshet)* and thereby creates various obligations, such as a duty of intimacy (onah) and certain prohibited sexual relations.[53] Subsequently, the act of *nissuin*, marriage, creates a framework of monetary obligations, such as spousal support. At the same time, a marriage may be viewed as a partnership between spouses.[54]

51. See *Le-Or Ha-Halakhah*, 330-5; R. S. Yisraeli, *Amud Ha-Yemini* 16:16-32. R. Zevin concurs that a person exercises decisional authority, even though he cannot be said to own his body; see *Le-Or Ha-Halakhah*, 327.

52. *Shulhan Arukh, Even Ha-Ezer* 26, 37, 38-39, 43-44.

53. "The woman becomes prohibited to all others in the same fashion as *hekdesh* (consecrated objects)." See *Kiddushin* 2b.

54. For authorities who view marriage as an economic partnership, see Resp. *Maharashdam, Hoshen Mishpat* 206; *Pesakim U-Ketavim*, vol. 9, *Hoshen Mishpat* 33; *Resp. Havalim Ba-Ne'imim*, vol. 5, *Even Ha-Ezer* 34; File No. 9061-21-1, Netanya Regional Rabbinical Court, Ploni v. Plonit, June 26, 2006; File No. 14850-1, Ashdod Regional Rabbinical Court, Plonit v. Ploni, September 19, 2010; File No. 347562-1, Tel Aviv-Yaffo Regional Rabbinical Court, Ploni v. Plonit, September 13, 2011; R. Shlomo Daichovsky, "Liquidating the Partnership and Dividing the Assets of the Spouse" (Hebrew), 16-17 *Shenaton Ha-Mishpat Ha-Ivri* (5750-5751): 501, 508; idem., "The *Halakhot* of Marital Partnership: Is it the Law of the Monarchy?" (Hebrew),18 *Tehumin* (5758) 18; *Piskei Din Rabbanayim* 11:116; this writer's, "A Comparative Analysis of a Wife's Capacity to Pledge her Husband's Credit for Domestic Necessities in Anglo-American Law and Jewish Law", 13 *The Jewish Law Annual* 213, 2000.

In R. Yisraeli's view, a Jewish couple's participation in an IVF program is a form of partnership together to sire a child.[55] In contrast to a commercial partnership, which is formed based upon pooling assets in a common purse through a written operating agreement, verbal commitment, or each partner undertaking to be the agent of the other,[56] the partnership of the progenitors is created by the commingling of the sperm and the egg.[57] Once that partnership has been created, neither partner may dissolve it prior to the expiration date or prior to attaining its objectives as provided in their agreement.

R. Yisraeli argues that a joint effort to sire a child is no different than any other partnership arrangement. Should there arise unforeseen circumstances (*ones*), such as disability or sickness, that make it impossible for one partner to continue to work, such circumstances are grounds for partnership dissolution.[58] Similarly, the unanticipated event of a couple becoming divorced should allow the husband to terminate the partnership agreement for preembryo implantation.[59]

Although he accepts the partnership model, R. Ariel disagrees with R. Yisraeli's conclusion.[60] R. Ariel compares the agreement between the husband and wife in this case to a sale between a seller and buyer, which is dependent on the intent of both (*taluy be-da'at sheneihem*).[61] In general, once a sale has been consummated, the buyer has no grounds to rescind the sale if he subsequently discovers a defect in the item.[62] The

55. *Resp. Havot Binyamin* 3:108, reprinted in Avraham Steinberg (ed.), *Encyclopedia Hilkhatit Refu'it* (1994), vol. 4, 37-44.

56. *Shulhan Arukh, Hoshen Mishpat* 176:2, 5; *Resp. Ha-Rivash* 71; *Sefer Ha-Levush, Hoshen Mishpat* 176:1; *Ra'avad, Hilkhot Sheluhin Ve-Shutafim* 4:2.

57. See supra n. 55.

58. According to one view, a partner is construed as an employee; see *Resp. Rabi* 219; *Tur, Hoshen Mishpat* 176:4; *Shakh, Hoshen Mishpat* 176:8. Consequently, a progenitors' agreement regarding preembryo disposition, which is akin to a labor contract, is either consummated by a symbolic act of undertaking an obligation(a *kinyan)* or through the commencement of work – that is, the commingling of the sperm and the egg. See *Bava Metzia* 76a, 83a; *Rema, Hoshen Mishpat* 333:2. Similarly, a partner, like an employee, may terminate the partnership due to an unforeseen circumstance (an *ones).* See *Bava Metzia* 77b; *Shulhan Arukh, Hoshen Mishpat* 333:5.

59. *Havot Binyamin,* supra n. 55; *Resp. Ateret Shlomo,* 2:151

60. R. Yoezer Ariel, "The Cessation of the IVF Process Upon Spousal Demand," (Hebrew) 77-78 *Assia* (5761), 102.

61. *Resp. Sho'eil U-Meishiv, Mahadura Kamma* 1:145, 197,199; *Resp. Nodah Be-Yehudah, Mahadura Kamma, Yoreh Deah* 69, *Mahadura Tinyana, Even Ha-Ezer* 130; *Resp. Maharsham* 3:82 and 5:5.

62. *Shulhan Arukh, Hoshen Mishpat* 176:1; *Rema,* ad loc.

sale would be voided only provided that two conditions are fulfilled – the buyer would not have agreed to the sale had he known that the defect would appear in a reasonable time after the purchase and the seller included among the terms of the sale that the transaction was contingent on the usefulness of the item. In the absence of both conditions, the sale is final even if a defect is found.[63]

Analogously, R. Ariel argues, the unforeseen event of divorce (*ones*) should not serve as grounds for failing to follow through with the partnership. Although the husband opposes continued participation in the IVF program, his wife does not agree with him, and her desire is given equal halakhic weight.

Thus, in the absence of a provision in the preembryo disposition agreement addressing contingency situations such as divorce, implantation should proceed as initially agreed upon by the gamete providers.[64]

In effect, R. Ariel views this partnership agreement as an agreement between two parties who undertake certain obligations.[65] Whereas, the argument of *ones* may be advanced regarding a unilateral agreement, for a sales agreement which is a bi-lateral agreement – such an argument cannot be raised.[66] Consequently, neither partner (progenitor) is empowered to retract from the agreed-upon arrangement unless both conditions of a standard sale's agreement have been obtained.

Although R. Yisraeli and R. Ariel disagree regarding whether a husband can oppose implantation in the case of divorce, both decisors invoke the commercial partnership paradigm to address how to deal with inter-spousal disputes regarding their human reproductive materials. Although the halakhic norms of commercial partnership focus on "the world of commodities," these authorities show no reluctance in applying *Hoshen Mishpat* concepts to "the world of the human body." Both realms focus on individuals who utilize their authority to make decisions – whether to execute business arrangements or regarding what to do with their reproductive materials.

63. *Tosafot, Bava Kamma* 110b; *Tosafot Ha-Rosh, Ketubot* 47b; *Netivot Ha-Mishpat, Hoshen Mishpat* 230:1.

64. For the effectiveness of a provision addressing *ones* instances, see *Sma, Hoshen Mishpat* 310:12; *Shakh, Hoshen Mishpat* 334:1.

65. *Taz, Hoshen Mishpat* 176:1; *Resp. Maharbil* 2:37-38.

66. *Tosafot, Ketubot 47b, s.v. shelo.*

Commodification and Privacy Interest

To address the issue of commodification, we will focus upon the propriety of a Jew donating his kidney to a fellow Jew. If kidney transplantation is permitted, ought one be compensated for his donation? We have articulated this question elsewhere:[67]

> The permissibility of a kidney transplant provides us with one of the many illustrations of the overarching and paramount significance of *pikuah nefesh*, i.e., the preservation of human life. *Pikuah nefesh* suspends all biblical prohibitions excluding idolatry, homicide, and certain sexual offenses... Here, we are dealing with the preservation of human life being effectuated by a surgical procedure which involves the sacrifice of a human organ. In effect, the procedure entails "*havalah*," i.e., wounding, which usually is prohibited whether it is self-inflicted or inflicted by others... Given that halakhic strictures are suspended for the purposes of preservation of human life, is the proscription against *havalah* equally set aside in the cases of kidney transplants?

In our analysis elsewhere, we offered three different approaches:

The permissibility or non-permissibility of transplants hinges upon determining the degree of risk associated with a nephrectomy as defined by medical assessment. As we have seen, whether risk will be determined simply based upon the arbiter's perception, state of medical technology, or societal willingness to accept the risk is subject to debate. Assuming that the procedure is "halakhically risk-free," then *pikuah nefesh* will override *havalah*.

On the other hand, other contemporary authorities assert that *pikuah nefesh* cannot suspend the proscription against *havalah*. Self-injury is proscribed and the prohibition against battery is construed as a stricture ancillary to the prohibition of homicide (*avizrayhu*). The situation is therefore defined as one of "*nefashot*" or "*safek nefashot*," a precarious or possibly precarious situation, which mandates the avoidance of jeopardizing one's life. Accordingly, a transplant will not be allowed. Alternatively, one can contend that this question is to be resolve through

67. See this writer's "Renal Transplantation: Living Donors and Markets for Body Parts –Halakha in Concert with Halakhic Policy or Public Policy?" 40:2 *Tradition* (2007): 14, 15.

the prism of "*havalah.*" Is wounding for the sake of rescuing human life permitted? Should the wounding be administered in a contentious matter (*derekh nitzahon*) or in a disrespectful fashion (*derekh bizayon*), then such action constitutes *havalah* and is prohibited. Consequently, if an individual is willing to sustain an injury in order to save the life of another, i.e., an action of respect, then this act is sanctioned as a case of privileged battery. Hence, a donor may undergo a transplantation procedure.[68]

Thus, according to one opinion, renal transplantation constitutes *havala* or *safek sakana* and is therefore prohibited. Others, however, contend either that *pikuah nefesh* suspends the prohibition against *havalah* or that *havalah* in a respectful fashion is permissible.[69]

According to the latter approach, we place a supreme value upon the *mitzvah* of preservation of life and it becomes the sole deciding factor. Even if the donor's motivation is commercial gain, it is an irrelevant consideration.[70] At first glance, such a conclusion appears problematic, as in general, one may not receive compensation for the performance of a *mitzvah.*[71] One rationale offered for this ruling is that one is unable to receive compensation for performing an action that entails the performance of a divine obligation, rather than a decision to benefit another person.[72] If, however, one is performing the *mitzvah* through his gainful employment (such as a physician),[73] or if societal needs dictate that compensation should be forthcoming in order to promote the saving of human life, remuneration is permissible.[74] Thus, even though a kidney is

68. Ibid., 17-21.

69. Ibid.

70. *Nishmat Avraham, Yoreh Deah* 349:3-4, in the name of R. Shlomo Z. Auerbach.

71. Mishnah *Bekhorot* 4:6; *Shulhan Arukh, Yoreh De'ah* 336:2.

72. Rambam, *Perush Ha-Mishnah, Nedarim* 4:2; Shakh, *Yoreh De'ah* 221:22, 246:5.

73. Sma, *Hoshen Mishpat* 264:19; *Shulhan Arukh, Yoreh Deah* 336:2.

74. *Shulhan Arukh, Hoshen Mishpat* 246:5; *Tiferet Yisrael, Nedarim* 4:2; *Resp. Mahari Bruna* 114; Resp. *Iggerot Moshe, Hoshen Mishpat* 1:103; R. Levi Y. Halperin, *Ma'aseh Hoshev*, vol. 4, 62-67; R. Mordechai Halperin, "Removal of Organs from a Live Donor: Halakhic Perspectives" (Hebrew) 45-46 *Assia* 34 (5749). Pursuant to Tosafot, *Pesahim* 65a, s.v. *ha-mekhabed*, R. Shabtai Rapoport argues that compensation is sanctioned provided that the primary motivation of the transplant is to save a life rather than to receive remuneration. See R. Shabtai Rappaport, "Sale of Organs: From Living Donor for Transplant – Motivation and Decision Making," in Alfredo Rabello (ed.), *An Equitable Distribution of Human Organs for Transplantation* (Jerusalem, 2003), 97, 107.

an essential body party and non-regenerative, many authorities permit the sale of a kidney, considering it no different than the sale of hair and blood, which are regenerative.[75]

The implications of allowing a market of human organs for life-saving or health-enhancing purposes reaffirms our thesis that man's relationship to his body and its components is marked by his dispositional authority, rather than recognition of the human body as a fungible item as akin to negotiable instruments and shares of common stock. Moreover, since most authorities agree that Halakhah does not treat a human organ as a piece of property, the value of the kidney may be based upon the actual value to the kidney donor, which may be beyond its market value.[76]

A person's decisional authority to sell his kidney is comparable to transferring a note of indebtedness (a *shtar hov)* to another person. A lender who holds a *shtar hov* against a debtor may choose to sell this *shtar* to a third party, who may then wish to sell it to someone else. *Netivot Ha-Mishpat* suggests that if the original transfer of the *shtar* to a third party was not properly recorded in the *shtar* or a separate document, as mandated,[77] the third party does not acquire the *shtar* for purposes of debt collection; he can only sell the nominal value of the worth of the paper of the *shtar.*[78] The third party does not own the *shtar*, but he is entitled to compensation for its paper value.[79]

Similarly, one might argue, although a person does not own his kidney, he may nevertheless sell the value of the kidney.

Other authorities disagree with this analysis, arguing that organ donation for financial gain is forbidden. Based on *Tosafot's* view that one

75. *Mishnah Nedarim* 9:5; *Nedarim* 65b; *Mishnah Arakhin* 1:4; *Arakhin* 7b.

76. Resp. *Beit Yitzhak, Hoshen Mishpat* 30; *Erekh Shai, Hoshen Mishpat* 386; *Resp. Helkat Yo'av* 3:91; *Resp. Mekor Hayyim* 31. Cf. *Shakh, Hoshen Mishpat* 72:128; *Netivot Ha-Mishpat* 148:1, 207:8.

77. *Shulhan Arukh, Hoshen Mishpat* 66:1-2.

78. *Netivot Ha-Mishpat* 66:12.

79. Others argue that the *shtar* actually belongs to the borrower; it is transferred to the lender for the purposes of proving that he may collect from the borrower the amount earmarked on the document. Consequently, upon transferring the *shtar* to a third party, the lender is transferring the right to collect the debt, rather than the right to sell the paper value of the *shtar*. See *Shakh, Hoshen Mishpat* 66:8; *Ketzot Ha-Hoshen* ad loc. The analogy to our case applies according to this understanding as well. Whether the third party has the right to sell the *shtar* for its paper value or the right to collect the debt it represents, the creditor has decisional authority regarding collecting the debt. Similarly, although a person's organs do not belong to him, he has the authority to sell them as he wishes. See R. Ya'akov Ariel, *Shut Be-Ohela Shel Torah*, 487.

is proscribed from committing self-inflicted harm for commercial gain,[80] R. Menashe Klein contends that selling a kidney, which involves battery, is an affront to human dignity.[81] Arriving at the same conclusion from a different perspective, R. Moshe Zorger acknowledges that if the world engages in such a practice and/or the donor requires the compensation for his living, marketing a kidney is permissible,[82] but he concludes that such a practice is "disgusting."[83] Those who argue that the proscription against *havalah* preempts transplantation would ban the marketing of kidneys ex ante (*le-khat'hila*). On the other hand, these authorities would uphold the validity of selling kidneys ex post facto (*be-diavad*).[84] Given the prohibited nature of transplantation, how can this be justified? There is a clear distinction between the prohibited act of battery and the two parties' willingness to execute their personal obligations – that is, the transfer of money for undergoing the act of battery. In the words of *Professor Silberg*, a renowned twentieth century Israeli jurist:[85]

> We see clearly that Jewish law does not establish a causal connection between the commission of an offense and the voiding of a civil contract... The violation of the law or morality is one thing, and the legal validity of the contract is another – to the extent that the fulfilling of the contract itself does not activate the offense... Precisely because Jewish law does not distinguish between law and morality, and that practically every performance of an obligation is at the same time a fulfillment of a religio-moral commandment – such as "the commandment" of repaying a debt of monetary obligation –the non-fulfillment of a contract entered into through a violation of law will only turn out to be an additional offense to supplement the original one committed by the transgressor.

80. *Tosafot, Bava Kamma* 91b, s.v. *ela*.
81. *Resp. Mishneh Halakhot* 4:245.
82. *Resp. Va-Yeshev Moshe* 93.
83. Ibid. 94.
84. See further, E. Shochetman, *Ma'aseh Haba Be'averah*, Jerusalem 5741, 184. Similarly, an agreement to have relations with a prostitute in exchange for money is valid ex post facto; see *Bava Kamma* 70b; *Tosafot, Bava Kamma*, ad loc., s.v. *ilu*; *Resp. Ha-Rashba* 1: 302; *Resp. Shevut Ya'akov* 2:136. Even though the act is prohibited, should the act be consummated, the undertaking of the duty to furnish compensation is enforceable. In the words of R. Yosef S. Nathanson, "this is clear as day;" see *Resp. Sho'eil U-Meishiv, Mahadura Revi'ah* 3:39.
85. Moshe Silberg, *Talmudic Law and the Modern State* (New York, 1973), 85.

In other words, even though there is a prohibition against the market of organs, since the agreement between the parties complies with the norms of the halakhic laws of obligations, the donor is entitled to payment for his kidney. Thus, despite the fact that these authorities fear that the dignity of the human being is diminished if the body is treated like a commodity, and they ban the sale of human organs accordingly, they nevertheless rule that ex post facto, the sale is valid.[86]

According to this view, after the commission of a prohibited act, money may be taken for a service based on a mutual agreement of the parties. *A fortiori*, compensation is permissible for services relating to the use of our bodies on a daily basis. Medical researchers take a salary, and writers work on commission under contract, frequently producing works of intellectual value. A factory worker commodifies the use of his body by using his brains and by moving his hands, and he receives a salary for this service. A teacher talks and uses her brains, mouth, and lungs, and she receives money for doing so. If to "commodify" means merely to accept a fee, the portions of *Hoshen Mishpat* that deal with the undertaking of these obligations would look askance at legitimating these relationships based upon an exchange of money. But such ties are, in fact, recognized, and the labor market – entailing the buying and selling of a person's labor – is not viewed as an affront to human dignity.[87]

Other areas of social endeavor that may be characterized as

86. Although the sale would be halakhically valid, there may be some halakhic public policy considerations that would militate against sanctioning such sales should they materialize.

87. Nevertheless, since employment based upon an hourly wage is construed as "enslavement" unless the employee requires a job for an income, one should refrain from being in the employ of one individual for more than three years. See *Rema, Hoshen Mishpat* 333:3, 16; *Shakh, Hoshen Mishpat* 333:16-17. Cf. *Ketzot Ha-Hoshen* 333:7. Others argue that a labor contract with a term of employment of more than three years is valid provided that the employee resides in his own home rather than living at his employee's domicile. See *Resp. Hemdat Shlomo* 7; *Resp. Lehem Rav* 81.

To avoid being enslaved to his job, an employee may rescind his contract of service at any time; see *Bava Metzia* 10a; *Bava Kamma* 116b; *Shulhan Arukh,Hoshen Mishpat* 333:3. However, should he execute an arrangement of nonrescission with his employer, such an agreement is valid; see *Resp. Zera Emet*, 2, *Yoreh De'ah* 97. Similarly, should an independent contractor (*kablan*) accept a project accompanied by the execution of a *kinyan*, he cannot withdraw from the job. See *Rema, Hoshen Mishpat* 333:1; *Shakh*, ad loc. 3. Cf. others who argue that even a standard employee cannot rescind his service if a *kinyan* was executed at the time of the commencement of work; see *Hiddushei Ha-Ritva, Bava Metzia* 75b; *Resp. Ha-Ritva* 117. Given that enslavement is frowned upon, some of these views are difficult to understand. See supra nn. 37, 42-43.

non-market matters are established through a "commodified understanding." For example, to ascertain a couple's firm resolve (*gemirat da'at*) to consummate a marriage pursuant to the dictates of Halakhah, an object is given by the prospective husband to his prospective wife.[88] Once married, the couple is allowed to engage in conjugal relations and mutually benefit from the pleasures of the other's body. Similarly, undertaking an obligation that entails the use of one's body parts, such as a partnership or a sale, is executed through the implementation of a *kinyan* (symbolic act of transfer), which may entail the use of an object to attest to the parties' resolve to engage in these matters. Decisors understood these *kinyanim* as modes of ascertaining the parties' intent.

In short, there is nothing wrong *per se* with taking money for the use of one's body, and formal recognition of that fact resonates in our norms of *Hoshen Mishpat.*

In light of the foregoing discussion, can we determine whether Halakhah recognizes a right to privacy regarding one's body and tissue? As we mentioned earlier, the rejection of property in the human body has led to the invocation of the right to privacy by American legal commentators.[89] Given that man's body belongs to God, does Halakhah recognize a zone of privacy? Clearly, the minority of decisors who oppose renal transplantation as a violation of battery recognize that there is a right to bodily integrity, or what we might call today a right to privacy. Certainly, there exist a plethora of *halakhot* that protect individual privacy, such as the laws barring a lender's entry into a borrower's home to collect a debt, the prohibition of eavesdropping, and the emphasis on domestic privacy (*hezek re'iyah*).[90] Renal transplantation may provide an additional illustration of this same category.

According to the authorities who define *havalah* as an act of wounding administered in a disrespectful fashion, if an individual is willing to sustain injury in order to save a life, the act is permissible. A kidney transplant is excluded from the prohibition not due to the benefit that accrues to the recipient, but rather because of the privileged nature of the act. Consequently, the donor does not enjoy a right to privacy or a

88. *Mishnah Kiddushin* 1:1.

89. See supra text accompanying notes 26-27 and Rao, supra n.12, at n. 15.

90. *Shulchan Arukh, Hoshen Mishpat* 97:16, 154:3, 7; Rema, *Hoshen Mishpat* 154:7; *Halakhot Ketanot* 1:276; *Piskei Din Rabbaniyim* 14:329. See further, N. Rakover, Protection of Individual Privacy (Hebrew), Jerusalem, 5730 and I. Warhaftig, "The Right to Privacy in Jewish Law," (Hebrew), *Mishpetei Eretz,* 2009.

right to bodily integrity when the *havalah* occurs for a constructive and beneficial purpose.

For the majority of authorities, however, the permissibility of a nephrectomy provides us with one of many illustrations of the overarching significance of *pikuah nefesh,* which suspends almost all prohibitions, including wounding. Most authorities rule that undergoing this procedure is a permissible act (*reshut*) or an act of piety (*midat hassidut*).[91] It is thus the donor's option whether he wants to retain his bodily integrity or not.[92]

Our presentation demonstrates that for both Halakhah and American law, property concepts merit attention as a flexible and eminently helpful intellectual tool to discuss the ownership and sale of human tissue. From the Jewish legal perspective, at first glance, the issue seems to be unusually lucid; as a religious legal system, Halakhah maintains that our bodies are owned by God. Upon further analysis, as we have shown, the landscape is by no means so neat and the indicators do not all point in one direction. Utilizing property concepts in the context of issues of bioethics and briefly invoking other realms of Halakhah, we encounter the notion that even a religious legal system will impart a degree of latitude, a zone of privacy and autonomy to members of a covenant-faith community.

91. See this writer, supra n. 67, at text accompanying nn. 7, 15, 16 and 20.

92. Interestingly, Dr. Avraham Steinberg (*Entzyklopedia Hilkhatit Refu'it* 3, col. 104, n.198) explains R. Ovadia Yosef's opinion, "A Responsum Regarding the Permissibility of a Kidney Transplant" (Hebrew), 7 *Dine Israel* (5736): 25; reprinted as *Resp. Yabia Omer* 9 *Hoshen Mishpat* 12, as describing organ donation as an obligatory mitzvah (*mitzvah hiyuvit*). Accordingly, the zone of privacy regarding one's body is trumped by the performance of the *mitzvah.*

Thus, the question of whether a right to bodily integrity exists is a subject of debate regarding how one understands the propriety or possible impropriety of undergoing a renal donation. However, Dr. Abraham S. Abraham (*Nishmat Avraham* 4, p. 122) disagrees and explains R. Ovadia Yosef 's opinion in line with most other authorities in describing organ donation as a permissible, yet highly praiseworthy activity.

Chapter 10

The Nature of the Halakhic Decision-Making Process – Monistic or Pluralistic?

IS THERE ONE REPLY or more to a halakhic issue? The threshold question which must be asked is: why did halakhic controversy arise? After all, given that we are dealing with a religious legal system, are we not engaging in the deliberation of divine truth? As such, ought such matters evoke unanimity rather than debate?

Explicitly or implicitly relying upon various exegetical interpretations of the Torah (Midrashim) and Talmudic passages,[1] we may conclude that the controversies emerged due to the fact that many halakhot were lost or forgotten. Consequently, doubts as to what the Halakhah ought to be, arose due to controversies between arbiters. As *Talmud Bavli Temurah* 16a states:

> R. Yehudah said in the name of Rav: When Moshe was about to depart this world... he told Yehoshua: Ask me about any uncertainties you have. Yehoshua responded: Have I ever left your presence for a moment?... Immediately, Yehoshua grew weak; he forgot 300 halakhot and 700 doubts arose in his mind... Hashem informed him: For Me to communicate the halakhot is impossible....

To state it differently, doubt arose in the universe of the halakhic-legal system due to forgetfulness, and it was a Jew's rather than Hashem's responsibility to reconstruct the traditions transmitted from the time of Moshe and divine revelation at Sinai.

1. *Midrash Shemot Rabba* 41:6; Talmud Yerushalmi *Horayot* 3:5;Talmud Bavli *Berakhot* 33a; *Nedarim* 33a; *Temurah* 15b, 16a.

Maimonides vehemently attacks this notion that attributes halakhic dispute to forgetfulness, categorically stating:[2]

> But as for their saying that when the students (of Hillel and Shammai) who had insufficiently studied increased, dispute increased, this matter is crystal clear, for when two individuals are similar in comprehension and in learning and knowledge of the principles based upon their study, there will not be any disagreement between them in what they study in one of the hermeneutic principles (13 middot through which one expounds the Torah)... just as we have encountered controversies between Hillel and Shammai other than a few halakhot, for their methodologies of study in all that they would learn by one of the principles were similar to one another, and also the correct principles which were espoused by one were endorsed by the other.

In contrast to the previous approach, for Maimonides, accompanying the tradition which was received from Moshe and transmitted to future generations, arbiters were halakhically authorized to introduce new interpretations of the Torah. Consequently, due to the emergence of new interpretations, doubt arose which led to halakhic debate. As Maimonides observes:[3]

> And when the study of their students (Hillel and Shammai) diminished and the methods of (halakhic) reasoning became weakened for them in comparison to Hillel and Shammai their teachers, controversies transpired during the exchange on numerous matters, due to the fact that each reasoned according to the level of his intellect and in pursuance to the principles known to him.... And in this fashion disagreement emerged, rather than that they erred in their receiving of tradition and one's tradition is true and the other's false...

Contrary to both the above views, Rabbi Avraham Ibn Daud, in his introduction to the classic medieval work, Sefer ha-Kabbalah, writes:[4]

---

2. Introduction to Commentary to the Mishnah, Y. Kapah, trans., Yerushalayim: Mossad Harav Kook, 1963, 20.

3. Ibid., 35.

4. *Sefer ha-Kabbalah,* The Book of Tradition ed. G. Cohen, Philadelphia, JPS,

> Now should anyone infected with heresy attempt to mislead you, saying: "It is because the rabbis differed on a number of issues that I doubt their words," you should retort bluntly and inform him that he is "a rebel against the decision of the court;" and that our rabbis of blessed memory never differed with respect to a commandment in principle, but only with respect to its details; for they heard the principle from their teachers, but had not inquired as to its details, since they had not waited upon their masters sufficiently. As a case in point, they did not differ as to whether or not it is obligatory to light the Sabbath lamp; what they did dispute was "with what it may be lighted and with what it may not be lighted".... This holds true for all their discussions.

Implicitly rejecting Midrash Shemot Rabba 41:6, Midrash Vayikra Rabba, Be'hukkotai 19:6 and Talmud Yerushalmi Pe'ah 1:1 which inform us that the details of Halakhah were not revealed to Moshe,[5] Rabbi Abraham Ibn Daud argues that both the details as well as the principles were transmitted by Moshe. However, controversy emerged due to the fact that, in the words of seventeenth century author Rabbi David Nieto:[6] "They studied insufficiently. They didn't remain with teachers who had ample time to receive the interpretation of the principles and therefore disagreement emerged." Whereas for Rabbis Nieto and Ibn Daud, the arguments in the Mishnah and Talmud could have been avoided had the students been attentive to their masters, for Maimonides the debates stemmed from their differing mental capacities and methods of interpretation.[7]

On the other hand, Rashi contends:[8]

> It is plausible to say, "these and those are the words of the Living Hashem" – sometimes this consideration is applicable and sometimes another consideration is applicable. For the relevant consideration reverses itself according to a change of things and situations....

1967, 3–4.

5. Cf. *Mekhilta, Shemot* 21:1 which contends that even the details were known by Moshe and transmitted to the Jewish people. On the other hand, *Tosafot Yom Tov* in his Introduction to the Mishnah claims that Moshe received everything but withheld certain matters.

6. *Matteh Dan,* 63.

7. Introduction to Commentary to the Mishnah, supra n. 2, 20–21, 35.

8. Talmud Bavli *Ketubot* 57a.

For Rashi, controversy is determined by the times.[9]

In short, forgetfulness and loss of halakhic tradition (*mesorah*), details of halakhot were not revealed to Moshe, differing times and differing mental capacities and methods of interpretation, have all been advanced as reasons for the emergence of controversy. The underlying premise of all of these varying positions is that there is only one answer to a halakhic issue. The fact that there is debate is due to extraneous reasons, e.g., forgetfulness and loss of *mesorah*, differing mental capacities and methods of interpretation.

Construing the halakhic system as monistic in character already was alluded to in medieval times by the author of the Sefer Ha-Hinnukh, who explains the rationale for preferring the adoption of the majority view rather than the absolute truth. As he observes:[10]

> It is better to suffer one error and all to be subservient to the understanding of the rabbis rather than for each of us to act as he thinks, for in that direction lays the destruction of religion... and the anarchy of the nation.

However, it is Rabbeinu Nissim (known by the acronym: Ran) who drives the point home, positing that one position in a particular debate reflects divine truth. As *Ran* teaches us:[11]

> Once Hashem transferred the power of decision-making to the Sages, whatever they would agree upon, that is what Hashem commanded regarding that issue....
>
> There is no other alternative fashion to understand this matter. For since the words of those who opine something ritually impure and those who rule it ritually kosher are contradictory,

9. For two other understandings offered by Rashi, see *Rashi*, supra n. 8. See also text surrounding infra n. 15.

10. *Sefer Ha-Hinnukh, Mitzvah* 408.

11. *Derashot ha-Ran,* nos. 3 and 5. For other perspectives of endorsing a halakhic view arising from a disagreement as reflective of one absolute truth, see Meiri, *Beit ha-Behirah, Avot* 5:19; *Ramban, Devarim* 17:11; *Ramban, Milhamot ha-Shem,* Introduction; Rabbi Yosef Karo, Kelalei Gemara in *Halikhot Olam,* Portnoy ed., Machon ha-Mishpat, 61; Maharal of Prague, *Be'air ha-Golah,* Be'air Rishon, Derekh ha-Hayyim, chapter 5, 259-260, *Netivot Olam,* chapter 15; *Resp. Havot Yair* 192; *Resp. Zivhei Tzedek,* YD 66; *Resp. Avnei Nezer* HM 92; *Rabbi Elhanan Wasserman, Kovetz Shiurim,* vol. 2, 109 (5), 112 (16); *Resp. Shema Shlomo* 1, EH 6 (14) in the name of Maharashdam. For Talmudic precedents for this posture, see Talmud Bavli *Eruvin* 13b, *Hagigah* 3b.

> it is impossible for both parties to the debate to conform to the truth...

Though there is no explicit mention that a halakhic resolution reflects truth, Rabbi Yisrael Salanter claims that halakhic disagreement entails arriving at the truth. Focusing upon the disputes between Beit Hillel and Beit Shammai, *Rabbi Salanter* states:[12]

> The Heavenly Voice told the people that each side genuinely felt objectively correct, and therefore even the rejected words of Beit Shammai are the words of the living Hashem, and one who studies them is studying the Torah of Hashem.

However, *Rabbi Salanter* observes:[13]

> Man does not have the power to arrive at the true intellect, totally dismembered and separated from the subliminal forces of the psyche.

Finally, given that in the context of a *beit din* proceeding we resolve matters in accordance with the majority, the underlying assumption for certain authorities (*Poskim*) is that their *psak din*, decision, reflects the truth and the minority view embodies falsehood.[14] In short, they have adopted a monistic view of Halakhah.

In contradistinction to this monistic perspective of Halakhah, there are authorities who advocate for the notion that the system is pluralistic in character, and therefore the presence of controversy entails a debate of multiple halakhic truths. *Rashi* expounds:[15]

> When two Talmudic scholars are arguing whether a matter is permitted or prohibited... then there is no falsehood.... Each one is arriving at his own conclusion. This individual submits the reason that it should be permitted while the other one gives the rationale that it ought to be prohibited. This person analogizes

12. *Ohr Yisrael*, 44–46.
13. Ibid.
14. *Tosafot Bava Kamma* 27b, s.v. *ka mashma lan*; Maimonides, Introduction to the Commentary of the Mishnah; *Tumim* 25, *Kitzur Tokfo Kohen* 123–124; *Hiddushei Rabbi Hayyim ha-Levi on Shas, Bava Kama* 27b, 129; *Resp. Hut Ha-Meshullash* 8; *Keli Yakar Devarim* 17:11; *Resp. Zivhei Tzedek* YD 26 in the name of Hida.
15. *Rashi*, supra n. 8.

> (*hekesh* – AYW) to a particular subject and this individual analogizes to another matter. Here we may state, "These and those are the words of the living Hashem."

Subsequently, many Rabbis, starting with some in medieval France, query: How is it possible for contradictory views to both represent the truth? Relying explicitly or implicitly upon midrashim and the Tosefta and the Talmud,[16] their reply was the following:[17]

> When Moshe ascended to receive the Torah, it was proven to him that every issue was subject to forty-nine leniencies and forty-nine stringent approaches. When he questioned the matter, Hashem responded that the arbiters of every generation were empowered to decide among these views in order to establish the normative Halakhah.

A few centuries later, adopting the model of multiple halakhic truths, Maharshal argues:[18]

> Everything that is contained in the words of the sages of the Torah... was given by one shepherd, and one should not wonder at the gulf separating the sages in their disagreements, one of them declaring impure, the other declaring pure; one of them forbidding, the other permitting; one of them disqualifying, the other allowing; one of them exempting, the other obligating; one of them distancing, the other drawing near—so long as their views are for the sake of heaven. In fact, the early authorities even went so far as to disregard a heavenly voice—and all are the words of the living God as if each and every one of them received [the Halakhah] directly from God via Moses—even though the matter was not at any stage issued forth by Moses, taking two opposing stances on the same subject.... And the kabbalists explained that all of the souls were at Mount Sinai, and they received via forty-nine channels... and all of Israel saw

16. *Pesikta Rabbati*, Pesika 21; *Tosefta Sotah* 7:11–12; Talmud Yerushalmi, *Sanhedrin* 4:2; *Eruvin* 13b; Talmud Bavli *Hagigah* 3b; Massekhet *Soferim* 15:6–7.

17. *Hiddushei ha-Ritva Eruvin* 13a. See also, *Tosafot Shantz, Eduyot* 1:5; *Teshuvot Binyamin Ze'ev* 144; *Resp. Yosef Omeitz* 51; *Yavin Shemu'ah*, 81b. *Yam shel Shlomo*, Introduction to Tractate *Bava Kamma*. Cf. Maharshal, ibid. that states: "Never did two opposite predicates for one subject escape the lips of Moshe!"

18. *Yam shel Shlomo*, supra n. 17.

> the voices—which [the kabbalists] understand as the opinions as they divided in the channel, each person seeing through his channel according to his capacity... this one distant from that one, to the effect that one arrives at [a determination of] pure, while the other arrives at [a determination of] impure, and a third is in the middle, far from the extremes—and everything is true; understand this.

Others have endorsed this model of multiple halakhic truths.[19]

Whereas Rashi, the French rabbis (and those who followed in their path) and Maharshal contend that the truths are equal, *Maharal of Prague* claims that they are unequal:[20]

> Each understood the Torah from his own vantage point according to his intellectual capacity as well as the... character of his individual soul. This accounts for the difference in comprehension, as one concluded that a thing was *tamei* (ritually impure) in the extreme, another viewed it as clearly *tahor* (ritually pure), while a third person contends the ambivalent state of the object is in question.... Consequently, the learned men stated that in a controversy amongst true scholars, all views represent a form of truth....

In his classic essay regarding this issue, *Rabbi Michael Rosensweig* eloquently formulates his analytical understanding of Maharal's position, elucidating the following:[21]

> There is often no one decisive response to the issue of *tahara* or *tuma*, for example, since overall proximity to the ideal form represented by the classic case rather than a specific combination of components determines this status. Thus, one may speak of approximately the ideal sufficiently but not fully, and by the same token substantially but not sufficiently, and consequently, a whole hierarchy of truths would emerge. Dilution of some components and combination with competing and

19. Talmud Yerushalmi, *Sanhedrin* 4:2; Talmud Bavli *Hagigah* 3b; *Va-Ya'as Avraham, Kuntres Pri ha-Aretz*, 506–510; *Resp. Ginat Veradim, HM* 5:9.

20. *Maharal*, supra n. 11.

21. "*Elu va-Elu Divre Elokim Hayyim*: Halakhic Pluralism and Theories of Controversy," *Tradition* 26:3 (1992), 13–14.

> undermining characteristics may also contribute to the creation of a quasi-status, whole ultimate fate in the realm of practical Halakhah is likely to be debated.

Utilizing an analogy, *Maharal* notes:[22]

> The tree, for example, is composed of four elements (water, earth, fire and air) but the principal component is air.... Likewise, though any single matter has various halakhic aspects associated with it – all endowed by Hashem – one of them is the most paramount, and that is the determining component, and that is the *Halakhah*.

In short, halakhic controversy is either a representation of multiple halakhic truths, or exists due to extraneous reasons such as forgetfulness and loss of halakhic tradition.[23]

The emerging question is: how do these two diametrically opposing perspectives regarding the nature of halakhic controversy impact on how one perceives halakhic doubt (*safek de'dina*) where there is a controversy as to what ought to be the proper halakhic position? If we adopt the notion that there is only one opinion in a halakhic debate which represents truth, then the opposing view is false, as it emerged by dint of extraneous factors such as forgetfulness or a loss in transmission of the *mesorah*. On the other hand, espousing the doctrine of multiple halakhic truths inexorably leads one to the conclusion that all the positions in a particular halakhic disagreement represent halakhic truth.[24] Consequently, it is unsurprising to encounter Rabbi Yitzhak Yosef, a

---

22. *Maharal*, supra n. 11.

23. A third approach, espoused by *Ketzot ha-Hoshen*, Introduction to Ketzot ha-Hoshen, and Rabbi Moshe Feinstein, *Resp. Iggerot Moshe*, YD 1:101, is that from the perspective of Hashem there exists one truth, while from the vantage point of the halakhic arbiter there is one truth which he is dutybound to fulfill, namely "the truth in rendering a ruling" (*emet le'hora'ah*). Consequently, if two decisors disagree regarding an issue, they are both "the words of the living God". However, only one position reflects the truth vis-à-vis heaven. See Shimshon Ettinger, "Controversy and truth-on-truth in the halakhic context," (Hebrew), 21 *Shenaton ha-Mishpat ha-Ivri* 37 (2000). Cf. A. Sagi who misconstrues their positions as adopting a pluralistic view. See *Elu va-Elu: A Study on the meaning of Halakhic Discourse*, Hakibbutz Hameuhad, 1996, 101, 105, 115.

24. Obviously, if the arbiter has erred in his position, depending on the type of error, this will impact on whether the *psak din*, civil ruling or ritual ruling, remains valid, or if it becomes null and void as a result. See Talmud Bavli *Sanhedrin* 33a.

contemporary authority, citing the following in the name of Rabbi Refael Hazan of eighteenth-century Izmir:[25]

> Hashem gave the determination of Halakhah to the scholars of Yisrael which Hashem showed to Moshe forty-nine leniencies and forty-nine prohibitions.... Therefore, if the decisors are in debate and the Halakhah was not decided, whoever practices in accordance with one of these opinions has whom to rely upon....

As such, even if one subscribes to the notion of the existence of multiple halakhic truths concerning a particular issue, lest one assume that a decisor (a *posek*) may refrain from performing due diligence in deciding which view to accept and choose the stringent view, Talmud Yerushalmi exhorts us:[26]

> Just as one is prohibited to purify the impure, similarly, one cannot declare that the pure is impure.

For example, one of the techniques to void a marriage is labeled "*kiddushei ta'ut*" (loosely translated: a marriage in error). Prior to invoking the tool of *kiddushei ta'ut* and claiming there was an error in the creation of the marriage, one of the preconditions that must be obtained is that the husband's defect must be a major defect (a *mum gadol*) such as sexual impotency, refusing to have children, insanity or homosexuality which preexisted the marriage, and that the husband failed to disclose this defect to his prospective wife prior to their marriage.[27] A review of our halakhic tradition will indicate that the classical restatements of Halakhah such as Alfasi, Rambam, Rosh, Tur, Shulhan Arukh and Rema do not address the propriety of utilizing this technique as a vehicle for voiding a marriage concerning a husband's defects.[28] However, there are over 90 responsa (*teshuvot*) which address the propriety of employing

25. *Resp. Ein Yitzhak*, 2:304.

26. Talmud Yerushalmi, *Terumot* 5:3; *Pnei Moshe*, ad locum; *Shakh*, SA YD 242, *Kitzur Be-Hanhagat Hora'ot Issur ve-Heter*, 9. See also *Berakhot* 28b. This approach emerges from *Piskei Ha-Rosh, Sanhedrin* 4:6.

27. See this writer's *Rabbinic Authority*, vol. 3, 134–176, 294–327; vol. 4, 184–201, 284–297.

28. The implicit premise is that *Shulhan Arukh* is an independent halakhic work rather than a vehicle to recall the judgments memorialized in the *Beit Yosef* which was authored by R. Yosef Karo. See Rema, *Ha-Mapah*, Hakdama. Cf. *Hakdamat Ha-Rav Yehoshua Volk Katz Le-Arba'at Sefarav*; *Netivot Olam Ha-Torah* 115.

this tool. A review of these responsa will demonstrate that over 50 authorities endorse this approach and more than 25 decisors prohibit it.[29] In light of the fact that the classical legists did not address this matter and there does not exist normative Halakhah addressing the legitimacy of utilizing this technique,[30] decisors teach us that the arbiter is empowered to employ his knowledge and skills to address, deliberate upon this matter and arrive at a well-grounded and reasoned decision.[31] Clearly, arbitrarily choosing to align with one position is in contravention to the aforesaid Talmud Yerushalmi's dictum.[32]

---

29. See this writer's *Rabbinic Authority*, vol. 3, 138, n. 4, 140, n. 8.

30. Though the majority of legists support utilizing this technique, nevertheless, applying the rule of following the majority ("*aharei rabbim le-hatot*") is limited to disputes transpiring in a *beit din* setting rather than intergenerational controversies. See *Beit Yosef* HM 13 (end) in the name of *Resp. Ha-Rashba* 2:104; *Resp. Ha-Rashba* 3:304, 5:126; *Get Pashut, Kelalim, kelal* 1:5; *Resp. Maharlbah* 147. Cf. *Resp. Torat Emet* in the name of *Tosafot Bava Kamma* 27b; *Resp. Ha-Ridvaz* 4:116. Even in accordance with the view that majority rule is applicable where there are authorities engaging in intergenerational disputes, *Sefer Ha-Hinnukh*, mitzvah 78 contends that the authorities need to possess the same level of halakhic proficiency. See also *Resp. Hikrei Lev, OH* 496:96; *Resp. Tzitz Eliezer* 2:24, 3:29. See further, this writer's *Rabbinic Authority*, vol. 1, 50–52. Secondly, whether one follows the majority or a minority who are greater in wisdom is subject to debate. See *Ran on Rif, Yoma* 4b; *Hiddushei Ha-Ramban Sanhedrin* 32a; *Shakh, SA* YD 242, supra n. 31, at 2. Finally, for the complexity in ascertaining a particular arbiter's proficiency, see *Resp. ha-Rid* 62. Consequently, the propriety of employing *kiddushei ta'ut* as a technique to void a marriage has and continues to this very day to be addressed and debated by arbiters throughout the centuries.

31. *Resp. Ha-Rashba* 2:322; *Sheilat David, Kuntres ha-Hiddushin*, 73–74; *Shakh*, supra n. 26, at 4; *Taz's* Introduction to *Shulhan Arukh, YD; Ketzot ha-Hoshen*, Introduction; *Resp. Iggerot Moshe*, Introduction to *Orah Hayyim, YD* 1:101, YD 3:88, OH 4:11, 39; *Dibrot Moshe Shabbat* 11.

32. Upon analyzing an issue, an arbiter must distinguish between staking out a position based upon the understanding of the Mishnaic and Talmudic sources as interpreted by post-Talmudic authorities as well as the invoking of public policy considerations of Halakhah. In other words, it may be that an arbiter sincerely accepts that a particular practice is permitted by the authorities but nevertheless chooses to prohibit it due the fact that it may create a desecration of God's name (a *hillul ha-Shem*), it may lead to people to engage in other prohibitions, it may undermine a certain revered halakhic institution or it may undermine another important halakhic value. See A. Frimer and D. Frimer, "Women's Prayer Services – Theory and Practice, Part 1," *Tradition* 32:2, 5, 39, 60–69 (1998) and this writer's *Rabbinic Authority*, vol. 4, 21–48. As such, an arbiter's decision grounded upon public policy considerations would not run afoul of the Talmud Yerushalmi's teaching, supra text accompanying n. 19.

Chapter 11

The Role of *Hekesh* (Analogical Reasoning) in the Rendering of a Rabbinic Decision

1. The Parameters of the Workings of a *Hekesh*

The ability to analyze and potentially overrule one's predecessor, whether he be the author of a *teshuva* or a *sefer psak*, requires that the arbiter (including a *mara de-atra* or a *dayan*) possess *yirat Shamayim* (religious piety) and scholarship. In his decision-making, he must weigh the significance of contrary precedent opinion and exercise logic as well. Clearly, many questions posed to an arbiter can be answered by simply opening *sifrei psak* and *teshuvot*. In order to address new questions, however, being conversant with these sources does not suffice. Borrowing Talmudic terminology, Rosh argues that an arbiter must engage in a special type of logic, "*medameh milta le-milta*," applying analogical inferences for the purpose of discerning the similarities and differences between cases in order to address new situations.[1] Implicitly relying upon Talmudic precedent, R. Avraham the son of Maimonides expounds upon the nature of this type of logic:[2]

> An arbiter who in his decisions follows only what is written and explicitly stated is weak... In every decision that he is considering,

1. *Res. Ha-Rosh*, kelal 55:9 and 78:3. There is an ongoing debate about which types of reasoning are permissible in halakhic decision-making. See, for example, *Resp. Ohr Zarua* 2:33; *Resp. Mahari Weil* 164; *Resp. Terumat Ha-Deshen* 16; *Resp. Mahari Bruna* 92; *Resp. Ha-Rashba* 2:322; *She'alat David, Kuntres Ha-Hiddushin*, 73.

For a contemporary implementation of *hekesh* to render halakhic judgments, see *Resp. Iggerot Moshe, Orah Hayyim* 1:33,39, *Yoreh Deah* 4:36, *Hoshen Mishpat* 2:69. For the dynamics of executing a "*hekesh*" in the halakhic decision-making of Maimondes, Ravad and Rosh, see R. Shlomo Daichovsky, *Lev Shomeia LiShlomo*, vol. 3, 130-132.

2. *Resp. Rabbeinu Avraham ben Ha-Rambam* 97.

> he should analogize his case to something that is similar to it and derive branches from those roots... They [Talmudic precedents] were preserved for a reason... in order that the wise man, hearing them frequently, will develop his ability to weigh the matters with discretion and render decisions properly.

The vitality and effervescence of the decision-making process is maintained when the arbiter seeks to resolve a problem by searching for examples that may serve as fruitful sources for comparison. In comparing these precedents to the case at hand, the arbiter analyzes the similarities and differences between them, deriving a tentative analogy that posits a logical relationship between the examples and the problem. Finally, the arbiter confirms the rule by inquiring whether it meets the guidelines for invoking an analogy in this particular situation.[3] In effect, the method of analogy, unlike ordinary open-ended reasoning, starts with the prior decisions of one's predecessors, rather the arbiter's own reasoning and intuition.

The practice of analogical reasoning reflects the ongoing dialectic between deference to early authorities and creative innovation. The spur to originality and creativeness, *ko'ah ha-hiddush*, is tempered by the commitment to thoroughly investigate a wealth of sources and the collaborative effort of numerous arbiters over time who may have addressed similar and/or identical problems. The weightiness of precedent opinion facilitates avoidance of flawed and misplaced reasoning. The engagement in "*medameh milta le-milta*" is thus concomitantly a stimulant and a depressant – a spur to creativity, but equally a motive for restraint.

As the Talmud informs us:[4]

> Once a person has asked and was informed that a Halakhah was to be taken as a guide for practical decisions, he may continue to give practical decisions accordingly, provided he draws no comparisons. But surely, in the entire domain of the Torah, comparisons are made! R. Ashi said: It is this that was meant:

3. For other examples, see this writer's, "The Investment Advisor: Liabilities and Halachic Identity," 58 *Journal of Halacha and Contemporary Society* (2009), 107; "Self-Dealing in the Not for Profit Board Room: An Inquiry into a Trustee's Multifaceted Halakhic Identity," 43 *Tradition* (Spring 2010), 7, and "The Multi-Faceted Halakhic Identity of a Jewish Investment Broker," 43 *Tradition* (Fall 2010), 51.

4. Talmud Bavli *Bava Batra* 130b.

> Provided one draws no comparisons in ritual questions related to *treifot* [diseased animals which, though ritually slaughtered, are forbidden to be eaten]....

The Talmud argues that the application of "*medameh milta le-milta*" is embedded and integrated within the entire corpus of Halakhah, allowing the arbiter to analogize from one branch to another. Upon further reflection, pursuant to R. Ashi's posture, extreme care must be given prior to comparing one case to another, lest one succumb to a mistaken analogy.[5] According to R. Yair Bachrach, a mistaken analogy is in fact subsumed in the category of a "*ta'ut be-devar Mishnah*," an error in black-letter Halakhah, which means that such a decision is null and void.[6]

While the Talmud employs this type of dialectic in the contexts of both *issura* (ritual law) and *mamona* (monetary matters),[7] the Talmud itself exhorts us not to draw an analogy between the two; "no analogy in a manner involving ritual law may be established from monetary matter,"[8] and conversely, "no analogy in a monetary matter may be established from a matter concerning ritual law."[9]

These statements leave us with many questions. Are there any situations in which one can derive a norm in monetary matters from a norm in ritual matters or vice versa? Is it possible to draw an analogy to ritual matters from a norm in a matter comprised of both ritual and monetary aspects, or an analogy to monetary matters from a norm in a matter comprised of both ritual and monetary characteristics? Can one draw an analogy between two commandments, two rules of Shabbat, two *minhagim* (customs), or two legal presumptions? Can we compare legal fictions from different spheres or permit a legal fiction based upon the use of analogy? Is it possible to draw an analogical inference when there is an explicit proof in the Talmud but later teachings lead to a contrary conclusion? Can one analogize from the portion of legal thinking that has no bearing on the conclusion (*obiter dictum*), or must such reasoning be limited to the reasoning essential to the conclusion (*ratio decidendi*)? In monetary matters, may one rely upon a minority lenient opinion in emergency circumstances, as is the case in ritual matters ("Rabbi X is

---

5. This conclusion is reiterated in Talmud Bavli *Gittin* 19a and 37a.
6. *Resp. Havot Ya'ir* 45.
7. Moshe Silberg, *Talmudic Law and the Modern State* (NY: 1973), 65–66.
8. Talmud Bavli *Berakhot* 19b.
9. Talmud Bavli *Ketubot* 46b.

worthy to be relied upon in a dire need")? Can one analogize from one piece of legislation to another, from *hilkhot mikveh* to *hilkhot Sukkot*?

These questions and many others pose significant challenges to the arbiter as he begins the process of reasoning by analogy. Given the penchant for analogical reasoning and that this reasoning is viewed as infinitely malleable, it is not surprising that the Talmud mandates that prior to invoking an analogy, the arbiter must seek advice from a colleague who is of greater scholarly stature than himself regarding the propriety of this reasoning.[10] The classical restatements, including Mishneh Torah, Tur, and Shulhan Arukh, reiterate this need for consultation.[11] Their positions have been understood as mandating this requirement even if the arbiter is free of doubt regarding how to resolve the case. In fact, according to certain authorities, even if he has consulted a greater scholar, he is obligated to confer with him again regarding a similar case, lest he assume that the second case is analogous to the first.[12]

Analogical reasoning coupled with the requirement of consultation with one's colleagues counteracts the errors of open-ended judgment. Reliance serves as a reason for the arbiter to align his own decisions to prior decisions of other arbiters.

Over-reliance on earlier opinions bereft of rationale equally has its pitfalls. As the Talmud Yerushalmi observes, "All agree that we do not learn the law from a previous ruling."[13] One of the commentators notes there:[14]

10. Talmud Bavli *Yevamot* 109b. Some argue that consultation with "the books" rather than a great scholar fulfills this obligation. See *Resp. Shevut Ya'akov* 64; *Urim Ve-tumim* 10, *Urim* 3; *Resp. Yabia Omer, Orah Hayyim* 1, Introduction, p. 10. Although the Talmud does not mandate consultation with another scholar for matters that do not involve the exercise of this type of reasoning, some authorities nevertheless require it; see *Resp. Maharshal* 35; *Resp. Ha-Mabit* 3:93.

11. *Mishneh Torah, Hilkhot Sanhedrin* 20:8, *Tur, Hoshen Mishpat* 10; *Beit Yosef, Hoshen Mishpat* 10:3; *Shulhan Arukh Hoshen Mishpat* 10:2. This requirement equally applies to a *mara de-atra*; see *Birkei Yosef, Hoshen Mishpat* 10:3.

12. Rashi, *Yevamot* 109b; *Bah, Hoshen Mishpat* 10:3; *Perishah, Hoshen Mishpat,* ad loc. Cf. *Nimmukei Yosef, Bava Batra* 58b (Rif pagination); *Ketzot Ha-Hoshen, Hoshen Mishpat* 14:1. One of the opinions cited by the *Hukkot Ha-Dayanim, Hoshen Mishpat* 3:3 extends the logic of this position by arguing that if the arbiter is personally confident in the cogency of his analogical reasoning, he may refrain from conferring with a greater scholar; see *Resp. Mishpetei Uziel, Hoshen Mishpat* 1:3.

13. Yerushalmi *Hagigah* 1:8.

14. *Korban Ha-Eidah,* ibid.

> If a scholar ruled on an issue of Halakhah, one should refrain from determining the Halakhah thereby, since one might be wrong regarding the scholar's reasons for that decision, since there are many who err in their studies.

Thus, conforming to past decisions that are devoid of reasoned judgments must be eschewed. Even reasoned judgments of predecessors cannot guarantee proper decision-making. As R. Yeshaya ben Yisrael Basan, an eighteenth century Italian scholar, elucidates:[15]

> All these arbiters who stick like glue (*to'ke'ah be-devar halakhah*) to a particular teshuvah without examining the roots of the manner are not arbiters at all. Rivash of Barcelona... in replying to someone who wanted to rely upon one of his rulings... answered that it should not be used as a precedent because he might have followed Rashba... since Barcelona was under his jurisdiction. And he may have... had his own reasons for deciding in this manner... Not everyone has the privilege of learning from responsa... since frequently their points are statements which do not form a necessary part of the scholar's ruling.

Hence, reliance on precedent should be weighed properly in the course of analogical reasoning.

2. A Parent's Decision to Withhold Medical Treatment From Children – A Case Study in Competing Analogies

The purpose of this study is to explore the dynamics of the analogical argument in the Jewish legal decision-making process through an analysis of a contemporary case. A range of cases that has gained increasing prominence recently centers around the parental responsibility to provide medical treatment for children. Interestingly enough, the Talmud is reticent regarding this issue. However, post-Talmudic decisors and respondents have suggested that the law of criminal omissions, norms of *tzedakah* (donation of charity) and the child support obligation may

15. Quoted in *Pahad Yitzhak*, part 1, 325; translation culled from Zerah Warhaftig, "Precedent in Jewish Law," in H. Ben-Menahem and N. Hecht (eds.), *Authority, Process, and Method* (London: 1998), 1, 22–23. This position has its Talmudic antecedent in *Bava Batra* 130b, which addresses the potential pitfalls of drawing erroneous conclusions from actual cases.

serve as the halakhic-legal categories for resolving this issue. Implicit in their suggestion of the relevancy of these categories for our case is the assumption that one can extend the rules governing criminal omissions, *tzedakah* and child support which are applicable to one set of fact patterns to our fact pattern (i.e., parental neglect of medical care) which are similar in relevant respects. Here, as in other instances, Halakhic legists resort to the use of "reasoning by analogy" to resolve a case.

Equally significant however, are the *consequences* of adopting a particular analogical argument. Every analogical argument leads to very different substantive results. Our case suggests many competing analogies and therefore the yielding of different outcomes. Yet aside from a decision of the Israeli Rabbinical Court, all authorities who invoke an analogy to resolve our case fail to examine either the consequences of adopting the particular analogical inference and/or the outcome of adopting a counter-analogy.

Our study will attempt to unravel the consequences of viewing a parent who withholds medical care as analogous to that of an individual who fails to rescue an endangered party, declines to give *tzedakah* or as a parent who neglects to support his child.

3. The Halakhah of Criminal Omissions

To fully understand the analogical argument suggested by the halakhic law of criminal omissions, let me begin with a brief presentation of the position of American law.

Our case presents a case of homicide by omission on the part of parents. This case in American law involves three issues: (1) a parent's legal duty to provide necessary medical attention and the imposition of criminal sanctions for failure to fulfill this duty, (2) the degree of negligence required for involuntary manslaughter, and (3) the circumstances under which an omission is deemed to proximately cause the death of the other.[16]

16. See e.g., Eaglen v. State, 249 Md. 144, 231 N.E. 2d 147 (1967); Craig v. State, 220 Md. 590, 155 A. 2d 684 (1959), and State v. Staples, 126 Minn., 148 N.W. 283 (1914). Commonwealth v. Barnhart, 345 Pa. Super. 10, 497 A. 2d. 616 (1985) appeal denied, 517 Pa. 620, J38 A. 2d. 874, cert. denied 109 S. Ct. 55 (1988) and Walker v. Superior Court, 47 Cal. 3d. 112,763 P. 2d. 852, 253 Cal. Rptr. 1 (1988). See also, 30 A.L.R. 2d 1138 & 52 A.L.R. 3d 118.

The adoption of a causation framework implies a commitment to one of the following theses: Either that the failure to avert harm, i.e., omission is the cause of the harm, i.e., negative causation. Or, by failing to avert harm, one is *blameworthy* and

Perhaps one of the most striking illustrations of the causation thesis as a ground for denying liability for homicide is exemplified by the case of Bradley v. State.[17] In Bradley, a minor, epileptic daughter had fallen into a fire during a seizure and received severe burns. On religious grounds, the father refused to treat the burns with medication. Suggesting that there was no causal relation between the father's omission and the child's death, the court exonerated the defendant of manslaughter stating:[18]

> Whatever motive may have prompted the father in failing and refusing to provide medical attention for his severely burned daughter, such failure and refusal, however reprehensible, does not appear to be within the letter or intent of the statute making "the killing of a human being, by the act, procurement or culpable negligence of another" a felony called manslaughter. It is not claimed that the allegations and proofs show that any 'act' or 'procurement' of the father caused the death of the child... Manifestly, the death of the child was caused by the accidental burning in which the father had no part...

In other words, the failure to avert harm is to be distinguished from causing harm. Since the child's death was caused by the accidental burning in which the father had no part, the father did not "cause the killing of the child". To borrow John Klenig's phraseology, his failure to act is

therefore the cause of the harm that occurs. See e.g., D'Arcy, *Human Acts*, Oxford: Oxford U. Press, 1903; Casey, "Actions and Consequences" in Casey ed. *Morality & Moral Reasoning*, London: Methuen, 1971; Harris, "The Marxist Concept of Violence" 3 *Philosophy & Public Affairs* 192 (1974); Harris, "Bad Samaritans Cause Harm" 32 *Philosophical Quarterly* 60,1982; Klenig, "Good Samaritanism" 5 *Philosophy & Public Affairs* 382, 1976.

For a critique of the causation theses in the context of criminal omissions, see e.g., Mack, "Bad Samaritanism & the Causation of Harm" 9 *Philosophy & Public Affairs* 230 ,1980; Weinryb, 30 *The Philosophical Quarterly* 1, 1980; Feinberg, *Harm to Others*, N.Y. Oxford U. Press, 1984, 171-186; Benditt, "Liability for Failing to Rescue" 1 *Law & Philosophy* 391, 396-400 (1982); Fletcher, *Rethinking Criminal Law*, Boston: Little Brown, 1978, 371; and Robinson, "Criminal Liability for Omissions: A Brief Summary & Critique of the Law in the U.S.", 29 *NYU School Law Review* 101, 110 ,1984.

17. 79 Fla. 651, 84 So. 677 (1920).
18. Id. at 655, 84 So. at 679.

"harm exacerbating rather than harm initiating."[19] Therefore, he should not be held liable for harm he failed to avert.[20]

Traditionally, the common law has refused to impose a general duty to rescue persons in peril. Nonetheless, many exceptions to this rule have developed in the form of "special relationships between two individuals" out of which affirmative duties emerge. The duty of rescue based on a special relationship is well settled when the individual needing medical care is a child and the person under a duty is the parent.[21]

Does the Bradley decision imply a recognition of humanitarian duties that "the law should reflect, reinforce..., at least the segment of shared morality which consists in moral duties owed to others"?[22] Rather, this decision reflects the judgment of Lord Atkin in the classic English case of Donohue v. Stevenson (1932) A.C. 562:

> The rule that you are to love your neighbor becomes in law, you must not injure your neighbor; and the lawyer's question, who is my neighbor? receives a restricted reply... lie answer seems to be persons who are so closely and directly affected by my act that I ought reasonably to have them in contemplation as being so affected when I am directing my mind to acts or omissions which we called in question.

Clearly, suggests Lord Atkin, the particular situation mandates that a parent rescue his child. Neither humanhood nor parenthood as moral duties become the source of the legal duty of care.[23] Whether a particular situation mandates a duty of care will be resolved by applying the rules of causation. Hence, the causation thesis is the justification for a duty of rescue based upon a "special relationship."

Does Halakhah analyze criminal omission in terms of "causation" and

19. Klenig, op. cit. 398.

20. One can assign liability for injury only for the proper amount of liability, i.e., causation of injury. See Epstein, "A Theory of Strict Liability" *2 Journal of Legal Studies* 151 ,1973.

21. See e.g., Commonwealth v. Breth, 44 Pa. C. 56 (Clearfield County Ct. 1915); State v. Walden, 306 N.C. 466, 293 S.E. 2d. 780 (1982); Nozza V. State, 288 $o. 2d. 560 (Fla. Dist. Ct. App. 1974); People v. Sealty, 136 Mich. App. 168, 356 N.W. 2d. 614 (1984). For other exceptions to the common law rule, see e.g., Jones v. U.S., 308 F. 2d. 307, 310 (D.C. Cir. 1962), People v. Beardsley, 150 Mich. 206, 113 N.W. 1128 (1907).

22. Hart & Honore, *Causation & the Law*, Oxford: Oxford U. Press, 1959, 34, 35 and 37.

23. Klenig, op. cit. 383.

thus insist on a causal link between omission and harm?[24] How does Halakhah analyze parental responsibility for medical care for its citizenry? A cursory reading of Talmudic discussions of homicide clearly indicates that the concept of causation is limited to affirmative acts, i.e., criminal commissions.[25]

If, according to Halakhah, the harm that the individual does not prevent from occurring cannot be regarded as a consequence of his refraining, since the required causal relation is absent, on what basis can one hold an individual responsible for his omission? Without recourse to a given causal framework, as suggested by American law, there exists in Jewish law a positive duty to every individual, a duty beyond the "negative" one of not causing harm to the individual. A parent's obligation to provide medical treatment has been suggested by various authorities as an example of this generalized duty of rescue, one that extends to strangers.[26]

Seemingly, the application of this duty of rescue analogy is ineffective in the sense that it is a somewhat toothless tiger since the failure to rescue lacks a halakhic-legal sanction.[27] Hence, given our case, a minor would have no legal redress against a recalcitrant parent who refuses to provide medical care.[28]

---

24. Our analysis is predicated upon two assumptions: (1) In contradistinction to other religious traditions, there is a Judaic obligation to seek conventional medical care. See generally, Bleich, "Ethico-Halakhic Considerations in the Practice of Medicine", 7 *Dine Israel* 87, 1976, reprinted as "Theological Considerations in the Care of Defective Newborns" in *Decisionmaking and the Defective Newborn* (ed. Swinyard, Thomas: Illinois, 1978) 512-561 and Rosner, *Modern Medicine & Jewish Ethics*, N.Y. Ktav, 1986, 7-22. Compare Rabbi (hereafter R.) Bornstein (19th Cent: Galicia), *Resp. Avnei Nezer, Hoshen Mishpat* 193. (2) The failure to provide medical treatment is an act of homicide by omission rather than a positive act of homicide. See R. Yosef Hayyim (19th Cent: Iraq), *Resp. Rav Pe'alim, Orah Hayyim* 3:36.

25. See Talmud Bavli, *Sanhedrin* 77a, 78a & 78b. Also, Genauer, The Treatment of Homicide in the Talmud, Dissert. Seattle, Wash. 1970.

26. See R. Waldenberg (20th Cent: Israel), *Resp. Tzitz Eliezer* 15:40; R. Navon (19th Cent: Kushta), *Resp. Beit Ephraim* 65; and R. Nathanson (19th Cent: Galicia), *Resp. Shoeil U-Meshiv, Mahadura Kamma* 3:140.

27. See e.g., Talmud Bavli. *Makkot* 15b, Maimonides (12th Cent: Spain), *Mishneh Torah, Hilk. Sanhedrin* 18:1-2; *Hilk. Rotze'ah U-Shemirat HaNefesh* 1:16.

28. The lack of halakhic legal sanction is limited to the situations which mandate a rescue based upon the halakhot of criminal omissions. However, situations which mandate a rescue based upon the halakhot of finders will be subject to judicial coercion. (This distinction between the halakhot of criminal omissions and halakhot of finders based upon the presence or absence of halakhic legal sanction is beyond the scope of this presentation). Nevertheless, rabbinically ("*mi-de-rabbanan*"), it

Countering this objection, Professor Aaron Kirschenbaum states:[29]

> It is a fact of history that in Jewish society..., non-prosecutable injunctions, by their sheer religious weight, were effective in their deterrent power. It would be misleading, though, to interpret the lack of judicial punishment in Jewish law for the innocent bystander who fails in his duty to come to the rescue of his fellowman in distress as indicating that the duty is merely moral. Rather, Jewish law views such failure as nonfeasance, a formal offense of inaction.., where action is a duty required by law.

Echoing a similar notion, Professor Ernst Weinrib writes:[30]

> To regard the talmudic duty as moral rather than legal, however, is to misconceive the talmudic position. The duty of rescue is not merely a matter of conscience... Because Jewish law embodies a jurisprudence of obligation, the legal character of the duty to rescue lies in its very existence as a duty, even if its breach is not subject to sanction...

Halakhah is primarily a system of duties owed rather than rights possessed. Hence, the individual's duty by itself mandates compliance.

This positive duty of rescue is based upon both a positive and a negative commandment: "And you shall restore him to himself" and "Do not stand idly by the blood of your neighbor."[31] Whereas the negative commandment biblically mandates aid for victims in peril, the former verse dealing with the restoration of lost property is interpreted by the Midrash to encompass the restoration of an individual's body.[32]

---

is permissible to compel compliance in cases of criminal omissions. See e.g., R. Hezekiah Medini (20th Cent: Israel), *Sedei Hemed*, Entry "M," Principle 106-110; R. Berlin (19th Cent: Lithuania), *Resp. Meshiv Davar* 4:11; and R. Pelaggi (19th Cent: Izmir) *Ginzei Hayim*, Entry "M", Malkot, section 87. `

For the applicability of the halakhot of finders & criminal omissions to the rescue operation, see discussion infra.

29. Kirschenbaum, "The Good Samaritan & Jewish Law," 7 *Dine Israel*, 17-18, 1976.

30. Weinrib, "Rescue & Restitution" 1 *S'vara* 59, 61, 1990.

31. See *Vayikra* 19:16 and *Devarim* 22:2.

32. *Sifrei Ki Tetzei* 22:2 (ed. Finkelstein, p. 256). Our implicit assumption is that the halakhot of finders mandates a rescue even in non life threatening situations. See e.g., Maimonides, Commentary on the Mishnah; ed. Kapah, *Nedarim* 4:4, 91

Seemingly, the positive and negative commandments are two sides of the same coin; the negative one has no intrinsic significance; it relates only to the omission of the positive, i.e., the failure to rescue.

However, the Talmud views the provisions regulating the duty to rescue as a resolution of the interplay between a positive and a negative commandment emerging from two different spheres of Jewish law, namely the law of finders and the rules of criminal omissions.[33] The Talmud states:[34]

> From where do we know that if a man sees his neighbor drowning..., he is bound to save him? From the verse, "Do not stand idly by the blood of your neighbor." But is it derived from this verse? Is it not rather from elsewhere? From where do we know (that one must rescue his neighbor from) the loss of himself? From the verse, "And you ought to restore him to himself." From that verse I might think that it is only a personal obligation, but that he is not bound to take the trouble of hiring men (if he cannot deliver him himself); therefore, this verse teaches that he must.

If the duty of rescue would have been governed exclusively by the halakhah of the finder, then the scope of a rescuer's involvement would have been limited to personal involvement.

The halakhah of criminal omissions mandates that an individual's duty in a rescue is not eclipsed by personal involvement. The rescuer, while attempting to render assistance to the endangered party, is obligated to incur the expenditures required for the rescue.[35] Thus, the halakhah of criminal omissions serves to expand the scope of the rescuer's liability beyond the obligation mandated by the halakhah of finders.[36] Hence,

---

and *Hamra VeHayei, Sanhedrin* 73a. Compare Schiff, "Opening a Clinic in a Condominium Against the Wishes of the Other Tenants" (Hebrew), in *Emek Halakha* (ed. Halperin), Jerusalem: Dr. F. Schlessinger Institute, 1985, 138-140.

33. See Kirschenbaum op. cit. 19-22. In addition, see R. Grossnass (20th Cent: England), *Resp. Lev Aryeh* 42; R. Tsirelson (20th Cent.), *Resp. Atzei Halevanon* 61; and *Beit Ephraim*, op. cit.

34. Talmud Bavli, *Sanhedrin* 73a.

35. For the scope of one's financial obligations, see e.g., R. Kook (20th Cent: Israel), *Resp. Mishpat Kohen* 144; R. Weinberg (20th Cent: Switzerland), *Resp. Seridei Esh*, Vol. 1, 313; R. Bachrach (17th Cent: Germany), *Resp. Havot Yair* 139; *Resp. Ha-Rivash* 387, and R. Sofer (19th Cent: Hungary), *Resp. Hatam Sofer, Hoshen Mishpat* 177.

36. Whereas, according to common law, there is an absence of a general legal

the extent of parental responsibility for providing a child's medical care comprises two elements: (1) personal involvement and (2) financial expenditures.

Viewing the provisions regulating the general duty of rescue as a resolution of the interplay between two diverse areas of Halakhah is reflected in post-Talmudic discussions. For example, what happens if an elderly father or a father well versed in Jewish law, capable of assisting, considers the rendering of a particular type of medical treatment undignified (e.g., personal treatment of a major hemorrhage of his child) and therefore declines to offer assistance? Since, according to the law of finders, under these circumstances the person would be exempt from his duty to restore lost property,[37] hence some post-Talmudic decisors conclude that he is equally exempt from the duty of rescue. However, the dominant school of thought argues that the law of criminal omissions mandates that there exists a general duty of rescue.[38] Therefore, an elderly father or father versed in Halakhah would remain dutybound to provide the necessary medical treatment for his child.

Inasmuch as Halakhah encourages the duty to rescue,[39] the halakhic-legal system (similar to many civil law systems) requires the rescuee to reimburse the rescuer for expenses that the rescuee would surely have authorized. However, according to a minority opinion, if the rescuee is impoverished and therefore cannot shoulder the costs of the rescue operation, the rescuer is exempt from his duty of rescue.[40] Consequently, it would seem that a father would be exempt from providing medical care to his dependencies who are bereft of financial resources. Alternatively,

---

duty to rescue persons in peril [see e.g., Ratcliffe (ed), *The Good Samaritan & the Law*, N.Y., Anchor 1966; D'Amato, "The Bad Samaritan Paradigm," 70 *Northwestern U. Law Review* 802 (1975); Weinrib, "The Case for a Duty to Rescue," 90 *Yale L.J.* 247 (1980) and Woozley, "Duty to Rescue: Some Thoughts on Criminal Liability," 69 *Virginia L.R.* 1273 (1983). Similarly, there is no legal obligation to secure and return lost property. (See Brown, The Law of Personal Property section 3.5 at 30 (3rd ed. 1970]. Under Halakhah, however, there exists a duty of restoring lost property as well as a duty of rescue. Moreover, the halakhah of finders may serve as a guideline in formulating the provisions regulating the rescue operation See discussion infra.

37. See Talmud Bavli, *Bava Metzia* 30a-b. For the varying definitions of an "elderly person," see e.g., Maimonides *Mishneh Torah, Hilk. Gezelah Va-Avedah* 11:13, and R. Ashkenazi (16th Cent: Egypt-Israel), *Shitah Mekubezet Bava Metzia* 30a.

38. See R.M. Plotski (20th Cent: Poland), *Kli Hemdah, Devarim, Ki Tetzei* pp. 186-188 and *Lev Aryeh*, op. cit.

39. See Kirschenbaum, op. cit., 59-80.

40. See Rakover, "The Saving of Life-Restitution for the Rescuer's Expenses" (Hebrew), Jerusalem: Ministry of Justice, No. 51, 1977, 13-16.

it might be argued that the case of a dependent child may be an exception to the rule.[41]

4. The Parameters of *Tzedakah*

A second analogical model suggested by contemporary decisors is to posit that parental responsibility to provide necessary medical treatment involves the fulfillment of a "*hiyuv*" (i.e., obligation), namely the *mitzva* (the duty) of *tzedakah*, i.e., charity.[42]

Seemingly, given the fact that *tzedakah* is "*mamon she'ain lo tov'in*", i.e., monies without determinate plaintiffs,[43] the failure to contribute is not justiciable. No potential recipient of tzedakah can demand anything from a donor as his due. Consequently, it would seem that a child has no legal redress against a recalcitrant parent who fails to provide medical care.

As the late Chief Rabbi of Israel, Rabbi Dr. Isaac Herzog, observes:[44]

> Right and its correlative duty are fundamental concepts in law... Thus, to give a sufficiently plain illustration, if A owes money to B, the right to recover the debt is vested in B and he is in legal language the owner of the right which avails against A... A, on the other hand, owes a duty to B. He is the person against whom the right of B avails, and upon whom the correlative duty lies... That these elemental concepts are present in Jewish law is, of course, self evident...

---

41. See R.S. de Medina (16th Cent: Salonica), *Resp. Maharashdam, Yoreh Deah* 204.

42. Decisions of the Rabbinical Courts of Israel (*Piskei Din Rabbani* hereafter cited as PDR) 10:220, 224.

43. See Talmud Bavli, *Bava Kamma* 36b & 93a, *Hullin* 130b; and *Nimukei Yosef, Bava Kamma* 93a. For responsa, see e.g., R.S. ben Aderet (13th Cent: Spain), *Resp. Ha-Rashba* 1:656 & 1256; R.Y. Perfet (14th Cent: Spain & North Africa), *Resp. Ha-Rivash* 465; and R.S. ben Z. Duran (15th Cent: N. Africa), *Resp. Ha-Tashbetz* 3:152, 303. Hence, the authority of the "*gabbai,*" i.e., collector of the "*kuppat tzedakah*," i.e., communal charity fund, is circumscribed. See *Resp. Ha-Rashba* 3:293 & 294; Resp. *Maharashdam, Yoreh Deah* 168; R.M. Issereles (16th Cent: Poland), *Resp. Ha-Rema* 31; *Mishneh Le Melekh, Mishneh Torah, Hilk. Malveh Ve-Loveh* 4: page 92:4, and R.Y. Lorberbaum (18th Cent: Poland), *Netivot Ha-Mishpat* 301:6. Compare Gulak, *History of Jewish Law — Law of Obligation & Its Guarantees* (Hebrew), Jerusalem: Hebrew U. Press, 1939, 90.

44. Herzog, *The Main Institutions of Jewish Law*, London: Soncino Press, 1967, vol. 1, 46.

Adopting the logical correlativity thesis, Halakhah posits that whenever someone has a right, it is a right held against some other individual and the latter has a corresponding duty to the right holder.[45]

Is the converse equally true? Is there a corresponding right whenever there is a duty? Jewish law argues that the converse of the thesis, however, turns out to be demonstrably false. Clearly, the duty of *tzedakah* may require one to contribute to one or to a number of determinate recipients (based on a system of priorities laid down by Halakhah),[46] yet not one of them can claim the contribution as his right.

As the Israeli Rabbinical Court notes:[47]

> The obligation of *tzedakah* is an obligation upon the individual, but he is not obligated to the recipient... There is a general obligation of *tzedakah*... without the existence of a creditor ("*ba'al hov*" — AYW) to whom he is duty-bound to pay his obligation...

Intrinsically, according to numerous authorities, the *mitzva* of *tzedakah* constitutes a "*hov*,"[48] i.e., debt, and possesses many of the characteristics associated with other types of debts recognized by Halakhah. *Tzedakah* is: (1) a legally enforced obligation;[49] (2) the evasion of a *tzedakah*

45. We are speaking in terms of "claim rights" rather than having a right in the sense of having a "liberty."

46. R. Issereles, Rema, *Yoreh Deah* 251:3. In certain respects, John Stuart Mill's notion of a "duty of imperfect obligation" is akin to our duty of *tzedakah*. Distinguishing between perfect and imperfect duties, Mill observes: "Duties of perfect obligation are those duties in virtue of which a correlative right resides in person or persons; duties of imperfect obligation are those moral obligations which do not give birth to any right." See *Utilitarianism*, N.Y. Hobbs-Merrill Co., 1961, 61. Yet whereas the duty of charity becomes "imperfect" in Mill's sense given the number of eligible recipients; in Halakhah, however, there exists a determinate recipient of *tzedakah* based upon a coordinated system of priorities for the allocation of funds.

47. PDR 1:145, 154, 155. 7.

48. There is a dual aspect involved in the *tzedakah* obligation: (1) "*mamona*," lit. monetary; (2) "*issura*," lit. prohibition. The aspect of "*issura*" is beyond the scope of this presentation.

49. See Talmud Bavli, *Ketubot* 86a-b, *Bava Batra* 8b and *Hullin* 110b. For the scope of coercion and its juridical basis, see e.g., *Tosafot, Ketubot* op. cit.; *Tosafot Bava Batra*, op. cit.; R. Abulafia (12th Cent: Spain), *Yad Ramah, Bava Batra* 8b; Maimonides, *Mishneh Torah, Hilk. Mattenot Aniyyim* 7:10; R.D. ben Zimra (16th Cent: Egypt), *Mishneh Torah*, loc. cit., R.Y. Ishbili (14th Cent: Spain), *Novellae of Ritba, Ketubot*, op. cit., *Bava Batra*, op. cit. and Rosh Hashanah 6a; R.Y. Perfet, Resp. Ha-Rivash, 260; R.Y. Kolon (15th Cent: Italy), *Resp. Ha-Maharik*, 148; R.Y. Karo (16th Cent: Israel), *Shulhan Arukh, Yoreh Deah* 248:1. For dissenting views, see R. Hai's

obligation creates a lien upon the property of a recalcitrant donor (i.e., *shi'bud nekhasim*),[50] and (3) *Tefisah* (lit. "the taking of possession" — "seizure") of *tzedakah* by the impoverished is legally effective.[51]

Yet, various decisors,[52] as well as an Israeli Rabbinical Court, note that since *tzedakah* is characterized as "*mamon she'ain lo tov'im,*" it is distinguished from the classical type of "*hov.*" Whereas, for example, the failure to repay a loan gives rise to a "*zekhut teviyah,*" i.e., claim and the initiation of halakhic-legal proceedings by a plaintiff, the evasion of one's *tzedakah* obligation, lacking a determinate recipient, fails to give rise to a correlative claim.

Seemingly, in our issue at bar, no halakhic-legal redress can be accorded to a minor attempting to initiate proceedings against a recalcitrant parent who fails to provide medical care.

Nevertheless, despite the absence of a determinate recipient with a correlative claim, the Rabbinical Court explains that a deserving, needy individual can approach the court, requesting of the *beit din*, "the father of orphans",[53] to compel the donor to fulfill his *tzedakah* obligation.[54]

---

ruling recorded by Rashba in *Otzar Ha-Geonim* ed. Lewin, Ketubot,130; R.Z. Ha-Levi (12th Cent: Provence), *Ba'al Ha-Maor, Bava Kamma*, Chapter 4; R. Tam (12th Cent: France), *Tosafot, Bava Batra* 8b. 9.

50. See e.g., *Yad Ramah*, op. cit.; Maimonides, op. cit.; R.D. ben Zimra, op. cit.; R.Y. Karo, *Kesef Mishneh, Mishneh Torah, Hilk. Nahalot* 11:11; *Shulhan Arukh, Yoreh Deah* 248:1; *Rema, Even Ha-Ezer* 71:2; R.S. Rapaport (17th Cent: Poland), *Shakh, Yoreh Deah* 248:4; R.E. of Vilna (18th Cent: Poland), *Be'ur Hagra, Yoreh Deah* 245:9, R.A.L. Heller (18th Cent: Galicia) *Ketzot Ha-Hoshen, Hoshen Mishpat* 39:1 and 290:15. For a dissenting opinion, see e.g., *Resp. Maharashdam, Yoreh Deah* 166. However, whereas regarding all debts, a beit din is empowered to recover the debt from the debtor's property even in the absence of the debtor; in the case of a recalcitrant donor, a beit din is authorized to recover from his property only in his presence, See e.g. R.Y. Karo, *Yoreh Deah* 248:1, *Shakh*, op. cit., subsection 4; R.S. Feibish (17th Cent: Poland) *Beit Shmuel, Even Ha-Ezer* 71:6. Compare, R.N. Gerondi (14th Cent: Spain), *Ran, Ketubot* 49b; R.D. Zimra, op. cit.; *Rema, Even Ha-Ezer* 71:2. For the parameters of "*eikul nekhasim*", i.e., the attachment of property, in cases of an individual's failure to meet his *tzedakah* requirements, see Shochetman, *Civil Procedure in Jewish Law* (Hebrew), Jerusalem: The Library of Jewish Law, 1988, 408-409.

51. See e.g., *Ohr Zarua, Hilkhot Tzedakah* 22, R.E. Navon, *Mahaneh Ephraim, Halakhot Zekhiyah U-Matanah* 9 & *Tzedakah* 1. For an analysis of the nature of "*tefisah*" in cases of *tzedakah*, see e.g., PDR 1:145, 156. 11.

52. *Resp. Ha-Rashba* 3:293, 294; *Resp. Maharashdam, Yoreh Deah* 168.

53. Talmud Bavli *Gittin* 37a and *Bava Kamma* 37a.

54. See PDR 1:145, 156. Implicit in this conclusion is that the system of priorities in the allocation of *tzedakah* as well as the obligation per se are halakhically-legally enforceable. See e.g. Maimonides, Commentary on the Mishnah, *Ketubot* 4:6; R.M. ben Hillel (13th Cent: Germany), Mordekhai, *Bava Batra* 8b, Sections 493-494; *Resp.*

Hence, in our situation, the minor may approach the *beit din* and demand compliance from his recalcitrant parent.

The question of the absence of a plaintiff in the context of *tzedakah* duties aside, the scope of *tzedakah* is quite limited when compared with the range of the halakhah of criminal omissions. Clearly, amounts of *tzedakah* were fixed at a tithe – limiting the potential donation. And, needless to say, the financial condition of the donor and recipient become relevant factors. Hence, a parent may be obligated to provide medical treatment only upon providing for his or her own needs.[55] In the case of parents without financial means, according to Halakhah, wealthy relatives must attend to his needs. If these resources are unavailable, then the communal charity funds may be tapped to provide medical care.[56] Or, if the child is financially independent, there would be no obligation to give *tzedakah*.[57] Consequently, adopting the analogical model of *tzedakah* has significant juridical consequences. There will be numerous situations where a minor will be bereft of medical care and become a public charge, dependent upon the community for his medical care.

5. The Scope of Child Support

A third analogical model suggested by a contemporary decisor and an Israeli Rabbinical Court is that the halakhic-legal basis for a parental obligation to provide medical care stems from "*mezonot yeladim,*" i.e., the child support obligation.[58] In other words, the fact of a familial relationship, juridically creates a special tie between parent and child, constituting the basis for a parent's liability to support their children,

---

Ha-Rashba 3:292; R.M. Mintz (15th Cent: Ashkenaz), *Resp. Maharam Mintz* 7 and 65; *Shulhan Arukh, Yoreh Deah* 251:4, & *Rema, Yoreh Deah* 251:4. For dissenting opinions, see e.g. R. Yeruham (14th Cent: Provence & Spain), *Sefer Meisharim, Netiv* 23, Part 5; and R.P. Horowitz (18th Cent.), *Sefer Hafla'ah, Ketubot* 71:2.

Hence, despite the impression of *beit din* coercion for this duty as well as the enforcement of a system of priorities for *tzedakah* allocation, the minor does not appear in the beit din as a plaintiff claiming his due.

55. *Shakh, Yoreh Deah* 240:5, 248:1; *Rema, Yoreh Deah* 251:3.

56. See Talmud Bavli *Nedarim* 65b; *Resp. Ha-Rashba* 3:292; *Shulhan Arukh, Yoreh Deah* 257:8.

57. See e.g., PDR 2:301, 7:136, 149-151. Similarly, a "wicked recipient" would not receive *tzedakah*. See e.g., *Shulhan Arukh, Yoreh Deah* 251:1, Shakh, op. cit. Conversely, accepting funds from a donor who is a "*mumar*" is questionable. See e.g., Rema, *Yoreh Deah* 254:10; *Shakh*, op. cit.; *Resp. Ha-Mabit* 2:214; and *Resp. Shevut Yaakov* 3:85.

58. *Resp. Minhat Yitzhak* 6:150; PDR 10:219.

including the provisions of medical treatment. In contrast to the analogical models of criminal omissions and *tzedakah* which focus upon the individual's duty to rescue and contribute respectively, the analogical model of the law of domestic relations invokes the relational interest of family status. Adopting the framework of criminal omissions and *tzedakah,* the parental obligation resides with the individual, and consequently both father and mother are equally responsible.[59] Adopting the rubric of domestic relations, the duty falls squarely upon the shoulders of the father qua parent.[60]

Conceptually speaking, what is the basis for the parental obligation to provide medical treatment? Though the Talmud does not address this question, the Israeli Rabbinical Court suggests that the scope of parental responsibility for medical care can be determined by ascertaining the scope of a husband's duty of medical care for his ailing wife. In other words, since the father's obligation to maintain his child stems from the duty to support his spouse;[61] consequently the scope of the paternal obligation to provide medical care will be identical with the requirements of a husband's duty of medical care, an element of spousal support.

What sort of medical attention must a husband provide for his ailing spouse? The talmudic response[62] is that he must provide "medical treatment without fixed cost" unqualifiedly. What constitutes "medical treatment with fixed cost," regarding which there is a discussion as to the conditions under which the husband must provide them? The Talmud is referring either to a brief illness or to an extended illness whereby there is a prior arrangement of the husband with the physician to pay a fixed amount to treat his wife in time of need.[63]

Since the obligation of providing "medical treatment without fixed cost" falls under the rubric of *mezonot,* i.e., spousal support,[64] therefore

59. Regarding criminal omissions, see Talmud Bavli *Bava Kamma* 15a. Concerning a mother's *tzedakah* duty, see e.g., R.Y. Eybeschutz, *Bnei Ahuvah*; Maimonides *Mishneh Torah, Hilk. Ishut* 21:16; *Resp. Yaskil Avdi, Even Ha-Ezer* 6:28 & 38; PDR 9:251, 263.

60. For a general overview, see B.Z. Schereschewsky, *Family Law,* 3rd ed., Jerusalem; Rubin Mass, 1984, 471-503.

61. For the basis of this approach, see discussion infra. See also this writer's, "Child Custody; A Comparative Analysis," 14 *Israel Law Review* 480, 486-487 (1979), reprinted in this writer's *Rabbinic Authority,* vol. 4, 109-129.

62. Talmud Bavli *Ketubot* 52b.

63. See *Shitah Mekubetzet Ketubot* 52b; Rashi, *Ketubot* 52b. For further discussion, see Cohn, "The Husband's Liability for the Medical Treatment of his Wife According to Jewish Law" (Hebrew) 7 *Dine Israel* 67 (1976).

64. Talmud Bavli, *Ketubot* 52b; Tosafot, *Ketubot* 52b; R. Yehiel (13th Cent:

it is incumbent upon a husband to provide this type of care to his sick wife. Hence (as we stated earlier, the scope of child support is dependent upon the scope of spousal support), it is a father's duty to provide care for children with extended illness and/or compensation to physicians for halakhically unenforceable medical expenses.

However, what type of medical care and/or compensation must a husband provide for an ailing spouse with a brief illness, i.e., "medical treatment with fixed cost"? One authority contends that this type of care is included in the husband's duty of redemption of his wife from captivity, i.e., *pidyon*. Others maintain, however, that there exists special legislation which rabbinically enjoins medical care.[65]

Seemingly, a father ought to be exempt from providing this type of medical attention for his children. Since there exists neither a parental duty of *pidyon* nor any special legislation which enjoins medical care, on what grounds can a minor expect to receive medical treatment for a brief illness or an extended illness whereby there was some prior arrangement regarding compensation for services rendered? Unable to offer a solution within the framework of domestic relations, the Israeli Rabbinical Court concludes that the relevant analogical models of the halakhah that are applicable are those of criminal omissions and the norms of *tzedakah*.[66]

However, a solution may be found within the framework of family law. R. David Meir Feder (known by the acronym: "Radam"), a nineteenth century decisor, writes:[67]

> One who obligated himself to maintain his daughter and son in-law according to the prevailing custom and the daughter became ill and died. Is the father allowed to deduct his daughter's medical expenses (which he incurred) from the obligation of support promised to his son-in-law?...
>
> Since it is customary for a father to provide for his daughter's illness during the course of the support period, when one undertakes an obligation, it is with awareness of this custom. However, a major illness and large medical expenditures does not occur every day... and it does not legally constitute a

---

Spain), *Piskei Ha-Rosh, Ketubot* 4:23.

65. See PDR 10:219, 221 Cohn, op. cit.

66. PDR 10:219, 224. The *Beit Din* arrives at this conclusion, albeit realizing the limitations of applying the category of *tzedakah* to multifarious situations

67. *Resp. Radam, Hoshen Mishpat* 4.

> "*minhag*" (i.e., custom) if it happens infrequently. And one cannot suggest a proof from the custom that a father remunerates medical fees for a slight illness. Clearly this is in the category of spousal support than instances of a large expenditure and major illness....

Accordingly, child support is governed by "halakhah" i.e., Jewish law and "*nohag*," i.e., usage or conventional custom.[68] Since it was customary and usual for a father to provide medical care for a brief illness which involves the incurring of minimal expenses, consequently R. Feder argues that this type of medical attention constitutes part of his support obligation. Hence, since the "*nohag*" did not indicate parental liability for major illness, therefore the father had no duty to provide such care. Thus, on the basis of this responsum, a father ought to provide for "medical treatment with fixed cost" for his children. Hence, parental responsibility for providing medical treatment for brief illnesses is predicated upon "*nohag*," a guideline for determining the scope of the "*mezonot*" obligation.

Adopting the analogical model of child support has significant juridical consequences. Whereas the halakhah of criminal omission is devoid of a halakhic legal sanction, a Beit Din can coerce compliance for paternal failure to fulfill one's support obligation. In contrast to the duty of *tzedakah*, where the financial conditions of the donor and recipient are relevant considerations, the duty of "*mezonot*" mandates support under all circumstances, even in a case of an indigent father and wealthy children.[69] Yet, according to the Talmud, the statutory requirement of "*mezonot*" ceases when the child attains the age of six. Upon reaching age six, the applicable rules of *tzedakah* would govern child support.[70] And as we have discussed earlier, numerous situations could arise which

68. For the distinction between "*minhag*" and "*nohag*," see M. Elon, *Jewish Law* (Hebrew), Jerusalem, 1988, 754-760.

69. See e.g., *Maimonides Resp.*, Blau ed, 190; R.M. of Rothenberg (13th Cent: Germany), *Resp. Maharam of Rothenberg*, Berlin ed. 2:249; *Piskei Ha-Rosh, Ketubot* 4:14; *Shulhan Arukh, Even Ha-Ezer* 71:1; PDR 3:299, 307; 6:225, 241; 8:325, 333. Compare *Resp. Ha-Rashba* 2:391.

70. Talmud Bavli, *Ketubot* 49b. Opinions vary whether the statutory requirement is enjoined by biblical law or rabbinical law. See e.g., Maimonides, *Mishneh Torah, Hilk. Ishut* 12:2 as interpreted by R. Algazi, *Ar'ah DeRabbanan*, 40, section 40b and PDR 7: 136, 143; *Piskei Ha-Rosh, Ketubot* 4:14; R. Karo, *Beit Yosef, Tur Even Ha-Ezer* 112, and R.E. of Vilna, *Be'ur Hagra, Even Ha-Ezer* 112:12. However, the child support obligation based upon *tzedakah* differs from the general rules of *tzedakah*. See Bazak, "The Mother's Obligation to Participate in Child Support According to Jewish Law" (Hebrew), 32 *HaPeraklit* 357 (1979).

would exempt a parent from a disbursement of funds. For example, the ability to provide one's own necessities will be one of the yardsticks for determining support eligibility. Since a child below age 15 is generally incapable of supporting himself, a father is liable for his maintenance. However, a father of a 15 year old is exempt from his parental duty of support if the child is financially independent or has the ability to find gainful employment.[71] Hence, a 15 year old who has the ability and yet refuses to work will be left without parental support, including provisions for medical care.

Nevertheless, the late Rabbi Moshe Feinstein, a contemporary decisor, argues that a child who resides at home and does not go to work until becoming married would be eligible for maintenance based upon the statutory requirement of *mezonot*.[72] Therefore medical care would be provided for a child until he actually gets married.

The foregoing analysis of the case of parental neglect of medical care is illustrative of the complex and pivotal role of the analogical argument in the decision-making process. As we have seen, the conceptual distinction between the competing analogies has significant juridical as well as functional consequences.

Summarizing the methodology of Jewish legal study, Justice Menachem Elon, the former Deputy President of Israel's Supreme Court, writes:[73]

> The student's endeavor is to uncover the roots of the subject and his main interest is in the analytical examination of the *sugya* (issue), through the views of Rishonim and Aharonim, their treatment of it, their approach to its study and comprehension...

71. See Schereschewsky op. cit., 484-485. In addition, see R. Uziel (20th Cent: Israel), *Resp. Mishpetei Uziel, Even Ha-Ezer* 74 and R. Hadaya, *Resp. Yaskil Avdi,* 6, *Even Ha-Ezer* 36.

72. *Resp. Iggerot Moshe Even Ha-Ezer* 1:106 and *Yoreh Deah* 1:143. For an analysis of R. Feinstein's position in light of the Talmudic statement, see e.g., R. S. Werner (20th Cent: Israel), *Resp. Mishpetei Shmuel* 9. Clearly, R. Feinstein adopts the Ran's approach to child support. See *Iggerot Moshe,* op. cit. and R. Spitz (20th Cent: Israel), *Minhat Tzvi,* vol. 3, 40-43. In 1944, the Rabbinical Supreme Court of the Land of Israel introduced legislation imposing a statutory duty to support children until the age of 15. See *Osef Piskei Din Shel Ha-Rabbanut le Eretz Yisrael,* ed. Warhaftig, 150 and *Resp. Mishpetei Uzziel, Even Ha-Ezer* 92; PDR 3, 306-307. For a differing interpretation of this legislation, see e.g., PDR 1:145, 154; 2:92-93 and 11:215-216.

73. See M. Elon, "More About Research in Jewish Law" in *Modern Research in Jewish Law,* ed. Jackson, Leiden: Brill, 1980, 89-90.

> On the other hand, the main interest of the *posek* is to give a ruling in the particular concrete problem before him... The researcher does not purport to act as a judge or *posek*, but merely desires to contribute to the comprehension and clarification of the Halakhah.

Deciding between competing analogies in our case will be the sole prerogative of the *posek*. The relative strength of each analogical argument applicable to our case, its effectiveness and plausibility will hopefully be tested within the framework and constraints of future *piskei din* (halakhic decisions).

Chapter 12

Jewish Noncompliance to Civil Law Constitutes a Halakhic Infraction[1]

A JEWISH COUPLE MARRIED in accordance with Orthodox Jewish law (Halakhah) on July 21, 2000, in Monsey, New York. The woman was born on July 25, 1985, as verified by her passport. As such, she had not reached the age of sixteen at the time of her marriage. From 1929 until 2017, New York State permitted 14 and 15 year old olds to marry, provided there was both civil court and parental approval.[2]

Given her age, upon requesting from the civil court to approve her marriage, the court failed to accede to her request. Nonetheless, the couple married in pursuance to Halakhah in violation of civil law. Subsequently, she refused to receive her *get* and thus was in violation of the sanction of excommunication (the *herem*) of Rabbeinu Gershom. Does Jewish noncompliance with civil law constitute a halakhic infraction?

According to Halakhah, minors are bereft of halakhic capacity to marry.[3] A man of majority age is an individual who attains the age of 13 years and a day.[4] A woman of majority age is an individual who attains the age of twelve and half years and one day.[5] In short, whereas pursuant to Halakhah, a 15 year old woman is of majority age and therefore may marry, in accordance with civil law she is proscribed from marrying without court approval and parental consent.

---

1. This is a hypothetical case which was discussed with two rabbinic colleagues.
2. New York Domestic Relations Law, section 15-a.

In 2017, New York State law was amended to allow 17 year olds to marry only if there was both court and parental consent. Otherwise, 18 is now the minimum age.

3. *Shulhan Arukh, Even Ha-Ezer* 43:1, 3; *Beit Shmuel* and *Helkat Mehokeik,* ad. locum.
4. *Mishneh Torah, Hilk. Ishut* 2:10.
5. *Mishneh Torah, Hilk. Ishut* 2:1-2.

Whether a father may marry off his minor daughter is subject to halakhic controversy and is beyond the scope of our presentation.

Based upon the foregoing, the emerging question is whether noncompliance with a civil law results in a halakhic prohibition. The implicit premise of our analysis is predicated upon the posture that "the law of the kingdom is the law" (*dina de-malkhuta dina*) applies in civil matters (*bein adam la'havero*) between two Jews, such as our case.[6] Secondly, it is known that in numerous places, the Talmud invokes the doctrine, "the kingdom of the land is the law".[7] Halakhah makes a material distinction between two types of subjects, namely religious norms (*issura*) and monetary norms (*mamona*).[8] Does "the law of the kingdom is the law" apply only to monetary matters or does it extend to ritual matters? If this doctrine encompasses only monetary matters, then the woman's decision to marry in violation of a civil norm does not entail a halakhic violation. However, if the doctrine has application to matters of ritual law such as the marital age of a woman, then her infraction of civil law regarding this issue entails a halakhic prohibition. Clearly, there are numerous authorities who argue that matters of ritual law do not fall under the rubric of this doctrine.[9] On the other hand, there are some decisors who claim that a matter of ritual law may be impacted upon by an infraction of civil law which neither modifies nor nullifies a religious norm resulting in the violation of a halakhic proscription.[10] Based upon the

---

6. Rashbam *Bava Batra* 55a; *Hiddushei Ha-Ritva, Bava Batra* 55a, *Resp. Ha-Ritva* 20, 38; *Hiddushei Ha-Ramban Bava Batra* 55a, *Resp. Ha-Rambam* 70; Ran, pages of Alfasi, *Gittin* 10b; Ran, pages of Alfasi, *Bava Batra* 55a; *Nimmukei Yosef*, pages of Alfasi, *Bava Batra* 55a; *Resp. Ha-Rashba* 1:895, 946, 3:66,79 (Cf. *Ha-Rashba* 2:2); *Resp. Ha-Rosh* 18:67; *Resp. Ha-Rivash* 52; *Resp. Ha-Tashbetz* 1:61; *Teshuvot Ha-Maharit* 2 *Hoshen Mishpat* 6; *Resp. Maharitz Ha-Hadashot* 32.

Cf. other authorities who argue that "the law of the kingdom is the law" is only applicable to matters of kingship. See *Hiddushei Ha-Ramban Bava Batra* 55a; *Ba'al Ha-Terumot Sha'ar* 46, *Helek* 8, *Siman* 5; *Resp. Ha-Maharik, shoresh* 66.

Whether civil law may nullify Halakhah is subject to debate. See *Shakh Hoshen Mishpat* 73:39; Rema *Hoshen Mishpat* 369:11

7. Talmud Bavli, *Nedarim* 28a; *Gittin* 10b; *Bava Kamma* 113a; *Bava Batra* 54b.

8. Mishnah *Yevamot* 15:3, *Eduyot* 1:12; *Tosefta Kiddushin* 3:8.

9. *Tosafot Rid, Gittin* 10b; *Sefer Ha-Terumot Sha'ar* 46, 8:5 in the name of Nahmanides; *Responsa* (hereinafter: Resp.) *Ha-Tashbetz* 1:158 (cf. 2:239); *Resp. Ha-Rambam* 210; *Resp. Maharam Mintz* 5,82; *Resp. Sha'ar Ephraim* 79; *Resp. Nahalat Shiva*, Resp. 31; *Magen Avraham, Orah Hayyim* 448:4; *Resp. Divrei Hayyim Orah Hayyim* 2:37; *Mishpat Shalom* 190:6; *Resp. Maharsham* 1:203; *Resp. Beit Shlomo , Hoshen Mishpat* 130; *Resp. Keter Kehuna* 1:8; *Resp. Binyan Tzion* 2:15; *Resp. Rosh Yosef, Hoshen Mishpat* 206:2; *Resp. Rosh Mashbir* 2:56; *Resp. Beit Shlomo Hoshen Mishpat* 130; *Resp. R. Akiva Eiger Mahadura Tinyana* 83; *Resp. Mishpetei Uzziel, Mahadura Tinyana*, 3, *Yoreh Deah* 92:5; *Resp. Knesset Yehezkel* 14.

10. *Ri Ha-Zaken Kiddushin* 8b; *Sefer Hashlama, Kelalei Yayin Nesekh* 18; *Resp.*

latter view, when the woman married in violation of civil law, in effect she was in noncompliance with the doctrine, "the law of the kingdom is the law," and thus was transgressing a halakhic prohibition.[11] In other words, the doctrine "the law of the land is the law" may apply to a matter of ritual law; however, the religious norm may neither be modified nor nullified.

What is the basis of recognizing the doctrine that "the law of the kingdom is the law"? Noteworthy is the theory offered centuries ago by Rabbi Samuel ben Meir (better known by the acronym: Rashbam) who writes the following:[12]

> All the taxes, levies and customs of the kings that are customarily announced in their kingdoms are the law because all the inhabitants of the kingdom accept upon themselves the laws of the King and his statutes and therefore it is binding law.

In short, Rashbam is arguing that compliance to the civil law is grounded in the "consent of the governed".[13] In other words, there is a social contract that the inhabitants of a particular country agree that compliance with the civil laws is a vehicle to establish stability lest anarchy occur.

Ma'sat Binyamin 97; *Resp. Panim Meirot* 2:52; *Resp. Hatam Sofer, Yoreh Deah* 314; *Resp. Lehem Yehudah, Yoreh Deah* 165; *Resp. Minhat Yehiel* 2:126; *Resp. Teshuva Mei'Ahava* 1:117; *Resp. Binyan Tzion* 1:2 (118-119); *Resp. Minhat Asher* 2:126.

Clearly, one cannot modify a religious norm or void a divine commandment. See *Mishneh Torah, Hilk. Melakhim* 3:9; *Tashbetz,* supra n. 8, 2:290; *Resp. Knesset Yehezkel, Orah Hayyim* 14

11. The accepted view is that failing to comply with the law of the land entails a biblical violation. See *Avnei Milluim* 28:2; *Resp. Hatam Sofer, Yoreh Deah* 127,314; *Resp. Dvar Avraham* 1:1; *Resp. Yehaveh Da'at* 5:64. Cf. others who claim it involves a rabbinic violation. See *Resp. Ba'alei Ha-Tosafot* 12; *Beit Shmuel, Even Ha-Ezer* 28:3; *Resp. Divrei Malkiel* 6:76.

Within the context of monetary matters, the ingredient of prohibition *(issur)* only comes into play after determining who has legal ownership of the object or is legally entitled to its possession. See *Tashbetz,* supra n. 8; R. S. Shkop, *Sha'arei Yosher* 5:1. This matter is beyond the scope of our presentation.

12. Talmud Bavli, *Bava Batra* 54b, s.v *ve'ha-amar Shmuel.*

13. See Ran, *Nedarim* 28a, s.v. *be-mokhes*; *Mishneh Torah, Hilk. Gezeilah Ve-Aveidah* 5:18; *Resp. Ohr Zarua* 705, 745; *Resp. Ha-Rashba Ha-Meyuhasot Le-Ramban* 22; *Resp. Ha-Rashba* 4:64; *Hiddushei Ha-Ritva* 46a; *Resp. Terumat Ha-Deshen* 441; *Yam shel Shlomo, Bava Kamma* 14:6; *Shulhan Arukh, Hoshen Mishpat* 369:2; *Resp. Hatam Sofer, Hoshen Mishpat* 5:44.

Alternatively, with the establishment of the civil law, one is halakhically obligated to comply with its tenets.[14]

Rabbi Elazar Fleckeles, a student of Noda Be-Yehudah,[15] addresses the following case dated 1797.[16] Pursuant to an eighteenth-century law, Jews were mandated to perform their *kiddushin* (loosely translated: marriage) in the presence of the rabbi of the community. In the event that the rabbi was absent from the ceremony, the question arose whether the marriage was void. Rabbi Yehoshua Reich, a colleague on the International Beit Din, cites in the *beit din* judgment the following excerpt from the responsum:[17]

> One who transgresses the directives of the king is akin to violating a divine commandment... and she requires a *get*... in this case the young man that betrothed her is prohibited to marry her as his wife since he has violated the king's mandate... and she requires a *get*...

To wit, given that the majority of authorities argue that compliance with "the law of the land is the law" is mandated on a biblical level ("*me'do-raita*"),[18] consequently the *kiddushin* is invalid. Implicit in R. Fleckeles' view is that concerning matters of prohibition (the prohibition of being a married woman – *issura*), the law of the land is effective.[19] Nonetheless, R. Fleckeles concludes that due to the failure to comply with the civil law, the man is obligated to give a *get* as a penalty rather than voiding the marriage.

Based upon the foregoing, the rabbi who officiated at the wedding, as well as the witnesses who attested to the act of *kiddushin*, were unaware of the woman's age and therefore both were invalid to participate in the ceremony due to their failure to comply with the civil law that requires that a fifteen year old woman receive prior authorization to marry from the civil authorities.[20]

---

14. See *Mishneh Torah, Hilk. Melakim* 4:1; *Ran*, supra n. 13; *Meiri, Sefer Beit Ha-Behira, Bava Kamma* 113a.

15. *Teshuva Mei'Ahava*, supra n. 10.

16. This case was suggested by one of my colleagues in order to address the pending matter.

17. International Beit Din File no. 2015/131.

18. See supra n. 10.

19. See supra n. 9.

20. Given that noncompliance with the civil law entails a biblical or rabbinic infraction (see supra n. 10), the officiating rabbi and the witnesses are invalid to

Given that this civil law is "the law of the kingdom," and in accordance with Shakh and others, this civil legal norm must be in harmony with Halakhah;[21] thus, there ought to have been compliance with the civil law. Given that in our case there was a civil infraction based on her marital age, the couple should not have been married under halakhic auspices and consequently the marriage held under the marital canopy (*hupah*) was invalid. After the *hupah* was performed, the woman had attained the age of sixteen and a civil marriage was executed.

Furthermore, as we will demonstrate, the halakhic norms of agency (*shelihut*) equally reach the same conclusion as we found regarding non-compliance with a civil legal norm undermining the doctrine "the law of the kingdom is the law". Agency is a doctrine authorizing a person, i.e., the principal to execute a legal act through another (the *shaliah* – the agent), in such a fashion that it will be recognized as the legal act of the principal.[22]

However, if a person appoints an agent to perform a forbidden act, then the agent is responsible, not the principal. The rule in marriage and divorce, as well as in other realms such as monetary matters, is "there is no agency for wrongful acts" (*ein shaliah li-devar averah*) – i.e., he who commits a wrongful act, under the direction of his principal, is himself responsible for it.[23] The rationale for this rule is that the authority of the principal cannot legitimate an act prohibited by the divine authority of Halakhah, or as the rabbis articulated it:"If the Master's (God's) words

---

serve as witnesses for the *kiddushin*. See *Piskei Halakhot* 1:158b; *Beit Shmuel, Even Ha-Ezer* 42:19.

21. *Shakh, Hoshen Mishpat* 73:39; *Levush Hoshen Mishpat* 369 (end); *Resp. Hakhmei Provence*, 426-427; *Netivot Ha-Mishpat* 104:3, 149:4.

However, if the civil law contradicts Halakhah, the doctrine of "the law of the kingdom is the law" is inapplicable. See *Beit Yosef, Hoshen Mishpat* 26 in the name of Rashba; *Resp. Maharam Mintz* 5, 82; *Shakh, Hoshen Mishpat* 73:14, 36, 39; 356:7 (10); *Nahalat Shiva*, Resp. 31; *Resp. Sha'ar Ephraim* 79; *Resp. Divrei Hayyim, Orah Hayyim* 2:37; *Magen Avraham, Orah Hayyim* 448:4; *Resp. Maharsham* 1:203.

22. Restatement of the Law, Second. Agency #1, St. Paul, Mn: American Law Institute, 1958.

23. Talmud Bavli *Kiddushin* 42b; Rema, *Hoshen Mishpat* 182:11.

Clearly, if during the process of executing the agency, a sin is committed incidentally, the agency isn't invalidated. For example, if the agency is performed on Shabbat, the agency is not invalidated. See *Mishneh Le'Melekh, Hilk. Geneivah* 3:6.

Secondly, there are some exceptions to the rule that the principal is responsible due to the agent's improper behavior. See Talmud Bavli *Kiddushin*, op. cit.; *Kiddushin* 43a; *Bava Metzia* 10b; *Mishneh Lemelekh, Hilk. Malveh Ve-Loveh* 5:14; *Nimmukei Yosef* on *Bava Metzia* 10b; *Shakh, Hoshen Mishpat* 388:67; *Mishneh Torah, Hilk. Avodat Kokhavim* 3:9.

conflict with the pupil's (the principal's) words, to whom should you listen?"[24] Consequently, in our case, should the officiating rabbi and witnesses who are serving as agents to supervise or establish respectively the act of *kiddushin* commit an offense concerning the *kiddushin* by allowing a fifteen year old woman to marry, thus the marriage is invalid.

The Noda Be-Yehudah, addressing the validity of a divorce that was given to a wife against her wishes by an agent in violation of the sanction of excommunication (the *herem*) of Rabbeinu Gershom, concludes that the principal is neither liable for the act of his agent nor is there validity to the agent's act, namely that the divorce conducted in such a manner is invalid.[25]

Regarding a case of a *kohen* who appointed an agent to betroth a divorced woman – this resulted in the invalidity of the *kiddushin* for two reasons. Firstly, there is no validity to the agency for commission of a sin since the appointment is defective. Moreover, the principal did not seriously intend to execute the agency since he believed that the agent would not agree to work with him.[26] Alternatively, the institution of agency is a halakhic innovation, and in the absence of this institution one could only operate personally. Given the innovation, one can only implement agency for permissive acts such as marriage and divorce as well as monetary issues. Therefore, prohibitive actions cannot be addressed via the institution of halakhic agency.[27] To state it differently, according to one opinion, the source for the absence of the effectiveness of "agency for a matter of sin" is not linked to the norms of agency but rather the expectation of the principal. The principal is not seriously considering the appointment of an agent since he does not believe that the agency will be executed. On the other hand, the second view advances that the source of the absence of the validity of "agency for a matter of sin" is related to

24. Talmud Bavli *Kiddushin* 42b.

25. *Resp. Noda Be-Yehudah, Even Ha-Ezer Mahadura Kamma* 64, 75; *Resp. Rashi* 177; *Tosafot, Bava Metzia* 10b, s.v. *de'amar* (second answer); Rema, *Yoreh Deah* 160:16; *Hazon Ish, She'vi'it* 24(4).

Cf. others who disagree. See *Tosafot, Bava Metzia* 10b, s.v. *de'amar* (first answer); *Hiddushei Ha-Ritva Kiddushin* 42b; *Shakh Hoshen Mishpat* 348:5; *Netivot Hamishpat* 162:1; *Mahaneh Ephraim, Hilk. Sheluhin Veshutafim* 9; *Resp. Hatam Sofer Even Ha-Ezer* 2, 1; *Resp. Maharsham* 2:242; *Resp. Har Tzvi Yoreh Deah* 123; *Resp. Yabia Omer* 8, *Hoshen Mishpat* 2(3) (numerous authorities).

26. *Sma, Hoshen Mishpat* 182:2.

27. *Pnei Yehoshua, Kiddushin* 42b, s.v. *ve'ha'tanya*; *Resp. Nodah Be-Yehudah, Mahadura Kamma, Even Ha-Ezer* 80.

the application of the halakhot of agency. In other words, these norms do not apply to prohibited actions.[28]

Similarly, in the cited case there was no validity to the executed *get* since it was given against her will. Analogously, in our case the officiating rabbi and the witnesses participating in the act of *kiddushin* are agents to the couple who permitted the civil offense of allowing the woman who was below the statutory age of sixteen to marry. As such, the act of *kiddushin* was invalid.

In sum, the voiding of the *kiddushin* was either because the rabbi and the witnesses were invalid due to their allowance to permit a fifteen year old woman to marry in violation of civil law or due to the fact that the rabbi and witnesses were agents who permitted the woman to marry, albeit being only fifteen years old.

---

28. M. Wygoda, H. Zafri, *Jewish Law for Israel: Agency* (Hebrew), The Jewish Legal Heritage Society, 2014, 32.

For example, if the agent is unaware that the action that he executes on behalf of the principal is prohibited, i.e., an instance of *shogeg*. As such, the agent will not hesitate to violate the wrong and therefore the principal will rely upon him. On the other hand, if one accepts that we don't recognize the rule "agency for a matter of sin," therefore, there is no difference whether he does it intentionally or unintentionally. See *Shakh, Hoshen Mishpat* 388:6; *Ketzot Ha-Hoshen* 388:12; Wygoda, op. cit., 33.

Chapter 13

The Giving of a *Get* and the Resolution of End of Marriage Matters: Which Precedes the Other?

FOR MANY YEARS, OUR Torah-observant community has encountered here and abroad, situations where a recalcitrant spouse chooses to condition the giving or the acceptance of a *get* upon a prior resolution of all end of marriage matters such as dividing marital assets and parenting arrangements and the execution of a civil divorce. Such conduct raises halakhic issues which we will address here in regard to the *get* recalcitrance husband.

To understand the ramifications of conditioning the giving of a *get*, let me share a few cases that I have encountered in recent years.

For example, a couple has been separated for over eighteen years and a civil divorce was executed 12 years ago and the husband claims that he is ready and willing to give his wife her *get* on the condition that she waive a post-divorce monetary claim against him. Such egregious conduct is not an isolated incident. In another case, after ten years of litigation in civil court and the subsequent issuance of a civil divorce, then the wife received her *get*. The delay in resolving the end of marriage matters such as the division of marital assets and alimony was due to the fact that on numerous occasions the husband changed his attorney. In other scenarios, albeit very common ones, from the time of the onset of litigation in a civil court the process takes one to two years or more to be completed before a civil divorce has been executed. And only then, does the wife receive her *get*.

During this period of litigation, generally American rabbinical courts do not address whether there is a duty of the husband to give a *get* to his wife. *Halakhah* recognizes two distinct grounds for obligating a *get*. Firstly, as we know, whether a husband is *obligated* to give a *get* generally speaking hinges upon whether there exists an *ilat gerushin*, a ground for divorce. The grounds for divorce *may* be subdivided into two categories. One type of a ground for divorce is a husband's physical defect such as the inability of a wife to have conjugal relations with her husband due to the fact that he is afflicted by a contagious and/or dangerous disease or by dint of her revulsion of his body odor which is linked to his occupation.[1]On the other hand, a husband's inappropriate behavior may serve as a justification for divorce. For example, spousal rape, refusal to cohabitate with his wife, physical and/or emotional divorce of his wife, or refusal to financially support her may serve under certain conditions as a claim for coercing or obligating a husband to give a *get*.[2]

Secondly, according to various authorities a *get* ought to be given in the wake of a couple being separated for over a year or eighteen months where there are no prospects for marital reconciliation.[3] Numerous contemporary Israeli rabbinical court rulings handed down under the Chief Rabbinate as well as some contemporary Israeli rabbis adopt this position.[4]

---

1. *Ketuvot* 77a ; *Yevamot* 65b.

2. *SA EH* 76:1,154:1, 6; *Rema SA EH* 154:3.

3. Rabbeinu Yeruham, *Sefer Meisharim* Netiv 23, Helek 8; *Resp. Radakh*, Bayit 3,s.v. u'le'ravha; *Resp. Hayyim ve- Shalom* 2:112; *Resp. Iggerot Moshe YD* 4:15(2). Should a *beit din* obligate a *get* based upon a marital separation of one year or eighteen months and should a husband fail to comply with the ruling, the wife is to be identified as a chained woman(an *agunah*).

Some contend that even if a particular *get* that was received by the wife poses certain *halakhic* issues and the husband demands money from his wife in order to execute a second *get* since that there is a fear that she will be without a *get* "many days", she is to be labeled an *agunah*. See *Resp. Pnei Yehoshua EH* 80; *Resp. Simhat Yom Tov* 12; *Resp. Maharsham* 3:251(1).In other words, the absence of having a *get* for a short period of time may label the woman as an *agunah*.

4. *PDR* 7:112-113, 11:364, 12:193-203, 13:267, 14: 183,194,19:52; File no. 4276-63, Beit Din ha-Rabbani ha-Gadol, November 11, 2003; File no. 3599-22-1, Tiberias Regional Beit Din, *Plonit v. Ploni*, November 24, 2004 (R. Yoezer Ariel's opinion); File No. 7479-21-1, Tel Aviv-Yaffo Regional Beit Din, November 18, 2007; File no. 8801-21-1, Tel Aviv Regional Beit Din, June 24, 2009; File no. 289477/1, Netanya Regional Beit Din, December 28, 2010; File no. 842462/1, Netanya Regional Beit Din, January 16, 2012; File no. 2487693, Netanya Regional Beit Din, *Ploni v. Plonit*, May 16, 2012; File no. 587739-6, Haifa Regional Beit Din, July 17, 2012; File no. 289799-1, Netanya Regional Beit Din, *Ploni v. Plonit*, January 2, 2013; File no. 862233-1, Tiberias Regional Beit Din, *Plonit v. Ploni*, January 8, 2013; File no. 901912/1, Haifa Regional Beit Din, May 7, 2013; File no. 8426111, Ashdod Regional Beit Din, *Plonit v. Ploni*, June 10, 2013 (R. Avraham Atiyah's opinion); File no. 284462-9, Netanya Regional Beit Din, May 14, 2014; File no. 764231-6, Haifa Regional Beit Din, May 25, 2014; File no. 869531/2, Netanya Regional Beit Din, July 31, 2014; File no. 849440/19, Tel Aviv-Yaffo Regional Beit Din, July 14, 2015; File no. 847350/3, Beit Din ha-Rabbani ha-Gadol, July 27,2015; File no. 1066559/1, Yerushalaym Regional Beit Din, October 30, 2016;File no. 1043346/1, Tel Aviv-Yaffo Regional Beit Din, May 8, 2017; File no.

Clearly, the American rabbinical courts may be espousing the opinion of others who argue that "a dead marriage" *per se* will not serve as grounds for obligating the husband to deliver a *get* to his wife.[5] As such, generally they refrain from issuing a divorce judgment based upon irretrievable marital breakdown. Yet, generally they equally refrain from rendering a divorce decision stemming from a ground for divorce.[6]

Even assuming a *beit din* would hand down a divorce decision that obligates a husband to give a *get* and the husband would be ready and willing to give one; in the wake of pending end of marriage matters can a *get* be given? In other words, the emerging issue is whether all the end of marriage issues such as awarding the value of the *ketubah*, parenting arrangements, child support and the division of marital assets must be resolved prior to the execution of the *get*? [7]Many American rabbinical courts (*battei din*) as well as American rabbis will counsel their clientele and constituents respectively that a *get* must be given only after all end

865704/1, Tzfat Regional Beit Din, May 8,2017; File no. 1011050/3, Tel Aviv-Yaffo Regional Beit Din, October 24, 2017; File no. 1083672/1, Haifa Regional Beit Din, January 25, 2018; File no. 1063300/10, Beit Din ha-Rabbani ha-Gadol, April 13, 2018; *Resp. Yabia Omer* 3, *EH* 18 (13); *Resp. Ateret Devorah* 2, *EH* 89.

5. *Resp. Divrei Malkiel* 3:144-145; *Resp. Divrei Shmuel* 3:145; *Resp. ha-Gaon Avraham Herzog EH* 154; A. Herzog, *Pesakim u-Ketavim* 7:133-134; *Resp. Tzitz Eliezer* 6:42,17:52; *Resp. Shema Shlomo* 3, *EH* 19; *PDR* 1:162, 4:112, 7:108–109, 112–113, 9:200, 211-212, 10:173, 11:362, 364; 12:206, 13:360, 14:183, 193; File no. 4827-21-2, Beit Din ha-Rabbani ha-Gadol, (R. I'zirer's opinion), July 3, 2005; File no. 172-21-1, Beit Din ha-Rabbani ha-Gadol, February 18, 2009; File no. 1750-21-1, Beit Din ha-Rabbani ha-Gadol, (R. I'zirer's opinion), May 5, 2009; File no. 290506/1, Netanya Regional Beit Din, November 21, 2010; File no. 77890/5, Be'air Sheva Regional Beit Din, May 29, 2014; File no. 698719/15, Yerushalayim Regional Beit Din, July 26, 2015; File no. 1083672/1, Haifa Regional Beit Din, January 25, 2018 (a supporting argument); File no. 1147208/2, Beit Din ha-Rabbani ha-Gadol, July 2, 2018.

6. There is a minority opinion that argues that rendering a judgment to obligate the giving of a *get* runs afoul of the strictures of a coerced *get* (a *get meuseh*) and on a biblical level according to the majority of authorities it is null and void. See *Resp. Yabia Omer* 2, *EH* 10; File no. 1083672/1, Haifa Regional Beit Din, January 25, 2018. In other words, just as a *get* compulsion order may run afoul of the strictures of a coerced *get*, similarly a *beit din* judgment to obligate a *get* may encounter the identical problem. It may be for this reason that some American *battei din* will only *recommend* to the husband that he give a *get* since such language does raise the fear of a coerced *get*.

For a list of decisors who contend that a coerced *get* is biblically null and void, see this writer's *Rabbinic Authority*, vol. 3, 30, n. 11.

7. For a lively exchange regarding this matter, see R. Menashe Klein and R. Shimon Ya'acobi, "The giving of a *get* and financial arrangements: which precedes the other?" (Hebrew), 22 *Tehumin* (5762)157.

of marriage issues have been resolved and/or a civil divorce has been executed. Consequently, it is unsurprising to encounter situations as the ones described above that a wife may remain *halakhically* married to her spouse despite the fact that the couple has been separated for years, a period marked by the absence of conjugal relations, no spousal support, and no prospects for marital reconciliation accompanied by years of divorce litigation. Yet relying upon the aforesaid rabbinic counsel under such circumstances, the woman will not expect that the *get* will be forthcoming.

The question is whether there is a basis for such a *halakhic* posture? Relying upon Mahari Mintz's guidelines for executing a *get*, states Rema,[8]

> And the scholar who is preparing the execution of the *get* says to her: 'Please know that you will be divorced with this *get* from your husband'. And the rabbi will inquire after the *ketubah* (the husband paying the value of the *ketubah*-AYW) that the husband will return the (value of the -AYW) *ketubah* or she will waive her right to it lest they start quarrelling due to the (value of the -AYW) *ketubah* with the result that the husband will say, 'on this condition I didn't divorce her'.

As such, given that that the *get* was given in error (a *get mut'eh*-AYW) the consequence will be a retroactive annulment of the *get*. Other *Poskim*, albeit only a few would concur with this position.[9]

Explaining this view, Rabbi Ya'akov Ettlinger writes,[10]

> Since not everyone is versed in *Halakhah*, Rabbi Mintz argues that there will always be slander if the husband shouts that he divorced her in error and therefore the *get* is null and her children will be *halakhic* bastards (*mamzerim*), even though the truth is otherwise.
>
> Based upon the fear of a wrongful *get*, we can understand

8. *Rema SA EH* 154:81.

9. *Resp. Maharam of Lublin* 122; *Mishkenot Ya'akov EH* 34.

Other decisors adopt this approach on the condition that the husband was misled prior to the giving the *get* and he was under the impression at that time that everything was to materialize as mutually agreed upon. See *Resp. Noda be-Yehudah*, Mahadura Kama, *EH* 11; *Resp. Helkat Yo'av EH* 25; *Ereh Shai EH* 134; *Resp. Malbushei Yom Tov* 2 *EH* 7; *Resp. Hessed le-Avraham*, Mahadura Kamma *EH* 42.

10. *Resp. Binyan Tzion* 144.

the position that all end of marriage issues ought to be resolved prior to executing a *get.*

However, the majority of authorities argue explicitly or implicitly that the *get* procedure (the *seder ha-get*) entails a husband's nullification of all prior conditions (*bittul moda'ot*).[11] Consequently there is no basis for a husband claiming that it was an erroneous divorce due to the fact that his wife reneged on an earlier commitment memorialized in a divorce agreement or had he known that a particular matter which was resolved after the execution of a *get* was to his detriment, therefore he never would have divorced her.

Even if one adopts the majority opinion that opposes the retroactive annulment of a *get* due to a breach of the divorce agreement or the resolution of a matter to the husband's detriment after the execution of the *get,* there is additional reason that all matters must be resolved before the giving of a *get.* Implicitly relying upon a letter of Rabbi Yisrael Isserelein that states that with the advent of the execution of a Jewish divorce "the husband and wife should not be bound by any connection or condition in the world,"[12] which has been understood to mean that neither spouse should file claim after the execution of the *get* lest the couple exposes themselves to committing a sexual prohibition.[13]

Upon a closer scrutiny of the *Halakhah,* we encounter a more nuanced approach how a divorced couple ought to conduct themselves. On one hand, to avoid the engagement in intimate relations, an ex-husband shall refrain from living with her in the same courtyard and to avoid social interaction the couple ought not to proceed to a *beit din* proceeding together.[14] However, according to certain opinions, should he enter a

11. *Taz SA EH* 145:6; *Beit Shmuel,* ad. locum. 16; *Resp. Ma'sat Binyamin* 76; *Resp. Bah ha-Hadashoth* 90-91; *Sma* and Levush, *Bah ha-Hadashot, ibid. Resp. Tzemah Tzedek EH* 290:1; *Noda be-Yehudah,* supra n. 86; *Beit Meir EH* 145:9; *Avnei Mi'luim* 10:2; *Resp. Mahariz Enzel* 81; *Resp. Divrei Hayyim* 1:84; *Aruch ha-Shulhan EH* 145:30; *Resp. Oneg Yom Tov* 154. For additional decisors who ascribe to this position, see *Resp. Ateret Devorah* 2:86.

For the requirement of nullifying all prior conditions prior to a husband's giving of the *get,* see *SA EH* 134:1-3; *Rema,* ad.locum.

12. *Resp. Mahari Mintz* 123.

13. *Resp. Ranah* 91, 96; Resp. *Teshuvot ve-Hanhagot* 1:784; *Resp. Mahari Katzpi* 14, Rabbi Menashe Klein, supra n. 7, 171; *Resp. Mishneh Halakhoth,* Mahadura Tinyana 357.

14. *SA EH* 119:7, 9; *Beit Shmuel,* ad. locum. 17; *Rema SA EH* 119:7; *Rema SA EH* 119:8; *Aruch ha-Shulhan EH* 119:31. Cf *Beit Yosef Tur EH* 119 in the name of Rosh and Tur who contends that this *halakhah* applies only to a divorcee whose husband

home or her house by chance there is no prohibition since he is not living her or interacting with her. And some are adopt a stricter opinion lest such meetings lead to the engagement in prohibitions.[15]

On the other hand, to minimize interaction with one's ex spouse, should a wife have lent money to her ex-husband, she should appoint an agent to demand its return.[16]Similarly, an ex-husband may support his ex-wife on the condition that he refrains from interaction with her and appoints an agent to implement support measures.[17] Though both Shulhan Aruch and Rema permit an ex-wife to file a claim in *beit din* for her dowry (*nedunyah*) or the value of her *ketubah*,[18] it is clear from their other rulings that such a claim must be filed through an agent so as to minimize interaction between the divorced couple.[19]

Consequently, it is unsurprising that there will be instances when the value of the *ketubah* will be paid to the wife *after* the *get* has been executed. As we know, accompanying a decision to obligate a *get* there is a decision to obligate the husband to pay the value of the *ketubah*.[20]Though numerous *Poskim* argue that the value of the *ketubah* ought to be paid prior to executing the *get*,[21]there are decisors who allow the *ketubah* to remain a debt which can be paid by the husband after the *get* is executed.[22] Others argue that if the husband is giving the *get* voluntarily then the value of the *ketubah* must be paid prior to the divorce. However, if the *beit din* is obligating him to give a *get* then the value of the *ketubah* may be paid after the execution of the *get*.[23] Finally, in a situation of a

---

is a *kohen* and a divorced woman who remarried.

For the prohibition of a divorced couple to reside in the same apartment or home, see *Tur SA EH* 111 and *SA EH* 119:7-11.

15. *Arukh Ha-Shulhan,* supra n. 14.

16. *SA EH* 119:8.

17. *Rema SA EH* 119:8.

18. *SA EH* 101:3-4; *Rema SA EH* 119:8.

19. *SA*, supra n. 16; *Rema*, supra n. 94.

20. *Resp. Ha-Rashba* 1:1192; *Hiddushei Ha-Ritva, Ketuvot* 76a; *Resp. Ha-Rivash* 127; *Resp. Ha-Tashbetz* 1:1; *Rema SA EH* 154:21; *Resp. Maharlbah* 33; *Resp. Ha-Maharit* 1:113; *Resp. Maharbil* 3:102; *Be'ur ha-Gra SA EH* 154:69; *Resp. Beit Meir* 39.

21. *Resp. Ha-Rashba* 1:1254; *Resp. Ha-Tashbetz* 3:227; *Beit Shmuel SA EH* 100:24, 119:6; *Helkat Mehokeik SA EH* 119:5; *Pri Hadash SA EH* 119:6; *Resp. Yismah Lev EH* 25 in the name of 26 authorities; *Hazon Ish EH* 69:13.

22. *Resp. ha-Rosh* 42:1;*Rema SA EH* 119:6 (Cf. *Rema SA EH* 154:21); *Helkat Mehokeik SA EH* 100:27; *Resp. ha-Ridvaz* 1:445, 3:566.

23. *Resp. ha-Tashbetz* 4, Hut *ha-Meshulash* 1:4; *Yad Aharon, Ha-Gahot* Beit Yosef 4; *Helkat Mehokeik SA EH* 119:5; *Get Pashut 119:18*; *Arukh Ha-Shulhan EH* 119:11-13.

second marriage for each spouse who despise each other, there are no prospects for marital reconciliation and each one wants to be divorced, one may rely upon those decisors who argue that divorce ought to occur immediately and the value of the *ketubah* may be paid after the couple is *halakhically* divorced.[24] In sum, under certain circumstances and in pursuance to certain decisors a husband may pay the value of the *ketubah* after the execution of the *get.*

In contemporary times, a cursory review of some of the rabbinical court judgments handed down by the courts under the Israeli Chief Rabbinate will show that in fact divorce judgments are rendered without being contingent upon a prior resolution of the outstanding financial issues and parenting arrangements of the divorcing couples. Regardless whether the claims are being dealt with in *beit din* or in civil court, the *beit din* issued decisions which recommend, obligate or coerce the giving of the *get.*[25]

Rather than advise divorcing couples that the arrangement of the *get* may await the resolution of all their monetary issues and the issuance of a civil divorce, American rabbinical courts and rabbis ought to follow the approach that once it is clear that there is a *halakhic* basis to give a *get,* its execution ought to transpire and any financial matters and parenting arrangements will be addressed afterwards.[26]

In effect, the American rabbinic network ought to adopt the practice

---

24. *Beit Shmuel SA EH* 119:6; *Resp. Ha-Ridvaz* 3:566; *Torot Emet* 119:6; *Resp. Lev Meivin EH* 116; *Resp. va-Yomeir Yitzhak EH* 179.

25. Collection of the Rabbinical Court Decisions of the Chief Rabbinate in Israel, ed. Z. Warhaftig, 97; *PDR* 1:129, 4:68, 9:94; File no. 47126/9, Ashkelon Regional Beit Din, June 18, 2012; File no. 289160/5, Netanya Regional Bei Din, September 19, 2012; File no. 901912/1, Haifa Regional Beit Din, May 7, 2013; File no. 965579/2, Netanya Regional Beit Din, July 23, 2015; File no. 514847/9, Haifa Regional Beit Din, December 28, 2015; File no. 8293/5, Ashdod Regional Beit Din, February 18, 2018; File no. 1103694/2, Yerushalayim Regional Beit Din, January 6, 2019.

For understanding these different types of divorce judgments, see supra n. 28.

26. Various contemporary *dayanim* have aptly noted that parenting arrangements that entail a third party's interest, namely a child's interest may not serve as a reason to delay the execution of a *get* which focuses upon claims which directly relate to a divorcing spouse such as the value of the *ketubah* and the division of marital assets. See S. Landesman, "Can a husband who is obligated to grant a divorce impose conditions?" (Hebrew), 2 *Divrei Mishpat* 145, 151-152; S. Daichovsky, "A husband who makes the granting of a divorce contingent on cancellation of his previous obligations," (Hebrew), 26 *Tehumin* 149,157(2005); File no. 029612306-68-1, Beit Din ha-Rabbani ha-Gadol, July 17, 2007, *ha-Din veha-Dayan*, gilyon 19,4-5; File no. 863382/4, Beit Din ha-Rabbani ha-Gadol, unpublished decision, November 9, 2013.

(*minhag*) employed by the rabbinical courts which serve under Israel's Chief Rabbinate which has been described in the following fashion:[27]

> "The common practice in the rabbinical courts in Israel is that before the giving of a *get* the *beit din* who executes the *get* (the *mesadeir ha-get*-AYW) informs the husband that he should know that there is no connection between the financial matters which were resolved and memorialized in an agreement which was signed and reviewed by the *beit din*...and the *get*. And the husband should be aware that if the wife breaches the entire agreement or portions of it, he still is giving the *get* voluntarily... unconditionally and he cannot say (due to the breach-AYW) I have not divorced her...Only after he understands and affirms his agreement, the *beit din* executes the *get*.
>
> The rabbinical courts make every effort to persuade the parties to resolve all the monetary issues and children (parenting arrangements- AYW) prior to the *get*. However, there are instances where it is impossible (to finalize these matters-AYW)...In such cases the *beit din* agrees that that each party shall retain his right to file a claim and they warn the husband that he is giving the *get* unconditionally even if it emerges that he erred. In other words, a claim which he intended to submit against his wife in the end was rejected in a proceeding which took place after the *get* or a claim advanced by the wife and he thought that according to *Halakhah* (or secular law if the claim is occurring in a civil court- AYW) that she will succeed and she won the suit...
>
> This determination "etched in stone" ("*nehe'rezeth*"- AYW) that all financial matters are to be completed prior to the *get* is a stringency that potentially may lead to a leniency...Delaying the arrangement of the *get* by a *beit din* when the parties are agreeable to wait until the monetary claims and children are completed...will cause many stumbling-blocks of being a married woman (potential of incestuous relationships- AYW) and God forbid the proliferation of bastards. And this occurs when the *beit din* delays the *get* and the husband stands and screams that he is willing to give a *get* unconditionally."

Clearly in the first case we mentioned, given the fact that husband was

27. *Rabbi Shimon Ya'acobi*, supra n. 7, 160.

a secular Jew he was only willing to give a *get* conditional upon the execution of a post-divorce agreement which provided that that both parties mutually agreed that all end of marriage issues have been resolved. The fact that he was separated from his wife since 1998 and a civil divorce was executed in 2006 did not propel him to date to give a *get* to his wife. Since he is irreligious, there is no interest in having the matter of the *get* adjudicated in a *beit din* setting. Regretfully, many divorcing husbands who identify themselves as being members of the Torah observant Jewish community would equally refuse to accede to their wives' request to address the matter of the *get* in a *beit din* setting prior to resolving all end of marriage issues. As such, the *get* hopefully will be given by the husband upon the resolution of financial claims and parenting arrangements.

Based upon the foregoing we have shown that there is a persuasive and strident *halakhic* tradition of resolving these outstanding matters after a *get* has been given. Following their Israeli counterpart, American rabbinical courts ought to be willing and ready to either to recommend the giving of a *get*, issue a judgment of "*mitzvah* to divorce" or obligate a *get* unconditionally to a divorcing couple who consent to their jurisdiction and will heed their rulings.[28] In the wake of a husband's refusal to

28. Whereas, coercing a *get* (*kofin lergaresh*) by a *beit din* may entail imprisonment, flogging, excommunication, or shunning, rendering a decision of obligating a *get* (*hiyuv legaresh*) involves verbal persuasion such as labeling the *get* recalcitrant husband as a sinner. See *Sefer Ha-Yashar, Resp.* 24; *Resp. Ha-Tashbetz* 2:8; *Rema SA EH* 154:21. Cf. *Piskei Ha-Rosh Yevamot* 6:11 who contends that the consequence of a failure to adhere to a ruling of obligating a *get* may result in a social ban (*niddui*). Notwithstanding the Rosh's posture, the level of sanctions differs when a *beit din* obligates a *get* rather than compels a *get*. Whereas in Israel, the *battei din* are empowered to coerce a *get* which may result in imprisonment for failure to adhere to the *beit din's* ruling, in the United States the rabbinical courts are legally authorized only to obligate a *get* which may result in verbal persuasion or according to certain arbiters in financial pressure by the *beit din* should the husband refuse to comply with the *beit din's* judgment. See *Resp. Ha-Rashba* 4:50, 7:414; *Resp. Ha-Mabit* 1:76(Cf. 3:41); *Resp. Maharashdam EH* 63.

In contradistinction to the *get* compulsion and obligating orders and in the wake of the concern for avoiding the specter of a coerced *get*, some American *battei din* may choose to recommend a *get* rather than obligate a *get*. Alternatively, in a case of an *agunah*, some rabbinic courts may decide to hand down a judgment directing the husband that there is a divine commandment to be divorced (*mitzvah legaresh*). See *Resp. Terumat Ha-Deshen, Pesakim u-Ketavim* 58; *Beit Yosef Tur EH* 134 in the name of Tashbetz; *Resp. Ma'amar Mordekhai* 2, *EH* 11.

Cf. *Resp. Ha-Rashbash* 411 who contends that the issuance of a *beit din* directive that under certain conditions there is a commandment to be divorced is employed

comply with their directive, the *beit din* ought to direct the community to religiously, socially and economically isolate him known in rabbinic parlance as "*harhakot of Rabbeinu Tam*".[29]

In the wake of a husband's refusal to appear in a *beit din* prior to the resolution of all end of marriage issues, American rabbis ought to function as arbiters of prohibitions and permissibility("*morei hora'ah*") as well as rabbinic courts ought to function as arbiters of prohibitions and permissibility and address the wife's inquiry whether there are grounds to give a *get.*[30]Should the arbiter determine that there is a ground for the husband to give a get and upon notification of that determination the husband refuses to give one, the rabbi or *beit din* ought to direct the community to religiously, socially and economically isolate him known in rabbinic parlance as "*harhakot of Rabbeinu Tam*".[31]

Failure to follow such a procedure **has** and will only continue to pose "many stumbling-blocks of being a married woman (potential of incestuous relationships- AYW) and God forbid the proliferation of bastards".

---

regarding a wife who is a sinner.

Once a *beit din* obligates a *get,* the giving of the *get* must be given unconditionally. In other words, a husband cannot argue that the giving of a *get* is contingent upon the resolution of certain end of marriage issues such as dividing marital assets and/or parenting arrangements. The execution of the *get* must be done immediately. See this writer's *Rabbinic Authority*, vol. 3, 55-81.

29. *Sefer Ha-Yashar*, supra n. 28; *Resp. Ha-Maharik*, Shorshim 133, 166; *Rema SA EH* 154:21.

30. In other words, whether a husband is obligated to give a *get* to his wife one may resolve this question of halakhoth of prohibitions and permissibility ("*issur veheter*") in the absence of the husband while being in the presence of one rabbi or a *beit din* functioning as arbiters of the laws of prohibitions and permissibility. See *Ketzot Ha-Hoshen, HM* 2:1; *Netivot Ha-Mishpat, HM* 3:1; *Resp. Yehuda* (Gordin), EH 51:2; *Resp. Hatam Sofer, OH* 51, *EH* 2:64; *Pithei Teshuva, EH* Seder *Ha-Get* 6,8; *Piskei Din Rabbanim* 6:265, 269; File 957-61, Beit Din Yerushalayim for Monetary Matters and Yuhasin, vol. 7, 515; File no. 448866/3, Tel-Aviv-Yaffo Regional Beit Din, July 11, 2013; File no. 1086123/1, Beer Sheva Regional Beit Din, December 20. 2018.

31. *Sefer Ha-Yashar*, supra n. 28; *Resp. Ha-Maharik*, Shorshim 133, 166; *Rema SA EH* 154:21

Chapter 14

The Application of Secular Law in a Beit Din Proceeding

THE FIRST ISSUE TO resolve is whether our matter will be adjudicated based upon halakhah or secular law? The Tovea requested that the decision be grounded in secular law and the Nitva desired halakha to serve as the basis of our decision.

Seemingly, the proposal to resolve this matter pursuant to secular law is fraught with perilous ramifications. To suggest this posture, seems to ignore the prohibition against recourse to *arka'ot shel akum*, i.e. litigating in non-Jewish courts. As Rabbi J. David Bleich notes,[1]

> Recourse to a gentile forum is tantamount to a declaration by the litigant that he is amenable to allowing an alien code of law to supersede the law of the Torah. Such conduct constitutes renunciation of the law of Moses…recourse to a gentile court to administer laws recorded in *Hoshen Mishpat*…is forbidden because…it enhances the status of an alien legal system…The litigant appears before the gentile courts because he accepts their authority and if they administer the law of Moses he accepts that law, not because he regards it as binding upon him by virtue of having been commanded by God, but because it has been endorsed and adopted by gentiles…
>
> The prohibition…is not limited to bringing a suit before a gentile court… The prohibition includes any judicial proceeding that negates the law of Moses. A judicial body composed entirely of judges who happen to be members of the Jewish community but who administer an alien system of law,

1. J. David Bleich, "Litigation and Arbitration before Non-Jews," 34 *Tradition* (Fall 2000), 58, 65-67 For an earlier treatment of this issue by the same author, see *Benetivot Hahalakhah*, (Hebrew), vol. 2, (N.Y.:1998), 170-171.

> is undoubtedly to be classified as within the halakhic category of *arka'ot shel akum* for the simple reason that the laws such a court administers are not those of the Torah.
>
> Since...acquiescence by both litigants does not serve to mitigate the prohibition...and since the prohibition applies even when the judges themselves are Jews, it follows that the parties are not entitled to accept the authority of a rabbinic court... but stipulate that the beth din shall apply the law of a secular state. Accordingly, if two parties...enter into a contract and stipulate that any dispute with regard to fulfillment of the terms of the contract is to be resolved by a rabbinic court in accordance with, for example, the laws of the State of Delaware, the stipulation is void by virtue of being inconsistent with biblical law (*matneh al mah she-katuv ba-Torah*).

Other contemporary poskim such as Rabbi Zvi Spitz[2] and Rabbi Zvi Gartner[3] concur in rejecting such agreements. As pointed out earlier, individuals are empowered to make agreements contrary to halakhah provided that these arrangements do not violate ritual law. At first glance it would seem, that such agreements should be a violation of the prohibition against litigating in civil courts.

Though such agreements have been met with trenchant criticism from *aharonim*,[4] nevertheless, there is a coherent and persuasive halakhic tradition commencing with Rashba, Giddulei Terumah, Sema, Netivot ha-Mishpat, Sanzer Rov, Rabbi Haym Kahane, dayan of Sigat and culminating with contemporary authorities such as Rabbis Avrohom Atlas, Ezra Batzri, Tzvi Y. ben Ya'akov, Shlomo Daichovsky, Zalman N. Goldberg, David Malka, Maimon Nahari, Shlomo Shaanan, Asher Weiss and Yitzchak Weiss of the Eidah ha-Haredith which lays the groundwork for the implementation of this type of an arrangement.[5] In fact, we have

2. *Teshuvot Minhat Zvi*, Laws of Neighbors, # 16.

3. R. Zvi Gartner, "In the Matter of *Arka'ot*," (Hebrew),11 *Yeshurun* (2002), 698-701.

4. See *Taz, Hoshen Mishpat* 26:3; *Be-ur Hagra, Hoshen Mishpat* 61:23; *Teshuvot Teshurat Shai*, 529.

5. *Teshuvot ha-Rashba*, 6:254. For our understanding of Rashba's position, see Eliav Shochetman, "The Halakhic Recognition of the Laws of the State of Israel," (Hebrew), 16-17 *Shenaton Hamishpat Haivri*, 417, 456 (1991); R. Zalman N. Goldberg, "In the Matter of *Arka'ot*," (Hebrew) 11 *Yeshurun* (2002), 702, Yona Reiss, "*Matneh al mah Shakatuv ba-Torah be-davar Mammon*," (Hebrew) 4 *Sha'arei Tzedek* 288 (2003) and 18 *Piskei Din Battei Hadin Harabbanayim* (hereinafter: PDR) 319, 324,

numerous *shtarot,* i.e. halakhic legal agreements dating back to the time of *rishonim* that attest to parties agreeing to have their matters resolved according to secular law.[6]

The validity of these agreements relating to monetary affairs is grounded in the discussion in Kiddushin 19b and Makot 3b regarding the ability of an individual to execute agreements in monetary matters in variance with halakhah. Implicitly drawing upon this Talmudic discussion, Rashba, Sma and others argue that if the spouses entering into this agreement to resolve their financial matters according to civil law are merely withdrawing from a privilege granted by the halakhic legal system and desirous to avail themselves of a *zechut,* i.e. a benefit in a particular situation rather than a wholesale affirmation that the norms of a secular legal system govern their lives, such an agreement is binding.[7] Such an

---

and see this writer's, "Varying Approaches towards the Division of Matrimonial Property upon Divorce", (Hebrew) *Hadarom,* Summer 2001.

For others who adopt Rashba's position, see *Resp. Ha-Tashbetz,* 3: 69; *Giddulei Terumah, Sefer Ha-Terumoth, Sha'ar* 62, *Helek* 1; *Sma Hoshen Ha-Mishpat* 26:11, 61:14; *Netivot Ha-Mishpat* 26:11; *Resp. Divrei Hayyim, Hoshen Ha-Mishpat* 2:30; *Divrei Gaonim* 25:3, 111:3; *Bnei Shmuel, Hoshen Mishpat* 26; *Maharitz Hahadashoth,* 22; *Resp. Yosef Ometz,* 4; *Birkei Yosef, Hoshen Mishpat* 26:3,8; *Tzedakah Umishpat, Orach Hayim,* 7; *Leket Shek'cha* found in *Karnei Re'em,* Section 4 Dayannim; File No. 1-24-053917464, Haifa Regional Rabbinical Court; R. Ezra Basri *Dine Mamonot,* vol. 3, 197; Shlomo Daichovsky, "The Halakhot of Marital Partnership: Is it the Law of the Monarchy?" (in Hebrew), 18 *Ha-Tehumin* 18 (5758); Z. N. Goldberg, "Acquisition in the Sale of Kidneys," (Hebrew), *Ateret Shlomo* (1997), 49, 52; Z.N. Goldberg, *Lev Hamishpat,* Volume 1, 286; Asher Weiss, 6 *Darchei Horo'ah* 111 (2007); *PDR* 18:314, 324; *Resp. Minhat Yizchak,* 9:112.

6. *Machzor Vitri,* pp. 551,562; *Ittur,* Ot 5, harsha'ah; *Sefer Maharil,* Minhagim (Likkutim) 17; *Resp. Ha-Rashba,* 2: 54, 127, 7: 400; *Resp. Ha-Ritva,*156; *Resp. Mahari ibn Lev,* 1: 120. Cf. *Resp. Harosh* 18:4 and *Resp Ha-Tashbetz,* 2:99 who interpret these *shtarot* differently.

7. See Rashba and *Sema,* supra n.6. An alternative rationale is that the rule that one cannot stipulate against what is written in the Torah, i.e. halakhah is limited to a situation in which one wants to nullify what is written there. However, if one stipulates for himself that he does not want to avail himself of a benefit accorded by halakhah such a stipulation is understood to mean that the individual waives a privilege accorded to him by halakhah and therefore such an agreement is valid. See Rashi, *Makot* 3b, s.v. *le-dede*; Rashbam, *Tosafot Makot* 3b s.v. *al menat*; *Resp. Ha-Tashbetz,* 1:94; *Tosafot Rabbeinu Elchanan, Ketubot* 56a-b; *Hiddushei Haritva* on *Kiddushin* 19b; *Hiddushei Harashba* on *Shita Mekubetzet, Ketubot* 56a. See also, *Sma, Hoshen Mishpat* 97:28; *Netivot Ha-Mishpat* 212:4. Whether *Sma* would reject an agreement between individuals to accept secular law is subject to debate. See *Ulam Hamishpat* 26; *Lev Hamishpat,* supra n. 6..

arrangement is no different than individuals who prior to marriage sign off on an agreement that their monetary affairs be governed by civil law.[8]

In short, there are grounds for the Tovea to request that he benefit from the norms of secular law which relate to his claims. Such a request must be mutually agreed upon by the opposing party accompanied by the execution of a *kinyan*. However, given that the Nitva insists that this matter be resolved according to the halakhot of Hoshen Mishpat, therefore this matter will be adjudicated accordingly.

Whether a community may agree to accept the entire laws of a secular system rather than specific ones which benefit themselves in a particular matter is subject to debate and beyond the scope of our discussion. See *Resp. ha-Rivash*, 52; *Resp. Ha-Tashbetz*, 1:61.

8. File no. 1-21-5035, Ploni v. Plonit, Tel Aviv Rabbinical Court. In fact, there are various prenuptial agreements relating to the division of marital property drafted by rabbinic authorities such as Rabbi Tzvi ben Ya'akov, a member of the Haifa Rabbinical Court which is based upon secular law.

II Rabbinic Authority
The Reality

Chapter 15

Decisions in *Even Ha-Ezer*

A. A HUSBAND WHO IS A PHILANDERER AND ADDICTED TO DRUGS: EVIDENTIARY REQUIREMENTS

The Facts of the Case

On February 24, 2014, Issac and Naomi were married in accordance with Orthodox Jewish law and until separation the couple lived in Monsey, New York. Both parties were married previously and sired children from their respective first marriages. The married couple did not have any children in common.

We were told by two men and one woman of the yeshiva community that Issac's divorce from his first wife was due to his drug addiction as well as being a philanderer (a *ro'eh zonot*). Regarding his drug addiction, we received a copy of a pharmacy's description of the drugs that he was taking during his first marriage. For example, during 2013, he was taking suboxone. It is our understanding that numerous people in the yeshiva community knew about his behavior. Nevertheless, Naomi as well as her children were raised and educated in a modern Orthodox Jewish environment and at the time of her marriage she was unaware of his behavior.

In August 2019, Naomi filed for civil divorce. A series of three summons (*hazmanot*) commencing with one on December 2, 2019, and culminating with being in contempt of *beit din* (a *seruv*) on July 1, 2020, regarding Naomi's request for the *get,* were issued by the Beth Din of America in New York City. We summoned Issac to appear at our *beit din* regarding the matter of the *get* and he refused to attend a hearing. On September 15, 2020, we conducted a hearing with Naomi.

Due to the COVID pandemic, on March 22, 2020, Issac left the marital home and traveled to Toronto, Canada. On July 10, 2020, the first order of protection was issued which precluded Issac from returning to the marital home. Two days later, he violated the order of protection by trying to enter the marital home. Subsequently, he attempted twice to return to the marital home. We have a copy of the order of protection as well as copies of the two police reports memorializing these two incidents.

Based upon Naomi's presentation to the panel, it is our understanding that she filed for divorce for three reasons. Firstly, based upon a submission of pictures of medicine bottles and copies of pharmaceutical records, Issac was regularly consuming amphetamines, clonazepam, oxycodone, suboxone and marijuana. In a text dated April 30, 2019, he admitted to smoking. His drug consumption made him temperamental, unpredictable and emotionally abusive. Due to his inability to function, Naomi assumed many of the domestic and parental responsibilities which conventionally would be performed by a husband and a father to his children.

Secondly, our panel received copies of dozens of text messages which advertised posts of escort services around the United States. In each post, there was a telephone number, a detailed description of the woman's physique and the cost for the service. In certain instances, the post had a picture of the woman and a list of the services being provided.

During January 2017, Naomi discovered that her husband's departure from the marital home for extended periods of time prior to 2017 was in order to have affairs with prostitutes. Primarily based upon a review of his text messages, according to Naomi, in 2019-2020 he was home approximately 30 to 60 days. During this time period he was in January and February 2019 in the Caribbean, May 2019 in Florida, June and July 2019 in Las Vegas and Canada, September 2019 in Canada, November 2019 in Florida, December 2019 in Canada, January 2020 through mid-March 2020 in Canada and from the end of March 2020 to early July 2020 in Canada. Prior to 2019, he had "one-night stands" with escorts in other places like New Jersey, Massachusetts and Israel. During their marriage, he had illicit affairs with a woman in Israel and a woman in Miami Beach, Florida. In numerous texts, though Naomi accuses of him of infidelity, he simply does not respond to her allegations. Yet, in two texts written in 2017 and one text in January 2019, Issac admits to his wife that he was spending time with hookers.

We received a copy of letter dated January 31, 2018, from a health care professional, where she directs Issac to avail himself of the services of an addiction counselor. In fact, on numerous instances, as attested by the text messages submitted to our panel, Naomi attempts to persuade him to proceed to a rehabilitation program. Though he sometimes promised that he would accede to her request, proceeding to a rehabilitation center never materialized for Issac. Subsequently, in October 2018, Naomi's OB-GYN strongly recommended that she should be checked for STD. As memorialized in a copy of a bill for lab work submitted to this panel, on October 29, 2018, Naomi tested negative for n. gonorrhea DNA and chlamydia trachomatis RNA.

Finally, Issac emotionally abused Naomi. For example, during December 2017, he threatened that he would send naked pictures of his spouse to her parents as well as post such photos on the internet. In fact, in Naomi's mind, he took these pictures at the outset of the marriage because he knew that one day he may need these pictures as "ammunition" to thwart any attempt by her to disenfranchise him in any fashion. Subsequently, in December 2017, he forwarded the pictures to her parents and continued to threaten her that these pictures would be released to the internet. Another example: there are unpaid bills relating to domestic expenses as well as his wife's medical expenses totaling over $110,000 which Issac refuses to pay. Though Naomi claims that he has the financial means to pay these bills, nevertheless, his nonpayment is a means of control that perpetuates the idea that she continuously needs something from him. In other words, despite his infidelity, drug addiction and meting out emotional abuse, it is Naomi's understanding that at the end of the day she should feel that he is needed. Other examples of emotional abuse are Issac's taking her keys and phone, unplugging the garage door opener resulting in her car being stuck in the garage for days, and walking around the house with an unregistered shotgun as a means of intimidation of his wife.

The husband's acts of infidelity, his drug addiction, and his abusive behavior all appear on the recordings and the text messages exchanged by the couple.

In her diary, on page 32 which was written during March 2018, Naomi writes:

> I am not myself. I cannot work. I cannot sleep. I barely go out. I am embarrassed to see people. I've gained weight.... What happened... I need to get out of this situation. It's debilitating.

On August 1, 2019, Naomi (hereafter: the plaintiff) filed for civil divorce.

To date, Naomi has yet to receive her *get* from Issac (hereafter: the defendant).

Discussion

1. The Evidentiary Significance of Recordings

Regarding the issue of the authenticity of recordings, what is the halakhic validity of a recording where the defendant has been identified in the recording by the *beit din* as admitting to acts of infidelity?

The preliminary question is the propriety of a *beit din* accepting a recording as evidence that has been obtained by the plaintiff through deception by concealing a recording device from the defendant.

The dilemma with which we are faced is whether the need to establish the truth outweighs the need to, ex post facto, allow evidence which was obtained unlawfully (i.e., in violation of the *halakhah*), or does protection of the public interest requiring that privacy be preserved override, in the case at hand, the need to reveal the truth?

The American, English and Israeli legal systems are adversarial systems in which the judge is supposed to be passive while the parties lay out their arguments before him. Accordingly, the judge does not endeavor to uncover evidence that the parties did not present. In accordance with this system, it was ruled that the proceedings in court have finality, since the process is a value in itself, even in cases where justice is not exhausted.[1]

On the other hand, a halakhic system requires the judge to be active regarding the involvement of the *beit din* in the procedural process,[2] and pursuant to the Talmud his function is to rule according to the truth:[3]

> Any judge who renders a judgment that is absolutely true, even [if he sits in judgment for only] one hour, is considered by Scripture as if he became a partner with the Holy One, Blessed is He, in the act of creation,

1. Herbert L. Packer, *Limits of the Criminal Sanction* (Stanford University Press, 1968).
2. *Mishneh Torah, Hilk. Sanhedrin* 21:10-11; *Hilk. To'ein ve-Nit'an* 6:1; *Hilk. Edut* 1:4-6, 2:1-5.
3. Talmud Bavli *Shabbat* 10a.

and elsewhere it is stated in the Talmud:[4]

> Any judge who renders a judgment that is not absolutely true causes the Divine Presence to depart from Israel.

Moreover, although the ruling in practice is that a breach of privacy constitutes a transgression, the halakhic principle is that the evidence that was obtained as a result of this violation is not to be disqualified.[5] This principle is learnt from the law pertaining to a person who for three consecutive years ate the halakhically-forbidden fruit of a particular field: these three years count for the purpose of a presumption of ownership, even though the eating of the fruit itself was forbidden.[6] According to this position, "evidence that was obtained unlawfully is admissible as evidence, and the prohibition does not detract from the right of the possessor."[7]

This principle derives from a wider principle that was articulated by Abaye in the following classical fashion:[8]

> Any act which the Divine Law forbids, if it has been done – it has a halakhic effect.

In other words, committing a prohibited act does not negate its legal consequences, for according to the *Halakhah*, there is a distinction between the sphere of prohibitions and the legal sphere, and therefore, an unlawful violation of privacy does not disqualify use of the evidence that was obtained by means of this violation.[9]

---

4. Talmud Bavli *Sanhedrin* 7a.

5. Concerning the matter of Rabbenu Gershom's prohibition against reading the letter of another without his knowledge, see *Responsa* (hereinafter: Resp.) *Maharam of Rothenberg* (Prague ed.) 1022; *Be'er Ha-Golah, Yoreh Deah*, end of no. 334; *Resp. Hikekei Lev* 1, *Yoreh Deah* 49; *Resp. Halakhot Ketanot* 1:276; *Resp. Torat Hayyim* 3:47. On the question of "*hezek reiyah*" [=damage caused by viewing the property of another] in relation to reading the material on another person's computer, there is a dispute regarding this matter, but it is beyond the scope of our presentation.

6. Talmud Bavli *Bava Batra* 36a (according to the reading of *Ba'al Halakhot Gedolot*, Rabbenu Hannanel and Rif); *Mishneh Torah, Hilk. To'ein ve-Nit'an* 12:12; *Arukh Ha-Shulhan, Hoshen Mishpat* 141:8; *Resp. Mishpetei Uziel* 4, General Matters 18; *Resp. Rabaz* 1 *Orah Hayyim-Yoreh Deah*, 54; *Resp. Mishneh Halakhot* 2:59, 17:183.

7. Eliav Shochetman, *Ma'aseh Haba Ba'avera* (5741) 111, n. 40.

8. Talmud Bavli *Temura* 4b.

9. For further discussion on this matter, see Shochetman, supra n. 7, at 104 ff.

Based upon the foregoing, wiretapping via a recording is an infringement of individual privacy and entails a severe infraction of Halakhah in the sphere of social relations. Nevertheless, a *beit din* isn't entitled to deprive an individual's right to submit evidence, albeit proof which was obtained ex post facto, by violating a prohibition in order to establish the person's justification of his claim. In other words, a *beit din* possesses the discretionary right to infringe the realm of individual privacy for the purpose of pursuing truth and such an incursion is not deemed a sinful act.

Authorities have dealt with the validity of voice recognition in monetary matters, criminal issues, and matters of prohibition.

Now let us address the significance of a recording as a halakhic form of evidence. On the one hand, Ketzot Ha-Hoshen states:[10]

> In criminal matters, voice recognition is ineffective and one can say that is not him.... Voice recognition is weak evidence.

In contrast, the Netivot Ha-Mishpat argues:[11]

> Voice recognition is ineffective in criminal matters due to the need for awareness and proof....

The point of contention among the authorities is that in pursuance to Netivot's opinion, voice recognition produces only awareness, whereas according to Ketzot, voice recognition "is a proof, albeit a weak one..."

On the other hand, Netivot and Ketzot are in agreement concerning the validity of voice recognition for matters of prohibitions.

Following in the footsteps of the Ketzot and Netivot, various authorities have endorsed their view.[12] Precedent for this position that one may rely upon recognition by voice in a situation of a prohibition was already articulated in the Talmud, where it states that a blind man is permissible to his wife on this basis![13]

In pursuance to the above posture, if two witnesses testify that they recognize the voice of an individual, their testimony is valid.[14]

10. 81:13.

11. 81:17.

12. *Resp. Divrei Hayyim*, 1: 32; *Resp. Avodat Ha-Gershuni* 110; *Resp. Bigdei Kehuna, Even Ha-Ezer* 7. Cf. *Resp. Shevut Ya'akov* 1:100.

13. Talmud Bavli *Gittin* 23a and *Hullin* 96a.

14. *Resp. Ri Migash* 149; *Birkei Yosef Hoshen Mishpat* 35:9.

Alternatively, in accordance with the Sefer Agudah, one may deem a husband a philanderer (*ro'eh zonot*) based upon his admission.[15]

Relying upon Ran on the Rif (*Kiddushin 29a*), *Tosafot Yevamot 88a*, and *Shulhan Arukh, Even Ha-Ezer 115:6*, silence is equated to admission on the condition that there is substance, a foundation ("*raglayim le'davar*") to the admission. As Shakh (*Hoshen Mishpat 81:17*) observes:

> ... one does not equate silence to admission. Everything depends on how the *beit din* understands the opinion of the silent one, such is determined.

Therefore, in our case, on the basis of recordings, text messages, and the plaintiff's diary, we are convinced that the defendant's silence attests to an admission regarding his philandering, drug addiction, and emotional abuse vis-à-vis the plaintiff.

In our case, one adult Jewish male knew the couple for six years, while the other adult Jewish male knew the plaintiff six years and knew the defendant for longer than six years. Both of them heard the voice of the couple on recording no. 9, dated November 6, 2017. In this recording, the plaintiff argues that the defendant is a philanderer and addicted to drugs, and the defendant does not respond to the allegations. However, on recording no. 14, dated November 15, 2018, in response to the plaintiff's allegations that her husband is a philanderer and emotionally abuses her, the defendant states that he is prepared to seek out therapy in order to rehabilitate himself with regard to ceasing both the abusive behavior as well as his acts of infidelity. Based upon the foregoing, there is an admission by the defendant based upon voice recognition of the defendant.

2. The Evidentiary Significance of Text Messages That Were Transmitted by a Mobile Phone

Additionally, there are many text messages that were written and exchanged between the parties in which one finds admissions by the defendant that he is a philanderer. For example, see the texts dated December 13, 2017, December 23, 2017, and May 17, 2019. There is also a text dated January 22, 2019, in which the defendant admits consuming

15. *Agudah* is cited by *Beit Yosef, Even Ha-Ezer* 154 and Rema, *Even Ha-Ezer* 154:1.

marijuana. May one rely upon text messages as proof that the defendant is a philanderer, emotionally abusive and addicted to drugs?

Seemingly, a text message, if it has the sender's name affixed to it, may be compared to a letter written by a person, where one can identify the handwriting in order to identify the author. As we know, according to Tur, Hoshen Mishpat 46, there are three ways to validate a handwritten document: (1) comparison of the handwritten document with another handwritten document. (2) The signatory of the document who testifies that he authored the document and (3) a third party who recognizes the handwriting of the signatory.

Clearly, regarding the handwritten diary authored by the plaintiff, we compared the writing of the diary with other handwritten documents penned by the plaintiff, and we concluded that the diary was indeed authored by the plaintiff. As such, we received a detailed picture of the state of the marriage during the years 2017-2018 as seen through the eyes of the plaintiff.

However, regarding the evidentiary value of the text message, File no. 851788-2, *Netanya Regional Beit Din*, 15 Iyar 5772 aptly observes:

> In our case, the husband's will is to submit text messages, we cannot rely upon what is written since the written word is electronic writing and clearly it is impossible to identify who authored the words. And even if you know from which telephone the texts originated and establish that the owner of the device sent it and therefore establish that the texts came from the wife's telephone and were written by her, it is clear that the fact that the information was written with the wife's device does not tell us that the owner of the device has sent the tests... Since the wife's cellular device was in the husband's hands, he could have written them... And even if the device was not in the husband's hands, in many places and many instances there is nothing preventing a third party from writing texts by using another person's device. So, who tells you that the wife authored the texts rather than somebody else wrote them. And the fact that the texts were found in her cellular device does not permit us to conclude that the wife wrote these texts.

Based upon the foregoing, one cannot conclude with certainty that the defendant himself was responsible for text messages which originated from his cellular phone and that he was the author of these texts. Now, despite the fact that we have arrived at the conclusion that one may not rely upon the texts as formal evidence, may we utilize them in order to arrive at the truth in our case?

As we have elucidated, the duty of the *beit din* is to proceed down every avenue in order to attain the truth. According to strict *Halakhah* (*shurat hadin*), one may rely upon an assessment (*umdana*) of a rabbinic arbitrator in determining the facts of the case. However, the mandate of requiring two witnesses was in order to deal with situations where the assessment is unclear. Moreover, there was a consensus amongst the rabbinical courts to refrain from implementing an assessment due to the fear that some courts may be halakhically unethical or devoid of halakhic proficiency.[16] Despite this policy, certain norms of *Halakhah* remained that were built upon assessment. For example, in the absence of the presence of men in a particular location, should there be women in the area, they would be considered trustworthy to submit information to the *beit din* in order to verify tort claims.[17]

Based upon the foregoing, the recordings which were submitted by the plaintiff are valid forms of evidence due to the rule of voice recognition. The implication of this conclusion is that based upon the recording, the defendant admitted to being a philanderer and engaging in emotional abuse vis-à-vis the plaintiff. Secondly, in every instance, one must check if one can rely upon the content of a text message in order to determine whether the owner of the phone in fact wrote the content of the text. In our case, it could not be determined whether the defendant sent the texts which originated from his cellular device. Finally, despite the fact that we were unable to determine whether the texts were admissible as evidence, nonetheless we utilized the texts in order to assist in determining the truth of what transpired. It was clear that the content of the texts were identical to the content describing the state of the marriage in general and the reasons of divorce in particular as memorialized in the recordings, the plaintiff's diary and the numerous supporting documentations furnished by the plaintiff to the *beit din*. Clearly, these texts serve as an example of a *beit din's* assessment of ascertaining the facts of the case (*umdana*).

16. Maimonides, *Mishneh Torah, Hilk. Sanhedrin* 24:1-2.

17. *Rema, Hoshen Mishpat* 35:14; Rabbi S. Daichovsky, "Wiretapping" (Hebrew), 11 *Tehumin*, 299, 304 (5759).

3. Does the husband's infidelity constitute a ground for divorce (*ilat gerushin*)?

1. REBELLIOUS WIFE DUE TO REVULSION

From the Talmud, it emerges that there are two types of claims of rebellion on the part of the wife regarding marital relations:[18]

a. Rebellion due to a dispute (She says, "I want him as a husband but I wish to torment him") – A wife who does not want to divorce, but refuses to engage in marital relations, in order to cause distress to her husband due to her dispute with him.[19] However, in *Tosafot,* the opinion of Rabbenu Tam is cited, according to whom the said rebellious wife is interested in divorcing without providing reasons, and she is tormenting her husband so that he will divorce her and pay out her *ketubah*.[20]
b. Rebellion due to revulsion ("He is repulsive to me") – the wife can no longer bear to engage in marital relations with her husband.[21]

In our view, the arguments of the plaintiff cannot be classified as rebelliousness of the first type, for she has no interest in causing her husband distress, neither due to any argument with him, nor so that he will pay out the value of her *ketubah*. On the other hand, the plaintiff is not claiming that her husband is repulsive to her regarding marital relations; rather, life together with him is repulsive to her, and she no longer wishes to be married to him. The question, therefore, is whether this second type of argument of rebellion due to revulsion is limited only to cases in which the woman can no longer bear having intimate relations with her husband, or whether it can also be made in circumstances in which the wife can no longer tolerate married life with her husband due to his conduct towards her.

Rabbi Aharon Sasson had doubts with regard to this question, particularly as pertains to the correct understanding of Maimonides' opinion,

18. Talmud Bavli *Ketubot* 63b.
19. *Mishneh Torah, Hilk. Ishut* 14:9; *Shulhan Arukh, Even Ha-Ezer* 77:2.
20. *Ketubot* 63b, s.v. *aval*. Said position also appears in *Perishah, Even Ha-Ezer* 77:18.
21. Rashi, *Ketubot* 63b, s.v. *aval amra*.

and he communicates a differing interpretation of the wife's plea, "he is repulsive to me":[22]

> When the *gemara* says, "He is repulsive to me,"... her claim is that she can no longer engage in sexual relations with him due to revulsion, like the precise understanding of the expression, "He is repulsive to me like the flesh of a pig, etc." But if her argument does not relate to revulsion at intercourse, then her argument is not that of, "He is repulsive to me", and even if she says, "I do not want him because I hate him," or, "He will no longer be called my husband," etc., as is said in this case, these statements do not indicate a claim of, "He is repulsive to me" etc., for it is possible that the hatred arises not due to revulsion but only because of a dispute with him, or something else, and then her claim is not one of revulsion.
>
> And it might also be possible to say the contrary, i.e., "He is repulsive to me" is one way of saying, "I hate him and I do not want to be with him," etc.... as is implied in Maimonides' words there: "She is not as a prisoner who is forced to have relations with one who is hateful to her," etc. The formulation, "He is repulsive to me" is not used [by Maimonides], from which we may deduce that hatefulness and repulsiveness are one and the same thing. And the reason that the *gemara* did not include hatred in general is because it wanted to be sure that there is an objective reason for the hatred.

And after discussing various proofs for each side of the argument he writes:

> In light of all this, I have doubts in the present matter, since I have not found a definitive answer in any of the *poskim*, or even the slightest indication of a preference in relation to any of these arguments. This may be because the matter was so clear to them that they did not feel the need to provide any definitive rulings. Therefore, my tendency is that wherever the wife says, "I do not want him and I hate him and he is no longer to be called my husband," we will apply the law of "He is repulsive to me."

Indeed, from the writings of a number of authorities, a distinction

22. *Resp. Torat Emet* 186.

emerges between the two possible claims of the wife that she is revolted by her husband, and according to this, only in relation to being revolted by intimate relations will the halakha of the rebellious wife ("*moredet*") due to revulsion be applied to the wife.[23]

R. Isaac Herzog defined revulsion by a medical analogy in a more narrowly focused manner and observed:[24]

> And one must further distinguish: the claim, "He is repulsive to me" is not just a matter of simple hatred, but deep revulsion at having relations with that body, and this is one of the deep secrets of the soul [in our days, the doctors have discovered a disease known as haphephobia – fear of being touched].

In any event, from the words of many other authorities it emerges that the claim of revulsion also applies in circumstances in which the wife is not interested in continuing to live with the husband, and there is not even a need for an explicit statement of revulsion, and explains that according to Maimonides and others, "Not only does this apply in relation to a claim of "He is repulsive to me," but in any case in which she claims a *get*, we give it to her immediately."[25] Maharashdam writes that the sanctions of Rabbenu Tam do not apply only to the claim, "He is repulsive to me," and cites various arbiters including R. Sasson discussing the case in which the claim was formulated in words other than "He is repulsive to me," which means that he ruled similarly.[26]

The position of these authorities was adopted in the rulings of the rabbinical courts in the State of Israel.[27]

The following appeared in the reasons for the judgment in File 284462/9 (Netanya Regional Beit Din) (9.4.2014):

> ... According to many of the authorities, and also according to Maimonides and the Shulhan Arukh, the definition of "repulsive"

23. *Hiddushei Ra'ah, Ketubot* 63b, s.v. *heikhi dami*; *Beit Ha-Behirah,* ad loc., s.v. *ugedolei hamehaberim.*

24. *Resp. Heikhal Yitzhak* 1:2.

25. *Resp. Mahari,* 102.

26. *Resp. Maharshdam Even Ha-Ezer,* 41 in the name of Mahari, supra. n. 25 and *Beit Shmuel, Even Ha-Ezer* 77:1. See also, *Resp. Tzemah Tzedek* (Lubavitch), *Even Ha-Ezer,* 262:11; *Resp. Pnei Moshe* 1:55.

27. PDR 5:154 (6 Nissan 5724), 157; PDR 8:124, 126 (8 Iyyar 5730); PDR 9:171 (30 Adar I 5733), 181-184; File (Ashdod Regional Beit Din) 32555/1 (9.5.2011); *Resp. Ateret Devorah* 1, *Even Ha-Ezer* 37.

> does not depend on this particular form, nor does it necessarily depend on marital relations; rather, the criterion is substantive, relating to the whole of the shared life, and insofar as it is clear to us that the woman hates her husband and does not want him, and in the opinion of the *beit din* her words are sincere and are based on clear pretexts, then it is as if she said, "He is repulsive to me," even though she does not insist that marital relations with him are repulsive to her. And as emerges clearly from the enactment of the law of the Academy [Geonim] (which is attributed to the *halakhah* of "He is repulsive to me," and as was proven also by Rabbi Sasson above, and nothing need be added), where it was clear that she was not claiming that he is repulsive to her due to sexual relations, nevertheless the halakhah of "he is repulsive to me" was applied.

Rabbi Sasson's understanding of "the plea of repulsion" as reflecting a wife's non-interest to continue to live with her husband may be traced back to *Tosafot Rid, Ketubot 64a,* and *Piskei Harosh, Ketuvot 5:34.* Subsequent to Rabbi Sasson's understanding of "the plea of repulsion," other authorities reaffirm his view.[28]

In the present case, the plaintiff did not say explicitly, "He is repulsive to me," but her words clearly express the revulsion she feels at the husband's infidelity, and her unwillingness to continue her married life with him.

We therefore rule in accordance with the opinion that the *halakhot* that apply to the rebellious wife due to her husband being repulsive to her also apply when the wife claims that she no longer wishes to live together with her husband.

2. THE EVIDENCE REQUIRED PROVING THE CLAIM: "HE IS REPULSIVE TO ME"

Although several authorities are of the opinion that accepting the claim, "He is repulsive to me" is conditional upon evidence being brought in relation to the cause of the revulsion,[29] many authorities hold that there

28. *Ba'er Hetev Even Ha-Ezer,* 77:12; *Resp. Pnei Moshe* (Beneviste), 1:55; *Resp. Divrei Shmuel,* 8; *Resp. Divrei Mordekhai,* 54; *Resp. Betzeil Ha-Kesef,* 2:10 in the name of Rabbi Metalon.

29. *Beit Ha-Behirah, Ketubot* 63b, in the name of Rambam; *Resp. Maharit, Even Ha-Ezer,* 40; *Resp. Divrei Malkiel* 3:145; *Hazon Ish, Even Ha-Ezer* 79:16; File

is no need for admissible proof for this purpose, and it is sufficient that her revulsion is evident from what she says or from the circumstances.[30] Alternatively, if she presents an explanation, a pretext [=*amtalah*], for her claim that he is repulsive to her – that will suffice.[31] There are indeed those who hold that there is no need for any explanation on the part of the wife, but the *halakhah* does not accord with that view.[32]

Regarding the "pretext": the majority of authorities are of the opinion that it is not sufficient simply to provide some sort of explanation for the claim, "He is repulsive to me," and what is necessary, according to them, is a "clear pretext."[33] In Israel, it has been established in rabbinic court judgments that there is no requirement of demonstrable proofs to ground "a plea of repulsion" akin to an argument to obligate a *get*, rather there is need of a substance ("*raglayim ledavar*") to persuade a *beit din* to negate other motivations, such as "possibly her eyes are cast on another."[34]

The assumption is that despite the emotional/psychological aspect of the claim, "He is repulsive to me", the wife who is suffering has the ability to express her feelings in a rational manner in front of the *beit din* by explaining the source or the reason for these feelings with a "clear pretext," and the *beit din* must determine whether there is a true, justified ground for divorce.

3. DISCRETION OF THE *BEIT DIN* IN ACCEPTING THE CLAIM, "HE IS REPULSIVE TO ME"

In fact, determination of whether the "clear pretext" is sufficiently strong

9922361/1 App. (Supreme Rabbincal Beit Din) (17.5.2015).

30. *Tosafot, Ketubot* 63b, s.v. *aval* – "Where there is a basis [for saying] that the husband is intolerable to her"; *Resp. Rashba*, cited in *Beit Yosef, Even Ha-Ezer*, 77, s.v. *uma she'amar sherabbi Meir*; *Resp. Maharimat* 2, *Even Ha-Ezer* 40. See also *Resp. Yabia Omer* 3, *Even Ha-Ezer* 18:2.

31. *Tosafot Ha-Rid, Ketubot* 64a; *Resp. Ha-Rosh 43:8* in the name of Maharam of Rothenberg; *Resp. Ha-Tashbetz* 4 (*Ha-Hut Ha-Meshulash*) col. 3:35; *Resp. Ha-Rashbash* 93.

32. *Resp. Rashba* attributed to Rambam 138; *Resp. Pri Tzedek* of Rabbi Raphael Tzror, 2, in the opinion of several Rishonim.

33. *Resp. Ha-Tashbetz* 4 (*Ha-Hut Ha-Meshulash*), supra n. 31; *Rema, Even Ha-Ezer* 77:3, and the super-commentaries; *Resp. Yabia Omer* 3, *Even Ha-Ezer* 18:3-4; File (Haifa Regional Beit Din) 1530/42, PDR 16:145 (Shevat 5750).

34. File no. 9807121/1, Haifa Regional Beit Din, 2 Mar Cheshvan 5775; File no. 1113846/2, Haifa Regional Beit Din, 28 Av 5777; File no. 113995/3, Be'air Sheva Regional Beit Din, 17 Tevet 5778.

to attract the application of the halakhot of the rebellious wife whose husband is repulsive to her is subject to the discretion of the *beit din*, in accordance with "what the *dayanim* see for themselves"(*ein lo la-dayan ella mah she-einav ro'ot*).[35] Thus, the *dayanim* assess the sincerity of the claim that the husband is repulsive.[36]

In other words, the *beit din* must believe that the wife is making the claim for real, relevant reasons, rather than as a trick or a tactic because "she had cast her eyes on another".[37] Thus, for example, if the woman waives collecting the money from her *ketubah*, the sincerity of her claim has a better foundation.[38]

Rabbi Kook defines, in his clear, articulate manner, the nature of the "clear pretext" as part of the investigation conducted by the *beit din*:[39]

> Where it is clear to the *beit din* that justice is on her side, and his bad deeds and conduct warrant his being repulsive to her, then her אונס (duress) is certain אונס, and there is no element of meanness. And because he caused all of this, there is no reason for her to lose anything, as long as he holds her back and does not give her a *get* ...

The plaintiff's claim that her husband, who is a philanderer, provides an example of a wife who argues that she is repulsed by her husband with a clear pretext.[40]

4. A PHILANDERER – "IS WORSE THAN THOSE MENTIONED IN THE CHAPTER OF HA'MADIR"

Notwithstanding our conclusion above, some authorities opine that if a wife claims she is repulsed by her husband, we do not coerce the giving of a *get*. In other words, one cannot define the behavior of a philanderer

35. For differing interpretations of the scope of the *dayan's* exercise of judicial discretion, see Talmud Bavli *Bava Batra* 130b, *Niddah* 20b and *Sanhedrin* 6b.

36. Rabbi Yitzhak Nissim, Rabbi Yosef Shalom Elyashiv and Rabbi Bezalel Zolty in App. (Supreme Rabbincal Beit Din) 139/5718, PDR 3:201 (30 Sivan 5719) at 206-207, and the opinion of the Supreme Rabbinical Court in App. File 5016, PDR 20:197 (14 Shevat 5751), at 200.

37. *Beit Ha-Behirah, Ketubot* 63a; *Resp. Ha-Rosh* 43:6.

38. *Resp. Maharit* 2, *Even Ha-Ezer* 40; *Hazon Ish, Even Ha-Ezer* 79:4.

39. *Resp. Ezrat Kohen* 56.

40. See File no. 8501006/2, Supreme Rabbinical Court, 14 Tevet 5772; File no. 113995/3, Be'air Sheva Regional Beit Din, 17 Tevet 5778.

within the framework of the *halakhot* of a plea of repulsion in general, and of advancing the plea of repulsion in a clear pretext in particular.[41]

However, regarding the matter of a philanderer, Rabbi Alexander Zuslin Ha-Kohen, in his *Sefer Ha-Agudah,* writes the following:[42]

> A matter once came before me: Leah claims about Reuven that he is a philanderer and he denies it. I ruled that if she brings witnesses that he is so – he must divorce her and pay out her the *ketubbah,* whether according to Scripture, or to the Talmud, or on rational grounds. Scripture – for it is written (Genesis 31:50): "If thou shalt take wives beside my daughters." The Talmud, for it says there: "A person may take more than one wife only when he is able to provide appropriately for all the needs," and in this context, it is written (Proverbs 29:3): "But he that keeps company with harlots wasteth his substance." And on rational grounds, since philandering is worse than all the grounds cited in *perek Ha-Madir* [Tractate Ketubot] for compelling a man to divorce his wife.
>
> But this is only when there are witnesses who saw him with the Aramean woman in the manner of adulterers; but if gentile women bring him children [claiming that he is their father], he is not forced [to divorce his first wife], because there have been several incidents in which [Jewish men] have been conspired against in this way.

Three reasons are brought in the above passage for the right of a woman to be divorced following infidelity on the part of the husband. First, intimate relations with another woman constitute a fundamental breach of the marriage, particularly nowadays, when there is a halakhic prohibition on marrying two wives. Second, when the husband is unfaithful, there is a very good chance that he will not be able to provide for his wife's needs. Third, if it is possible to compel a man to give his wife a *get* when he emits a bad odor, *a fortiori* can he be compelled to give a *get* in a case in which he is unfaithful to his wife!

In the nineteenth century, hundreds of years after the appearance of the Sefer Ha-Agudah, Rabbi Yehiel Michel Epstein suggests additional reasons for compelling a philandering husband to give a *get:*[43]

---

41. *Sefer Ha-Agudah, Yevamot* 77 and *Rema, Even Ha-Ezer* 77:3.
42. See supra n. 41.
43. *Arukh Ha-Shulhan, Even Ha-Ezer* 154:16.

> [Rema] wrote further, that if a person is a philanderer, and his wife complains, if there is evidence that he was seen with adulterers or that he confessed, there are those who say [*yesh omrim*] that he is compelled to divorce… and even though in relation to other sins which have no direct bearing on the woman he is not compelled to divorce, in the case of philandering, however, we do compel him, for in this case the sin does have a direct bearing upon her. First, it affects her right to sexual gratification, for philanderers "despise that which is permitted to them and are attracted by the sweetness of stolen waters;" second, there is no doubt that he is certainly repulsive in her eyes, and finally, he might even pose a danger to her. And this is true not only according to Maimonides, who maintains that if a wife complains that her husband is repulsive to her, he is compelled to divorce her, but even those who disagree with him would admit that in this case [compulsion is justified]. The Talmud explains that a person who refuses to fulfill conjugal duties is compelled [to divorce], and how much more so a philanderer, who is of course worse. All this applies when the truth of the matter has been thoroughly investigated.

According to the above, the husband is liable, due to his infidelity, to refrain from intimate relations with his wife. His infidelity causes him to be repulsive to his wife. Finally, a husband who lives with another woman poses a danger to his wife (presumably referring to the risk of contracting a sexually transmitted disease).

The common denominator of the reasons offered by Sefer Ha-Agudah and Arukh Ha-Shulhan in support of this ground for divorce isn't linked to the transgression of adultery itself, but rather in the destruction of family life caused by the husband as a result of these actions, and the wife is therefore entitled to demand a *get*.[44]

In such circumstances, not only is there cause for obligating the husband to give a *get*, but he may even be compelled to do so, as we already pointed out in explaining the words of the Sefer Ha-Agudah and Arukh Ha-Shulhan, and as implied or explicit by other arbiters.[45]

44. *Resp. Mishpatekha Le-Ya'akov* 6, 4:108.

45. As implied by *Resp. Mahari Bruna* 168, and as ruled by a string of *Aharonim*, see *Tur, Even Ha-Ezer* 154; *Erekh Lehem, Even Ha-Ezer* 154, end of no. 20; *Biur Ha-Gra, Even Ha-Ezer* 154:65; *Resp. Mahane Hayyim* 2, *Even Ha-Ezer*, 45 (on condition that there are witnesses who so testified); Rabbi Eliyahu of Tarla, *Resp. D'var Eliyahu*

Similarly, Rema Even Ha-Ezer 154:1 rules:

> A person who engages in adultery and his wife complains about him, if there is testimony concerning the matter, that he has been seen with adulteresses or he admitted, some say we coerce a *get*...

It is clear in pursuance to the view of Rabbi Zuslin Ha-Kohen and Rabbi Moshe Issereles that the halakhah of a hooker does not provide an example of a woman who claims a repulsion plea with a clear pretext but rather it is to be understood as noted by the words of the Sefer Ha-Agudah as a matter which is "worse than all the others which are mentioned in the chapter of Hamadir."

To state it differently, according to the author of the Sefer Ha-Agudah, a husband's infidelity is more severe than all the grounds for divorce which mandate *get* coercion that are memorialized in the list in Tractate Ketubot, such as a husband who has polyps or a tanner that spreads bad smell which a woman cannot tolerate.[46] There is nothing worse for a woman, or more repulsive in her eyes, than when her husband lives with other women, and consequently we coerce a *get*.

In the language of Rabbi Shmuel Werner:[47]

> Repulsion is a subjective matter according to her claim and she is unable to overcome her feeling regarding it. And she is incapable of uprooting her feeling towards it and she is unable to remove the repulsion and disgust and ill-suited to live with him and engage in conjugal relations, even in an attempt to restore marital peace.

In addition to his repulsive behavior, in the wake of the spread of AIDS today, given that an increased risk of contracting this condition is a potential consequence of his conduct, we may coerce an adulterous husband to give a *get* since "with a danger we are more stringent than with a prohibition."[48]

73; *Arukh Ha-Shulhan*, ibid.; *Resp. Noseh Ha-Ephod* 32; File (Tel Aviv Regional Beit Din) 7831/27, and PDR 8:254, 256-7*)*.

46. Talmud Bavli *Ketubot* 77a.

47. *Resp. Mishpetei Shmuel* 22:3.

48. *Resp. Mayyim Amukim* in the name of Rabbi Eliyahu Mizrahi 19; *Resp. Mas'at Moshe* 1, *Even Ha-Ezer* 17.

In light of the halakhic controversy as to whether there is a basis to impose *get* compulsion in the case of an adulterous husband, we may obligate the giving of a *get*.[49]

Therefore, we obligate a *get* under these particular circumstances due to the following reasons:

1. The wife's plea of repulsion is accompanied by a clear pretext.
2. The wife's claim of the repugnance of her husband's conduct as such that she is unable to continue to live with him.
3. It is a danger for the wife to continue to live with her husband.

4. Drug Consumption – A Ground for Divorce

In accordance with professional literature, a person addicted to drugs feels:[50]

> ... loss of control, fear, inability to function... tired, lack of motivation... impact to various psychological functions,... depression,... loss of mental stability... as it relates to the entire interaction of life between him and his wife, the children, and the family... and also it happens that drug addiction impacts the engagement in the entire network of intimate relations...

In our issue at bar, the plaintiff argues that divorce is required since the defendant is a drug addict. As such, we state that we are in effect dealing with a wife's plea of repulsion accompanied by a clear pretext. Since in the eyes of the *beit din* we recognize that he is a drug addict and cannot live with the plaintiff, and *beit din* is convinced that there exists no fear of "possibly she has cast her eyes on somebody else," therefore he is obligated to give a *get*.

Decision

Based upon the foregoing, we obligate the defendant to give a *get* immediately to the plaintiff. In light of the *beit din's* determination of

---

49. PDR 1:139, 141; *Resp. Yaskil Avdi* 6, *Even Ha-Ezer* 106; File no. 1-21-8991, *Ha-Din Veha-Dayan* 4, 10 (5764).

50. A. Atlas, I. Shahor and D. Domb, "*Get* Coercion for a Drug Addict and the Scope of He is Repulsive," 2 *Divrei Mishpat*, 135, 136, 5756.

"obligating a *get*" (a *hiyyuv get*), the defendant is not entitled to stipulate any condition(s) in exchange for his consent to give the *get*.[51]

Should Issac refuse to give a *get* within two weeks of receipt of this decision (*psak din*), we declare that in pursuance of Halakhah, we direct the Jewish communities of Monsey, NY, and Toronto, Canada, to practice the isolating measures of Rabbenu Tam. As such, every man and woman in Yisrael is forbidden to do business with him; to provide him with food and drink; to interact with him; to visit him during his time of illness; and bury him in a Jewish cemetery.[52] Additionally, he should not receive *kibbudim* and *aliyot* in any *beit knesset*.[53]

51. *Resp. Ha-Rashba* 4:156; *Bedek Ha-Bayit, Beit Yosef, Tur Hoshen Mishpat* 143; *Shulhan Arukh Even Ha-Ezer* 143:21.

52. *Sefer Ha-Yashar of R. Tam, Responsa* 24; *Rema, Even Ha-Ezer* 154:21. For decisors who endorsed the isolating measures of R. Tam, see *Resp. Binyamin Ze'ev* 88; *Sefer Ha-Agudah Ketubot* 107; *Resp. Ha-Maharik, shoresh* 102, 133, 134; *Levush, Even Ha-Ezer* 154:10; *Resp. Tzel Ha-Kessef* 1, *Yoreh Deah* 45.

53. Supreme Rabbinical Court, January 28, 2016.

B. THE CONSEQUENCES OF A VIOLATION OF AN ORAL PRENUPTIAL AGREEMENT

The Facts of the Case

On June 18, 2017, the plaintiff married the defendant in accordance with Orthodox Jewish law. This was a second marriage for both of them.

Prior to their marriage, the couple negotiated various matters relating to the conduct of their married life. In the framework of an oral prenuptial agreement between them, it was agreed that both would contribute equally to payment of the rent for the apartment, payment of utilities, and domestically related expenses such as the purchase of groceries.

However, during the initial 21 months of the marriage, although the defendant admitted (in a written document submitted to this Beit Din and marked exhibit no. 18) that there was a prenuptial agreement whereby he would share in these expenses, most of the time he refused to pay his share.[1]. As per a document written on October 31, 2019, the

1. The plaintiff's daughter lived in the apartment that the defendant had rented prior to the marriage, while the defendant and his two girls lived in the plaintiff's apartment with the plaintiff and her son. The agreement, as confirmed by one of the plaintiff's friends, was that the defendant would continue to pay for the rent, utilities and Wi-Fi in his apartment, and the plaintiff would pay for the rent, utilities and Wi-Fi in her apartment until her daughter left for Israel. Then, according to the agreement, he would give up his apartment, and he would contribute half of the household expenses and half of the rent of the plaintiff's apartment in which the plaintiff resided prior to marriage. However, he refused to give up his apartment while the plaintiff's daughter was in Israel, and did not contribute to payment of the rent, utilities and Wi-Fi in the plaintiff's apartment. In effect, he reneged on his prenuptial agreement to pay his share of the five months of rent of the plaintiff's apartment during the time he extended his lease on his apartment. However, the defendant's parents paid the plaintiff for two months (only) of those five months of rent which the defendant did not cover while the plaintiff's daughter was in Israel, and he paid $100 extra for three payments he owed, and then stopped paying altogether. In September 2018, the plaintiff moved to a small apartment in the neighborhood in order to be near her family, in an area she knew, and the defendant finally gave up his premarital apartment. During this period, the defendant contributed $800 towards the plaintiff's rent, and another $100 towards the utilities and Wi-Fi. He paid this amount until February 2019. The bills for the utilities and for food far exceeded $200 per month for a family of 5 people. It was then agreed that they would contribute equally to the ongoing costs: water, gas, electricity, Wi-Fi, food and other ongoing costs of running the home, but not including payments for home-help (in the event

defendant's claim in relation to the non-payment was that he earned an annual salary of only $14,256 from teaching in a Yeshiva, as stated in his signed income and expense declaration dated February 13, 2020, and therefore was unable to share in the domestic **expenses.** As such, it is no surprise that the plaintiff's bank statements for this period show that she covered these expenses. Due to the defendant's refusal to share in these expenses, she required the financial assistance of her father and her in-laws in paying the school fees as well as other expenses.

However, the defendant's credit card statements show the following: from March 2019 through December 2020, his average monthly credit card bill was approximately $3700. Clearly, as Sarah (the plaintiff) argues, a person earning $14,256 annually is financially incapable of paying a monthly amount such as this. In fact, in February 2020, the defendant paid the credit card company the sum of $10,000 in four payments towards his outstanding credit card debt, and his statement included a debit of $2,784 to Drew Wood Products. Subsequently, in May 2020, in order to cover his credit card debt, he paid $9,000 in four payments, and his statement included a debit of $1,791 to an automobile company.

In addition, an examination of the transactions in the said period, among them the transaction with Drew Wood Products, reveals that the defendant was paying for materials for cabinetry work, which suggests that he was earning an income from this work. Indeed, exhibit no. 8 submitted to this Beit Din by the plaintiff contains statements and a copy of purchase orders from five clients who paid the defendant for his cabinetry work.

Finally, a forensic accountant's findings dated October 7, 2020, show that the defendant's annual cash flow was $71,464, or $5,955 per month for the year ending December 31, 2019:[2] This is five times the annual amount that the defendant declared.

To this must be added that the defendant's wife from his first marriage, which lasted for more than five years, was a housewife, and it was he who provided for that family. The Beit Din received a document attesting to the fact that the defendant, together with his first wife, bought

---

that additional costs would be incurred, they would be split between the couple), as appears in a screen shot from March 17, 2019.

2. Due to his concealment of his earned income, the Court viewed the plaintiff as the main breadwinner who earned $87,915 in 2018 and $88,719 in 2019, and therefore on August 3, 2020, ordered the plaintiff to pay the defendant monthly maintenance in the amount of $800.

a house for $693,600. Within 6 months of the purchase his first marriage ended, without him supporting his first wife.

Although the couple in the present case had agreed prior to the marriage to open a joint bank account to be used exclusively for payment of their respective shares of the domestic expenses as suggested by the plaintiff's father, it was only in March 2019, a year and half after they married, that the defendant – at the behest of a rabbi whom he/the couple had consulted – began paying his share of these expenses, and only at that time was the joint account opened.

The prenuptial agreement addressed not only financial but also non-financial matters. For example, since the plaintiff was an extrovert and the defendant was an introvert, the prospective couple agreed that once a week, the defendant would take the plaintiff on a date. Here again, as confirmed by one of the plaintiff's friends, he frequently reneged on his promise. Also, on various occasions he refused invitations from his in-laws and friends for Shabbat daytime meals at their respective homes. Finally, prior to the marriage the couple agreed that normally, the plaintiff would cover her hair with a hat or scarf ("*tichel*"). However, on special occasions such as Shabbat, job interviews or engaging in certain work-related activities, she would wear a wig ("*sheitel*"). Nevertheless, with the beginning of the marriage, the defendant started commenting on the color and length of the wig, and finally he questioned the propriety of wearing a wig.

In the wake of these marital conflicts and hoping to save the marriage, in March 2019 the plaintiff insisted that they attend marital therapy on a weekly basis. During the therapy sessions, the plaintiff communicated to both the therapist and the defendant that she did not feel "safe in her marriage," due to the defendant's deceptions, such as failing to keep numerous prenuptial promises. Furthermore, the defendant did not allow her to express her opinions without humiliating her and/or he was not sensitive to her feelings. At first, the defendant heeded the therapist's advice, but eventually he stopped listening to him. This led to a deterioration in the couple's relationship, and it jeopardized the continuation of their family unit. The plaintiff then made it abundantly clear to the defendant that the marriage would end. In the course of October 2019, the marital therapy sessions ended.

Although the plaintiff admired the defendant's "passion for learning Torah, for praying and for Judaism as well as the fact that he was very sexual" (the plaintiff's words), nonetheless, due to his failure to fulfill many of his premarital commitments and not feeling safe with him physically, psychologically, and emotionally, she was unable to remain married to him. Consequently, on October 24, 2019, after the defendant threw a trash-can at the plaintiff, she contacted the police. As noted in the police report, the parties were instructed to separate, and the defendant left the marital home. On November 12, 2009, the plaintiff filed for civil divorce.

Although the plaintiff was well aware, prior to their marriage, that the defendant was not an American citizen, and that he had been summoned to appear before the US Immigration court to be "pardoned" for lying about his marital status on his immigration application, it was only after they separated that she discovered that the defendant had two different names (Allen and Ilan), two different social security numbers and two different driver's license numbers.[3] Upon discovering these facts, the plaintiff turned to a firm of investigators to investigate his records, and the same results emerged. On October 7, 2020, the investigator from Discovery Groups, LLC wrote as follows:

> In my experience, when multiple and distinct identities are attributed to the same person, this can usually be attributed to one or more of the following reasons: defrauding creditors, hiding assets from spouses and/or business partners, tax evasion,[4]... avoiding deportation... money laundering.....

Shortly after filing for a civil divorce, the plaintiff also applied to the local *beit din* to execute a *get*. However, the defendant refused to give one. There were various attempts by our Beit Din to set a date for arranging the *get*, but the defendant refused to attend a hearing. On August 18, 2020, we conducted a hearing with the plaintiff. On September 8, 2020, we ordered the defendant to give a *get* to the plaintiff. To date, he has refused to do so.

We shall now examine whether there are grounds to void the marriage in the circumstances described above and to permit the plaintiff to remarry without receiving a *get* from the defendant.

3. See report issued by Lexis Nexis dated January 7, 2020. Additionally, some of this information was received by the plaintiff in a telephone conversation with the IRS and from a search of their apartment upon the defendant's departure.

4. The plaintiff also claims that he was guilty of tax evasion.

Deliberations

A. The Husband's Lies and Misrepresentations as Grounds for Invalidating the *Kiddushin*

According to what we have described, the defendant lied to the plaintiff and misled her both in his undertakings in the pre-nuptial agreement with her, and in relation to his financial position; he also misled her about his identity, and about his acts of forgery and his deceptions vis-à-vis the state authorities. We must examine two questions that arise from such conduct. The first: is such conduct considered to be a major defect that justifies invalidation of the *kiddushin*? And secondly: does the very fact of his misrepresentation with regard to his person, his identity and his financial and personal situation justify the invalidation of the *kiddushin,* in light of the fact that the plaintiff agreed to marry him based on the financial and personal situation that he presented to her?

There is a difference between the two issues. A defect is a matter of an objective claim, such as in a mistaken transaction where the product is defective, and it clear that a person is not prepared, nor does he intend to purchase, a defective product – the defect being defined objectively according to the accepted standards in society at that time. So too with *kiddushin:* a woman is not prepared, nor does she intend to be married to, a person with a major defect. Misrepresentation, on the other hand, is a matter of a subjective argument, in which one party to the transaction or the *kiddushin* believes that the situation with which he is presented is the true situation, whereas the misrepresenting party knows that the true situation is totally different. Another important difference stems from this matter, i.e., that in relation to a defect, there is no need for an express statement or condition that the husband does not have a defect, whereas in a claim of misrepresentation as to the personal or financial situation of the husband, an express condition or statement is required, so that it is clear to the beit din that the woman is marrying only on the basis of the assumption that this is the situation of the husband.

Another difference deriving from this is that invalidation of *kiddushin* on the claim of defect does not require any sort of misrepresentation: this claim is valid even if the husband himself was unaware of his defect, as long as it is clear and proven that the defect existed prior to the marriage. As opposed to this situation, a claim of misrepresentation is entirely based on deliberate concealment of the situation at the time of the marriage. True, in the cases discussed by the authorities, the claim of defect usually has an aspect of misrepresentation as well, as the husband usually knows of his defect and conceals it; however, because the aspect of misrepresentation does not add anything to the assessment of the mistake on the part of the wife, it has been accorded less consideration by the authorities in cases of a claim of defect (but see, e.g., the words of R. Stern below).

B. Invalidation of *Kiddushin* on Grounds of Mistake and Misrepresentation

Invalidation of *kiddushin* on grounds of the wife's claim of mistake due to a defect may be considered upon the fulfillment of three preconditions:

1. The defect of the husband must be serious (Examples of serious defects discussed by the authorities include: impotence, insanity, homosexuality, exposure of the wife to a dangerous disease such as AIDS, etc.);
2. The defect must have existed prior to the marriage, and the woman must have been unaware of the defect at the time of the wedding;
3. The wife did not accept the defect when she discovered it after they were married.

Similarly, in a claim of invalidity of the *kiddushin* due to misrepresentation, three preconditions must obtain:[5]:

1. The existence of a significant disparity between the declared situation of the husband at the time of the wedding and his true situation, where it is clear that the woman would not have married the husband had she known of his true situation.
2. The true situation of the husband existed prior to the marriage, and the woman did not know of it when she married him.
3. The wife did not agree to continue living with the husband when she discovered his situation after they were married.

We will first discuss the question of whether the husband's conduct falls within the bounds of a major **defect (a *mum gadol*)**.

---

5. See this writer's *Rabbinic Authority*, vol. 2, 134-157; supra chapter 3.

1. MISREPRESENTATION, UNFOUNDED PROMISES, DECEIT

Our Sages said: "Four classes of people will not meet the Divine Presence," and one of these is "the class of liars" (*Sotah 42a*). The Holy One Blessed be He hates a person who says one thing with his mouth and another in his heart (*Pesahim 113b*), and it is better that a person should humiliate himself and sell carcasses than that he should lie (ibid.). R. Yona Ha-hassid of Girondi, a 13th-century Spanish sage, wrote that "a lie, apart from the damage it causes, is a Divine abomination, as it is written (*Proverbs 12:22*): 'Lying lips are an abomination to the Lord.'"[6]

R. Yona continues to devote significant attention to the halakhic-moral obligation of a Jew to keep his promises, writing as follows:[7]

> A person who promises to do something for the benefit of another, and he lies and goes back on his word: when a person has said that he will benefit another in the form of a promise, and the other trusted him, he may not break his promise, for this is the way of lying, and he is as a person who breaches a covenant, as it is said (*Zephaniah 3:13*): "The remnant of Israel shall not do iniquity, nor speak lies; neither shall a deceitful tongue be found in their mouth…." Similarly a person who says that he will give his fellow a small gift, even though he did not expressly promise… and also a person who boasts in public that he will give a person a gift, and he is praised for his generosity, this is like a promise, and it is not right that he should go back on his word after he was accorded credit and respect for this, as it is written (Proverbs 25:14): "As vapors and wind without rain, so is he that boasteth himself of a false gift": just as people are upset if there are signs of rain but these are not followed by rain – so too with a person who boasts of a false gift, because boasting of a thing is a sign of the existence of the thing, and therefore the person to whom the gift was promised will be upset, because he was disappointed….

In other words, breaking a promise, too, constitutes lying. And even though there are cases where it can be halakhically valid for a person who makes an oral promise to renege on his promise, generally speaking

6. *Sha'arei Teshuvah* 3:179.
7. Ibid., 183.

– from a halakhic of view, he must keep his promise. This is the normative *Halakhah.*[8]

According to the *Shulhan Arukh*:[9]

> A person who conducts negotiations orally only ought to stand by his word... and a person who goes back on his word, whether the buyer or the seller... he is one who is not trustworthy, and the Sages are displeased with him.

A person reneges on an oral agreement, who is called "untrustworthy," is in violation of a rabbinic prohibition,[10] and the rabbi or the *beit din* has the authority to publish his name in order to shame him.[11]

A promise relating to something that is not tangible, even if there was a formal act of acquisition, is not *halakhically e*nforceable, but the promissor [who breaks his promise] is called untrustworthy. An example could be one who promised another that he would perform the circumcision (*brit*) for that person's son.[12] This is also the *halakhah* that applies to a person who writes to another that he will do something particular, such as a promise to pay; even if there was an act of acquisition, as an oral acquisition has n*o halakhic* validity.[13] However, he is forbidden to renege, due to untrustworthiness.

Even more serious is a promise that a person made but did not intend to fulfill from the outset, and only outwardly demonstrated an intent to keep it. Apart from the lie inherent in such a promise, as R. Yona said, this is also a case of deceit (*genevat da'at*) and a breach of trust vis-à-vis the person who relied on the promise.[14]

Maimonides wrote as follows with regard to deceit:[15]

> A person is forbidden to act in a smooth-tongued and luring manner. He should not speak one thing outwardly and think

8. *Piskei Ha-Rosh, Bava Metzia* 4:12; *Shulhan Arukh, Hoshen Mishpat* 204:3; Rema, ibid,11.

9. *Shulhan Arukh, Hoshen Mishpat* 204:7.

10. *Resp. Ra'anah* 1:118.

11. *Resp. Maharam Mintz* 101; *Sefer Ha-Agudah, Bava Metzia* 4:66 citing Ra'aviya; *Resp. Nehpa Ba-Kessef* 2:260-62.

12. *Resp. Maharam of Rothenberg,* Prague ed., 949; *Resp. Rosh* 12:3; 102:10; Rema, *Yoreh Deah* 264:1; *Shakh,* ibid., 7.

13. *Bava Batra* 3a; *Shulhan Arukh, Hoshen Mishpat* 157:2.

14. *Bava Metzia* 29a.

15. *Mishneh Torah, Hilk. De'ot* 2:6

> otherwise in his heart. Rather, his inner-self should be like the self which he shows to the world. What he feels in his heart should be the same as the words on his lips.
>
> It is forbidden to deceive people, even a non-Jew. For example, one should not sell a gentile the meat of an animal which has not been ritually slaughtered as if it were ritually slaughtered meat...

Based on the discussion in the Talmud,[16] Maimonides rules that the deceit which is prohibited refers to a situation in which the other person is led to think that the first has done something good for him, whereas in fact that was not the intention.[17] In other words, this act constitutes misrepresentation.[18]

In the present case, the defendant lied, misrepresented, advanced false promises, and deceived the plaintiff. The defendant made oral promises relating to future actions, which he did not fulfill, nor did he intend to fulfill them. True, these promises were not made in the formal language of an obligation (a *hiyyuv*), they were not accompanied by an act of acquisition and they were not made in the presence of two witnesses, and therefore they are halakhically unenforceable, but they suffice to define the defendant as untrustworthy.[19] Moreover, the defendant deceived the plaintiff in that he concealed material facts concerning his identity and his activities vis-à-vis the immigration and tax authorities.

Based on the foregoing the question, therefore, is whether this conduct on the part of the defendant constitutes a "major defect," which may serve as grounds to void the marriage?[20]

---

16. Talmud Bavli *Hullin* 94a.

17. R. Fleischmann, *Mishpetei Yosher* 1:12-18.

18. The words of the Talmud and the examples memorialized in Hullin 94a imply that fraud is when a seller sells a person a defective product, whereas misrepresentation occurs even if he sells a product that is not defective, e.g., he sells a non-kosher animal to a non-Jew and tells him that it is a kosher animal; even though this makes no difference for the non-Jew, this is misrepresentation. See R. Yaakov Hildesheim, *Keter, Studies in Economics and Law According to the Torah,* Part 3 (5761-2001), 28 note 4, citing R. Zalman Nehemiah Goldberg.

19. See supra chapter 5.

20. From the *halakhot* of misrepresentation in relation to cancelling marital matches (*shiddukhin*) an analogy can be drawn to our matter of voiding *kiddushin*. In other words, in relation to the ways in which it is permissible to conceal a defect for the purpose of a match and in what ways may a defect not be concealed and when does prohibited concealment of a defect constitute grounds for cancelling the match. This matter is beyond the scope of our presentation.

2. VOIDING OF *KIDDUSHIN* ON GROUNDS OF MISREPRESENTATION

A person's misrepresentation of his identity and his situation at the time of the *kiddushin* is liable to constitute grounds for their invalidation.

The Mishnah deals both with cases of a man who misled the woman and a woman who misled the man at the time of the *kiddushin* regarding their lineage or their personal economic or family situation:[21]

> If one said to a woman: Be betrothed to me on the condition (*al menat*) that I am a priest, and he was found to be a Levite; or if he said: a Levite, and he was found to be a priest; or if he said: on the condition that I am a Gibeonite, and he was found to be *a mamzer* (a halakhic bastard – AYW) or he said: a *mamzer*, and he was found to be a Gibeonite; or if he said: on the condition that I am a resident of a small town, and he was found to be a resident of a large city; or if he said: a resident of a city, and he was found to be a resident of a town; or if he said: on the condition that my house is close to the bathhouse, and it was found to be far; or he said: far from the bathhouse, and it was found to be close; or if he said, on the condition that he has a grown daughter or a maidservant, and he does not have one, or on the condition that he does not have one and he has one; or on the condition that he has no sons, and he has sons, or on the condition that he has sons and he does not have sons, then... in all these cases, despite the fact that she later stated: I intended to become betrothed to him, nevertheless she is not betrothed. And similarly, if it was she who misled him.

Another Mishnah describes the cases in which there is no misrepresentation:[22]

> With regard to one who betroths a woman and later says: I thought that she was the daughter of a Priest, and it turned out that she is the daughter of a Levite, or if he claims that he thought she was the daughter of a Levite and she is actually the daughter of a Priest, or if he claims that he thought she was poor

21. *Kiddushin* 2:3.
22. *Kiddushin* 3:5, and see *Tosefta, Kiddushin* 3:3-9.

> and she is wealthy; or wealthy and she is poor, in all of these cases she is betrothed, because she did not mislead him...

These Mishnaic rules reflect normative *Halakhah,* and both the husband and the wife are equal with respect to them (*Mishneh Torah, Hilk. Ishut* 8; *Shulhan Arukh, Even Ha-Ezer* 38:24-33; *Resp. Hatam Sofer* 3:82), and as we learn from the Babylonian Talmud (*Kiddushin* 48b--49b) and the commentators (the main basis for this is the principle that mental reservations have no halakhic-legal validity (*"devarim she-balev einam devarim"*). In other words, the intention regarding whether to marry or not must be clear and explicit.

3. HALAKHOT GOVERNING CONDITIONS OR THE HALAKHOT OF MISTAKE

The question therefore arises as to whether the basis for these *halakhot* lies in the *halakhot* of conditions or in the *halakhot* of mistake. On the one hand, in cases in which the *kiddushin* are void, there is an express stipulation, formulated as "*al menat* – on condition that..."; on the other hand, in cases in which the *kiddushin* are not void, neither the man nor the woman said anything at all, but claimed "I thought that...", i.e., they made a mistake, or deceived themselves, as to the true situation. Therefore, the question arises as to the *halakhah* in a situation in which there were not only mental reservations, but an explicit presentation of the personal or financial situation of the person, although without the formulation of a condition.

R. Moshe Sofer formulated this question as follows:[23]

> At first glance it would appear that in accordance with the opinion stated by Tosafot, which is cited as authoritative in *Hoshen Mishpat 207,* there are various instances in relation to which we accord halakhic validity to mental reservations, and as a result we will accept as sufficient any indication as to such reservations. And it would appear to me at first sight that marriage is one such instance, and this also emerges from the language of the Mishnah in *Kiddushin* 62a: one who marries a woman and says, I thought that she was the daughter of a Kohen etc., rich but she is poor, she is betrothed because she did not mislead him. In other words, she never said or expressed herself saying

23. *Resp. Hatam Sofer, Even Ha-Ezer* 3:82.

> that she is the daughter of a Kohen or that she is rich; he simply thought so himself, and she did not mislead him, and she is betrothed. However, if she misled him, even though she did not say anything at the time of the kiddushin to the effect that indeed that is what she is, then she is not betrothed, for his mental reservation has halakhic effect. But it would appear from the Mishnah in *Kiddushin 48b and 49b,* [a person who says] *al menat* (on the condition) that I am rich etc., *al menat* that I am a Priest etc.: there would appear to be a basis for the opposite conclusion, that is, only when the condition was articulated at the time of the *kiddushin,* but a simple claim of mental reservation is insufficient to undo the *halakhic* effect of the *kiddushin.* To a certain extent this would also appear to be the import of the statement of the *Talmud in Kiddushin* 50a, and therefore we have two conflicting Mishnaic inferences.

The authorities disagreed regarding this question. *R. Shimon b. Zemah Duran* discussed the case of a person who deceived a particular woman in that he made it known that he was rich when in fact he was poor, and she married him.[24] He ruled that the *kiddushin* may be voided due to misrepresentation, provided that the formulation was in terms of "*al menat*:"[25]

> This question contains three arguments for voiding the *kiddushin*: Firstly, that he misled her in the matter of his wealth.... and this first argument is not enough to invalidate the *kiddushin,* for surely if he had said to her at the time of the *kiddushin,* "You are hereby consecrated to me with this ring *al menat* that I am rich" or "that I have so and so much money" and he was found to be poor or that he had no money, the *kiddushin* would be invalid... but here he did not marry her upon this condition, but simply let it be known that he was rich and that he had such and such an amount of money, and she believed him and married him, and for such a statement we do not void *kiddushin*....

24. *Resp. Ha-Tashbetz* 1:130.

25. Regarding the *halakhot* of conditions, some authorities hold that the formulation "*al menat*" is required, see: *Resp. Ha-Rosh* 81:1, citing Ri and Rabbenu Tam; *Tur, Even Ha-Ezer* 38, citing Rabbenu Hananel. There are also authorities who argue that when the formulation "*al menat*" is used, there is no need for all the *halakhot* of conditions. See *Shulhan Arukh, Even Ha-Ezer* 38:3.

In other words, in the case of a clear statement on the part of the deceiving party, the *kiddushin* are valid, because it is still considered to be a mental reservation that is not deemed to be deception. However, in the case of conditional *kiddushin*, this statement will be considered deception and the *kiddushin* will be invalid.

This is also the opinion of R. Yitzhak Schmelkes (*Resp. Beit Yitzhak 1, Even Ha-Ezer 106*), in the case of a man who deceived a woman and told her prior to the *kiddushin* that he had a house registered in his name, and that he had no children; after the *kiddushin* it became known that he had two sons, that he had many creditors and that he was poor. R. Schmelkes ruled that the *kiddushin* were valid: "It is clear that the woman is married, and there are no grounds for doubt at all, since there was no explicit condition that immediately preceded the *kiddushin*."

However, according to some authorities, these cases are in no way connected to the *halakhot* of conditions, but rather, to the *halakhot* of mistake, and for the purposes of these *halakhot*, a statement is sufficient. This is the opinion of our colleague, *R. Yehoshua Reich* citing R. Michael Dov ben Issachar[26] in the case of a person selling produce who, in answer to the purchaser's question, assured him that it would be clean. R. Reich states as follows:[27]

> And in my humble opinion, the *halakhot* of conditions are irrelevant to the case at hand since, as elucidated in Resp. Haram Alshcikh citing the *Petah Ha-Bayit (2:2, 8)*, if it is clear that the fulfillment of the condition is of primary importance, and the execution of the halakhic act is secondary to it, then we do not need to adhere to all the fine points of the *halakhot* of conditions. The same rule applies to the purchase of clean grain, i.e., if it is evident that the absence of impurities is the dominant consideration rather than the actual purchase of the grain, the *halakhot* of conditions can be ignored. Moreover, we find that according to many authorities, when it comes to monetary matters a mere statement of intent has greater halakhic effect than an imperfect condition (*Petah Ha-Bayit 2:12*). Upon further examination, it transpires that someone who married a woman on condition that she be the daughter of a Kohen but she turns out to be a mere Israelite, or if he married her on condition that she be free of vows and she turns out to be burdened by them, he is

26. *Resp. Agudat Ezov Midbari, Hoshen Mishpat* 10
27. International Beit Din, Case no. 246.

> not required to prove that his condition was a "double one," since the precise fulfillment of the *halakhot* of conditions is unnecessary in a case involving deception. Proof for this proposition may also be garnered from *Kiddushin (62a)*: "If one betrothed a woman and subsequently said that he had thought that she was the daughter of a Kohen but she turned out to be the daughter of a Levite, the *kiddushin* are valid since she did not mislead him." From this it may be inferred that had she had misled him, the marriage would be invalid even if his condition was not a "double one." It may certainly be argued that our case is analogous to one in which the wife misled her husband; hence, we do not require adherence to the "double condition" rule, or for that matter, to any of the *halakhot* governing the making of valid conditions in the *Halakhah.*

Based on this principle, R. Moshe Sofer too held that in principle, it is possible to invalidate *kiddushin* in a case of misrepresentation since there is no need for a condition, but an explicit statement is sufficient:[28]

> .... In *Kiddushin 62a* it states that a person who marries a woman and says, I thought that she was the daughter of a Kohen etc., that she was rich but she is poor – she is consecrated because she did not deceive him. This is when she never said or made it known in any way that she is the daughter of a Kohen or rich, but he simply thought so, and she never deceived him, and she is consecrated; but if she deceived him, even if she did not say at the time of the *kiddushin* "*al menat*" that she is so and so, then she is not married, for this expression has *halakhic* force.

And at the end of his responsum he writes: "And if the esteemed rabbis and the sages of their holy city will examine our words and will agree with us, each one would take a chip of the beam, and this woman ... will be permitted to marry anyone she desires."

R. Yosef ibn Ezra rules similarly:[29]

> And it would appear that incidentally, we are also being informed of a novel proposition, i.e., that if the woman said to the man marrying her that she is the daughter of a Priest and he

28. *Hatam Sofer*, supra n. 23.
29. *Atzmot Yosef, Kiddushin* 62a.

> married her, and he did not specify "*al menat...*," and it emerges that she is the daughter of a Levite, she is not married, for it is likely that he married her on the basis of what she said even though he did not specify, and she deceived him.

Based on the foregoing, we learn that there is no need for a specific condition, but it must be evident to the *beit din* that there is a clear connection between the intention to marry the person and the explicit statement of the deceiving party as to the situation.

As *Atzmot Yosef* states:

> ...for it is likely that he married her on the basis of what she said, and Hatam Sofer also wrote *(ad loc.)* that "it is likely that the woman would not be content to be betrothed to a person from a distant land had he not deceived her that he is rich and a scholar, and because he made an explicit statement and she was deceived, the *kiddushin* are invalidated."

4. EXPRESS STATEMENT PRIOR TO THE MARRIAGE

Is misrepresentation a ground for invalidation of *kiddushin* only when there was an express misrepresentation at the time of the *kiddushin,* or also when this misrepresentation preceded the *kiddushin*?

R. Yom Tov Lipman Heller ruled in accordance with the position of the Hatam Sofer that the *kiddushin* are invalidated in a case of an express statement, even if it was not formulated in terms of a condition.[30] Moreover, he is of the opinion that the *kiddushin* are invalid even if the misrepresentation preceded the marriage, and there was no condition at the time of the *kiddushin,* nor any express statement:

> It is not that he made a full condition at the time of the *kiddushin* "*al menat* that I am a Priest," but he said to her in a definitive fashion prior to the *kiddushin,* "I am a Priest, and *al menat ken* – on this condition – I wish to marry you, I am rich and *al menat ken* I am marrying you, or I am poor and *al menat ken* I am marrying you," and she accepted him and married unconditionally.... If so, this would appear to be the law with respect to [a person who says] "*al menat* that I am rich etc.," even if he

30. *Resp. Malbushei Yom Tov, Even Ha-Ezer* 2.

> did not state and stipulate at the time of the *kiddushin*. If there was an earlier express statement that *al menat ken* he wished to marry her, and it emerged that there was misrepresentation; this is mistaken *kiddushin,* and not a matter of invalidating a condition.

This conclusion is also the implication from the above words of the *Hatam Sofer,* who wrote:[31]

> ".... which means that she never made an express statement at any time that she is (the daughter of) a Priest or rich...," hence, if she said "at any time" that this was the case, even before the *kiddushin,* this is a matter of misrepresentation that justifies the invalidation of the *kiddushin.*

5. RULING LENIENTLY IN RELATION TO A PERSON WHO DID NOT ACT PROPERLY IN THE KIDDUSHIN

R. Itzhak Rappaport Hakohen discusses the case of a person who forged letters of reference in praise of himself, which said that "he was a respected person from a well-connected family and here he owns many houses and much property," and "we promise that this is a very good match"; the man also pretended to be someone known as "a very wealthy, established person who owns houses and fields." This person went from place to place and married several women in several places, taking money from them, and after much effort he was caught and put in prison. A question was discussed that concerned one of the women he deceived and to whom he refused to give *a get,* even though "at the time of the *kiddushin* there was no condition or articulation of *al menat,* but simply a straightforward *kiddushin*."

R. Rappaport elucidated:[32]

> And I would add that it is a great *mitzvah* for all the authorities to seek a mechanism by which to free her so that such evil people will not continue to persecute daughters of Israel with such acts, and how much did our Sages do in such matters, as stated in Bava Batra 48b, that even though he underwent *kiddushin,*

31. *Hatam Sofer,* supra n. 23.
32. *Resp. Mahari Ha-Kohen, Mahadura Tinyana, Even Ha-Ezer* 13.

> the rabbis invalidated the *kiddushin,* because he acted improperly and therefore they acted "improperly" with him and they annulled the *kiddushin,* and they expropriated the monies of the *kiddushin (hefker)* and his acts of intimacy were rendered acts of promiscuity. How far they went to suppress these evil acts. And see how far they are prepared to go and develop strategies in order to uproot such evil conduct, and although we do not have the power to do the same.... And the underlying logic here, in my opinion, is that ability to annul the *kiddushin* derives from the principle that whoever marries does so on condition that the marriage is rabbinically approved, and even though the marriage was tainted by sinfulness, and therefore should not receive rabbinic approval, the actual act *of kiddushin w*as performed in accordance with rabbinical directives, i.e., in accordance with the *halakhot* of Moses and Israel. And since the institution of marriage is based upon the enactments of the earlier rabbis, we are unable to uproot them. Nevertheless, there would have been some basis for claiming that in these circumstances, the earlier rabbis would have nullified the marriage, and therefore we ought to be able to do the same thing.

The source of the *Halakhah* regarding the annulment of *kiddushin* on which R. Rappaport bases himself lies in the Talmud which discusses a person who married a woman against her will. According to Mar bar Rav Ashi,[33] in that case, the rabbis annulled the *kiddushin* on the grounds that "he acted improperly in that he forced her, and therefore we shall act towards him improperly, exceeding the bounds of the law."[34] And R. Rappaport, Mahari Ha-Kohen, ruled in the circumstances of the above case, that apart from the reasons for invalidating the *kiddushin,* this is a case of "improper *kiddushin,*" although not a case of coerce*d kiddushin,* for the husband's deception is an evil act that justifies annulment of the *kiddushin.*

Apart from the actual use of the mechanism of annulment of the marriage in such a case of misrepresentation, it emerges from his words that even if the misrepresentation perpetrated by the husband occurred before the act of *kiddushin,* this is considered to be an improper act that justifies the annulment of the *kiddushin,* despite the fact that in the

33. *Bava Batra* 48b.
34. Rashi, s.v. *Mar Bar Rav Ashi.*

talmudic source of the rule the "improper *kiddushin*" is the actual act of *kiddushin.*

R. Abraham Yudelovitch discusses a case in which the husband did not disclose his defect to the wife prior to the marriage. She demanded that he tell her the reason for his sadness and fatigue, but he concealed the reason from her and assured her that he was healthy. In the circumstances of this particular case, in which the *kiddushin* were conducted in front of a single witness, and relying also on the above responsum of the *Tashbetz,* who held that the rationale of annulling the *kiddushin* of a person who acted improperly allows for adopting a lenient position in the dispute of the authorities relating to *kiddushin* with one witness, R. Yudelovitch ruled that the woman could be released from the marriage without *halitzah,*[35] writing as follows:[36]

> ...And I would say that the second reason follows from the words of the *Tashbetz (Resp. 1:130)* who wrote concerning a person who married a woman before a single witness, and also misled her by publicly announcing that he was rich when he was poor: after he explained at length that the great later Authorities (*Aharonim*) agreed with the early Authorities (*Rishonim*) that a person who marries a woman in front of a single witness is not deemed to be married – even if both of the couple affirm – and therefore there is no concern about *kiddushin* in front of one witness, and there is no place for any concern, he wrote, and how much more in this case.... that he surely acted improperly in deceiving her by announcing that he was rich when he was poor, and we find that there were rabbis in the Talmud who would invalidate fully constituted *kiddushin* in relation to a person who acted improperly, as it says in *perek Hezkat* (*Bava Batra 48b*), in relation to a woman who was hung up until she agreed to be betrothed, Rav Ashi said that the *kiddushin* are not valid, even though in the case of a seller who was hung up until he consented to sell, the sale is valid: they said the reason was that he acted improperly [by forcing the woman to accept the betrothal] and therefore they [the Rabbis] acted with him improperly and they abrogated his [technically valid] betrothal,

35. On the question of the possibility of drawing an analogy between the halakhot of *halitzah* and the halakhot of marriage, see *Resp. Yabia Omer* 8, *Even Ha-Ezer* 38:2.

36. *Resp. Beit Av Shevia'i* 14:3

> and *a fortiori* we will not adopt a stringent approach to these *kiddushin* because they were in any case mistaken... Hence, I maintain that as in our case the *kiddushin* were witnessed by a single witness only, and since he acted improperly and misled her and promised that he was healthy like other people, therefore we should not rule strictly in the case of *kiddushin* with one witness, and this wife should not be made an *agunah*, and she is hereby permitted to marry any person.

In another responsum R. Yudelovitch discusses the case of a woman who was left "alone and chained, bewailing her bitter fate with no one to save her," and he ruled that the *kiddushin* were to be invalidated due to the deception of the wife by the husband with respect to his personal and financial position, in addition to the fact that one of the witnesses to the *kiddushin* was ineligible because he was a sinner.

He stated as follows:[37]

> ...And concerning the woman... who married a man who came there from another city, and after the wedding he was with her for about a month and he took her money and ran away from her; four years have now passed and his whereabouts are unknown... and it is now known that this man already had a wife and three children in the city of Boston, and he left them too...
>
> And therefore in our case where he married her unconditionally, and she did not know about his defect, i.e., that he had a wife and three children, which is a major defect from her perspective. If she had known of this, it is patently clear that she would absolutely not have wanted to marry him, because it is against State law, and this man would be punished by the law: where is the young woman who would give herself in marriage to a man against the laws of the state? What is more, the enactments (rabbinic legislation) of Rabbenu Gershom extend to the wife and she is *a* halakhic-abiding woman and listens to her father, who is a person of integrity, and to her family, who would protest; and in addition, how is it at all possible that she would become betrothed to a man who she herself sees is cruel and has no mercy for his wife or his three children, and he is a thief and a murderer? How is it possible that she would marry him, and how could she trust him – all her life she would hear his words

37. *Resp. Beit Av*, supra n. 36, at 28.

> saying that he will love her, but he is a person who is not to be trusted, and what he says is in the spirit of deception, and even if he really does love her now, who knows what will be over time, and is it not possible that in a flash he will switch his affections to another and send her away as well?

Also relevant is another case in which the husband did not tell his wife before the wedding that he was suffering from testicular cancer, and when she asked for a *get* he refused and demanded large sums of money in order to free her from the chains of *iggun*. R. Shmuel Tuvia Stern held that the case was one of mistaken *kiddushin* due to the defect, and he regarded the misrepresentation as particularly severe, which lent additional weight to the claim of mistake. In his words:[38]

> Therefore there was certainly a mistaken transaction, and also mistaken *kiddushin,* and even worse, there was false *kiddushin...* and I therefore issue a practical ruling to invalidate these *kiddushin* and to release the woman to marry any man who turns up, and she does not require a *get.*

C. Credibility of the Wife Regarding Ignorance of the Husband's True Situation at the Time of the Marriage

The second condition for invalidating *kiddushin* is that the defect, or the husband's true situation, existed prior to the marriage, and the wife did not know about it at when she married him.

The plaintiff claims that prior to the wedding, she knew only that the defendant had lied to the authorities with respect to his personal status in his application to migrate to the USA, and nothing more. And since she did not know about his other deceptions and misrepresentations, she has grounds for voiding the *kiddushin* due to mistake.

Can we believe the plaintiff's claim that she did not know at the time of the wedding that the defendant had acted deceitfully in the past and refrained from keeping his promises? This is a matter of forbidden sexual relations and testimony directed at removing the presumption of marriage, and even though a single witness is believed in relation to prohibitions in general, surely the evidence of less than two witnesses is unacceptable in our case!

38. *Resp. Ha-Shavit* 7:30.

All agree that a single witness in a matter involving a sexual prohibition in a case in which the prohibition is established is not believed, but the authorities disagree in a case in which the said prohibition has not been established. There are those who hold that a single witness is not believed in matters of forbidden sexual unions, even when the prohibited union has not been established,[39] and some claim that he is believed.[40] Many of the later authorities (*Aharonim*) agreed that he is believed, contrary to the opinion of Nahmanides.[41]

In the present case, where the testimony of the wife concerning the defect and the deception goes to the very validity of the *kiddushin*, this is defined as testimony in a situation where the prohibition concerning the forbidden union has not been established, since the existence of the forbidden union has been negated by the testimony, and as the *Noda Be-Yehuda* stated:[42]

> In all events, where it has not been established, he is certainly credible, and it may not be said that the rule should be different because we are dealing with the prohibition of a married woman, for this applies to a witness who testifies about divorce or about the death of the husband, which is intended to release the woman from the status of a married woman, but here, our concern is with the force of the *kiddushin* – whether or not they are valid – and therefore there is not yet a presumption that the woman is married: quite the contrary, the presumption of being unmarried pertains.

The *Shev Shema'teta* elucidated in a similar vein:[43]

> It therefore seems that the inference from the analogy of words (*gezerah shavah*) based upon the repetition of the word *davar* in the context of the evidentiary requirements concerning both monetary and sexual matters is only applicable to a case which clearly falls within the rubric of sexual offenses, for example,

39. *Hiddushei Ha-Ramban, Gittin* 2b, s.v. *ha amrinan davar she-be-erva.*

40. *Resp. Maharik, shoresh* 72; *Resp. R. Akiva Eiger* 107, citing *Tosafot, Gittin* 2b, s.v. *havi.*

41. *Resp. Noda Be-Yehudah, Mahadura Kamma,* 54; *Mahadura Tinyana,* 75; *Resp. R. Akiva Eiger* 97 (as an additional argument); *Resp. Ahiezer, Even Ha-Ezer* 6; *Resp. Minhat Asher* 1:73.

42. *Noda Be-Yehudah,* 2nd ed., 59.

43. *Shema'teta* 6, chap. 3.

> where the prohibition in question has already been established; however, if it is not clear that the matter before us does involve a clear-cut sexual prohibition and one witness testifies that there was no forbidden union, as in the case of an agent who testifies that the betrothal he effected was not to himself but to the principal, then the prohibition is downgraded to that of a regular offense, in relation to which one witness is credible.

In our case, too, the import of the testimony of the plaintiff is that in fact, she was never married to the defendant, and we therefore rule that the plaintiff's testimony that she did not know prior to the marriage about the defects and about the true condition of the defendant is credible.

D. Delay and Non-Acceptance in Respect of the Defects

The third condition for invalidating the *kiddushin* is that the wife did not reconcile herself to the defect when she found out about it after the wedding.

The question of whether the wife remaining with the husband after she discovers his defect constitutes acceptance on her part is a point of disagreement amongst the authorities. Although according to the majority of authorities,[44] the wife must leave him immediately upon discovering the defect, nevertheless, according to other decisors, if she had justified reasons for staying with the husband, her remaining with him does not imply acceptance of the defect.[45] For example, where the defect was one that the woman thought was curable, and attempts were made to cure it: if it emerges ultimately that the defect was incurable, such as in a case of insanity where counseling and psychiatric treatment do not help, then the fact that the wife remains with the husband during the course of the treatments does not constitute acceptance. However, if she remains after it becomes clear that the treatments do not help, this would constitute acceptance, according to this view as well.

Now, according to the first view, invalidation of the *kiddushin* is unjustified, because the wife first became aware of the husband's defect in

44. *Tur* and *Beit Yosef, Even Ha-Ezer* 154; *Helkat Mehokeik, Even Ha-Ezer* 39:9; *Beit Shmuel, Even Ha-Ezer* 39:16; *Resp. Ha-Maharik, shoresh* 24; *Resp. R. Akiva Eiger,* 2nd ed., 57.

45. *Resp. Iggerot Moshe, Even Ha-Ezer* 3:45, 48; 4:113) and Dayyanim R. Goldschmidt and R. Bablicki File (Tel Aviv-Yaffo Region) 3899/5713, PDR 1:5 (9 Shevat 5714), 11-12; see also *Resp. Sha'arei Zion* 3, *Even Ha-Ezer* 4.

2017, and they separated only in October 2019, and therefore it must be said that she "considered and accepted," in that she continued to live with him – despite the defect – for some two years thereafter. But according to the second view, since she had justified reasons for not leaving him as soon as she found out about his defects, and she tried for seven months to attend marital therapy with him in order to rehabilitate the marriage, there has been no acceptance, particularly since this is a second marriage for her. Moreover, she also thought that her husband would repent, and that they would be able to continue their life together, but ultimately, after the failure of the therapy, when she understood that there was no chance of him changing, and their life together had reached a dead end – especially after the incident of his physical abuse of her – she despaired of her life together with the defendant and left him, despite her strong physical attraction to him.

Relying upon the ruling of the Tiv Kiddushin, the thinking behind the second approach is clearly explained in the responsum of *R. Osher Weiss*:[46]

> Indeed, it appears as stated by the Tiv Kiddushin that we are witnesses that the way in which a person reacts depends on the individual. And it is very common that when a person discovers defects in a spouse, he or she does not react immediately for various reasons, sometimes due to sadness and shock and sometimes in order to preserve his or her discretion or in order to consider how not to hurt the feelings of the other, and this is not evidence that she has accepted, or does not care ...
>
> But it appears that even if a person really regrets her marriage, she might nevertheless make an attempt to make things work through adoption etc., but if all the attempts fail, we go back to the first position, that this is a case of mistaken *kiddushin.*[47]

---

46. *Tiv Kiddushin* 39:12; *Resp. Minhat Asher* 1:73:4.

47. Apparently, proof from the above responsum cannot be brought for our case, for there, it was a question of *mamzerut* (halakhic bastardy), and as is known, it is permissible in that context to invoke lenient views to allow the children to become part of the community of Israel (see, e.g., in the *Kovetz Teshuvot* 4:164). However, in the precise words of R. O. Weiss, and from the mention of the view of the *Tiv Kiddushin* together with the logic of the matter, there is nothing that says that this ruling applies only to the question of *mamzerut.* Moreover, in *Resp. Minhat Asher* (3:85:2), R. Weiss was prepared to invalidate the *kiddushin* (upon the fulfillment of additional conditions), if there was a good reason for the delay, but in the circumstances of that case (which did not involve *mamzerut)* there was no justification for

In the present case, we rule that the behavior of the plaintiff and her delay do not constitute acceptance of the defect.

Conclusion

On the basis of the above, the plaintiff is free to marry any Jewish man other than a Kohen.

---

the delay. In other words, this responsum proves that in his opinion, it is possible to apply the above logic in all cases of "mistaken *kiddushin*," even if there is no question of *mamzerut*!

C. MISTAKEN *KIDDUSHIN* DUE TO MISREPRESENTATION

Leah approached us and asked us as *morei hora'ah*, qualified expositors of *Halakhah* (and not as *dayanim* sitting in judgment), to void her *kiddushin* and to permit her to marry any other Jew without receiving a *get* from her husband.[1]

Answer

Prior to their marriage, the couple courted for three months. Given the fact that in her previous marriage of 15 years, her ex-husband was the breadwinner and she was a mother and housekeeper, Leah was very concerned that her prospective husband would earn a living and that he had not incurred financial debt. During their courtship, Leah raised these concerns with Joseph and he assured her that he was earning a living and had not incurred any debt. Additionally, since Leah retained custody of two of her children from her first marriage, and Joseph allegedly had custody of his daughter from his first marriage, Leah's concerns regarding financial stability were understandable. In short, Leah was seeking a marriage marked by financial transparency as well as financial security.

Based upon Joseph's assurances, as well as on Leah's impressions that he was "a quiet and gentle individual" and "cool, calm, and collected" (her words), on September 5, 2016, they married in accordance with Orthodox Jewish law. Before the act of the *kiddushin* under the *huppah* was to take place, the ring for the *kiddushin* could not be found,

1. In other words, this is a question of *halakhic* laws of prohibitions and permissibility (*dinei issur ve-heter*) regarding whether a husband is obligated to give a *get* to his wife. The question may be resolved in front of three rabbis in the absence of the husband. As we know, there is a disagreement as to whether matters of divorce such as obligating or compelling the giving of a *get* may only be resolved in front of a *beit din* of three rabbis, or in front of one rabbi, or in the presence of only an individual Jew. See *Yam shel Shlomo, Bava Kamma* 3:9; *Helkat Mehokeik, Even Ha-Ezer* 17:78; *Taz, Even Ha-Ezer* 17:56; *Biur Ha-Gra Even Ha-Ezer* 17:131; *Ketzot Ha-Hoshen, Hoshen Mishpat* 3:1, 2; *Netivot Ha-Mishpat, Hoshen Mishpat* 3:1; *Resp. Yehudah* (Gordin), *Even Ha-Ezer* 51:2; *Resp. Ma'aseh Hiyah* 24; *Resp. Hatam Sofer, Orah Hayyim* 51, *Even Ha-Ezer* 2:64-65, *Hoshen Mishpat* 177; *Resp. Avnei Nezer, Even Ha-Ezer* 167:1, 178:2; PDR 6:265, 269; Beit Hora'ah File 957-61, Jerusalem Beit Din for Civil Matters and Status Clarification, vol. 7, 515; File 448866/3, 7.11.13, Tel Aviv-Yaffo Regional Beit Din; File no. 1086123/1, Be'er Sheva Regional Beit Din, 12.20.18. In the present matter, three rabbis convened to decide an issue of ritual *halakhah*.

and therefore the wedding ring of Joseph's mother was used. Having understood that the ring had been given only for use at the time of the *huppah,* Leah returned the ring to her mother-in-law a few days after the wedding. Pictures were submitted to our panel showing that the ring was initially on her mother-in-law's finger; later, however, during the time of the *huppah,* the ring was not on her finger, as it was used for the *kiddushin.*

Shortly after the wedding, Leah began receiving warrants in the mail for Joseph's arrest due to his failure to pay taxes for his business, and a warrant for his arrest due to non-payment of $23,000 in child support for his daughter from his first marriage. There was also an outstanding bill for $766 for failure to pay tolls, an AT&T suspension notice for failure to pay $828 in telephone bills, and a notice of over $50,000 which was owed to one of Joseph's electrical suppliers. The outstanding debt of over $50,000 related to transactions dated from August 24, 2017 through April 16, 2018. All of the above outstanding debts were confirmed by supporting documentation.

Joseph had promised Leah during their courting days that he would support her during the marriage, but she did not know prior to her marriage that Joseph had failed to support his first wife – as reported to us by the first wife. During their two years of living together, Joseph paid the rent for their home and their domestic necessities sporadically. On the other hand, Leah used the annual amount of $75,000 which she received from her divorce settlement and monies from her family (a combination of gifts and loans) to pay the mortgage and property tax for her newly-acquired home, as well as for domestic necessities such as food, clothing, summer camp, her stepdaughter's tuition fees and *bat mitzvah* expenses. Joseph claimed that he did not have the financial means to cover all the domestic expenses and that his boss was withholding part of his salary,[2] but Leah submitted documentation that showed that in one of his check cashing statements, Joseph had deposited $70,000 worth of checks from his clients and had received cash for them. When Joseph ceased paying for the domestic expenses and Leah's funds were depleted, the marriage began to "unravel" (the words of a relative).

Joseph's misrepresentation extended to non-financial matters. With the assistance of a lawyer, Leah discovered that his first wife had legal and physical custody of their daughter. Moreover, Joseph had claimed

2. His 2016 federal tax return states that he earned $20,000. If in fact, this was his earnings and he was not hiding his assets, on what basis did he promise Leah in 2016 that she would be financially secure during the marriage?

that he did not possess a passport because he had failed to renew it, but in fact he could not obtain a passport due to his failure to pay child support. Furthermore, according to Leah, Joseph claimed that both of his wives were psychologically unstable and cheated on him.[3] Finally, though he presented himself to Leah prior to the marriage as a licensed electrician, in reality he never had a license.

All of the above ought to have served as red flags, but Joseph offered explanations for his behavior and therefore, as a loyal wife, Leah initially believed what he said. Moreover, at first she thought that the cause of his untoward behavior was his daughter's emotional state. Leah surmised that his eleven-year-old daughter from his first marriage was a victim of abuse and suffered from emotional problems. For example, the mother sent gifts and letters to her daughter, but Joseph never gave them to her. Another example: an image of Leah's daughter, with the words "She will die" written above her head, was posted by Joseph's daughter on her social media.[4] Leah therefore decided to assume the role of parent and sent the girl to therapy; she also took care of her, which included doing homework with her. In order for the girl to be eligible for therapy, Leah, with the consent of Joseph's first wife, applied and received sole custody of her stepdaughter. Moreover, Leah – in the role of therapist – tried "to mend the fences" between Joseph and his daughter by talking to Joseph about his daughter's needs. Exchanges between the two of them, recorded in text messages, demonstrate Leah's concern for her stepdaughter's mental wellbeing.

However, as time progressed, Leah realized that the problems in the marriage extended beyond her stepdaughter. Joseph began to curse her in the presence of her children, and once threatened to hit her in front of the children. He would often disappear from the marital home for the whole night, and he would then claim that he had gone to visit a Rebbe's grave and that he fell asleep in the cemetery. During the month of June 2018, two months before their separation, she was scheduled to meet Joseph at Harriman State Park before it closed at 11:00 PM. Leah turned up at the park, but Joseph did not show. Though Leah, who was pregnant at the time, called him dozens of times to pick her up from the park,

3. But, in fact we received pictures dated August 29, 2018, showing Joseph partying with other women. Also, Leah claims that her stepdaughter communicated to her that her father was having dates with a single woman who had a child and was excited to go on these dates with the woman's child.

4. Photo was submitted to the panel.

he ignored her calls and went to sleep at their home.[5] Leah eventually found her way out of the park. During the same month, the skeleton image of Leah's daughter with the words "she shall die" written above her head was posted by his thirteen-year-old daughter on her social media. During this period, too, Leah found a wedding picture of Joseph and her in her stepdaughter's drawer, with a red line drawn across her neck. In view of these events, Leah told Joseph that if his stepdaughter did not begin therapy, she would leave home. Since Joseph refused to comply with Leah's demand, he and his daughter left the home during June 2018, and he returned home only a few times in order to pick up his belongings.

Due to complications with her pregnancy and the birth, Leah remained in the hospital for two months beginning in July 2018.

In August 2018, a baby boy was born to Leah and Joseph. Owing to Joseph's threatening behavior when visiting Leah in the hospital, the hospital denied him the right to visit his new-born son.[6] We have a recording from Joseph in which he says that he walked into a synagogue, opened the ark and prayed that Leah or the baby would die.[7] Upon returning to the marital home, Leah discovered that during her hospital stay, multiple electrical wires in the home had been tampered with (excluding Joseph's daughter's room). Moreover, the boiler was no longer functioning. A professional inspection revealed that the malfunctioning of the boiler was caused by insulating material having been stuffed above the flue. Two technicians confirmed that this stuffing was intentional, and had it not been discovered, it potentially could have caused the emission of carbon monoxide poisoning into the home.[8] Additionally, there was a malfunctioning light switch, a jammed front door, the shower could not be used, and the wiring of a Jacuzzi tub was disconnected. One person informed us that Joseph admitted to him that he had tampered with the wires and the boiler. Given that nobody else was in the home when Leah was staying in the hospital, it was clear to another person who was very familiar with the operation of their home that Joseph had sabotaged all these facilities. Prior to leaving the hospital, due to the above sabotage,

5. One of the text message exchanges between the couple mentions this incident.

6. The incident was confirmed in a report filed by the hospital staff.

7. Two Jewish males who were non-relatives testified that the voice on the recording belongs to Joseph. See *Resp. Ha-Ri Migash* 149; *Birkei Yosef, Hoshen Mishpat* 35:9; *Ketzot Ha-Hoshen* 81:13 citing *Mayim Hayyim* regarding the effectiveness of testimony about someone's voice. Whether Joseph meant seriously what he was saying, we leave as an open question.

8. Copies of technicians' bills were submitted to our panel.

she applied for an order of protection to be issued against Joseph which precluded him from entering the house.

In the wake of these conflicts and hoping to save their marriage, nine months into the marriage, Leah insisted that they speak with rabbis and also undergo marital therapy. For a period of eight months, the couple attended weekly therapy sessions conducted by certified American therapists.

However, Leah was unhappy with the counseling, and therefore she chose to seek the services of a Canadian psychologist. She proposed to Joseph to join her in therapy, but he refused to attend. After four months of therapy conducted by this psychologist, the couple separated.

Prior to being released from the hospital, Leah requested a *get*. After receiving custody of her new-born son, on March 20, 2019, she filed for divorce. A series of three summons (*hazmanot*), and finally a *ktav seruv* [order of contempt] dated August 24, 2020, regarding Leah's request for the *get*, were issued by the Beth Din of America.[9] On November 30, 2020, we conducted a hearing with Leah. To date, Leah has not received her *get*.

Deliberations

1. Use of the Borrowed Ring for Establishing the Act of *Kiddushin*

As is known, there is a debate amongst the authorities on the question of whether *kiddushin* with a borrowed ring are valid.[10] Others hold that this is a case of doubtful marriage (*safek kiddushin*), and she must perform the marriage ceremony again.[11]

9. Although Joseph claims in a text message that Leah never requested a *get*, his claim is unfounded in light of the fact that the text message was sent at the time that he was being summoned to the Beth Din of America to execute or address the matter of the *get*.

10. On the one hand, R. Avigdor Katz (cited in *Resp. Ha-Rosh* 35:2), *Tur Even Ha-Ezer* 28, *Shulhan Arukh Even Ha-Ezer* 19, and *Resp. Hatam Sofer, Even Ha-Ezer* 1:106 rule that *kiddushin* with a borrowed ring are valid. On the other hand, Rosh (*Resp. Ha-Rosh*, 35:2; cf. *Piskei Ha-Rosh, Kiddushin* 1:2), Rashba, *Resp. Ha-Rashba* 4:273; 6:2, *R. Shabtai b. Shmuel, Resp. Maharam of Rothenburg*, Levov edition 504 and following them many other *Aharonim*. See *Resp. Maharshah* 31; *Resp. Avnei Nezer, Even Ha-Ezer* 136; *Resp. Hiddushei Ha-Rim, Even Ha-Ezer* 20; *Resp. Tzemah Tzedek* 98; *Resp. Hasaba Kadisha, Even Ha-Ezer* 13; *Resp. Iggerot Moshe, Even Ha-Ezer* 1:90, all rule that the *kiddushin* are invalid.

11. See *Avnei Nezer*, supra n.10 citing *Beit Yitzhak*.

2. The Ring – "A Gift that is to be Returned"

In the present case, the plaintiff understood that the ring was given to her solely for use at the time of the *huppah,* and she therefore returned the ring to her mother-in-law several days after the ceremony.

Rosh rules as follows:[12]

> …And since the use of the word "borrow" is unsuitable, use must be made of the word "gift", but it must be a gift that is to be returned. In such a case the marriage is valid, and the ring may be taken back and returned after the wedding.

Following those authorities who are of the opinion that the act of *kiddushin* is invalid if performed with a borrowed ring, Rosh holds that there is a presumption that the lender intended to give him the ring as a gift, and that he wants the ring to be returned to him. Other authorities ruled in accordance with the position of Rosh.[13]

When a gift is given that is to be returned, the object (namely, the ring) belongs to the recipient (namely, the groom) for the duration of the time that it is in his possession on condition that he will return the gift to the giver. The giver allows the recipient to give the gift to another on condition that the third party return the gift to the recipient.[14]

In the present case, it is clear that the intention of the giver was that Joseph would give the ring to Leah for the act of *kiddushin,* that later Leah would return the ring to Joseph, and that he would return it to the giver, or that Leah would return the ring directly to the giver.

As is known, due to the strictness of the prohibitions against forbidden relationships, the *Halakhah* rules that a gift is valid only if it was executed according to the provisions of the "rules of conditions," i.e., that there was a double condition – the positive preceded the negative, the condition preceded the act and it was something that was possible to fulfill.[15]

In the present case, it is clear that the giver and the recipient of the

12. *Piskei Ha-Rosh, Kiddushin* 1:20.

13. *Resp. Maharam Padua* 77; *Resp. Ha-Tashbetz* 3:240; *Shulhan Arukh, Even Ha-Ezer* 28:19-20; *Resp. Sho'eil U-Meishiv, Mahadura Tinyana* 3:147; *Resp. Hatam Sofer, Even Ha-Ezer* 1:106; *Resp. Torat Hessed* 2:24.

14. *Mishneh Torah, Hilk. Nedarim* 7:16; *Bah, Hoshen Mishpat* 207.

15. *Hiddushei Ha-Ramban, Bava Batra* 137; *Mishneh Torah, Hilk Ishut* 6:14; *Drisha, Tur, Hoshen Mishpat* 217:3; *Tur, Even Ha-Ezer* 38 citing Rosh; *Shulhan Arukh, Even Ha-Ezer* 38:2.

gift (namely Joseph) did not specify conditions between them prior to the act of *kiddushin*.

If the rules of conditions are not fulfilled properly, there are authorities who hold that to the extent that an assessment exists whereby it is evident to the external onlooker that the giver wishes the gift to be executed on condition that it is "a gift that is to be returned, the transfer of the gift is valid."[16]

There are authorities who insist on the application of the rules of conditions in order to validate the transfer of a gift: invoking the assessment does not serve as an alternative for them.[17]

In order to receive a gift from the giver, the recipient must perform an act of *kinyan* (acquisition). For example, a gift of a chattel (such as a ring) is acquired by lifting (*hagbaha*) or pulling (*meshikhah*), or by other methods known as *sudar, kinyan agav or kinyan yad*.

The recipient of the gift who performed an act of acquisition vis-à-vis the object and did not know that it was a gift, but thought that the object had become his property, acquires it because there is no requirement that the recipient intended to receive a gift. The reason for this *halakhah* is that the giver intends to cause him to acquire it.[18]

In our case, however, the giver of the gift (namely, Leah's mother-in-law) was unaware of the laws of acquisition in general, and the law of the giver intending to cause the recipient to acquire in particular, and therefore the recipient (namely, Joseph/the groom) did not acquire the gift.

Secondly, contrary to the view of some authorities,[19] many authorities rule that at the time of the return, the recipient (namely, the groom) must perform an act of acquisition vis-à-vis the giver whereby this gift, which was given in order to be returned, was acquired by the recipient. Therefore, in the absence of an acquisition upon the return, the ring remains in the possession of the recipient.[20]

16. *Tosafot, Ketubot* 93, s.v. *zavin*; *Tosafot Kiddushin* 6 s.v. lo.

17. *Hiddushei Ha-Rashba, Gittin* 75; *Ran on Rif, Kiddushin* 21; *Maggid Mishneh, Mishneh Torah, Hilk. Ishut* 6:14.

18. *Netivot Ha-Mishpat* 197:4; *Resp. Avnei Nezer, Orah Hayyim* 342:2, *Hoshen Mishpat* 134; *Resp. Hatam Sofer, Even Ha-Ezer* 1:106-107; *Yoreh Deah* 313; *Resp. Maharit* 1:150; *Resp. R. Akiva Eiger* 1:37.

19. *Tosafot Ha-Rid, Sukkah* 41; *Resp. Ha-Ri Migash* 42; *Avnei Milu'im* 28:53.

20. *Hiddushei Ha-Ritva, Kiddushin* 6b; *Resp. Hatam Sofer, Orah Hayyim* 119 citing Ritva; *Piskei Ha-Rosh, Sukkah* 3:30; *Rema, Shulhan Arukh, Orah Hayyim* 658:5; *Resp. Maharam Shick, Orah Hayyim* 330 citing the *Hatam Sofer*; *Resp. Sho'eil U-Meishiv*, 1st ed., 1:266.

Furthermore, as opposed to Maharit and the Hatam Sofer,[21] there are several authorities who cite Rashba,[22] to the effect "that a woman does not know how to make a *kinyan*," the source of which is *Gittin* 10b-21a, and therefore, according to the Amira Tinyana 100:84 and also Resp. Pri Ha-Aretz 1:4, in such circumstances the woman is not married. Secondly, in accordance with others, if the recipient of the gift says, "Give it to me," the recipient has acquired the property as a gift.[23] Thirdly, if Leah's mother-in-law had performed a *kinyan yad*, but did not say explicitly, "I give this ring to Joseph", the acquisition would not take effect.[24]

In the present context, to the extent that a *kinyan yad* was performed, there was no statement on the part of the giver of the gift (namely Leah's mother-in-law). And he did not say, "give it to me", and therefore the "implied giving" (i.e., application of the assessment) is not effective, unless the giver says specifically that he (in this case – she) is giving the object as a gift.[25]

In short, the wedding ring must belong to the groom (Joseph) and he must have acquired it in a full act of acquisition.[26] It is not possible to use a ring that has not been acquired by the groom, such as one that is stolen.[27] And even if the wedding was preceded by formal *shiddukhin* [commitment to marry], according to the view of Rema, if the groom had not paid for the ring – she is not married.[28] And in the present context, the plaintiff never caused the ring to be acquired by the defendant, and therefore he is deemed to have married her with a stolen ring!

3. Mistaken *Kiddushin* Due to Misrepresentation

Before the mechanism of mistaken *kiddushin* can be applied to invalidate the *kiddushin* and to argue that there was a mistake in the creation of the marriage, three preconditions must be met:

---

21. *Resp. Ha-Maharit* 2:49; *Resp. Hatam Sofer, Even Ha-Ezer* 1:86.

22. *Otzar Ha-Poskim, Even Ha-Ezer* 29:2:9-12.

23. *Resp. R. Akiva Eiger, Mahadura Tinyana* 45, *Sefer Gevurat Anashim* 5 citing *Beit Meir* and *Mishneh Le-Melekh, Hilk. Ishut* 3.

24. Rema, *Hoshen Mishpat* 241:1; *Sefer Me'irat Einayim, Hoshen Mishpat* 241:5; *Arukh Ha-Shulhan, Hoshen Mishpat* 241:1; *Pithei Hoshen, Kinyanim* 1:7.

25. *Resp. Ginat Veradim, Hoshen Mishpat* 200:12; *erekh shin, Hoshen Mishpat* 88:12; *Sha'arei Zion* 1:1:4:5 citing the *Nodah Be-Yehudah*.

26. *Tur, Even ha-Ezer* 28.

27. *Shulhan Arukh* and *Rema, Even Ha-Ezer* 28:1.

28. *Even Ha-Ezer* 29:2, citing Ran.

A. The defect must be one such as: impotence, insanity, homosexuality or exposure of the wife to a dangerous illness such as AIDS. All these are examples of "serious defects" and have been mentioned in the rabbinical responsa.

Our Sages said, "Four classes of people will not meet the Divine Presence," and one of these is "the class of liars".[29] The Holy One Blessed be He hates a person who says one thing with his mouth and another in his heart,[30] and it is better that a person should humiliate himself and sell carcasses than that he should lie.[31] R. Yona Hahassid of Girondi, a 13th-century Spanish sage, wrote that "a lie, apart from the damage it causes, is a Divine abomination, as it is written (*Proverbs* 12:22): 'Lying lips are an abomination to the Lord.'"[32]

It is therefore not surprising that subsequently, *R. Yona* devotes significant attention to the halakhic-moral obligation of a Jew to keep his promises, writing as follows:[33]

> A person promises to do something for the benefit of another, and he lies and goes back on his word: when a person has said that he will benefit another in the form of a promise, and the other trusted him, he may not break his promise, for this is the way of lying, and he is as a person who breaches a covenant, as it is said (*Zephaniah* 3:13): "The remnant of Israel shall not do iniquity, nor speak lies; neither shall a deceitful tongue be found in their mouth...." Similarly, a person who says that he will give his fellow a small gift, even though he did not expressly promise.... and also a person who boasts in public that he will give a person a gift, and he is praised for his generosity, this is like a promise, and it is not right that he should go back on his word after he was accorded credit and respect for this, as it is written (*Proverbs* 25:14): "As vapors and wind without rain, so is he that boasteth himself of a false gift": just as people are upset if there are signs of rain but these are not followed by rain – so too with a person who boasts of a false gift, because boasting of a thing is a sign of the existence of the thing, and therefore the person

29. *Sotah* 42a.
30. *Pesahim* 113b.
31. Ibid.
32. *Sha'arei Teshuvah* 3:179.
33. *Sha'arei Teshuvah* 3:183.

> to whom the gift was promised will be upset, because he was disappointed....

In general, a person who breaks his promise is deemed to be a Jew who lies. Therefore, even though there are cases where, halakhically speaking, a person may go back on an oral promise, generally speaking – from a halakhic point of view, he must keep his promise. As R. Yona noted, misrepresentation is a manifestation of the conduct of a liar, who said he would benefit the other in terms of a promise, and the other person trusted him: he must not "break his promise." As our Sages said, "A person who conducts negotiations orally only ought to stand by his word... and a person who goes back on his word, whether the buyer or the seller... he is one who is not trustworthy, and the Sages are displeased with him...."[34]

A person who is called "untrustworthy" is guilty of violating a rabbinic prohibition,[35] and the rabbi or the *beit din* has the authority to publish his name in order to shame him.[36]

A promise relating to something that is not tangible, even if there was a formal act of acquisition, is not halakhically enforceable, but the promissor [who breaks his promise] is called untrustworthy. An example of this would be if he promised another that he would perform the circumcision at the *brit* (circumcision) for that person's son.[37] This is also the halakha that applies to a person who writes to another that he will do something particular, such as a promise to pay; even if there was an act of acquisition, as an oral acquisition has no halakhic validity.[38] However, he is forbidden to renege, due to untrustworthiness.[39]

A fortiori, in the present case, where there is an oral promise relating to future actions, but the required language of obligation (*me'akhshav*

34. *Mishneh Torah, Hilk. Mekhira* 7:8 and *Piskei Ha-Rosh, Bava Metzia* 4:12; *Shulhan Arukh, Hoshen Mishpat* 204:3; *Rema*, ibid., 11 ruled accordingly.

For additional examples, see Itamar Warhaftig, *The Obligation: Validity, Nature and Types* (5761-2001), (Heb.), pp. 393-94, 403, 411, 413, 415, 438-45, 451.

35. *Resp. Ra'anah* 1:118.

36. *Resp. Maharam Mintz* 101; *Sefer Ha-Agudah, Bava Metzia* 4:66 citing Ra'aviya; *Resp. Nehpa Ba-Kesef* 2:260-62

37. *Resp. Maharam of Rothenberg*, Prague ed., 949; *Resp. Ha-Rosh* 12:3; 102:10; Rema, *Yoreh Deah* 264:1; *Shakh, Yoreh Deah* 264:7.

38. *Bava Batra* 3a; *Shulhan Arukh, Hoshen Mishpat* 157:2

39. *Darkhei Moshe Yoreh Deah* 264 in the name of Rosh; *Tosafot Reim* 6.

– "from now"), an act of acquisition, and the presence of two witnesses, are all lacking.[40]

As R. Yona noted, in general a person who breaks his promise is deemed a Jew who lies. Moreover, the Talmud states that untrustworthiness relates to a person who says one thing but thinks otherwise, and his external presentation differs from what is in his heart.[41] In other words, the person is not only a liar, but he deceives other people. *Maimonides* wrote as follows in relation to deceit:[42]

> A person is forbidden to act in a smooth-tongued and luring manner. He should not speak one thing outwardly and think otherwise in his heart. Rather, his inner self should be like the self whom he shows to the world, and he must not deceive others, not even a gentile. For example, one should not sell a gentile the meat of an animal which has not been ritually slaughtered as if it were ritually slaughtered meat....

Based on the discussion in Talmud Bavli *Hullin* (94a), Maimonides rules that the deceit which is prohibited refers to a situation in which the other person is led to think that the first has done something good for him, whereas in fact that was not the intention.[43] In other words, this is misrepresentation or misleading.[44]

In the present case, Joseph's conduct in his misrepresentation as to his financial stability and his ability to support his wife, as well as his concealment of personal information, constitutes a breach of trust, misrepresentation and deceit.

The question arises as to whether there is a basis for invalidating the *kiddushin* due to misrepresentation. As is known, there is a rabbinical tradition according to which *kiddushin* can be invalidated due to a major

---

40. *Tur, Hoshen Mishpat* 245; *Shulhan Arukh, Hoshen Mishpat* 245:4; *Resp. Ha-Mabit* 2:26; *Resp. Maharshakh* 3:84; *Knesset Ha-Gedolah Hoshen Mishpat, Mahadurah* 2, 61, *Hagahot* 2.

41. Talmud Bavli *Bava Metzia* 29a.

42. *Mishneh Torah, Hilk. De'ot* 2:6.

43. *R. Yossef Fleischmann, Mishpetei Yosher* 1:12-18.

44. The words of the Talmud and the examples in *Hullin* (94a) imply that fraud is when a seller sells one a defective product, whereas misrepresentation occurs even if he sells a product that is not defective, e.g., he sells a non-kosher animal to a non-Jew and tells him that it is a kosher animal, even though this makes no difference for the non-Jew: this is misrepresentation. See R. Yaakov Hildesheim, *Keter, Studies in Economics and Law According to the Torah*, Part 3 (5761-2001), p. 28 note 4, citing R. Zalman Nehemiah Goldberg.

defect that existed prior to the marriage, where the wife did not know of the defect at the time of the marriage.[45] In other words, a husband who failed to disclose to his wife prior to the wedding that he does not keep his promises, that he is a liar and deceives people – does such conduct constitute a "major defect" and constitute misrepresentation such that the *kiddushin* may be invalidated?[46]

The *Mishnah* rules as follows:[47]

> With regard to one who betroths a woman and later says: I thought that she was the daughter of a Priest, and it turned out that she is the daughter of a Levite, or if he claims that he thought she was the daughter of a Levite and she is actually the daughter of a Priest, or if he claims that he thought she was poor and she is wealthy; or wealthy and she is poor, in all of these cases she is betrothed, because she did not mislead him.

The inference from the Mishnah is that in circumstances in which the wife did mislead her husband, she is not married, and indeed, according to the opinions of some tannaitic and amoraic sages, *kiddushin* may be voided in a case of misleading behavior.[48]

In the above sources, there is no distinction between a man who makes a condition vis-à-vis the wife at the time of the kiddushin "*al menat* ['on condition that'] I am rich" and he was found to be poor, or a false statement without the formulation of a condition – "marry me because I am rich" – and he was found to be poor: in other words, there is no difference between a condition and a description of a situation.

The common denominator of these sources is that misleading as a ground for invaliding *kiddushin* is limited to concealment that occurred <u>at the time of the act of *kiddushin*</u>. In other words, the main basis is the principle that "unarticulated matters have no effect": the intention to marry or not to marry requires clear, explicit articulation.

The question therefore arises as to whether the basis for these *halakhot* lies in the laws of conditions or in the laws of mistake? On the one

---

45. *Resp. Iggerot Moshe, Even Ha-Ezer* 1:79-80, 3:45, 4:19; *Resp. Beit Av* 7:27; *Resp. Maharsham* 3:16, 6:160; *Resp. Har Tzvi* 1:99, 2:181.

46. An analogy can be drawn from the laws of misrepresentation in relation to cancelling formal commitments to marry (*shiddukhin*) to our matter of invalidating *kiddushin*, i.e., in relation to the ways in which it is permissible to conceal a defect for the purpose of a match and in the ways in which a defect may not be concealed.

47. *Kiddushin* 3:5.

48. Mishnah *Kiddushin* 2:2-3; *Tosefta Kiddushin* 3:8-9; *Kiddushin* 48b-49b.

hand, in cases in which the *kiddushin* are invalid, there is an express stipulation, formulated as "*al menat* – on condition that..."; on the other hand, in cases in which the *kiddushin* are not invalid, neither the man nor the woman said anything at all, but claimed, "I thought that...", i.e., they made a mistake, or deceived themselves, as to the true situation. Therefore, the question arises as to the law in a situation in which there were not only mental reservations, but an explicit articulation of the personal or financial situation of the person, although without the formulation of a condition.

On the one hand, in a case in which a man misled a woman in that he made it known that he was rich whereas he was poor, and she married him, *R. Shimon b. Tzemah Duran* ruled that the *kiddushin* may be invalidated due to misrepresentation, provided that the formulation was in terms of "*al menat*":[49]

> This question contains three arguments for invalidating the *kiddushin*: the first, that he misled her in the matter of his wealth.... and this first argument is not enough to invalidate the *kiddushin*, for surely if he had said to her at the time of the *kiddushin*, "You are hereby consecrated to me with this ring *al menat* that I am rich" or "that I have so and so much money" and he was found to be poor or that he had no money, the *kiddushin* would be invalid... but here he did not marry her on this condition, but simply let it be known that he was rich and that he had such and such an amount of money, and she believed him and married him, and for such a thing we do not invalidate *kiddushin*....

This is also the opinion of R. Yitzhak Schmelkes in the case of a man who deceived a woman and told her prior to the *kiddushin* that he had a house registered in his name, and that he had no children; after the *kiddushin* it emerged that he had two sons, that he had many creditors and that he was poor. R. Schmelkes ruled that the *kiddushin* was valid: "It is clear that the woman is married, and there are no grounds for doubt at

49. *Resp. Ha-Tashbetz* 1:130. Regarding the laws of conditions, some authorities hold that the formulation "*al menat*" is required; see: *Resp. Ha-Rosh* 81:1, citing Ri and Rabbenu Tam; *Tur, Even Ha-Ezer* 38, citing Rabbenu Hananel. There are also authorities who hold that when the formulation "*al menat*" is used, there is no need for all the laws of conditions – see: *Shulhan Arukh, Even Ha-Ezer* 38:3.

all, since there was no explicit condition that immediately preceded the *kiddushin*."[50]

On the other hand, *R. Moshe Sofer* formulated this question as follows:[51]

> .... In *Kiddushin* 62a it states that a person who marries a woman and says, I thought that she was the daughter of a Kohen etc., that she was rich but she is poor – she is consecrated because she did not deceive him. This is when she never said or made it known in any way that she is the daughter of a Kohen or rich, but he simply thought so, and she never deceived him, and she is consecrated; but if she deceived him, even if she did not say at the time of the *kiddushin* "*al menat*" that she is so and so, then she is not married, for this expression has legal force....

And at the end of his responsum he writes: "And if the esteemed rabbis and the sages of their holy city will examine our words and will agree with us, each one would take a chip of the beam, and this woman ... will be permitted to marry anyone she desires."

As opposed to the *Tashbetz*, according to the Hatam Sofer, an explicit articulation has halakhic force to invalidate *kiddushin*.

As is known, the halakhot of mistaken *kiddushin* are derived in the halakhot of mistaken transactions.[52]

Therefore, the position of the Hatam Sofer is based on the halakhot of mistaken transaction, as determined by *R. Yosef Karo*:[53]

> But a person who sold unconditionally, even if his inner thought was that he is selling for a particular reason, even if it would appear that he did not sell except in order to do a particular thing, which was not done, it cannot be retracted, because he performed an explicit act, and mental reservations have no force; and even though prior to the sale he said that he was selling in order to do something particular, because he did not specify at the time of the sale, he cannot retract.

50. *Resp. Beit Yitzhak* 1, *Even Ha-Ezer* 106.

51. *Resp. Hatam Sofer Even Ha-Ezer* 3:82.

52. For example, see *Resp. Ein Yitzhak* 1:24 (39); R. Zalman Nehemiah Goldberg, "Exemption from Maintenance and the Claim of Mistaken Transaction Due to Mental Illness," 4 *Shurat Hadin* 54. See supra chapter 3.

53. *Shulhan Arukh, Hoshen Mishpat* 207:4.

R. Moshe Alsheikh (*Resp. Maharam Alsheikh 38*) wrote as follows:

> And even though he said to the agent, I wish to go up to the Land of Israel, talk to X, that he should buy my property, and the agent went and spoke to him, and the sale was made. And we nevertheless say that because he did not mention this at the time of the sale, we pay no attention to it, and similarly in this case, since there was no formal condition, then we do not consider his intention to have been articulated.

The opinion of the *Turei Zahav* is as follows:[54]

> It is an everyday matter that a person sells an object to another, and says: They gave me such and such an amount and I did not want to sell it at that price. And it later emerges that there was no buyer at the price that he mentioned, and because of this the sale should be nullified, but perforce as I have explained, we need a clear articulation that he was making the sale dependent upon what others were offering.

On the basis of the above, we can understand the position of the *Ketzot Ha-Hoshen*:[55]

> Where there is a clear articulation, we do not need any formal condition.

According to R. Yosef Karo, a clear articulation is sufficient, and the formulation in terms of condition is not required.[56]

As noted by R. Ariel Holland, a member of the International Beit Din panel, the effectiveness of a clear articulation lies in its equivalence to "*al menat*".[57]

R. Malkiel Tennenbaum wrote as follows:[58]

> As Ran wrote in Kiddushin chap. 3, a double condition is

54. *Hoshen Mishpat* 332:4.
55. 319:1.
56. *Shulhan Arukh,* supra n. 53.
57. *Pithei Teshuvah, Even Ha-Ezer* 38:14; *Resp. Sha'arei Tzion* 1, *Even Ha-Ezer* 20.
58. *Resp. Divrei Malkiel* 1:86.

> unnecessary where there is a clear articulation, and if she misled him, the *kiddushin* are invalid.

Is the invalidation of *kiddushin* in the case of the person saying, "I am rich..." a function of the laws of condition, or of misleading in a transaction? As R. Yehoshua Reich, member of the International Beit Din, wrote:[59]

> It is written in *Agudat Ezov Midbari, Hoshen Mishpat 10*: "And in my humble opinion, the present case has nothing to do with the laws of conditions... when it is clear that he is mainly concerned with the condition and not with the legality of the act, we do not need to follow all the laws of conditions... and we have found that in the opinion of many authorities, in monetary matters a clear articulation by itself is preferable to a condition that is not properly formulated." Therefore, the basis for invalidating the act is because she misled him, and not due to a condition, and the laws of conditions are not applicable to our case. This is clear from the words of *Maimonides, Hilk. Ishut 8:6*:
>
>> When a man consecrates a woman and says, "I thought she was from a priestly family, and instead she is from a family of Levites...," "from a family of Levites, and instead she is from a priestly family...," "poor, and instead she is rich...," or "rich, and instead she is poor," she is consecrated, for she did not mislead him.
>>
>> Similarly, if she says, "I thought he was a priest, and instead he is a Levite...," "a Levite, and instead he is a priest...," "poor, and instead he is rich," or "...rich, and instead he is poor," she is consecrated, for he did not mislead her.

In other words, *kiddushin* may be invalidated due to misleading that stems from a clear articulation, and not only from a condition.

The *Atzmot Yosef* rules similarly:[60]

> And incidentally it would appear that there is a novel point here, that if the woman said to the man who was marrying her that

59. File no. 2020/263.
60. Talmud Bavli *Kiddushin* 62b.

> she is from a priestly family, and he married her and did not specify [a condition], and she was found to be from a family of Levites – she is not consecrated, because it is evident that he married her on the basis of her word, even though he did not specify [a condition], and she misled him.

The ruling of R. Yom Tov Lipman Heller was similar to that of Hatam Sofer, according to which the *kiddushin* are void even in a case in which the deception occurred other than at the time when the *kiddushin* transpired:[61]

> We are not dealing with a case in which there was a properly formulated condition at the time of the *kiddushin*, "*al menat* that I am a Kohen," but he said to her prior to the *kiddushin*: "I am a Kohen, and on that condition ("*al menat ken*") I wish to marry you, or "I am rich and *al menat ken* I will marry you," or "I am poor and *al menat ken* I will marry you, and she accepted this and married him unconditionally... it therefore seems that this is the law with respect to "*al menat* that I am rich" etc.; even if this is not a case where he said this at the time of the *kiddushin*, but there was a prior articulation that *al menat ken* he wishes to marry her, and it emerges that this is not the situation – this is a case of mistaken *kiddushin*, and is not due to cancellation of the condition.

This also applies in a case in which prior to the marriage, the husband did not disclose his defect to her, and she demanded that he tell her the reason for his sadness and fatigue, and he concealed the truth from her and promised her that he was healthy. Relying on the above responsum of the Tashbetz, R. Abraham Yudelovitch ruled that one of the reasons that he permitted the woman to be released from the marriage without *halitzah* (the halakhic alternative to levirate marriage)[62] was as follows:[63]

> And I would say that the second reason follows from the words of the *Tashbetz (1:130)* who wrote concerning a person who married a woman before a single witness, and also misled her

61. *Resp. Malbushei Yom Tov, Even Ha-Ezer* 2.

62. On the issue of the possibility of drawing an analogy between the halakhot of *halitzah* and the halakhot of marriage, see *Resp. Yabia Omer* 8, *Even Ha-Ezer* 38:2.

63. *Resp. Beit Av Shevia'i* 14:3.

> by publicly announcing that he was rich when he was poor: after he explained at length that the great *Aharonim* agreed with the *Rishonim* that a person who marries a woman in front of a single witness is not deemed to be married – even if both of the couple affirm – and therefore there is no concern about *kiddushin* in front of one witness, and there is no place for any concern, he wrote, and how much more in this case…, that he surely acted improperly in deceiving her by announcing that he was rich when he was poor, and we find that there were rabbis in the Talmud who would invalidate fully constituted *kiddushin* in relation to a person who acted improperly, as it says in Perek Hezkat (Bava Batra 48b), in relation to a woman who was hung up until she agreed to be betrothed, Rav Ashi said that the *kiddushin* are not valid, even though in the case of a seller who was hung up until he consented to sell, the sale is valid: they said the reason was that he acted improperly [by forcing the woman to accept the betrothal] and therefore they [the Rabbis] acted with him improperly and they abrogated his [technically valid] betrothal, and *a fortiori* we will not adopt a stringent approach to these *kiddushin* because they were in any case mistaken... Hence, I maintain that as in our case the *kiddushin* were witnessed by a single witness only, and since he acted improperly and misled her and promised that he was healthy like other people, therefore we should not rule strictly in the case of *kiddushin* with one witness, and this wife should not be made an *agunah*, and she is hereby permitted to marry any person.

In another responsum R. Yudelovitch discusses the case of a woman who was left "alone and chained, bewailing her bitter fate with no-one to save her," and he invalidated the *kiddushin* due to the deception of the wife by the husband and due to a defect in the *kiddushin* ceremony. He wrote as follows:[64]

> And concerning the woman… who married a man who came there from another city, and after the wedding he was with her for about a month and he took her money and ran away from her; four years have now passed and his whereabouts are unknown… and it is now known that this man already had a wife and three children in the city of Boston, and he left them too …

64. *Resp. Beit Av*, ibid. 28.

And thus, in our case where he married her unconditionally, and she did not know about his defect, i.e., that he had a wife and three children, which is a major defect from her perspective. If she had known of this, it is patently clear that she would absolutely not have wanted to marry him, because it is against State law, and this man would be punished by the law: where is the young woman who would give herself in marriage to a man against the laws of the state? What is more, the enactments of Rabbenu Gershom extend to the wife and she is a law-abiding woman and listens to her father, who is a person of integrity, and to her family, who would protest; and in addition, how is it at all possible that she would become betrothed to a man who she herself sees is cruel and has no mercy for his wife or his three children, and he is a thief and a murderer? How is it possible that she would marry him, and how could she trust him – all her life she would hear his words saying that he will love her, but he is a person who is not to be trusted, and what he says is in the spirit of deception, and even if he really does love her now, who knows what will be over time, and is it not possible that in a flash he will switch his affections to another and send her away as well?

4. Ruling Leniently in Relation to a Person Who Acted Improperly Concerning *Kiddushin*

R. Itzhak Rappaport Ha-Kohen discusses the case of a person who forged letters of reference which made women believe that he was a good, eminent person, and he went from place to place and married several women in those places in order to take their money; he was finally caught and put in prison, but he refused to give a *get*. *R. Rappaport* ruled:[65]

> And I would add that it is a great *mitzvah* for all the authorities to seek a mechanism by which to free her so that such evil people will not continue to persecute daughters of Israel with such acts, and how much did our Sages do in such matters, as stated in *Bava Batra* 48b that even though he underwent *kiddushin*, the rabbis invalidated the *kiddushin*, because he acted improperly and therefore they acted "improperly" with him and they annulled the *kiddushin*, and they expropriated the monies of the *kiddushin* (*hefker*) and his acts of intimacy were rendered acts of promiscuity. How far they went to suppress these evil acts. And

65. *Resp. Mahari Ha-Kohen, Mahadura Tinyana, Even Ha-Ezer* 13.

> see how far they are prepared to go and develop strategies in order to uproot such evil conduct, and although we do not have the power to do the same....
>
> And the underlying logic here, in my opinion, is that the ability to annul the *kiddushin* derives from the principle that whoever marries does so on condition that the marriage is rabbinically approved, and even though the marriage was tainted by sinfulness, and therefore should not receive rabbinic approval, the actual act of *kiddushin* was performed in accordance with rabbinical directives, i.e., in accordance with the laws of Moshe and Israel. And since the institution of marriage is based upon the enactments of the earlier rabbis, we are unable to uproot them. Nevertheless, there would have been some basis for claiming that in these circumstances, the earlier rabbis would have nullified the marriage, and therefore we ought to be able to do the same thing.

In other words, the respondent refers the reader to the talmudic discussion of the woman who was consecrated when she was a minor. When she reached majority, the man was prepared to marry her but she was kidnapped, and she underwent *kiddushin* with the kidnapper. According to Mar bar Rav Ashi, her *kiddushin* are not valid, since the sages annulled them so that she would not be married against her will to someone whom she did not want.[66]

Relying on this position of annulling *kiddushin* that were performed in improper circumstances, R. Rappaport decided in the circumstances before him that these *kiddushin* had been performed in "improper circumstances" of misrepresentation, and they should be invalidated. In other words, although the "improper *kiddushin*" occurred in the framework of the creation of an act of *kiddushin* through fraud, an analogy may be drawn to the case discussed by Mahari Ha-Kohen which involves non-disclosure (i.e., misrepresentation) on the part of the husband that occurred prior to the act of *kiddushin*.

And in our time too, in the case in which the husband did not tell his wife prior to the *kiddushin* that he has cancer, and in particular, testicular cancer, and when she asked for a *get* he refused, and asked for large sums in order to release her from the chains of *igun*, R. Shmuel Tuvia Stern ruled that the husband misled the wife:[67]

66. *Bava Batra* 48b.

67. *Resp. Ha-Shavit* 4:30.

> ... This was certainly a mistaken transaction, and mistaken *kiddushin*, and what is worse, the *kiddushin* were fraudulent.

B. In order to invalidate the *kiddushin*, it must be clear that the defect existed prior to the marriage, and the wife did not know of the defect prior to the marriage.

With regard to Leah's awareness of the defect, the question arises as to whether she can be believed that she did not know prior to the marriage that Joseph was accustomed to acting fraudulently and breaking his promises. Can we believe a woman as "a single witness who is credible in matters of prohibited unions" in her claim that she only became aware of his tainted behavior after the wedding? Is it not that her testimony is not credible because in matters of forbidden sexual unions, the testimony of two witnesses is required?

Following her argument that she was not married to Joseph on the grounds that these were mistaken *kiddushin* or they are doubtful *kiddushin*, she is not considered to be a married woman, and therefore one witness is deemed to be credible in matters of prohibitions, even if of a sexual nature.[68]

There are indeed those who hold that a single witness is not believed in matters of forbidden sexual unions, even when the prohibited union has not been established.[69] However, several *Aharonim* opposed this view.[70]

In the present case, where the testimony of the wife concerning the defect and the deception goes to the very validity of the *kiddushin*, this is defined as testimony in a situation where the prohibition concerning the forbidden union has not been established, since the existence of the forbidden union has been negated by the testimony, and as the *Noda Be-Yehudah* elucidates:[71]

> In any event, where it has not been established, he is certainly credible, and it may not be said that the rule should be different because we are dealing with the prohibition of a married woman, for this applies to a witness who testifies about divorce

68. *Resp. R. Akiva Eiger* 107 citing *Tosafot Gittin* 2, s.v. *hu*; *Resp. Maharik, shoresh* 72.

69. *Hiddushei Ha-Ramban, Gittin* 2b, s.v. *ha-amrinan davar she-be-erva.*

70. *Resp. Noda Be-Yehudah, Mahadura Kamma*, 54; *Mahadura Tinyana*, 75; *Resp. R. Akiva Eiger* 97 (as a supporting argument); *Resp. Ahiezer, Even Ha-Ezer* 6; *Resp. Minhat Asher* 1:73.

71. *Noda Be-Yehudah*, supra n. 70, at 59.

> or about the death of the husband, which is intended to release the woman from the status of a married woman, but here, our concern is with the force of the *kiddushin* – whether or not they are valid – and therefore there is not yet a presumption that the woman is married: quite the contrary, the presumption of being unmarried pertains.

The *Shev Shema'teta* states in a similar vein:[72]

> It therefore seems that the inference via the analogy of words (*gezerah shava,* based upon the repetition of the word *davar* in the context of the evidentiary requirements concerning both monetary and sexual matters) is only applicable to a case which clearly falls within the rubric of sexual offenses, for example, where the prohibition in question has already been established; however, if it is not clear that the matter before us involves a clear-cut sexual prohibition, and one witness testifies that there was no forbidden union, as in the case of an agent who testifies that the betrothal he effected was not to himself but to the principal, then the prohibition is downgraded to that of a regular offense, in relation to which one witness is credible.

In our case, too, the import of Leah's testimony is that in fact she was never married to the defendant, and we therefore rule that her testimony, that she did not know prior to the marriage about Joseph's defects and his true condition, is credible.

C. Delay and Non-Acceptance in Respect of the Defects

The question of whether Leah should have left Joseph as soon as she became aware that there was a major defect is a point of disagreement amongst the authorities. Although according to the majority of authorities she ought to have left him immediately upon discovering the defect,[73] nevertheless, according to some authorities, including R. Feinstein, she could have remained in the marriage if she had justified reasons for doing so.[74] However, if in the final analysis it is impossible to solve the

---

72. *Shema'teta* 6, chap. 3.

73. *Tur* and *Beit Yosef, Even Ha-Ezer* 154; *Helkat Mehokeik, Even Ha-Ezer* 39:9; *Beit Shmuel,* ad loc. 16; *Resp. Ha-Maharik* 24; *Resp. R. Akiva Eiger,* 2nd ed., 57.

74. *Resp. Iggerot Moshe, Even Ha-Ezer* 3:45, 48; 4:113; PDR 1:5 (9 Shevat 5714), 11-12; see also *Resp. Sha'arei Tzion* 3, *Even Ha-Ezer* 4.

problems, e.g., in a case in which the husband is insane and medical or psychiatric treatment or medication do not help, the wife must leave the husband.

Moreover, despite the fact that the wife did not protest immediately upon discovering the defect, in reliance upon the ruling of the Tiv Kiddushin,[75] R. Osher Weiss held that the delay *per se* after discovering the defect does not prevent the wife from later claiming a mistaken transaction:[76]

> For we are witnesses that the way in which a person reacts depends on the individual. And it is very common that when a person discovers defects in a spouse he or she does not react immediately for various reasons, sometimes due to sadness and shock and sometimes in order to preserve his or her discretion or in order to consider how not to hurt the feelings of the other, and this is not evidence that s/he has accepted, or does not care ...
>
> But it appears that even if a person truly regrets her marriage, she might nevertheless make an attempt to make things work through adoption [the defect in the case under discussion was related to the husband's infertility] etc., but if all the attempts fail, we go back to the first position, that this is a case of mistaken *kiddushin*....

In the present case, Leah did not accept the defect.

However, as R. Yosef Sharabi comments, insofar as we are dealing with a claim of misleading in connection with the husband's behavior as a serial liar and breaker of promises, the moment that the wife knows that there was misrepresentation, there is no room for justifying delay. For example, in the present case, shortly after the wedding Leah began receiving notices in the post, arrest warrants for Joseph due to non-payment of taxes, an arrest warrant for non-payment of child support and other notices for non-payment of debts, and she understood that he was a liar and deceiver of people: could she wait to see if her spouse would become a person who told the truth? What had happened through the fraud had already happened, and it could not be changed. Therefore, apparently her remaining with her husband could be deemed acceptance.

Indeed, all of the above ought to have set off a warning light for Leah.

75. 39:12.

76. *Resp. Minhat Asher* 1:73 (4). See also, *Sha'arei Tzion* 3, *Even Ha-Ezer* 4 (1, 3).

But Joseph offered explanations for his behavior, and therefore, as a loyal wife, she initially thought that his untoward conduct was a result of the psychological state of his daughter. As we mentioned, Leah surmised that the daughter was a victim of abuse and suffering from psychological problems. Consequently, Leah decided to take upon herself the role of parent and sent her for psychological counseling, and she also took care of her, including doing homework with her. In addition, Leah sought and received sole custody of her stepdaughter. Leah tried to rehabilitate the relationship between Joseph and his daughter, but eventually, she understood that the problems in her marriage extended beyond the stepdaughter, and she began to focus on the deceit of her husband, and that she had been the victim of psychological abuse on the part of her husband.

On the basis of the above, Leah is permitted to marry any Jewish man other than a Kohen.

D. IS THERE A REQUIREMENT TO EXECUTE A *GET* UPON THE DISSOLUTION OF A CIVIL MARRIAGE?

Response to a Question

Question

Judy wed her husband in a civil ceremony on January 22, 2007. The couple had no children, and on May 18, 2015, they divorced civilly. Subsequently, the husband married a woman in accordance with Jewish law, and the *mesadeir kiddushin* (the rabbi who officiated at the wedding ceremony) did not require a *get* before performing the *kiddushin*. As of 2018, Judy has asked her husband three times to give her a *get*, but to date he has refused to do so. The International Beit Din asked the husband to give a *get*, but he has not complied with our request. To the best of our knowledge, the wife is a Conservative Jew (and not observant in the full sense of the word) in general, and does not observe the *halakhot* of ritual purity (*niddah*) in particular.

Judy petitioned us as rabbinical decisors to permit her to marry any Jew without having obtained a *get* from her civilly married husband.[1]

Response

The validity of civil marriage from the point of view of *halakhah* is in

1. In other words, this is a question of *halakhic* laws of prohibitions and permissibility (*dinei issur ve-heter*) regarding whether a husband is obligated to give a *get* to his wife. The question may be resolved in front of three rabbis in the absence of the husband. As we know, there is a disagreement as to whether matters of divorce such as obligating or compelling the giving of a *get* may only be resolved in front of a *beit din* of three rabbis, or in front of one rabbi, or in the presence of only an individual Jew. See *Yam shel Shlomo, Bava Kamma* 3:9; *Ketzot Ha-Hoshen, Hoshen Mishpat* 3:1,2; *Netivot Ha-Mishpat, Hoshen Mishpat* 3:1; *Resp. Yehudah* (Gordin), *Even Ha-Ezer* 51:2; *Resp. Ma'aseh Hiyah* 24; *Resp. Hatam Sofer, Orah Hayyim* 51, *Even Ha-Ezer* 2:64-65, *Hoshen Mishpat* 177; *Resp. Avnei Nezer, Even Ha-Ezer* 167:1, 178:2; PDR 6:265, 269; Beit Hora'ah File 957-61, Jerusalem Beit Din for Civil Matters and Status Clarification, vol. 7, 515; File 448866/3, 7.11.13, Tel Aviv-Yaffo Regional Beit Din; File no. 1086123/1, Be'er Sheva Regional Beit Din, 12.20.18. In the present matter, three rabbis convened to decide an issue of ritual *halakhah*.

accordance with the position taken by Rivash which was endorsed by many authorities.[2]

Rivash's responsum deals with the marriage of a Jewish couple who converted to Christianity, who lived together as a married couple and were known to all as such. Eventually, she returned to the Jewish religion after her husband left her, and she wished to marry a Jew in accordance with *halakhah*. In those circumstances, Rivash permitted the woman to marry without having received a *get*, with no concern for the presumption that "a person does not have intercourse as an act of fornication" when intimacy occurred within the framework of *kiddushin*, for several reasons.

First, since this was a case of a female apostate who married a male apostate in accordance with the Christian law at a time of persecution of the Jewish community, in the island of Majorca, and their acts proved that their Christian marital bond was enough for them, therefore it cannot be assumed that they intended to undergo halakhic *kiddushin*. A summary of Rivash's position appears as the *halakhah* in Shulhan Arukh, as follows:[3]

> A man and a woman who were forced into apostasy dues to the decrees, who married each other according to the laws of the nations, even though they are intimate with each other every day, and this is public knowledge, there is no concern that there has been *kiddushin*.

The same position is adopted by Rema:[4]

> A male apostate who married a female apostate in accordance with the Christian law and they later converted (to Judaism) – there has been no *kiddushin* at all, and she is permitted to leave him without a *get*; even though she had been with him for several years, this was nothing more than mere fornication.

Others concurred with this view.[5]

According to the above reasons, undergoing a civil ceremony is deemed to be an expression of the fact that the parties do not intend to undergo halakhic *kiddushin*.[6]

2. *Resp. Ha-Rivash* 6.
3. *Even Ha-Ezer* 149:6.
4. *Even Ha-Ezer* 26:1.
5. *Resp. Terumat Ha-Deshen* 209; *Resp. Ha-Ridbaz* 1:351.
6. Ridbaz of Slutzk, *Maariv* New York Volume, 5664-1904 at 125; *Resp. Pri*

Another reason mentioned by Rivash for releasing the wife lies in the scope of the Talmudic presumption that "a person does not have intercourse as an act of fornication."[7] According to Rivash, this presumption should only be applied to a couple in a relation to whom it can be assumed that they refrain from violating Torah prohibitions in general, and the *halakhot* applying to *niddah* in particular.

In light of this reason, civil marriage usually involves couples who are far removed from observing *mitzvot* and who are not scrupulous about observance of the *halakhot* of *niddah*. In the present case, the couple is not Torah-observant generally, and they do not keep the *halakhot* of *niddah* particularly.

In short, the position of most contemporary authorities is that a civil marriage that the parties undergo freely is not defined as a halakhic marriage, and therefore a *get* is not required, and the children who are born of this union are not deemed *mamzerim* (halakhic bastards).[8]

There is a minority of authorities who subscribe to the view that upon undergoing a civil marriage, a *get mi-safek* (a *get* due to doubt) is required, because of the concern that the public will mistakenly think that "a married woman is leaving the marriage without a *get*".[9] Others rule that a doubt arises regarding the question of whether such a marriage can be considered as *kiddushin* executed by the medium of a deed.[10] According to a third view, undergoing such a wedding ceremony engenders a concern about *kiddushin* being consummated via sexual relations (*bi'ah*).[11] In other words, the *Halakhah* does not recognize civil marriage, but merely is concerned about doubtful *kiddushin* due to external acts in the wedding ceremony or thereafter that create a halakhic doubt. In the framework of the Rabbinate in the Land of Israel, in accordance with the rulings of some of the leading halakhic authorities, the common practice in the rabbinical courts is to obligate those who have married in a civil ceremony to divorce with a *get le'humra* (a *get* for the sake of stringency), due to all the doubts that were raised by the above halakhic sages ("to deal more comprehensively with the matter").[12]

Ha-Sadeh 3:9; *Resp. Ohalei Aharon* 2:50-52; *Mishpetei Uziel* 59; *Resp. Kol Mevasser* 1:22; *Resp. Beit Zevul* 1:27.

7. Talmud Bavli *Ketubot* 72a; *Gittin* 81b.

8. R. Hayyim E. Grodzinski, *Kovetz Iggerot* 30; *Mishpetei Uziel, Even Ha-Ezer* 1:49, 2:54-56; *Resp. Heikhal Yitzhak, Even Ha-Ezer* 2:31; *Resp. Tzitz Eliezer* 1:27, 15:37; *Resp. Har Tzvi, Even Ha-Ezer* 74-76.

9. *Yevamot* 88b; *Resp. Ma'arkhei Lev* 87.

10. *Ma'arkhei Lev*, ibid.; *Levush Mordekhai* 2:40; *Resp. Minhat Yehiel* 3:60.

11. *Resp. Tzofnat Pane'ah*, Dvinsk edition, 1-4; *Perushei Ibra* 1:4.

12. B. Schereschewsky & M. Corinaldi, *Family Law in Israel* (Hebrew), Tel Aviv: 2016, 206.

Rabbi Moshe Feinstein ruled the following: "Even in the case of those who do not care about the *halakhah*, one should nevertheless rule stringently in light of Rabbi Henkin's view."[13]

However, in the Tel Aviv-Jaffo Regional ruling, it states the following:[14]

> There is no room for halakhic recognition of a couple as married if their union was through a civil ceremony only; however, for the sake of dealing more comprehensively with the matter, it is the practice of the rabbinical courts to require a "*get le'humra,*" which effectively means that if one of the couple wishes to divorce, the rabbinical court will call upon the spouses to divorce with a *get le'humra* for the sake of stringency, but if the court should encounter any sort of difficulty, for example, if one of the spouses is not prepared to give or receive a *get*, the court will permit the spouses to marry others even without a *get*.

Similarly, Rabbi Roth states simply:[15]

> And for the sake of good practice, a *get* should be required *ab initio* due to the concern about a married woman [marrying another man], where the *get can* be easily obtained, but when there is even a slight chance of *igun*, this concern need not be considered.

Other decisors agreed with this position.[16] As we noted, four years ago the wife asked for her *get*, and the husband has not responded to our request that he give a *get*, and to date she has not received a *get* from her husband.

On the basis of the above, the *halakhah* is thus according to the majority of lenient authorities and a minority of the stringent authorities in relation to civil marriage. Therefore, Judy is permitted to enter into a halakhic marriage with any Jew, even a *Kohen*, without receiving a *get* from her husband.

---

13. *Resp. Iggerot Moshe, Even Ha-Ezer* 1:74.
14. File 448866/3, Tel-Aviv-Yaffo Regional Rabbinical Court, 4 Av, 5773.
15. *Resp. Kol Mevasser* 2:4.
16. *Resp. Helkat Ya'akov* 119; *Resp. Ezrat Kohen* 38-39; *Perushei Ibra*, supra n. 9; *Resp. Melamed Le-Hoe'il, Even Ha-Ezer* 2; *Resp. Tzitz Eliezer* 9:37; *Resp. Iggerot Moshe, Even Ha-Ezer* 1:75.

E. A MISTAKEN MARRIAGE: A HUSBAND WHO REFUSES TO HAVE CHILDREN

Following the approach of Rashbash and Me'il Tzedakah, I will not render a final decision but state, "if the facts are such as presented to me, the applicable halakhah is thus".[1]

The Facts of the Case

During January 2015, I met with Rachel to hear about her situation. The couple married during the summer of 2007. During the period of their courting, there was no mention by the husband that he didn't want to have children. From the time of the marriage, the wife alleges that from time to time her husband physically abused her.

Upon hearing that she was pregnant in March 2008, he told her for the first time that he didn't want any children and began to hit her in the stomach and these assaults continued. Subsequent to these events, Aharon admitted in writing as well as to a local rabbi that he physically abused his wife. The latter was communicated to me by the local rabbi. His aggressive behavior in part is corroborated by a police report dated September 2009 that states that the police entered his home and found two handguns and a rifle.

In June 2008, she experienced first trimester bleeding and her mother

1. See *Resp. Ha-Rashbash* 230; *Resp. Meil Tzedakah* 253 cited by *Pithei Teshuva Hoshen Mishpat* 7:5.

In other words, this is a question of *halakhic* laws of prohibitions and permissibility (*dinei issur ve-heter*) regarding whether a husband is obligated to give a *get* to his wife. The question may be resolved in front of three rabbis in the absence of the husband. As we know, there is a disagreement as to whether matters of divorce such as obligating or compelling the giving of a *get* may be resolved either in front of a *beit din* of three rabbis, in front of one rabbi, or in the presence of an individual expert Jew. See *Yam shel Shlomo, Bava Kamma* 3:9; *Helkat Mehokeik, Even Ha-Ezer* 17:78; *Taz, Even Ha-Ezer* 17:56; *Biur Ha-Gra Even Ha-Ezer* 17:131; *Ketzot Ha-Hoshen, Hoshen Mishpat* 3:1,2; *Netivot Ha-Mishpat, Hoshen Mishpat* 3:1, *Biurim* 25:4; *Resp. Yehudah* (Gordin), *Even Ha-Ezer* 51:2; *Resp. Ma'aseh Hiyah* 24; *Resp. Hatam Sofer, Orah Hayyim* 51, *Even Ha-Ezer* 2:64-65, *Hoshen Mishpat* 177; *Resp. Avnei Nezer, Even Ha-Ezer* 167:1, 178:2; PDR 6:265, 269; *Hazon Ish, Negaim* 4:9; Beit Hora'ah File 957-61, Jerusalem Beit Din for Civil Matters and Status Clarification, vol. 7, 515; File 448866/3, 7.11.13, Tel Aviv-Yaffo Regional Beit Din; File no. 1086123/1, Be'er Sheva Regional Beit Din, 12.20.18. In the present matter, one rabbi convened to decide an issue of ritual *halakhah*.

told Aharon to take Rachel to a doctor. Aharon was supposed to take her to the hospital because previously he had told her parents and Rachel that he carried health insurance for her. But, in fact he drove Rachel to a clinic. At that time, Rachel told her mother that he had no medical insurance because he didn't want to spend the money and therefore Rachel ended up at a clinic. At that time, Aharon disclosed to her that he was unemployed.

In January 2009, the baby was born prematurely. The baby was placed in the ICU due to bleeding in the brain and problems with his bladder, kidney and liver. He was shredding his blood platelets and required numerous blood transfusions. Rachel submitted medical documentation of the above. Additionally, a doctor submitted a report that stated that the mother underwent a caesarean section due to a deficiency in amniotic fluid along with fetal stress. The placenta revealed old evidence of separation and reattachment that was consistent with a decreased ability to nourish the child. In the doctor's estimation, the infracted placenta, poor fetal growth and subsequent delivery may all trace traced back to the physical abuse she has described. In his words, "although this is not an absolute, it is a strong possibility." I take this physician statement to mean that one can never make absolute determinations regarding such matters.

Four months later, on July 28, 2008, she fled the marital home which was located in Staten Island, NY, due to his abusive behavior and moved back to her parents' home in Los Angeles, California, never to return to Aharon. As of today, though their end of marriage issues have been resolved and a civil divorce was executed (in the summer of 2013), he continues to refuse to give her a *get*. In fact, she requested a *get* well over five years ago. Additionally, she pursued the matter of the *get* with various *battei din* as well as with ORA (The Organization for the Resolution of Agunot), with the net result that a *get* was never forthcoming from Aharon.

Discussion

Given that the couple has been separated for over seven years and a civil divorce was executed over two years ago, Aharon is obligated to give a *get*.[2] Based upon information submitted at the hearing, there are no prospects for marital reconciliation (*shalom bayit*).[3]

2. *Resp. Hayyim Ve-Shalom* 2:112; *Resp. Iggerot Moshe, Yoreh Deah* 4:15 (2).
3. File no. 4827-21-2, Supreme Rabbinical Court, July 3, 2005 (R. Daichovsky's

In the time of the Talmud or in subsequent periods of Jewish history where there was the legal as well as halakhic option to physically coerce a husband to give a *get*, Rachel may have very well received her *get*. However, today, at least in the Diaspora where such an option is legally prohibited (and when the attempts to receive a *get* by other avenues have been unsuccessful),[4] as well-respected authorities have argued and others have observed, we need to explore whether there would be grounds to void a marriage (*bittul kiddushin*) based upon *kiddushei ta'ut*, i.e. an erroneous betrothal (or loosely translated marriage).[5]

Prior to a wife invoking the tool of *kiddushei ta'ut* to void a marriage retroactively and claim there was an error in the creation of the marriage; three preconditions must have been obtained:

1. The husband's defect must be a major one (a *mum gadol*) such as insanity, homosexuality, apostasy, a marital expectation communicated by the prospective husband prior to the marriage which turns out to be a misrepresentation, engaging in criminal behavior such as business fraud, or exposing one's mate to a contagious disease such as syphilis or HIV, a flaw which must have been existent prior to the onset of the marriage.

   One of the rudimentary purposes of halakhic marriage is to sire children. In fact, the first *mitzvah* is to "be fruitful and multiply," and upon entering heaven, one of the three questions that is asked is: "have you engaged in being fruitful and multiplying?" Consequently, it is unsurprising to find various authorities who argue that if a husband is sexually impotent this is a major flaw, and if so, under certain conditions the marriage may be voided.[6] Similarly, if the husband has been castrated or

---

opinion).

Alternatively, the basis for *get* coercion is due to the fact that he acted improperly to her. See *Resp. Ha-Rosh* 35:2; *Beit Shmuel, Shulhan Arukh, Even Ha-Ezer* 117:24; *Piskei Din Rabbanayim* 1:5, 7-8.

4. *Resp. Iggerot Moshe Even Ha-Ezer* 4:52.

5. *Resp. Ein Yitzhak 1, Even Ha-Ezer* 24; *Resp. Dvar Eliyahu* 48; *Resp. Har Tzvi, Even Ha-Ezer* 2:181; *Resp. Iggerot Moshe, Even Ha-Ezer* 1:79.

6. *Resp. Ha-Tashbetz* 1:1 (prohibited voiding the marriage due to the fact that the impotency may have occurred after the onset of the marriage); *Resp. Havot Yair* 221 (in theory); *Resp. Sheilat Yitzhak, Mahadura Tanina* 174; *Ein Yitzhak*, supra n. 5 (*halitzah* case); *Dvar Eliyahu*, supra n. 5; *Resp. Yabia Omer, Even Ha-Ezer* 7, 7 (7); *Resp. Iggerot Moshe, Even Ha-Ezer* 1:79, 4:52; *Resp. Beit Av* 27; *Har Tzvi*, supra n. 5; *Resp. Shevet Me-Yehudah*, 2, Even Ha-Ezer 25.

if the wife's genital organ is closed, under certain conditions the marriage may also be voided.[7]

Therefore, if a husband refuses to engage in procreation, he is undermining one of the bases of entering into a marriage. His situation is analogous to the husband who is sexually impotent. Lest one contends that castration, sexual impotence, sterility and closure of a genital organ entails a physical defect whereas refusing to have children entails the opinion of the husband in our situation, it should be noted that just as Rabbi Feinstein, under certain conditions voided a marriage due to sexual impotency, he equally voided a marriage where a husband did not want to sire children.[8] As *R. Feinstein* emphatically rules:[9]

> To marry a sterile husband is a major shortcoming and women who have the ability to sire children, and *a fortiori* a husband who has the capacity to sire children and refuses to have due to stupidity and cruelty and the like they will not marry him... and this is a major defect... and this is marriage in error (*kiddushei ta'ut*).

In short, refusal to engage in procreation is a "*mum gadol*".

Based upon the cumulative evidence submitted to me, it is clear that Aharon did not want to engage in procreation. The evidence for this conclusion is the following:

a. After Rachel informed him that she was pregnant, he told her for the first time that he did not want children. In fact, a rabbi informed me that he heard that Aharon didn't want children. Months later on August 18, 2008, Aharon admits in an e-mail communication that he didn't want to have a family.
b. Upon finding out about her pregnancy, the frequency of the physical abuse spiraled and Rachel's allegation that Aharon hit her in the stomach is corroborated as per the clinic's report regarding the bleeding which transpired during the first trimester as well as the doctor's assessment that the ensuing

7. Resp. Rabbi A. Gutmacher 2:4-5; *Resp. Rosh Besamim* 340; *Resp. Maharsham* 3:16, 295.

8. *Resp. Iggerot Moshe, Even Ha-Ezer* 1:79, 4:13.

9. *Resp. Iggerot Moshe, Even Ha-Ezer* 4:13.

medical problems of their newborn child was directly linked to his acts of battery.

c. In a copy of a declaration authored by Aharon, in section 39 it states that he requested a paternity test due to the fact that the baby's weight was low for an infant who was born nearly full-term and because Rachel did not allow him to see the baby's birth certificate.

His representation is open to a question. In written documentation dated August 18, 2008, authored by Aharon, he admits taking money out of his wife's assets without prior authorization and lying about bad checks. And in various e-mail exchanges with Rachel during the summer of 2008, Aharon promises that he will repay monies that were taken without authorization.

Given the questionability of the husband's credibility, I was unprepared to accept his rationale(s) for requesting a paternity test. In effect, in my estimation the request for the test was made in the hope that the results would demonstrate that he was not the father of the child, because it is my understanding that he did not want to have a family.

4. The wife must be unaware of the defect prior to the inception of the marriage and only have discovered it after the marriage. On the other hand, if for example, during the marriage a husband commits adultery or contracts Alzheimer's, though both may be characterized as a *mum gadol* that significantly impairs the matrimonial relationship, nevertheless since the conduct or disease respectively occurred after the onset of the marriage, there would be no grounds for a wife's claim that the marriage was consummated in error.

Based upon the cumulative evidence submitted, we find that prior to the marriage Aharon did not communicate to Rachel that he wanted to have children.

5. Finally, upon a wife's awareness of the major latent defect, she must decide to leave the marriage. Regarding this condition, whether she must immediately leave the marriage or not is subject to debate. Though in accordance with certain authorities, upon discovery of a major latent defect one must leave the marriage immediately or refrain from remaining in the marriage for an extended period of time, nonetheless, in pursuance to Rabbi Moshe Feinstein, Dayanim E. Goldschmidt, S. Karelitz,

> Y. Bavliki, and others she may continue to live with him provided she offers a reasonable explanation for remaining in the marriage.[10]

There is a twofold reason why Rachel chose to remain in the marital home during the first trimester of her pregnancy. Firstly, experience has shown that Orthodox Jewish women are generally intent in trying to save their marriage, which in this case was less than one year old. There was a hope that she could persuade her husband to welcome the child and discontinue his abusive behavior. Secondly, as one rabbi told me, after becoming pregnant and given Aharon's behavior, Rachel came to him and requested counsel how to handle the situation. And his response was that she should leave the marital home and get an order of protection against him. Following his advice, she left him and subsequently received an order of protection. In fact, in September 2008, two years into the marriage in an e-mail communication to Aharon, she wrote him that she had no intention to return to "an unsafe environment."

Both these reasons are reasonable explanations for the delay in leaving the marital home and therefore the marriage may be voided in light of the *mum gadol.*

In sum, all three conditions have been met prior to employing the instrument of *kiddushei ta'ut.*

Ruling[11]

I declare that Rachel's marriage to Aharon is void and that she is free to marry any man, even a *Kohen.*

10. In pursuance to some authorities, upon discovery of a major defect in her spouse, if a wife delays her decision to bolt the marriage for a reason(s) which is acceptable to the *beit din,* the marriage may be voided. See *Ein Yitzhak,* supra n. 5; *Resp. Ha-Maharik Ha-Hadashot* 24; *Resp. Iggerot Moshe, Even Ha-Ezer* 3:45 ("*ta'am hagun" or "teirutzim nekhonim"*), 48, 4:113; *Piskei Din Rabbanayim* 1:5, 11-12.

11. Please note that a renowned rabbinic authority approved of this decision provided that one could demonstrate that the husband did not want children.

F. VOIDING A MARRIAGE FOR A DIVORCEE MARRYING A *KOHEN*

Response to a Question

Question

Joseph Kaplan and Hannah Cohen were married on June 10, 2018, in accordance with Orthodox Halakhah and were divorced via the execution of a *get*, a writ of Jewish divorce on October 13, 2021.

Ms. Cohen approached me and requested from me as an expositor of *Halakhah* ("*moreh hora'ah*"[1]) to void her *kiddushin* (loosely translated: marriage) to Joseph Kaplan and permit her to marry a *kohen*. As we know, a *kohen* is proscribed by an explicit prohibition in the Torah to marry a divorcee and the ban is memorialized in the various restatements of *Halakhah*.[2]

Response:

1. Facts of the Case

As attested by Joseph's mother:[3]

---

1. In other words, this is a question of halakhic laws of prohibitions and permissibility (*dinei issur ve-heter*) whether matters of divorce such as voiding a marriage may be resolved by a *beit din* of three, a single rabbi or an individual Jew. See *Yam shel Shlomo, Bava Kamma* 3:9; *Helkat Mehokeik, Even Ha-Ezer* 17:78; *Taz, Even Ha-Ezer* 17:56; *Biur Ha-Gra Even Ha-Ezer* 17:131; *Ketzot Ha-Hoshen* 3:1-2; *Netivot Ha-Mishpat, Hoshen Mishpat* 3:1; *Resp. Ma'aseh Hiyah* 24; *Resp. Hatam Sofer, Even Ha-Ezer* 2:64-65, *Hoshen Mishpat* 177; *Resp. Avnei Nezer Even Ha-Ezer* 167:1; Rabbi Z. N. Goldberg, *Lev Mishpat* 1, 149-150. For additional sources, see this writer's *Rabbinic Authority*, vol. 5, 271, n. 1.

Following the approach of Rashbash and *Me'il Tzedakah,* I will not render a final decision but state "if the facts are such as presented to me, the applicable halakhah is thus." See *Resp. Ha-Rashbash* 230; *Resp. Meil Tzedakah* 253 cited by *Pithei Teshuva Hoshen Mishpat* 7:5.

2. See *Vayikra* 21:7; *Tur Even Ha-Ezer* 13; *Shulhan Arukh Even Ha-Ezer* 6:1; Rema 13:10, 26:1.

3. A signed letter dated October 25, 2021.

> When Joseph was a child, he was more tired than his peers… I tried changing his diet and had him eliminate certain foods in an attempt to curtail his fatigue… Throughout Joseph's time in college, he struggled with fatigue and insomnia… This led him to undergo two separate sleep studies over the span of a few years. Each sleep study did not reveal any significant findings. No medical treatment was recommended. This took place before Hannah came into our lives.
>
> I personally never discussed Joseph's sleeping issues with Hannah before they married…. He had no formal diagnosis and neither of us (Joseph and his mother – AYW) could have imagined that his symptoms would have spiraled the way they did.
>
> The first time that Joseph obtained a formal diagnosis was when he was married to Hannah… His official diagnosis was upper airway resistance syndrome, a sleep breathing disorder.

Prior to the marriage Hannah wasn't told by Joseph or a third party about his symptoms of suffering from exhaustion, insomnia and difficulty in staying awake, nor were the symptoms obvious to her, since her premarital interaction with Joseph was in a few hour increments. Upon the inception of their marriage, Hannah became aware that he rarely slept, and if he slept it was irregular and in an erratic fashion, and she heard his breathing obstructions during the time of his sleeping. After the formal diagnosis of his condition in late 2016 by Dr. Steven Park, a physician specializing in the upper airway diagnosis (hereafter: UARS),[4] the disorder was addressed in the following medical and dental fashion performed between 2017 and 2019:[5]

First year of marriage
frenotomy – multiple surgeries
turbinectomy – surgery
tonsillectomy – surgery
epiglottectomy – surgery
palate surgery – multiple surgeries

4. As per the medical report dated November 24, 2020.

5. Information of his medical history was corroborated by documentation. His first surgery was on November 3, 2016, four months after their marriage, and the balance of surgeries were between 2017-2019.

Second year of marriage
palate surgery – multiple surgeries
frenotomy – multiple surgeries
DNA (dental) appliance
ALF (dental) appliance
AGGA (dental) appliance

Third year of marriage
palate surgery – multiple surgeries
double jaw surgery – surgery
tracheostomy – surgery

The foregoing shows that some of the surgeries such as frenotomy and palate were performed multiple times in the span of three years.

In addition to the performance of various surgeries during the third year of marriage, Joseph was allegedly taking medications against anxiety, sleeping medication, stimulants to remain awake and antidepressants, as well as receiving myofunctional therapy.

In the couple's discussion on November 3, 2021, with their attorney, Hannah and Joseph agreed that their marriage ended as a result of Joseph's medical complications and the stress placed upon them as a couple.[6] One of the stresses was that Joseph barely worked during the marriage. His first job began in January 2018, five months prior to their marriage and he stopped working approximately in January 2019. During 2018, he attempted working part-time, which lasted two to four weeks before he quit. During their marriage, the couple's income was the following:[7]

2016: Hannah – $36,609.15 / Joseph – $27,081.10
2017: Hannah – $49,817.13 / Joseph – $5,617.67
2018: Hannah – $53,774.08 / Joseph – $575.89
2019- Hannah – $71,338.03 / Joseph – no income

Clearly, with the emergence in late 2016 of the diagnosis of his suffering UARS and the commencement of multiple surgeries, Joseph was unable to hold down a job. Finally, from the onset of their marriage, Hannah

6. As per the attorney's letter dated September 7, 2020.
7. As per copies of the yearly form 1099 submitted to the IRS.

observes that there were issues with intimacy which were related to his newly discovered medical disorder.[8]

In a letter dated July 23, 2021, admitting to a deteriorating quality of life which had left him homebound and with no energy, Joseph admitted (*hoda'ah*) he was suffering from: "an extremely severe case of upper airway resistance syndrome/obstructive sleep apnea and chronic fatigue syndrome."

Due to his physical ailments, Joseph felt that his life was not worth living.[9] After failed suicide attempts, Hannah says that Joseph applied for voluntary assisted suicide in Switzerland. On December 22, 2021, Joseph died by means of voluntary assisted suicide, which took place in Switzerland. At the time of his suicide, Joseph was accompanied by his mother.

2. Mistaken *Kiddushin* (*Kiddushei Ta'ut*) due to Upper Airway Resistance Syndrome/ Obstructive Sleep Apnea and Chronic Fatigue Syndrome

Before the mechanism of mistaken *kiddushin* can be implemented in order to invalidate the *kiddushin* and claim that there was a mistake prior to the inception of the marriage, three pre-conditions must be fulfilled:

1. The defect must be serious, e.g., impotence, insanity, homosexuality or exposure of the wife to a dangerous disease such as AIDS.

In a judgment of Israel's Supreme Rabbinical Court, Rabbi Shlomo Daichovsky, the presiding Dayan of the Supreme Rabbinical Court, stated as follows regarding the definition of defects on the part of the husband:[10]

> The matter of defects for which a woman may sue for her *get* is not scripturally ordained law, but reason and logic, as Maimonides writes (Hilk. Ishut 25:2): "These matters are concepts that reason dictates; they are not decrees of the Torah." The whole subject of defects is a matter of human reason, and

8. See https://doctorstevenpark.com/sleep-apnea-basics/upper-airway-resistance-syndrome.

9. As per a signed letter that Joseph sent to his family.

10. App. (Sup. R.C.) 1-22-1510, 7.9.2004.

> the emotional unwillingness of one spouse to endure an intolerable situation on the part of the other spouse. For this reason we have the halakhah of "he assessed and accepted" or "she assessed and accepted." It is possible to say that if the general opinion concerning a particular defect changes, then it may not be said that "she assessed and accepted" on the basis of her past acquiescence...

UARS may produce a significant disease with symptoms, alter quality of life and cardiovascular morbidity. UARS patients may also report insomnia.[11] UARS (upper airway resistance syndrome) is characterized by the occurrence of excessive daytime sleepiness due to the fact the person doesn't experience deep sleep and therefore the body cannot rejuvenate itself and deal with conventional life experiences.

The combination of both UARS and sleep apnea created a situation of a husband who could not function on a daily basis, i.e., was incapable of working during their marriage, experienced chronic fatigue, was severely depressed, feeling faint, having headaches, a decreased sex drive, weaker erections, excessive daytime sleepiness and insomnia. The fact that he committed suicide due to his inability to live under such conditions in effect post-validated Hannah's unwillingness to remain living with such a person and thus she divorced him.

It seem quite clear that his medical condition constituted a major defect.

Though prior to the marriage, Joseph may not have had upper airway resistance syndrome/ obstructive sleep apnea and chronic fatigue syndrome, nevertheless there were symptoms which were precursors to having these disorders, and halakhically these precursors suffice to voiding their marriage based upon *kiddushei taut*.[12] Appended to this *beit din* judgment is Rabbi B. Be'eri's note (see page 80) that in this decision a marriage was voided due to the fact that the husband failed, intentionally or unintentionally, to disclose his *premarital precursors* to schizophrenia. This conclusion was approved by well-known Rabbis H. Izirer, A. Sherman, S. Fischer and H. Zimbalist.

---

11. See Perin et al. Respiration 2012, 83:559-566. Dr. Park confirmed in a conversation with the couple that a symptom of UARS is decreased sex drive and weaker erections. See https://doctorstevenpark.com/sleep-apnea-basics/upper-airway-resistance-syndrome.

12. File no. 8701275, Haifa Regional Beit Din, December 29, 2014.

2. The wife must have been unaware of the defect prior to the inception of the marriage

Rabbi Yitzhak Elhanan Spektor states as follows:[13]

> And therefore, the halakhah is that where she did not know at the time of the marriage that he has a major defect, the marriage is certainly invalidated as a result of the defect, in the same way that any transaction involving defective property is a nullity (Ketubot 73b). The same halakhah applies to defects in the wife...

The wife must have been unaware of the defect prior to the inception of the marriage and it must have only been discovered after the marriage commenced. On the other hand, if for example, during the marriage it emerged that Joseph was suffering from UARS and sleep apnea, though such conditions may be characterized as a major flaw that significantly impairs the marital relationship, nevertheless since the condition(s) occurred after the onset of the marriage, there would be no grounds for a wife's claim that the marriage was consummated in error.[14]

Based upon the foregoing, Joseph's mother claims that her daughter-in-law was unaware of his condition prior to the marriage. And Hannah only became aware of the disorder after the onset of the marriage. And in fact, the first time there was a diagnosis given was a few months after the marriage.

The emerging question is whether one can trust Hannah and her mother-in-law that Hannah was unaware of the existence of the defect prior to the inception of the marriage? Assuming there are grounds to void the marriage and therefore she is not construed as a married woman (*eishet ish*), will we trust her as "one witness is trustworthy regarding prohibitions" in a matter of licentiousness (*davar she'be'ervah*) to argue that she only became aware of her husband's condition after the onset of the marriage? Seemingly, she is not to be trusted even if she is not viewed as a married woman.[15] Relying upon some authorities, Rabbi

13. *Resp. Ein Yitzhak, Even Ha-Ezer* 24:6:38.

14. See also, *Resp. Ahiezer* 3:19.

15. Rashi, *Yevamot* 88; *Hiddushei ha-Ramban, Gittin* 2b; *Hiddushei ha-Rashba,* ibid.

Osher Weiss concludes that she is believed in a matter of licentiousness even if she is not viewed as a married woman.[16]

3. A wife's delay in separating from her husband

Given that the diagnosis of Joseph's condition was given towards the end of 2018 and the couple got divorced in October 2021, the outstanding question remains that it seems she became reconciled to the situation (*savra ve'kibla*) despite the existence of the major defect, and therefore she cannot claim that her marriage was a mistaken marriage (*kiddushei ta'ut*).

In response to this: firstly, the existence of a major flaw in the husband is not subject to the rule, "she considered and accepted" (*savra ve'kibla*).[17] Secondly, though according to numerous authorities one must leave her husband immediately upon discovering the defect, there are some arbiters who contend that if one has a reasonable explanation(s) for delaying her departure,[18] there can still be grounds to void the marriage.[19]

Clearly, upon discovering his disorders in late 2018, and despite the endless number of surgeries during the span of three years, Hannah hoped that the matter would be addressed. In response to her husband's statement of hopelessness concerning recovery, a friend heard Hannah say to Joseph: "Don't say that, there's another surgery coming up and the doctor said that this one is very promising and will fix it."

However, after having cared for him full-time during the three years of marriage (while trying to work at the same time), and after the performance of invasive surgery in 2019 which failed to assist him, Hannah realized that there were no prospects for recovery and therefore she got divorced due to the situation, as memorialized in the attorney's letter.[20] Upon the divorce, Joseph moved in with his mother who cared for him.

16. *Tosafot Gittin* 2b; *Resp. Maharik, shoresh* 72; *Resp. R. Akiva Eiger* 176; *Resp. Nodah Be-Yehudah, Mahadura Kamma Even Ha-Ezer* 54; *Resp. Ohr Sameach* 1; *Resp. Ahiezer Even Ha-Ezer* 6; *Resp. Minhat Asher* 1:73 [3].

17. *Beit Shmuel, Even Ha-Ezer* 39:9; *Hamiknah, Kuntres Aharon* 39; *Resp. Iggerot Moshe Even Ha-Ezer* 3:45.

18. *Tur* and *Beit Yosef, Even Ha-Ezer* 154; *Beit Shmuel Even Ha-Ezer* 39:17; *Helkat Mehokeik, Even Ha-Ezer*, ad. locum. 9; *Resp. Ha-Maharik, shoresh* 24; *Resp. R. Akiva Eiger, Mahadurah Tinyana* 57.

19. *Iggerot Moshe*, supra n. 17; *Tiv Kiddushin* 39:12; *Resp. Minhat Asher* 1:73 (5), *Piskei Din Rabbanayim* 1:5, 11.

20. Text supra accompanying n. 4.

Additionally, it should be noted in this context that Pulmonary and Sleep Specialists in Baltimore, MD. write:[21]

> In the middle of that spectrum exists several moderately harmful sleep disorders, which will certainly worsen over time if they are not treated. Upper airway resistance syndrome (UARS) is one such sleep disorder that begins simply, but can become especially dangerous over time if it is not addressed.

As Rabbi Meir Arik and others state, some diseases intensify over time and therefore the rule of "she considered and accepted" is inapplicable.[22]

3. In the Wake of a Voided Marriage, After a Divorce, is the Divorcee Permitted to Marry a *Kohen*?

Shulhan Arukh rules:[23]

> If a *kohen* marries a divorcee, even if she is a *safek gerushah* (there is a halakhic doubt whether she is a divorcee), he must leave her... and even *rei'ah ha-get* (the fragrance of the *get*) invalidates her to a *kohen*...

Rema adds:[24]

> Even if she became divorced only because of *kol kiddushin* (loosely translated: a rumor of marriage – AYW), even though it is clear that there is no *mamash* (no substance) in the *kiddushin* and the *get* was given only because of a *humra be-alma* (a halakhic stringency), nonetheless she is invalidated to marry a *kohen*).

As we know, a *get* can be executed pursuant to the law (*min ha-din*), which means that a *beit din* will determine the grounds for a divorce, such as a husband's impotency, unwillingness to support his wife, or engaging in spousal abuse—physical or emotional. Alternatively, if a

21. https://pccab.com/services/sleep-disorders/upper-airway-resistance-syndrome/
22. *Resp. Imrei Yosher* 2:119; *Resp. Ha-Mabit* 3:212; *Resp. Divrei Hayyim* 1:51.
23. *Even Ha-Ezer* 6:1.
24. *Even Ha-Ezer* 6:1.

couple has been separated for either a minimum of a year or 18 months and it is clear that we are dealing with "a dead marriage" and there are no hopes for marital reconciliation, according to certain *dayanim* today, such a situation would be grounds to either obligate or coerce a *get*. Aside from mandating a *get min ha-din*, on rabbinic grounds one can direct the issuance of a *get le'humra* (a precautionary stringency). For example, according to most decisors today, in the case of a couple who only underwent a civil marriage, should they dissolve their relationship, a *get le'humra* is required. In short, for Rema, regardless of whether the execution of the *get* is *mei-ikar hadin* or *le'humra*, the divorcee is prohibited from marrying a *kohen* due to the Talmudic label of "*rei'ah ha-get*". And in fact, there are numerous *Poskim* (authorities) who would endorse Rema's opinion and argue that one cannot nullify a *kol kiddushin*.[25]

The source reference in Rema's ruling is a responsum of the Rashba. Though the source reference was not authored by Rema, nonetheless, authorities assume that Rema's position is based upon this responsum. As such, we will refrain from understanding Rema's view independently of Rashba's opinion.

The following question was posed to Rashba. Reuven arranged for a *shidduch* (a marital engagement) for his daughter and subsequently the *shidduch* failed to materialize. Upon the voiding of the *shidduch*, they said to the father of the prospective bride that the prospective groom ought to give a *get* to the woman, lest the public assume that she was betrothed to him. The groom was halakhically ignorant and heeded their advice and gave a *get* to the woman, despite there having been no rumor that she was in fact betrothed to him. Subsequently, Reuven wanted to marry off his daughter to a *kohen* and the question arose whether such an action is permissible. In such a situation, Rashba, a dominant authority in this matter, rules that the notion of "*rei'ah ha-get*" was applicable and therefore prohibited the *shidduch*.[26]

However, some decisors astutely note that a subsequent responsum penned by Rashba[27] contradicts the above responsum.[28] The question posed in this responsum involved Reuven who betrothed the daughter of a Jew. Subsequently, Shimon cast aspersions upon this betrothal by

25. *Resp. Hut Ha-Meshullash, Tur Bet* 12; *Helkat Mehokeik, SA Even Ha-Ezer* 47:11; *Beit Shmuel*, ad. locum 14; *Resp. Divrei Rivot* 5; *Resp. Pnei Moshe* 2:130.

26. *Resp. Ha-Rashba* 1:550.

27. *Resp. Ha-Rashb*a 4:304.

28. *Beit Yosef, Tur Even Ha-Ezer* 13; *Helkat Mehokeik, Shulhan Arukh Even Ha-Ezer* 6:2, *Beit Shmuel*, ad. locum., *Knesset Ha-Gedolah Even Ha-Ezer* 6:5, 10:2; *Resp. Lehem Rav* 33.

arguing that his son was already betrothed to the woman. The father of the betrothed woman and the woman denied the veracity of Shimon's words. Though Rashba didn't fear that the betrothal transpired, nevertheless he mandated the giving of the *get* because he feared that Shimon's animosity to Reuven may result in the hiring of witnesses who would falsely testify that the betrothal took place. In other words, since the *get* was executed for no reason, she doesn't have to wait 3 months before marrying somebody else. Given that the *get* was given due to a halakhic stringency, the divorcee wasn't prohibited to a *kohen*. In short, there is a contradiction in Rashba's responsa whether the prohibition for a divorcee to marry a *kohen* is in place when dealing with a halakhic stringency regarding the giving of the *get*.

In light of the contradiction in Rashba's responsa, many decisors have determined that the ruling cited by Rema reflects his earlier position, whereas Beit Yosef is citing his later view.[29] The proof given for this conclusion is based upon a read of the later responsum, where Rashba counters the proofs that he had brought to buttress his decision in the earlier responsum. In effect, Rashba, similar to earlier arbiters such as Rambam and Rosh, change their mind and both the original position and their final decision are memorialized in their collection of rulings. The net result is that for Rashba, in a situation where it is factually clear that the act of betrothal never transpired and a *get* was executed, the divorcee is permitted to marry a *kohen*.

Alternatively, one may argue that there is no contradiction in the Rashba's decisions. In the earlier decision of Rashba which serves as the basis for Rema's position, we are dealing with a situation where the wife did not deny that the betrothal transpired. Consequently, we construe her silence as an admission that the betrothal occurred, and the *get* is given due to the fact that there is a doubt regarding the betrothal. Under such circumstances, we execute a *get* based on halakhic stringency, and therefore we are concerned about "the fragrance of the *get*," and the divorcee is prohibited to marry a *kohen*. On the other hand, in the Rashba's subsequent judgment, where the act of betrothal is denied by the woman and nevertheless, the *get* was executed due to a halakhic stringency, there is no reason to prohibit her from marrying a *kohen*.[30]

29. *Resp. Yabia Omer*, 6 *Even Ha-Ezer* 1 (4); *Resp. Sha'arei Tzion* 1, *Even Ha-Ezer* 2 (20); *Resp. Tzitz Eliezer* 4:19; *Resp. Shema Shlomo*, 1, *Even Ha-Ezer* 2; *Resp. Shemesh U-Magen*, 3 *Even Ha-Ezer* 13.

30. See Dayan R. A. Yanai, "A divorcee's who is civilly married requests to marry a *kohen*" (Hebrew), *Heker Ha-Mishpat*, vol. 1, 75, 81-83, 5781.

Based upon the foregoing, in the wake of voiding a marriage (*bittul kiddushin*) after the execution of a *get*, are there grounds for the divorcee to marry a *kohen*? In pursuance to Rema's posture and his few adherents,[31] regardless of whether the execution of *get* is *min hadin*[32] or is a *get le'humra* (a halakhic stringency) and whether or not we are dealing with a definitive act of *kiddushin*, we are dealing with *rei'ah ha-get* (the fragrance of the *get*) and consequently under all these circumstances, the divorcee is prohibited from marrying a *kohen*. However, as *Rabbi Refael A. Kobo* aptly notes:[33]

> And numerous authorities have disagreed with them... and also Rashba in another responsum... contradicts himself...

Finally, the Lehem Mishneh observes that since the second responsum of Rashba[34] and Rosh's ruling[35] is absent from Shulhan Arukh, this demonstrates that Rabbi Yosef Karo is relying upon the more lenient responsum of Rashba which he cites in his Beit Yosef![36] In short, in this response to Hannah's question, I am concurring with Rashba's second responsum (a position supported by other early sources) and as we will demonstrate, one that also emerges from contemporary authorities, who contend that *rei'ah ha-get* is inapplicable in a situation where the act of betrothal (*kiddushin*) never transpired properly. As such, we need to address some of the situations where the act of betrothal did not halakhically occur and thus failed to establish a valid halakhic marriage and see whether decisors permitted the divorcee to marry a *kohen*.

However, it seems that the implementation of "*kiddushei ta'ut*" after a *get* was executed runs afoul of a ruling by Rabbi Mordechai Eliyahu. In a case that came before him, a couple married, and after the onset of the marriage she discovered that he was mentally dysfunctional and later divorced him. Subsequently, she married a *kohen* civilly and then married him in accordance with *Halakhah* based upon rabbinic advice that the

31. Mordekhai, *Kiddushin* 531 in the name of Tosafot Rabbi Eliezar Me-Beham; *Resp. Ha-Rosh* 35:14, *Tur Even Ha-Ezer* 48.

32. According to the rulings of *Shulhan Arukh Even Ha-Ezer* 154 or *Resp. Iggerot Moshe Yoreh Deah* 4:15.

33. *Resp. Sha'ar Asher* 1:30. See also, *Resp. Shemesh U-Magen* 3, *Even Ha-Ezer* 14 in the name of Rabbi O. Yosef.

34. *Resp. Ha-Rashba* 4:560.

35. Rosh, supra n. 31.

36. *Resp. Lehem Rav* 33; *Resp. Yabia Omer*, 6, *Even Ha-Ezer* 1:4; *Shemesh U-Magen*, supra n. 33 in the name of Rabbi O. Yosef.

first marriage was a case of "*kiddushei ta'ut.*" Addressing this case, Rabbi Eliyahu was unwilling to invoke this technique to void their marriage due to the fact that he was unsure whether the *get* was executed *min ha-din* or as a *get le'humra.*[37] In our situation, the *beit din* executed a *get* for the Kaplans and did not address whether the *get* ought to be executed *min ha-din* or as a *get le'humra.*[38]

Clearly, our review of responsa did not reveal to us why the *get* was given in a particular case, and nevertheless the various decisors determined *post facto* that the execution of the *get* was rabbinically mandated as a *humra* (a stringency), and consequently there were grounds to permit the divorcee to marry the *kohen*. For example, one case involved a *kohen* who divorced his wife and afterwards returned to engage in conjugal relations, with children having been sired from that relationship after the divorce. Subsequently, they became *ba'alei teshuva,* but it was discovered that one of the witnesses was a public transgressor of Shabbat. So the question posed to Dayan Rabbi Boyaron was whether they could remarry in accordance with *Halakhah*? Without even addressing the matter of the children, the *get* was identified as a *get le-humra* due to the witness disqualification and therefore the rule of "*rei'ah ha-get*" is inapplicable, and consequently he is allowed to remarry his former wife.[39]

Moreover, addressing the case of a couple who separated and originally were married by a Reform rabbi, Rabbi Amar ruled that the divorcee would be permitted to marry a *kohen.* Notwithstanding Rabbi Feinstein's view that the act of *kiddushin* never transpired at a wedding ceremony which is officiated by a Reform rabbi, for those decisors who rule that a *get le'humra* is required, he concludes that the divorcee may marry a *kohen.*[40] In another case, there was a *kol kiddushin* (but clearly there was no basis for claiming that the *kiddushin* ever happened), a *get* was executed and subsequently a *kohen* married her and they had children. The question posed to Rabbi Waldenberg was whether the *kohen*

37. *Resp. Ma'amar Mordekhai* 2, *Even Ha-Ezer* 1.

38. In fact, R. O. Yosef approved of invoking *kiddushei ta'ut* after a *get* was executed. As such, the *get* was executed as a matter of stringency (*get le'humra*). See *Kovetz Ha-Torani Beit Hillel,* Memorial Volume for R. O. Yosef, Adar 2 5774, 94.

In other words, should it be clear that the *get* was executed due to stringency factors (*get le'humra*), Halakhah allows the marriage to be voided should the proper halakhic conditions have been obtained. See *Resp. Maharshal* 25; *Resp. Nediv Lev, Even Ha-Ezer* 24; *Resp. Moshe Ha'Ish Even Ha-Ezer* 6; *Resp. Yabia Omer* 2, *Even Ha-Ezer* 5.

39. *Resp. Sha'arei Tzion, Even Ha-Ezer* 1:2, 2:9, 12.

40. *Resp. Shema Shlomo, Even Ha-Ezer* 1:2

could remain married to his wife or must he divorce her? Here again, the ruling was that he may remain married to her, and the same line of reasoning as advanced by Rabbis Amar and Boyaron was argued by Rabbi Waldenberg.[41] A similar fact pattern to the one that we found by Rabbi Waldenberg was equally posed by Rabbi Pinchas Zevichi, and he arrived at the identical conclusion.[42]

Finally, notwithstanding the majority of authorities who contend that a civil marriage does not constitute a halakhic marriage, the Rogatchover, Ma'arkhei Lev, *Melamed le-Ho'il,* Rabbi Henkin, Hazon Ish, and Rabbi Elyashiv mandate the execution of a *get le-humra.* The question emerges: if a couple who was only civilly married and a *get le-humra* was issued, can that divorcee marry a *kohen*? On the one hand, adopting Rema's view, *Menahem Meishiv* and Rabbi Dovid Cohen ruled that the divorcee would be proscribed from marrying a *kohen.*[43] On the other hand, relying upon the Rashba's ruling cited by Beit Yosef and rejecting Rema's position, Rabbi Ya'akov Breisch ruled that she can marry a *kohen.*[44] And Rabbi O. Yosef as well as others adopt the same argumentation and concur with Rabbi Breisch.[45]

4. The Contemporary Status of *Kohanim*

As a supporting argument (a *senif*), there are authorities who claim that the genealogical claims of contemporary kohanim are uncorroborated and therefore remain in doubt.[46]

As such, the prohibition of divorcee to marry a *kohen* is inapplicable.

Based upon the foregoing, in the wake of her marriage being in error (*kiddushei taut*), Hannah is permitted to marry a *kohen.*

41. *Resp. Tzitz Eliezer* 4:19.

42. *Resp. Ateret Paz, Even Ha-Ezer* 3:3.

43. *Resp. Menahem Meishiv* 34; Rabbi David Cohen, *Shurat Ha-Din,* vol. 8, 259.

44. *Resp. Helkat Ya'akov Even Ha-Ezer* 33

45. *Resp. Yabia Omer,* 6, *Even Ha-Ezer* 1; *Ateret Paz,* supra n. 42; *Shema Shlomo,* supra n. 40.

46. *Resp. Maharashdam Even Ha-Ezer* 235; *Yam shel Shlomo, Bava Kamma* 5:35; *Resp. Mahari Weil 193; Resp. Beit Ephraim, Orah Hayim* 6; *Zevah Todah, Zevahim,* chapter 13; *Pithei Teshuva Even Ha-Ezer* 7:2 in the name of Rivash; *Resp. Shevet Ha-Levi* 10:224-225; *Resp. Yabia Omer,* 11, *Even Ha-Ezer* 25-27, 29, 30, 33-34.

G. "A DEAD MARRIAGE" AND ITS HALAKHIC AND LEGAL AFTERMATH

Facts of the Case

Abraham and Esther were married on December 23, 2008, according to Orthodox Jewish law. Since October 20, 2021, the couple has been separated.

In June 2022, we summoned Abraham to appear in *beit din*. We convened two hearings with the couple, one on September 7, 2022, and a second on September 12, 2022. To date, Esther is requesting her *get* while Abraham wants to reconcile with Esther.

Discussion

Based upon the information and evidence submitted at the two hearings, there are no prospects for marital reconciliation *(shalom bayit)*. Given that the couple has been separated for more than a year, Abraham is obligated to give a *get* to Esther.[1]

Rabbi Yeruham, a renowned authority rules the following:[2]

> And my teacher Avraham ben Ashmael writes that it seems to him that the wife who says she does not find her husband pleasing... and the husband says that he likewise does not find her pleasing, but does not want to give a *get*... we wait twelve

1. In order to execute to arrange a *get*, the couple must be living in separate homes or there should be a separate entrance to the living quarters where each quarter leads to a separate yard. See *Resp. Ha-Rashba* 1:209; *Shulhan Arukh, Even Ha-Ezer* 119:4; *Taz, Even Ha-Ezer* 157:3; *Bi'ur Ha-Gra Even Ha-Ezer* 157:21; *Get Pashut* 41; *Resp. Ateret Devorah* 3:31, 63.

Whether a couple may live together when a *get* is being obligated by a *beit din* is a subject to debate. See R. Herzog, *Pesakim Ve-Ketavim* 7; 139, File no. 681773/5, Jerusalem Regional Beit Din, 2 Tammuz 5779; File. no. 1363653/2, Jerusalem Regional Beit Din, 30 Marheshvan 5783; R. Ushinski, *Orot Mishpat* 4:272.

2. *Sefer Meisharim, helek* 8, *netiv* 23. For earlier discussion of R. Yeruham's view, see S. Zilberberg and A. Radzyner, "The Revival of the Cause of 'Death of Marriage': The View of Rabbeinu Yeruham in the Rabbinical Court" (Hebrew), 49 *Mishpatim* 113, 5779; this writer's *Rabbinic Authority*, vol. 2, 200-223.

> months regarding the *get*, because possibly she will reconcile. After the year, we force him to divorce her...

As noted by *Israeli Dayan Uriel Lavi*,[3]

> There is no difference which spouse is guilty and therefore responsible for the separation and who is responsible for the present situation that the couple is separated...

As observed by the late *dayan* of Israel's Supreme Rabbinical Court, *Rabbi H. Shlomo Sha'anan*:[4]

> We have not found authorities who disagreed with R. Yeruham.

As stated by *Dayan Refael ben Shimon*:[5]

> Clearly here we have the logic of R. Yeruham that we are avoiding chaining the woman (*igun*).

And in our case, we are trying to equally avoid *igun*. Numerous rabbinical courts in contemporary times have endorsed R. Yeruham's opinion.[6]

Based upon the foregoing, we obligate Abraham to give a *get* immediately and unconditionally.[7]

---

3. File no. 862233/1, Tiberias Regional Rabbinical Court, January 8, 2013.
4. Piskei Din Rabbanayim (hereinafter: PDR) 14:183, 193.
5. File no. 920384/1, Netanya Regional Rabbinical Court, June 18, 2015.
6. PDR 6:13, 8:323, 11:95, 255, 13:264, 14:183, 19:57; *Iyunim Be-Mishpat, Even Ha-Ezer* 237–240; File no. 7479-21-1, Tel Aviv-Jaffa Regional Beit Din, November 18, 2007; File no. 26259-21-2, Tiberias Regional Beit Din, March 17, 2008; File no. 854682-1, Supreme Beit Din, Ploni v. Plonit, June 28, 2012; File no. 587739-6, Haifa Regional Beit Din, Plonit v. Ploni. July 17, 2012.
7. Once a *beit din* obligates the giving of a *get*, no preconditions can be advanced by the husband prior to executing the *get*. See *Resp. Ha-Rashba* 4:156; *Shulhan Arukh, Even Ha-Ezer* 143:21.

H. MAY A FATHER DISINHERIT ONE OF HIS SONS?

Response to a Question*

A couple was married in accordance to Orthodox Jewish law. Decades later, the father, who was suffering from dementia vascular, decided to divide equally his estate among two of his three sons and a non-Torah heir, while the third son would receive nothing.

The threshold question to be posed is what ought to be the halakhic result if the above division and disinheritance have transpired prior to his contracting this debilitating mental illness?

1. What is the Halakhah when the testamentary disposition of assets was written and executed prior to contracting this debilitating disease?

Based upon the possibility that the testamentary disposition of assets was written and executed prior to suffering from dementia, there emerge various questions. Firstly, was the gifting which was executed prior to the father's demise halakhically appropriate? Secondly, in the father's testamentary disposition, was it halakhically proper to disinherit one of his sons and give the money to a non-Torah heir? In his testamentary disposition, was it proper for the father to refrain from transferring assets to one of his sons? Finally, ought the non-Torah heir return his distribution in order to remove the sin from the father who transferred the assets?

The Torah's Order of Hereditary Succession entails the prohibition (the issur of) disinheriting the halakhic heirs (avurei ahsanta) and "there is no undertaking of a symbolic obligation" (a kinyan after death)

Inheritance occurs by itself. Upon a person's demise, human ownership

1. Following the approach of Rashbash and *Me'il Tzedakah*, I will not render a final decision but state: "if the facts are such as presented to me, the applicable halakhah is thus." See *Resp. Ha-Rashbash* 230; *Resp. Me'il Tzedakah* 253 cited by *Pithei Teshuvah Hoshen Mishpat* 7:5.

ceases and halakhic succession law determines who will inherit his estate. As Rabbeinu Gershom notes, the heir automatically receives his ancestor's inheritance without anyone giving it to him.[1] There is no transfer of assets between the testator and his heirs via the implementation of a *kinyan*, i.e., a symbolic act of transfer such as an exchange of money or the writing of a halakhic-legal document (a *shtar*). As the Talmud states,[2] and as it is restated in the *Shulhan Arukh*:[3]

> There is no halakhically bona fide document (a *shtar*) after death.

The signing of a *shtar* is an example of a *kinyan* that may serve as a vehicle to transfer assets, provided that the person is alive. Upon death, the person is incapable of transferring assets, or as the rabbinical authorities (the *Poskim*) state:[4]

> There is no undertaking of a symbolic obligation of acquisition (a *kinyan*) after death.

In the words of the late *Dayan Grunfeld* of London, England:[5]

> ... In Jewish law we have the rules... There is no gift after death and... There is no effective document after death... The logical consequence of this is that any money in the hands of a beneficiary of a will under the law of the land, which as far as Jewish religious law is concerned, belongs to a different person, namely, the proper heir in accordance with the Jewish law of inheritance, has to be returned to that heir.

Unlike secular law, which permits a transfer of assets upon death, according to Halakhah, the moment of death preempts this possibility. The halakhic system, rather than transferring the property via the effectuation of a *kinyan*, creates the transfer of an inheritance. Pursuant to

---

1. Talmud Bavli *Bava Batra* 141b.
2. Talmud Bavli *Ketubot* 55b; *Bava Batra* 152a. However, a deceased retains ownership of his estate. For further discussion, see J. David Bleich, "*Do the Deceased Enjoy Property Rights?*" 47 *Tradition* 71, 82–88 (2014).
3. *Hoshen Mishpat* 250:9.
4. Ibid., 250:17.
5. Dayan I. Grunfeld, *The Jewish Law of Inheritance*, New York: Feldheim, 1987, 53-55.

the Mishnah,[6] upon demise of the decedent, i.e., the father, the order of succession is as follows: (1) the sons, (2) their descendants, (3) the daughters, (4) their descendants, (5) the father, (6) the brothers, (7) their descendants, (8) the sisters, (9) their descendants, (10) the grandfather, (11) the brothers of the father, (12) their descendants, (13) the sisters of the father, (14) their descendants, etc.

After presenting the halakhot of succession, the Torah concludes by stating that the order of hereditary succession is a statute of judgment (*hukat mishpat*). The description of the Jewish law of inheritance as a law whose rationale is unknown(a *hok*) implies, among other things, that these halakhot, despite dealing with monetary matters, are immutable.[7] Generally speaking, Halakhah allows individuals to determine their own monetary relationships, provided that the arrangement complies with a proper form, i.e., *kinyan*, and is not violative of any prohibitions, such as theft or the interdict against taking interest, known as *ribbit*.[8]

One of the exceptions to this rule is the laws of inheritance. As *Maimonides* states:[9]

> A man cannot cause his estate to descend to someone who is not potentially his heir; nor can he deprive the heir of the inheritance even though this is a money matter. For it says... "And it shall be for the children of Israel a statute of judgment".... That means, this statute cannot be altered and no stipulation can affect it.

6. Talmud Bavli *Bava Batra* 88b. And a son(s) rather than a daughter(s) inherits the estate. See *Bava Batra* 108a, 110b–111a.

7. *Mishneh Torah, Hilk. Ishut* 12:9; *Hilk. Nahalot* 6:1; R. *Yisrael Moshe Hazan, Nahala Le-Yisrael*, Vienna, 1851, 49.

8. *Kiddushin* 19b; *Beit Yosef, Tur, Hoshen Mishpat* 305:4; *Shulhan Arukh, Even Ha-Ezer* 38:5, *Hoshen Mishpat* 291:17, 305:4; *Rema, Hoshen Mishpat* 344:1.

9. *Mishneh Torah, Hilk. Nahalot* 6:1. See *Piskei Ha-Rosh, Bava Batra* 5:3; *Resp. Maharam of Rothenberg*, Prague ed., 998; *Resp. Ha-Maharit, Hoshen Mishpat* 6; *Resp. Maharashdam Hoshen Mishpat* 336; *Resp. Maharsham* 7:12; *Resp. R. Akiva Eiger, Mahadura Tinyana* 83; *Resp. Maharshach* 2:164; *Resp. Zera Emet* 2:110; *Resp. Tzemah Tzedek, Hoshen Mishpat* 42.

Even if a little has been retained by the Torah heir(s), such behavior is prohibited. See *Maharam of Rothenberg*, op. cit.; *Resp. Hatam Sofer, Hoshen Mishpat* 151; *Arukh Ha-Shulhan Hoshen Mishpat* 282:2. Cf. others who sanction leaving a portion for the Torah heir(s). See *Resp. Ha-Tashbetz* 3:147; *Resp. Ha-Rivash* 168; *Resp. Maharshal* 49; *Taz, Even Ha-Ezer* 113:3; *Birkei Yosef, Yoreh Deah* 249,15; *Resp. Iggerot Moshe, Hoshen Mishpat* 2:49.

In other words, stipulating that assets are to be distributed to a non-halakhic heir falls in the category of stipulating against what is stated in the Torah, his condition is nullified (*matneh al ma shekatuv ba-Torah tena'o batel*),[10] and therefore a testator is not empowered to stipulate that a non-Torah heir should inherit him,[11] and it is prohibited to execute such an arrangement.[12] Moreover, according to many *arbiters*, the Torah

---

10. *Kiddushin*, supra n. 8. Whereas Maimonides argues that an estate distribution at variance with Halakhah is a violation of "*hukat mishpat*," others contend that the execution of such planning presumes that the assets of the testator during his lifetime can be designated as his inheritance (*yerusha*). But, in fact, during the testator's lifetime these are his assets. It is only upon the testator's demise that Halakhah determines that these assets are now designated as *yerusha*, are no longer in the testator's possession, and automatically the Torah heirs receive their rightful distribution. See *Hiddushei Ha-Rashba*, *Bava Batra* 113b. Alternatively, since the *yerusha* belongs to the heir only upon the testator's demise, during his lifetime he cannot execute an arrangement at variance with the Torah order of *yerusha*. See *Ran* on *Rif*, *Ketubot* 41a.

Though *Shulhan Arukh*, *Hoshen Mishpat* 282:1 states that diverting a share of the estate to a non-Torah heir is characterized as a transaction that merely does "not find pleasure in the eyes of scholars," decisors construe such conduct as a formal prohibition. See *Resp. Ha-Rosh* 85:3; *Resp. Maharam Mi-Padua* 60; *Resp. Maharbil* 3:93; *Resp. Maharashdam*, *Hoshen Mishpat* 336; *Resp. Ranah* 1:118. Cf. *Ha-Tashbetz* 2:177; *Sma*, *Hoshen Mishpat* 366:3.

11. *Resp. Ha-Ridvaz* 1:543; *Resp. Mishpetei Shmuel* 103; *Resp. Maharashdam*, *Even Ha-Ezer* 110, *Hoshen Mishpat* 304; File no. 8820-41-1, Supreme Beit Din, *Ploni v. Attorney General*, November 23, 2009. Prior to the testator's demise, whether a Torah heir can waive his right to his share is subject to controversy. See *Yad Rama*, *Bava Batra* 126b; *Hiddushei Ha-Ritva*, *Bava Batra* 126b; *Resp. Havot Yair* 50.

12. Talmud Yerushalmi, *Bava Batra* 8:6; *Rashbam*, *Bava Batra* 133b, s.v. *ma*; *Piskei Ha-Rosh* 8:37; *Resp. Ha-Rosh* 85:3; *Maharam Me-Padua*, supra n. 10; *Maharashdam*, supra n. 10; *Ranah*, supra n. 10; *Resp. Hatam Sofer*, *Hoshen Mishpat* 151; *Resp. Maharasham* 7:12; *Resp. Ha-Maharit* 1:29; *Resp. Zera Emet*, 2:110; *Mishpat Ha-Yerusha*, Livorno, 1878, 25a. Cf. others who argue that it is improper rather than a prohibition to engage in disinheritance. See *Beit Ha-Behirah*, *Ketubot* 53a; *Resp Ha-Tashbetz* 2:177; *Shulhan Arukh*, *Hoshen Mishpat* 282:1; *Sma*, ad locum. 2; *Resp. Divrei Malkiel* 1:103; *Resp. Agudat Eizov*, *Hoshen Mishpat* 15.

Nevertheless, according to many authorities, one may distribute assets to non-Torah heirs if a significant share of the estate (fifty percent or twenty percent) is distributed to Torah heirs, or according to others, if even a nominal amount is distributed to Torah heirs. See *Ohr Zarua* 3, *Bava Batra* 127; *Sefer Ha-Ittur*, *Matnat Shekhiv Mera* 59b (p. 118); *Resp. Ha-Tashbetz*, 3:147; *Resp. Ha-Rivash* 168; *Resp. Maharshal* 49; *Taz*, *Shulhan Arukh*, *Even Ha-Ezer* 113:1; *Resp. Maharsham* 7:12 in the name of *Rema*; *Resp. Beit David*, *Hoshen Mishpat* 137; *Hiddushei Ha-Rashash*, *Bava Batra* 133b, s.v. *avurei ahsanta*; *Zerah Emet*, supra n. 12; *Resp. Pnei Moshe* 1:70; *Resp. Avkat Rokhel* 92; *Resp. Ha-Rema* 92 (as understood by *Taz*, *Even Ha-Ezer* 113:1) and *Resp. Shoeil U-Meishiv*, *Mahdura Batra*, 1:1 (in the name of Resp.

heirs are entitled to the entire estate and there is a prohibition to transfer any portion from the Torah heirs to non-Torah heirs.[13] For example, if a father is survived by a son and a daughter, the son, the Torah heir, will inherit his entire estate.

Moreover, should a non-Torah heir retain the assets, it would constitute stealing from the rightful heir.[14] Consequently, a civil will that provides an estate distribution to a non-Torah heir ought to be null and void. Barring any halakhically sanctioned arrangement that allows an estate to be distributed to non-Torah heirs,[15] it should be of no surprise to find that many authorities, both past and present, have invalidated a civil will due to the rule that "there is no gift after death" and because compliance with a secular will may lead to disinheriting a Torah heir.[16]

Ha-Rema 92); *Nahalat Shiva* 21:4, 6; *Resp. Agudat Eizov, Hoshen Mishpat* 15; *Ketzot Ha-Hoshen* 282:2; *Resp. R. Akiva Eiger, Shulhan Arukh, Hoshen Mishpat* 16; *Birkei Yosef, Yoreh Deah* 249:15; *Resp. Iggerot Moshe, Even Ha-Ezer* 1:110, *Hoshen Mishpat* 2:49–50; *Resp. Shevet Ha-Levi* 4:216; Rabbi Z. N. Goldberg, 2 *Shurat Ha-Din* 360, n. 11, 5754.

Pursuant to one opinion, as long as some of the same property that is distributed to a non-Torah heir(s) is given to the Torah heir, there is no violation of *the laws of inheritance.* See *Resp. Pnei Moshe* 1:70.

One exception to the rule is that one cannot withhold a portion of the *firstborn*'s double share. See *Resp. Ha-Geonim,* Harkavi ed. 260; *Shulhan Arukh* and *Rema, Hoshen Mishpat* 281:4. For exceptions to this rule, see this writer's *Rabbinic Authority: The Vision and the Reality* (hereinafter: *Rabbinic Authority*) *vol. 2,* 62.

The fact that the distribution of a portion to a Torah heir and the balance to a non-Torah heir does not contravene a proscription, cannot be taken as proof that a distribution based upon a civil will would be recognized by the above decisors.

13. *Rosh,* supra n. 12; *Piskei Ha-Rosh, Bava Batra* 8:37; *Maharashdam,* supra n. 9; *Resp. Ha-Maharit* 1:29, 2, *Hoshen Mishpat* 5; *Resp. Mahari Ibn Lev* 3:31,93; *Hatam Sofer,* supra n. 12; *Resp. Yashiv Moshe* 2:236.

14. *Resp. Ha-Rivash* 160; *Resp. Hatam Sofer, Hoshen Mishpat* 142; *Resp. Mahari Ha-Levi* (Ettinger) 2:86; *Resp. Sha'ar Asher* 2, *Hoshen Mishpat* 29; *Resp. Maharsham* 2:15; *Shakh, Shulhan Arukh, Hoshen Mishpat* 282:1; *Dinei Mamonot, vol.* 3:208. Cf. this writer's *Rabbinic Authority, vol. 2,* 61, n. 80.

15. For a discussion of various halakhic-sanctioned techniques that allow one to transfer one's possessions to non-Torah heirs, see Judah Dick, "Halacha and the Conventional Last Will & Testament," 3 *The Journal of Halacha and Contemporary Society* 5 (1982); Feivel Cohen, *Kuntres Me-Dor Le-Dor*; *Mattisyahu Schwartz, Mishpat Hatzava'ah,* vols. 1–2, "A Systematic Summary of Disinheriting from Torah Heirs"(Hebrew) 10 *Kovetz Beit Aharon Ve-Yisrael,* vols. 58-61, pp. 86, 90, 92, 95.

For drafting a halakhic will and the validity of a revocable living trust, see this writer's *Rabbinic Authority, vol. 2,* 286–317.

16. *Rosh,* supra n. 12; *Maharashdam,* supra nn. 10–11; *Maharit,* supra n. 13; *Mahari ibn Lev,* supra n. 13; *Resp. Maharam Galante* 13; *Resp. Maharshach* 146; *Resp. Lehem Rav* 219; *Hatam Sofer,* supra n. 12; *Resp. Lev Aryeh* 2:57; *Resp. Heishiv*

Alternatively, given that death divests the testator of title and automatically transfers title to the Torah heirs,[17] can one disinherit or diminish the assets of the Torah heirs during one's lifetime? According to certain authorities, by making a gift in a halakhically effective manner during one's lifetime – *matnat bari*, the gift of a healthy person – one can divest himself of his assets so that upon death, the title to the property will not automatically vest with the Torah heirs.[18]

Based upon the foregoing, was the gifting which was executed prior to the father's demise halakhically appropriate? Clearly, by making a gift in a halakhically effective manner during one's lifetime –the gift of a healthy person (*matnat bari*) – the father can divest himself of his assets.[19] However, the disadvantage in utilizing gifting is that it is effective for transferring property[20] and chattel only.[21] Currency, bank accounts, promissory notes and mortgages cannot be transferred in this fashion.[22] Hence, in our situation, the father could not arrange for gift transfers of his financial instruments.

To argue differently, in his testamentary disposition, was it proper for the father to refrain from transferring assets to one of his sons?

Moshe, Hoshen Mishpat 90, 164; *Resp. Minhat Yitzhak* 2:95, 6:164–165; Cohen, supra n. 14, at 3–7; R. Zalman N. Goldberg, "Inheritances & Wills," (Hebrew) 5, *Ha-Yashar Ve-Ha-Tov* 3, 7 (5768).Cf. this writer's *Rabbinic Authority, vol. 2*, 44-80.

17. *Bava Batra 135b.*

18. *Piskei Ha-Rosh* 85:3; *Tur Hoshen Mishpat* 246; *Knesset Ha-Gedolah, Hoshen Mishpat* 282:10; Netziv, *Ha'amek Sheilah, Parshat Va-Yetzeh, Sheiltah* 21. See this writer's *Rabbinic Authority, vol. 1*, 294-298. Cf. *Resp. Maharashdam, Hoshen Mishpat* 311; *Resp. Hatam Sofer, Hoshen Mishpat* 151; *Resp. Tzemah Tzedek, Hoshen Mishpat* 42; *Resp. Zera Emet* 2:110.

19. *Sefer Ha-Orah, Parshat Hayei Sarah, Parsha* 25; *Knesset Ha-Gedolah, Hoshen Mishpat* 282:10; *Resp. Rema* 92; *Resp. Ha-Rosh* 85:3; *Resp. Hatam Sofer, Even Ha-Ezer* 147, *Hoshen Mishpat* 151; *Peri Ha-Adamah, Mishneh Torah, Hilk. Nahalot* 6:11. See supra text accompanying note 18.

To state it differently, the will exemplifies the acquisition element of a gift with the consequence being that the asset is transferred to the beneficiary during the lifetime of the testator via a *kinyan*, whereas the use of it is only transferred to him after the testator's demise. See *Mishneh Torah, Hilk. Zekhiyah U-Mattanah* 12:13, 15; *Shulhan Arukh Hoshen Mishpat* 257:1, 258:1; *Resp. Maharam Padua* 52; *Resp. Ha-Mabit* 2:160; *Resp. Ginat Veradim Hoshen Mishpat* 5:8.

20. *Sefer Ha-Orah, Parshat Hayei Sarah, Parsha* 25 in the name of the *Levush*; *Resp. Maharit* 2, *Hoshen Mishpat* 6; *Resp. Maharashdam Hoshen Mishpat* 311; *Resp. Maharsham* 7:12.

21. *Piskei Ha-Rosh* 85:3; *Mordekhai, Bava Batra* 620.

22. *Shulhan Arukh, Hoshen Mishpat* 190:1, 195:1, 203:1; *Pithei Hoshen*, vol. 8, 170, n. 2.

Clearly, changing the testator's instructions regarding dividing up the estate resulting in the existence of unequal shares between sibling sons is prohibited.[23] *A fortiori*, transferring the entire portion of one son to another son(s) is prohibited.[24]

On one hand, if has three sons, but none of them are firstborns, the testator may bequeath all of his property to one or to two of them, see Shulhan Arukh Hoshen Mishpat 281:1.

On the other hand, given that it is a prohibition for the father, the testator, to disinherit a Torah heir, ought he retract his share? Interpreting the view of Rabbi Eliyah ben Hayyim, a sixteenth century decisor from Constantinople,[25] R. *Matisyahu Schwartz*, a renowned contemporary authority on halakhic inheritance, states:[26]

> It is preferable that he should live with his prohibition and refrain from changing one's mind and transfer from the non-Torah heir to the Torah heir... even though there exists a prohibition, (the testator) should not retract the transfer due to the absence of negotiating in good faith (*mehusar amana*).

Whether a *mehusar amana* may be coerced to comply with his promise to distribute the estate properly is subject to debate. On one hand, there are authorities who argue that coercion is a remedy.[27] Even if the promise is unenforceable by a *beit din*, nonetheless, the public may proclaim and shame him that he has reneged on an oral commitment.[28] A Jew who told his friend that he will give a gift in a manner such that his

23. Rashbam, *Bava Batra* 133b, s.v. *be avurei ahsanta*; *Sdei Hemmed Hashalem, Ma'arekhet* 30, *Kelal* 3, subsection 7 in the name of Rashbam; *Tur, Hoshen Mishpat* 282; *Beit Yosef, Hoshen Mishpat* 282; Schwartz, 10 *Kovetz Beit Aharon Ve-Yisrael*, vol. 58, 97 in the name of Tur and Beit Yosef; *Resp. Maharitz Ha-Hadashot* 70.

24. *Sefer Ha-Ittur, Matnat Shekhiv Me-Ra*, 118; *Resp. Ha-Tashbetz* 3:147; *Resp. Ha-Rivash* 168; *Resp. Minhat Yitzhak* 3:135.

25. Ranah, supra n. 10.

26. Schwartz, supra n. 15 at *Kovetz Beit Aharon Ve-Yisrael*, vol. 61, 102-103.

27. See Rashi, *Ketubot* 86a; *Mordekhai, Bava Metzia* 451 in the name of *Ittur*; *Resp. Pri Yitzhak* 1:51.

28. See *Mordekhai, Bava Metzia* 4:451; *Resp. Maharam Mintz* 39,101; *Sefer Ha-Agudah, Bava Metzia* 66; R. Schwadron, *Mishpat Shalom, Hoshen Mishpat* 204.

Noncompliance of a promise involves a violation of "the remnant of Israel shall not commit a sin." See *Bava Metzia* 106b; *Sha'arei Teshuva Le-Rabbeinu Yona, Sha'ar* 3, 6:183; *Resp. Maharam of Rothenberg*, Prague ed., 949 in the name of R. Tam; *Nimmukei Yosef, Bava Metzia* 29a; R. Z. N. Goldberg, "The Validity of an Obligation to Sell in a Preliminary Agreement" (Hebrew), 12 *Tehumin* 279, 291-292, 5751.

friend relied upon him, is prohibited from retracting his offer. And if he retracts his offer, he is labeled a *mehusar amana*. Consequently, if he orally promised to give a small gift, since it is logical that he will keep his word, his friend will rely upon him and therefore he is prohibited from retracting his promise. However, if he orally promised to give a large gift which his friend will not rely upon, he is not deemed a *mehusar amana* if he retracts his promise.[29]

On the other hand, in our case, the testamentary disposition was written and as such even if he retracted a large gift, he is labeled a *mehusar amana*.[30] To state it differently, as *Hazon Ish* aptly notes:[31]

> The major principle in undertaking obligations (*kinyanim*) is that he must firmly resolve in his heart to transfer the item to his friend and his friend must have intention to acquire it.

In halakhic nomenclature, there is a requirement of the testator's resolution to transfer an asset in a testamentary disposition, i.e., *gemirat da'at*.[32] As such, even if he retracted a large gift, he is labeled a *mehusar amana*.

Moreover, concerning divesting a portion or the entire portion of the Torah heir's share and transferring it to another Torah heir, the Talmud and post-Talmudic authorities note:[33]

---

29. Talmud Bavli *Bava Metzia* 49a; *Mishneh Torah, Hilk. Mehirah* 7:9; *Shulhan Arukh Hoshen Mishpat* 204:8.

Gemirat da'at is determined objectively in accordance with the assessment of rabbinic authorities. See *Hiddushei Ha-Ramban, Kiddushin* 26a; *Hiddushei Ha-Ran, Kiddushin* 13a.

Therefore, whether the testator's oral testamentary disposition in his eyes was viewed as a major gift or a small gift is a decision of the arbiters. Given that our case is dealing with a written estate disposition, we will refrain from dealing with this issue. See infra text accompanying nn. 29-31.

30. Schwartz, supra n. 26.

31. *Hoshen Mishpat* 22. See also, *Hazon Ish, Even Ha-Ezer* 38:7.

32. Talmud Bavli *Yevamot* 52b; *Kiddushin* 26a; *Tur Hoshen Mishpat* 189, *Beit Yosef*, ibid., *Bah*, ibid.; *Avnei Milluim* 27:9; *Sha'arei Yosher, Sha'ar* 7, *Perek* 12; *Resp. Tuv Taam ve-Da'at* 1:269; *Tziyunim La-Torah* 39; *Resp. Ramatz, Yoreh De'ah* 76; *Resp. Devar Yehoshua*, vol. 3, *Hoshen Mishpat* 13 (3).

33. Talmud Bavli *Ketubot* 53b; *Bava Batra* 133b; *Resp. Ha-Rosh* 84:1; *Ranah*, supra n.9; *Resp. Maharashdam Hoshen Mishpat* 336; However, numerous authorities disagree with this opinion. See *Mishneh Torah, Hilk. Mekhirah* 7:8; *Mordekhai, Bava Metzia* 4:312; *Resp Maharam of Rothenberg*, Prague ed. 949; *Resp. Ha-Tashbetz* 1:94; *Resp. Maharam Mintz* 101; *Sma, Hoshen Mishpat* 216:14; *Resp. Ein Yitzhak*, 1:34 (37). For additional sources, see supra n. 22. Cf. *Knesset Ha-Gedolah, Hoshen Mishpat* 282:9.

> Samuel said to Rabbi Judah; keep away from transfers of inheritance even though they be from a bad son to a good son.... and from a son to a daughter...

Clearly as in our case, adding or detracting from one Torah heir's portion and transferring to another Torah heir is governed by Rabbi Schwartz's position which states, as cited above:[34]

> It is preferable that he should live with his prohibition and refrain from changing one's mind and transfer from the non-Torah heir to the Torah heir... even though there exists a prohibition, (the testator) should not retract the transfer due to the absence of negotiating in good faith (*mehusar amana*).

In sum, though the testator's divesture of his son's inheritance entails a halakhic violation; nonetheless, the inheritance remains with those who received it.[35]

To expound upon R. Schwartz's position, we submit the following rationale of the ruling offered by *Rabbi Ya'akov Y. Bloi* who wrote the following:[36]

> Even if he acted improperly and divested the inheritance effectively (in accordance with the law of *kinyanim* – AYW)... the Torah heirs benefited from what was given to them. See Shulhan Arukh 282:1. And though he transgressed a prohibition... it is obvious for which reason one can nullify the gift that was executed with the proper *kinyan* and the transaction that was consummated by engaging in a prohibition is valid. And from the words of Ranah no. 118 it seems that even if one is able to retract, it is improper to retract... it is preferable that he will continue with the transgression of disinheritance rather than engage in another prohibition...

Such a position provides another example of how the halakhic system distinguishes between the commission of a prohibited act and the undertaking of an agreement in accordance with the norms of

34. *Schwartz,* supra n. 26.

35. *Shulhan Arukh, Hoshen Mishpat* 282:1; *Sma,* ad. locum. 3; R. Bloi, *Pithei Hoshen, Yerusha & Ishut,* 4:3 (11).

36. See supra n. 35.

undertaking an obligation (*kinyan*).[37] As *Professor Moshe Silberg*, the late Israeli Supreme Court judge, jurisprudentially observes the halakhic bifurcation:[38]

> We see clearly that Jewish law does not establish a causal connection between the commission of an offense and the voiding of a civil contract... The violation of the law or of morality is one thing, and the legal validity of the contract is another – to the extent that the fulfilling of the contract itself does not activate the offense... Precisely because Jewish law does not distinguish between law and morality, and practically every performance of an obligation is at the same time a fulfillment of an obligation at the same time a fulfillment of a religio-moral commandment-as [in the case of] "the commandment" of repaying a debt of monetary obligation – the non-fulfillment of a contract entered into through a violation of law will only turn out to be an additional offense to supplement the original one committed by the transgressor.

Despite the testator's transgression-failure to live up to the prescribed halakhic directives regarding inheritance, agreements that are premised upon disinheritance must, on the strength of the duty to comply with one's agreements, be enforced.

2. The Testamentary Disposition of Assets Was Written and Executed While Suffering From Dementia

Based upon the possibility that the testamentary disposition of assets was written while the testator was suffering from dementia, the emerging question is whether his decision to disinherit one of his sons is valid.

---

37. For another example, see this writer's "Contractual Consequences of Cohabitation in American Law and Jewish Law," 20 *The Jewish Law Annual*, 279, 334-335, 2013.

38. Moshe Silberg, *Talmudic Law and the Modern State*, N.Y. 1973, 82.

For the grounds for Prof. Silberg's position, see *Temurah* 4b-6b; Ramban, *Sefer Hamitzvot*, Negative Commandment 227; *Hiddushei Ha-Rashba Kiddushin* 67b, s.v. *eimah*; *Resp. Ha-Rosh* 7:4; *Resp. Ha-Ridvaz* 6:2068; *Resp. Maharshakh* 2:79; *Resp. Hatam Sofer, Yoreh Deah* 6; *Resp. Nodah Be-Yehudah, Mahadura Tinyana, Even Ha-Ezer* 129; *Mishneh La-Melekh, Hilk. Malveh Ve-Loveh* 8:1.

The locus classicus for our inquiry is a Talmudic passage which teaches us the following:[39]

> Our Rabbis instructed: Who is deemed mentally dysfunctional (a *shoteh*)? One who goes out alone at night [risking personal danger], sleeps overnight in the cemetery and tears his garments. Rabbi Huna said: He must do all three [to be labeled mentally dysfunctional]. And Rabbi Yohanan stated: If he has one of the characteristics of being mentally dysfunctional he is established as a *shoteh*.

And the classical authorities have adopted R. Yohanan's position.[40]

What is the scope of these characteristics memorialized in the Talmud? Since the Talmud specified these examples of *shoteh*-like behavior, it is unsurprising that some decisors endorse the position that only these examples define the individual as a *shoteh*.[41]

On the other hand, *Maimonides* defines *shoteh* and other examples of mental dysfunction in terms of their validity to submit testimony:[42]

> Not only is he insane (a *shoteh*) when he walks around naked, destroys articles and throws stones, but anyone who is mentally deranged so that his judgment is always impaired in any matter, even though he speaks and responds appropriately in other matters, is disqualified and categorized as insane.

By defining a *shoteh* as "anyone who is mentally deranged so that his judgment is always impaired in any matter, even though he speaks and responds inappropriately in other matters," Maimonides is widening the scope of who is subsumed in the category of a *shoteh*. Namely, in pursuance to Maimonides's words, anybody who lost the capacity to render

39. Talmud Bavli *Hagigah* 3b.

40. *Resp. Rav'yah* 805; *Piskei Ha-Rosh Hullin* 1:4; *Tur Yoreh Deah* 1; *Shulhan Arukh, Yoreh Deah* 1.

41. R. Simha Speyer, *Resp. Maharam Ben Baruch* 455; *Resp. Ha-Rashba* 765; *Resp. Beit Yosef* 119; *Resp. Ha-Maharik, shoresh* 19 in the name of Avigdor Katz; *Resp. Zikhron Yosef* 10; *Resp. Divrei Hayyim* 53,74-75.

42. *Mishneh Torah, Hilk. Edut* 9:9. For others who subscribe to Rambam's approach to expand the definition of a *shoteh* beyond the Talmudic parameters, see *Sma, Hoshen Mishpat* 35:21; R. Yehezkel Abramsky, *Otzar Ha-Poskim*, vol. 2, endnotes p. 22 in the name of R. Chaim Soloveitchik; *Resp. Iggerot Moshe, Even Ha-Ezer* 1:120.

decisions in a particular area, albeit he is capable of speaking and asking questions to the point concerning other matters, is deemed a *shoteh.*

Clearly, a *shoteh* is an individual who is not mentally functioning (a *bar da'at*) and according to certain authorities his behavior cannot be explained logically.[43] Given that we are dealing with a testator who is transferring ownership of an estate to his sons, we need to briefly explain the means to establish obligations (*hiyuvim*). As Hazon Ish aptly notes:[44]

> The major principle in undertaking obligations (*kinyanim*), the primary purpose of undertaking an obligation is that he must firmly resolve in his heart to sell the item to his friend and his friend must have intention to acquire it.

In halakhic nomenclature, there is a requirement of the seller's and buyer's resolution to transfer an object, i.e., *gemirat da'at.*[45]

For example, Avraham without informing Yitzhak gives to Ya'akov a gift for Yitzhak. Upon Ya'akov's performance of an act of acquisition (a *kinyan*), the asset belongs to Yitzhak, even if the latter is unaware that Ya'akov has received a gift on his behalf. Upon Ya'akov's acquisition, Avraham can no longer demand that the gift be returned to him, since it is no longer his.[46]

The acquisition of the gift for another was finalized due to the fact that the donor intended to transfer it (*da'at aheret makne lo*).[47] According to a few decisors, if another party verbally transfers the gift, the recipient acquires it even if there was no intention to acquire it.[48] If the donor

43. *Yad David, Piskei Halakhot* 1(167); *Iggerot Moshe*, supra n. 141. For the psychological basis for this definition of a *shoteh*, see Y. Strauss, "The *Shoteh* and Psychosis in Halakhah through the Prism of Modern Clinical Medicine" (Hebrew), *Kenas Ha-Dayanim* 5774, 267, 268.

44. *Hoshen Mishpat* 22. See also, *Hazon Ish, Even Ha-Ezer* 38:7.

45. Talmud Bavli *Yevamot* 52b; *Kiddushin* 26a; *Tur Hoshen Mishpat* 189, *Beit Yosef*, ibid., *Bah*, ibid.; *Avnei Milluim* 27:9; *Sha'arei Yosher, Sha'ar* 7, *Perek* 12; *Resp. Tuv Ta'am Ve-Da'at* 1:269; *Tziyunim La-Torah* 39; *Resp. Ramatz, Yoreh De'ah* 76; *Resp. Devar Yehoshua*, vol. 3, *Hoshen Mishpat* 13(3).

46. *Shulhan Arukh, Hoshen Mishpat* 243:1. The presentation below and many of the sources cited below may be found in Baruch Kahane, *Laws of Gift*: Section 6, Jerusalem: The Library of Jewish Law.

47. *Hiddushei Ha-Rashba Gittin* 20b; *Hiddushei Ha-Ritva, Yevamot* 52b; *Resp. Avnei Nezer, Orah Hayyim* 342; *Resp. Beit Ephraim, Orah Hayyim* 41; *Nimmukei Yosef, Bava Batra* 22b, Rif Pagination in the name of Ra'avad; *Resp. Maharit* 1:150; *Resp. Divrei Hayyim, Even Ha-Ezer* 1:53.

48. *Shitah Mekubetzet Bava Batra* 41a, s.v. *od* in the name of Ra'avad; *Resp.*

failed to state, prior to the execution of the *kinyan,* that he is giving the object to a particular individual, the transaction is invalid even if he intended to give it to him, since the articulation of the individual who is transferring the acquisition is required.[49] Alternatively, should the recipient articulate "give me the object as a gift" while the donor is silent, the transaction is valid.[50] The performance of the *kinyan* transpires an abundant time after the statement that this is a gift is ineffective, i.e., the gift has not been acquired.[51] Finally, similar to other agreements, the language of the donor must be formulated properly.[52]

On the other hand, other authorities argue that the recipient does not acquire the gift if he had no intention to buy it, even if he executed a *kinyan* and if the donor intended to transfer ownership to him.[53]

Based upon the foregoing, we submitted a presentation, albeit a brief one, regarding the halakhot applicable to the rule that the acquisition of the gift by a third-party beneficiary was finalized due to the fact that the donor intended to transfer the gift (*da'at aheret makne lo*).Clearly, this rule epitomizes the definition of the word Halakhah suggested by the author of the Sefer Ha-Arukh, i.e. the path that the Jewish community walks. One example of "the path" is the scope of this rule *da'at aheret makne lo* which mandates that every member of our covenant Jewish community must be mentally functional in order to be able to render personal decisions regarding when the rule is applicable in a particular situation. Said conclusion is applicable in other realms of Halakhah. For example, a Jew may be appointed to be an agent and appoint an agent on the condition that he is mentally functional.[54]

The emerging question is whether a testator who is suffering from vascular dementia may transfer an estate to his children.[55] Pursuant to

---

Hatam Sofer, Yoreh Deah 313; *Netivot Ha-Mishpat* 197:4. Cf. *Shitah Mekubetzet,* op. cit. in the name of Rashba.

49. *Resp. Ha-Maharit* 1:127; *Avnei Milluim* 27:9; *Pithei Hoshen, Kinyanim* 1 (1).

50. *Arukh Ha-Shulhan Hoshen Mishpat* 241:1.

51. *Resp. Beit Yitzhak, Yoreh Deah* 2:81.

52. See supra chapter 5.

53. *Yad Rama, Bava Batra* 3:224; *Resp. Ha-Rashbash* 288.

Notwithstanding receiving a gift in his hand, most types of *kinyan* are ineffective if the recipient has no intent to acquire it. See *Resp. Havazelet Hasharon* 1, *Even Ha-Ezer* 61. However, certain *kinyanim* such as the yard (*hatzer*), pulling the object towards you (*me'shikhah*) and raising the object (*hagbaha*) may be executed without intent to acquire the object. See *Ma'adanei Melekh,* 134-138.

54. *Pnei Yehoshua Gittin* 64b, s.v. *na'arah*; *Shulhan Arukh, Hoshen Mishpat* 188:2.

55. We received three professional diagnoses of the testator, and all three agreed

the information provided by John Hopkins Medicine, Mayo Clinic, and Weill Institute for NeuroScience: Memory & Aging Center, among the symptoms of those suffering from this end-stage dementia is that the person possesses reduced ability to organize his thought or actions and demonstrates a decline in ability to analyze a situation, develop an effective plan and communicate to others.

In the words of the Mishnah, he is a *shoteh* since he is devoid of mental functioning (*da'at*).[56] On the one hand, since the *shoteh* has no "hand" to acquire a gift;[57] he may not benefit from the receipt of a gift even though *da'at aheret makne.*[58] In fact, even if he possessed the capacity to acquire it, given his need to be able to know if the donor was gifting it in a proper halakhic fashion, he would have to understand the dynamics of the *da'at aheret makne,* a comprehension beyond the mind of the donor who is a *shoteh.* On the other hand, in our case, the testator, as a victim of dementia, generally speaking was psychologically incapable to address whether the process of the testamentary disposition was following the norms of Halakhah.[59] As such, any testamentary dispositions were invalid.

In short, given that the father is a shoteh, his testamentary disposition is null.[60] As such, pursuant to a ruling, the estate disposition ought to follow the Torah's order of hereditary succession. Given that the testator is a *shoteh* and we therefore are unaware of how he desires to divide his estate; therefore, the three Torah heirs ought to receive equal shares of the estate.[61]

---

that he is suffering from vascular dementia.

56. *Arakhin* 1:1.

57. *Ketzot Ha-Hoshen* 243:5; *Resp. Beit Ephraim, Hoshen Mishpat* 8.

58. *Mishneh Torah, Hilk. Zekhiyah & Matanah* 4:7; *Shulhan Arukh, Hoshen Mishpat* 243:17.

59. *Mishneh Torah, Hilk. Mekhirah* 29:4; *Shulhan Arukh, Hoshen Mishpat* 235:20. However, *da'at aheret makne lo* is effective if the *shoteh* has a partial understanding and comprehends the execution of the *kinyan*. See *Sma, Hoshen Mishpat* 243:29; *Resp. Ha-Rim, Even Ha-Ezer* 24.

60. If there is even a doubt whether he is suffering from dementia, the testamentary disposition is void. See *Resp. Maharsham* 1:201; *Pithei Hoshen, Yerusha and Ishut,* 4:28 (64).

61. As we have shown, if the testamentary disposition of the father's assets which entailed disinheritance of a Torah heir would have been executed prior to contracting dementia, the disinheritance would have been final. On the other hand, in our case of the testamentary disposition being arranged and executed during the time the father was suffering from dementia, the disinheritance was not viewed as final, and the assets were redistributed among the Torah heirs. In other words, the differing outcome is due to the father's mental state at the time of the testamentary disposition. In the situation of the testator being mentally functional at the time

I. DIVIDING UP A FAMILY ESTATE BETWEEN SIBLINGS

A *beit din* having been chosen by the parties as arbitrator pursuant to an arbitration agreement between Sarah Levy and Abraham Cohen ("plaintiffs") and Isaac Cohen ("defendant") to submit their disputes to the *beit din* with respect to financial losses due to the defendant's alleged mismanagement of the family's irrevocable trust, having given said matters due consideration, having reviewed written submissions accompanied by detailed exhibits during the hearing and post-hearing phase and having heard all parties and their legal counsel testify as to the facts of said disputes and differences, including four witnesses, does decide as follows:

Facts

Plaintiffs and defendant are siblings, whose mother was Rivka Cohen ("Settlor"). Settlor owned a family business, Cohen Liquors, where defendant was an employee. Settlor also owned two commercial properties, as well as a residential apartment building. Prior to August 30, 1996, the family business utilized the two commercial properties as a storage facility and a showroom to service its ongoing business.[1] During this period, Cohen Liquors paid rent, utilities, real estate taxes and insurance, maintenance and repairs on these properties. Although defendant managed all the properties, he received management fees only with respect to one of the properties which was sold in 2003. The clothing business continues to utilize the other commercial property and the residential apartment building.

On August 30, 1996, Rivka Cohen, along with each of her four children, Issac Cohen, Murray Cohen, Abraham Cohen and Sarah Levy, executed an agreement titled, "Operating Agreement of Cohen Properties, LTD" (the "Agreement") establishing Cohen Properties, LTD as a limited liability company (the "LLC"). Pursuant to the terms of the Agreement,

---

of the disposition, though the disinheritance was prohibited; the division of estate assets was final. The firm resolution in the testator's mind (*gemirat da'at*) was determinative. However, in our case, the testator is mentally dysfunctional and incapable of rendering decisions (a *shoteh*); consequently, the disinheritance was nullified, and the estate was redistributed equally in accordance with Halakhah, namely among the Torah heirs.

1. We have chosen to decline identifying the two commercial properties as well as the rental property.

Rivka Cohen was the Member-Manager with a 100% interest in the LLC's income. The LLC became a holding company for the properties.

At some time thereafter, Rivka Cohen (the "Settlor") executed the "Rivka Cohen Irrevocable Trust Agreement" (the "trust"), and gifted a portion of the LLC to the trust. The parties dispute what portion of the LLC was granted to the trust. The beneficiaries of the trust were the Settlor's four children.

In July 2003, the Settlor executed a power of attorney to the defendant. The document was witnessed by one of the plaintiffs, Sarah Levy.

On September 5, 2003, at a family meeting addressing other family matters, the defendant distributed to his siblings a packet of materials including copies of the trust agreement.

On July 5, 2005, Rivka Cohen passed away.

Plaintiff's Claims

Plaintiff claims that Rivka Cohen gifted 99% of her entire capital and membership interest in Cohen Properties LTD, and her entire interest in Cohen Liquors, to the trust. As the initial trustee of the trust, the defendant had a fiduciary responsibility to manage the assets of the trust held in the trust, for the benefit of the trust's beneficiaries, namely his siblings and himself. Any self-dealing by the defendant is a breach of his role as a trustee. Summarizing the plaintiff's argument in legal terms, we may state that the trustee may justify a self-dealing transaction only by demonstrating (1) that the beneficiaries agreed, (2) that their consent was given after disclosure of all the facts relating to the transaction, and (3) that the transaction was reasonable. But, in fact, until September 5, 2003, the defendant never disclosed the existence of the trust to his siblings, much less his management of the trust's assets. Moreover, for almost eight years, the defendant engaged in self-dealing by authorizing Cohen Liquors to pay a rental charge which was below the fair market rental value of the properties, charged excessive management fees for maintaining said properties and paid his wife's monthly car lease payment with trust assets.

In addition, Article 1, paragraph 1 of the trust agreement contemplated the division of the trust into four separate trusts and the appointment of trustees as of December 31, 2001. Despite the requirements set forth in the trust agreement, defendant failed to comply with the aforesaid division and trustee appointment.

The plaintiffs request that the defendant reimburse the siblings in a proportionate amount for all gifts or excessive fees taken from the Settlor, including but not limited to the $30,000 gift taken a few days prior to the Settlor's demise. Plaintiffs also request the payment to Abraham Cohen of $7,500, representing a gift to him that was promised by Rivka Cohen but never paid out.

Plaintiffs also seek to recover $55,000 in GRNA loans and $12,000 in loans to one of the commercial properties paid to the defendant, rental income from the other commercial property and fair rental market value of the rental property, overcharge of management fees for commercial properties and overcharge in car lease payments.

Plaintiffs also request that defendant relinquish control of the real estate, allow the plaintiffs to sell the properties or manage the real estate, and receive control of Cohen Liquors, Ltd. Furthermore, plaintiffs seek to be indemnified for any future costs related to Murray Cohen and the IRS and seek recovery of beit din fees.

Finally, plaintiffs request that defendant pay all costs and attorney fees with pre- and post-judgment interest, as a result of defendant's bad faith breach of his fiduciary duty. In sum, plaintiffs' monetary claim is $1,285,219.00.

Defendant's Response and Counterclaims

Defendant states that on the one hand, the Settlor wanted to distribute all her assets equally to her offspring and allow them to reap the estate tax benefits of the trust structure that her attorneys devised. On the other hand, during her lifetime, the Settlor wanted to maintain control of and retain income from these assets and therefore designated the defendant, her son who had been in the family business since the 1980s, to look after her interests. The Settlor's conflicted feelings regarding this matter are best summed up in Eli Schwartz's testimony. He testified that it was his impression that after discovering the implications of executing a trust instrument, i.e., loss of Settlor's control of her assets, Rivka Cohen signed the document with a great degree of reluctance. Following the establishment of the trust and conveyance of the properties into the trust, the properties continued to be managed, and income therefrom was distributed, in the same manner that they were managed prior to the institution of the trust, with Rivka Cohen's assent. Defendant points to this as evidence that Rivka Cohen never intended to change the ownership structure of her assets.

In addition, defendant contends that despite signing the LLC operating agreement in 1996 and knowing about the trust at least since 2003, the plaintiffs never approached the Settlor regarding any issues relating to the trust and never objected to defendant's handling of any matters relating to the trust.

The defendant claims that if the beit din determines that the plaintiffs are entitled to back rent and management fees, those amounts should be offset by monies paid by Cohen Liquors from 1996-2008 for mortgage payments, real estate taxes, utility expenses, general maintenance and repairs and security maintenance relating to the two commercial properties.

Defendants also object to the respective $9.25 per square foot and $8.00 per square foot rental appraisals for the commercial properties that were set forth in the realty appraisal. Defendants contend (without supporting documentation) that the fair market rental values are $7.50 per square foot and $6.50 per square foot, respectively.

In reply to plaintiffs' representation, based upon Rivka Cohen's tax returns, that defendant received $104,450.00 in management fees for managing the 2120 Property, the defendant argues that he received only $45,200.00 for management fees for said property. He claims the balance represents other unrelated payments that were distributed through Cohen Liquors. In response to plaintiff's claim for loan repayment, defendant argues that the loans were repaid.

In response to Sarah's representation that her mother gifted her a ring, pearl necklace and earrings, the defendant argues that said jewelry was appropriated and belongs to all the siblings.

Furthermore, defendant requests that he be allowed to purchase 80% of the 2199 Property at its fair market value, and that upon closing the siblings shall receive their share of proceeds. Additionally, defendant requests that the clothing business be allowed to remain on the premises of one of the commercial properties for six months.

Finally, defendant requests that the beit din recognize the indemnity clauses of the LLC operating agreement and trust and recover all legal and court fees associated with the civil litigation including but not limited to certain criminal matters.

In a post-arbitration brief, defendant requested an offset for management fees of the total rent for his management of the commercial properties.

Discussion

1. Choice of Law

The arbitration agreement executed between the parties provides that the rights and obligations of the parties in this case are to be determined according to Ohio law. Parties who agree in an arbitration agreement to the application of secular law do so as a means of applying a particular benefit (in the words of the *Sma*, a "*zekhut*") set forth in a provision of secular law, so that such provision becomes the choice of law provision to govern the resolution of the matter before the beit din. Such private ordering does not constitute their acceptance of the norms of a secular legal system as governing their affairs. See *Sma Hoshen Mishpat; Resp. Avnei Hefetz* 74 in the name of *Shakh* 22; *Netivot Ha-Mishpat*, Hoshen Mishpat 66:34; *Tur Hoshen Mishpat* in the name of *Sefer Ha-Terumot*, Sha'ar 62 (4); *Beit Yosef*, Hoshen Mishpat 26 in the name of *Resp. Ha-Rashba*; *Levush Hoshen Mishpat* in the name of Rashba 6:254; *Tumim 26:4*; *Resp. Teshurat Shai* 529; Piskei Din Rabbanayim 18:319, 324; Rabbi Zalman Nechemiah Goldberg, *Lev Hamishpat*, vol. 1, page 286; S. Karelitz, "On the Matter of Local Custom,"(Hebrew) 6 *Masoret*, 117-118, 1979; Rabbi Ezra Batzri, *Dinnei Mamonot*, vol. 3, page 197; Resp. *Ateret Devorah* 3:14; File no. 133004/5, Be'air Sheva Regional Court October 10, 2021.[2] Given such motivation, said agreement is valid and is not a violation of the prohibition of litigating in secular courts.

In this case, the parties limited the choice of law provision to apply only "so long as Ohio law is consistent with the obligations of the beit din under the laws of Halakhah." For example, being halachically constrained from applying secular law includes payment of prohibited interest (*ribbit*), since *ribbit* may not be paid under Jewish law even if parties agree to do so. In other words, *Halakhah* allows parties to

2. For the halakhic propriety of executing a civil will and rendering a *beit din* decision based upon secular law, see further this writer's *Rabbinic Authority: The Vision & the Reality*, vol. 1, pp. 195-199, vol. 2, 44-80. Cf. *Resp. Ha-Rosh* 18:2; *Taz, Hoshen Mishpat* 26:3; *Bi'ur Ha-Gra, Hoshen Mishpat* 61:23; *Hazon Ish, Sanhedrin* 15:4; R. Avraham Sherman, "The Halakhic Principles regarding Proceeding to Non-Jewish Courts to Issue Inheritance Directives and other Claims" (Hebrew), 12 *Sha'arei Tzedek*, 402-411, 5771.

Cf. *Sma Hoshen Mishpat* 369:20 who permits parties to a business deal agree to resolve their future differences in accordance with the norms of civil law. However, parties appearing at a *beit din* hearing are proscribed from executing such an arrangement.

prescribe their own rules as governing their business relationship, even if those terms depart from the baseline *halakhah.*[3]

But matters actually prohibited under Jewish law (*issur ve'heter*), such as the collection of *ribbit*, are prohibited regardless of any contract or waiver between the parties. See *Kiddushin* 19b; *Shulhan Arukh, Even Ha-Ezer* 38:5; *Shulhan Arukh, Hoshen Mishpat* 291:17; *Beit Yosef, Tur, Hoshen Mishpat* 305:4; *Shulhan Arukh, Hoshen Mishpat* 305:4; *Rema, Hoshen Mishpat* 344:1.

It is worth noting that Ohio law would govern in this matter even absent an Ohio choice of law provision in the arbitration agreement. By virtue of executing the trust agreement, Rivka Cohen and the defendant conferred rights to the beneficiaries of the trust, and the contours of

3. To state it differently, though it is prohibited to litigate a pending case in civil court even if the parties agreed, if the parties undertook the obligation (executed a *kinyan*) and litigated there, the parties must comply with the judgment after the fact (*be'di-avad*). See *Shulhan Arukh, Hoshen Mishpat* 26:1; *Responsa Ha-Tashbetz* 3:68; *Responsa Ha-Rashbash* 331; *Tumim, Shulhan Arukh* 26:1; *Yeshuot Yisrael, Shulhan Arukh* 26; *Responsa Maharsham* 1:89; *Birkei Yosef, Hoshen Mishpat* 26:3; On the other hand, as we have shown, we permit ex ante (*le'kha-tehillah*) parties to litigate their claims in *beit din* based upon the norms of civil law.

Such a position provides another example of how the halakhic system distinguishes between the commission of a prohibited act and the undertaking of an agreement in accordance with the norms of undertaking an obligation (*kinyan*). As Professor Moshe Silberg, the late Israeli Supreme Court judge, jurisprudentially observes this halakhic bifurcation: "We see clearly that Jewish law does not establish a causal connection between the commission of an offense and the voiding of a civil contract... The violation of the law or of morality is one thing, and the legal validity of the contract is another – to the extent that the fulfilling of the contract itself does not activate the offense... Precisely because Jewish law does not distinguish between law and morality, and practically every performance of an obligation is at the same time a fulfillment of an obligation at the same time a fulfillment of a religio-moral commandment-as [in the case of] 'the commandment' of repaying a debt of monetary obligation – the non-fulfillment of a contract entered into through a violation of law will only turn out to be an additional offense to supplement the original one committed by the transgressor." See Moshe Silberg, *Talmudic Law and the Modern State*, N.Y. 1973, 82.

For the grounds for Prof. Silberg's position, see *Temurah* 4b-6b; Ramban, *Sefer Hamitzvot*, Negative Commandment 227; *Hiddushei Ha-Rashba Kiddushin* 67b, s.v. *eimah*; *Responsa Ha-Rosh* 7:4; *Resp. Ha-Ridvaz* 6:2068; *Resp. Maharshakh* 2:79; *Resp. Hatam Sofer, Yoreh Deah* 6; *Resp. Nodah Be-Yehudah, Mahadura Tinyana, Even Ha-Ezer* 129; *Mishneh La-Melekh, Hilk. Malveh Ve-Loveh* 8:1.

Despite the parties' engagement in the prohibition of litigating in civil courts, on the strength of the duty to comply with one's agreements via the execution of a *kinyan, ex post facto* the civil decision is enforced.

those rights are defined by the terms of the trust agreement. Paragraph 6 of Article III of the trust agreement provides that, "this agreement is governed by the law of the State of Ohio." Accordingly, Ohio law should be used in any determination regarding the defendant's conduct as trustee in this case.

2. Legal Recognition of a Trust.

Based upon the cumulative evidence submitted to the panel, it is our opinion that an irrevocable trust was created by Rivka Cohen on December 31, 1996.

Legally, with the inception of the family trust, the defendant, as the initial trustee, had a fiduciary responsibility to manage and administer the trust's assets for the exclusive benefit of those having a beneficial interest in it, without regard to the fiduciary's own interests. The fiduciary is required to keep the beneficiaries duly informed, to maintain records, and to render accounts to the beneficiaries of the estate. One Ohio court has ruled:

> The law is clear that self-dealing or breach of good faith on the part of the trustee can not be excused on the ground that the instrument creating the trust and making him trustee has given him broad authority and unlimited discretion in the administration of the trust... unless express authorization is contained in the instrument creating the trust or in a provision of law... (*Cleveland Trust Co. v. Eaton*, 11 Ohio Misc. 151, 229 N.E. 2d 850 [Ct. App. 1967])

Regarding the issues at bar, a family trust was created with all its attendant legal consequences, and based upon the cumulative evidence presented to this panel we conclude that the defendant as trustee was remiss in some of his fiduciary duties towards his siblings.[4]

3. Litigation in Secular Courts

A Jew who summons another Jew against his or her will to civil court to litigate a noncriminal matter that may fall under the jurisdiction of a beit din, where the defendant incurs expenses as a result of that

4. For the grounds for recognizing a trust, see this writer's *Rabbinic Authority: The Vision & the Reality*, vol. 1, 305-317.

summons, is liable to pay for said expenses. See *Tur, Hoshen Mishpat* 26:7; *Responsa Ha-Mabit* 3:12; *Divrei Hayyim*, vol. 2, *Hoshen Mishpat* 1. Matters regarding inheritance and the administration of trusts can be litigated in a *beit din*, and plaintiffs were therefore proscribed from litigating this matter in civil court. Consequently, plaintiffs are liable to reimburse defendant for his legal and court expenses.

A defendant must provide a record of such expenses in order to receive such relief. See *Responsa Ridvaz* 1:172.

4. The *Beit Din*'s Basis for Its Calculations

The calculation of fair market rental rate for the commercial properties is based upon a triple net (NNN) rent structure as outlined in the Realty appraisal report. Given this rental rate structure, defendant is entitled to a credit for his mortgage payments for said properties but is not entitled to receive remuneration for expenses relating to operating expenses such as utility expenses, real estate taxes and insurance, general maintenance and repairs, security maintenance and management fees.

The calculation of the fair rental value for the rental property is based upon the actual rent taken for said property as memorialized in Rivka Cohen's tax returns. The outlay for car expenses and net rental income of the rental property is based upon Rivka Cohen's tax submissions.

Based upon the cumulative evidence, given that the amount of management fees taken by the defendant for the rental property is unclear, pursuant to the provisions of the arbitration agreement that this matter may be resolved based upon norms of *beit din*-mediated settlement in accordance to Jewish law ("*peshara kerova ledin*"), we are assuming that two-thirds of the $104,450.00 amount memorialized in Rivka Cohen's tax returns was taken for management fees and the balance was a distribution for other purposes.

Based upon the cumulative evidence, given that the issue of whether the loans were repaid is a matter of dispute, Halakhah would require the defendant to swear that the loans were repaid. Since, in contemporary times, the common practice is to abstain from imposing the obligation of swearing, based upon *peshara kerova ledin*, a governing provision of this arbitration agreement, we credit the plaintiffs with one-third of the amount of the loans. See *Shulhan Arukh, Hoshen Mishpat* 12:2; *Responsa Shevut Ya'akov* 2:145.

Plaintiffs shall receive a one-third credit for the various loans and one-third credit for car lease payments.

Decision

The dollar amounts calculated by the beit din, pursuant to the decision below, are based in part on the financial statements and financial representations which were communicated to the beit din by the parties during the arbitration proceeding hearings and the post-hearing phase. If any of such statements or representations is proven to have been materially false, the beit din shall have the right to modify its decision accordingly.

1. For the period January 1997 through December 2008, the total fair market rental value of the 2113 Property owed by the defendant (after subtracting rent income already distributed) is $243,017.
2. For the period January 1997 through December 2008, the total fair market rental value of the 2199 Property owed by the defendant (after subtracting rent income already distributed) is $117,330. This figure represents 80% of the amount which is due.
3. For the period January 1997 through July 2006, the plaintiffs are entitled to receive $16,997.97 for the overcharge in car lease payments.
4. The commercial property is jointly owned by the plaintiffs (eighty per cent) and by the defendant (twenty per cent). For the period January 1997 through December 2008, the defendant paid $209,981.52 for mortgage payments for one of the commercial properties. The defendant is entitled to a credit of $167,985.22 which represents eighty per cent of the mortgage payments.
5. For the period January 1997 through July 2006, the net rental income for the 2120 Property was $72,875.00 (after subtracting losses declared on 2004, 2005 and 2007 tax returns). Plaintiffs are entitled to a reimbursement of $72,875.00 from said property belonging to them.

   The gross rental income for said property for the aforementioned period was $856,195.00 and the defendant took $69,693.03 in management fees for said property (after subtracting monies distributed to Murray Cohen – see below). Based upon 6% of the total fair market rental of said property, the defendant was entitled to receive $51,371.70 in management fees.

Therefore, the plaintiffs are credited $18,321.33 in overcharge of management fees.

6. The defendant shall have the option to purchase the plaintiff's 80% interest in one of the commercial properties. The option may be exercised by written notice from the defendant to the plaintiff delivered within two months of the date of this decision. Such written notice shall contain a purchase price offer, which plaintiff may accept or reject. If plaintiff rejects such offer, plaintiff shall have seven (7) days to present a counteroffer, which the defendant may accept or reject. If the defendant rejects such offer, the parties shall arrange for an appraisal of the property by a third-party property appraiser agreed upon by the parties. The parties shall then reasonably proceed to close on the purchase at the agreed-upon price or the price set by the appraiser, as the case may be. If the defendant does not exercise his purchase option, the parties may agree to rent the property to the defendant, to rent it to a third party, or to sell it. Any differences and disputes regarding the appraisal process, purchase option process and sale of the property shall be resolved by the beit din. Effective immediately, the defendant should resign as manager of said property in favor of the plaintiffs.
7. Defendant shall have the option to continue to operate the clothing business on the commercial property until no later than October 1, 2009. After the defendant vacates the premises, the plaintiffs and defendant may agree to continue to rent the property or sell it. All outstanding obligations regarding expenses relating to the commercial property dating from January 2009 until the vacating of the property by the defendant shall be resolved by the parties at the time the defendant vacates said premises. Any differences and disputes regarding said sale shall be resolved by the beit din.
8. Commencing January 2009 and until the defendant's purchase of one of the commercial properties or the date he ceases to occupy the property and defendant's vacating the other commercial property, defendant shall pay rent in the amount of $1,850.67 per month for the other commercial property, and, for plaintiffs' 80% share of rent for one of the commercial properties, $2,169.06 per month. These calculations are based on fair market rental valuations calculated for 2008.
9. During this period, real estate payments, property insurance, utility bills, security maintenance and repairs shall be paid by

the defendant. Any maintenance of said properties during this period which exceeds $1,500 requires prior written authorization from the plaintiffs. Plaintiffs shall respond to any requests for authorization via e-mail to the defendant within five working days. Should there arise the need for an emergency repair which exceeds $1,500, defendant shall call at least one of the plaintiffs to receive authorization. If the defendant fails to receive authorization, the emergency repair shall be done. Any differences of opinion regarding these matters shall be resolved by the beit din.

10. Defendant shall pay $20,000 to the plaintiffs as reimbursement of his pro rata share of the gift transfer to the defendant's personal bank account, which was executed a few days prior to their mother's demise.
11. Defendant shall pay Abraham Cohen $7,500.00.
12. Plaintiff shall pay $48,181.00 to the defendant for court and legal fees associated with the civil litigation.
13. Sarah Levy shall receive her mother's ring, pearl necklace and earrings.
14. In the event that there are future costs relating to the defendant's settlement with Murray, the parties shall submit the matter to the beit din for a determination regarding whether the defendant shall be required to indemnify the plaintiffs.
15. The parties are encouraged to consult with tax counsel to advise them regarding any tax consequences of this decision or the transactions contemplated by this decision. Any disputes among the parties regarding the apportionment of tax liabilities occasioned by this decision shall be submitted to the beit din.
16. The 22 gold coins shall be equally divided among the siblings based upon a written appraisal of their market value. If the siblings are unable to divide the coins equally, the coins shall be sold and the revenue from the sale shall be divided equally among the siblings.
17. Offsetting Credits and Debits:
    a. Plaintiffs' Credits:
        1. $243,017 for fair market rental value of one of the commercial properties
        2. $117,330 for fair market rental value of the other commercial property
        3. $18,321.33 for defendant's overcharge in management fees for rental property

4. $72,875.00 for net rental income of rental property
5. $22,333.33 for loan repayment
6. $20,000 for defendant's gift transfer
7. $7,500.00 for Abraham Cohen
8. $16,997.97 for defendant's car lease payments

Total Credit for Plaintiffs: $518,374.63

b. Defendant's Credits:

1. $48,181.00 for court and legal fees relating to civil litigation
2. $167,985.22 for mortgage payments for the commercial properties

Total credit for Defendant: $216,166.22

Defendant shall hereby pay $294,708.41 to plaintiffs and $7,500.00 to Abraham Cohen.

The schedule of payments shall be as follows:

By July 24, 2009, defendant shall hereby pay $147,354.21 to plaintiffs and $7,500.00 to Abraham Cohen.

By September 24, 2009, defendant shall hereby pay $73,677.10 to plaintiffs.

By December 23, 2009, defendant shall hereby pay $73,677.10 to plaintiffs.

Any lateness in any payment obligates the defendant to pay the entire outstanding balance at the time of the late payment.

18. All other applications and claims are hereby denied.

The obligations set forth herein shall be enforceable in any court of competent jurisdiction, in accordance with the arbitration agreement.

Any provision of this decision may be modified only with the consent of both parties.

J. A MENTALLY DYSFUNCTIONAL HUSBAND*

Question

I was asked as a *moreh hora'ah*, a qualified expositor of Halakhah (and not as a *dayan* sitting in judgment) to render a *teshuva* (responsum) in order to ascertain whether there are grounds to void a certain woman's *kiddushin* (*bittul kiddushin*) and to permit her to marry any other Jew without a *get* from her husband.

1. The Facts of the Case

After ten to twelve minutes talking to Ya'akov, Rochel told her parents that "he was a good match." It was an arranged marriage and consequently they never spoke about any substantive matter before the marriage. After Pesach 2015, the two of them became engaged and the couple was married during the following November 2015 in accordance with Halakhah.

During the four and a half years that the couple lived together they gave birth to three children. During this period, Ya'akov was administered with a regimen of drugs which treated some of his psychological disorders such as schizophrenia, OCD, ADHD, and bipolar disorder. There are numerous prescriptions that have been given based upon the findings of the health care professionals concerning the determination of whether this particular individual ought to be treated with a particular medication.[1] For accepting such evidence in medical matters, see the authorities cited above (in n. 1), as well as R. Herzog, Teshuvot Pesakim u-Ketavim EH 105. Implicit in our acceptance of these psychological findings is that it is based upon a professional assessment.[2]

Concurrently with the above, Ya'akov was treated psychiatrically in various hospitals from January 2021 until August 2023. Some of his psychic disorders may be read in the hospital files and his physician records, they are also mentioned in family accounts, and they may be distilled

1. See *Resp. Beit Yitzhak, EH* 1:5; *Resp. Parshat Mordekhai* 26; *Resp. Levushei Mordekhai*, EH 80; *Resp. Hayyim shel Shalom* 2:19; *Resp. Maharam Schick*, EH 2–3; *Resp. Teshurat Shai* 1:384; PDR 3:353, 360.

2. See *Gittin* 72b; *Kiddushin* 73b-74a; *Sanhedrin* 75a.

from the medications he was taking during the marriage and up until September 2022.

After four and a half years of marriage, Rochel requested that he give her a *get*. Upon his *get* recalcitrance, Rochel summoned him to Badatz Mishpitei Yisroel, Rabbinical Court Ezer Mishpat, Bais Din Sharei Mishpat, Beis Din Beis Yoseph, Rabbinical Court of Kiryas Joel and Beth Din of America. Whereas the aforementioned five *battei din* each issued "a *ktav seruv*" (a statement declaring him to be in contempt of *beit din*) against him, the Beth Din of America recommended that he give a *get* to his wife. To date, she has not received her *get*.

Answer

The threshold question is: Does a person exhibiting psychic disorders such as schizophrenia, OCD, ADHD, and bipolar disorder fall into the halakhic category of a *shoteh* (halakhically mentally dysfunctional)? The Tosefta and Talmud define four characteristics of a *shoteh*: one who goes out alone at night, he who spends the night in a cemetery, one who tears his clothes and one who loses what is given to him.[3] Hakhmei Provencia, Rambam, Mahari Weil, Tur, Shulhan Arukh, Rema and others rule that the Talmudic list is not exhaustive of *shoteh* conduct and therefore a person can be classified as a *shoteh* even if his behavior did not exemplify one of the four characteristics of a *shoteh* as enumerated in the Talmud.[4]

(It is debated whether Rambam would deem an individual a *shoteh* when exhibiting behavior which is not one of the four characteristics mentioned in the Talmud only with regard to submitting testimony or in all other realms. See Rabbi Yehezkel Landau, Ohr ha-Yashar 30; Resp. Ba'al ha-Tanya 25; Zikhron Yosef, op. cit.; Tevuot Shor 1:29.)

3. See *Tosefta Terumot* 1:3; *Hagigah* 3b. It should be noted that, in contrast to the views cited in the text above, some authorities take the contrary view that the list in the Talmud is closed or comprehensive. These include Rabbeinu Simhah, Rabbi Avigdor, Rabbi Moshe Sofer in the name of Rashba, Rabbi Yosef Steinhardt, Rabbi Schneersohn and the Sanzer Rov. See *Resp. Ha-Rashba* 1:765, 4:201; *Beit Yosef, Tur EH* 119 in the name of Rabbeinu Simhah; *Resp. Ha-Maharik, shoresh* 19 in the name of Rabbi Avigdor; *Resp. Hatam Sofer EH* 2:24 in the name of Rashba; *Resp. Zikhron Yosef* 10; *Resp. Tzemah Tzedek, EH* 153; *Resp. Divrei Hayyim EH* 53, 74. See also *Resp. Ha-Rivash* 20; *Resp. Ha-Tashbetz* 2:132; *Shakh SA YD* 1:24; *Taz SA YD* 1:12.

4. See *Resp. Hakhmei Provencia* 57; *Mishneh Torah* (hereafter: MT), *Edut* 3:3; *Resp. Mahari Weil* 52; *Tur HM* 35; *Shulhan Arukh YD* 1:5, *HM* 35:8 (Cf. *YD* 1:5); *Darkhei Moshe ha-Arokh Tur EH* 119:5, 121; *Sma, SA HM* 35:21; *Beit Shmuel, SA EH* 121:9 and *Torat Gittin* 121:5.

Addressing the situation of a mentally dysfunctional wife, Rabbi Tzvi Pesah Frank argues that living with a *shoteh,* a spouse who is mentally impaired and is viewed halakhically as a *shoteh,* is an illustration of the Talmudic observation, "one does not live together with a snake in the same basket."[5] As the Talmud explains, the reason it has been halakhically legislated that marriage cannot be consummated by a *shoteh* is because "one does not live together with a snake in the same basket."[6] Secondly, a fundamental requirement for a stable marriage is a husband's respect for his wife.[7] Consequently, if a man was *shoteh* at the time of executing the act of *kiddushin* and this was intentionally or unintentionally hidden from her before the *kiddushin,* if his wife desires to receive a *get* – should he refuse to give one, then the marriage is deemed a *kiddushin* in error (*kiddushei ta'ut*) and the marriage may be voided.[8] However, in our situation there is no evidence to demonstrate that Ya'akov was mentally dysfunctional at the time of the establishment of the *kiddushin.*

Our foregoing presentation, based upon the physician and hospital records, was conveyed regarding the husband's mental state and lack of respect for his spouse ***during*** the marriage. What we have here is a violation of the rabbinic directive, "that a man ought to respect his wife more than himself and love her like himself... and he should not instill excessive fear, and his speaking should be calm rather than be sad or angry."[9] Such a violation is an example of: "one does not live together with a snake in the same basket." As such, in accordance with Rabbi Shalom Schwadron and Rabbi Tzvi Pesach Frank, we may void the marriage based upon the clear expectation of *umdana demukhah* (hereinafter: *umdana*) of – "*ada'ata dehakhi lo kidshah nafshah.*"(on this understanding she did not betroth him).[10] For example, "had I known that my husband would have become a *mumar* (an apostate Jew), become a criminal or would have become mentally dysfunctional during our years of marriage, I never would have married him," may serve as illustrations of a wife invoking an *umdana* – a major inference from assessed expectations – which, if proven, may serve as grounds to

5. *Resp. Har Tzvi* EH 1:14.

6. *Yevamot* 112b.

7. *Ohr Zarua, Bava Kamma* 161; *Resp. Maharam of Rothenburg,* Cremona ed., 291, Prague ed. 81; *Resp. ha-Rashba ha-Meyuhasot la-Ramban* 102.

8. See *Resp. Maharsham* 7:160 (contingent upon the sanction of two Torah scholars); *Resp. Iggerot Moshe EH* 1:80; File no. 870175/4, Haifa Regional Beit Din, 3 Tevet, 5775.

9. *MT Ishut* 16:19; *Be'air Ha-Golah, SA EH* 154:10.

10. *Resp. Maharsham* 7:95; *Resp. Har Tzvi EH* 2:133.

void a marriage without the giving of a *get*.[11] In accordance with their view, invoking the *umdana* creates a situation of a *safek kiddushin*, a doubtful *kiddushin*, and for some *Poskim* such as *Teshuvot Maharbil* 1:17 one should refrain from being more lenient in *kiddushei safek* than a doubtful divorce. Nonetheless, others follow the view of Ran in the first chapter of Tractate Kiddushin that *safek kiddushin* creates a *hezkat penuyah*, a presumption of a single woman *me'deoraita*, on a Biblical level, and the rabbis ruled stringently due to the prohibition related to her status of *eishet ish* (as a married woman) and therefore she requires a *get*.[12]

Finally, the invoking of *umdana* as an avenue to void a marriage seemingly runs afoul of the ruling of the Shulhan Arukh. As we know, for an *umdana* to be effective is dependent upon both parties. For example, a sales transaction involves the agreement of parties, the seller and the buyer: "*taluy be-da'at shenehem*."[13]

The voiding of the sale with the appearance of a defect subsequent to purchase would be predicated upon two conditions:[14]

1. The buyer would not have consummated the deal if he had realized that the item sold would be defective within a reasonable time. As Shulhan Arukh states:[15]

> If one sells another land, a slave, a domesticated animal, or other moveable property, and a defect, of which the

11. For examples of various *umdanot* which serve as a basis to void a marriage, see *Tosafot Ketuvot* 47b, s.v. *shelo*; *Resp. Maharam of Rothenburg*, Prague ed., 1022; *Resp. Beit Ha-Levi* 3:3; *Resp. Hesed le-Avraham, Mahadura Tinyana, EH* 55; *Resp. Torat Hesed, EH* 26; *Resp. Radakh, Bayit* 9; *Resp. She'eilot Moshe EH* 2 (*halitzah*); *Resp. Zikhron Yehonatan* 1, *YD* 5; *Resp. Avnei Hefetz* 30; *Resp. Sha'arei Ezra* 4 *EH* 26; *Resp. Divrei Malkiel* 4:100; *Resp. Tzvi Tiferet* 4; *Resp. Meishivat Nefesh EH* 73–77; *Resp. Divrei Hayyim* 1, *EH* 3; *Resp. Maharsham* 7:95 (a matter of a wife's mental dysfunction); D. Meisels, *Resp. Radad EH* 40; *Resp. Iggerot Moshe, EH* 1:80, 4:121; *Resp. Har Tzvi EH* 2:133. Cf. *Resp. Avodat Ha-Gershuni* 35, *Resp. Beit Yitzhak* 1:106; *Resp. Nishmat Hayyim* 129; *Resp. Maharsham* 2:110; *Resp. Heikhal Yitzhak EH* 2:25; File no. 861974/1, Tzfat Regional Beit Din, January 21, 2013 (R. Y. Ariel's opinion).

12. *Resp. Maharik, shoresh* 171, *Pri Hadash*, YD 110 (end) dealing with Sefek Sefeika, *Resp. Maharsham* 8, EH 239, *Resp. Sha'arei Tzion* 3, EH 4, 22–24.

13. *Resp. Shoeil u-Meishiv, Mahadura Kamma* 1:145, 197; *Resp. Noda be-Yehudah, Mahadura Kamma*, YD 69, Mahadura Tinyana, EH 80; Resp. Maharsham 3:82, 5:5.

14. See *Tosafot Ketuvot* 47b, s.v. shelo; *Netivot Ha-Mishpat HM* 230:1.

15. *Hoshen Mishpat* 232:3.

> buyer did not know, is found in the purchase, the buyer may return it (to the seller and receive his money back) even if a number of years (have elapsed since the transaction), since this transaction was based upon fundamental error, provided that the buyer did not continue to use the item after he became aware of the defect. If, however, the buyer continued to use the item after he saw (or became aware of) the flaw, he has (by his behavior) renounced (his right of rescission) and cannot return (the defective item and receive his money back).

2. The seller would negotiate the sale contingent upon the utility of the item being sold. In other words, the voiding of the sales transaction is dependent upon the existence of both the seller's and buyer's implied conditions. The requirement of "*taluy be-da'at shenehem*" as a precondition prior to the invoking of an *umdana* equally applies to marriage which is based upon the consent of both a man and a woman. For example, if a husband is engaged in criminal activity while married, the fact that a wife would exclaim, "had I known he would become a criminal, I never would have married him," would seem to offer no basis for voiding the marriage, since a similar statement must have either been articulated by the husband or be presumed on the husband's behalf. The husband's declaration would be – "If I become a criminal after the onset of the marriage, my marriage is invalid." In fact, the husband may not want to void the marriage in order to avoid his sexual intercourse being redefined as *be'ilat zenut*, an act of fornication. However, in contradistinction to the above view, adopting the views of Rabbis Mordekhai Hillel, Zvi Ashkenazi, Yehezkel Landau, Hayyim Halberstam, Zvi Shapiro, Moshe Zweig, Moshe Feinstein, Ezra Batzri and others, in cases of a major *umdana* or what has been labeled as an *umdana demukhah*, a major inference from assessed expectations expressed by one person suffices in order to void a commercial transaction and according to certain Poskim a marriage or a *halitzah* may be equally voided.[16]

16. See *Mordekhai, Yevamot* 4:29; *Resp. Hakham Tzvi* 41; *Resp. She'ailat Yitzhak*, 174, 186 (R. Stern's opinion); *Resp. Noda be-Yehudah, Mahadura Kamma, YD* 69, *Mahadura Tinyana EH* 80, 135; *Resp. Ohel Moshe* 1:62, *Mahadura Tlitai* 123; *Ha-Beit Meir, Tzal'ot ha-Bayit* 6; *Resp. She'eilot Moshe EH* 2 (4); D. Meisels, *Resp. Radad EH* 40; R.Y. Frankel, *Derekh Yesharah, be-Din Halitzah* in the name of R. Feinstein; *Resp. Iggerot Moshe, EH* 4:121; *Resp. Avnei Hefetz* 30; *Teshuvot Sha'arei*

In light of the *umdana* that one cannot reside with a husband who is suffering from mental disorders, Rochel is free to remarry without a *get* any Jew, even a *Kohen*.

* One may resolve this question of whether a husband is obligated to give a *get* to his wife, or for that matter voiding a marriage, as these are "halakhot of prohibitions and permissibility" ("*issur ve-heter*"). In the absence of the husband (i.e., either a husband who was summoned to a hearing but refuses to appear, or one who was not summoned to the hearing), there is a debate as to whether one rabbi or three rabbis functioning as arbiters of these halakhot of *issur ve-heter* may issue a *hora'ah* (instruction) of a scholar (a *rav*) rather than a *beit din*. See *Ketzot Ha-Hoshen, HM* 3:1–2; *Netivot ha-Mishpat, HM* 3:1, Biurim 25:4; *Teshuvot Yehuda* (Gordin), EH 51:2; *Teshuvot Hatam Sofer, OH* 51, *EH* 2:64; *Pithei Teshuvah, SA EH Seder Ha-Get* 6, 8; *Hazon Ish, Nega'im* 4:9; *Piskei Din Rabbanayim* 6:265, 269; File 957-61, Beit Din Yerushalayim for Monetary Matters and Yuhasin, vol. 7, 515; File no. 448866/3, Tel-Aviv-Yaffo Regional Beit Din, July 11, 2013; File no. 1086123/1, Be'er Sheva Regional Beit Din, December 20. 2018. Notwithstanding scrutinizing witnesses for which one requires a *beit din*, Rabbi Zalman N. Goldberg writes, "However, in questions of Even Haezer such as divorce and *mamzerut* and the like, it seems that there is no need for a *beit din*... From the halakhot of *agunah*, one cannot prove that one needs a *beit din* in questions of Even Haezer." See *Lev Ha-Mishpat* 1, 149-150.

Whether the individual Jew must be knowledgeable in Halakhah is subject to controversy. See *Yam shel Shlomo, Bava Kamma* 3:9; *Teshuvot Ma'aseh Hiyah*, 24; *Ketzot Ha-Hoshen HM* 3:1; File no. 448866/3, op. cit.

In the present case, the issues have been resolved by a *moreh hora'ah* who is guided by the rule: "if the matter is such, the halakhah is thus and thus" (*Teshuvot Ha-Rashbash* 230). In other words, if the determination of the facts is made in a given manner, the relevant Halakhah ought to be applicable. Secondly, in the absence of one party, this ruling of the *rav* may be rendered in a decision regarding *igun*, provided that the participating party is known to possess integrity and would not lie. See *Knesset Ha-Gedolah*, Tur *HM* 17:19.

Ezra 4:26 and others.

Chapter 16

Decisions in *Hoshen Mishpat*

A. THE STATUS OF A SUBTENANT AS A BAILEE: A COMPARATIVE ANALYSIS

The Beit Din having been chosen by the parties as arbitrators pursuant to an Agreement to Arbitrate (the "Arbitration Agreement"; attached hereto as Exhibit A), dated as of November 12, 2009, between Issac Prager, ("Plaintiff") and Max Louis ("Defendant") for a binding decision with respect to monies allegedly owed in connection with the property located at 3333 Henry Hudson Parkway, Bronx, New York (the "Apartment"), with each party claiming financial and other claims against the other, and the parties having acknowledged that the Beit Din is authorized to resolve all such disputes, having given said matters due consideration, having heard all parties testify as to the facts of said disputes and differences, and having reviewed additional written submissions made by the parties following those hearings, does decide as follows:

Facts

Plaintiffs, shareholders in Whitehall co-operative ("Whitehall"), sublet the Apartment to Defendant. With the permission of Whitehall, Plaintiff executed two subleases between Plaintiff and Defendant. Pursuant to clause nine of the sublease agreement, Defendants obligated themselves to "take good care of the Apartment and... not permit or do any damage to it." On December 4, 2005, a water main broke. Tenants at Whitehall were notified that the main would be shut down, and no water was to be used before the main was turned back on. Nevertheless, during the shut-off, Defendant's five-year-old daughter turned on a bathroom faucet.

When the main was turned back on, water flooded the Apartment and caused damage to the Apartment.

Defendant immediately notified Plaintiff regarding the damage caused by the flood. As required by Whitehall's Proprietary Lease and House Rules, Plaintiff maintained in full force, throughout the term of the two subleases and thereafter, a public liability and property damage insurance policy. Nonetheless, Plaintiff failed to submit a claim for the incurred loss in a timely fashion. When Plaintiff later made an insurance claim, the insurance company denied the Plaintiff's claim based on its lateness.

The term of the second sublease of the Apartment expired on February 9, 2008. Nevertheless, Defendant continued to occupy the Apartment after the expiration of said term. Due to Defendant's occupation of the Apartment without the consent of Whitehall, Whitehall evicted them in August 2009.

Plaintiffs' Claims

Plaintiff's claim is that as of the date of Defendant's eviction from the Apartment, they are owed two months' rent, totaling $6,700, and reimbursement for a utility bill, totaling $600. In addition, Plaintiffs claim that Defendant removed from the Apartment a new oven range and refrigerator that was purchased by Plaintiffs, with a total value of $915. Plaintiffs also claim an unspecified amount for Defendant's allegedly unauthorized removal of two air conditioners from the Apartment.

Due to the initial damage sustained by Plaintiff as a result of the flood, Plaintiff originally claimed $4,500.00. Due to the subsequent loss incurred by the buckling of the floors in the master bedroom and second bedroom as well as damage to the carpet in the foyer, Plaintiff now claim an additional $2,000 to $3,000 from Defendant.

Finally, Plaintiff maintain that at all times it was Defendant who obtained permission from Whitehall to sublease the Apartment from Plaintiff, and Defendant accepted the responsibility of obtaining such consent to any sublease renewals. Following Defendant's failure to file an application with Whitehall to extend the sublease after the expiration of the second lease, Whitehall brought suit against Plaintiffs to terminate the proprietary lease and essentially end Plaintiffs' possessory interest in the Apartment. Plaintiff incurred legal expenses of $24,722.23 defending their right to keep their Apartment, as well as $1,492.28 for legal fees billed to them by Whitehall relating to this matter.

Defendant's Defenses and Counterclaims

Defendant acknowledges liability in the amount of $3,350.00 for unpaid rent, and $600 for the unpaid utility bill. Defendant denies any liability for the refrigerator and oven range, claiming that both were left in the Apartment by Defendant in good working order at the end of the tenancy.

Defendant claims that the air conditioning units were in poor condition and unserviceable. Since disposing of these items was authorized, Defendant maintains that Plaintiff is not entitled to any compensation.

Defendant asserts a number of defenses to his liability for the damages caused by the flood. First, pursuant to halakha, there is no liability for damage caused by a tortfeasor who is a *katan* (a minor). Second, given that *karka* (immovables) such as an apartment is not subject to *hilkhot shemirah* (law of bailment), Defendant cannot be construed as a *shomer* (bailee) and is therefore not liable for the damages caused by the flood. Finally, Defendant asserts that since he notified Plaintiff in a timely fashion regarding the flood and the resultant damage, he is not liable for any of the damage incurred by Whitehall, or Plaintiff. Had Plaintiffs filed a claim with the insurance company in a timely fashion, the insurance company would have covered the cost of the repairs. Defendant argues that given that the Plaintiffs were contractually obligated to Whitehall to carry liability insurance, the lease agreement between Plaintiffs and Defendant contains an implied term that the tenant is exempt from any tort liability covered by the insurance policy. Therefore, Defendants are liable neither for the losses relating to the flood which were suffered by Plaintiffs nor for payment of Plaintiffs' legal fees relating to the Whitehall litigations.

Defendant claims reimbursement for (i) $7,500 paid to Whitehall in settlement of the Whitehall Damage Suit and (ii) $3,350.00, representing the security deposit being held by Plaintiffs.

Discussion

1. Liability for the Acts of a Minor

Upon the attainment of majority age (for a girl, 12 years and a day; for a boy, 13 years and a day), an individual becomes responsible for his or her own financial affairs. Prior to attaining majority age, a child is viewed as a *katan* (minor) without *da'at* (rational capacity for decision making).[1] Consequently, minors are represented by their parents who serve as *apotroposim* (guardians)[2] entrusted to manage their children's interests, including their appearances in *beit din* on their behalf relating to matters of *nezikin* (torts).[3] Consequently, for a plaintiff to advance a claim against a minor, the arbitration agreement must designate the minor as a defendant and state that the parent is representing the minor in this proceeding. In addition, a *katan* is generally exempt from tort liability for the damages that he or she caused,[4] and a *beit din* would refrain from invoking extra-halakhic penal measures against a minor tortfeasor.[5]

Nevertheless, a parent is responsible for any damages incurred by a minor child.[6] Therefore, although the minor child is not a party to the arbitration agreement and would, in any event, be exempt from liability on the basis of his or her status as a minor, this *beit din* is empowered to assess liability to the parents of the minor child.

2. Subtenant's Status as a *Shomer*

One of the avenues for establishing a *mafkid-nifkad* (bailor-bailee) relationship is by the bailee's verbal acceptance to guard a particular asset. The Talmud states that if the owner of an asset requests an individual to guard his property and the bailee replies "leave it with me," we construe such words as an agreement to be a *shomer*.[7] Alternatively, if a *shomer* states "I will accept it," we interpret such language as consenting to be a shomer.[8] In our case, although there was no verbal declaration, there is a written confirmation of the Defendant's willingness to become a *shomer*. Paragraph 9 of the sublease agreement provides that, "[y]ou will take good care of the Apartment and will not permit or do any damage

1. Additionally, for the male, there is a requirement of two pubic hairs and for the female she needs to have *simanim*. See *Tosefta Nidah* 6:2; *Nidah* 45b-46a. For the absence of *da'at*, see *Hagiga* 2b.

2. The father on the grounds of his legal standing as a natural guardian and the mother by virtue of her appointment by a *beit din* or by virtue of living with her child. See *Resp. Ha-Rosh* 82:2, 87:4, 96:2; *Resp. Ha-Rashba* 2:49.

3. Mishnah *Bava Kamma* 4:4; *Bava Kamma* 39a.

4. *Shulhan Arukh, Hoshen Mishpat* 424.

5. *Shulhan Arukh, Hoshen Mishpat* 343:9; *Resp. Ha-Ridvaz* 1:432.

6. *Tosafot Bava Kamma* 21b, s.v. *adam*; *Nimmukei Yosef*, 9b [as per Rif pagination], s.v. *adam*.

7. Talmud Bavli *Bava Metzia* 80b; *Shulhan Arukh, Hoshen Mishpat* 291:2.

8. *Pithei Teshuva, Hoshen Mishpat* 291:2.

to it..." By signing this agreement, Plaintiffs and Defendant agreed that Defendant would act as a *shomer* of Plaintiffs' property.

Numerous authorities hold that contracts that are enforceable under secular law are recognized under Jewish law as well, based upon the doctrine of *kinyan situmta* (the acceptability of such an agreement in standard commercial practice), even absent the performance of an actual formal *kinyan* (symbolic act under Jewish law to effect an obligation).[9] Consequently, a signed sublease agreement is enforceable under Jewish law provided that it is enforceable according to secular law.[10] In addition, many decisors of Jewish law do not mandate the performance of any *kinyan* altogether in order to establish a bailment relationship and make the bailee liable for losses relating to the object entrusted in his care.[11] For these authorities, it is sufficient that the bailee agree to guard the item, and that the bailor communicate to the bailee that he is entrusting him with the asset and withdraw from guarding the asset.

Alternatively, should one require a *kinyan*[12] and challenge the efficacy of *kinyan situmta* regarding *karka* (real property),[13] the fact that Defendant utilized the premises suffices as a means for creating the *mafkid-nifkad* relationship.[14] Accordingly, *shemirah* is established in our case either based upon the terms of the sublease agreement or Defendant's use of the property.

3. Liability of Subtenant for Damages

A. UNDER HALAKHAH

Generally, a *shomer*'s monetary liability with respect to a leased apartment would only extend to *metaltelin* (movables), such as appliances

9. *Resp. Hatam Sofer, Hoshen Mishpat* 66; *Resp. Ahiezer* 3:79, Sec. 7; *Resp. Maharsham*, 5:45; *Resp. Tzemah Tzedek* (Lubavitch), *Yoreh Deah* 233; PDR 6:202, 216; 9:16, 40; 16:133, 138.

10. PDR 12:279, 291; 18:108, 112.

11. *Tosafot, Bava Metzia* 99a, s.v. *kakh*; *Piskei Ha-Rosh, Bava Metzia* 6:16; *Tur, Hoshen Mishpat* 307:1; *Be'ur Hagra, Hoshen Mishpat* 291:13.

12. *Mishneh Torah, Hilk. Sekhirut* 2:8; *Shulhan Arukh, Hoshen Mishpat* 303:1; *Shakh, Hoshen Mishpat* 291:13; *Tumim* 72:54; *Netivot Hamishpat* 306:1; *Erekh Shai, Hoshen Mishpat* 291:5; *Resp. Divrei Malkiel* 5:215.

13. *Bah, Hoshen Mishpat* 201:2.

14. *Ketzot Ha-Hoshen* 153:3, 189:1; *Netivot Ha-Mishpat* 192:6, 306:1; *Mahaneh Ephraim, Hilk. Sekhirut* 1; *Resp. Devar Avraham* 2:17; *Resp. Hikekei Lev*, Vol. 2, *Hoshen Mishpat* 48; *Hazon Ish, Even Ha-Ezer* 147:3.

and furniture.[15] The walls,[16] ceilings and flooring of a leased apartment are subsumed in the category of *karka'ot* (immovables) and therefore are exempt from the halakhot of bailment. However, according to Rambam, a *shomer* who is *posheia* (negligent) is viewed as a *mazik* due to the fact that he or she accepted to guard the asset and the bailor relied upon him or her to be a *shomer* and ceased to guard it.[17] Some Jewish law decisors endorse Rambam's conclusion that a *shomer* is monetarily responsible for damages caused by his or her negligence.[18] Nonetheless, most Jewish law decisors reject Rambam's view.[19] In their eyes, negligence is an example of *grama* (indirect cause) and one is exempt from liability for indirectly caused damage.[20] As such, one might conclude that Defendant ought to be exempt from liability for the ensuing loss. Yet, even according to the majority opinion, a *shomer* who damages *karka* is liable due to the fact that the bailor relied upon the bailee and the bailee promised to act responsibly with his bailment.[21]

In this case, Section 20(A) of the sublease agreement expressly provides that Defendant is liable for any damage to the Apartment. Accordingly, Defendant is liable even for acts of *grama* to *karka* or *metaltelin*.[22]

Defendant's liability, whether resulting from default halakhic rules that emanate from his *shomer* status or from his liability pursuant to the terms of the sublease agreement, exists notwithstanding the fact that Plaintiffs maintained insurance coverage for the damage that occurred. According to most halachic decisors, personal liability for damage inflicted exists independent of the sustained loss. Accordingly, even if the tort victim is compensated for the loss incurred by collection of insurance proceeds, the tort victim is entitled to claim additional payments

---

15. *Shemot* 22:6, 9; *Bava Metzia* 57b.

16. *Tosafot, Shavuot* 42b, s.v. *shomeir*. Cf. *Ittur, Ot Ayin – Iska Vehov* 20b, who construes walls as movable.

17. *Resp. Ha-Rashba* 5:166; *Even Haezel, Mishneh Torah, Hilk. Sekhirut* 2:3; *Mahaneh Ephraim, Hilk. Shomrim* 7; *Arukh Ha-Shulhan, Hoshen Mishpat* 291:2.

18. *Shakh, Hoshen Mishpat* 66:126, 95:3; *Resp. She'elat Ya'avetz* 1:85; *Resp. Hatam Sofer, Hoshen Mishpat* 94.

19. Ra'avad, *Mishneh Torah, Hilk. Sekhirut* 2:3; *Resp. Harif* 97; *Teshuvot Ha-Rosh* 39:2; *Shulhan Arukh, Hoshen Mishpat* 95:1; *Rema, Hoshen Mishpat* 66:40, 301:1; *Hiddushei Rabbi Akiva Eiger, Hoshen Mishpat* 308:7; *Tumim, Hoshen Mishpat* 96:2; *Resp. Pnei Yehoshua* 2:106.

20. *Piskei Ha-Rosh, Bava Metzia* 4:21; *Resp. Ahiezer* 3:37.

21. *Beit Yosef, Hoshen Mishpat* 66:41 (in the name of Ritva).

22. *Mahaneh Ephraim,* supra n. 17, at 9.

for damages directly from the *mazik* (tortfeasor).[23] Hence, in our case, even if Plaintiffs would have received compensation for losses incurred from their insurance company, they would still retain the right to demand additional payment for damages caused by Defendant.

This halakhic recognition of a "double indemnity" principle would allow Plaintiffs to advance a claim for damages even if they had received compensation from the insurance company. *A fortiori*, in our case, where no insurance proceeds were collected, Plaintiffs' claim for recovery is valid.

B. UNDER COMMON COMMERCIAL PRACTICE AND SECULAR LAW

In addition to the conclusion reached through an analysis of Jewish law in this matter, since the Apartment is located in New York and the parties entered into a standard New York form sublease for co-op apartments, it is quite possible that the expectation of the parties was for their sublease relationship to be governed by standard commercial practice in New York, as determined by New York law.[24] An inquiry into New York law on this matter is therefore appropriate.

Typically, when attorneys negotiate the provisions of a lease, they aim to coordinate the insurance, subrogation, indemnity and casualty provisions of the lease so that any damage to the property is covered by insurance, and neither party has any liability, regardless of fault. This is accomplished by expressly setting forth each party's liability with respect to damage to the property, and obligating the liable party to obtain insurance coverage for such liability and waivers of subrogation that prevent the insurer from seeking restitution from the other party for claims paid.[25]

Secular courts have addressed the issue of whether the existence of insurance coverage works to shield a tenant from liability for damage covered by the insurance, in the absence of an express provision to that effect. Some cases have dealt with situations where a lease requires a landlord to maintain insurance and the landlord collects under the policy to repair damage for which the tenant is liable under the lease.

23. *Ohr Sameah, Hilk. Sekhirut* 7:1; *Resp. Shoeil U-Meishiv, Mahadura Tinyana,* 3:129, *Mahadurah Tlitai,* 1:223; *Resp. Maharsham* 4:7; *Kovetz Shiurim, Ketubot, Simanim* 217-218; *Sha'ar Hamishpat, Hoshen Mishpat* 72:12; *Resp. Minhat Yitzchak* 3:126; *Resp. Mishneh Halakhot* 2:10.

24. See *Resp. Iggerot Moshe, Hoshen Mishpat,* 1:72.

25. See Friedman on Leases, §38:2 (2010).

Courts have held that because the lease required the landlord to maintain insurance, part of the rent paid by the tenant is effectively a reimbursement of the insurance premiums paid by the landlord. As a result, the tenant is treated as a "co-insured" and the landlord may not sue the tenant under the lease for the damage incurred if the landlord has already collected insurance proceeds under its policy.[26] At least under these circumstances, secular courts have declined to adopt the "double indemnity" theory discussed above.

Another line of cases has dealt with the issue of subrogation of claims. In these cases, one party to the lease damages the leased property. The other party maintains insurance for that damage, and receives insurance proceeds to repair the damage. The insurance company then seeks to subrogate, and recover its losses by bringing an action against the party that damaged the property. New York courts have held that such subrogation claims are viable, and the party that damaged the property may not claim that they are "immune from subrogation as an implied co-insured" under the insurance policy.[27]

In all of the cases where courts imputed a "co-insurance" arrangement to shield a tenant from liability based on the existence of an insurance policy held by the landlord, the leases have expressly required the landlord to maintain insurance or have not contained express language making the tenant liable for the damage incurred.[28] In this case, however, the sublease agreement could not be clearer as to the liability of Defendant regardless of any insurance coverage held by Plaintiffs. Section 20(A) of the sublease agreement obligates Defendant to "reimburse Owner for any of the following fees and expenses incurred by Owner... making

---

26. See Am. Nat'l Bank & Trust Co. v. Edgeworth, 618 N.E.2d 899 (Ill. Ct. App. 1993) (landlord acquired insurance, and was paid insurance proceeds; landlord has duty to apply proceeds to repair, even if the lease provides that tenant must repair).

27. Viacom Intern., Inc. v. Midtown Realty Co., 235 A.D.2d 332 (App. Div. 1st Dept. 1997). To be sure, some jurisdictions have adopted the "Sutton doctrine", which states that even absent an explicit waiver of subrogation, an implied waiver exists that shields the tenant from liability to the insurer. See Sutton v. Jondahl 532 P.2d 478 (1975). These courts have held that "the law considers the tenant as a co-insured of the landlord absent an express agreement between them to the contrary." Id. at 482. However, even those jurisdictions which have adopted the Sutton doctrine have held that where explicit language in the lease agreement makes the tenant liable for the damage, no waiver of subrogation can be implied. For a broader discussion about the Sutton doctrine, see Friedman on Leases, §9:11.1 (2010).

28. For additional citations to relevant case law, see C. R. McCorkle, "Liability of tenant for damage to the leased property due to his acts or neglect," 10 A.L.R.2d 1012, §3 and Friedman on Leases, id.

any repairs to the Apartment or the Building, including any appliances in the Apartment, which result from misuse or negligence by You, the Permitted Occupants of the Apartment, persons who visit the Apartment or work for You." Also, Section 33 of the sublease agreement states that Defendant "acknowledges that Owner may not be required to maintain any insurance with respect to the Apartment."

Given these explicit sublease provisions, secular case law generally provides that Defendant is liable for damage to the Apartment, regardless of the fact that Plaintiff maintained insurance. Accordingly, applying standard commercial practice as informed by secular law, Defendant is liable for the damage to the Apartment. Since both secular law and Jewish law reach the same result regarding this issue, we need not decide which set of laws governs this case.

4. The Subtenant's Liability for Sub-landlord's Property

Both the landlord and the tenant are proscribed from changing the appearance of the leased property without their mutual consent and upon expiration of the term of the lease, the tenant must return the property to the landlord in the condition that he initially received it.[29] Should a doubt arise between the parties regarding the terms of the lease arrangement or issues arising due to the arrangement, given that the landlord is the *muhzak* (the possessor), "*yad ha-maskir al ha-elyona*" (the landlord is at an advantage).[30] Hence, the burden of proof is upon the tenant to validate his claim. Analogously, this halakha will equally apply to our case of a sub-landlord-subtenant relationship.

Consequently, in our case, due to the doubts regarding whether the Defendant is obligated to remunerate the Plaintiffs for the appliances and due to Defendant's inability to prove his claim, we accept the position of the Plaintiffs regarding these matters. Hence, Defendant is obligated to pay for the oven, refrigerator and the air conditioners.

5. The Recovery of Legal Fees

The prevailing party in a *din Torah* is generally not entitled to reimbursement of legal fees and other litigation costs, because such a claim is construed as *grama* (indirect damage).[31] Consequently, Plaintiff's claim

29. *Shulhan Arukh, Hoshen Mishpat* 212:6; *Sma*, ad. locum. 16.
30. *Shulhan Arukh* and *Rema*, *Hoshen Mishpat* 312:16.
31. *Shulhan Arukh, Hoshen Mishpat* 14:5.

for recovery of legal fees regarding their proceedings with Whitehall relating to damage to the Apartment is a claim for an act of *grama* and therefore we deny relief.

On the other hand, if one must defend oneself in court due to the improper behavior of the opposing party, such an act is labeled *garmi* (direct damage) and therefore, a defendant is entitled to recover his legal fees.[32] In our case, Defendant acted improperly in failing to file an application with Whitehall to extend the sublease after the expiration of the second lease. As a result of Defendant's omission, Plaintiff was required to be party to a civil proceeding which entailed the incurring of legal expenses. Consequently, Plaintiffs are entitled to recoup their legal costs relating to this civil proceeding.

Decision

Based on the foregoing, we decide as follows:

1. Defendant shall pay $6,700 to Plaintiffs for outstanding two months' rent.
2. Defendant shall pay $600 to Plaintiffs for outstanding utility bill.
3. Defendant shall pay $915 to Plaintiffs for Plaintiffs' purchase of an oven and refrigerator.
4. Defendant shall pay $100 to Plaintiffs for the air conditioning units.
5. Defendant shall pay $4,500 to Plaintiffs for the initial losses due to the flood.
6. Defendant shall pay $1,500 to Plaintiffs due to the subsequent loss incurred by the buckling of the floors in the master bedroom and second bedroom as well as the carpet in the foyer.
7. Defendant shall pay $26,214.51 to Plaintiffs for recovery of Plaintiffs' legal fees relating to Whitehall's civil suit regarding Defendant's failure to file an application to renew their sublease after the expiration date of the second lease.
8. Defendants are entitled to a set-off of one month's rent in the amount of $3,350 representing the security deposit being held in escrow by Plaintiffs.
9. All other applications and claims are hereby denied.

32. *Be'ur Hagra, Hoshen Mishpat* 14:30; *Piskei Din, Battei Hadin Harabbanayim* 10:3, 16.

Total Credit to Plaintiff: $40,529.51

Total Credit to Defendant: $3,350.00

Net to Plaintiffs: $37,179.51

The schedule of payments shall be as follows:

No later than June 1, 2011, Defendant shall pay $20,179.51 to Plaintiffs.

No later than August 1, 2011, Defendant shall pay $17,000.00 to Plaintiffs.

If Defendant fails to remit the amount due by June 1, 2011, the entire remaining balance shall become immediately due.

The parties are encouraged not to speak disparagingly of each other.

The obligations set forth herein shall be enforceable in any court of competent jurisdiction, in accordance with the Rules and Procedures of the Beth Din of America and the Arbitration Agreement.

Any request for modification of this award by the arbitration panel shall be in accordance with the Rules and Procedures of the Beit Din and the Arbitration Agreement.

Any provision of this decision may be modified with the consent of both parties.

All of the provisions of this decision shall take effect immediately.

B. RECOVERY OF REAL ESTATE BROKERAGE FEE COMMISSION

Facts

In June 2005, a New York licensed real estate broker (hereinafter: the Plaintiff) entered into a written brokerage agreement with his client (hereinafter: the Defendant), whereby he would show prospective NY commercial properties for sale to the Defendant and would receive a seven per cent commission to be shared equally between the buyer and seller on any consummated sale. Pursuant to this agreement, the Defendant was shown several properties by the Plaintiff. Subsequently, in May 2007, the Defendant purchased one of those properties for three million dollars. Defendant refused to pay the seven per cent commission on the transaction.

In August 2005, the Defendant placed an ad in the local newspaper that he was interested in selling a piece of NY residential property. Upon reading the ad, the Plaintiff secured a buyer for the Defendant's property and the Defendant sold it. Inadvertently, the Plaintiff forgot about the transaction and eighteen months later he remembered about it. At that time, the Plaintiff billed him but the Defendant refused to pay the broker commission regarding this transaction.

Plaintiff's Claims

Based upon the written agreement executed between the parties, Defendant argues that he is entitled to a brokerage fee for his services rendered.

Regarding the purchase of the residential property, even though there was no express brokerage agreement between the parties, Defendant claims that services were rendered and based upon commercial practice he is entitled to a broker's commission fee of six per cent.

In both transactions, the Defendant accepted the benefits of the Plaintiff's services, and therefore he is entitled to a commission

Defendant's Reply

Given that there was no express written brokerage agreement between the parties regarding the purchase of the residential property, according to commercial practice Defendant is not entitled to a commission for services rendered. Moreover, even if Plaintiff is entitled to payment, given that New York state's statute of limitations for filing a lawsuit regarding unpaid real estate commission is six years, the time limit on pursuing a remedy has expired and therefore, commercial practice dictates that Plaintiff is not entitled to recover his commission.

Regarding the purchase of the commercial property, Defendant admits that the Plaintiff provided the services as promised but his rate of commission memorialized in the brokerage agreement is above the market rate for property sold for three million dollars and therefore is entitled to a maximum of 6% brokerage commission.

Discussion

The broker, i.e., *metavekh* or *sarsur,* whether he be a real estate broker [or a marital broker, i.e., *shadkhan*] is duty-bound to comply with the halakhot of *hiyuvim* [obligations]. Halakhah recognizes the following rules which serve as the groundwork for clients to remunerate a broker for his services: namely, the *zeh neheneh ve-zeh haser* rule and *minhag hasochrim.*

1. The *Zeh Neheneh Ve-zeh Haser* Rule

Halakhah recognizes that if someone benefits from someone else and the latter sustains a loss due to the benefit conferred, the beneficiary is liable to pay. The grounds for liability are either that the beneficiary is viewed as a *gazlan* (a thief) who is benefiting without remitting payment or a *mazik* (tortfeasor) of the assets of another.[1] Prior to imposing monetary liability for what secular law labels "unjust enrichment," one must define the loss caused to the benefactor. In our scenario, real estate brokers invest their time in order to identify a property which best fits their clients' needs and budgets. They obtain listings and execute agreements with owners to place properties for sale with the real estate company. They compare the listed property with similar properties that recently sold, to determine the market value of the property. A broker may meet frequently with prospective buyers to discuss and visit available properties. When buying property, brokers arrange for title searches to verify ownership and for meetings between a seller and potential buyer during

1. *Tur, Hoshen Mishpat* 371:10; *Ohr Sameah, Hilk. Nizkei Mamon* 1:2.

which they agree to the details of the transaction. A broker also acts as an intermediary in price negotiations between a buyer and seller. In some instances, they may assist in arranging financing from a lender for the prospective buyer, which may be the catalyst "to close the deal". There is ample evidence in the record that the Tovea (Plaintiff) acted as the broker on this transaction of residential property. No expenses are being reimbursed for advertising, licensing and transportation expenses, or other overhead expenses. This outlay of expenses is covered by a broker's market commission. In short, the consummation of a sale without the broker receiving a commission for his time investment constitutes a loss for the broker and therefore is illustrative of the rule *zeh neheneh ve-zeh haser.* In the absence of a written or verbal agreement to provide services, *Rema* rules,[2]

> An individual who performs an action or benefit for his friend, he cannot say that it was done gratis since you didn't tell me to do it and he must compensate him.

Numerous legists endorse Rema's view,[3] arguing that an individual is entitled to a fee for services rendered regardless of whether the individual was duly empowered by another to perform these actions, or he performed these services on his own initiative provided that the beneficiary of the work did not direct him to stop working or communicated to him that he would not receive remuneration for his services[4].

2. *Hoshen Mishpat* 264:4. See also, *Rema, Hoshen Mishpat* 246:17. Cf. *Rema, Hoshen Mishpat* 363:10.

On the other hand, *Rema* contends that certain actions such as expressing a willingness to be an *arev* (guarantor on a loan) without performing a *kinyan* (symbolic act of undertaking an obligation) is not an action which one customarily receives compensation, hence, under these circumstances a failure to pay the *arev* will not allow the *arev* to recover from the borrower a fee for his services. See *Rema Hoshen Mishpat* 129:22. For the rationale of Rema's ruling, see *Resp. Ha-Rosh* 64:3.

3. See the list in *Resp. Maharam Alsheich* 70; *Resp. Maharitz,* 2, *Even Ha-Ezer* 21; *Resp. Maharashdam, Hoshen Mishpat* 345; *Resp. Havot Yair* 134; *Beth Shmuel, Even Ha-Ezer* 70:28; PDR 11:278, 282-283. Given the contradictory rulings in Rema [see supra n. 2], some *aharonim* view this matter as a halakhic doubt and therefore, one cannot extract money from the beneficiary. See *Bah, Tur, Hoshen Mishpat* 363; *Resp. Nodah Be-Yehudah, Mahadurah Tinyana, Hoshen Mishpat* 34; *Resp. Hatam Sofer, Hoshen Mishpat 119; Resp. Doveiv Meisharim* 1:42.

4. Talmud Bavli *Bava Metzia* 101b; *Tur, Hoshen Mishpat* 375:1 (in the name of Rosh); *Beit Yosef, Tur Hoshen Mishpat* 375:1; *Resp. Mahari Halevi,* 2:151. Cf. *Hiddushei Ha-Rashba, Bava Metzia* 101b; *Hiddushei Ha-Ramban, Bava Metzia* 101b;

Pursuant to some authorities, the basis for Rema's position is reflected in the Talmudic case of the planted trees:[5]

> A man came before Rav. Rav said to the owner of the field, "Go and assess it for him." The owner said he did not want the trees. Rav said to him "Go and assess it for him".... But the owner said, "I do not want the trees" Subsequently, he fenced the trees in and was guarding it. Rav said to the owner, "You have revealed your mind that you desire it. Go and make an assessment for him and the planter shall be at an advantage.

On one side, we have the improver who plants trees without the owner's permission and requests remuneration. On the other side, we encounter the owner's repeated assertions that he does want these improvements. Yet, subsequently, by fencing in and guarding the trees, the owner admitted that he did want them. Hence, Rav directed him to pay for the plantings. Failure to remit compensation for work rendered is subsumed in the category of "encroaching upon another's property without permission and plants".[6] As such, even in the absence of an agreement between the parties, a broker should receive compensation for his services.[7] In effect, a broker's performance is a quasi-contract based upon unjust enrichment, i.e. *zeh nehene ve-zeh haser*.[8] Hence, if a broker furnished his services and the buyer changed his mind and withdrew from the deal, the buyer is obligated to pay a full commission.[9]

2. *Minhag Hasochrim* (Commercial Practice) as a Basis of Obligation

One of the issues at bar is whether New York commercial practice allows for the recovery of a brokerage commission in connection with a broker's efforts to procure a buyer for a residential property. Significantly,

Resp. Peri Tevuah 58; *Resp. Maharash Engel*, 3:15.

5. Talmud Bavli *Bava Metzia* 101a.
6. *Bi'ur Hagra, Hoshen Mishpat* 87:117, 185:13, based on *Bava Kamma* 101a.
7. *Resp. Iggerot Moshe, Hoshen Mishpat* 2:49; PDR 13:34 (*Resp. Tzitz Eliezer* 15:67); *Resp. Halikhot Yisrael* 1.
8. *Resp. Shoeil U-Meishiv, Mahadura Tilitaah* 3:7 *Resp. Halikhot Yisrael* 14.
9. *Resp. Sha'ar Ephraim, Hoshen Mishpat* 150. This position is endorsed by numerous *Aharonim* including *Resp. Bnei Hayei, Hoshen Mishpat* 185: *Misgeret Hashulhan* 185:21; *Mishkenot Haro'im*, ot 60 *Sirsur* 120; *Resp. Mayim Rabim, Hoshen Mishpat* 27.

Plaintiff does not allege that it had an express agreement with Defendant to perform brokerage services with him for this property; however, New York commercial practice as memorialized in New York judgments would entitle him to such compensation.

Even in the absence of an express agreement, New York case law clearly supports giving a broker commission. In one case which occurred in 2002, a broker sought recovery of a commission for finding a tenant for a property, the court stated the following:[10]

> (T)he contract of employment may be established either by proof of an express and original agreement that the services should be rendered, or by facts showing, in the absence of such express agreement, a conscious appropriation of the labors of the broker." Indeed, "the contract may be established in some cases by the mere acceptance of the labors of a broker."

This holding is reflective a series of earlier NY case law dating back to 1881 that a broker is entitled to commission based upon facts showing, in the absence of an express agreement, a conscious appropriation of the labors of the broker by the client, i.e., an implied contract of employment.[11]

Though neither party is knowledgeable in New York law,[12] nevertheless their respective expectation was to resolve their differences based upon *minhag hasochrim* (commercial practice). In matters relating to monetary affairs, Halakhah imparts recognition to such an expectation. As Hazon Ish states:[13]

10. Joseph P. Day Realty Corp. v. Chera 308 A. D. 2d 148, 152, 762 N.Y.S. 373, N.Y. A.D., 2003.

11. Sibbald v. Bethlehem Iron Co., 83 NY 378, 380 (1881); Colvin v. Post Mortgage & Land Co., 225 NY 510 (1919); Greene v. Hellman, 51 NY2d 197,205-206 (1980); Gronich & Co. v. 649 Broadway Equities Co., 169 AD2d 600 (1991). For other grounds for recovery, see Ficor, Inc. v. National Kinney Corp., 67 AD2d 659, 659-660 (1979); Helmsley-Spear, Inc. v. NY Blood Center, 257 AD2d 64, 67 (1999).

12. See infra n. 16.

13. *Hazon Ish, Hoshen Mishpat, Likkutim* 16:1. Interestingly enough, Hazon Ish finds precedent for his position in the Rabad's ruling cited by Shakh, *Hoshen Mishpat* 73:36. However, a review of his ruling indicates that the invoking of the *umdana* is limited to instances when the Halakhah fails to address a situation and the resolution of the situation can be realized by invoking an *umdana*. However, Hazon Ish argues that it is inconceivable that there is a gap in Halakhah. Halakhah as a religious-legal system has the capacity to address all situations based on its own sources and rules of interpretation. As such, by citing Rabad's position, Hazon Ish

> The law of the kingdom [i.e. civil government] determinates the expectation of people; And since customarily, we abide by the law of the kingdom under certain prescribed conditions, nevertheless the law influences people who then decide to rely on civil law... and therefore when we apply secular law, we [i.e., beit din] judge we are in actuality following our Halakhah rather than their laws.

For example, one of the pieces of Israeli civil legislation is "the Law for Tenant Protection." When a tenant rents an apartment from a landlord, Rabbi Shlomo Karelitz argues in the name of his uncle, the Hazon Ish, that absent any agreement to the contrary, there is implicit expectation, an *umdana* that the terms of the tenancy will be based on civil law.[14] However, *Hazon Ish* adds that, in the absence of a clear indication that the parties are desirous to adopt civil law, the assumption is that Halakhah is the governing system.[15] The invoking of this *umdana* regarding tenancy law has been endorsed by others.[16] In effect, Halakhah may be predicated upon the expectations of people to follow halakhic

---

extends Rabad's affirmation of the workings of an *umdana* even if the Halakhah provides a contrary solution! Cf. others who limit the Rabad's ruling to situations where the Halakhah regarding a particular matter is subject to diverse opinions. See *Resp. Maharsham,* 3:128.

14. *Resp. Ateret Shlomo* (Shlomo Karelitz), Vol. 1, p. 360.

15. *Hoshen Mishpat Sanhedrin Likkutim* 16:1, 5, 9.

16. *Resp. Minhat Yitzchak* 2:86; PDR 16:312. On the other hand, others focus upon the assumption that the parties were desirous of following the *nohag* which is to adopt secular law rather than invoking the notion of *umdana.* See *Resp. Maharash,* Vol. 6, no. 19; *Resp. Iggerot Moshe, Hoshen Mishpat,* 1:72.

According to many poskim the efficacy of *nohag,* i.e., usage, is its existence regardless of whether the spouses knew the provisions of civil law, is subject to debate. See *Resp. Ha-Rosh* 68:12; *Tur* and *Shulhan Arukh Hoshen Mishpat* 61:5; *Shakh, Hoshen Mishpat* 42:36, 61:9, 71:33; *Biur Ha-Gra,* ad. locum 29, *Even Ha-Ezer* 66:48; *Resp. Re'im,* 16; *Pithei Hoshen, Hilk. Sekhirut,* p. 149. Should one contend that one must know of the usage, then if one party claims that he is unfamiliar with the expectation that people want to follow secular law regarding dividing up marital assets, then it becomes the other party's responsibility to demonstrate that such an expectation in fact exists. See *Shakh, Hoshen Mishpat* 42:36, 61:5 in the name of Rashba; *Erekh Shai, Even Ha-Ezer* 50:7; Michael Wygoda, *Agency Law* (Hebrew), Section 5, Israel's Ministry of Justice, n. 390.

If everyone is following the *nohag,* then claiming that one does not subscribe to it will be no defense. However, in monetary matters, should there be a minority who fails to follow the *nohag,* then such a claim will be accepted. See *Resp. Nahal Yitzchak,* 1, *Hoshen Mishpat,* 61.

tenancy law. Secular law may cause a change in the expectation which originally entailed adhering to halakhic tenancy law and now desires to follow secular law. Consequently, the Halakhah changes due to the change in the *umdana*.[17] At first glance, such an understanding of Hazon Ish's stance seemingly contradicts the notion of Halakhah's immutability. But, in fact the underlying rationale for legitimating this approach is that *umdana* is construed as equivalent to parties having agreed to resolve their issues according to their expectations which in our situation means following secular law.[18] In the words of Rabbi Moshe Feinstein,[19]

> They operate on the strength of the custom of the city, for having this in mind is equivalent to having specifically agreed to this arrangement.

Given that the custom of the locale reflects civil law, therefore the parties' expectation to follow this law is analogous to having accepted such an arrangement between themselves. Such a rationale should equally apply to *umdana*. In other words, the assessed expectation of the parties is no different than parties executing a contract and providing for a choice of law provision which states that their differences should be resolved by applying secular law.

Does that mean that if the parties have expectations which entail the transgression of *issurim*, i.e., ritual law, Halakhah will validate such mutual intent? Obviously, nothing could be further from the truth. In fact, the Talmud instructs us that "an individual may stipulate contrary to what is written in the Torah" only with regard to monetary matters.[20] As such, should parties expect to resolve their matters which entail violations of

---

17. Yoezer Ariel, *The Laws of Borerut* (in Hebrew), Jerusalem; 5765, p. 68. For an extensive list of contemporary decisors who subscribe to this view, see Dov Frimer, "The Influence of Israeli Law upon Jewish Law" (Hebrew), 39 *Jewish Studies* (1999), 133.

Rabbi Sherman challenges this conclusion by arguing that an *umdana* rooted in non-Jewish practices is ineffective. See Avraham Sherman and Shlomo Daichovsky, "The Law of Marital Partnership- Non-recognition in Jewish Law" (Hebrew), 19 *Tehumin* 205, 210-211 (5759).

Cf. this writer's "Varying Approaches towards the Division of Matrimonial Property upon Divorce" (Hebrew), *Hadarom*, Summer 2001, n. 46. which provides a list of responsa which affirm a reliance upon non-Jewish practices in monetary matters.

18. See supra notes 16-17.

19. *Iggerot Moshe*, supra n. 16. In effect, the *minhag* reflects civil law. See *Resp. Divrei Yosef* 21.

20. *Kiddushin* 19b.

theft and *ribbit* (exacting prohibited interest), such arrangements would be halakhically unenforceable. Yet, parties' expectations that general broker-client relations should be governed by commercial practice are enforceable provided that the mutually-agreed upon arrangements do not entail the violation of *issurim* (prohibitions).

In short, pursuant to the halakhic law of obligations as well as the invoking of an *umdana* based upon the parties' expectations that their issues be resolved in accordance with *minhag hasochrim,* we find that despite the absence of an express agreement between the parties regarding the Plaintiff's entitlement to a commission for his efforts in identifying and procuring the residential property, the Defendant is obligated to remit compensation to the Defendant. The fact that the newspaper ad announcing the availability of the residential property for sale failed to mention that brokers are not requested fails to be grounds for exempting the Nitba'at (Defendant) from payment. As mentioned, there is ample evidence in the record that demonstrates that the Defendant undeniably accepted the benefit of his services and the Defendant's efforts were instrumental in consummating the sale. As Rabbi Grossman argues, by dint of the negotiations between the broker and the seller, we have *"hoda'at ba'al din ke'me'ah edim damya"* (a man's own admission of guilt is akin to the power of one hundred witnesses) that the Nitba'at wants a broker and he gave his implicit consent to his appointment and therefore he is obligated to pay.[21] Alternatively, Rabbi Blau contends that we invoke *umdana*, i.e., the expectations of the parties. In other words, if Plaintiff rendered brokerage services on the transaction, then he is entitled to remuneration.[22] Accordingly, Plaintiff should be entitled to a market commission for his efforts.

3. The Amount of a Brokerage Commission

When the parties' agreement is silent as to the specific amount of the commission or, as in our case, where no agreement was executed regarding brokerage services, how does one determine the rate? Addressing this issue, Rabbi Ya'akov Halevi Ettinger of seventeenth century Salonika contends that the resolution of this matter is contingent upon the scope of the Talmudic rule *dina de'malkhuta dina* (the law of the kingdom is the law).[23] The question is whether the regulation of real estate matters

21. *Resp. Halikhot Yisrael* 39.
22. *Pithei Hoshen, Sekhirut,* 336.
23. Talmud Bavli *Nedarim* 28a, *Gittin* 10b, *Bava Kamma* 113a-b, *Bava Batra*

can be validated based upon this rule. As Rabbi Ettinger elucidates, this question depends on whether we accept the Rema's ruling or the Shakh's view regarding the parameters of this rule. In the opinion of Rema, all matters which are "*le'takanat bnei hamedinah*" (for the benefit of its citizens) which is understood by Rema as referring to any issues relating to social interaction, may be governed by civil law.[24] Vigorously disagreeing with Rema, Shakh argues that if the particular secular law contradicts Halakhah, *dina de'malkhuta dina* will not govern.[25] Regarding our instance, as we will show, there is no conflict between halakha and civil law, therefore even Shakh would concur that the rule is applicable. Hence, in our issue at bar, the Plaintiff is entitled to a commission.

Nevertheless, in instances where civil law would contradict Halakhah, given that there is halakhic doubt whether we should follow the view of Rema or Shakh,[26] Rabbi Ettinger suggests that we resolve the rate of a brokerage commission based upon *minhag* (commercial custom). Many decisors have endorsed his opinion regarding a real estate broker and *shadchan* (marriage broker) alike.[27]

Based upon the foregoing, Plaintiff is entitled to receive the customary six percent commission received in New York at the time of the sale of the residential property.

4. The Validity of a Mutually-Agreed Upon Commission Which is Above the Market Rate

In the contract between the parties regarding the commercial property, the parties agreed that the brokerage commission would be seven

44b-45a.

24. *Darkhei Moshe, Tur, Hoshen Mishpat* 369; Rema, *Hoshen Mishpat* 73:14, 369:11.

25. *Hoshen Mishpat* 73:39. Interestingly enough, though normative halakha today is to follow Shakh's view, nevertheless, there are some *rishonim* and the majority of *aharonim* who adopt the Rema's posture. See *Aliyot De'rabbeinu Yonah, Bava Batra* 55a; *Resp. Ha-Rashba Ha-meyuhasot Le-Ramban*, 22; *Levush Iyr Shushan Hoshen Mishpat* 369:11; *Resp. Divrei Emet* 12; *Resp. Doveiv Meisharim* 1:76.

26. Other *aharonim* have the same hesitancy See *Resp. Hatam Sofer, Hoshen Mishpat* 65; *Erekh Shai, Hoshen Mishpat* 73:14; *Resp. Havatzelet Ha-Sharon, Hoshen Mishpat* 8.

27. *Resp. Maharshach* 1:79; *Resp. Ginat Veradim, Hoshen Mishpat* 1:1 *Resp. Vayeshev Moshe* 38; *Mishpat Shalom, Hoshen Mishpat* 185; *Resp. Beit Yitzhak Even Ha-Ezer* 1:115; *Resp. Betzeil Hahokhmah* 3:28; *Resp. Panim Meirot* 2:63; *Resp. Rabaz, Even Ha-Ezer* 62; PDR 10:278, 284; *Resp. Iggerot Moshe Hoshen Mishpat* 2:57.

percent of the purchase price of the commercial property. Given that the rate of compensation is linked to local custom standards, Defendant alleges the mutually-agreed upon rate is above the market standard which is between four to six percent, and consequently, he should pay less than the agreed rate stipulated in the contract.

At first glance, this question hinges upon the following debate. Relying upon the Maharam's ruling, Rema, Shakh and others claim, given that the client can always allege that he was jesting ("*hashata*") and therefore never seriously intended to pay such a rate, the broker is limited to receiving a commission which reflects the market rate.[28] Even if it is clear that the client was serious and not jesting, he still is only obligated to pay the market rate.[29] Should the client voluntarily pay the rate he promised after the consummation of the transaction, he has no grounds for advancing a claim of 'jesting' and therefore the entire sum belongs to the broker.[30] On the other hand, even if the rate exceeds the market standard, the majority of authorities opine that the broker is entitled to receive the agreed-upon amount.[31] Pursuant to one of the canons of decision-making, one follows the majority opinion and therefore we would affirm that the parties' agreement to pay a brokerage commission rate which exceeds the customary one is valid.

However, in our scenario, even those decisors who contend that a broker's remuneration cannot exceed the customary rate concede that once the parties sign off on a contract, the client is bound to the terms of the agreement including paying the agreed-upon commission. In effect, the execution of a *kinyan* (the symbolic act of undertaking an obligation) which entails *gemirat da'at* (firm resolve of the parties) preempts the advancement of 'the jesting' argument.[32]

Alternatively, should the local practice be that one compensates

28. *Mordekhai, Bava Kamma* 172 (in the name of Maharam); *Resp. Maharam of Rothenberg*, Berlin ed., 498, 499, 952; Rema, Hoshen Mishpat 264:7; *Shakh*, ad. locum 15; *Resp. Maharil Hadashot* 158; *Resp. Beit Yitzhak, Hoshen Mishpat* 76. Many sources in this section have been culled from Yosef Goldberg, "A Broker's Claim for Wages Exceeding the Market Rate" (Hebrew), 8 *Shurat Hadin* 183 (5763).

29. *Resp. Ha-Rosh* 64:3. Cf. *Ketzot Ha-Hoshen* 81:4; *Mahaneh Ephraim, Hilkh. Sekhirut* 15.

30. *Resp. Ha-Rashba* 1240; *Shulhan Arukh Hoshen Mishpat* 264:8.

31. *Resp. Maharah Ohr Zarua* 3; *Resp. Maharbil* 1:99; *Resp. Divrei Rivot* 396; *Resp. Mishpat Tzedek* 3:71; *Resp. Hikrei Lev, Hoshen Mishpat* 2:135, *Imrei Yosher, Hilkhot Dayanim* 18.

32. *Rosh*, supra n. 29; *Shakh Hoshen Mishpat* 81:6; *Netivot Ha-Mishpat, Hoshen Mishpat* 264:8; *Ketzot Ha-Hoshen* 129:8, 264:4; *Resp. Shevut Ya'akov* 2:157; *Mishpat Shalom, Hoshen Mishpat* 185.

whatever amount that the client promises, we follow the *minhag* (custom) and he is obligated to remit whatever he promised.[33] The rationale for this view is that the existence of *minhag* implicitly assumes that there is *gemirat da'at* (firm resolve) to comply with one's duty to remit payment. In effect, pursuant to the Shulhan Arukh and Rema, a *minhag* unaccompanied by rabbinic or communal sanction entailing monetary matters has an independent status even if the result will be to extract money from *muhzakim* (owners).[34]

5. A Brokerage Real Estate Agreement – An Example of *Kinyan Situmta*

The implicit premise of the aforementioned conclusion is that the signing of a brokerage agreement is regarded as a real agreement (*kinyan*) and hence binding upon the parties and therefore, the Defendant is obligated to remit a brokerage commission which exceeds the prevailing market rate. This conclusion requires further elaboration.

There are two components required in the undertaking of an obligation: effectuating a *kinyan* involves a physical act such as a *suddar* (by handing a handkerchief or any other article by the one party undertaking the obligation to the other party undertaking the obligation) and *gemirat da'at* (firm resolve of the parties).[35] Given that the commission is *davar she-lo ba la'olam* (something which is not yet in existence) at the time the *kinyan* was executed, the *kinyan suddar* was ineffective in obligating the Defendant to pay the brokerage fee for the commercial property.[36] Numerous authorities view the language of undertaking an obligation such as "I will pay" as merely a promise to execute a future action and therefore falls in the category of a *kinyan devarim*, i.e., an act that fails to create an enforceable duty.[37] Among the terms of our brokerage agreement are the following:

> Owner agrees to pay a commission of seven percent of the sale

33. *Resp. Edut Be-Yehosef* 2:35; *Resp. Maharshach*, supra n.27.

34. *Shulhan Arukh, Hoshen Mishpat* 176:10, 218:19, 229:2, 230:10, 232:6, 330:5, 331:12; *Resp. Ha-Rema* nos. 19-20; Rema, *Shulhan Arukh, Hoshen Mishpat* 72:5.

35. *Hazon Ish, Hoshen Mishpat* 22; R. Yehezkel Abramsky, *Dinei Mamonot* (Hebrew), Bnei Brak, 5731.

36. *Shulhan Arukh, Hoshen Mishpat* 60:6,209: 4-7. Cf. *Ketzot Ha-Hoshen* 332:6.

37. *Bava Batra* 3b, 148b; *Shulhan Arukh Hoshen Mishpat* 245:1, 253:3; *Resp. Maharbil* 1:59; *Resp. Lehem Rav* 147; PDR 11:131. See this writer's "Breach of a Promise to Marry," 17 *Jewish Law Annual* (2007), 267.

> price if you procure a buyer who is ready, willing and able to purchase the premises.
>
> If the property is sold... the commission provided for herein shall be due and payable...

Such language is illustrative of a *kinyan devarim* wherein owner consents to remit payment based upon the occurrence of a future event. To overcome this *kinyan devarim*, an agreement should incorporate language of *hit'hayevut* (obligation) such as "I obligate myself to pay" or "I obligate myself now to pay." By utilizing this terminology, a monetary obligation is created, and the parties become debtors, in contrast to having merely exchanged mutual promises to carry out a future action.[38] Hence, it would seem that a clause providing for payment in the future of a commission, even if it reflects the market rate, ought to be a *kinyan devarim* and therefore unenforceable.

However, the halakhic law of obligations recognizes the execution of a contract as binding by virtue of *situmta* (lit. a seal).[39] It is important to note that the basis of imparting validity to *kinyan situmata* is the implied *gemirat da'at* (firm resolve of the parties) to undertake an obligation in accordance with *minhag*.[40] Whereas agreements implementing a *kinyan suddar* are valid *min hadin* (based upon the formal laws of obligations), contracts which are characterized by language which runs afoul of *kinyan devarim* such as surety agreements, preliminary agreements, contract to sell a house, arbitration agreements, divorce agreements, and the like are binding by virtue of the fact that such agreements are valid based upon *minhag hasochrim*.[41] Thus, a real estate brokerage agreement is no different than the other aforementioned agreements. Consequently, a contractual term providing for a *davar she-lo ba la'olam* such as a payment of a commission in the future regardless of whether it reflects the market standard or exceeds it is valid and binding.[42] Therefore, Plaintiff is entitled to receive a seven per cent commission on the sale of the commercial property.

---

38. *Sma, Hoshen Mishpat* 243:12.

39. *Resp. Maharshach* 3:8; *Resp. Hatam Sofer, Hoshen Mishpat* 66; *Resp. Maharsham* 5:45; *Mishpat Shalom, Hoshen Mishpat* 194:2; *Resp. Ahiezer* 3:79.

40. *Responsa Ha-Rosh* 55:10; *Responsa Ha-Rashba* 2:268; *Responsa Maharsham, Hoshen Mishpat* 380; *Resp. Hatam Sofer, Yoreh Deah* 314, *Hoshen Mishpat* 66; *Resp. Shoeil U-Meishiv, Mahadurah Kamma* 2:39.

41. See supra n. 37; PDR 16:40, 16:133,18:354.

42. Rema, *Hoshen Mishpat* 129:6; *Sma*, ad. locum. 15; *Shakh*, ad. locum. 13.

6. "Mishpetei Hatenaim"

In addition to the requirements under *Halakhah* for solemnizing an agreement between parties that are discussed above, *Halakhah* requires that the terms of an agreement incorporate certain stipulations which are referred to as the "*mishpetei hatenaim*" (laws of conditions) in order to be binding.[43] In our case, the brokerage agreement should have been drafted in the following fashion:

> If the broker renders his services properly, he is entitled to a commission; if the broker fails to render his services properly, he would not be entitled to a commission.

However, normative *Halakhah* argues that the parties' intent to establish terms of a commercial contract trumps any failure to comply with the "*mishpetei hatenaim.*" Accordingly, notwithstanding the agreement's failure to properly employ the formal language of stipulation mandated under *Halakhah*, an agreement that sets forth terms will be binding upon the parties.[44]

7. Statute of Limitations Regarding Outstanding Debt

Even if Plaintiff is entitled to a commission on the residential property, Plaintiff argues that in the state of New York, there exists a statute of limitations law which places a time limit on pursuing a legal remedy in relation to an unpaid real estate commission. In New York, after the passage of six years, the injured person loses the right to file a lawsuit seeking money damages or other relief. Given that Plaintiff filed a lawsuit regarding the unpaid commission after more than six years, commercial practice dictates that Plaintiff be precluded from receiving any relief.

Given that the mere lapse of time may suffice to impugn the credibility of the evidence in support of such a claim, had the Defendant casted doubt about the existence of such a debt, Halakhah would be suspicious of the reliability of Defendant's claim. If a claim for an outstanding debt was advanced after a considerable delay in time, and if the *beit din*

43. *Tur Hoshen Mishpat* 207:3; *Netivot Ha-Mishpat,* ad. locum., 7; *Shulhan Arukh, Even Ha-Ezer* 38:2.

44. *Shulhan Arukh, Hoshen Mishpat* 61:16; *Bi'ur Hagra,* ad. locum. 39; *Sma,* ad. locum. 26.

believes that there was fraud, then the panel would find on behalf of the Defendant.[45]

However, in our instance, in the absence of fraud, other than a few exceptions,[46] a lapse of time does not extinguish the right to advance a claim for an outstanding debt. As Tosefta states:[47]

> A creditor may recover a debt at any time, even if it has not been mentioned.

And the Shulhan Arukh rules accordingly:[48]

> When the creditor submits a note of indebtedness which is authenticated, the *beit din* says to the borrower; "pay!" Even if there was a lapse of a few years and he did not advance a claim, we do not say that he waived it....

Unless a creditor has explicitly waived his right of collection,[49] the consensus of authorities is to reject a statute of limitations regarding unpaid debts.[50] Nonetheless, in a locale where there was no existent *minhag* of paying brokerage fees such as in nineteenth century Munkatch, Rabbi Avraham Alkali raised a doubt as to whether a lapse of time should not be viewed as *mehilah* (a waiver of debt).[51] However, today, when there

45. *Resp. Ha-Rosh* 68:20, 85:10; *Tur, Hoshen Mishpat* 61:16-17; *Shulhan Arukh, Hoshen Mishpat* 61:9, 98:2; *Resp. Ha-Maharik* 190; *Resp. Divrei Rivot* 109; *Resp. Ha-Mabit* 2:142; *Resp. Maharashdam, Hoshen Mishpat* 73; Rabbi Hayyim Shabbtai, *Resp. Torat Hayyim*, 1, *Hoshen Mishpat* 44.

46. For example, in family law matters, there is a statute of limitations regarding a widow who failed to advance a claim for payment of her *ketubah* or for support for an extended period of time. or a daughter who failed to claim one tenth of her father's estate for her wedding. See *Ketubot* 68b; 96a, 104a. In monetary affairs, if a dayan accepted a bribe and the giver does not claim its return, some construe his silence as waiving his right of recovery. See *Bah, Tur Hoshen Mishpat* 9:2; *Levush, Hoshen Mishpat* 9:1.

47. *Tosefta Ketubot* 12:3.

48. *Shulhan Arukh, Hoshen Mishpat* 98:1, See also, *Shulhan Arukh Even Ha-Ezer* 101:3; Rema, *Hoshen Mishpat* 163:2.

49. *Shakh, Hoshen Mishpat* 98:2, *Sma*, ad. locum. 2; *Yam Shel Shlomo, Bava Kamma* 2:17; *Resp. Helkat Ya'akov* 3:134.

50. *Resp. Ha-Rashba* 2:26; *Resp. Ha-Rivash* 404; *Resp. Ha-Tashbetz* 3:85; *Resp. Maharam Alsheich* 17; Rabbi Shmuel Aboav, *Resp. Devar Shmuel* 41; *Kezot Ha-Hoshen* 104:2; *Resp. Avodat Ha-Gershuni* 7; *Resp. Maharsham* 2:15; *Resp. Imrei Yosher* 1:107; *Resp. Shoeil U-Meishiv, Mahadurah Kamma*, 1:50.

51. *Zekhor Le-Avraham Hoshen Mishpat*, 3, *erekh sakhar*.

is a common practice to pay for such services, unless there is an explicit waiver, Rabbi Ovadia Yosef argues, the right of collection will not be withdrawn due to the lapse of time.[52]

Yet, historically *rishonim* as well as *aharonim* inform us that there were commercial practices that recognized a statue of limitations concerning outstanding debts, with some authorities validating such customs.[53] For example, Rosh informs us,[54]

> If an announcement appears, that anyone who has a claim and lien regarding land, he should now inform us and advance his claim, and if he remains silent without protest, all his rights will be null since this is the practice and this is the law of the land.

The rationale for such a view is that any creditor which remains silent after the issuance of such a public announcement has implicitly decided to waive his right to the outstanding debt. And in the sixteenth century, Shulhan Arukh endorses this procedure.[55] Such a practice continued to exist between the seventeenth and nineteenth century Polish communities and was subscribed to by some decisors.[56] For these decisors, the practice of recognizing a statute of limitations was either to be validated based upon the fact that it is the *minhag*, the common practice in the locale; it has been incorporated into a *takanat hakahal* (a communal ordinance) or pursuant to the norms of civil law.

Such a conclusion is problematic and therefore open to serious challenge. The common denominator of invoking *minhag*, *takanat hakahal* or *dina de'malkhuta dina* is that it calls for a nullification of a right of entitlement of a broker, who is considered a *kablan* (a contractor for certain services[57]) for his real estate services rendered.[58] In effect, by asserting the expiration of the right to collect an outstanding debt, we are sanctioning the act of *gezelah* (misappropriating) from a creditor based

52. PDR 13:34, 43.

53. For an extensive review of this issue, see Menachem Elon, "The Statute of Limitations in Jewish Law," (Hebrew) 14 *Hapraklit* (5718), 179, 243.

54. *Resp. Ha-Rosh* 79:13.

55. *Hoshen Mishpat* 104:2.

56. *Mazkeret Hashulhan, Hoshen Mishpat* 61:16; *Ateret Zvi, Hoshen Mishpat* 61:16; *Resp. Shevut Ya'akov* 3:182; *Netivot Hamishpat* 61:18; *Kesef Hakodshim, Hoshen Mishpat* 61:9.

57. *Magid Mishneh, Sekhirut* 9:4; *Rema, Hoshen Mishpat* 333:5.

58. *Resp. Halikhot Yisrael* 1-2.

upon the application of *minhag, takanat hakahal* or *dina de'malkhuta dina*.

The act of *gezelah* is an illustration of one of many *issurim* (ritual prohibitions) regarding which Halakhah mandates our compliance. As such, even though in the realm of *mamon* (monetary matters), under certain prescribed conditions, we invoke the notion that *minhag mevatel halakha* (custom nullifies Halakhah),[59] yet, in the sphere of *issur*, we are powerless to permit what Halakhah prohibited. For example, a *minhag* not to cancel debts in the sabbatical year has no validity.[60] Moreover, though Halakhah recognizes civil legal provisions in many areas of monetary matters, nevertheless, should a civil law entail an element of *issur*, Halakhah will decline to impart recognition to the particular secular law.[61] For example, should there be a civil law which allows for the collection of *ribbit* (prohibited interest), one is proscribed from following it.[62] Finally, the power of the Jewish community to legislate matters for their citizens is limited to the sphere of *mamon*. However, the community cannot legislate in variance with a norm of *issur*.[63] For example, pursuant to many arbiters, one is prohibited to imprison a Jew due to his delinquency in repaying a debt and therefore any communal legislation sanctioning this form of punishment is invalid.[64] In short, grounding the validation of a statute of limitations based upon the fiat of a communal ordinance or civil law or by dint of the authority of commercial custom is untenable.

Consequently, it is unsurprising to hear Rabbi Uziel's trenchant

59. Talmud Bavli *Bava Metzia* 83a-b.Talmud Yerushalmi, *Bava Metzia* 7:1.
60. *Resp. Ha-Rosh* 64:4.
61. *Resp. Ha-Tashbetz* 1:158.
62. *Resp. Avnei Nezer, Yoreh Deah* 133.
63. *Resp. Ha-Tashbetz* 2:132; *Resp. Ha-Rivash* 178, 185.
64. *Resp. Ha-Rosh* 68:10; *Resp. Ha-Rivash* 484; *Shulhan Arukh Hoshen Mishpat* 97:15.

Lest one argue that a community is not empowered to pass legislation which involves misappropriating a citizen's assets resulting in profit for one citizen and financial loss for another, such a conclusion applies only if the legislation is directed against a particular individual(s). See *Nahalat Shiva* 27:13; *Resp. She'erit Yosef* 9. However, if a piece of legislation is passed for the benefit of the community, and subsequently an individual incurs a loss due to its passage, such an ordinance is binding. See Rema, *Hoshen Mishpat* 2; *Nahalat Shiva* 27:13; *Resp. Ha-Maharit* 1:237. Seemingly, the communal passage of a statute of limitations which addresses the community at large should be valid.

Yet, in our case, it is the element of *issur* rather than the incurring of individual loss which invalidates the legislation.

criticism of those arbiters, who invoked commercial practice and civil law as validating a statute of limitations:[65]

> And our matter is different from a custom adopted wherein we accept modes of *kinyanim* (symbolic acts of transfer) such as *situmta* or *minhag hasochrim* which are binding pursuant to custom but there is no sanction to steal due to customary practice.... it falls under the rubric of the law of theft, and theft is not permitted due to custom.

Based upon the foregoing, we find that the Plaintiff's right to recover his compensation remains intact until this very day and never expired due to the lapse of time.

Decision

1. The Defendant is hereby obligated to pay a seven per cent commission as a brokerage fee for the sale of the commercial property
2. The Defendant is hereby obligated to pay a six per cent brokerage commission regarding the sale of the residential property.

65. *Resp. Mishpetei Uziel Hoshen Mishpat* 28.

C. THE HALAKHIC AVENUES FOR REMUNERATION FOR PROFESSIONAL SERVICES RENDERED

Facts

Defendant paid $1200 to Plaintiff for accounting services relating to the fiscal year ending December 31, 2007, including bank reconciliations, maintenance of a general ledger and sales tax returns.

Subsequently, Plaintiff and Defendant entered into an engagement letter signed by the Plaintiff on September 25, 2008, and by Defendant on November 7, 2008 (the "Engagement Letter"). The Engagement Letter provided that Plaintiff would perform the same tasks as he did for the 2007 fiscal year, again for a fee of $1200. The Engagement Letter also provided for preparation of year-end adjustments, analyses, closing entries, year-end closing of the books and tax returns, for an additional $500. The Engagement Letter also stated that the covered services included, "Any items incidental to the above accounting services, which did not require a substantial amount of additional time." It further stated that, "items not included and subject to additional billing will be tax audits, special projects, etc."

In 2009, Plaintiff submitted the following invoices for work done in connection with the 2008 fiscal year: (i) $600 for preparation of year-end adjustments, analyses, closing entries, year-end closing of the books and tax returns, (ii) $600 for changing from a "one-write check writing system" to the conventional check with stub system, (iii) $200 for preparation of two quarterly sales tax returns and two quarterly corporate 2009 income tax estimates and (iv) $1200 for preparation of projections relating to a tax matter, conferences with the owner of the corporation and reclassification of various entries and revisions in the closing of books and preparation of tax returns due to "Defendant's error" regarding the actual number of receivables.

Defendant paid $800 to Plaintiff, for services mentioned in items (i) and (iii) above. Defendant did not submit payment for the services mentioned in items (ii) and (iv) above. Plaintiff claims the balance of $1800 from Defendant.

At the *din Torah* (rabbinical court proceeding), Plaintiff stated that he bills at the rate of $200 per hour for his work and $80 per hour for his assistant's work for matters not covered under the fixed price arrangement set forth in the Engagement Letter.

Defendant argued the invoiced services mentioned in item (iv) above were incidental and did not require a substantial amount of additional time, and therefore should have been covered under the fixed rate arrangement.

Regarding the change from a "one-write check writing system" to the conventional check with stub system, Defendant claimed that Plaintiff was aware of this change at the time that they executed the Engagement Letter[1] and the increase of monthly recurring services which were billed out at $600 in the fiscal year ending December 31, 2007, to $1200 for the fiscal year ending December was due to Plaintiff's need to invest additional time in providing services utilizing the conventional check with stub system.[2] Hence, Defendant is not liable to pay $600 for this matter.

Finally, Defendant requested that Plaintiff immediately return any and all records in his possession.

Discussion

Pursuant to the terms of the signed Arbitration Agreement, this matter will be addressed within the context of *din* (the law) and the context of *pesharah kerovah ledin*:

Pursuant to the *din*, an agreement between two parties which calls for future performance is characterized by the Talmud and by post-Talmudic decisors as a *kinyan devarim* (a symbolic undertaking in words of an obligation) and therefore unenforceable. See Talmud Bavli *Bava Batra* 3a; Rashi, ad. locum., s.v. *kinyan devarim hu*; *Mishneh Torah Hilk. Mekhirah* 5:14, *Shulhan Arukh Hoshen Mishpat* 157:2; *Resp. Ha-Rosh* 12:3, 102:10; Rema *Yoreh Deah* 264:1; *Resp. Ha-Rashba* 2:41; *Resp. Maharashdam Hoshen Mishpat* 274; *Resp. Maharam Lublin* 108; *Resp. Perah Matteh Aharon* 13-14. The Engagement Letter arguably is a *kinyan devarim*.

Alternatively, said agreement is enforceable under Halakhah based upon *minhag* (i.e., mercantile custom grounded in the norms of *kinyan situmta*, i.e., the law that deals with seals. See *Resp. Maharashdam Hoshen Mishpat* 380; *Resp. Maharshach* 3:8; *Resp. Hatam Sofer Hoshen Mishpat* 66; *Resp. Maharsham* 5:48; *Resp. Ahiezer* 3:73 (7)).

1. The claim is that he was aware of this change and therefore the intent of both parties was that it was included in the fixed price arrangement.

2. The labor costs increase when using the conventional check with stub system.

An agreement is enforceable as a *kinyan situmta* provided it complies with the norms of secular law and is enforceable. See PDR 12:279, 291, 18:108, 112. Halakhically, it is viewed as a contractual obligation. See *Mishneh Torah, Hilk. Mekhirah* 11:15; *Shulhan Arukh Hoshen Mishpat* 60:6; R. Zalman N. Goldberg, "Contract" (Hebrew), *Otzar Hamishpat* 683. Others validate a modern-day contract based upon "the law of the kingdom is the law" *(dina de'malkhuta dina).* See *Resp. Shoeil U-Meishiv, Mahadura Kamma* 1:18; *Rema Hoshen Mishpat* 207:15.

Even in the absence of an express agreement between the parties, Plaintiff would be entitled to be remunerated for professional services rendered. According to *Rema Hoshen Mishpat* 246:17, 264:4, an individual is entitled to be paid for services rendered regardless of whether the individual was duly empowered by another to perform these actions, or if he performed these services on his own initiative. Failure to remit compensation for services rendered is subsumed in the category of "encroaching upon another's property without permission." See Talmud Bavli *Bava Metzia* 101a; *Piskei Ha-Rosh Bava Metzia* 8:22; *Shulhan Arukh Hoshen Mishpat* 375:1; *Sma*, ad. locum. 13; *Netivot Ha-Mishpat* 375:3. Finally, such remuneration is based upon a doctrine of unjust enrichment, i.e., *zeh nehene ve-zeh haser*. Liability stems either that the one who derived benefit is viewed as a tortfeasor or a thief. See *Resp. Maharit Even Ha-Ezer* 21; *Resp. Nodah Be-Yehudah*, Mahadurah Tinyana *Hoshen Mishpat* 24; *Piskei Ha-Rosh Bava Kamma* 2:8; *Tur Hoshen Mishpat* 371:10; *Bi'ur Ha-Gra Hoshen Mishpat* 363:14.

However, we are authorized under the terms of the Arbitration Agreement to resolve a case in accordance with *pesharah kerovah ledin.* See *Resp. Divrei Malkiel* 2:133 which states that the definition of *pesharah kerovah ledin* is measured in qualitative terms, i.e., the rendering of a fair and equitable decision.

Based on the testimony submitted at the hearing, it is unclear to what extent the services mentioned in item (iv) above were incidental and whether the services mentioned in item (ii) above were discussed initially among the parties and intended to be included in the fixed price arrangement. In addition, we find that Plaintiff's hourly rates should have been communicated to Defendant earlier than July 31, 2009. In any event, considering that the accounting fees for the entire year were to be $1800, it is reasonable to expect that prior to incurring an additional $1800 in fees, Plaintiff would first notify Defendant that the services mentioned in item (iv) above were to be performed at standard professional rates, and submit an estimate for that work. Given the difficulty in precisely valuating the amount owed by Defendant to Plaintiff considering the factors mentioned above, we have determined that an equitable resolution under the rubric of *pesharah kerovah ledin* is appropriate.

Decision

The Beit Din decides as follows:

1. Defendant shall immediately pay $800 to Plaintiff for the services mentioned in items (i) and (iii) above.
2. Defendant shall immediately pay $800 to Plaintiff for the services mentioned in items (ii) and (iv) above.
3. Plaintiff shall immediately return any and all records in his possession.

Any provision of this decision may be modified with the consent of both parties.

All of the provisions of this decision shall take effect immediately.

Rabbi Warburg's Publications

Books

Rabbinic Authority: The Vision and the Reality, 2024

Rabbinic Authority: The Vision and the Reality: The Double Halakhic Doubt in Marriage and Divorce, 2020.

Rabbinic Authority: The Vision and the Reality: The Halakhic Family, the Child's Welfare & the Agunah, 2018.

Rabbinic Authority: The Vision and the Reality: Halakhic Divorce & the Agunah, 2017

Rabbinic Authority: The Vision and the Reality, 2016

Rabbinic Authority: The Vision and the Reality, 2013

English & Hebrew Articles

"The Giving of a *Get* and the Resolution of End of Marriage Matters: Which Precedes the Other?" *Hakirah* (2024)

"Who has the Authority to Void a Marriage: Giants of the Generation or Qualified Rabbinic Decisors," (Hebrew) *Hama'ayan* (Tevet 5784)

"Criminal Proceedings Against a Jew in a Non-Jewish Court for *Get* Refusal: The Effect on the Validity of the *Get*," (Hebrew) *Emunat Itecha* (Nissan, 5783)

"Criminal Proceedings Against a Jew in a Non-Jewish Court for *Get* Refusal: The Effect on the Validity of the *Get*" 32 *Hakirah* 247 (2022)

"The Beth Din of America Prenuptial Agreement: *Halakhic* Foundations," (Hebrew) 27 *Hakirah* 5 (2019)

"The Role of Detrimental Reliance in the Law of Obligations: A Comparative Analysis," in *Studies and Halakhah: Menahem Elon Memorial Volume,* 2018, 3.

"A Divorcee's Relief from the Consequences of an Exploitative Divorce Agreement," 48 *Tradition* 24 (2015)

"The Propriety of a Conditional Divorce," 47 *Tradition* 31 (2014)

"An Employer's Vicarious Liability for an Employee's Sexual Misconduct," 47 *Tradition* 41 (2014)

"May a *Beit Din* render a Tort Award for an *Agunah*," (Hebrew) 34 *Tehumin* 430 (5774)

"The Propriety of a Civil Will" 15 *Hakirah* 165 (2013)

"Contractual Consequences in Living Arrangements: Jewish & American Legal Perspectives," 20 *Jewish Law Annual* 279 (2012).

"Harnessing the Authority of *Beit Din* to deal with Cases of Domestic Violence," 45 *Tradition* 37 (2012)

"The Propriety of Awarding a *Nezikin* Claim by *Beit Din* on behalf of an *Agunah*," 45 *Tradition* 55 (2012)

"The Ownership & Market of Human Tissue," in And You *Shall Surely Heal, Albert Einstein College of Medicine Synagogue Compendium* 199 (2012).

"The Practice of Gender Separation on Buses in the Ultra-Orthodox Community in Israel: A View from the Liberal Cathedral," 44 *Tradition* 19 (2011)

"Tenure Rights of an Employee and Rights to Severance Pay upon Termination: The *Beth Din* Experience as a Case Study," 12 *Hakirah* 89 (2011)

"The Tort of Negligent Misrepresentation of Investment Planning: A Comparative Analysis," 19 *The Jewish Law Annual* 141 (2011)

"The Theory of Efficient Breach: A Jewish Law Perspective" in ed. Aaron Levine, *Judaism and Economics,* Oxford University Press: 2010

"The Multi-Faceted *Halakhic* Identity of an Investment Broker"- 43 *Tradition* 51 (2010)

"Self-Dealing in the Not-for-Profit Boardroom: An Inquiry into a Trustee's Multi-faceted *Halakhic* Identity," 43 *Tradition* 7 (2010)

"Drafting a Halakhic Will," 10 *Hakirah* 73 (2010).

"Collaborative Reproduction: Unscrambling the Conundrum of Legal Parentage" in *And You Shall Surely Heal, Albert Einstein College of Medicine Synagogue Compendium*, 57 (2009)

"Toward Recovery for Spousal Emotional Stress: Proposed Relief for a Modern-Day *Agunah*" 18 *Jewish Law Annual* 13 (2009)

"An Investment Advisor: Liabilities and Halachic Identity," *Journal of Halacha & Contemporary Society*, 107 (2009)

"Toward Recovery for Spousal Emotional Stress: Proposed Relief for a Modern-Day *Agunah*: A Working Proposal" *Journal of Halacha & Contemporary Society*, Spring 2008

"Renal Transplantation: Living Donors & Markets in Body Parts: *Halakha* in Concert with Halakhic Policy or Public Policy?" 40 *Tradition* 14 (2008)

"May One Destroy Neighbor's Property in order to Save One's Life & Its Contemporary Implications for the Incorporation of Jewish Law into the Israeli Legal System"- *Turim: Dr. Bernard Lander Festschrift*, 331 (2007)

"The Nature of the Promise to Marry in Jewish Law," 17 *Jewish Law Annual* 267 (2007)

"Corporal Punishment in School: A Study in the Interaction of Contemporary American Law & Jewish Law with Social Morality," 37 *Tradition* 57, (2003)

"Solomonic Decisions in Frozen Preembryo Disposition: Unscrambling the Jewish Legal Conundrum," 36 *Tradition* 31 (2002)

"Varying Approaches towards the Division of Matrimonial Property upon Divorce" (Hebrew) 71-72 *Hadarom*, 129 (2001)

"A Comparative Analysis of a Wife's Capacity to Pledge Her Husband's Credit for Domestic Necessities in Anglo-American Law & Jewish

Law" 13 *Jewish Law Annual* 213 (2000)

"G-d Bless the Child: The Role of the Religious Factor in the Dynamics of Custody Decision-Making in Jewish & American Law," *Touro Jewish Law Report*, December 1997

"The Aliyah of Minors: Competing Paradigms in the Laws of *Keriat ha-Torah*," in *Hazon Nahum*, Festschrift in honor of Dr. Norman Lamm, 669 (1997)

"Parental Withdrawal of Medical Treatment from Children" 17 *Dine Israel* 35 (1993-1994)

"Some Reflections on the Jewish Criminal Process" 8 *The Jewish Lawyer* 11 (1991)

"In the Courts: Kidney Transplantation in Jewish Law" Touro Law School, *Institute of Jewish Law Newsletter*, June 1989

"A Wife Pledges her Husband's Credit for Necessaries" Touro Law School, *Institute of Jewish Law Newsletter*, February 1989

"Judicial Immunity in Jewish Law: A Chapter in Procedure or Torts?" Touro Law

School, *Institute of Jewish Law Newsletter*, May 1988

"Surrogate Parenting-Legal Issues under Jewish Law" *New York Law Journal*, March 11, 1988, page 1

"Preventive Detention: A Jewish Legal Perspective" Touro Law School, *Institute of Jewish Law Newsletter*, December 1987

"A Bibliographic Guide to Jewish Law" 1 *National Jewish Law Review* 59 (1985-1986)

"Child Custody: A Comparative Analysis" 14 *Israel Law Review* 480 (1979) cited in Israeli Supreme Court Decision *Nir v. Nir*, 35 (1) P.D.518 (1980)